standard catalog® of
CADILLAC
1903-2000

Edited by James T. Lenzke

Published by

700 E. State Street • Iola, WI 54990-0001
Telephone: 715/445-2214

Please call or write for our free catalog.
Our toll-free number to place an order or obtain a free catalog is 800-258-0929
or please use our regular business telephone 715-445-2214
for editorial comment and further information.

Library of Congress Catalog Number: 91-61301
ISBN: 0-87341-925-1

Printed in the United States of America

CONTENTS

CATALOG STAFF

EDITOR: . . . . James T. Lenzke

COVER DESIGN: . . . . Clay Miller

COLOR GALLERY DESIGN: . . . . Tom Nelsen

PAGE DESIGN: . . . . .Kay Sommerfeld

FOREWORD

The concept behind Krause Publications' *Standard Catalog of American Cars* series has been to compile massive amounts of information about motor vehicles and present it in a standard format that the hobbyist, historian, collector, or professional dealer can use to answer some commonly asked questions.

These questions include: What year, make, and model is the vehicle? What did it sell for new? How rare is it? What is special about it? Some answers are provided by photos and others by the fact-filled text.

Chester L. Krause, founder of Krause Publications, is responsible for the concept of creating the *Standard Catalog* series covering American automobiles. David V. Brownell undertook preliminary work on the project while serving as editor of *Old Cars Weekly* during the 1970s. Then-editor John A. Gunnell assumed the project in 1978. The first *Standard Catalog*, covering post-World War II models (1946-1975), was originally published in 1982 and is now in its fourth (1997) edition. Beverly Raye Kimes researched and wrote *Standard Catalog of American Cars 1805-1942*, which was first published in 1985 and is now in its third (1996) printing. Edited by Gunnell and first published in 1987, *Standard Catalog of American Light-Duty Trucks 1896-1986* was reprinted in 1993. Further spin-offs in the *Standard Catalog* series have subsequently included *American Motors 1902-1987, Imported Cars 1946-1990, Independents,* and marque-specific *Catalogs* covering all Chevrolet and Ford products, as well as Buick, Chrysler, Oldsmobile, and Pontiac.

Currently, the *Standard Catalog* series enjoys excellent sales (as evidenced by the frequent reprintings of its individual titles) in the old-vehicle hobby and provides a wealth of detailed information that car and truck collectors, hobbyists, restorers, and investors will not find offered by any other publishing house.

The scope of these *Catalogs* has been to cover the major manufacturers that have survived to the end of the millennium—DaimlerChrysler, Ford, General Motors, BMW, and others—as well as companies that they have absorbed and companies no longer with us today. Independent carmakers such as Checker, Hudson, Kaiser-Frazer, Nash, Packard, Studebaker, and Willys are included in the earlier *Catalogs*, as well as more than 200 producers of low-volume nameplates from Airscoot to Yenko. In each case the information compiled encompasses a physical description, list of known equipment and original specifications, technical data, historical footnotes, and—in most cases—an indication of the car's current "ballpark" value.

For each *Catalog*, compilations were made by an experienced editorial team consisting of the automotive staff of Krause Publications and numerous other contributors who are recognized experts on various marques or specific areas of automotive history. A major benefit of combining teamwork with expertise has been the gathering of many siginificant facts about each model.

No claims are made that these *Catalogs* are history textbooks or encyclopedias. Nor are they repair manuals. They are, rather, intended as contributions to the pursuit of knowledge about many of the wonderful cars and trucks that have been produced by the primary industrialized nations of the world since 1805. They are much larger in size, broader in scope, and more deluxe in format than any previously published collectors' guides, buyers' digests, or pricing guides.

The long-range goal of Krause Publications is to make all of these *Catalogs* as nearly perfect as possible. At the same time, we expect such reference works will always raise new questions and bring forth new facts that were not previously unearthed in the countless hours of research by our team. All contributors are requested to maintain an ongoing file of new research, corrections, and additional photos that can be used to refine and expand future editions.

We thank the editors and contributors to the three-volume *Standard Catalog of American Cars* series for providing much of the material contained herein. We also thank the 15 contributing authors whose selected articles—previously published in Krause Publications' journal of the collector-car hobby, *Old Cars Weekly*—appear within these pages under the headings of "Cadillac . . . Standard of the World" and "Gee, Our Old LaSalle Ran Great." It is through the research and editing efforts of all of these that we produce this *Standard Catalog of Cadillac 1903-2000* with the assurance that the great bulk of information from those three *Catalogs* combined here is accurate and well-researched.

Should you have access to expanded information that you wish to share, please don't hesitate to contact the editors, in care of Krause Publications, *Standard Catalog of Cadillac 1903-2000*, 700 E. State St., Iola, WI 54990-0001.

Other Catalogs currently available include: *Standard Catalog of American Cars 1805-1942, Standard Catalog of American Cars 1946-1975, Standard Catalog of American Cars 1976-1999, Standard Catalog of American Light-Duty Trucks 1896-1986, Standard Catalog of 4x4s 1945-1993, Standard Catalog of Chevrolet 1912-1998, Standard Catalog of Ford 1903-1998, Standard Catalog of American Motors 1902-1987, Standard Catalog of Independents,* and *Catalogs* dealing specifically with Buick (1903-1999), Chrysler (1914-2000), Oldsmobile (1897-1997), and Pontiac (1926-1995).

For ordering information and current prices, please call 1-800-258-0929, Code AUBR, or write to Krause Publications, Automotive Books Dept. AUBR, 700 E. State St., Iola, WI 54990-0001

COVER PHOTO CREDITS

In addition to those photos provided by Cadillac Division of General Motors, four of our cover illustrations depict cars owned by subscribers to *Old Cars Weekly*. They are: (front cover) 1959 Cadillac Eldorado Biarittz convertible owned by Rick Case, of Hillsboro Beach, Florida; 1937 LaSalle 37-50 coupe owned by Johnny and Adele Johnston, of Yates Center, Kansas; 1936 Cadillac 36-90 V-16 convertible sedan owned by Frank Nicodemus, of Wappingers Falls, New York; and (back cover) 1954 Cadillac Eldorado convertible owned by Dave Lindsay, of Manawa, Wisconsin.

ABBREVIATIONS

A/C . . . . Air conditioning
A.L.A.M. . . . Assoc. of Licensed
Automobile Mfgs.
Adj . . . . Adjustable
Aero . . . . Fastback
AM, FM, AM/FM . . . Radio types
Amp. . . . . Ampere
Approx . . . . Approximate
Auto. . . . . Automatic
Auxil. . . . . Auxiliary
Avail. . . . . Available
Avg. . . . . Average
BxS . . . . Bore x Stroke
Base . . . . Base (usually
lowest-priced) model
Bbl. . . . . . . Barrel (carburetor)
B.H.P. . . . . Brake horsepower
BSW . . . . Black sidewall (tire)
Bdrcl. . . . . Broadcloth
Bus. . . . . Business
(i.e. Business Coupe)
C.C. . . . . Close-coupled
Cabr. . . . . Cabriolet
Carb. . . . . Carburetor
Cass. . . . Cassette (tape player)
CB . . . . Citizens Band (radio)
CEO . . . Chief Executive Officer
C.I.D. . . Cubic inch displacement
Clb. . . . . . Club (Club Coupe)
Clth. . . . . . Cloth-covered roof
Col. . . . . Colonnade
(coupe body style)
Col. . . . . Column (shift)
Conv/Conv. . . . . . Convertible
Conv. Sed . . Convertible Sedan
Corp Limo Corporate Limousine
Cpe . . . . Coupe
C.R. . . . . . . Compression ratio
Cu. In. . . . . Cubic Inch
(displacement)
Cust. . . . . Custom
Cyl. . . . . Cylinder
DeL. . . . . DeLuxe
DFRS . . Dual facing rear seats
Dia . . . . Diameter
Disp . . . . Displacement
Dr. . . . . Door
Ea . . . . Each

E.D. . . . . Enclosed Drive
E.F.I. . Electronic Fuel Injection
E.W.B. . . . Extended Wheelbase
Eight . . . Eight-cylinder engine
8-tr . . . . Eight-track
Encl. . . . . Enclosed
EPA . Environmental Protection
Agency
Equip. . . . . Equipment
Exc. . . . . Except
Exec. . . . . Executive
F . . . . Forward
(3F = 3 forward speeds)
F.W.D. . . . . Four-wheel drive
Fam. . . . . Family
Fml . . . . Formal
"Four" . . . Four-cylinder engine
4WD . . . . . Four-wheel drive
4-dr. . . . . Four-door
4-spd. . . . . Four-speed
(transmission)
4V . . . . Four-barrel carburetor
FP . . . . Factory Price
Frsm . . . . Foursome
Frt . . . . Front
FsBk . . . . Fastback
Ft. . . . . Foot/feet
FWD . . . . . Front-wheel drive
GBR . . . Glass-belt radial (tire)
Gal. . . . . Gallon
GT . . . . Gran Turismo
G.R. . . . . Gear Ratio
H . . . . Height
H.B. . . . . Hatchback
H.D. . . . . Heavy Duty
HEI . . . . High Energy Ignition
H.O. . . . . High-output
H.P. . . . . Horsepower
HT/HT Hdtp. . . . . . . Hardtop
Hr . . . . Hour
Hwg . . . . Highway
I . . . . Inline
I.D. . . . . Identification
In . . . . Inches
Incl. . . . Included or Including
Int. . . . . Interior
Lan . Landau (coupe body style)
Lb. or Lbs. . Pound-feet (torque)

LH . . . . Left hand
Lift. . . . . Liftback
Limo . . . . Limousine
LPO . Limited production option
Ltd. . . . . Limited
Lthr. Trm. . . . . . Leather Trim
L.W.B. . . . . . Long Wheelbase
Mag. . . . . Wheel style
Mast. or Mstr. . . . . . Master
Max. . . . . Maximum
MFI . . . . . Multi-port Injection
M.M. . . . . Millimeters
MPG . . . . . Miles per gallon
MPH . . . . . Miles per hour
N/A . . . . Not Available
(or not applicable)
NC . . . . No charge
N.H.P. . . . . . Net horsepower
No. . . . . Number
Notch or N.B. . . . . Notchback
OHC . . Overhead cam (engine)
OHV . . Overhead valve (engine)
O.L. . . . . Overall length
OPEC . . . . Organization of
Petroleum Exporting Countries
Opt . . . . Optional
OSRV . . . Outside rear view
O.W. or O/W . . . Opera Window
OWL . Outline White Letter (tire)
Oz. . . . . Ounce
P . . . . Passenger
PFI . . . . Port fuel injection
Phae . . . . Phaeton
Pkg. . . . . Package
Prod. . . . . Production
Pwr. . . . . Power
R . . . . Reverse
RBL . . . Raised black letter (tire)
Rbt. . . . . Runabout
Rds . . . . Roadster
Reg . . . . Regular
Remote . . . . . Remote control
Req. . . . . Requires
RH . . . . Right hand drive
Roch. . . Rochester (carburetor)
R.P.M. . Revolutions per minute
RPO Regular production option

R.S. or R/S . . . . . Rumbleseat
RV . . . . . Recreational vehicle
RWL . . Raised white letter (tire)
S.A.E. . . . Society of Automobile
Engineers
SBR . . . . . Steel-belted radials
Sed . . . . Sedan
SFI . . . Sequential fuel injection
"Six" . . . . . Six-cylinder engine
S.M. . . . . Side Mount
Spd . . . . Speed
Spec . . . . Special
Spt. . . . . Sport
Sq. In. . . . . Square inch
SR . . . . Sunroof
Sta. Wag. . . . . Station Wagon
Std. . . . . Standard
Sub. . . . . Suburban
S.W.B. . . . . Short Wheelbase
Tach . . . . Tachometer
Tax. . . . Taxable (horsepower)
TBI Throttle body (fuel) injection
Temp. . . . . Temperature
3S . . . . Three-seat
Trans. . . . . . . Transmission
Trk. . . . . Trunk
2-Dr. . . . . Two-door
2 V . . . . Two-barrel (carburetor)
2WD . . . . . . Two-wheel drive
Univ . . . . Universal
Utl. . . . . Utility
V. . . . . . . Venturi (carburetor)
V-6, V-8 . . . . . Vee-type engine
VIN . . . . . Vehicle Identification
Number
W . . . . With
W/O . . . . Without
Wag. . . . . Wagon
w (2w) . Window (two window)
W.B. . . . . Wheelbase
Woodie . . . . Wood-bodied car
WLT . . . . White-letter tire
WSW . . . White sidewall (tire)
W.W. . . . . Whitewalls
W. Whl. . . . . Wire wheel

PHOTO CREDITS

Whenever possible, throughout this Catalog, we have striven to illustrate all cars with photographs that show them in their most original form. Each photo caption ends in an alphabetical code that identifies the photo source. These codes are interpreted below.

The editor wishes to extend special thanks to the editors of all previous editions of Krause Publications' *Standard Catalog of American Cars* series for their original research and for obtaining many of these photos of Cadillac products over the years.

(AA) Applegate & Applegate
(DW) "Dick" Whittington
(GM General Motors

(HAC) Henry Austin Clark, Jr.
(JAC) John A. Conde
(OCW) Old Cars Weekly

HOW TO USE THIS CATALOG

APPEARANCE AND EQUIPMENT: Word descriptions identify cars by styling features, trim and (to a lesser extent) interior appointments. Most standard equipment lists begin with the lowest-priced model, then enumerate items added by upgrade models and option packages. Most lists reflect equipment available at model introductions.

I.D. DATA: Information is given about the Vehicle Identification Number (VIN) found on the dashboard. VIN codes show model or series, body style, engine size, model year and place built. Beginning in 1981, a standardized 17 symbol VIN is used. Earlier VINs are shorter. Locations of other coded information on the body and/or engine block may be supplied. Deciphering those codes is beyond the scope of this catalog.

SPECIFICATIONS CHART: The first column gives series or model numbers. The second gives body style numbers revealing body type and trim. Not all cars use two separate numbers. Some sources combine the two. Column three tells number of doors body style and passenger capacity ('4-dr Sed-6P' means four door sedan, six-passenger). Passenger capacity is normally the maximum. Cars with bucket seats hold fewer. Column four gives suggested retail I price of the car when new, on or near its introduction date, not including freight or other charges. Column five gives you the original shipping weight. The sixth column provides model year production totals or refers to notes below the chart. In cases where the same car came with different engines, a slash is used to separate factory prices and shipping weights for each version. Unless noted, the amount on the left of the slash is for the smallest, least expensive engine. The amount on the right is for the least costly engine with additional cylinders. 'N/A' means data not available.

ENGINE DATA: Engines are normally listed in size order with smallest displacement first. A 'base' engine is the basic one offered in each model at the lowest price. 'Optional' describes all alternate engines, including those that came with a price listed in the specifications chart. (Cars that came with either a six or V-8, for instance, list the six as 'base' and V-8 'optional'). Introductory specifications are used, where possible.

CHASSIS DATA: Major dimensions (wheelbase, overall length, height, width and front/rear tread) are given for each model, along with standard tire size. Dimensions sometimes varied and could change during a model year.

TECHNICAL DATA: This section indicates transmissions standard on each model, usually including gear ratios; the standard final drive axle ratio (which may differ by engine or transmission); steering and brake system type; front and rear suspension description; body construction; and fuel tank capacity.

OPTIONAL EQUIPMENT LISTS: Most listings begin with drivetrain options (engines, transmissions, steering/suspension and mechanical components) applying to all models. Convenience/appearance items are listed separately for each model except where several related models are combined into a single listing. Option packages are listed first, followed by individual items in categories: comfort/convenience, lighting/mirrors entertainment, exterior, interior, then wheels/tires. Contents of some option packages are listed prior to the price: others are described in the Appearance/Equipment text. Prices are suggested retail, usually effective early in the model year. ('N/A' indicates prices are unavailable.) Most items are Regular Production Options (RPO), rather than limited-production (LPO), special-order or dealer-installed equipment. Many options were available only on certain series or body types or in conjunction with other items. Space does not permit including every detail.

HISTORY: This block lists introduction dates, total sales and production amounts for the model year and calendar year. Production totals supplied by auto-makers do not always coincide with those from other sources. Some reflect shipments from the factories rather than actual production or define the model year a different way.

HISTORICAL FOOTNOTES: In addition to notes on the rise and fall of sales and production, this block includes significant statistics, performance milestones, major personnel changes, important dates and places and facts that add flavor to this segment of America's automotive heritage.

1958 CADILLAC

SERIES 62 — (V-8) — Cadillacs for 1958 were basically carryover models with a face lift on all but the Brougham. There was a new grille featuring multiple round 'cleats' at the intersection of horizontal and vertical members. The grille insert was wider and the bumper guards were positioned lower to the parking lamps. New dual headlamps were seen throughout all lines and small chrome fins decorated front fenders. Tailfins were less pronounced and trim attachments were revised. The word Cadillac appeared, in block letters, on the fins of Series 62 base models. On the sides of the cars there were five longer horizontal windsplits ahead of the unskirted rear wheel housings; front fender horizontal moldings with crests placed above at the trailing edge and no rocker sill trim. The convertible, Coupe DeVille and Sedan DeVille used solid metal trim on the lower half of the conical projectile flares, while other models had a thin ridge molding in the same location. On Series 62 Eldorados, a V-shaped ornament and model identification script were mounted to the deck lid. The two luxury Cadillacs also had 10 vertical chevron slashes ahead of the open rear wheel housings and crest medallions on the flanks of tailfins. Broad, sculptured beauty panels decorated the lower rear quarters on Eldorados and extended around the wheel opening to stretch along the body sills. Standard equipment was the same as the previous year. All new was an extended deck Series 62 sedan, which was 8.5 inches longer than other models.

CADILLAC I.D. NUMBERS: Serial numbers now used a three symbol prefix. The first pair of numerical symbols '58' designated the 1958 model year. A one-letter alphabetical code (included as part of model number in charts below) indicated model and series. Each prefix was followed by the consecutive unit number, which started at 000001 and up. The serial number was located at the front of the left-hand frame side bar. Engine serial numbers again matched and were found on the center left-hand side of the block above the oil pan.

SERIES 62

Model Number	Body/Style Number	Body Type & Seating	Factory Price	Shipping Weight	Production Total
58K-82	6239(X)	4-dr HT Sed-6P	4891	4675	13,335
58K-62	6239(X)	4-dr Exp Sed-6P	4891	4675	204
58N-62	6239E(X)	4-dr Ext Sed-6P	5079	4770	20,952
58L-62	6239EDX	4-dr Sed DeV-6P	5497	4855	23,989
58G-62	6237(X)	2-dr HT Cpe-6P	4784	4630	18,736
58J-62	6237DX	2-dr Cpe DeV-6P	5231	4705	18,414
58F-62	6267X	2-dr Conv Cpe-6P	5454	4845	7,825
58-62	62	Chassis only	—	—	1

SERIES 62 ELDORADO SPECIAL

Model Number	Body/Style Number	Body Type & Seating	Factory Price	Shipping Weight	Production Total
58H-62	6237SDX	2-dr HT Cpe Sev-6P	7500	4910	855
58E-62	6267SX	2-dr Biarritz Conv-6P	7500	5070	815
58-62	6267SSX	2-dr Spl Eldo Cpe-6P	—	—	1

NOTES: The export sedan was shipped in completely-knocked-down (CKD) form to foreign countries. The Special Eldorado Coupe was a special order model built in limited quantities. Five specially equipped Eldorado Biarritz convertibles were also built (see Historical Footnotes for details). The symbol 'X', in brackets after Body/Style Number, indicates power windows and seat optional; without brackets indicates these features are standard. Style Number 6239E(X) is the new Extended Deck Sedan (Listed above as 4-dr Ext Sed-6P).

SERIES 62 ENGINE

Same general specifications as above except for following changes: Brake horsepower: 355 at 4800 R.P.M. Carburetors: Three (3) Rochester two-barrel Model 7015801.

SERIES 62 ELDORADO SPECIAL ENGINE

V-8: Overhead valves. Cast iron block. Displacement: 365 cubic inches. Bore and stroke: 4 x 3.625 inches. Compression ratio: 10.25:1. Brake horsepower: 310 at 4800 R.P.M. Five main bearings. Hydraulic valve lifters. Carburetor: Carter AFT four-barrel Model 2862S.

CHASSIS FEATURES: Wheelbase: (Series 62) 129.5 inches; (Series 60S) 133 inches; (Series 70) 126 inches; (Series 75)149.7 inches. Overall length: (58K) 216.8 inches; (58G, 58J and 58F) 221.8 inches; (58N and 58L) 225.3 inches; (58M) 225.3 inches; (58H and 58E) 223.4 inches; (58R and 58S) 237.1 inches. Front and rear tread: (All models) 81 inches. Tires: (Series75) 8.20 x 15 six-ply blackwall; (Series 62 Eldorado) 6.20 x 15 whitewall; (Series 70) 8.40 x 15 high-speed thin whitewall; (Other models) 8.00 x 15 blackwall.

CONVENIENCE ACCESSORIES: Radio with antenna and rear speaker ($164). Radio with rear speaker and remote control on Series 75 only ($246). Automatic heating system for Series 75 ($179); for other models ($129). Posture seat adjuster ($81). Six-Way seat adjuster ($103). Power window regulators ($108). E-Z-Eye Glass ($46). Fog lamps ($41). Automatic headlamp beam control ($48). Five sabre spoke wheels ($350). White sidewall 8.20 x 15 four-ply tires ($55). Gold finish grille on Eldorado (no charge); on other models ($27). Four-door door guards ($7). Two-door door guards ($4). Remote control trunk lock ($43). License plate frame ($8). Air conditioning ($474). Series 75 air conditioner ($625). Eldorado engine in lower models ($134). Air suspension ($214). Electric door locks on coupes ($35); on sedans ($57). Local dealer options: Utility kit ($15). Monogram ($12). Blue Coral waxing ($25). Undercoating ($5). Lubrication agreement ($34).

HISTORICAL FOOTNOTES: Five special Eldorado Biarritz convertibles were built with completely automatic top riser mechanisms and metal tonneaus and incorporated humidity sensors, which activated the top riser mechanism in case of rain. These cars had four-place bucket seating and custom leather interior trims including driveshaft tunnel coverings. The 1958 Eldorado Brougham is a certified Milestone Car.

BODY STYLES

Body style designations describe the shape and character of an automobile. In earlier years automakers exhibited great imagination in coining words to name their products. This led to names that were not totally accurate. Many of those "**car words**" were taken from other fields: mythology, carriage building, architecture, railroading and so on. Therefore, there was no "correct" automotive meaning other than that brought about through actual use. Inconsistencies have persisted into the recent period, though some of the imaginative terms of past eras have faded away. One manufacturer's "sedan" might resemble another's "coupe." Some automakers have persisted in describing a model by a word different from common usage, such as Ford's label for Mustang as a "sedan." Following the demise of the true pillarless hardtop (two- and four-door) in the mid-1970s, various manufacturers continued to use the term "hardtop" to describe their offerings, even though a "B" pillar was part of the newer car's structure and the front door glass may not always have been frameless. Some took on the description "pillared hardtop" or "thin pillar hardtop" to define what observers might otherwise consider, essentially, a sedan. Descriptions in this catalog generally follow the manufacturers' choice of words, except when they conflict strongly with accepted usage.

One specific example of inconsistency is worth noting: the description of many hatchback models as "three-door" and "five-door," even though that extra "door" is not an entryway for people. While the 1976-1999 domestic era offered no real phaetons or roadsters in the earlier senses of the words, those designations continue to turn up now and then, too.

TWO-DOOR (CLUB) COUPE: The Club Coupe designation seems to come from club car, describing the lounge (or parlor car) in a railroad train. The early postwar club coupe combined a shorter-than-sedan body structure with the convenience of a full back seat, unlike the single- seat business coupe. That name has been used less frequently in the 1976-99 period, as most notchback two-door models (with trunk rather than hatch) have been referred to as just "coupes." Moreover, the distinction between two-door coupes and two-door sedans has grown fuzzy.

TWO-DOOR SEDAN: The term sedan originally described a conveyance seen only in movies today: a wheeless vehicle for one person, borne on poles by two men, one ahead and one behind. Automakers pirated the word and applied it to cars with a permanent top, seating four to seven (including driver) in a single compartment. The two-door sedan of recent times has sometimes been called a pillared coupe, or plain coupe, depending on the manufacturer's whim. On the other hand, some cars commonly referred to as coupes carry the sedan designation on factory documents.

TWO- DOOR (THREE-DOOR) HATCHBACK COUPE: Originally a small opening in the deck of a sailing ship, the term "hatch" was later applied to airplane doors and to passenger cars with rear liftgates. Various models appeared in the early 1950s. but weather-tightness was a problem. The concept emerged again in the early 1970s, when fuel economy factors began to signal the trend toward compact cars. Technology had remedied the sealing difficulties. By the 1980s, most manufacturers produced one or more hatchback models, though the question of whether to call them "two-door" or "three-door" never was resolved. Their main common feature was the lack of a separate trunk "Liftback" coupes may have had a different rear-end shape, but the two terms often described essentially the same vehicle.

TWO-DOOR FASTBACK: By definition, a fastback is any automobile with a long, moderately curving, downward slope to the rear of the roof. This body style relates to an interest in streamlining and aerodynamics and has gone in and out of fashion at various times. Some (Mustangs for one) have grown quite popular. Others have tended to turn customers off. Certain fastbacks are, technically, two-door sedans or pillared coupes. Four-door fastbacks have also been produced. Many of these (such as Buick's late 1970s four-door Century sedan) lacked sales appeal. Fastbacks may or may not have a rear-opening hatch.

TWO-DOOR HARDTOP: The term hardtop, as used for postwar cars up to the mid-1970s, describes an automobile styled to resemble a convertible, but with a rigid metal (or fiberglass) top. In a production sense, this body style evolved after World War II, first called "hardtop convertible." Other generic names have included sports coupe, hardtop coupe or pillarless coupe. In the face of proposed rollover standards, nearly all automakers turned away from the pillarless design to a pillared version by 1976-77.

COLONNADE HARDTOP: In architecture, the term colonnade describes a series of columns, set at regular intervals, usually supporting an entablature, roof or series of arches. To meet federal rollover standards in 1974 (standards that never emerged), General Motors introduced two- and four-door pillared body types with arch-like quarter windows and sandwich type roof construction. They looked like a cross between true hardtops and miniature limousines. Both styles proved popular (especially the coupe with louvered coach windows and canopy top) and the term colonnade was applied. As their "true" hardtops disappeared, other manufacturers produced similar bodies with a variety of quarter-window shapes and sizes. These were known by such terms as hardtop coupe, pillared hardtop or opera-window coupe.

FORMAL HARDTOP: The hardtop roofline was a long-lasting fashion hit of the postwar car era. The word "formal" can be applied to things that are stiffly conservative and follow the established rule. The limousine, being the popular choice of conservative buyers who belonged to the Establishment, was looked upon as a formal motorcar. So when designers combined the lines of these two body styles, the result was the Formal Hardtop. This style has been marketed with two or four doors, canopy and vinyl roofs (full or partial) and conventional or opera-type windows, under various trade names. The distinction between a formal hardtop and plain pillared-hardtop coupe (see above) hasn't always followed a strict rule.

CONVERTIBLE: To Depression-era buyers, a convertible was a car with a fixed-position windshield and folding top that, when raised, displayed the lines of a coupe. Buyers in the postwar period expected a convertible to have roll-up windows, too. Yet the definition of the word includes no such qualifications. It states only that such a car should have a lowerable or removable top. American convertibles became extinct by 1976, except for Cadillac's Eldorado, then in its final season. In 1982, though, Chrysler brought out a LeBaron ragtop; Dodge a 400, and several other companies followed it a year or two later.

ROADSTER: This term derives from equestrian vocabulary where it was applied to a horse used for riding on the roads. Old dictionaries define the roadster as an open-type car designed for use on *ordinary* roads, with a single seat for two persons and, often, a rumbleseat as well. Hobbyists associate folding windshields and side curtains (rather than roll-up windows) with roadsters, although such qualifications stem from usage, not definition of term. Most recent roadsters are either sports cars, small alternative-type vehicles or replicas of early models.

RUNABOUT: By definition, a runabout is the equivalent of a roadster. The term was used by carriage makers and has been applied in the past to light, open cars on which a top is unavailable or totally an add-on option. None of this explains its use by Ford on certain Pinto models. Other than this inaccurate usage, recent runabouts are found mainly in the alternative vehicle field, including certain electric-powered models.

FOUR-DOOR SEDAN: If you took the wheels off a car, mounted it on poles and hired two weightlifters (one in front and one in back) to carry you around in it, you'd have a true sedan. Since this idea isn't very practical, it's better to use the term for an automobile with a permanent top (affixed by solid pillars) that seats four or more persons, including the driver, on two full-width seats.

FOUR-DOOR HARDTOP: This is a four-door car styled to resemble a convertible, but having a rigid top of metal or fiberglass. Buick introduced a totally pillarless design in 1955. A year later most automakers offered equivalent bodies. Four-door hardtops have also been labeled sports sedans and hardtop sedans. By 1976, potential rollover standards and waning popularity had taken their toll. Only a few makes still produced a four-door hardtop and those disappeared soon thereafter.

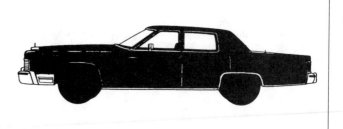

FOUR-DOOR PILLARED HARDTOP: Once the "true" four-door hardtop began to fade away, manufacturers needed another name for their luxury four-doors. Many were styled to look almost like the former pillarless models, with thin or unobtrusive pillars between the doors. Some, in fact, were called "thin-pillar hardtops." The distinction between certain pillared hartops and ordinary (presumably humdrum) sedans occasionally grew hazy.

FOUR-DOOR (FIVE-DOOR) HATCHBACK: Essentially unknown among domestic models in the mid-1970s, the four-door hatchback became a popular model as cars grew smaller and front-wheel-drive versions appeared. Styling was similar to the original two-door hatchback, except for — obviously — two more doors. Luggage was carried in the back of the car itself, loaded through the hatch opening, not in a separate trunk.

LIMOUSINE: This word's literal meaning is "a cloak." In France, limousine means any passenger vehicle. An early dictionary defined limousine as an auto with a permanently enclosed compartment for 3-5, with a roof projecting over a front driver's seat. However, modern dictionaries drop the separate compartment idea and refer to limousines as large luxury autos, often chauffeur-driven. Some have a movable division window between the driver and passenger compartments, but that isn't a requirement.

TWO-DOOR STATION WAGON: Originally defined as a car with an enclosed wooden body of paneled design (with several rows of folding or removable seats behind the driver), the station wagon became a different and much more popular type of vehicle in the postwar years. A recent dictionary states that such models have a larger interior than sedans of the line and seats that can be readily lifted out, or folded down, to facilitate light trucking. In addition, there's usually a tailgate, but no separate luggage compartment. The two-door wagon often has sliding or flip-out rear side windows.

FOUR-DOOR STATION WAGON: Since functionality and adaptability are advantages of station wagons, four-door versions have traditionally been sales leaders. At least they were until cars began to grow smaller. This style usually has lowerable windows in all four doors and fixed rear side glass. The term "suburban" was almost synonymous with station wagon at one time, but is now more commonly applied to light trucks with similar styling. Station wagons have had many trade names, such as Country Squire (Ford) and Sport Suburban (Plymouth). Quite a few have retained simulated wood paneling, keeping alive the wagon's origin as a wood-bodied vehicle.

LIFTBACK STATION WAGON: Small cars came in station wagon form too. The idea was the same as bigger versions, but the conventional tailgate was replaced by a single lift-up hatch. For obvious reasons, compact and subcompact wagons had only two seats instead of the three that had been available in many full-size models.

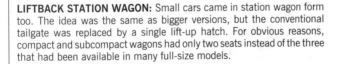

DIMENSIONS

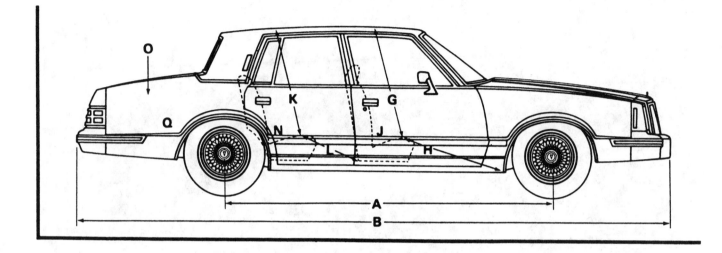

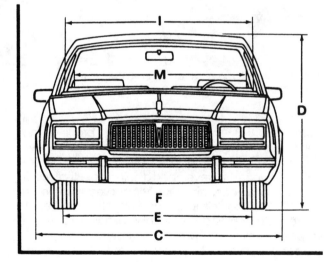

Exterior:

- A Wheelbase
- B Overall length
- C Width
- D Overall height
- E Tread, front
- F Tread, rear

Interior — front:

- G Headroom
- H Legroom
- I Shoulder room
- J Hip room

Interior — rear:

- K Headroom
- L Legroom
- M Shoulder room
- N Hip room
- O Trunk capacity (liters/cu. ft.)
- P Cargo index volume (liters/cu. ft.)
- Q Fuel tank capacity (liters/gallons)

CADILLAC
1903-2000

The first Cadillac was built in a small Detroit factory in 1902. A crowd of mechanics and factory employees looked on anxiously as the car was started and driven for the first time. (OCW)

Henry Martyn Leland was born to Quaker parents in Vermont in 1843. As an adult, he learned precision machining with Samuel Colt in Connecticut and with Brown and Sharpe, makers of tools and machinery in Rhode Island, for whom he developed a hair clipper that made a barber's work considerably easier for years thereafter.

In 1890 he took his family and his talents to Detroit, where fine machining was virtually unknown and where he allied himself with wealthy lumberman Robert C. Faulconer and tool designer Charles H. Norton in the formation of Leland, Faulconer, and Norton. The firm reduced by one in 1894 when Norton struck out on his own, later to become a successful manufacturer of crankshaft grinders. Precision gear making was the Leland and Faulconer specialty initially, though by 1896 the firm was into the manufacture of steam engines for Detroit street cars and gasoline units for marine use.

In June 1901, contracted by Olds Motor Works to produce engines for the curved dash Oldsmobile, Leland came up with a refined version that developed 23 percent more horsepower, but which was rejected by Olds people because retooling for it would further delay production already delayed by a factory fire in March. But

a year later Henry Leland was in the automobile business . . . courtesy of Henry Ford.

In August 1902 William Murphy and Lemuel W. Bowen, who were among the financial backers behind Ford's automotive venture, which to their dismay seemed to produce little more than racing cars, called in Leland as a consultant to appraise the automobile plant and equipment so they could sell it and get out. Leland showed them the engine rejected by Olds and suggested they stay in. Thus was born the Cadillac Automobiule Company named for Le Sieur Antoine de la Mothe Cadillac, the French explorer who had founded Detroit in the early eighteenth century.

The first Cadillac was completed on Oct. 17, 1902 and was given its maiden test drive by Alanson P. Brush, the 24-year-old Leland and Faulconer engineeer who had contributed substantially to the car's design and who would later build the Brush runabout.

In January the Cadillac was taken to the New York Automobile Show where company sales manager William E. Metzger (formerly of Olds Motor Works, later the "M" of E-M-F) took orders for an astounding 2,286 cars before declaring mid-week that the Cadillac was "sold out."

Tradition has it that Cadillacs began with this car, the first Cadillac built, which was completed October 20, 1902. Known as the Model A roadster, this 1,320-pound automobile with a 76-inch wheelbase was driven by a one-cylinder, 10-hp engine at speeds from five to 25 mph. It was sold for approximately $750. (OCW)

What made the Model A Cadillac such a best-seller, in addition to Metzger's super-salesman technique, was its refinement. Though the 10 hp developed by its single-cylinder, copper-jacketed engine was exemplary, its two-speed planetary transmission and center chain drive via a Brown-Lipe differential was conventional. Still, in a day when many automobile productions had a machine shop look to them, the Cadillac, comparatively, looked like a jewel from Tiffany's. And the price was just $750.

The deal made with the former Ford backers called for Leland and Faulconer merely to supply engines, transmisssions, and steering gears for the Cadillac, and that part of the operation moved with Leland-like precision. But at the Cadillac factory on Cass Avenue, chassis and body assembly lagged woefully behind. In October 1905, the Cadillac and Leland and Faulconer operations were merged into a new Cadillac Motor Car Company, with Henry Leland—now in his 60s—as general manager, his son Wilfred as assistant treasurer under Murphy.

The single-cylinder Cadillac would be built for half a dozen years in America, but its most significant historical achievement occurred in England during 1908. It was the idea of F.S. Bennett, the London importer for Cadil-

lac who had fielded the car successfully in hill climbs and endurance trials since 1903.

1906 Cadillac Model M Light Touring Car (HAC)

At Brooklands in 1908, under Royal Automobile Club supervision, Bennett directed in the dismantling of three single-cylinder Cadillacs, the scrambling of their parts, and the reassembly thereafter of the three cars, which were then run on the Brooklands track. The concept of precision manufacturing of interchangeable parts was a new one for the automobile industry.

1908 Cadillac Model G Limousine (HAC)

The Cadillac achievement in demonstrating the concept won the company the Dewar Trophy—the first ever for an American car—in 1908, and was the basis for the Cadillac slogan, "Standard of the World." The first four-cylinder Cadillac—with 28/30-hp vertical in-line engine mounted up front under a hood, planetary transmission (revised to selective in 1907), and shaft drive—had arrived for the 1905 model year, followed for 1909 by the Model Thirty, a refinement of the four that would advertise "1/1000th of an inch is the standard measurement."

Shortly after the announcement of the Model Thirty, there was another announcement that Cadillac had been bought by General Motors for over $5.5 million. This was undoubtedly the most substantial, and probably the wisest, purchase William C. Durant made for his new empire, and Durant was smart enough to keep the Lelands on board in complete charge.

In 1910, when Durant's free-spending had plunged GM into financial disaster, it was the persuasion of the Lelands and the strength of Cadillac that saved the corporation from possible dissolution. Closed coachwork—which had been introduced with the Osceola coupe model in 1906—became prominent in Cadillac catalogs from 1910 which, while not pacesetting, did represent an early focus on closed cars as standard productions.

was the beginning of a revolution that opened the use of the automobile to everyone, including women. (OCW)

In 1912 Cadillac became "The Car That Has No Crank" with the introduction of the Delco self-starter and electric lights developed by Charles F. Kettering. Cadillac tried hard for the Dewar Trophy that year, but didn't succeed, the Dewar Committee electing to award no prize at all in 1912. Interestingly, in October Cadillac inaugurated the slogan "Standard of the World," which may indicate that the company fully expected to recieve the award.

Amusingly, the Dewar Trophy was awarded to Cadillac in 1913 both for its "improved" starting-lighting-ignition system and its new two-speed rear axle. Unfortunately regarding the latter, Austin Automobile Company of Grand Rapids, which had earlier that year introduced its own version, sued for patent infringement in late 1914 and won in January 1915.

As a result, Cadillac dropped mention of the two-speed axle as concomitant to its second winning of the Dewar and indeed was so embarrassed that the 1913 award was hardly mentioned at all.

Later the company would choose to fudge by noting that "the 1912 electrics had led to the second Dewar", which was not entirely untrue. Wholly meritorious during this period was the new Cadillac V-8. Introduced in September 1914, three months later *The Automobile* would comment that it had "ushered in an epoch." Neither the world's first V-8 (Clement Ader's Paris-Madrid race car of 1903 was a V-8, and De Dion's V-8 of 1910 was first in series production) nor America's (Hewitt and Buffum preceding), the Cadillac version nonetheless was epochal.

Inspired by the De Dion unit, Cadillac refined the V-8 concept into an engine of supreme sophistication and one that would become the hallmark of Cadillac for generations thereafter, far outliving its many competitors. Introduced in four open and four closed body styles ranging in price from $1,975 to $3,600, the cars were most attractively priced and more than 20,000 were sold in 1915.

This 1912 Cadillac was the first car to use C.F. "Boss" Kettering's newly invented self-starter, and

During World War I, Cadillac went to war as the official staff car for the United States Army. Shown here is General John J. Pershing stepping out of his 1917 Cadillac Limousine. (OCW)

In January that year "The Penalty of Leadership," written by Theodore MacManus for Cadillac and one of the most celebrated advertisements in automobile history, was published in *The Saturday Evening Post*. During World War I, more than 2,000 Cadillac V-8s were sent overseas as staff cars, and it was during World War I, also, that the Lelands left Cadillac. According to William C. Durant, they were fired, principally because their personal egos now foreshadowed their interest in General Motors.

According to the Lelands, they resigned because Durant refused to build the Liberty aero engine. Following their leavetaking, Cadillac did proceed into Liberty manufacture, as did the Lelands who organized the Lincoln Motor Company for that purpose. For a number of years after the Lelands' departure Cadillac management was in some turmoil. Immediately succeeding as general manager was former Buick man Richard H. Collins, who left in 1921 for Peerless, taking with him chief engineeer Benjamin H. Anibal who had succeeded D. McCall White who, incidentally, was now building a V-8 called the Lafayette in Indiana for Charles Nash.

But by 1923, Ernest Seaholm, who had been on Anibal's design staff, was officially made chief engineer and would remain so until World War II. And in 1925, following the unremarkable tenure of Herbert H. Rice, who had replaced Collins, Lawrence P. Fisher assumed the Cadillac presidency for a decade-long run. (As legend has it, all seven of the Fisher brothers had filed into Rice's office to complain one after the other about his management, and he resigned soon after.) By the mid-'20s things had settled down nicely at Cadillac. Continuing refinements of the V-8 had brought detachable cylinder heads for 1918, an inherently balanced crankshaft in the V-63 of 1924 (which also introduced four-wheel abrakes), and detail changes in the interim 85.5-hp Series 314 V-8, which endured until 1936 when Cadillac's new 165-hp V-8 introduced unit block construction and featured downdraft carburetion in a design that would survive until 1949. By the '20s, Cadillac's price range was up in the $3,000-$5,000 league, but the cars were selling well, generally in the 20,000s annually, a figure that would nearly double in 1928.

The Series 341 cars for '28 were the first Cadillacs designed by Harley J. Earl, and they bore a distinct resemblance to the smashing LaSalle, Cadillac's companion car introduced the year before. Cadillacs for 1929 pioneered the synchromesh transmission and introduced safety glass. In January 1930 the V-16 Cadillac made its debut, followed in September by the V-12. Both engines (their design credited to Owen Nacker) were overhead-valve units, developing 165 hp and 135 hp respectively at introduction, though the V-12 was up to 150 hp and the V-16 to 185 hp for 1934. By that model year the V-16's wheelbase was stretched to a mammoth 154 inches making Cadillac America's lengthiest production car.

The Harley Earl-designed and Fleetwood-built bodies, on the V-16 particularly, were elegant and included the very striking and provocatively named Madam X. The lavish and luxurious excess of multi-cylinders made sense when they were developed by various manufacturers during the Roaring '20s. Ultimately arriving on the market as they did after the stock market crash and as the Great Depression took hold, there was no real rationale for these cars. But, alone among manufacturers offering twelves or sixteens, Cadillac did surprisingly well, selling 15,207 of them in a decade, far more than anyone else. Meanwhile, Cadillac's engineering department, justifiably renowned in the industry, came up with ride control for '32, no-draft ventilation for '33, and independent front suspension for '34.

By 1935 the Fisher all-steel turret top had arrived, and by now Nicholas Dreystadt was occupying Cadillac's general managership chair, having slid into it in June 1934 when Lawrence Fisher moved on to another GM assignment. Though Cadillac had not suffered as horrendously as many other manufacturers during the depths of the Depression, the company was nonetheless hurting. Dreystadt's formula for easing the pain was to streamline operations and to cut costs. This resulted in 1938 in the discontinuation of the ohv V-16 and V-12, which were replaced by a new flat-head V-16 generating the same 185 hp of its predecessor, but a less troublesome engine and more economical to build.

For 1930 Cadillac offered the industry's first V-16 engine. Equipped as such, this seven-passenger sedan represented the ultimate in luxury and power. (OCW)

1929 Cadillac 341-B Sport Phaeton (OCW)

Nineteen thirty-eight also saw Cadillac go to a steering-column-mounted gearshift lever a year before other GM cars--and the new V-8 Sixty Special with notched back, no running boards, and a spunky new look courtesy of a young designer on Harley Earl's staff named Bill Mitchell. Nineteen forty-one saw the final rationalization of the Dreystadt streamlining program with the Cadillac V-16 and the LaSalle dropped, and production concentrated on seven V-8 models mounted on three wheelbases and offering as options air conditioning (following Packard's lead of 1940) and Hydra-Matic fully automatic transmissions (introduced by Oldsmobile for 1940).

Cadillac sales for 1941 approached 60,000 cars, the best in the company's history. In 1942 Cadillac, along with the rest of the auto industry, turned to war production. Postwar, GM's premier division would enjoy its best production year ever, amid some further pacesetting Cadillac cars.

1941 Cadillac Series 61 Touring Sedan (OCW)

The years 1946-1975 were good ones for Cadillac. The company entered postwar times selling about 30,000 updated 1942 models each year and competing, with Packard, for the top rank in America's luxury car market. The battle was a short one. The famous, aircraft-inspired tailfin look debuted on selected 1948 models and, from then on, Cadillac became the style innovator in the high-priced field. Sales hit 100,000 units in 1950, passing those of other prestige makes and remaining out front for more than 25 years. By 1975, Cadillac's annual sales volume was some 265,000 cars.

1949 Cadillac Series 62 Coupe (OCW)

Trendsetting engineering seemed, always, to be part and parcel of the motoring masterpieces turned out, with remarkable consistency, by the Cadillac styling studio. In 1949, a compact, but exceptionally sturdy, over-

head valve V-8 became the brand's new power source. It was an engine that would last some 30 years without growing stale, becoming always more monstrous in size and output as time rolled by. Tailfins and big engines would characterize the marque, year after year, right through the early 1960s, but annually reblended in a product that seemed constantly new and ever more exciting.

The Golden Era of the automotive stylist is a good way to describe the early 1950s, a period that gave birth to such Cadillac innovations as the Florentine Curve roof, bumper tip dual exhaust exits, purposeful-looking "egg crate" grilles, and the simulated air vent rear fenderline treatment.

Derived from the Motorama parade of futuristic dream machines, the Cadillac Eldorado convertible became a production-line reality in 1953. This "Eldo", like many top dollar Cadillacs, came only fully equipped. It featured a profile that belonged more to a sports car than an elegant convertible. Exactly 532 buyers had the foresight to place orders for a copy, while 109,000 others made their picks from the balance of Cadillac's 1953 fleet. New that season was the bullet-shaped bumper/grille "bomb", which saw immediate popularity and imitation.

After celebrating its 50th season as an automaker, in 1952, Cadillac marked its 40th consecutive year of V-8 availability in 1954. A far cry from the 70-bhp Type 51 engine of 1914, the 1954 powerplant had a 331-cubic-inch piston displacement, four-barrel carburetion, 8.25:1 compression ratio, and 230 "horse" output rating. Unlike other manufacturers, the company did not enlarge engine size each year, but usually managed a power boost through compression or induction refinements. The cars themselves, however, did tend to grow a bit larger annually.

1954 Cadillac Series 62 Convertible (OCW)

Sales for 1955 peaked at a record 141,000 deliveries. The product line started at the rich level and included the traditional, long-wheelbase limousines for upper crust society. Features like automatic transmission and power brakes were taken for granted. Power seats, steering, and window lifts came at no additional cost in some models. Air conditioning was far from rare. For several years the Eldorado was marketed with styling touches that the rest of the line would adopt a year or two hence. This allowed the company to test forthcoming design changes, before putting them into full production.

After 1955, this system was also used on the Eldorado's closed-bodied counterpart, the super luxurious Seville hardtop coupe. At this point in time Packard was gasping its final breaths, Imperial was having an identity crisis, and Lincoln was just incubating its fabulous Continental Mark II. Meanwhile, Cadillacs found 155,000 buyers, virtually dominating the top rung of the domestic market spectrum.

The big news for 1957 was all-new styling and technology combined with the release of another show car come to life. The Eldorado Brougham, with its advanced airplane fuselage styling, was priced above $13,000 and came with every conceivable option, plus a few features never before seen on any car.

The 1958-1960 era has been called the "Wurlitzer Jukebox" period of automotive design and, like other carmakers, Cadillac was guilty of excessive use of towering tailfins, unnecessary tinsel, and overpowering size. To some, the "Batmobile" look of 1959 will always be regarded as the ultimate of this era. On the other hand, the cars of this vintage are precious to collectors now.

Like the Edsel, the 1959 Cadillac has come to represent a cultural symbol of its day. The immediate following model, however, though somewhat similar in appearance, was clearly a move towards the more sophisticated styling of the 1960s.

Clean, crisp lines and a modest attempt at downsizing characterized the 1961 model year. Slowly, but surely, the tailfin started to descend back towards earth. Sculptural body feature lines took the place of unneeded bright metal sweep spears. Increasing emphasis was placed on more attractive roofline treatments, interior design reflecting subdued elegance, and the creation of cars equipped for safer, more comfortable, and ultra-convenient driving. Cadillac's 1964 introduction of the Comfort-Control heating and air-conditioning system set a new industry standard.

1963 Cadillac Eldorado Convertible (OCW)

Finless rear fenders appeared on a long, low and even more luxurious line of Cadillacs for 1965. A new Fleetwood Brougham, with a vinyl-covered roof as standard equipment was introduced. Outstanding performance was, as usual, an accepted fact. The latest V-8, of 340 hp, came with the best power-to-weight ratio of any engine used as base equipment in a domestic car. Sales climbed to nearly 200,000 units, a barrier level that finally fell by the wayside during 1966.

The highlight of model year 1967 was a radically new front-wheel-drive Eldorado coupe aimed at the growing sports/personal car segment of the high-priced field. Its slotted wheel covers, hidden headlamps, and long-hood/short-deck configuration quickly endeared the sporty new Cadillac to the wealthy who were young

at heart. By 1968, the Eldorado was attracting over 25,000 buyers a year, while the more conventional Cadillacs continued to follow a conservative pattern of annual styling and engineering refinements that won more customers each season. Between 1963 and 1968, Cadillac Division established a new sales record each year.

This ever-upward trend was temporarily broken in 1969, the year in which the front vent window disappeared. This was not a very popular styling change and may have accounted, in some measure, for the modest drop in sales. In 1970, however, Cadillac bounced back with a massive 500-cid engine and deliveries of a record 239,000 units.

A growing emphasis on safety keynoted the completely restyled Cadillacs of 1971, which were also larger than ever before. Even the Eldorado was dressed in entirely new sheetmetal that further accented the "big car' look. In coupe form, it could now be had with a sun roof, a feature not seen on Cadillacs since 1941. Two long-standing models, the deVille sedan and convertible, passed from the scene as the company adapted to a more streamlined marketing program for its seventh decade. Convertibles were now available only on the front-wheel-drive Eldorado platform and the so-called "Sedan" deVille was actually a four-door hardtop. To keep a watchdog government happy, Cadillac adopted massive front safety bumpers and a 8.5:1 compression ratio to permit utilization of low-lead or lead-free gasoline.

To celebrate its 70th anniversary, in 1972, Cadillac built and sold 267,000 cars for the calendar year. One of these—a Fleetwood Eldorado Coupe—became a gift to the late Leonid Brezhnev from US President Richard M. Nixon. Although the Cadillac image changed little, from year-to-year, in the early 1970s, sales continued to climb. The company had abandoned its former role as innovator and was now virtually an institution—the King of the luxury car market. A degree of conservatism seemed to go with the new role.

The King, of course, reigned supreme. More than 300,000 Cadillacs were sold in 1973, a year in which a white Eldorado convertible paced the 57th running of the Indianapolis 500 Mile Race. Not since 1937 had a Cadillac product been given this particular honor.

Modern technology was very obvious in the facelifted Cadillacs presented to buyers in the 1974 model year. Not only was a digital dashboard clock standard equipment, but an expanded list of options included the air bag safety restraint system, steel-belted radial tires, High-Energy electronic ignition systems, and pulsating windshield wipers. In addition, a number of extremely high-priced luxury option packages were offered. They could convert various models into ultraelegant Cabriolet, d'Elegance, or Talisman editions. Sales, however, took a plunge to the 242,000-unit level as a result of the Arab nations' embargo upon the flow of oil to the United States. Of course, this eco-political situation affected all automakers and Cadillac wound up with a larger market share, even though volume sales were off.

In 1975, Cadillac's superiority over competitors in the prestige class was once again demonstrated when Chrysler Corporation announced that it was discontinuing production of the Imperial (later revived). This left the top of the market to Cadillac and Lincoln, both of which had seen a nearly tenfold increase in sales since 1946. Yet, in terms of overall volume, Cadillac continued to play the King's role by outselling the "fancy Ford" by a wide margin.

A seasonal highlight was the mid-year release of an international-sized Seville on a 114-inch-wheelbase platform. A completely new concept, the "baby" Cadillac found more than 16,000 buyers waiting. For the big cars, another mid-year innovation was the offering of an optional, electronic fuel-injection setup on the 500-cid V-8.

From the beginning, Cadillac had been nearly synonymous with luxury. People spoke of countless products as "The Cadillac of (whatever)." Through the tailfinned postwar years, Cadillacs had been poshly (sometimes gaudily) appointed, gargantuan in size, and powered by some of the biggest V-8s around. However, the models built by Cadillac Division in the first 30 years after World War II were, for the most part, outstanding machines that maintained the brand's traditional position as the "Standard" of the automotive world. Owning one was viewed as a milepost, a demonstration that one had "arrived."

As the 1976 model year began, signs were already appearing that change was imminent; that Cadillac's position might even be in jeopardy one day. For the moment, though, it was business as usual. Only Lincoln competed in the American-car luxury market, as Chrysler had abandoned its Imperial. Beneath all full-size Cadillac hoods was the biggest V-8 of modern times, a 500-cid behemoth, fully appropriate for the car's enormous length. On the other hand, the 1975 model year had brought the emergence of a much different kind of Cadillac—the compact Seville, powered by a comparatively tiny, fuel-injected 350-cid V-8. Unlike the soft American ride and slushy handling typified by big Cadillacs, Seville delivered control more appropriate in a European sedan.

Amid massive publicity, the "final" front-drive Eldorado convertible came off the line in 1976, selling for astounding mark-ups to speculators before finally leveling off in price. The bottom-ranked Calais was in its final year, soon to leave only Fleetwood and deVille to attract full-size coupe/sedan devotees. Luxury-minded customers had plenty to choose from, however, including three special editions: d'Elegance, Talisman, and Cabriolet models. Yet this was the final season for the mammoth Seventy-Five limousine and nine-passenger sedan. Led by Seville's popularity, Cadillac set records for both sales and production.

In 1977, Cadillac's 75th anniversary year, the full-size models were downsized, losing almost half a ton each. Who would have believed it? Eldorado kept its former huge form a while longer, but all models (except Seville) now carried a new, smaller, 425-cid V-8 instead of the giant 500. Eldorado, now without a convertible offering, added a special edition—the Custom Biarritz—with padded Elk Grain cabriolet roof. The pillarless four-door hardtop was also gone, as all sedans now had pillars and framed door glass. Downsizing didn't hurt, apparently, as sales and production scored gains once again.

Not much happened for 1978, except for new deVille Phaeton (coupe or sedan) and Seville Elegante special editions. Dunlop wire wheels were now available. Sevilles could be ordered with Oldsmobile's diesel V-8 engine. And, for the third consecutive year, sales set a record.

Eldorado finally got its own downsizing for 1979, along with a modest 350-cid V-8 under the hood, and independent rear suspension. Bigger Cadillacs kept the 425-cid V-8, and all models could be equipped with the Olds diesel. As usual, quite a selection of special editions was offered, some of which may appeal to later enthu-

siasts: Brougham and Seville d'Elegance, deVille Custom Phaeton, Seville Elegante, and Eldorado Biarritz.

1979 Cadillac Coupe deVille (OCW)

While Brougham and deVille got a moderate restyling for 1980, Seville changed drastically. Not everyone adored the new "bustleback" body and long hood, or the razor-edge contours reminiscent of mid-century Rolls-Royce bodies. The new Seville had front-wheel drive and, in a surprising move, a standard diesel engine. Other Cadillacs turned to a 368-cid gas V-8. A fuel-injected version was standard on Eldorado, available for Seville. Later in the year came more shocking powerplant news—a Buick-built V-6 under Cadillac hoods. Sales dropped sharply, and would do so again in 1981, but these were bad years for the industry as a whole.

A different kind of powerplant emerged for 1981, one that would bring Cadillac nothing but grief. The variable displacement (V-8-6-4) engine may have seemed like a good idea at the time, capitalizing on a rising interest in economy, but in real life it was trouble. It lasted only one year (though limousines kept it several years longer). The Buick V-6 continued as an underhood alternate.

If the compact "international size" Seville had startled traditionalists back in 1975, what might they make of the latest Cadillac offering for 1982, the subcompact Cimarron? On the whole, not much. Cimarron never managed to catch on, perhaps because it was perceived as little more than a glorified (and costly) Chevrolet Cavalier.

1982 Cadillac Seville Eleganté four-door sedan (OCW)

Four-cylinder engines and manual gearboxes couldn't attract either former or new Cadillac buyers in significant numbers. A new aluminum-block 249-cid HT-

4100 V-8 replaced the troublesome V-8-6-4 as standard engine in other models. Seville abandoned the standard diesel—another idea that never caught hold. Eldos added a special-edition Touring Coupe with special suspension and wide blackwall tires, in yet another shift away from the traditional. Sales rose for 1982, and again in 1983, which was a year without major change. Rear-drive Cadillacs, the biggest standard cars available, remained popular, and customers also seemed to like the HT-4100 engine a lot better than its predecessor. Cimarron introduced a d'Oro edition with black body and goldtone accents, which didn't exactly sparkle in the sales race.

In a move sparked by Chrysler Corp. in 1982, Eldorado returned a Biarritz convertible to its line for 1984, as sales rose once again. This was the final season for the rear-drive deVille, as front-drive versions were coming. The 1985 deVille and Fleetwood were two feet shorter than their rear-drive forerunners, powered by a transverse mounted V-6 or V-8. Even the Fleetwood limousines were front-drive, but Brougham carried on with rear-wheel drive, still finding quite a few customers. Cimarron could now have a V-6 engine (from Chevrolet).

1984 Cadillac Cimarron four-door sedan (OCW)

Brand-new Eldorado and Seville bodies arrived for 1986, far more similar to each other than before. Sales of both fell sharply. No convertible was available, though Eldo could have a Biarritz option, Seville an Elegante. deVille had an important new option: anti-lock braking. Touring Coupe and Sedan models came with a stiffer suspension to please performance-minded buyers. Diesel engines were gone completely. Limousines finally dropped the V-8-6-4 engine. Fleetwood Brougham stuck around in rear-drive form, powered by a 5.0-liter V-8, enjoying a resurgence in sales. For the future, Cadillac was concentrating on its new Allanté two-seater, due out in 1987.

The "final" 1976 Eldorado convertibles weren't nearly so rare as promoters suggested, though collectors might still be interested since prices have fallen to more sensible levels. Naturally, the 1980s ragtops are also worth a look. So are many of the attractive special editions: d'Elegance, Elegante, Biarritz. Some models that attracted little interest when new will find a future among enthusiasts later, but Cimarron isn't likely to be among them. The razor-edge Sevilles, on the other hand, seem to look more appealing with each passing year, especially since later Sevilles lost their unique styling touches. Two-tone Sevilles with their striking accent moldings and Elegante extras may well be worth consideration.

Cadillac's introduction of the Allanté in 1987 highlighted what was called the "New Spirit of Cadillac." In an effort to focus customer attention on the virtues of specific models, Cadillac subdivided its "spirit" into five sections. The Cadillac with a "Sporting Spirit" was the Cimarron, which had a more powerful 125-hp engine, an improved front suspension, and the composite, tungsten headlights previously used on the 1986 d'Oro model.

The "Contemporary Spirit" was found in the deVille and Fleetwood models that were slightly longer for 1987. The deVille touring coupe and sedan models were continued. Both the deVille and Fleetwood series were identified by their restyled grille, new hood header molding, and revised side markers.

Both the Eldorado—Cadillac's "Driving Spirit" model—and the "Elegant Spirit" Seville were virtually unchanged for 1987. As with all its 1987 models, Cadillac warranted the Seville and Eldorado against rust-through for five years or 100,000 miles. The Seville/Eldorado braking system also carried a five-year or 50,000-mile warranty. Larger Goodyear tires were fitted on the standard Seville and Eldorado. Replacing the conventional speedometer on both models was a new system using electric signals generated at the transmission by a speed sensor. The body computer module had a nonvolatile memory circuit that retained odometer information if the battery was disconnected.

The surprising popularity of the "Classic Spirit" Brougham (its sales had increased by over 30 percent during the 1986 model year) indicated that a significant market continued to exist for the last remaining rear-drive Cadillac.

Neither the carry-over Series Seventy-Five models nor the revised Series Sixty sedan received a Cadillac Spirit label. The Sixty Special's return suggested that Cadillac's efforts to reassert its status as a premier-quality vehicle would entail both a forward-looking perspective and the reincarnation of concepts that had previously been successful.

The Allanté had originated in 1982 in what was identified as the LTS or Luxury Two Seater project. In contrast to the criticism leveled at the Cimarron for its close proximity to less expensive versions of the J-car, the Allanté was recognized as a unique vehicle. The Allanté was based upon the GM-30 platform used for the Eldorado, Buick Riviera, and Oldsmobile Toronado. But the specific engineering of the Allanté plus the role of Pininfarina in its manufacture justified its unique status among Cadillacs.

Indicative of the influence General Manager John O. Grettenberger was exerting upon Cadillac was its declaration in 1988 that "we are guided by one vision—to design, build, and sell the world's finest luxury automobiles." Although Cadillac's share of the luxury market fell almost two percent in 1987 to 28.9 percent from 30.8 percent in 1986, it could still declare itself "America's luxury car leader for 39 consecutive years."

Once again, Cadillac's price structure was capped by the Allanté, which Cadillac noted made use of German steel and Swiss aluminum. Cadillac also underscored the Allanté's international character by reminding the public that its coachwork was by Pininfarina who was also the "designer of Ferraris and Rolls-Royce Camargue." Although some critics had been uncomfortable with Cadillac's depiction of the Cimarron as the "Cadillac of small cars," few grumbles were heard about the claim that the "Allanté brings Cadillac comfort to two-passenger automobiles." As in 1987, the Allanté's only option was a cellular telephone.

Cadillac's best-selling Sedan deVille model was touted as possessing an "uncanny ability to reflect today's new approach to luxury." Like the other front-wheel-

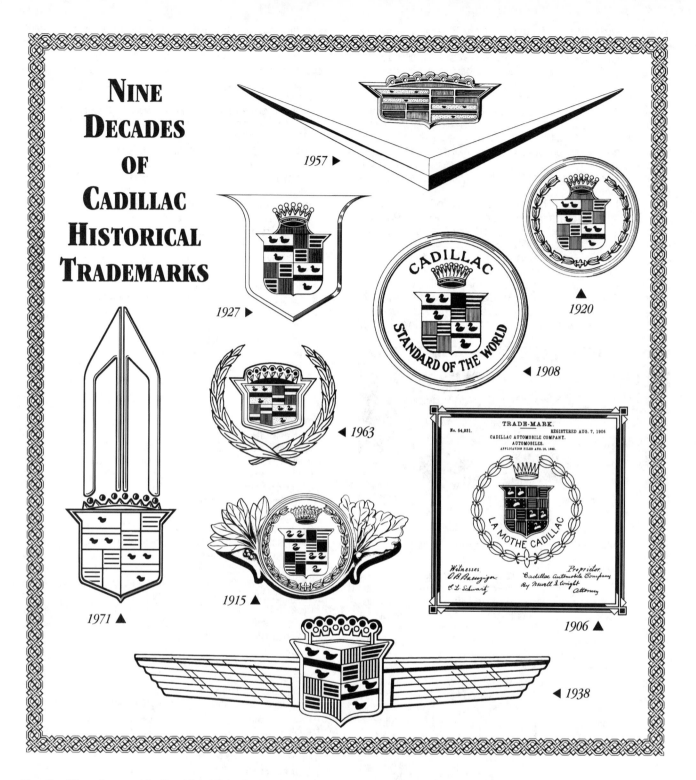

Nine Decades of Cadillac Historical Trademarks

1957 ▶

1927 ▶

▲ 1920

◀ 1908

◀ 1963

1915 ▲

1971 ▲

1906 ▲

TRADE-MARK.
No. 54,931. REGISTERED AUG. 7, 1906
CADILLAC AUTOMOBILE COMPANY.
AUTOMOBILES.
APPLICATION FILED AUG. 18, 1905.

LA MOTHE CADILLAC

Witnesses   Proprietor
O.B. Barrington   Cadillac Automobile Company
E.L. Schwartz   By Merrill S. Wright
                                                    Attorney

◀ 1938

drive Cadillacs (except for the Allanté) both deVille models were powered by a more powerful V-8 engine, which, with over one million miles of reliability testing, was backed by a six-year/60,000-mile powertrain warranty.

Helping customers appreciate the higher trim level and exclusive nature of the Fleetwood models, Cadillac reminded them that the "Fleetwood name has always been reserved for very special Cadillacs."

The Eldorado shared a new "powerdome" hood with the Seville. The Eldorado also received a new roof treatment and vertical taillights that helped reinforce the link that Cadillac was intent on reforging with earlier Eldorados.

The Cimarron was destined to be discontinued after the 1988 model year, but in its final form it was at the peak of its performance and appeal. Only one version was offered with color-keyed body side moldings. The optional three-speed automatic transmission now had a torque converter clutch.

Apparently possessing interminable appeal, the Brougham, said Cadillac, "continues to be among the luxury cars most in demand."

Aware, however, of the need to attract younger buyers, Cadillac was not relying on the Brougham to serve as its attention-getter for buyers oriented toward vehicles with highly visible technical features and engineered to provide road feel, taut handling, and precise control. Instead, it opted to publicize such features as the optional anti-lock brake system. In this context, Cadillac noted that it "offers anti-lock braking on more models than any other American company."

Also tilting Cadillac marketing toward a younger audience was the availability of the Touring Sedan version of the Sedan deVille and the Touring Suspension option for both the Seville and Eldorado.

Cadillac also provided its customers with its "Gold Key Delivery System," which continued a company policy dating back to 1926. This program offered nationwide automotive service, an audio cassette of information about the specific Cadillac model purchased, a full tank of fuel, two sets of 23-karat gold-plated keys, and a personalized Gold Key Identification Card. Cadillac also offered an exclusive, no-cost, Gold Key vehicle inspection of the new Cadillac at the owner's convenience.

With the elimination of the Cimarron in 1989, Cadillac returned to its traditional position of offering automobiles powered exclusively by V-8 engines. Among the new model year highlights were longer, restyled deVille/Fleetwood models, a more powerful Allanté, and new functional and convenience features for the Seville, Eldorado, and Brougham. Among these items introduced in 1989 were an express-down driver's window, electrochromic inside rearview mirror, ElectriClear windshield and an oil life indicator.

Cadillac's manufacturing operations included five separate units that either assembled vehicles for Cadillac and other GM divisions or provided parts, components, and assemblies for GM plants in North America and overseas, as well as for outside companies.

The success of the 1989 models provided Cadillac with a strong plan for its 42nd consecutive year as America's No. 1 luxury-car company. Among the highlights for 1990 were full-time traction control on the Allanté (a first for a domestic manufacturer), antilock brakes on every model, and, except for the Brougham, driver side supplemental inflatable restraints on all Cadillacs, a 25-hp increase to 180 for Eldorado, Seville, deVille and Fleetwood, and an optional 5.7-liter V-8 on the Brougham.

Cadillac's six distinct product lines, which ranged from highly expensive luxury vehicles such as the Allanté to the more conservative Brougham, marked the 75th anniversary of the introduction of the V-8 engine in Cadillac automobiles. This advantage over some of its foreign and domestic competition was compounded by the popularity of the newly styled and lengthened deVille and Fleetwood models whose 1989 model year sales had been up more than 15 percent compared to 1988 levels. Sales of the Seville and Eldorado also posted strong gains in 1989. Deliveries were up 13.7 and 14.1 percent, respectively, for the two models compared to 1988.

In 1989, Cadillac also became the first domestic manufacturer to offer a Tourist Delivery Program. Under this program, which was continued for 1990, European buyers could order a new Cadillac through the General Motors International Export Sales office in their home country and save up to 15 percent by taking delivery of the vehicle in the United States. Cadillac arranged for shipment.

Cadillac's commitment to quality enabled it in 1989 to continue to lead all domestic, and many leading import manufacturers, in customer satisfaction. From 1987 to 1989 Cadillac led all domestic automakers in quality.

For 1990 Cadillac also enhanced its image as a safety-conscious company. The structural integrity of the deVille/Fleetwood, Eldorado, and Seville were improved. In addition to producing better overall ride characteristics, improvements were made in roof crush performance, door operation after a crash, occupant kinetics, and vertical steering column. The changes included longer side rail reinforcement in the engine compartment, additional welding at the upper front corners of the engine compartment, reinforced windshield and hinge pillars, and heavier reinforcement in the front floorpan.

All Cadillacs offered anti-lock brakes as standard equipment in 1991. The following year saw all-new Seville and Eldorado models, Cadillac's first new offerings since the automaker was reorganized in 1987 as an autonomous General Motors division.

Cadillac observed its 90th Anniversary in 1993 in a big way, as the pioneering Northstar engine, with limp-home capability, was introduced. This was also the final year of production for the Allanté two-seater convertible (no longer offered as a convertible hardtop) as well as the Fleetwood series. The Fleetwood name would survive, though, being affixed to the former Brougham sedan. This last-year Allanté convertible (which also was selected to pace the Indianapolis 500) was powered by the Northstar V-8. This trifecta of convertible, racing heritage, and abundant power should keep the '93 version of the luxury two-seater on collectors' lists in years to come.

1993 Cadillac Brougham d'Elegance four-door sedan (OCW)

As early as 1994, all Cadillacs were meeting 1997 federal standards for dynamic side impact protection. It was a leaner Cadillac lineup that year, with a four-series, seven-model offering compared to six series and nine models in 1993.

The Northstar engine of 1995, powering all Cadillacs except the Sedan deVille and Fleetwood, helped to mark the 80th Anniversary of the Cadillac V-8. The following year saw final production of the Fleetwood and Fleetwood Brougham sedans—Cadillac's last remaining front-engine/rear-drive models.

Catera, the Cadillac that "zigged," debuted in early 1996 as a 1997 model. The all-new, rear-drive sports sedan was a joint venture product of Cadillac and Adam Opel AG, and was constructed in Ruesselsheim, Germany. Powered by a V-6, it was the first time Cadillac offered an engine other than a V-8 since 1988.

1998 Cadillac deVille d'Elegance four-door sedan (OCW)

Cadillac continued refinement of its automobiles through the end of the decade, but the big news of 1999 focused on the Escalade, a sport utility vehicle that was Cadillac's first truck-based offering in its 96-year history. In other big news, Cadillac stunned the motorsports world when it announced it would return to sports car competition with a factory-backed effort to compete in the 24 Hours of LeMans. It had been since the 1950s that Cadillac (a privateer effort) had competed in France's day-long race.

Cadillac's millennium-ending 2000 lineup featured completely restyled full-size deVille sedans built on a much stiffened platform shared with some other GM marques. The end results were somewhat shorter and slightly narrower than the '99 models, but rode on a 1.5-inch longer wheelbase. Catera received a face-lift and the addition of a Sport version distinguished by 17-inch wheels and other exterior styling fillips. Eldorado and Seville remained largely unchanged in appearance, but received tweaks to their Northstar V-8 engines. While Cadillac's impressive Evoq concept car hinted at future styling for the marque, the year's production models were characterized by technological razzle-dazzle such as a thermal-imaging Night Vision system, updates to StablilTrak that included automatic shock-absorber dampening adjustment on individual wheels, LED taillights, Ultrasonic Rear Parking Assist, and a system that prevented front and side passenger air bags from deploying if the seat was unoccupied or contained a small child.

1903 CADILLAC

1903 Cadillac, runabout with tonneau, OCW

CADILLAC — ONE: Note: Cadillac did not use the "A" designation in 1903. However, later Cadillac publications combined references to 1903 "Cadillac" and "1904 Model A" and used "Model A" in reference to all single-cylinder cars with two front springs and angle steel frame.

Chassis: Angle steel frame. Two half-elliptic springs front and rear. Straight, tubular front axle. Right-hand, wheel steering. Controls to right. Adjustable rack and pinion steering gear. Single tube tires, wood wheels.

Engine: Leland & Faulconer "Little Hercules." Horizontal single cylinder mounted to the left under front seat. Water-cooled, impeller pump circulation through finned tube front-mounted sloping radiator. Detachable, special alloy, cast iron cylinder with copper water jacket. Detachable combustion/valve chamber. Valves vertical, in-line and perpendicular to the cylinder bore. Exhaust, at bottom, is operated by rocker and push rod from cam on gear-driven half-speed shaft in crankcase. Inlet, at top, is operated by rocker that is operated by a sliding cam driven by an eccentric on the half-speed shaft. The fulcrum for the sliding cam is adjustable by movement of a lever on the steering column, giving variable lift to the inlet valve and, thus, throttle adjustment for the engine. Fuel is gravity fed from a tank under the driver's seat to an updraft mixer that automatically delivers the amount of fuel demanded by the inlet valve opening. Internal lubrication by splash from single-pipe, gravity feed oiler. External points, including mains, lubricated by grease and oil cups. Cranking from right or left side of vehicle through jackshaft and chain to crankshaft.

Driveline: Two speed planetary transmission. Low speed on left foot pedal. High and reverse on controller lever at right. Single chain to spur gear differential.

Brakes: Foot pedal operated mechanical on inboard ends of rear half axles. Engine can be used for additional braking by easing controller lever into reverse.

Body: Two-passenger runabout convertible to four-passenger by bolting on rear entrance tonneau. Sloping, curved dash. Body can be lifted from chassis without disconnecting any wiring, plumbing, or controls.

Note: Alanson P. Brush, of Leland & Faulconer, held patents on copper water jacket, variable lift inlet valve, mixer, planetary transmission, and adjustable rack and pinion steering. By 1906, the impact of Brush patents would start a drastic change in Cadillac design.

I.D. DATA: Serial numbers were not used. Engine numbers were stamped two places on crankcase: 1. Top, right edge of cylinder flange, near water outlet. 2. Right, front face, just below top cover. (Blank spaces on patent plate are for additional patent dates, not engine number.) Engine No.: 1-2500 (Includes three prototypes built in 1902.)

Model No.	Body Type & Seating	Price	Weight	Prod. Total
NA	Runabout-2P	750	1370	Note 1
NA	W/Tonneau-4P	850	1450	Note 1

Note 1: Cadillac model year total was 2,497.

ENGINE: Horizontal, with cylinder to rear. One cylinder. Cast iron cylinder, with copper water jacket. B & S: 5 x 5 in. Disp.: 98.2 cu. in. Brake H.P.: "Higher than advertised or calculated H.P." Advertised H.P.: 6-1/2. (ALAM, NACC, SAE H.P. calculated by identical formulae.) (ALAM first used formula in 1908.) Main bearings: Two. Valve lifters: Mechanical (See "Description"). Carb.: Updraft mixer, manufactured by Cadillac.

CHASSIS: W.B.: 72 in. O.L.: 9 ft. 3 in. Height: 5 ft. Front/Rear Tread: 54-1/2 in. Tires: 28 x 3 single tube.

TECHNICAL: Planetary transmission. Speeds: 2F/1R. (3:1 low, rev. direct high). Controls: low — foot pedal. Rev., high — lever to right. Low, rev. — bands. High — disc clutch. Chain drive. Spur gear differential. Overall ratio: 3.1:1 to 5:1 (see drivetrain options). Mechanical brakes on two wheels — contracting on inboard drums. Wood wheels — 12 spoke (14 spoke on prototype). Wheel size: 22 in.

Drivetrain Options: Different combinations of 9 or 10 tooth driving sprocket with 31, 34, 38, 41, or 45 tooth driven sprocket gave ten possible ratios from 3.1:1 to 5:1. Lower ratios for runabout to be run on smooth, level roads to higher ratios for loaded delivery to be run on rough, hilly roads. Instructions for changing sprockets were furnished to owners, but the change involved disassembly of the transmission and rear axle, definitely not a "quick-change" set-up.

OPTIONS: Tonneau ($100.00). Leather top w/side curtains and storm apron (50.00). Rubber top w/side curtains and storm apron (30.00). Lights.

HISTORICAL: Advertised November 1902, but was not at auto shows until January 1903. Innovations: Interchangeable parts. Calendar year sales and production: 2,497. Model year sales and production: 2,497. The president of Cadillac was C.A. Black.

Although period photos exist of stripped single-cylinder Cadillacs in speed contests, the as-delivered cars were only fast enough to travel at reasonable speeds on the roads of the time.

However, the cars soon gained a reputation for reliability, ease and economy of maintenance, and remarkable pulling and climbing capability. Publicity shots show Cadillacs pulling heavily loaded wagons up slopes and climbing the steps of public buildings.

The first Cadillac exported to England was entered by its promoter, F.S. Bennett, in the July 1903 Sunrising Hill Climb — "The worst hill in England." The entry finished seventh in a field of 17, being the only one-cylinder in a field otherwise made up of two- and four-cylinder cars with up to four times the displacement of the Cadillac. The same car was entered in the September 1903 One Thousand Mile Reliability Trial in England and finished fourth in its price class on total points but first in its price class on reliability scoring.

1904 CADILLAC

1904 Cadillac, Model B, touring, OCW

1904 Cadillac, Model B, runabout, JAC

CADILLAC — MODEL A — ONE: Continuation of 1903, delivery body with detachable top added. Horsepower rating upped to 8-1/4. Clincher tires now standard equipment. Optional 60 in. tread available. Pressure fed multiple oiler introduced.

CADILLAC — MODEL B — ONE: Same as Model A except:

Chassis: Pressed steel frame and axles. Front axle girder style (not available in wide tread). Single transverse half-elliptic front spring. Cranking (counterclockwise) at left side only. Compression relief provided for cranking. Safety device to prevent crank from being inserted when spark control lever is in advanced position. Horsepower rating upped to 8-1/4 — more a question of confidence than any engine design changes.

Body: Inverted box replaces sloping, curved dash. Radiator vertical and below frame. Joint in body at dash allows body to be slid off with no lifting. Surrey body style added — side entrance detachable tonneau. Delivery top no longer detachable. Weight of all body styles reduced by as much as 70 pounds. Prices increased $50.

I.D. DATA: Serial numbers were not used for Model A or B. Engine numbers were stamped two places on crankcase: 1. Top, right edge of cylinder flange, near water outlet. 2. Right, front face, just below top cover. (Blank spaces on patent plate are for additional patent dates, not engine number.) Model A engine Nos.: 3500 — 4018 with B. 8200 — 8350 with CEF (1905). 13501 — 13706 with CEF (1905-special). Model B engine Nos.: 2500 — 3500. 3500 — 4018 with A. 4200 — 5000 with EF.

Model No.	Body Type & Seating	Price	Weight	Prod. Total
Model A				
NA	Rbt.-2P	750	1370	—
NA	W/Tonneau-4P	850	1450	—
NA	Del.-2P	850	1525	—
Model B				
NA	Rbt.-2P	800	1300	—
NA	Tr.-4P	900	1420	—
NA	Surrey-4P	900	1400	—
NA	Del.-2P	900	1525	—

ENGINE: Horizontal, with cylinder to rear. One. Cast iron cylinder, with copper water jacket. B & S : 5 x 5 in. Disp.: 98.2 cu. in. Brake H.P.: "Higher than advertised or calculated H.P." Advertised H. P.: 8-1/4. (ALAM, NACC, SAE H.P. calculated by identical formulae.) (ALAM first used formula in 1908.) Main bearings: Two. Valve lifters: Mechanical (see "Description"). Carb.: Updraft mixer, manufactured by Cadillac.

CHASSIS: (Model A, except Delivery) W.B.: 72 in. O.L.: 9 ft., 3 in. Height: 5 ft. Front/Rear Tread: 54-1/2 in. (60 optional). Tires: 28 x 3 Clincher. (Model A Delivery) W.B.: 72 in. O.L.: 9 ft., 3 in. Height: 7 ft., 1 in. Front/Rear Tread: 54-1/2 in. Tires: 28 x 3 Clincher. (Model B, except Delivery) W.B.: 76 in. O.L.: 9 ft., 4 in. Height: 5 ft. Front/Rear Tread: 54-1/2 in. Tires: 30 x 3 Clincher. (Model B Delivery) W.B.: 76 in. O.L.: 9 ft., 4 in. Height: Approx. 7 ft. Front/Rear Tread: 54-1/2 in. Tires: 30 x 3-1/2 Clincher.

TECHNICAL: Planetary transmission. Speeds: 2F/1R (3:1 low, rev. direct high). Low-foot pedal, rev., high — lever to right. Low, rev. bands, High disc clutch. Chain drive. Spur gear differential. Overall ratio: 3.1:1 to 5:1 (see drivetrain options). Mechanical brakes on two wheels — contracting on inboard drums. Wood wheels — 12 spoke (14 spoke on prototype). Wheel size: (Model A) 22 in. (Model B) 24 in., (Delivery) 23 in.

Drivetrain Options: Different combinations of 9 or 10 tooth driving sprocket with 31, 34, 38, 41, or 45 tooth driven sprocket gave ten possible ratios from 3.1:1 to 5:1. Lower ratios for runabout to be run on smooth, level roads to higher ratios for loaded Delivery to be run on rough, hilly roads. Instructions for changing sprockets were furnished to owners, but the change involved disassembly of the transmission and rear axle, definitely not a "quick-change" set-up.

OPTIONS: Model A: same as 1903. Model B: Bulb horn. Lights. Leather top w/sides and storm apron ($50.00). Rubber top w/sides and storm apron (30.00). Deck to replace tonneau on touring or surrey (10.00).

HISTORICAL: Model A introduced 1903. Model B introduced January 1904. Calendar year sales and production, Model A & B: 2,319. Model year sales and production: same. The president of Cadillac was C.A. Black.

Note: Factory burned in the spring of 1904, reducing production to almost nothing for 45 days. Deposits on 1,500 orders were returned. Volume of sales still exceeded those of any other make in the country.

When the street was muddy, cars with rear entrance tonneau were backed in perpendicular to the sidewalk so passengers needn't walk in the mud. The side-entrance surrey ended this inconvenience.

1905 CADILLAC

1905 Cadillac, rear entrance tonneau, OCW

CADILLAC — MODEL B — ONE: Unchanged from 1904. Horsepower now rated at 9. Optional wide tread, not available on Model B in 1904, is now made available by use of tubular axle with 61-inch tread to replace pressed steel axle with standard tread.

CADILLAC — MODEL C — ONE: Mid-year offering, at reduced prices, of Model B with Model F "hood" and radiator. Cadillac called the Model C "an accommodation to customers who want a detachable tonneau." The Model F was non-detachable. This may be interpreted as "a program to move out the remaining Model B chassis."

CADILLAC — MODEL D — FOUR: Body: Five-passenger touring with side entrance tonneau doors. Wood body. Aluminum skin available at extra cost. Runningboards. Aluminum dash, carrying lubricator and running fuel tank with gravity feed to mixer. Storage fuel tank at rear of chassis — fuel transfer to running tank by exhaust pressure.

Chassis: Emphasis on strength and durability. Pressed steel frame. Two half-elliptic springs in front, platform spring in rear. Right hand steering, controls to right. Brake lever operates service brakes on rear drums. Foot pedal operates emergency brake on drive shaft. Application of either brake system disengages flywheel clutch through an interlock. Engine and transmission mounted in tubular subframe. Patented double syphon muffling system.

Driveline: Three-speed planetary transmission (3:1, 2:1, direct). Progressive shift — all speeds on single lever. Twin disc clutch in flywheel, disc clutch and three bands on transmission, emergency brake drum behind transmission. Shaft drive (two U-joints) to bevel gear. Live rear axle with spur gear differential.

Engine: Four-cylinder vertical in-line L-head, counterclockwise cranking. Individual cylinders with copper water jackets, heads detachable with factory equipment. Two-piece crankcase — lower section carrying mains and patented sloping-trough splash lube system that ensures lubrication to each cylinder regardless of grade. Horizontal commutator shaft projects forward into cavity in radiator — commutator is serviced from front of vehicle. With number one cylinder over the front axle and a stretched out accessory section on the front of the engine, the radiator extends forward of the front tires. The hood is one-quarter the length of the car.

Engine throttle control is a complicated variation of the one-cylinder throttling arrangement. The L-head valves are operated by in-line pushrods and roller tappets riding on extra wide cams on a spring-loaded, sliding camshaft. Exhaust cams are of constant cross section but inlet cams are cone shaped to effect a varying lift and timing as the camshaft is moved along its axis. Axial motion of the camshaft against its return spring is by hydraulic piston that receives pressure from an engine-driven pump. The throttle control on the steering column operates a bypass valve in the hydraulic loop. Position of this valve regulates the percentage of system pressure acting on the camshaft piston, thus the nominal axial position of the camshaft. Governor action is automatic due to interaction between engine driven pump speed, hydraulic pressure, and cam position (overspeed increases pressure and drives cam back to a lower speed position). As on the one-cylinder, inlet valve opening automatically determines the amount of fuel supplied by the mixer — identical to the one-cylinder mixer except for the addition of an auxiliary air intake valve.

Note: In addition to patents pertaining to one-cylinder cars, Alanson Brush also held patents on the splash lubrication system and the muffler system used on Model D. Although not patented, counterclockwise cranking was a Brush "trademark."

1905 Cadillac, Model E, runabout, HAC

CADILLAC — MODEL E — ONE: Same as 1904 except: more normal looking "hood" with sharp corners and side louvers. Radiator raised to fit shape of "hood." Detachable tonneau not available. Front axle now tubular, arched, with truss. Rocker shaft between front axle and spring introduced mid-year. Balanced linkage on transmission bands,

Note: E, F, K, M, S, T are not six distinct models. E, K, S are runabouts; F, M, T all other body styles.

CADILLAC — MODEL F — ONE: Same chassis as Model E except two-inch longer wheelbase. Body styles: first Cadillac one-cylinder touring car with non-detachable tonneau and two side doors for tonneau entrance. Delivery.

I.D. DATA: Serial numbers were not used on any of these models. Engine numbers were stamped two places on crankcase. 1. Top, right edge of cylinder flange, near water outlet. 2. Right, front face, just below top cover. (Blank spaces on patent plate are for additional patent dates, not engine number.) Model B engine Nos.: 4200-5000 with EF (1904). Model C engine Nos.: 6600-8200 with EF, 8200-8350 with AEF, 13501-13706 with AEF-special. Model D engine numbers were stamped on top of crankcase — in front of and to the left of number one (front) cylinder. Starting: 10001. Ending: 10156. Model E engine Nos.: 4200-5000 with EF (1904), 5000-6600 with F, 6600-8200 with CF, 8200-8350 with ACF, 13501-13706 with ACF-special. Model F engine Nos.: 4200-5000 with BE (1904). 5000-6600 with E, 6600-8200 with CE, 8200-8350 with ACE, 13501-13706 with ACE special, 13728-14200.

Model No.	Body Type & Seating	Price	Weight	Prod. Total
Model B				
NA	Tr.-4P	900	1450	—
NA	Sur.-4P	900	1450	—
Model C				
NA	Rbt.-2P	750	1330	—
NA	Tr.-4P	850	1450	—
Model D				
NA	2-dr. Tr.-5P	2800	2600	156
Model E				
NA	Rbt.-2P	750	1100	—
Model F				
NA	2-dr. Tr.-4P	950	1350	—
NA	Del.-2P	950	1400	—

ENGINE: Models B, C, E, F: Horizontal, with cylinder to rear. One cylinder. Cast iron cylinder, with copper water jacket. B & S: 5 x 5 in. Disp.: 98.2 cu. in. Brake H.P.: "Higher than advertised or calculated H.P." Advertised H.P. 9. (ALAM, NACC, SAE H.P. calculated by identical formulae.) (ALAM first used formula in 1908). Main bearings: Two. Valve lifters: mechanical (See "Description"). Carb.: Updraft mixer, manufactured by Cadillac. Model D: Vertical, in-line, L-head. Four cylinder. Cast iron cylinders, cast singly, copper water jacket. B & S: 4-3/8 x 5 in. Disp.: 300.7 cu. in. Advertised H.P.: 30. Main bearings: Five. Valve lifters: Mechanical, roller tappets, variable lift inlet. Carb.: Cadillac updraft mixer with auxiliary air valve.

CHASSIS: (Model B) W.B.: 76 in. O.L.: 9 ft., 4 in. Height: 5 ft. Front/Rear Tread: 56-1/2 (61 opt). Tires: 30 x 3 Clincher. (Model C) W.B.: 76 in. O.L.: 9 ft., 4 in. Height: 5 ft. Front/Rear Tread: 56-1/2 in. Tires: 30 x 3 Clincher. (Model E) W.B.: 74 in. O.L.: 9 ft. Height: 4 ft., 8 in. Front/Rear Tread: 56-1/2 (61 opt.) Tires: 28 x 3 Clincher. (Model F Touring) W.B.: 76 in. O.L.: 9 ft., 4 in. Height: 5 ft., 4 in. Front/Rear Tread: 56-1/2 (61 opt.) Tires: 30 x 3-1/2 Clincher (Model F Delivery) W.B.: 76 in. O.L.: 9 ft., 4 in. Height: approx. 7 ft. Front/Rear Tread: 56-1 /2 in. Tires: 30 x 3-1/2 Clincher. (Model D) W.B.: 100 in. O.L.: approx. 12 ft., 10 in. Height: approx. 5 ft., 9 in. Front/Rear Tread: 56-1/2 in. Tires: 34 x 4-1/2 Dunlops.

TECHNICAL: Models B & C: Planetary transmission. Speeds: 2F/1R (3:1 low, rev. — direct high). Controls: low foot pedal, rev., high lever to right low, rev. bands, high — disc clutch. Chain drive. Spur gear differential. Overall ratio: 3.1:1 to 5:1 (see drivetrain options). Mechanical brakes on two wheels contracting on inboard drums. Wood wheels 12 spoke. Wheel size: 24 in.

Drivetrain Options: Different combinations of 9 or 10 tooth driving sprocket with 31, 34, 38, 41, or 45 tooth driven sprocket gave ten possible ratios from 3.1:1 to 5:1. Lower ratios for runabout to be run on smooth, level roads to higher ratios for loaded delivery to be run on rough, hilly roads. Instructions for changing sprockets were furnished to owners, but the change involved disassembly of the transmission and rear axle, definitely not a "quick-change" set-up.

Model D: Planetary transmission. Speeds: 3F/1R. Right-hand drive, controls to right. Clutch: twin disc in flywheel, disc and three bands on transmission. Shaft drive. Live axle, bevel drive, spur gear differential. Mechanical brakes on two wheels — service-lever-rear drums — emergency-pedal-drive shaft. Wood artillery wheels, 12 spoke. Wheel size: 25 in. Model E: Planetary transmission. Speeds: 2F/1R (3:1 low, rev. direct high). Controls: low — foot pedal, rev., high — lever to right. Low, rev. — bands. High disc clutch. Chain drive. Spur gear differential. Overall ratio: 3.1:1 to 5:1 (see drivetrain options). Mechanical brakes on two wheels — contracting on inboard drums. Wood wheels — 12 spoke. Wheel size: 22 in.

Drivetrain Options: Model E: Same as Models B & C. Model F: Planetary transmission. Speeds: 2F/1R, (3:1 low, rev. — direct high). Controls: low — foot pedal, rev., high — lever to right. Low, rev. bands, High — disc clutch. Chain drive. Spur gear differential. Overall ratio 3.1:1 to 5:1 (see drivetrain options). Mechanical brakes on two wheels contracting on inboard drums. Wood wheels — 12 spoke (14 spoke on prototype). Wheel size: 23 in.

Drivetrain Options: Same as Models B & C.

OPTIONS: (Model B) Bulb horn. Lights. Rear deck to replace tonneau ($10.00). (Models C & F) Bulb horn. Lights. (Model E) Bulb horn. Lights. Leather top w/sides and storm apron (50.00). Rubber top w/sides and storm apron (30.00)

HISTORICAL: Model B: Introduced 1904. Calendar year sales and production: 4029 with C, E, F. Model year sales and production: same. Model C: Introduced summer 1905. Calendar year sales and production was a limited percent of 4,029 with B, E, F. Model year sales and production: same. Model D: Introduced January 1905. Innovations: Three speed planetary transmission. Governed throttle. Variable lift inlet valve gear on multi-cylinder engine. Calendar year sales and production: 156. Model year sales and production: same. The president of Cadillac was C.A. Black.

Note: After designing the one-cylinder and Model D Cadillacs, Alanson Brush left L&F/Cadillac and extracted lump sum and royalty payments for use of his patents. This action triggered a plan to purge Cadillac design of Brush influence.

Model E: Introduced January 1905. Calendar year sales and production: 4,029. Model year sales and production: same.

Note: Cadillac Automobile Co. and Leland & Faulconer merged in October 1905 to form Cadillac Motor Car Co. Henry Leland became general manager of the new company. Maximum production capability one car every ten minutes of each ten-hour working day.

Model F: Introduced January 1905. Calendar year sales and production: 4,029 with B, C, E. Model year sales and production: same.

Note: The new front end styling was recognized as a desirable improvement. Not only did Cadillac update Model Bs with the Model F "hood" and radiator (Model C), but owners of As and Bs had the new nose grafted to their cars. There was even an aftermarket supplier of update kits.

1906 CADILLAC

CADILLAC — MODEL K — ONE: Chassis same as 1905 except spark control now on steering column and oiler has mechanical feed from a cam on the hub of the flywheel. Straight-side Dunlop tires are now standard equipment. Bodies restyled. All 1906 one-cylinder passenger car bodies now victoria style. Dash now pressed steel and corners of "hood" rounded. This "hood" and dash treatment was used through 1908. 1906 cars can be identified by long muffler and severe cant to the nose of the front fenders. Tops were not shown in catalogs but undoubtedly were available. Cadillac was setting up its own top department and would be offering Cadillac-made tops for 1907.

1906 Cadillac, Model M, touring, OCW

CADILLAC — MODEL M — ONE: Same as 1906 Model K except for body styles and two-inch longer wheelbase.

CADILLAC — MODEL L — FOUR: Based on 1905 Model D.

Bodies: Cadillac's first offering of a limousine body. Cadillac's first use of auxiliary (rear facing) seats in touring tonneau to give seven-passenger seating capacity.

Engine: Bore increased from 4-3/8 to 5 in.; mixer replaced by throttled, float feed, jet type carburetor; hydraulic governor replaced by centrifugal ring-type governor linked to carburetor throttle butterfly; variable lift inlet valve feature dropped, commutator shaft changed from horizontal to vertical.

Chassis: Change in commutator drive allowed for shorter hood, dash now pressed steel; wheelbase lengthened to 110 in.; service and emergency brakes both act on rear drums.

1906 Cadillac, Model H, coupe, HAC

CADILLAC — MODEL H — FOUR: Same as Model L except no limousine offered; touring is five-passenger; runabout and first production Cadillac coupe offered. Wheelbase 102 in.; tires 32 x 4; rear springs 3/4 elliptic.

Note: Early ads, advance catalogs, and the 1906 ALAM Handbook listed the wheelbase of the Model H as 100 in. rather than the actual 102 in.

I.D. DATA: Model K & M serial numbers on plate on rear of body (with engine number). Engine numbers were stamped two places on crankcase: 1. Top, right edge of cylinder flange, near water outlet. 2. Top surface of left, front mounting leg. Also on plate on rear of body (with serial number). (Blank spaces on patent plate are for additional patent dates, not engine or serial number.) Engine Nos.: 8350-10000 with M, 20001-21850 with M, 21851-22150 with M (1906-1907). Model L serial numbers on plate on rear of body or on dash (with engine No.). Engine numbers were stamped on top surface of crankcase — in front of and to the left of number one (front) cylinder. Model H serial numbers on plate on rear of body or on dash (with engine No.). Engine numbers were stamped on top surface of crankcase — in front of and to the left of number one (front) cylinder. Engine Nos.: 10201-10709 (1906-1908).

Model No.	Body Type & Seating	Price	Weight	Prod. Total
Model K				
NA	Vic. Rbt.-2P	750	1100	—
Model M				
NA	2-dr. Vic. Tr.-4P	950	—	—
NA	Delivery-2P	950	—	—
Model L				
NA	2-dr. Tr.-5/7P	3750	2850	—
NA	2-dr. Limo.-7P	5000	3600	—
Model H				
NA	2-dr. Tr.-5P	2500	2400	—
NA	Rbt.-2P	2400	—	—
NA	2-dr. Cpe.-2P	3000	2500	—

Note: The weight of the Model K victoria runabout is approximate.

ENGINE: Models K&M: Horizontal, with cylinder to rear. One. Cast iron cylinder. With copper water jacket. B & S: 5 x 5 in.

Disp.: 98.2 cu. in. Brake H.P.: "Higher than advertised or calculated H.P." Advertised H.P.: 10. (ALAM, NACC, SAE H.P. calculated by identical formulae.) (ALAM first used formula in 1908). Main bearings: Two. Valve lifters: Mechanical (see "Description") Carb.: Updraft mixer, manufactured by Cadillac. Model L: Vertical, in-line, L-head. Four. Individual cast iron cylinder, copper water jacket. B & S: 5 x 5 in. Disp.: 392.7 cu. in. Advertised H.P.: 40. Five main bearings. Valve lifters: mechanical. Carb.: throttled, float feed, jet type made by Cadillac. Model H: Vertical, in-line, L-head. Four. Individual cast iron cylinder, copper water jacket. B & S: 4-3/8 x 5 in. Disp.: 300.7 cu. in. Advertised H.P.: 30. Main bearings: Five. Valve lifters: Mechanical. Carb.: throttled, float feed, jet type made by Cadillac.

CHASSIS: (Model K) W.B.: 74 in. O.L.: 9 ft., 2 in. Height: 4 ft., 6 in. Front/Rear Tread: 56 in. (61 opt). Tires: 28 x 3. (Model M Touring) W.B.: 76 in. O.L.: 9 ft., 7 in. Height: 5 ft., 6 in. Front/Rear Tread: 56 in. (61 opt). Tires: 30 x 3-1/2. (Model M Delivery) W.B.: 76 in. Front/Rear Tread: 56 in. Tires: 30 x 3-1/2. (Model L Touring) W.B.: 110 in. O.L.: approx. 13 ft., 3 in. Height: approx. 6 ft., 3 in. Front/Rear Tread: 56-1/2 in. Tires: 36 x 4 front, 36 x 4-1/2 rear. (Model L Limousine) W.B.: 110 in. O.L.: approx. 13 ft., 6 in. Height: approx. 7 ft., 5 in. Front/Rear Tread: 56-1/2 in. Tires: 36 x 4 front, 36 x 5 rear. (Model H) W.B.: 102 in. Front/Rear Tread: 56-1/2 in. Tires: 32 x 4.

TECHNICAL: Model K&M: Planetary transmission. Speeds: 2F/1R (3:1 low, rev. — direct high). Controls: low — foot pedal, rev., high — lever to right. Low, rev. — bands, High — disc clutch. Chain drive. Spur gear differential. Overall ratio: 3.1:1 to 5:1 (see drivetrain options). Mechanical brakes on two wheels — contracting on inboard drums. Wood wheels 12 spoke. Model K wheel size: 22 in. Model M: 23 in.

Drivetrain Options: Different combinations of 9 or 10 tooth driving sprocket with 31, 34, 38, 41, or 45 tooth driven sprocket gave ten possible ratios from 3.1:1 to 5:1. Lower ratios for runabout to be run on smooth, level roads to higher ratios for loaded delivery to be run on rough, hilly roads. Instructions for changing sprockets were furnished to owners, but the change involved disassembly of the transmission and rear axle, definitely not a "quick-change" set-up.

Model L&H: Planetary transmission. Speeds: 3F/1R. Right-hand drive, controls to right. Clutch: Twin disc in flywheel, disc and three bands on transmission. Shaft drive. Live axle, bevel drive, bevel differential. Mechanical brakes on two wheels — service and emergency on rear drums. Wood artillery wheels, 12 spoke. Wheel size (Model L): 28 front, touring rear 27, limousine rear 26 in. (Model H) 24 in.

OPTIONS: Model K: Bulb horn. Lights. Rubber top with sides and storm apron ($30.00). Leather top with sides and storm apron (50.00). Model M: Bulb horn. Lights. Cape cart top for Touring (75.00). Model L: Bulb horn. Lights. Touring top (150.00). Model H: Bulb horn. Lights. Touring top (125.00). Runabout top (50.00).

HISTORICAL: Models K & M: Introduced January 1906. Calendar year sales and production: 3,650 K & M. Model year sales and production: same. Model L: Introduced January 1906. Calendar year sales and production: Unknown — probably limited. Model year sales and production: same. The president of Cadillac was C.A. Black.

Note: Except for the V-16s, the Model L engine displacement was not equalled in a production Cadillac engine until 1964. Wm. K. Vanderbilt, Jr., owned a Model L Cadillac, but this type of customer was rare. Cadillac needed high production to make the concept of interchangeable parts pay off.

Model H: Introduced January 1906. Calendar year sales and production: 509 (1906-1908). Model year sales and production: same.

Note: Purge of Alanson Brush design features started. Mixer and variable inlet valve opening no longer used on four-cylinder Cadillacs. The real start of the purge was the design of the Model G for 1907.

1907 CADILLAC

CADILLAC — MODEL G — FOUR: Although the Model L Cadillac limousine had a planetary transmission and 5 x 5 bore and stroke like the single-cylinder Cadillac runabout, the two models were entirely opposite in concept. The single-cylinder was a horseless carriage for the masses, the Model L a Nabob's throne-on-wheels. Whether due to the Alanson Brush patent squabble, acute marketing perception, or both, Cadillac came up with a four-cylinder design that met the expectations of customers who wanted just a bit more than the best one-cylinder car could offer — an inexpensive, easily maintained, long lasting, precision built car — a "single-cylinder Cadillac with four cylinders" — the Model G.

1907 Cadillac, Model K, light runabout, HAC

CADILLAC — MODEL M — ONE: Chassis same as Model K except for two-inch longer wheelbase. Additional body styles offered. Straight-line touring again available. Folding tonneau new, tonneau folds to look like runabout but this body not available on shorter Model K chassis. First production one-cylinder coupe offered.

I.D. DATA: Model G & H serial numbers on plate on rear of body or on dash (with engine No.). Engine numbers were stamped on top surface of crankcase — in front of and to the left of number one (front) cylinder. Model G engine Nos.: 30003-30425 (1907), 30426-30500 (1907-1908). Model H engine Nos.: 10201-10709 (1906-1908). Model K & M serial numbers on plate on rear of body (with engine No.). Engine numbers were stamped two places on crankcase. 1. Top, right edge of cylinder flange, near water outlet. 2. Top surface of left, front mounting leg. Also on plate on rear of body (with serial number). (Blank spaces on patent plate are for additional patent dates, not engine or serial number.) Engine No. 2185122150 with M (1906-1907), 22151-24075 with M, 24075-24350 with M, S, T.

1907 Cadillac, Model M, victoria touring, OCW

Engine: Four cylinder, 4 x 4-1/2 in., L-head, 20 H.P.; cylinders cast singly, copper water jackets, detachable combustion valve chamber, main bearings replaceable without removing crankshaft; interchangeable inlet and exhaust valves operated by pushrod and roller cam follower on single gear driven camshaft; belt driven fan, water pump, and oiler; splash lubrication; three-point engine suspension; float-feed carburetor controlled by foot throttle or automatic ring-type governor; clockwise cranking.

Chassis: Pressed steel frame; two half-elliptic front, two full-elliptic rear springs; foot brake internal, hand brake external on rear drums; worm and sector steering mechanism.

Driveline: Leather-faced cone clutch; selective sliding gear transmission, independently attached to frame; single universal in driveshaft to bevel driveline rear axle with spur gear differential.

Bodies: Two-door, five-passenger touring and three-passenger (single rumble) runabout, both with wooden dash. Cadillac-built tops available at extra cost.

CADILLAC — MODEL H — FOUR: Same as 1906 Model H except body lines of touring simplified and five-passenger limousine offered.

CADILLAC — MODEL K — ONE: Chassis same as 1906 except muffler much shorter with outlet at front rather than side, oiler drive changed from cam to pulley and belt, and engine/transmission drip pan added. Runabout bodies remained the same as 1906 but front fenders were changed — nose of fender was now flattened and an inside skirt was added (early 1907 catalogs still showed the canted fender). For the first time, a factory-installed-only victoria style top was offered, as well as a buggy top.

Model No.	Body Type & Seating	Price	Weight	Prod. Total
Model G				
NA	2-dr. Tr.-5P	2000	—	—
NA	Rbt.-2P	2000	—	—
NA	Rbt.-3P	2000	—	—
Model H				
NA	2-dr. Tr.-5P	2500	—	—
NA	2-dr. Limo.-6P	3600	—	—
NA	Rbt.-2P	2400	—	—
NA	2-dr. Cpe.-2P	3000	—	—
Model K				
NA	Vic. Rbt.-2P	800	1100	—
NA	W/Vic. top	925	—	—
Model M				
NA	2-dr. Straight line Tr.-4P	950	1350	—
NA	2-dr. Vic. Tr.-4P	950	—	—
NA	Folding Tonneau-4P	1000	—	—
NA	2-dr. Cpe.-2P	1350	—	—
NA	Del.-2P	950	—	—

Note: Weights are approximate.

ENGINE: Model G & H: Vertical, in-line, L-head. Four. Individual cast iron cylinder, copper water jacket. (Model G) B & S: 4 x 4-1/2 in. (Model H) B & S: 4-3/8 x 5 in. Model G Disp.: 226.2 cu. in. Model H Disp.: 300.7 cu. in. Model G advertised H.P.: 20. Model H advertised H.P.: 30. Main bearings: five. Valve lifters: mechanical. Carb.: throttled, float feed, jet type made by Cadillac. Models K & M: Horizontal, with cylinder to rear. One cylinder. Cast iron cylinder, with copper water jacket. B & S: 5 x 5 in. Disp.: 98.2 cu. in. Brake H.P.: "Higher than advertised or calculated H.P." Advertised H.P.: 10. (ALAM, NACC, SAE H.P. calculated by identical formulae.) (ALAM first used formula in 1908.) Main bearings: two. Valve lifters: mechanical. Carb.: updraft mixer, manufactured by Cadillac.

CHASSIS: (Model K) W.B.: 74 in. O.L.: 9 ft., 2 in. Height: 5 ft., 6 in. Front/Rear Tread: 56 in. (61 opt). Tires: 30 x 3. (Model M Touring) W.B.: 76 in. O.L.: 9 ft., 7 in. Height: 5 ft., 2 in. Front/Rear Tread: 56 in. (61 opt). Tires: 30 x 3-1/2. (Model M other bodies) W.B.: 76 in. Front/Rear Tread: 56 in. (61 opt). Tires: 30 x 3-1/2. (Model G) W.B.: 100 in. Front/Rear Tread: 56 in. Tires: 32 x 3-1/2. (Model H) W.B.: 102 in. Front/Rear Tread: 56-1/2 in. Tires: 32 x 4.

TECHNICAL: Model G: Selective sliding gear transmission. Speeds: 3F/1R. Right-hand drive, controls to right, Leather-faced cone clutch. Shaft drive. Live axle, bevel drive, spur gear differential. Mechanical brakes on two wheels — service and emergency on rear drums. Wood artillery wheels, 10 spoke front, 12 spoke rear. Wheel size: 25 in. Model H: Planetary transmission. Speeds 3F/1R. Right-hand drive, controls to right. Twin disc in flywheel. Disc and three bands on transmission. Shaft drive. Live axle, bevel drive, bevel differential. Mechanical brakes on two wheels — service and emergency on rear drums. Wood artillery wheels, 12 spoke. Wheel size: 24 in. Models K & M: Planetary transmission. Speeds: 2F/1R (3:1 low, rev. direct high). Low — foot pedal, rev., high — lever to right. Low, rev. bands, high — disc clutch. Chain drive. Spur gear differential. Overall ratio: 3.1:1 to 5:1 (see drivetrain options). Mechanical brakes on two wheels — contracting on inboard drums. Wood wheels — 12 spoke. Model K wheel size: 24 in., Model M: 23 in.

Drivetrain Options: (Model K & M) Different combinations of 9 or 10 tooth driving sprocket with 31, 34, 38, 41, or 45 tooth driven sprocket gave 10 possible ratios from 3.1:1 to 5:1. Lower ratios for runabout to be run on smooth, level roads to higher ratios for loaded delivery to be run on rough, hilly roads. Instructions for changing sprockets were furnished to owners, but the change involved disassembly of the transmission and rear axle, definitely not a "quick-change" set-up.

OPTIONS: Model G: Bulb horn. Lights. Cape cart top for touring ($120.00). Note: Tops now being manufactured by Cadillac. Model H: Bulb horn. Lights. Touring top ($150.00). Model K: Bulb horn. Lights. Rubber top w/side curtains and storm apron (40.00). Leather top w/side curtains and storm apron (70.00). Model M: Bulb horn. Lights. Rubber cloth cape cart top for touring (100.00).

HISTORICAL: Model G: Introduced January 1907. Calendar year sales and production: 1,030 (1907-1908). Model year sales and production: same. President of Cadillac was C.A. Black. Model G was first Cadillac without major Alanson Brush design influence. Model H: Introduced 1906. Calendar year sales and production: 509 (1906-1908). Model year sales and production: same. Models K & M: Introduced 1906. Calendar year sales and production: 2,350 with M, K, S, T. Model year sales and production: same. In February-March 1908, three late 1907 Model Ks successfully completed the Royal Automobile Club's Standardization Test. As a result of these test results, the Cadillac Automobile Company was awarded the Dewar Trophy for 1908 (actual award date was February 1909). The Dewar Trophy was an annual award for the most important advancement of the year in the automobile industry.

1908 CADILLAC

CADILLAC — MODEL G — FOUR: Same as 1907 Model G except; limousine added to the line; one-or two-passenger rumbleseats available, of different pattern than the single rumble of 1907.

Note: There were no changes in the Model G engine for 1908, but the advertised horsepower rating was increased from 20 to 25. This was due to the newly instituted ALAM horsepower formula, which gave the Model G a horsepower rating of 25.6. Cadillac had always been conservative in horsepower ratings. The ALAM rating was also conservative, and gave the same rating to every engine with the same bore and number of cylinders. There was no allowance for design, accuracy or precision of manufacture, superior

practice in fits and tolerances, etc. Cadillac, although having had a voice in establishing the ALAM formula, soon took exception to being rated the same as the least sophisticated manufacturer. Although engines were tested for actual developed horsepower, it was to be many years before horsepower curves were publicized.

1908 Cadillac, Model G, limousine, HAC

CADILLAC — MODEL H — FOUR: Same as 1907 Model H except: coupe body dropped from the line; touring body now similar to Model G, with continuous molding across center of doors. Engine speed governor and interlock between brakes and clutch no longer supplied. Tire size increased to 34 x 4.

CADILLAC — MODEL M — ONE: Offered as delivery only. Same as 1907 delivery except that prices now include two oil side lamps, an oil tail lamp, and a bulb horn. Headlamps would not be included as standard equipment on Cadillacs until 1910. Does not have longer wheelbase or runningboards of Models S & T.

CADILLAC — MODEL S — ONE: Chassis same as 1907 except wheelbase on all body styles increased to 82 in., and full runningboards replaced step plates. Single and double rumbleseat options on straight line or victoria styles were available on runabouts. If rumbleseat passengers were to be carried regularly, tire size increase from 30 x 3 to 30 x 3-1/2 was recommended.

CADILLAC — MODEL T — ONE: Chassis same as Model S except coupe did not have runningboards. Bodies were same as 1907 Model M except folding tonneau was dropped. Victoria style top now available for tonneau of victoria touring.

I.D. DATA: Model G & H serial numbers on plate on rear of body or on dash (with engine Nos.). Engine numbers were stamped on top surface of crankcase — in front of and to the left of number one (front) cylinder. Model G engine Nos.: 30426-30500 (1907-1908), 30501-31032 (1908). Model H engine Nos: 10201-10709 (1906-1908). Model M, S, & T serial numbers on plate on rear of body with engine number. Engine numbers were stamped two places on crankcase: 1. Top, right edge of cylinder flange, near water outlet. 2. Top surface of left, front mounting leg. Also on plate on rear of body (with serial number). (Blank spaces on patent plate are for additional patent dates, not engine or serial number.) Model M engine Nos.: 24075-24350 with K, S, T (1907). Model S engine Nos.: 24075-24350 with K, M, T (1907), 24351-25832 with T. Model T engine Nos.: 24075-24350 with K, M, S (1907), 24351-25832 with S.

Model No.	Body Type & Seating	Price	Weight	Prod. Total
Model G				
NA	2-dr. Tr.-5P	2000	—	—
NA	2-dr. Limo.-5P	3000	—	—
NA	Rbt.-3P	2000	—	—
NA	Rbt.-4P	2025	—	—
Model H				
NA	2-dr. Tr.-5P	2500	—	—
NA	2-dr. Limo.-6P	3600	—	—
NA	Rbt.-2P	2400	—	—
Model M				
NA	Delivery-2P	950	—	—
Model S				
NA	Straight Line Rbt.-2P	850	—	—
NA	Vic. Rbt.-2P	850	—	—

NA	Vic. Rbt. w/single rumble	875	—	—	
NA	St. Line Rbt. w/double rumble	885	—	—	
Model T					
NA	2-dr. St. Line Tr.-4P	1000	—	—	
NA	2-dr. Vic. Tr.-4P	1000	—	—	
NA	2-dr. Cpe.-2P	1350	—	—	

1908 Cadillac, Model S, runabout with rumble, HAC

ENGINE: Model H: Vertical, in-line, L-head. Four. Individual cast iron cylinder, copper water jacket. (Model G) B & S: 4 x 4-1/2 in. (Model H) B & S: 4-3/8 x 5 in. Model G Disp.: 226.2 cu. in. Model H Disp.: 300.7 cu. in. (Model G) ALAM H.P.: 25.6. Advertised H.P.: 25. (Model H) ALAM H.P.: 30.625. Advertised H.P. 30. Main bearings: five. Valve lifters: mechanical. Carb.: throttled, float feed, jet type made by Cadillac. Models M, S, & T: Horizontal, with cylinder to rear. One. Cast iron cylinder, with copper water jacket. B & S: 5 x 5 in. Disp.: 98.2 cu. in. Brake H.P.: "Higher than advertised or calculated H.P." Advertised/ALAM H.P.: 10. (ALAM, NACC, SAE horsepower calculated by identical formulae.) (ALAM first used formula in 1908.) Main bearings: two. Valve lifters: mechanical. Carb.: updraft mixer, manufactured by Cadillac.

CHASSIS: (Model M Delivery) W.B.: 76 in. Front/Rear Tread: 56. Tires: 30 x 3-1/2. (Model S) W.B.: 82 in. O.L.: 10 ft., 1 in. Height: 5 ft., 4 in. Front/Rear Tread: 56 in. (61 opt) Tires: 30 x 3. (Model T Touring) W.B.: 82 in. O.L.: 10 ft., 2 in. Height: 5 ft., 4 in. Front/Rear Tread: 56 in. (61 opt). Tires: 30 x 3-1/2. (Model T Coupe) W.B.: 82 in. Front/Rear Tread: 56 in. (61 opt). Tires: 30 x 3-1/2. (Model G) W.B.: 100 in. Front/Rear Tread: 56 in. Tires: 32 x 31/2 (34 x 4 limousine). (Model H) W.B.: 102 in. Front/Rear Tread: 56-1/2 in. Tires: 34 x 4.

TECHNICAL: Model G: Selective sliding gear transmission. Speeds: 3F/1R. Right-hand drive, controls to right. Leather-faced cone clutch. Shaft drive. Live axle, bevel drive, spur gear differential. Mechanical brakes on two wheels — service and emergency on rear drums. Wood artillery wheels, 10 spoke front, 12 spoke rear. Wheel size: Touring and roadster 25 in., Limousine 26 in. Model H: Planetary transmission. Speeds: 3F/1R. Right-hand drive, controls to right. Twin disc in flywheel, disc and three bands on transmission. Shaft drive. Live axle, bevel drive, bevel differential. Mechanical brakes on two wheels — service and emergency on rear drums. Wood artillery wheels, 12 spoke. Wheel size: 26 in. Models M, S & T: Planetary transmission. Speeds: 2F/1R (3:1 low, rev. — direct high). Low — foot pedal, rev., high — lever to right. Low, rev. — bands, high — disc clutch. Chain drive. Spur gear differential. Overall ratio: 3.1:1 to 5:1 (see drivetrain options). Mechanical brakes on two wheels — contracting on inboard drums. Wood wheels — 12 spoke. Models M & T wheel size: 23 in., Model S: 24 in.

Drivetrain Options: (Models M, S, & T) Different combinations of 9 or 10 tooth driving sprocket with 31, 34, 38, 41, or 45 tooth driven sprocket gave ten possible ratios from 3.1:1 to 5:1. Lower ratios for runabout to be run on smooth, level roads to higher ratios for loaded delivery to be run on rough, hilly roads. Instructions for changing sprockets were furnished by owners, but the change involved disassembly of the transmission and rear axle, definitely not a "quick-change" set-up.

OPTIONS: Model G: Headlights. Rubber, leather, and mohair tops in three-bow, cape cart, and victoria styles ($90.00 to 200.00). Model H: Headlights. Lined cape cart top for touring (150.00). Model M: Headlights. Model S: Headlights. 30 x 3-1/2 tires on runabouts with rumble (50.00). Rubber top with side curtains and storm apron (60.00). Leather top with side curtains and storm apron (80.00). Victoria style top (factory installed only) (175.00). Storm front w/windows to replace storm apron (15.00). Model T: Headlights. Cape cart top (115.00). Victoria style top (factory installed only) (175.00).

HISTORICAL: Model G: Introduced November 1907. Calendar year sales and production: 1,030 (1907-1908). Model year sales and production: same. The president of Cadillac was C.A. Black.

Note: The bulky, complicated, planetary transmission, luxury fours were too great a first leap from the single cylinder, which had become passé. The compromise Model G design formed a solid basis for the "Thirty," which was to be the single line for Cadillac through 1914. Had Brush design concepts been perpetuated, the company might well have failed. Its move into a firm position in the luxury car field was to wait another seven years.

Model H: Introduced June 1907. Calendar year sales and production: 509 (1906-1908). Model year sales and production: same.

Note: The last of the planetary transmission fours and the last of counterclockwise cranking for Cadillac. The only remaining Brush features were to be the copper water jacket and the splash lube system; both of these were in use by Cadillac through 1914.

Model M: Introduced 1906. Model year production: Included with 1907. Models S & T: Introduced November 1907. Calendar year sales and production: 1,482 with S & T. Model year sales and production: same.

Note: Several hundred of the approximately 16,000 single-cylinder Cadillacs produced still exist in the hands of collectors all over the world. A prominent Australian collector visiting Hershey remarked, "Anyone wanting to restore, drive, and enjoy a one-cylinder car best find a Cadillac" — no argument, mate.

See page 6 for "How to Use This Catalog"

1909 CADILLAC

1909 Cadillac, Thirty, touring, OCW

CADILLAC — MODEL "THIRTY" — FOUR: After an inauspicious trial in the luxury car field, and recognizing the disappearing market for the single-cylinder cars that made their reputation, Cadillac settled down with a design that had originated in 1906 (the 1907-1908 Model G). With inhouse mass production of a single line, Cadillac was able to offer a high quality automobile at a moderate price: $1,400 for the Model "Thirty" as compared to $2,000 for the Model G.

The "Thirty" differed from the Model G as follows:

Bodies: No closed bodies offered. Detachable tonneau once again available. Steel doors and cowl on roadster and demi-tonneau. Flaring, twisted front fenders replaced by flat fenders with filler between fender and frame. Full runningboards and runningboard dust shields on all bodies. No louvers in hood. Bodies finished (painted) by Cadillac.

Chassis: 3/4 platform rear spring system. Single dropped frame. Wheelbase lengthened to 106 in. In mid-year, brake drum diameter was increased to 12 in.

Driveline: Transmission refined and mounted at three points to frame cross members rather than at four points to frame side rails. Universal joint housed in ball joint at rear of transmission. Rear axle with bevel gear differential made by American Ball Bearing.

Engine: Drive for water pump (gear type) and oiler changed from external belt to internal gears. Gear driven accessory shaft allows for optional magneto. Speed governor no longer used.

I.D. DATA: Serial numbers on plate on rear of body or on dash (with engine No.). Engine numbers were stamped on top surface of crankcase — in front of and to the left of number one (front) cylinder. Starting: 32002. Ending: 37904.

Model No.	Body Type & Seating	Price	Weight	Prod. Total
NA	2-dr. Touring-5P	1400	—	—
NA	2-dr. Demi-Tonneau-4P	1400	—	—
NA	Roadster-3P	1400	—	—

ENGINE: Vertical, in-line, L-head. Four. Individual cast iron cylinder copper, water jacket. B & S: 4 x 4-1/2 in. Disp.: 226.2 cu. in. Brake H.P.: 30. ALAM H.P.: 25.6. Main bearings: five. Valve lifters: mechanical-pushrod-roller cam followers. Carb.: float feed; made by Cadillac.

CHASSIS: W.B.: 106 in. Front/Rear Tread: 56 in. (61 opt.) Tires: 32 x 3-1/2.

TECHNICAL: Selective, sliding gear transmission. Speeds: 3F/1R. Right-hand drive, controls to right. Leather-faced cone clutch. Shaft drive. Plain live rear axle, bevel drive, bevel gear differential. Overall ratio: tour., demi-tonn. 3.5:1, roadster 3:1. Mechanical brakes on two wheels — Service/foot/contracting — emergency/lever/expanding. Wood artillery wheels, 10 and 12 spoke, quick detachable rims. Wheel rim size: 25 in. Optional final drive ratios: 3:1, 3.5:1, 4:1.

OPTIONS: Seat covers ($45.00-75.00). "Rubber," mohair, or leather tops (55.00-125.00). Bosch, Dow, Eisemann, or Splitdorf magnetos (100.00-126.00). Rushmore style B headlamps with Rushmore No. 1 generator (46.50); with Prest-O-Lite style B tank (59.50). Mezger windshield (50.00). Gabriel horns, styles 1, 2, 3, 4 (15.00-35.00). Stewart & Clark speedometer (15.00-40.00).

HISTORICAL: Introduced December 1908. Calendar year sales and production: 5,903. Model year sales and production: same. The president/general manager of Cadillac was Henry Leland. On July 29, 1909, Cadillac Motor Car Co. became a wholly owned subsidiary of General Motors Co., and Henry Leland became president and general manager of Cadillac Motor Car Co.

1910 Cadillac, Thirty, limousine, HAC

CADILLAC — MODEL "THIRTY" — FOUR: Same as 1909 except: basic price increased to $1,600.

Bodies: Only open cars advertised before April 1910. Limousine in early catalog, coupe added in later catalog. Closed bodies by Fisher. Touring body of wood, large (rear) panel of demi-tonneau and all doors of steel.

Chassis: Gas headlamps now standard. Wheelbase lengthened to 110 in. (120 in. on limousine).

Driveline: In mid-year, rear axle was changed to Timken semi-floating.

Engine: Bore increased to 4-1/4 in. Dual ignition consisting of new Delco four coil system and low tension magneto. Mid-year change to centrifugal water pump.

I.D. DATA: Serial numbers on plate on rear of body or on dash (with engine No.). Engine numbers were stamped on top surface of crankcase — in front of and to the left of number one (front) cylinder. Starting: 40001. Ending: 48008.

Model No.	Body Type & Seating	Price	Weight	Prod. Total
NA	2-dr. Touring-5P	1600	—	—
NA	2-dr. Demi-Tonneau-4P	1600	—	—
NA	Roadster-2P	1600	—	—
NA	Roadster-3P	1600	—	—
NA	2-dr. Limo.-7P	3000	—	—
NA	2-dr. Coupe-3P	2200	—	—

ENGINE: Vertical, in-line, L-head. Four. Individual cast iron cylinder, copper water jacket. B & S: 4-1/4 x 4-1/2 in. Disp.: 255.4 cu. in. Brake H.P.: 33. ALAM H.P.: 28.9. Main bearings: five. Valve lifters: mechanical-pushrod-roller cam followers. Carb.: float feed — made by Cadillac.

CHASSIS: All except limousine W.B.: 110 in. Front/Rear Tread: 56 in. (61 opt). Tires: 34 x 4. Limousine. W.B.: 120 in. Tires: 34 x 4-1/2.

TECHNICAL: Selective, sliding gear transmission. 3F/1R. Right-hand drive, controls to right. Leather-faced cone clutch. Shaft drive. Live; bevel drive; bevel gear differential; ABB plain/Timken semi-floating. Overall ratio: 3.5:1 (limousine 4:1). Mechanical brakes on two wheels. Service/foot/contracting — emergency/lever/expanding. Wood artillery wheels, 10 and 12 spoke, quick detachable rims. Wheel size: 26 in. (limousine 25 in.). Optional final drive ratios: 3:1, 4:1.

OPTIONS: Seat covers ($40.00-60.00). "Rubber" or mohair tops (55.00-95.00). Prest-O-Lite style B tank (25.00). Windshield (30.00). Jones speedometer No. 29, 33, 34 (25.00-35.00). Foot rail (3.50).

HISTORICAL: Introduced November 1909. Innovations: Delco ignition system. Model year sales: 8,008. Model year production: 8,008. President and general manager of Cadillac was Henry Leland.

Note: In the early days of automobiling in America, open cars and poor travel conditions precluded winter motoring. Manufacturers displayed samples at the winter auto shows and took orders for spring and summer delivery. Cadillac's model year coincided with the calendar year and the year's production was presold.

In 1910, Cadillac got more heavily into closed cars and had a solid reputation for quality and value. With a ready demand for their full factory capacity, they introduced the 1911 models in late summer of 1910 and had delivered a significant percentage of the 1911 model production by the start of the calendar year. Cadillac was now producing below demand and customers were willing to accept delivery at any time or wait as long as necessary for delivery.

1911 CADILLAC

1911 Cadillac, Thirty, touring, OCW

CADILLAC — MODEL "THIRTY" — FOUR: Same as 1910 except: basic price increased to $1,700.

Bodies: First front (fore) door on an open Cadillac body — left side only on fore-door touring and torpedo. Torpedo body all steel on wood frame. Limousine body interchangeable with touring and coupe body interchangeable with demi-tonneau (an inducement to year-round motoring).

Chassis: Wheelbase lengthened to 116 in. Brake drum diameter increased to 14 in. Double dropped frame.

Driveline: Rear axle changed to Timken full floating, with torsion arm and two universal joints in the driveshaft.

Engine: Bore increased to 4-1/2 in. Schebler Model L carburetor used. Bosch high tension magneto and Delco single coil system used for dual ignition.

I.D. DATA: Serial numbers on plate on dash (with engine No.) Engine numbers were stamped on top surface of crankcase — in front of and to the left of number one (front) cylinder. Starting: 50000. Ending: 60018.

Model No.	Body Type & Seating	Price	Weight	Prod. Total
NA	2-dr. Touring-5P	1700	—	—
NA	2-dr. Demi-Tonneau-4P	1700	—	—
NA	3-dr. Fore-door Tr.-5P	1800	—	—
NA	3-dr. Torpedo-4P	1850	—	—
NA	Roadster-2P	1700	—	—
NA	Roadster-3P	1700	—	—
NA	2-dr. Limo.-7P	3000	—	—
NA	2-dr. Coupe-3P	2250	—	—

ENGINE: Vertical, in-line, L-head. Four. Individual cast iron cylinder, copper water jacket. B & S: 4-1/2 x 4-1/2 in. Disp.: 286.3. cu in. ALAM H.P.: 32.4. Main bearings: five. Valve lifters: mechanical-pushrod-roller cam followers. Carb.: float feed: Schebler Model L.

CHASSIS: All except limousine W.B.: 116 in. Front/Rear Tread: 56 in. (61 opt). Tires: 34 x 4. Limousine tires: 36 x 4-1/2.

TECHNICAL: Selective, sliding gear transmission. Speeds: 3F/1R. Right-hand drive, controls to right. Leather-faced cone clutch. Shaft drive. Full-floating rear axle, bevel drive, bevel gear differential. Overall ratio: 3.43:1 (roadster 3.05:1, limousine 3.66:1). Mechanical brakes on two wheels — Service/foot/contracting — emergency/lever/expanding. Wood artillery wheels, 10 and 12 spoke, quick detachable rims. Wheel size: 26 in. (limousine. 27 in.). Optional final drive ratios: 3.43:1, 3.66:1.

OPTIONS: Seat covers ($40.00-60.00). Mohair tops (65.00-90.00). Prest-O-Lite style B tank (25.00). Windshield (40.00). Jones electric horn, with storage battery (40.00).

HISTORICAL: Introduced August 1910. Model year sales: 10,019. Model year production: 10,019. The president and general manager of Cadillac was Henry Leland.

1912 CADILLAC

1912 Cadillac, Four, roadster, HAC

1912 CADILLAC — FOUR: Same as 1911 except: basic price increased to $1,800.

Bodies: Demi-tonneau and fore-door touring replaced by phaeton. Coupe accommodates extra passenger on folding seat. The only fully enclosed standard four-cylinder limousine. Open bodies of steel, closed bodies of aluminum. Full set of doors on all body styles. Hoods once again louvered. Runningboard dust shields cover frame and runningboard brackets. Exterior trim nickel plated. Electric side lights have external wiring. All controls inside except brake lever on open bodies.

Chassis: Brake drum diameter increased to 17 in.

Driveline: No significant change.

Engine: New carburetor, made by Cadillac to C.F. Johnson patents. Delco 6/24 volt starting-lighting-twin ignition system.

I.D. DATA: If serial numbers were used they were on the plate on dash (with engine No.). Engine numbers were stamped on top surface of crankcase — in front of and to the left of number one (front) cylinder. Starting: 61001. Ending: 75000.

Model No.	Body Type & Seating	Price	Weight	Prod. Total
NA	4-dr. Touring-5P	1800	—	—
NA	4-dr. Phaeton-4P	1800	—	—
NA	4-dr. Torpedo-4P	1900	—	—
NA	2-dr. Roadster-2P	1800	—	—
NA	4-dr. Limo.-7P	3250	—	—
NA	2-dr. Coupe-4P	2250	—	—

ENGINE: Vertical, in-line, L-head. Four. Individual cast iron cylinder, copper water jacket. B & S: 4-1/2 x 4-1/2 in. Disp.: 286.3 cu. in. Brake H.P.: 40 plus. ALAM H.P.: 32.4. Main bearings: five. Valve lifters: mechanical pushrod-roller cam followers. Carb.: float feed, made by Cadillac to C.F. Johnson patents.

CHASSIS: W.B.: 116 in. Front/Rear Tread: 56 in. (61 opt). Tires: 36 x 4.

TECHNICAL: Selective, sliding gear transmission. Speeds: 3F/1R. Right-hand drive, controls to right. Leather-faced cone clutch. Shaft drive. Full-floating rear axle, bevel drive, bevel gear differential. Overall ratio: 3.92:1 (phaeton and torpedo 3.66:1, roadster 3.43:1). Mechanial brakes on two wheels — service/foot/contracting — emergency/lever/expanding. Wood artillery wheels, 10 and 12 spoke, quick detachable rims. Wheel size: 28 in. Optional final drive ratios: 3.05:1, 3.43:1, 3.66:1.

OPTIONS: Front bumper ($18.00). Clock (15.00). Seat covers (32.00-50.00). Mohair tops (60.00-90.00). Windshields (35.00-40.00). Trunk rack (10.00). Kamlee No. 1000 trunk (30.00). Demountable rims (25.00). Electric horn (25.00). Power tire pump (35.00). Handy lamp (2.00).

HISTORICAL: Introduced September 1911. Innovations: Electric starting-ignition-lighting system. Model year sales: 13,995. Model year production: 13,995. The president and general manager of Cadillac was Henry Leland.

1912 Cadillac, Four, touring, JAC

1913 CADILLAC

1913 CADILLAC — FOUR: Same as 1912 except: basic price increased to $1,975.

Bodies: Smoother, more integrated appearance. All controls inside. Cowls on all bodies except coupe. Reverse curve in front fenders. Top and windshield standard equipment. Sidelight wiring concealed.

Chassis: Wheelbase lengthened to 120 in.

Driveline: No significant change.

Engine: Major changes in lower end. Stroke increased to 5-3/4 in. Main bearings now in upper half of crankcase — lower half becomes an oil pan. Camshaft and accessory shaft chain driven. Engine mounting points moved to top of crankcase. Engine suspended from arched cross members. Valve stems enclosed. Starter/generator simplified (six volt only) and more compact. Ring governor used once more, but for

spark control, not speed control. Engine-driven tire pump optional.

I.D. DATA: If serial numbers were used, they could be found on plate on the dash (with engine No.). Engine numbers were stamped on top surface of crankcase — in front of and to the left of number one (front) cylinder). Starting: 75001. Ending: 90018.

1913 Cadillac, Four, touring

Model No.	Body Type & Seating	Price	Weight	Prod. Total
NA	4-dr. Touring-5P	1975	—	—
NA	4-dr. Torpedo-4P	1975	—	—
NA	4-dr. Touring-6P	2075	—	—
NA	4-dr. Phaeton-4P	1975	—	—
NA	2-dr. Roadster-2P	1975	—	—
NA	4-dr. Limo.-7P	3250	—	—
NA	2-dr. Coupe-4P	2500	—	—

ENGINE: Vertical, in-line, L-head. Four. Individual cast iron cylinder, copper water jacket. B & S: 4-1/2 x 5-3/4 in. Disp.: 365.8 cu. in. Brake H.P.: 40-50. ALAM H.P.: 32.4. Main bearings: five. Valve lifters: mechanical-pushrod-roller cam followers. Carb.: float feed, made by Cadillac to C.F. Johnson patents.

CHASSIS: W.B.: 120 in. Front/Rear Tread: 56 in. (61 opt.). Tires: 36 x 4-1/2.

TECHNICAL: Selective, sliding gear transmission. Speeds: 3F/1R. Right-hand drive, controls to right. Leather-faced cone clutch. Shaft drive. Full floating rear axle, bevel drive, bevel differential. Overall ratio: 3.43:1 (roadster 3.05:1, limousine 3.66:1). Mechanical brakes on two wheels — service/foot/contracting — emergency/lever/expanding. Wood artillery wheels, 10 and 12 spoke. Demountable rims. Wheel size: 27 in. Optional final drive ratios: 3.43:1, 3.66:1, 3.92:1.

OPTIONS: Front bumper ($15.00). Clock (35.00). Seat covers (32.50-65.00). Runningboard trunk (33.00). Tire trunk (16.50). Electric horn (25.00). Power tire pump (25.00). Handy lamp (2.00). Weed chains (8.00).

HISTORICAL: Introduced August 1912. Model year sales: 15,018. Model year production: 15,018. The president and general manager of Cadillac was Henry Leland.

Note: "Standard of the World" first used in the fall of 1912, in ads for the 1913 cars.

1914 CADILLAC

1914 CADILLAC — FOUR: Same as 1913 except:

Bodies: Torpedo body no longer available. Landaulet treatment on coupe. Five-passenger "inside drive limousine" (actually a center-door sedan) is a new style. Hinged steering wheel and hinged driver's seat cushion facilitate entrance and exit for front seat passengers at right side of car. With smaller side lamps, bodies now have the appearance of enclosing the occupants and all the machinery.

1914 Cadillac, Four, landaulet coupe, HAC

Chassis: Hinged steering wheel. Speedometer drive located in left steering knuckle.

Driveline: Rear axle changed to Timken two-speed.

Engine: Second ignition system for auxiliary use only. One distributor, one set of spark plugs. Fuel tank moved to rear of chassis. Hand pump on dash to pressurize tank for starting, camshaft driven pump for running. Power tire pump standard equipment.

I.D. DATA: There were no serial numbers for the 1914 Cadillac. Engine numbers were stamped on top surface of crankcase — in front of and to the left of number one (front) cylinder. Engine Nos.: 91005-99999; A-1 A-5008.

Model No.	Body Type & Seating	Price	Weight	Prod. Total
NA	4-dr. Touring-7P	2075	—	—
NA	4-dr. Touring-5P	1975	—	—
NA	4-dr. Phaeton-4P	1975	—	—
NA	2-dr. Roadster-2P	1975	—	—
NA	2-dr. Landaulet Coupe-3P	2500	—	—
NA	4-dr. Standard Limo.-7P	3250	—	—
NA	2-dr. Inside Drive Limo.-5P	2800	—	—

1914 Cadillac, Four, seven-passenger touring, JAC

ENGINE: Vertical, in-line, L-head. Four. Individual cast iron cylinder, copper water jacket. B & S: 4-1/2 x 5-3/4 in. Disp.: 365.8 cu. in. Brake H.P.: 40-50. N.A.C.C. H.P.: 32.4. Main bearings: five. Valve lifters: mechanical-pushrod-roller cam followers. Carb.: float feed, made by Cadillac to C.F. Johnson patents.

CHASSIS: W.B.: 120 in. Front/Rear Tread: 56 in. (61 opt). Tires: 36 x 4-1/2. Special chassis. W.B.: 134 in.

TECHNICAL: Selective, sliding gear transmission. Speeds: 3F/1R. Right-hand drive, controls to right. Leather-faced cone clutch. Shaft drive. Full floating rear axle, two speed, bevel drive, bevel gear differential. Overall ratio: 3.67:1/2.5:1. Mechanical brakes on two wheels. Service/foot/contracting — emergency/lever/expanding. Wood artillery wheels, 10 and 12 spoke. Demountable rims. Wheel size: 27 in. Optional final drive dual ratio: 4.07:1/2.5:1.

OPTIONS: Seat covers ($32.50-65.00). Handy lamp (2.00).

HISTORICAL: Introduced July 1913. Innovations: Production two-speed rear axle. Model year sales: 14,003. Model year production: 14,003. The president and general manager of Cadillac was Henry Leland.

Note: The last four-cylinder Cadillac for 67 years, and the final use by Cadillac of Alanson Brush design features.

Note: A 1914 Cadillac touring (engine number 92,524) was awarded the 1913 Dewar Trophy as a result of electrical and two-speed axle performance during a 1,000-mile test conducted in September/October 1913.

1915 CADILLAC

1915 Cadillac, Type 51, landaulet coupe, OCW

CADILLAC — TYPE 51 — EIGHT: Bodies: Similar to 1914 bodies except: sidelights smaller. Hood top panels blend smoothly into hood side panels. Shape of doors changed. Three-piece "Rain Vision" windshield used on closed cars. Roof line of closed cars raised at front. Cadillac "one-man" top with inside operating curtains that open with the doors is standard equipment. Top fastened to windshield, eliminating straps. Four-passenger phaeton replaced by two-door salon with passageway between individual front seats (right front seat revolves). "Inside Drive Limousine" of 1914 now designated "Five-Passenger Sedan." Berline enclosed drive limousine added. The designation "Imperial" used with "sedan" (or "brougham", "suburban", etc.) denotes a regular sedan with a glass partition added between front and rear compartments.

Chassis: First left-drive Cadillac (right-drive available as an option). Tread: 56 in. (61 in. optional wide tread still available). Wheelbase 122 in. (145 in. chassis available without body). Wood wheels with 10 spokes in front, 12 spokes in rear. Speedometer drive changed to right steering spindle. Rear springs three-quarter platform, front springs half-elliptic, six inches longer than in 1914. Ladder-type frame changed to six-inch deep "H" frame with three cross members.

Driveline: Multiple disc, dry plate clutch with 15 steel plates, 7-3/4 in. diameter. Alternate plates faced with wire mesh asbestos. Selective sliding gear transmission. Aluminum case in unit with engine. Tubular driveshaft with two universal joints. Torque arm. Spiral bevel drive in full floating rear axle.

Engine: Ninety degree L-Head V-8; B & S: 3-1/8 x 5-1/8 in. Disp.: 314 cu. in. Cast iron cylinders in two blocks of four located exactly opposite on aluminum-copper alloy crankcase. Water jackets and combustion chambers integral. Water circulation and temperature control is by an impeller-type pump with thermostat for each block of cylinders. Three 1-7/8 in. diameter bearings on crankshaft with four throws all in one plane. Fork and blade connecting rods. Rod bearings available standard, .005 under, and .020 under. Three rings, solid wall pistons and cylinder blocks available standard, first, and second oversize. Single camshaft with eight cams. Camshaft and generator shaft driven by silent chain. Motor/generator/distributor at rear, two-cylinder power tire pump at front, inside engine vee. Updraft carburetor, water-heated intake manifold, and log-type exhaust manifolds located inside vee. Dual exhaust system with no balance pipe. Valves 1-9/16 in. diameter, 5/16 lift. Exhaust valves flat, intake valves tulip shaped. Valves actuated by adjustable tappets that are activated by rocker arms with roller riding on cams. Firing order is: 1L-2R-3L-1R-4L-3R-2L-4R, where R(right) and L(left) are as viewed from the rear, and each bank is numbered one through four from the front. Valve chamber caps are stamped H, L, or LL for high or low compression ratios. Engine has three-point suspension. Ball and socket at front and solid at rear, forming an additional frame cross member. Before Engine No. A-7710, oil relief valve is cast integral with starter gear housing. Starting with Engine No. A-7710, oil relief valve is a separate unit mounted on angular face of crankcase. The lubrication system is recirculating, pressure fed from a gear-type oil pump. The pump draws oil from the crankcase and forces it through a header pipe running inside the crankcase. Leads run from this pipe to the main bearings and thence through drilled holes in the crankshaft to the connecting rod bearings. Pistons, cylinders, etc., are lubricated by oil thrown from the lower ends of the connecting rods. Oil from the rear end of the header pipe runs to the pressure relief valve. Overflow from this valve is gravity fed to the camshaft and chains, then drains back to the crankcase.

I.D. DATA: Serial numbers were not used. Engine numbers stamped on the crankcase just back of the right hand bank of cylinders, and on a plate on the dash. Starting: A-6000. Ending: A-19001.

Style No.	Body Type & Seating	Price	Weight	Prod. Total
NA	4-dr. Touring-7P	1975	—	—
NA	4-dr. Touring-5P	1975	—	—
NA	2-dr. Salon-5P	1975	—	—
NA	2-dr. Roadster-2/4P	1975	—	—
602	2-dr. Landaulet Coupe-3P	2500	—	—
601	2-dr. Sedan-5P	2800	—	—
583	4-dr. Limo.-7P	3450	—	—
NA	4-dr. Berline Limo.-7P	3600	—	—
715	4-dr. Imperial Sedan-5P	—	—	—

Note: Through 1919, Cadillac sometimes referred to touring cars and roadsters as "Seven-Passenger Car," "Five-Passenger Car" or "Two-Passenger Car." The designations "Touring" and "Roadster" are used herein for clarity.

ENGINE: Ninety degree V-8. L-head. Heads not detachable. Cast iron blocks of four on aluminum crankcase. B & S: 3-1/8 x 5-1/8 in. Disp.: 314.5 cu. in. C.R.: 4.25:1. Brake H.P.: 70 @ 2400 R.P.M. (60 advertised). S.A.E./N.A.C.C. H.P.: 31.25. Main bearings: three. Valve lifters: rockers with roller cam follower acting on mechanical lifters. Carb.: float feed, auxilary air control; manufactured by Cadillac under C.F. Johnson patents. Torque (compression) 180 lb.-ft. @ 2000 R.P.M.

1915 Cadillac, Type 51, seven-passenger touring, HAC

CHASSIS: (Type 51) W.B.: 122 in. Front/Rear Tread: 56 in. (61 opt.). Tires: 36 x 4-1/2. (Special Chassis) W.B.: 145 in.

TECHNICAL: Selective sliding gear transmission. Case in unit with engine. Speeds: 3F/1R. Left drive, center control (rhd opt). Multiple disc, dry plate, 15 discs. Shaft drive. Spiral bevel, full floating rear axle. Overall ratio: 4.44:1. Mechanical brakes on two wheels, one external, one internal. Wood artillery wheels, demountable rims (wire wheels optional). Wheel size: 27 in. Optional drive ratio: 3.94:1, 5.07:1.

HISTORICAL: Introduced September 1914. Innovations: High production V-8 engine. Model year sales: 13,002. Model year production: 13,002. The president and general manager of Cadillac was Henry Leland.

1916 CADILLAC

1916 Cadillac, Type 53, victoria, HAC

CADILLAC — TYPE 53 — EIGHT: Bodies: Similar to Type 51 except: hood line raised so that transition in cowl is less abrupt. Roof line of closed bodies raised again at front so that entire roof line is one gentle curve. Door shape changed. Five-passenger touring dropped. Salon now has four doors. Victoria body replaces landaulet coupe. Four-passenger coupe built by Cadillac added in mid-year. Five/seven-passenger brougham replaces two-door sedan. (The seating arrangement 7P denotes two folding auxiliary seats facing forward in the rear compartment. The seating arrangement 5/7P denotes two emergency "seats" in the rear compartment. These "seats" are rear-facing upholstered shelves hinged down out of the back of the front seat.) Touring body on special 132-inch chassis offered. Police patrol, ambulance, and hearse bodies on special 145-inch chassis offered.

Chassis: Same as Type 51 plus 132-inch chassis also available.

Driveline: Power tire pump moved from engine to transmission.

Engine: Distributor moved from rear to front of engine. Fan blades curved. Exhaust manifolds redesigned with curved connector pipes feeding into collector.

I.D. DATA: Serial numbers were not used. Engine numbers were stamped on the crankcase just back of the right-hand bank of cylinders, and on a plate on the dash. Starting: A-20000. Ending: A-38003.

Style No.	Body Type & Seating	Price	Weight	Prod. Total
NA	4-dr. Touring-7P	2080	—	—
NA	4-dr. Salon-5P	2080	—	—
NA	2-dr. Roadster-2/4P	2080	—	—
1517	2-dr. Victoria-3P	2400	—	—
NA	2-dr. Coupe-4P	2800	—	—
1518	4 dr. Brougham-5/7P	2950	—	—
1744	4 dr. Limo.-7P	3450	—	—
1519	4-dr. Berline-7P	3600	—	—
NA	4-dr. 132-inch Touring	—	—	—
NA	Ambulance	3455	—	—
NA	Police Patrol	2955	—	—
NA	Hearse	3880	—	—

ENGINE: Ninety degree V-8. L-head. Heads not detachable. Cast iron block of four on aluminum crankcase. B & S: 3-1/8 x 5-1/8 in. Disp.: 314.5 cu. in. Brake H.P.: 77 @ 2600 R.P.M. (60 plus advertised). S.A.E./N.A.C.C. H.P.: 31.25. Main bearings: three. Valve lifters: rockers with roller cam follower acting on mechanical lifters. Carb.: float feed, auxiliary air control; manufactured by Cadillac under C.F. Johnson patents.

CHASSIS: (Type 53) W.B.: 122 in. Front/Rear Tread: 56 in. (61 opt). Tires: 36 x 4-1/2. (Special Chassis) W.B.: 145 in., 132 in.

TECHNICAL: Selective sliding gear transmission. Case in unit with engine. 3F/1R. Left drive, center control (rhd optional). Multiple disc, dry plate clutch, 15 discs. Shaft drive. Spiral bevel, full-floating rear axle. Overall ratio: 4.44:1. Mechanical brakes on two wheels, one external, one internal. Wood artillery wheels, demountable rims (R-W wire wheels optional). Wheel size: 27 in. Optional drive ratio: 3.94:1, 5.07:1.

OPTIONS: Seat covers ($35.00-65.00).

HISTORICAL: Introduced July 1915. Model year sales: 18,004. Model year production: 18,004. The president and general manager of Cadillac was Henry Leland. In May 1916, Erwin G. "Cannonball" Baker and Wm. F. Sturm drove a V-8 Cadillac roadster from Los Angeles to New York City in seven days, 11 hours, 52 minutes. They bettered their previous time, driven in another make of car by three days, 19 hours, 23 minutes.

1917 CADILLAC

1917 Cadillac, Type 55, touring, OCW

CADILLAC — TYPE 55 — EIGHT: Bodies: Similar to Type 53 except: new crown fenders and elimination of molding on hood panels and around doors give smoother appearance overall. Phaeton and roadster have six degree slope to windshield. Salon replaced by phaeton with bench seat in front. Club roadster added. Convertible touring (a four-door hardtop) manufactured by Cadillac and having a vee windshield is introduced. Coupe with cast aluminum body is also manufactured by Cadillac. Victoria is now five-window with fixed top and removable pillars. Berlin/berline is now called Imperial (undoubtedly due to nasty connotation of "Berlin" at the time). Landaulet body style added. One listing of closed body styles by Fisher mentions "Touring Couplet," with no description. Previous round, plain door (rim) of headlights now embellished with stylized outline of shield and crown.

Chassis: Frame depth increased to eight inches, and two tubular cross members added. Wide tread no longer available.

Driveline: Number of clutch plates increased to 17.

Engine: Lighter pistons of "belted" design with large oil return holes in the piston walls. Exhaust manifolds have shorter connector pipes. Split, tapered collars used to retain valve spring feet.

I.D. DATA: Serial numbers were not used. Engine numbers were stamped on the crankcase just back of the right hand bank of cylinders, and on a plate on the dash. Engine No.: 55-A-1 through 55-A-1000; 55-B-1 through 55-B-1000, etc., through 55-S-2.

Style No.	Body Type & Seating	Price	Weight	Prod. Total
NA	4-dr. Touring-7P	2240	—	—
NA	4-dr. Phaeton-4P	2240	—	—
NA	2-dr. Roadster-2/4P	2240	—	—
NA	2-dr. Club Roadster-4P	2240	—	—
NA	2-dr. Conv. Victoria-4P	2710	—	—
NA	2-dr. Coupe-4P	2960	—	—
NA	4-dr. Conv. Touring-7P	2835	—	—
2460	4-dr. Brougham-5/7P	3110	—	—
2450	4-dr. Limo.-7P	3760	—	—
2440	4 dr. Imperial-7P	3910	—	—
2620	4 dr. Landaulet-7P	3910	—	—
2470	Touring Couplet	—	—	—
NA	Ambulance	3760	—	—
NA	Police Patrol	3160	—	—
NA	Hearse	4040	—	—

Note: Prices $160 less previous December 14, 1916.
Note: Touring Couplet may be same as Convertible Victoria.

ENGINE: Ninety degree V-8. L-head. Heads not detachable. Cast iron blocks of four on aluminum crankcase. B & S: 3-1/8 x 5-1/8 in. Disp.: 314.5 cu. in. S.A.E./N.A.C.C. H.P.: 31.25. Main bearings: three. Valve lifters: rockers with roller cam follower acting on mechanical lifters. Carb.: float feed, auxiliary air control, manufactured by Cadillac under C.F. Johnson patents.

CHASSIS: (Type 55) W.B.: 125 in. Front/Rear Tread: 56 in. Tires: 36 x 4-1/2. (Type 55 limousine, landaulet, imperial) W.B.: 132 in. Front/Rear Tread: 56 in. Tires: 37 x 5. (Special Chassis) W.B.: 145 in.

TECHNICAL: Selective sliding gear transmission. Case in unit with engine. Speeds: 3F/1R. Left drive, center control (rhd optional). Multiple disc, dry plate clutch, 17 discs. Shaft drive. Spiral bevel, full-floating rear axle. Overall ratio: 4.44:1. Mechanical. brakes on two wheels, one external, one internal. Wood artillery wheels, demountable rims (R-W or Houk wire wheels optional). Wheel size: 27 in. Optional drive ratio: 3.94:1, 5.07:1.

HISTORICAL: Introduced August 1916. Model year sales: 18,002. Model year production: 18,002.

Note: General Motors Corp. was incorporated October 13, 1916, in Delaware. General Motors Co. was taken over by General Motors Corp. August 1, 1917. General Motors Corp. was then an "operating" company and Cadillac Motor Car Co. became a Division of General Motors.

Henry Leland left Cadillac in June 1917 and Richard H. Collins became president and general manager.

1918 CADILLAC

1918 Cadillac, Type 57, touring, OCW

CADILLAC — TYPE 57 — EIGHT: Bodies: Similar to Type 55 except: top line of hood and cowl now a continuous straight line to the windshield on most body styles. Headlight reflectors tilted by mechanical linkage to lever on steering post. Nine hood louvers tilted six degrees. Windshield on all open cars tilted six degrees. Club roadster, coupe, convertible touring, and touring couplet dropped from the line. Town limousine and town landaulet added. The main compartment of these two bodies was approximately four inches narrower than on the standard limousine. Suburban added in mid-year.

Chassis: No significant change from Type 55.

Driveline: Transmission redesigned and is not interchangeable with Types 51, 53, 55.

Engine: Detachable cylinder heads. "Belted" pistons replaced by ultra lightweight pistons.

I.D. DATA: Serial numbers were not used. Engine numbers were stamped on the crankcase just back of the right-hand bank of cylinders, and on a plate on the dash. Also stamped on the fan shaft housing. Engine Nos.: 57A-1 through 57-Z-1000 with 1919.

Style No.	Body Type & Seating	Price	Weight	Prod. Total
NA	4-dr. Touring-7P	2590	4035	—
NA	4-dr. Phaeton-4P	2590	3925	—
NA	2-dr. Roadster-2/4P	2590	3865	—
2750	2-dr. Conv. Victoria-4P	3075	3970	—
2730	4-dr. Brougham-5/7P	3535	4290	—
NA	4-dr. Brougham-7P	4145	—	—
2740	4-dr. Limo.-7P	4085	4425	—
2820	Limo.	—	—	—
2680	4-dr. Town Limo.-6P	4100	4295	—

Style No.	Body Type & Seating	Price	Weight	Prod. Total
3110	U.S. Govt. Limo.	—	—	—
2760	4-dr. Imperial-7P	4285	—	—
2770	4-dr. Landaulet-7P	4235	4510	—
2840	4-dr. Twn. Land.-6P	4250	4350	—
2910	4-dr. Suburban-7P	4090	4350	—
NA	Police Patrol	3850	—	—
NA	Ambulance	4350	—	—
NA	Hearse	4685	—	—

Note: Prices increased several times during the war years, partly due to war taxes. The lowest prices for the body style are given.

ENGINE: Ninety degree V-8. L-head. Heads detachable. Cast iron blocks of four on aluminum crankcase. B & S: 3-1/8 x 5-1/8 in. Disp.: 314.5 cu. in. S.A.E./N.A.C.C. H.P.: 31.25. Main bearings: three. Valve lifters: rockers with roller cam follower acting on mechanical lifters. Carb.: float feed, auxiliary air control manufactured by Cadillac under C.F. Johnson patents.

CHASSIS: (Type 57) W.B.: 125 in. Front/Rear Tread: 56 in. Tires: 35 x 5. (Type 57 Roadster) W.B.: 125 in. Front/Rear Tread: 56 in. Tires: 34 x 4-1/2. (Type 57 limousine, imperial, landaulet, town limousine, town landaulet) W.B.: 132 in. Front/Rear Tread: 56 in. Tires: 35 x 5. (Special Chassis) W.B.: 145 in.

TECHNICAL: Selective sliding gear transmission. Case in unit with engine. Speeds: 3F/1R. Left drive, center control (rhd optional). Multiple disc, dry plate clutch, 17 discs. Shaft drive. Spiral bevel, full-floating rear axle. Overall ratio: 4.44:1. Mechanical brakes on two wheels, one external, one internal. Wood artillery wheels, demountable rims (R-W wire wheels optional). Wheel size: 25 in. Optional drive ratio: 3.94:1, 5.07:1.

HISTORICAL: Introduced August 1917. Model year sales: 45,146 with 1919. Model year production: 45,146 with 1919. The president and general manager of Cadillac was Richard H. Collins.

1919 CADILLAC

1919 Cadillac, Type 57, touring, OCW

CADILLAC — TYPE 57 — EIGHT: Similar to 1918 Type 57, with the following exceptions:

Bodies: Twenty-five vertical hood louvers. Phaeton 1-1/2" lower. Victoria no longer "convertible" and has aluminum rather than leather roof and rear quarter. Brougham replaced by sedan with full width front seat and no emergency seats. Town limousine renamed town brougham. Landaulet, town landaulet, and hearse dropped. As Fisher made minor changes in details on the vctoria, suburban, and sedan, the bodies were identified as 57-A and 57-B. This was a body designation only, not a Type designation. There was no Type 57-B Cadillac. The 57-B bodies had a square effect at body, door, and window corners, and the lower edge of the windshields followed the curve of the cowl.

Chassis: No significant change.
Driveline: No significant changes from 1918.
Engine: No significant changes from 1918.

I.D. DATA: Serial numbers were not used. Engine numbers were stamped on the crankcase just back of the right-hand bank of cylinders, and on a plate on the dash. Also stamped on the fan shaft housing. Engine Nos.: 57-A-1 through 57-Z-1000 with 1918, and 57-AA-1 through 57-TT-146.

Style No.	Body Type & Seating	Price	Weight	Prod. Total
NA	4-dr. Touring-7P	3220	4035	—
NA	4-dr. Phaeton-4P	3220	3925	—
NA	2-dr. Roadster-2/4P	3220	3865	—
3040	2-dr. Victoria-4P	3990	3970	—
3050	4-dr. Sedan-5P	4215	—	—
3260	Imperial Sedan	—	—	—
3210	4-dr. Limo.-7P	4520	4425	—
NA	4-dr. Imperial-7P	4620	—	—
NA	4-dr. Twn. Brougham-6P	4520	4295	—
2830	Limo.-8P	—	—	—
3140	4-dr. Suburban-7P	4465	4350	—
3140-PI200	Imp. Suburban	—	—	—
NA	Police Patrol	4050	—	—
NA	Ambulance	4550	—	—

Note: Some overlap existed on new or deleted body styles for 1918 and 1919.

ENGINE: Ninety degree V-8. L-head. Heads detachable. Cast iron blocks of four on aluminum crankcase. B & S: 3-1/8 x 5-1/8 in. Disp.: 314.5 cu. in. S.A.E./N.A.C.C. H.P.: 31.25. Main bearings: three. Valve lifters: rockers with roller cam follower acting on mechanical lifters. Carb.: float feed, auxiliary air control, manufactured by Cadillac under C.F. Johnson patents.

CHASSIS: (Type 57) W.B.: 125 in. Front/Rear Tread: 56 in. Tires: 35 x 5. (Type 57 roadster) W.B.: 125 in. Front/Rear Tread: 56 in. Tires: 34 x 4-1/2. (Type 57 Limousine Suburban) W.B.: 132 in. Front/Rear Tread: 56 in. Tires: 35 x 5. (Special Chassis) W.B.: 145 in.

TECHNICAL: Selective sliding gear transmission. Case in unit with engine. Speeds: 3F/1R. Left drive, center control (rhd optional). Multiple disc, dry plate clutch, 17 discs. Shaft drive. Spiral bevel, full-floating rear axle. Overall ratio: 4.44:1. Mechanical brakes on two wheels, one external, one internal. Wood artillery wheels, demountable rims (R-W wire wheels optional). Wheel size: 25 in. Optional drive ratio: 3.94:1, 5.07:1.

OPTIONS: Front bumper ($12.50). Rear bumper (12.50). Cigar lighter (5.00). Seat covers (13.50-125.00). Spotlight (7.50). Set of five Rudge-Whitworth wire wheels (150.00). Tire chains (9.00). Rear view mirror (3.75).

HISTORICAL: The 1919 Type 57 was a continuation of 1918 Type 57. Model year sales: 45,146 with 1918. Model year production: 45,146 with 1918. The president and general manager of Cadillac was Richard H. Collins.

1920-1921 CADILLAC

1920 Cadillac, Type 59, town car, HAC

CADILLAC — TYPE 59 — EIGHT: Similar to Type 57, with the following exceptions:

Bodies: General lines slightly straighter and fuller. Cowl lengthened on phaeton and roadster. Windshield on limousine and town brougham tilted slightly. Lower section of windshield fixed; ventilation to lower part of front compartment provided by vent in top of cowl. Hood hinge concealed. Narrow beading added on cowl at joint with hood. Smaller sidelights, closer to windshield. Shield-shaped pattern on headlight doors changed to narrow bead with curved sides; detachable emblem at top. Headlights and sidelights optionally available in full nickel. Touring on 132 in. wheelbase. Two-passenger coupe new — this and town brougham dropped in mid-run but picked up again for Type 61.

Chassis: Front wheels changed from 10 to 12 spoke. Frame stiffened by lengthening the deep section. Radiator water condenser moved to outside of frame. Extra length chassis not available.

Driveline: Speedometer drive moved from front axle to transmission.

Engine: Intake manifold heated by exhaust gases. Timing chains adjustable, from outside crankcase. Crankshaft diameter increased to 2 in. New-style four-pole motor-generator used.

I.D. DATA: Serial numbers were not used. Engine numbers were stamped on the crankcase just back of the right-hand bank of cylinders, and on a plate on the dash. Engine Nos.: 59-A-1 through 59-Z-1000 and 59-AA-1 through 59-BB-12.

Style No.	Body Type & Seating	Price	Weight	Prod. Total
1st Design				
	4-dr. Tr.-7P	3740	—	—
	4-dr. Phae.-4P	3590	—	—
	2-dr. Rds.-2/4P	3590	—	—
4000	2-dr. Vict.-4P	4340	—	—
	2-dr. Cpe.-2P	4290	—	—
4010	4-dr. Sed.-5P	4750	—	—
4020	4-dr. Sub.-7P	4990	—	—
4030	4-dr. Limo.-7P	5090	—	—
4050	4-dr. Imp. Limo.-7P	5190	—	—
4040	4-dr. Twn. Brgm.-7P	5090	—	—
2nd Design				
	4-dr. Tr.-7P	3940	—	—
	4-dr. Phae.-4P	3790	—	—
	2-dr. Rds.-2/4P	3790	—	—
4130	2-dr. Vict.-4P	4540	—	—
	2-dr. Cpe.-2P	—	—	—
4140	4-dr. Sed.-5P	4950	—	—
4120	4-dr. Sub.-7P	5190	—	—
4150	4-dr. Limo.-7P	5290	—	—
4170	4-dr. Imp. Limo.-7P	5390	—	—
4160	4-dr. Twn. Brgm.-7P	5290	—	—

Style No.	Body Type & Seating	Price	Weight	Prod. Total
3rd Design				
	4-dr. Tr.-7P	3940	—	—
	4-dr. Phae.-4P	3790	—	—
	2-dr. Rds.-2/4P	3790	—	—
4290	2-dr. Vict.-4P	4540	—	—
	2-dr. Cpe.-2P	—	—	—
4270	4-dr. Sed.-5P	4950	—	—
4300	4-dr. Sub.-7P	5190	—	—
4360	4-dr. Limo.-7P	5290	—	—
4350	4-dr. Imp. Limo.-7P	5390	—	—
	4-dr. Twn. Brgm.-7P	5690	—	—

NOTE: Coupe and town brougham dropped for 1921.

Note 1: Some Fisher references designate 1st, 2nd, 3rd designs as 59-A, 59-B, 59-C. These designs differ only in detail and are not significant styling changes. The -A, -B, -Cs refer only to bodies, not "type" — there was no Type 59-A, Type 59-B, or Type 59-C Cadillac.
Note 2: The two-passenger coupe appeared only in early Type 59 catalogs. If produced at all as a Type 59 body style, this coupe was dropped by April 1920 but was picked up as a Type 61 style.
Note 3: The April 1, 1920, price list advanced all prices by $200 (two-passenger coupe not listed). The only price change on May 1, 1920, was an advance to $5,690 for the town brougham. This body style was not shown in the later (1921) catalogs, but was picked up as a Type 61 style.
Note 4: Job (Body) number is stamped on right front door sill.

ENGINE: Ninety degree V-8. L-Head. Cast iron blocks of four on aluminum crankcase. B & S: 3-1/8 x 5-1/8 in. Disp.: 314.5 cu. in. S.A.E./N.A.C.C. H.P.: 31.25. Main bearings: three. Valve lifters: rockers with roller cam follower acting on mechanical lifters. Carb.: float feed, auxiliary air control manufactured by Cadillac under C.F. Johnson patents.

CHASSIS: (Type 59 phaeton, roadster, victoria, coupe, sedan) W.B.: 125 in. Front/Rear Tread: 56 in. Tires: 34 x 4-1/2. (Others) W.B.: 132 in. Front/Rear Tread: 56 in. Tires: 35 x 5.

TECHNICAL: Selective sliding gear transmission. Case in unit with engine. Speeds: 3F/1R. Left drive, center control (rhd optional). Multiple disc, dry plate clutch. Shaft drive. Spiral bevel, full-floating rear axle. Overall ratio: 4.44:1, 5.07:1. Mechanical brakes on two wheels, one external, one internal. Wood artillery wheels, demountable rims, 12 spoke. Wheel size: 25 in. Optional drive ratio: 3.94:1.

OPTIONS: All nickel headlamps, sidelamps, and hubcaps. R-W wire wheels.

HISTORICAL: Introduced January 1920. Model year sales: 24,878. Model year production: 24,878. The president and general manager of Cadillac was Richard H. Collins (H.H. Rice as of May 1921).

Note: The general state of the postwar economy, shortages of materials, railway strikes, and the completion and occupation of a new factory resulted in a production slump at Cadillac during 1920-1921. With the outstanding war record of the Type 57, with long waiting lists of eager customers, and with reconstruction pressures in the nation and in the company — Cadillac built the new Type 59 for two years without significant styling or mechanical changes.

1921 Cadillac, Type 59, limousine, JAC

1922-1923 CADILLAC

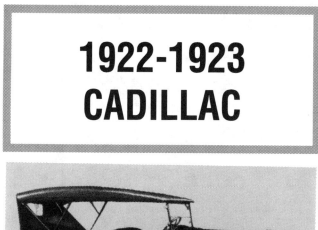
1922 Cadillac, Type 61, touring, HAC

CADILLAC — TYPE 61 — EIGHT: Similar to Type 59, with the following exceptions:

Bodies: Higher radiator. Shoulders of hood raised. Lower center of gravity with same ground clearance. Hood made of aluminum. Exterior door handles on all but front doors of limousine. Soft-type roof construction on closed cars. Leather-covered, fixed visor on closed cars. Trunk rack, vertical bars on rear of body, and runningboard kick plates on five-passenger sedan and phaeton. Headlights mounted by single post rather than fork. Shield shaped bead on headlight door has straight rather than curved sides. Optional nickel-plated lights and radiator shell offered. Horn moved under hood. New steering wheel, without hinge. Windshield cleaner and rear view mirror standard equipment. Two-passenger coupe and town brougham revived. Five-passenger coupe new. Landau sedan new for 1923. Victoria for 1923 had roomier interior and doors hinged at front.

Chassis: Smaller wheels, giving lower center of gravity. All bodies on 132 in. wheelbase. Self-lubricating bushings at many points in brake and clutch linkage. New piston-type grease cups at other lube points.

Driveline: Rear axle housing redesigned to maintain road clearance with smaller wheels. Final drive ratios now 4.50:1, 4.91:1, and 4.15:1 (special). Transmission lock provided.

Engine: Camshaft drilled to provide internal oil passage and replace oil tube. Two-pole generator replaced four-pole.

I.D. DATA: Serial numbers were not used. Engine numbers were stamped on the crankcase just back of the right-hand bank of cylinders, and on a plate on the dash. Engine Nos: 61-A-1 through 61-Z-18006.

Style No.	Body Type & Seating	Price	Weight	Prod. Total
1st Design				
	4-dr. Tr.-7P	3940	4025	—
	4-dr. Phae.-4P	3790	3955	—
	2-dr. Rds.-2/4P	3790	3920	—
4420	2-dr. Vict.-4P	4540	4115	—
4470	2-dr. Cpe.-2P	4540	3980	—
4440	2-dr. Cpe.-5P	4690	4130	—
4430	4-dr. Sed.-5P	4950	4220	—
4400	4-dr. Sub.-7P	5190	4420	—
4450	4-dr. Limo.-7P	5290	4400	—
4460	4-dr. Imp. Limo.-7P	5390	4450	—
4480	4-dr. Town Brgm.-7P	—	—	—
5160	4-dr. Land. Sed.-5P	—	—	—
2nd Design				
	4-dr. Tr.-7P	3150	4025	—
	4-dr. Phae.-4P	3150	3955	—
	2-dr. Rds.-2/4P	3100	3920	—
4430	2-dr. Vict.-4P	3875	4115	—
5080	2-dr. Cpe.-2P	3875	3980	—
5050	2-dr. Cpe.-5P	3925	4130	—
5040	4-dr. Sed.-5P	4100	4220	—
4410	4-dr. Sub.-7P	4250	4420	—
5060	4-dr. Limo.-7P	4550	4400	—
5070	4-dr. Imp. Limo.-7P	4600	4450	—
	4-dr. Town Brgm.-7P	—	—	—
	4-dr. Land. Sed.-5P	—	—	—
3rd Design				
	4-dr. Tr.-7P	2885	4025	—
	4-dr. Phae.-4P	2885	3955	—
	2-dr. Rds.-2/4P	2885	3920	—
5090	2-dr. Vict.-4P	3675	4115	—
	2-dr. Cpe.-2P	—	3980	—
	2-dr. Cpe.-5P	3750	4130	—
	4-dr. Sed.-5P	3950	4220	—
5030	4-dr. Sub.-7P	3990	4420	—
	4-dr. Limo.-7P	4300	4400	—
	4-dr. Imp. Limo.-7P	4400	4450	—
	4-dr. Town Brgm.-7P	—	—	—
	4-dr. Land. Sed.-5P	3950	—	—

Note: Introductory prices were much the same as for Type 59. In January 1922 came a drastic price reduction, followed by a smaller reduction in December 1922. These were the first price reductions for Cadillac and followed an industry trend. Increased production schedules, higher efficiency in the new manufacturing facilities, and economic pressures combined to make the reductions possible as well as necessary.

1923 Cadillac, Type 61, touring, OCW

ENGINE: Ninety degree V-8. L-head. Cast iron blocks of four on aluminum crankcase. B & S: 3-1/8 x 5-1/8 in. Disp.: 314.5 cu. in. Brake H.P.: 60 plus advertised. S.A.E./N.A.C.C. H.P.: 31.25. Valve lifters: rockers with roller cam follower acting on mechanical lifters. Carb.: float feed, auxiliary air control manufactured by Cadillac under C.F. Johnson patents.

CHASSIS: (Type 61) W.B.: 132 in. Front/Rear Tread: 56 in. Tires: 33 x 5.

TECHNICAL: Selective sliding gear transmission. Case in unit with engine. Speeds: 3F/1R. Left drive, center control (rhd optional). Multiple disc, dry plate clutch. Shaft drive. Spiral bevel, full-floating rear axle. Overall ratio: 4.50:1, 4.91:1. Mechanical brakes on two wheels, one external, one internal. Wood artillery wheels, demountable rims, 12 spoke. Wheel size: 23 in. Optional drive ratio: 4.15:1.

OPTIONS: All nickel headlamps, sidelamps, hubcaps, and radiator shell. R-W wire wheels.

HISTORICAL: Introduced September 1921. Model two-year sales: 41,001. Model two-year production: 41,001. The president and general manager of Cadillac was Herbert H. Rice.

1924 CADILLAC

CADILLAC V-63 EIGHT: Similar to Type 61, with the following exceptions:

Bodies: Longer hood. One-inch higher radiator. Roof and rear quarter lines of closed cars softened. Liberal use of non-functional landau bars (buggy bows). Two-passenger coupe has blind quarters. More interior room. Lower seating position in closed cars. Ventilator door set flush in cowl. 1-1/2 in. narrower windshield posts. Full width, curved division windows. Automatic, vacuum-operated windshield cleaner. Bowl shape replaced bell shape of headlight bodies. Five-passenger sedan with Imperial division offered. New seven-passenger sedan offered mid-year.

Chassis: Front wheel brakes added. Service brake pedal acts on rear external and front internal bands. Emergency brake lever acts on rear internal bands. Front axle/steering knuckle design changed to reversed Elliott type. New tie rod with adjustable ball and socket ends moved from front to rear of axle. Two cross members added to frame. 145 in. wheelbase special chassis once more made available.

Driveline: No significant changes.

Engine: The engine is much the same as in the Type 61 cars except for the new harmonized and inherently balanced two-plane crankshaft and the revisions dictated by this system. Firing order changed to: 1L-4R-4L-2L-3R-3L-2R-1R. Flywheel weight reduced as a result of increased flywheel effect of compensators and larger (2-3/8 in. diameter) crankshaft. Sixteen cams on camshaft. Rocker arms and plate redesigned. Chain adjustment no longer needed — a result of 1/4 in. wider chains and greater smoothness of engine.

I.D. DATA: There were no serial numbers used on the Cadillac V-63. Engine numbers were stamped on the crankcase just back of the right-hand bank of cylinders, and on a plate on the dash. Starting: 63-A-1. Ending: 63-H-1550.

1924 Cadillac, V-63, Suburban, HAC

Style No.	Body Type & Seating	Price	Weight	Prod. Total
NA	4-dr. Touring-7P	3085	4280	—
NA	4-dr. Phaeton-4P	3085	4200	—
NA	2-dr. Roadster-2/4P	3085	4190	—
5490	2-dr. Victoria-4P	3275	4380	—
5380	2-dr. Coupe-2P	3875	4270	—
5280	2-dr. Coupe-5P	3950	4370	—
5270	4-dr. Sedan-5P	4150	4480	—
5290	4-dr. Landau Sedan-5P	4150	4480	—
5460	4-dr. Imperial Sedan-5P	4400	4600	—
5260	4-dr. Suburban-7P	4250	4560	—
5310	4-dr. Imp. Suburban-7P	4500	4640	—
5470	4-dr. Sedan-7P	3585	4610	—
5300	4-dr. Limousine-7P	4600	4640	—
5370	4-dr. Twn. Brougham-7P	4600	4530	—

Note: All Cadillac V-8s up to this time had been designated Type 51, Type 53, etc., through Type 61; with no -A, -B, etc. to designate the first or second year of a two-year production run (57, 59, 61). For 1924-1925, the designation became V-63; not Type V-63, not Series V-63, just V-63. However, some Cadillac master parts books covering V-63 plus Type 59 and Type 61 do refer to Type 63. Further, these parts books refer to 63-A and 63-B in reference to early vs. late or 1924 vs. 1925 V-63 chassis as well as body differences.

ENGINE: Ninety degree V-8. L-head. Cast iron blocks of four on aluminum crankcase. B & S: 3-1/8 x 5-1/8 in. Disp.: 314.5 cu. in. Brake H.P.: 80 plus advertised. S.A.E./N.A.C.C. H.P.: 31.25. Main bearings: three. Valve lifters: rockers with roller cam follower acting on mechanical lifters. Carb.: float feed, auxiliary air control; manufactured by Cadillac under C.F. Johnson patents.

CHASSIS: (V-63) W.B.: 132 in. Front/Rear Tread: 56 in. Tires: 33 x 5. (Special Chassis) W.B.: 145 in. Front/Rear Tread: 56 in. Tires: 33 x 5.

TECHNICAL: Selective sliding gear transmission. Case in unit with engine. Speeds: 3F/1R. Left drive, center control (rhd. optional). Multiple disc, dry plate clutch. Shaft drive. Spiral bevel, full-floating rear axle. Overall ratio: 4.50:1, 4.91:1. Mechanical brakes on four wheels. Wood artillery wheels, demountable rims, 12 spoke. Wheel size: 23 in. Optional drive ratio 4.15:1.

OPTIONS: All nickel headlamps, radiator shell, and hubcaps. Wire wheels. Disc wheels. Five balloon tires on disc wheels ($140.00). Six balloon tires on disc wheels, plus double carrier for spares (215.00). Five balloon tires on wire wheels (225.00). Six balloon tires on wire wheels, plus double carrier for spares (315.00).

HISTORICAL: Introduced September 1923. Innovations: Compensated, inherently balanced, two-plane crankshaft. Four wheel brakes. Model year sales: 35,500 with 1925 Model V-63. Model year production 35,500 with 1925 Model V-63. The president and general manager of Cadillac was Herbert H. Rice.

1925 CADILLAC

CADILLAC — V-63 — EIGHT: A continuation of the 1924 line, expanded to include the "Custom" line introduced in October 1924. Five "Custom" bodies were shown in the catalog, but a total of eight were listed by job number. The new line was custom to the extent that the customer could choose from 24 color harmonies and 10 upholstery patterns. The introduction of Duco finishes signaled the start to a color explosion that hit Cadillac in the next few years. Nickel-plated radiator shell and lights became standard. The scrolled radiator shell, first exclusive to the "Custom" line, was adapted to the standard line. The "Custom" line was distinguished by sloping windshields and double belt molding. A two-door, five-passenger coach body was added to the standard line.

I.D. DATA: Serial numbers were not used. Engine numbers were stamped on the crankcase just back of the right-hand bank of cylinders, and on a plate on the dash. Starting: 63-H-1551. Ending: 63-M-2572.

1925 Cadillac, V-63, two-door coach, OCW

Style No.	Body Type & Seating	Price	Weight	Prod. Total
Standard Body Styles				
1149	4-dr. Touring-7P	3185	—	—
1150	4-dr. Phaeton-4P	3185	—	—
1151	2-dr. Roadster-2/4P	3185	—	—
5690	2-dr. Victoria-4P	3485	—	—
6150	4-dr. Sedan-5P	3835	—	—
5700	4-dr. Landau Sedan-5P	3835	—	—
5680	4-dr. Sedan-7P	3885	—	—
6030	4-dr. Imp. Sedan-7P	4010	—	—
6010	2-dr. Coach-5P	3185	—	—
"Custom" Body Styles				
5750	4-dr. Sedan-5P	4550	—	—
5720	4-dr. Suburban-7P	4650	—	—
NA	4-dr. Imp. Sedan-5P	—	—	—
5760	4-dr. Limousine-7P	—	—	—
5730	4-dr. Imp. Suburban-7P	4950	—	—
5770	4-dr. Twn. Brougham-7P	—	—	—
5740	2-dr. Coupe-5P	4350	—	—
5710	2-dr. Coupe-2P	3975	—	—

ENGINE: Ninety degree V-8. L-head. Cast iron blocks of four on aluminum crankcase. B & S: 3-1/8 x 5-1/8 in. Disp.: 314.5 cu. in. Brake H.P.: 80 plus advertised. S.A.E./N.A.C.C. H.P.: 31.25. Main bearings: three. Valve lifters: rockers with roller cam follower acting on mechanical lifters. Carb.: float feed, auxiliary air control; manufactured by Cadillac under C.F. Johnson patents.

CHASSIS: (All standard body styles and custom two-passenger coupe) W.B.: 132 in. Front/Rear Tread: 56 in. Tires: 33 x 5. Special chassis. W.B.: 145 in. Front/Rear Tread: 56 in. Tires: 33 x 5. (All custom body styles except two-passenger coupe) W.B.: 138 in. Front/Rear Tread: 56 in. Tires: 33 x 5.

1925 Cadillac, V-63, Imperial sedan, JAC

TECHNICAL: Selective sliding gear transmission. Case in unit with engine. Speeds: 3F/1R. Left drive, center control (rhd optional). Multiple disc, dry plate clutch. Shaft drive. Spiral bevel, full-floating rear axle. Overall ratio: 4.50:1, 4.91:1. Mechanical brakes on four wheels. Wood artillery wheels, demountable rims, 12 spoke. Wheel size: 23 in. Optional drive ratio: 4.15:1, 5.55:1.

OPTIONS: Black radiator shell. Wire wheels. Disc wheels. Five balloon tires on disc wheels ($140.00). Six balloon tires on

disc wheels, plus double carrier for spares (215.00). Five balloon tires on wire wheels (225.00). Six balloon tires on wire wheels, plus double carrier for spares (315.00).

HISTORICAL: The 1925 Cadillac V-63 was a continuation of 1924 ("Custom" line introduced October 1924). Innovations: Duco finish. Model year sales: 35,500 with 1924 model V-63. Model year production: 35,500 with 1924 Model V-63. The president and general manager of Cadillac was Herbert H. Rice (L.P. Fisher as of May 1925).

1926 CADILLAC

1926 Cadillac, Series 314, touring, OCW

"THE NEW NINETY DEGREE CADILLAC" — SERIES 314 — EIGHT:
Bodies: Open cars transferred to "Custom" line with 138 in. wheelbase except roadster, which retained 132 in. wheelbase. Two-passenger "Custom" coupe transferred to Standard line, keeping 132 in. wheelbase. Window added in rear quarter. Coach renamed brougham. Landau sedan, limousine, and town brougham dropped. Semi-commercial chassis now 150 in. wheelbase. Cadillac offered funeral coaches and ambulance (bodies by Superior) plus armored car.

Narrower, higher radiator with thermostatically controlled shutters. Moto-meter on "Custom" cars. Greater distance radiator to windshield. Long sweeping front fenders containing battery and tool boxes. One-piece windshield on all cars. Windshield swinging from pivot at top on open cars. Vertical "V-V" windshield on closed cars. Fourteen louvers to rear of hood. New nickel-plated radiator shell with emblem set on badge-shaped background. All front doors now hinged at windshield post. No sidelights. New drum-shaped headlights contain parking bulb plus double filament bulb for tilting beam. Small (9 in.) drum on standard line, large (10 in.) drum on "Custom" line. Rear lamp on left fender instead of on tire carrier. Bumpers on "Custom" line. Motor-driven horn attached to left-hand headlight bracket instead of intake manifold.

As of end of 1925: "Custom" closed bodies once more had sloping (V-V) windshield (more angle than on V-63). Triangular side glasses added forward of windshield posts.

In spring of 1926 at Chassis Unit Number 1-25000, battery and tool boxes moved from front fenders back to location behind runningboard dust shields.

Mid-year 1926: Cabriolet (leather-backed) version of "Custom" closed cars added to line.

By June 1926: "Custom" touring available on order with fender wells, six wire wheels and trunk rack at $360 extra.

Chassis: Rear springs now semi-elliptic with ball and socket rear shackles. Spring seats no longer oscillate on rear axle housing. Spring covers on "Custom" line. Torque arm relocated from right to left side and connected to frame through fabric hanger. Radiator now cellular instead of tube and plate, and second radiator-to-cowl brace added. Balloon tires on split rims with no side rings. Brake drums bell-shaped to give clearance for balloon tires. Watson stabilators replace Gabriel snubbers. "American" ("National") threads replace special (Cadillac) threads. Chassis weight reduced by 263 lbs. (130 lbs. of this in engine weight reduction). In spring of 1926, at Steering Gear Unit Number 1-23500, steering changed from worm and sector type to split nut type.

Driveline: Axle shafts have 14 drive teeth instead of 6 lugs.

Engine: Crankcase ventilation system to eliminate dilution and condensation (this feature was used on the last 2,000 V-63s). Oil filter added. Oil level indicator on right side of crankcase instead of inside vee. Oil filler cap screw type instead of hinged. Camshaft bearings fed full oil pressure, not overflow from regulator. Rocker arms eliminated. Valves and tappets placed at an angle to the cylinder bores to line up directly with cams. One water pump, at left. Detachable water elbow on cylinder heads. Oil pump at right front corner of crankcase, in place of second water pump. Oil and water pumps driven directly from cross shaft. Starter and generator separate units for first time on Cadillacs. Starter vertical at top of flywheel housing, driving through teeth on rear face of flywheel. Generator at front, in vee. Generator/fan driven by belt, eliminating one chain. Tension on single chain maintained by idler sprocket. Front cover of engine made of steel instead of aluminum. Intake manifold now a separate piece.

1926 Cadillac, Series 314, four-door sedan, AA

I.D. DATA: Serial numbers were not used. Engine numbers were stamped on crankcase immediately above the base of the oil filler spout and on plate on dash. Starting: (1925) 100001. (1926) 114250. Ending: (1925) 114249. (1926) 142020.

Up to the Series 314, Cadillac had used the engine number as the key identifying number for the vehicle, and all changes made during a model production run were recorded by engine number. Parts orders listing the part and the engine number ensured receipt of the correct version of the part, including correct paint color, if applicable.

Starting with the Series 314, a "unit and car number" scheme was put into effect. Each car was assigned an engine number, which was stamped on the engine and on a plate on the firewall just before the car was shipped. This engine number, as before, was the identifying number of the vehicle — to be used for registration, etc.

However, changes were recorded, for the most part, by unit number, vehicle was the number stamped on each main assembly of the vehicle as that assembly was completed. Engine number and engine unit number bore no relation to each other. A change made at engine unit number 138009 might or might not have been included on the car carrying engine number 138009.

Various Cadillac manuals and parts books detail the various changes by unit number or, in rare cases, by engine/car number; but no cross reference exists. If the factory kept any cross reference of unit numbers against engine/car numbers, they did not pass it along with the car. Dealers were urged to make a unit number record for each of their customer's cars, so as to be able to service and supply parts for the car according to the exact requirements of the particular configuration of that vehicle.

Engine numbers for Series 314 cars consist of six digits, starting with the figure 1. Unit numbers for Series 314 cars consist of

the figure 1, followed by a dash, followed by one to five digits. The generator and starter carried Delco serial numbers.

The various numbers are located as follows:

Engine/Car Number — On the crankcase at the base of the oil filler and on the patent plate on the front face of the dash.

Engine Unit Number — On top of left-hand crankcase support arm (rear).

Chassis/Frame Unit Number — On the upper surface of the left-hand side bar, opposite the steering gear.

Body Unit Number and Job/Style Number — On right front sill or on metal plate on the front face of the dash.

Steering Gear Unit Number — On housing, near lubrication fitting.

Transmission Unit Number — On top of flange holding brake and clutch pedal bracket.

Clutch Unit Number — On front and rear retaining plates.

Front Axle Unit Number — On upper surface of axle I-beam.

Rear Axle Unit Number — On rear surface of the housing, just to right of cover plate.

Carburetor Unit Number — On left-hand rear face of flange by which carburetor is attached to intake header.

Generator Unit Number — On side of generator.

Starter Unit Number — On side of starter.

Style No.	Body Type & Seating	Price	Weight	Prod. Total
Standard body styles				
6400	2-dr. Brougham-5P	2995	4075	—
6430	2-dr. Coupe-2P	3045	4040	—
6490	2-dr. Victoria-4P	3095	4115	—
6420	4-dr. Sedan-5P	3195	4155	—
6410	4-dr. Sedan-7P	3295	4240	—
6440	4-dr. Imperial-7P	3435	4360	—
"Custom" body styles (August 1925)				
1154	4-dr. Touring-7P	3250	4300	—
1155	4-dr. Phaeton-4P	3250	3960	—
1156	2-dr. Roadster-2/4P	3250	3920	—
6460	2-dr. Coupe-5P	4000	4190	—
6470	4-dr. Sedan-5P	4150	4190	—
6450	4-dr. Suburban-7P	4285	4250	—
6480	4-dr. Imp. Suburban-7P	4485	4355	—
"Custom" closed body styles (January 1926)				
replacing closed bodies of August 1925 (sloping windshield)				
6680	2-dr. Coupe-5P	4000	4465	—
6690	4-dr. Sedan-5P	4150	4465	—
6670	4-dr. Suburban-7P	4285	4580	—
6700	4-dr. Imp. Suburban-7P	4485	4615	—
Mid-year additions to "Custom"				
6680-L	2-dr. Cab. Coupe-5P	—	—	—
6690-L	4-dr. Cab. Sedan-5P	—	—	—
6670-L	4-dr. Cab. Sub.-7P	—	—	—
6700-L	4-dr. Imp. Cab. Sub.-7P	—	—	—
Semi-commercial line				
NA	5-dr. Cus. Limo. Funeral Coach	—	—	—
NA	5-dr. Imp. Limo. Ambulance	—	—	—
NA	5-dr. Imp. Limo. Funeral Coach	—	—	—
NA	3-dr. Armored Car	—	6500	—

Note: The weight of the three-door armored car is approximate.

ENGINE: Ninety degree V-8. L-head. Cast iron blocks of four on aluminum crankcase. B & S: 3-1/8 x 5-1/8 in. Disp.: 314.5 cu. in. Brake H.P.: 80 plus advertised. S.A.E./Taxable/N.A.C.C. H.P.: 31.25. Main bearings: three. Valve lifters: mechanical lifters with roller acting directly on cams. Carb.: float feed, auxiliary air control, manufactured by Cadillac under C.F. Johnson patents.

CHASSIS: (All Standard cars plus Custom roadster) W.B.: 132 in. Front/Rear Tread: 56 in. Tires: 33 x 6.75 low pressure. (All Custom cars except roadster) W.B.: 138 in. Front/Rear Tread: 56 in. Tires: 33 x 6.75 low pressure. (Semi-commercial) W.B.: 150 in. Front/Rear Tread: 56 in. Tires: 33 x 6.75 low pressure.

TECHNICAL: Selective sliding gear transmission. Case in unit with engine. Speeds: 3F/1R. Left drive, center control (rhd optional). Multiple disc clutch. Shaft drive. Spiral bevel, full-floating rear axle. Overall ratio: 4.91:1, 4.5:1, 4.15:1. Mechanical brakes on four wheels. Wood artillery wheels, split rim, 12 spoke (wire and disc optional). Wheel size: 21 in. Optional drive ratio: 5.33:1 (Standard on armored car).

OPTIONS: Front bumper for Standard cars ($24.00). Rear bumper for Standard cars (24.00). Heater (32.00). Spring covers for Standard cars (20.00). 33 x 5 tires on wooden wheels (NC). Tonneau windshields (90.00-120.00). Trunks (56.00-72.50).

Note: Cadillac still took the stand that its cars were complete and ready for entirely acceptable service as built. However, accessories were recognized and dealers were encouraged to handle this business. Accessory catalogs were published by factory branches and the factory put out bulletins to dealers. It would be a few more years before the factory put out an accessory catalog directly to the public.

HISTORICAL: Introduced August 1925. Innovations: Crankcase ventilation. Calendar year sales: (1925) 14,249, (1926) 27,771. Calendar year production: (1925) 14,249, (1926) 27,771. Model two-year sales: 50,619 (August 1925 through September 1927). Model two-year production: 50,619 (August 1925 through September 1927). The president and general manager of Cadillac was Lawrence P. Fisher.

Other notes: With increasing consistency, Cadillac promotional material had mentioned the model designation alongside the name "Cadillac." For 1924/1925, practically every ad, catalog, manual, etc., carried the designation "V-63." Suddenly, in August 1925, all mention of a model designation was withheld from promotional material. The public would learn to think "Cadillac," not "Model," and would be presented "The New Cadillac" periodically for many years to come. However, for practical considerations in the area of Parts and Service, a system of model designation was still required. The "New Cadillac" for 1926/1927 was known to insiders as Series 314, based on engine displacement.

1927 CADILLAC

1927 Cadillac, Series 314, Fleetwood Imperial seven-passenger sedan, OCW

"THE NEW NINETY DEGREE CADILLAC" — SERIES 314 — EIGHT: August 1926 (Chassis Unit Number 1-29675. Steering Unit Number 1-30501):

Body: Sport coupe and sport sedan added to Standard line. Convertible coupe and double cowl (sport) phaeton added to "Custom" line. Custom bodies by Fleetwood, Brunn, Willoughby, and others available. Wheelbase on Standard seven-passenger sedan and Imperial now 138 in. Standard victoria made five-passenger by removing parcel compartment. New radiator shell with sharp corner between top and front surfaces and with round emblem on black background. Roadster and phaetons have forward folding windshields. Monogram panel on touring and phaetons extended to cowl, and vertical molding in front of rear door

moved to back of door. Light controls moved from instrument panel to steering wheel. New instrument panel of walnut with silver inlay effect. "Custom" cars and Standard sport models have nickel cowl band and sidelights. All cars have large (10 in.) headlights; black body on Standard, all nickel on "Custom." Horn of vibrator type, with bent trumpet. Fender wells standard on sport coupe and sedan, and on sport phaeton. Bumpers and moto-meter standard on "Custom" line and Standard sport models.

Chassis: At Steering Gear Unit Number 1-44906, steering gear was changed back to worm and sector type.

Driveline: 4.9:1 was only final drive ratio offered.

Engine: Early 1927, at Engine Unit Number 1-41001 (Chassis Unit Number 1-40994), practically everything on the outside of the engine, except the carburetor, was relocated. The overall appearance, except for the location of the starter, now resembled the soon to be introduced 303 LaSalle engine. Generator and water pump were moved to lower right front corner of engine and were driven by a common chain. The fan was once more on a separate bracket, still belt driven. The distributor went from the rear to the front of the engine and onto a common shaft with the oil pump, now inside the engine. The fuel pressure pump was now at the rear of the engine, driven by a connecting rod. The starter was moved forward and now driven through gear teeth cut on the front face of the flywheel.

1927 Cadillac, Series 314, sport sedan, JAC

I.D. DATA: Serial numbers were not used on the 1927 Cadillac. Engine numbers stamped on crankcase immediately above the base of the oil filler spout and on plate on dash. Starting: 142021. Ending: 150619.

Style No.	Body Type & Seating	Price	Weight	Prod. Total
Standard body styles				
6970	2-dr. Brgm.-5P	2995	4170	—
6980	2-dr. Cpe.-2P	3100	4105	—
7000	2-dr. Sport Cpe.-2P	3500	4460	—
7030	2-dr. Vic.-5P	3195	4190	—
6990	4-dr. Sed.-5P	3250	4270	—
7040	4-dr. Spt. Sed.-5P	3650	4590	—
7050	4-dr. Sed.-7P	3400	4370	—
7010	4-dr. Imp.-7P	3535	4480	—
"Custom" body styles				
7020	2-dr. Conv. Cpe.-2/4P	3450	4300	—
6680	2-dr. Cpe.-5P	3855	4465	—
6690	4-dr. Sed.-5P	3995	4465	—
6670	4-dr. Sub.-7P	4125	4580	—
6700	4-dr. Imp.-7P	4350	4615	—
6680-L	2-dr. Cab. Cpe.-5P	3955	—	—
6690-L	4-dr. Cab. Sed.-5P	4095	—	—
6670-L	4-dr. Cab. Suburban-7P	4225	—	—
6700-L	4-dr. Cab. Imp.-7P	4450	—	—
1165	2-dr. Rds.-2/4P	3350	4220	—
1164	4-dr. Phae.-4P	3450	4275	—
1164-B	4-dr. D.C. Phae.-4P	3975	4465	—
1163	4-dr. Tr.-7P	3450	4285	—
Fleetwood body styles				
2891	Limo. Brgm.	5525	—	—
2925	Twn. Cab. (seats forward)-7P	5750	—	—
3200	Twn. Cab. (opera seats)-7P	5500	—	—
3202	Coupe with rumble-2P	4775	—	—
3260	Imp.-5P	4975	—	—
3260-5	Sed.-5P	4875	—	—
3261	Imp. Cab.-5	5125	—	—
3261-5	Sed. Cab.-5P	4975	—	—
3275	Imp.-7P	5150	—	—

Style No.	Body Type & Seating	Price	Weight	Prod. Total
3275-5	Sed.-7P	4975	—	—
3276	Imp. Cab.-7P	5375	—	—
3291	Limo. Brgm.	5525	—	—
3078	Cabr.-7P	—	—	—
3012	Trans. Cab.-7P	—	—	—
2950	Conv. Cab.-7P	—	—	—
Brunn body styles				
1810	Collapsible Cab.-4P	—	—	—
1836	Sed.-4P	—	—	—
1915	Sed. Lan.-6P	—	—	—
NA	Twn. Cabr.	4800	—	—
Willoughby body styles				
NA	Twn. Cabr.	4800	—	—

Semi-commercial line: Continuation of 1926.

1927 Cadillac, Series 314, four-door phaeton, JAC

ENGINE: Ninety degree V-8. L-head. Cast iron blocks of four on aluminum crankcase. B & S: 3-1/8 x 5-1/8 in. Disp.: 314.5 cu. in. S.A.E./Taxable/N.A.C.C. H.P.: 31.25. Main bearings: three. Valve lifters: mechanical lifters with roller acting directly on cams. Carb.: float feed, auxiliary air control; manufactured by Cadillac under C.F. Johnson patents.

CHASSIS: All Standard cars except seven-passenger sedan and Imperial. Custom roadster and convertible coupe. W.B.: 132 in. Front/Rear Tread: 56 in. Tires: 33 x 6.75 low pressure. Semi-commercial. W.B.: 150 in. Front/Rear Tread: 56 in. Tires: 33 x 6.75 low pressure. All Custom cars except roadster and conv. coupe. Standard seven-passenger sedan and Imperial. W.B.: 138 in. Front/Rear Tread: 56 in. Tires: 33 x 6.75 low pressure.

TECHNICAL: Selective sliding gear transmission, case in unit with engine. Speeds: 3F/1R. Left drive, center control (rhd optional). Multiple dry disc clutch. Shaft drive. Spiral bevel, full-floating rear axle. Overall ratio: 4.91:1. Mechanical brakes on four wheels. Wood artillery wheels, split rim, 12 spoke. (See Note). Wheel size: 21 in.

Note: Disc wheels standard on Standard sport coupe and sedan. Wire wheels standard on Custom sport phaeton.

OPTIONS: Front bumper for Standard cars ($25.00). Rear bumper for Standard cars (25.00). Tire cover(s) (6.25-17.50). Black radiator shell (NC). Heater (40.00). Trunk rack (50.00). Trunks (55.00-91.00). Armrest on Standard line (25.00). Motometer on Standard line (10.00). Cowl lamps on Standard line (75.00). Nickel headlights on Standard line (10.00). 33 x 5 high pressure tires (NC). Disc wheels set of five (NC). Disc wheels set of six w/dual carrier (25.00). Wire wheels set of five (140.00). Wire wheels set of six, w/dual carrier (175.00). Six wire wheels, fender wells (350.00). Six disc wheels, fender wells (240.00). Six wood wheels, fender wells (200.00).

HISTORICAL: The 1927 Cadillac Series 314 was a continuation of 1926 models. Some new body styles introduced August 1926. Calendar year sales: (1927) 8,599. Calendar year production: (1927) 8,599. Model two-year sales: 50,619 (August 1925 through September 1927). Model two-year production:

50,619 (August 1925 through September 1927). The president and general manager of Cadillac was Lawrence P. Fisher.

1927 Cadillac, Series 314, convertible coupe, JAC

Note: "Fifty body styles and types — Five hundred color and upholstery combinations" was Cadillac's catch phrase for its new program to individualize the motor car. Change was constant; everything was tried; and pilot models were sold but not cataloged. The catalog was but a starting point — the customer could pick almost any combination of bits and pieces and have a unique motor car without the expense of a full custom. Authenticity of surviving cars may be in question because of the multitude of possible variations. In the final analysis; if it has a vertical starter motor, it's most likely a 314.

1927 Cadillac, Series 314, Fleetwood limousine brougham, JAC

1928 CADILLAC

CADILLAC — SERIES 341-A — EIGHT: General Motors now owned 100 percent of Fisher and had purchased Fleetwood and made it a division of Fisher. Practically all of Fleetwood's output was now on Cadillac/LaSalle chassis, and most Cadillac/LaSalle catalog or full customs were by Fleetwood. By using several variations and combinations of treatment above the belt line on a few basic body shells, Fleetwood was able to satisfy most customer's special desires and still offer short delivery (three to seven weeks). For the few who wanted something truly unique, Fleetwood produced full customs to order (four months delivery).

The Fisher and Fisher "Custom" lines were merged. The victoria was dropped. The two-door brougham was replaced by the four-door town sedan. Funeral coaches, ambulances, and a combination of the two were offered on the new 152 in. wheelbase chassis; bodies by Superior. All passenger car bodies were on a 140 in. chassis.

1928 Cadillac, Series 341-A, Imperial cabriolet, OCW

The longer wheelbase and underslung rear springs allowed for long, low-slung body lines. The deep, narrow, cellular radiator slung low in the frame and the slatted metal cover sweeping down over the fuel tank contributed to this effect, but the kick panels under the doors detracted somewhat.

Massive 12 in. bullet-type headlights were mounted on a crossbar between the fenders. A monogram rod was attached between the headlights and nickeled wire-conduit stanchions were placed between headlights and frame. Matching sidelights were mounted on the cowl. Dual ball-shaped rear lights were fender mounted. The top of the hood and radiator shell were flattened and 30 narrow louvers were set toward the rear of the side panels. Dual ventilator doors were in the top of the cowl on open cars and in the sides on closed cars.

The wind split on the lights was also featured in panels and moldings on the hood and cowl. An extra wide single-belt molding blended into the cowl and hood, as well as the pillars. The monogram panel on four-door open bodies was back to rear-doors-only. Fleetwood bodies featured a molding sweeping down and forward on the sides of the cowl, except on the transformables, which had a bold molding sweeping up the cowl and forward across the top of the hood.

Other body details included 3-1/2 inch wider rear compartment (rear tread had been increased by two inches), adjustable front seats on all but Imperials, and bumpers as standard equipment on all cars.

Chassis: Front brake drums increased from 16 to 17 in. in midyear. Rear springs under-slung. Fuel tank filler neck extended outside frame side rail. Hydraulic shock absorbers. Rear tread only increased to 58 in.

Driveline: New twin disc clutch, cast iron transmission housing, torque tube drive.

1928 Cadillac, Series 341-A, four-door sedan, JAC

Engine: New dimensions of 3-5/16 x 4-15/16 were the first change for the Cadillac V-8 since the Type 51. The transition that had started with the final version of the Series 314 engine was now complete; the 341 Cadillac engine and the 303 LaSalle engine were practically identical in configuration.

The 341 now had offset blocks, side by side connecting rods, single exhaust system, horizontal starter along right side of transmission, oil filter mounted on engine, oil level indicator behind right-hand block, manifold vacuum plus vacuum pump operating fuel feed system and windshield wipers. Aside from differences due to displacement and power, the only noticeable difference was the enameled heat deflector over the Cadillac carburetor.

I.D. DATA: There were no serial numbers used. Engine numbers were stamped on plate on front of dash and on crankcase just below the water inlet on the right side. Starting: 300001. Ending: 320001.

Style No.	Body Type & Seating	Price	Weight	Prod. Total
Fisher — 140 in. wheelbase:				
1173	2-dr. Roadster-2/4P	3350	4590	—
1171	4-dr. Touring-7P	3450	4630	—
1172	4-dr. Phaeton-4P	3450	4640	—
1172-B	4-dr. Sport Phaeton-4P	3950	5145	—
7920	2-dr. Coupe-2/4P	3295	4820	—
7980	2-dr. Conv. Coupe-2/4P	3495	4665	—
7970	2-dr. Coupe-5P	3495	4760	—
7950	4-dr. Sedan-5P	3595	4880	—
7960	4-dr. Town Sedan-5P	3395	4875	—
7960-L	4-dr. Town Sedan-5P	3395	4875	—
7930	4-dr. Sedan-7P	3695	4965	—
7990	4-dr. Imp. Sedan-5P	3745	4925	—
7990-L	4-dr. Imp. Cabriolet-5P	3745	4925	—
7940	4-dr. Imp. Sedan-7P	3895	5025	—
7940-L	4-dr. Imp. Cabriolet-7P	3895	5025	—
Semi Commercial — 152 in. wheelbase:				
NA	Limo. Funeral Coach	—	—	—
NA	Limo. Amb.	—	—	—
Fleetwood — 140 in. wheelbase				
8020	4-dr. Sedan-5P	4095	5120	—
8020-L	4-dr. Sedan (leather back)-5P	—	—	—
8030	4-dr. Imp. Sedan-5/7P	4245	5085	—
8030-L	4-dr. Imp. Sedan (leather back)-5/7P	—	—	—
8025	4-dr. Sedan Cabriolet-5P	4095	5120	—
8035	4-dr. Imp. Sed. Cab.-5/7P	4245	5085	—
8045	4-dr. Sedan Cabriolet-5P	4095	5120	—
8045-C	4-dr. Coll. Landau-5P	4795	—	—
8055	4-dr. Imp. Sed. Cab.-5/7P	4245	5085	—
8055-C	4-dr. Coll. Landau-5/7P	4945	—	—
8000	4-dr. Sedan-7P	4195	5040	—
8000-L	4-dr. Sedan (leather back)-7P	—	—	—
8010	4-dr. Imperial-7P	4445	5180	—
8010-L	4-dr. Imp. (leather back)-7P	—	—	—
8005	4-dr. Sedan Cabriolet-7P	4195	5040	—
8015	4-dr. Imp. Cab.-7P	4445	5180	—
3525	4-dr. Trans. Twn. Cab.-7P	5500	5180	—
3525-C	4-dr. Tr. Twn. Coll. Land.-7P	6200	—	—
3512	4-dr. Trans. Twn. Cab.-5/7P	5000	5180	—
3512-C	4-dr. Tr. Twn. Coll. Land.	5700	—	—
3520	4-dr. Trans. Twn. Cab.-7P	5500	5180	—
3520-C	4-dr. Tr. Twn. Coll. Cab.-7P	6200	—	—
3591	4-dr. Tr. Limo.Brougham-7P	5500	5180	—
3591-C	4-dr. Tr. Coll. Limo.Brgm.-7P	—	—	—
3550	Full Coll. Cab. (on order)	—	—	—
3550-C	(Twn. Car w/full coll top-7P)	—	—	—

Note: The following body styles are listed as Fleetwood 341, 341-A, 341-B, but are unconfirmed. All are on 140 in. wheelbase except as noted. Included must be full customs and one-off variations of catalog customs.

1928/1929 Cadillac Series 341-A, 341-B

Style No.	Body Type & Seating	Price	Weight	Prod. Total
3015	Limo.-7P (138" wb)	—	—	—
3097	Limo.-5P	—	—	—
3133	All Weather Touring-5P	—	—	—
3135	Special Town Cabriolet	—	—	—
3144	Sedan-4P (132" wb)	—	—	—
3174	Sport Cabriolet-5P	—	—	—
3185	Sedan-7P	—	—	—
3199	Coupe-2P	—	—	—
3208	Imperial Cabriolet-5P (152" wb)	—	—	—
3238	Club Cabriolet-5P	—	—	—
3274	Sport Cabriolet Sedan-5P	—	—	—
3300	Convertible Cabriolet-7P	—	—	—
3360	Sedan-5P	—	—	—
3360-5	Imperial-5P	—	—	—
3361	Sedan-5P	—	—	—
3361-5	Imperial-5P	—	—	—
3375	Sedan-7P	—	—	—
3375-5	Imperial-7P	—	—	—
3376	Sedan-7P	—	—	—
3412	Town Car-7P (152" wb)	—	—	—
3435	Town Car-7P (152" wb)	—	—	—
3475	Limo.-7P	—	—	—
3512-P	Town Car-5P	—	—	—
3512-C-P	Town Car-5P	—	—	—
3515	Limo.-7P	—	—	—
3520-P	Town Car-5P	—	—	—
3520-C-P	Town Car-7P	—	—	—

Style No.	Body Type & Seating	Price	Weight	Prod. Total
1928/1929 Cadillac Series 341-A, 341-B				
3525-P	Town Car-7P	—	—	—
3525-C-P	Town Car-7P	—	—	—
3591-P	Town Car-7P	—	—	—
3591-C-P	Town Car-7P	—	—	—
3885	Convertible Sedan	—	—	—
3891	Imperial Sedan-7P	—	—	—

ENGINE: Ninety degree V-8. L-head. Eight. Cast iron block on copper/aluminum crankcase. B & S: 3-5/16 x 4-15/16 in. Disp. 341 cu. in. C. R.: 4.8:1 standard, 5.3:1 optional. SAE/Taxable/N.A.C.C. H.P.: 35.1. Main bearings: three. Valve lifters: mechanical, with rollers riding on cams. Carb.: float feed, auxiliary air control; manufactured by Cadillac under C.F. Johnson patents. (Compression) 90-92 PSI @ 1000 RPM., 105-107 PSI @ 1000 RPM with high compression heads.

1928 Cadillac, Series 341-A, Fleetwood transformable town cabriolet, JAC

CHASSIS: (Series 341-A) W.B.: 140 in. O.L.: 213-1/4 in. Front/Rear Tread: 56/58 in. Tires: 32 x 6.75 (7.00-20). (Series 341-A Commercial Chassis) W.B.: 152 in. Front/Rear Tread: 56/58 in. Tires: 32 x 6.75 (7.00-20).

TECHNICAL: Selective transmission. Speeds: 3F/1R. Left-hand drive, center control (rhd optional). Twin disc clutch. Shaft drive (torque tube). Full-floating rear axle. Spiral bevel drive. Overall ratio: 4.75:1 standard; 4.39:1, 5,08:1 optional. Mechanical brakes on four wheels. 16 in. rear drums. 16 in. front drums (17 in. front mid-year). Artillery wheels (wire and disc optional).Wheel size: 20 in.

OPTIONS: Folding trunk rack ($25.00). Step plate (3.25 ea.). Tire mirrors (30.00). Wind wings (15.00-30.00). Trunks (65.00-

100.00). Herald ornament (12.00). Seat covers (5.25). Spotlight (35.00). Tire covers (10.00). Tonneau windshield (120.00). Natural wood wheels (10.00 extra). Five disc wheels (20.00). Six disc wheels, fender wells, two spares (175.00). Five wire wheels (95.00). Six wire wheels, fender wells, two spares (250.00). Fender wells for wood wheels, two spares (140.00).

HISTORICAL: Introduced: September 1927. Model year sales: 20,001. Model year production: 20,001. The president and general manager of Cadillac was Lawrence P. Fisher.

See page 6 for "How to Use This Catalog"

1929 CADILLAC

1929 Cadillac, Series 341-B, roadster, OCW

1929 Cadillac, Series 341-B, roadster, JAC

CADILLAC — SERIES 341-B — EIGHT: Similar to 1928 Cadillac Series 341-A except:

Bodies: Sidelights moved to fenders. Security-Plate safety glass used in all windows and windshields. All brightwork chrome plated. Electric windshield wipers used. Fleetwood introduced the all weather phaeton. Fleetwood showed the sweep panel across cowl and hood on all body styles.

Chassis: Duplex-mechanical brakes with all shoes internal used.

Driveline: Synchromesh transmission introduced.

Engine: Connecting rods drilled to give pressure lubrication to small ends. Metric spark plugs introduced mid-year.

I.D. DATA: There were no serial numbers used, engine numbers were stamped on plate on front of dash and on crankcase just below the water inlet on the right side. Starting: 320002. Ending: 338104.

1929 Cadillac, Series 341-B, Fleetwood sport cabriolet, JAC

1929 Cadillac, Series 341-B, town sedan, JAC

Style No.	Body Type & Seating	Price	Weight	Prod Total
Fisher — 140" wb				
1182	4-dr. Touring-7P	3450	4774	—
1183	4-dr. Phaeton-7P	3450	4635	—
1183-8	4-dr. Sport Phaeton-4P	3950	5110	—
1184	2-dr. Roadster-2/4P	3350	4678	—
8620	4-dr. Sedan-7P	3795	5145	—
8630	4-dr. Imp. Sedan-7P	3995	—	—
8640	4-dr. Sedan-5P	3695	5027	—
8650	4-dr. Imp. Sedan-5P	—	—	—
8660	4-dr. Town Sedan-5P	3495	5028	—
8670	2-dr. Coupe-5P	3595	4887	—
8680	2-dr. Conv. Coupe-2/4P	3595	4796	—
8690	2-dr. Coupe-2/4P	3295	4909	—
Semi-Commercial — 152" wb				
NA	Limo. Funeral Coach	—	—	—
NA	Limo. Ambulance	—	—	—
Fleetwood — 140" wb				
3830	4-dr. Imperial-5P	4345	5130	—
3830-S	4-dr. Sedan-5P	4195	5120	—
3830-C	4-dr. Coll. Imp.-5P	5045	—	—
3830-SC	4-dr. Coll. Sedan-5P	4895	—	—
3830-L	4-dr. Imp. (leather back)-5P	445	—	—
3830-SL	4-dr. Sedan (leather back)-5P	4295	—	—
3861	4-dr. Imp. Twn.(club) Sed.-5P	—	—	—
3861-S	4-dr. Club Cabriolet-5P	4395	5120	—
3861-C	4-dr. Coll. Imp. Club. Cab.-5P	—	—	—
3861-SC	4-dr. Coll. Club Cab.-5P	5095	—	—
3855	4-dr. Imp. Cabriolet-5P	4345	5130	—
3855-S	4-dr. Sedan Cab.-5P	4195	5120	—
3855-C	4-dr. Coll. Imp. Cab.-5P	5045	—	—
3855-SC	4-dr. Coll. Sedan Cab.-5P	4895	—	—
3875	4-dr. Imperial-7P	4545	5210	—
3875-S	4-dr. Sedan-7P	4295	5200	—
3875-C	4-dr. Coll. Imp.-7P	5245	—	—
3875-L	4-dr. Imp. (leather back)-7P	4645	—	—
3875-SL	4-dr. Sedan (leather back)-7P	4395	—	—
3875-SC	4-dr. Coll. Sedan-7P	4995	—	—
3875-X	4-dr. Imp. (full leather quarter)-7P	4795	—	—
3875-SX	4-dr. Sed. (full leather quarter)-7P	4545	—	—
3180	All Weath. Phaeton-5P	5750	5130	—
3880	4-dr. Imp. A-W Phaeton-5P	5995	5140	—
3512	4-dr. Trans. Twn. Cab.-5/7P	5250	5180	—
3512-C	4-dr. Coll. Tr. Twn. Cab.-5/7P	5950	5180	—
3520	4-dr. Trans. Twn. Cab.-7P	5500	5180	—
3520-C	4-dr. Coll. Tr. Twn. Cab.-7P	6200	5180	—
3525	4-dr. Trans. Twn. Cab.-7P	5500	5180	—
3525-C	4-dr. Coll. Tr. Twn. Cab.-7P	5500	5180	—
3591	4-dr. Tr . Limo.Brougham-7P	5500	5180	—
3591-C	4-dr. Coll. Tr. Land. Brhm.-7P	6200	5180	—
3550	4-dr. Full. Coll. Tr. Cab.-7P	6700	—	—

ENGINE: Ninety degree V-8: L-head. Eight. Cast iron block on copper/aluminum crankcase. B & S: 3-5/16 x 4-15/16 in. Disp.: 341 cu. in. C.R.: 5.3:1 std.; 4.8:1 opt. Brake H.P.: 90 plus advertised. SAE/Taxable/N.A.C.C. H.P.: 35.1. Main bearings: three. Valve lifters: mechanical, with rollers riding on cams. Carb.: float feed, auxiliary air control; manufactured by Cadillac under C.F. Johnson patents. Compression: 90-92 PSI @ 1000 RPM, 105-107 PSI @ 1000 RPM with high compression heads.

CHASSIS: (Series 341-B) W.B.: 140 in. O.L.: 213-1/4 in. Front/Rear Tread: 56/58 in. Tires: 7.00-20 (32 x 6.75). (Series 341-B Commercial Chassis) W.B.: 152 in. Front/RearTread: 56/58 in. Tires: 7.00-20 (32 x 6.75).

TECHNICAL: Selective synchromesh transmission. 3F/1R. Left drive, center control (rhd optional). Twin disc clutch. Shaft drive (torque tube). Full-floating rear axle, spiral bevel drive. Overall ratio: 5.08:1 std.; 4.75:1, 4.39:1 opt. Duplex-mechanical brakes on four wheels. All shoes inside drums. 16-1/2 in. drums. Wood artillery wheels (wire and disc optional). Wheel size: 20 in.

OPTIONS: Folding trunk rack ($25.00). Step plate (3.25 ea.). Tire mirrors (30.00). Wind wings (15.00-30.00). Heater (32.00). Trunks (65.00-100.00). Herald ornament (12.00). Seat covers. (25.25). Spotlight (35.00). Tire covers (10.00). Tonneau windshield (120.00). Natural wood wheels (10.00 extra). Five disc wheels (20.00). Six disc wheels, fender wells, two spares (175.00). Five wire wheels (95.00). Six wire wheels, fender wells; two spares (250.00). Fender wells for wood wheels, two spares (140.00).

HISTORICAL: Introduced August 1928. Innovations: Synchromesh transmission. Safety glass. Model year sales: 18,103. Model year production: 18,103. The president and general manager of Cadillac was Lawrence P. Fisher.

1929 Cadillac, Series 341-B, sport phaeton, JAC

1930 CADILLAC

1930 Cadillac, Series 353, seven-passenger sedan, OCW

CADILLAC — SERIES 353 — EIGHT: An extension of the Series 341-B, with the following changes:

Bodies: Fisher ("Fisher Custom") line reduced to seven closed bodies, including convertible coupe. Fleetwood ("Fleetwood Special Custom") line consolidated into 11 basic bodies, with many variations.

Louvers carried well to the front of the hood. Fleetwood roadster had louvers in the sides of the cowl. Wider radiator. Larger headlights (12 in. lens, 13 in. overall). Windshield slopes a few degrees. Short, cadet-type visor. Valance across rear of car covers fuel tank and frame, and joins rear fenders. With wider rear tread, rear cushions made 4 in. wider. All but a few bodies were prewired for radio, with an aerial built into the top.

Chassis: Ball and socket spring shackles no longer used. Front tread increased from 56 in. to 59 in. Rear tread increased from 58 in. to 59-1/2 in. Third rear shoe for emergency brake dropped; lever now operates rear service brake shoes. Fan shaped end on exhaust tail pipe. Demountable wood wheels offered as an extra cost option.

Driveline: All cars have 3/4 floating rear axle.

Engine: Bore increased 1/16 inch. Reduction type starter used. Fan lubricated by engine oil return pressure. Cover used over spark plugs. New distributor has wires out rear, into single conduit.

I.D. DATA: There were no serial numbers on the 1930 Cadillac Series 353. Engine numbers were stamped on crankcase just below the water inlet on the right-hand side. Starting: 500001. Ending: 511005.

Style No.	Body Type & Seating	Price	Weight	Prod. Total
Fisher				
30152	4-dr. Twn. Sed.-5P	3495	5040	—
30158	2-dr. Cpe.-2/4P	3295	4955	—
30159	4-dr. Sed.-5P	3695	5070	—
30162	4-dr. Sed.-7P	3795	5170	—
30163	4-dr. Imp.-7P	3995	5210	—
30168	2-dr. Conv. Cpe.-2/4P	3595	4860	—
30172	2-dr. Coupe-5P	3595	4945	—
Fleetwood built-to-order				
4150	4-dr. Full Coll. Trans. Twn. Cab.	—	—	—
4157	4-dr. Tour.-7P	—	—	—
4160	4-dr. Spt. Phae.-5P	—	—	—
4160-A	4-dr. Spt. Phae.-5P	—	—	—
4160-B	4-dr. Spt. Phae.-5P	—	—	—
4161	4-dr. Sed. or Imp. Spt. Cab.-5P	—	—	—
4164	4-dr. Trans. Brougham-5P	—	—	—
4164-B	4-dr. Trans. Brougham w/cane work-5P	—	—	—
4176	2-dr. Spt. Sta. or Conv. Cpe.-2P	—	—	—
4185	2-dr. All Weather Cpe.-4P	—	—	—
3350	Trans. All Weather Phae. (152 in. wb)-7P	—	—	—
3950	Twn. Car w/Full Collapsible Top-7P	—	—	—
3902	2-dr. Rds.-2/4P	3450	4625	—
3930	4-dr. Imp.-5P	4395	5220	—
3930-5	4-dr. Sedan-5P	4195	5150	—
3930-C	4-dr. Collapsible Imp.-5P	5195	—	—
3930-SC	4-dr. Collapsible Sed.-5P	4995	—	—
3955	4-dr. Imp. Cabr.-5P	4445	5240	—
3955-5	4-dr. Sed. Cabr.-5P	4245	5200	—
3955-C	4-dr. Collapsible Imp. Cabr.-5P	5195	—	—
3955-SC	4-dr. Collapsible Sed. Cabr.-5P	4995	—	—
3975	4-dr. Imp.-7P	4595	5320	—
3975-5	4-dr. Sed.-7P	4295	5280	—
3975-C	4-dr. Collapsible Imp.-7P	5395	—	—
3975-SC	4-dr. Collapsible Sed.-7P	5095	—	—
3975-P	4-dr. Imp. (plain hood)-7P	4845	—	—
3981	4-dr. Sedanette Cabr.-5P	4500	5070	—
3982	4-dr. Sedanette-5P	4595	5070	—
3980	4-dr. All Weather Phae.-5P	4700	4990	—
3912	4-dr. Transformable Twn.Cabr.-5/7P	4995	5230	—
3912-C	4-dr. Coll. Trans. Twn. Cabr.-5/7P	5745	—	—
3920	4-dr. Twn. Cab. (quarter window)-7P	5145	5150	—
3920-C	4-dr. Coll. Twn. Cab. (quarter window)-7P	5945	—	—
3925	4-dr. Trans. Twn. Cab. (no quarter window)-7P	5145	5150	—
3925-C	4-dr. Coll. Tr. Twn. Cab. (no quarter window)-7P	5895	—	—
3991	4-dr. Trans. Limo. Brougham-7P	5145	5320	—
3991-C	4-dr. Coll. Tr. Limo. Brougham-7P	5945	—	—

1930 Cadillac, Series 353, Fleetwood transformable limousine brougham, JAC

ENGINE: Ninety degree V-8. L-head. Cast iron on silicon/aluminum crankcase. B & S: 3-3/8 x 4-15/16 in. Disp.: 353 cu. in. C.R.: 5.05:1 std., 4.92:1 opt. Brake H.P.: 96 @ 3000 R.P.M. SAE/Taxable H.P.: 36.45. Main bearings: three. Valve lifters: mechanical, with rollers riding on cams. Carb.: float feed, auxiliary air control; manufactured by Cadillac under C.F. Johnson patents.

CHASSIS: (Series 353) W.B.: 140 in. Length: app. 210-5/8 in. Front/Rear Tread: 59/59-1/2 in. Tires: 7.00-19. (Commerical Chassis) W.B.: 152 in.

TECHNICAL: Selective, synchromesh transmission. Speeds: 3F/1R. Left drive, center controls (rhd optional). Twin disc clutch. Shaft drive (torque tube). 3/4 floating rear axle spiral bevel gears. Overall ratio: 5.08:1 std.; 4.39:1, 4.75:1 opt. (4.75:1 made standard in mid-year). Safety-mechanical brakes on four wheels. (16-1/2 in. drums). Wood artillery wheels (disc, wire, wood demountable optional). Wheel size: 19 in.

1930 Cadillac, Series 353, Fleetwood Imperial phaeton, JAC

OPTIONS: Tire cover(s) ($6.50-30.00). Wind Wings (25.00-55.00). Tonneau Shield (185.00). Radio (175.00). Heater (42.50). Radiator ornament (25.00). Trunks (80-115.00). Seat covers (26.75-230.25). Spotlight/driving lights (15.50-80.00). Tire mirrors (32.00/pair). Five wire wheels (70.00). Six wire wheels w/fender wells, trunk rack (210.00). Five demountable wood wheels (50.00). Six demountable wood wheels w/fender wells, trunk rack (190.00). Five disc wheels (50.00). Six disc wheels w/fender wells, trunk rack (190.00).

HISTORICAL: Introduced September 1929. Innovations: radio available. Most bodies pre-wired for radio, with aerial built into top. Model year sales: 14,995. Model year production: 14,995. The president and general manager of Cadillac was Lawrence P. Fisher.

1930-1931 (V-16) CADILLAC

1930 Cadillac, V-16, roadster, OCW

CADILLAC — SERIES 452/452-A — SIXTEEN: Bodies: Although full-custom bodies were built by Fleetwood, Murphy, Waterhouse, Saoutchik, Vanden Plas, Pinin Farina, and others; most were "catalog customs" by Fleetwood. A few cars had Fisher bodies. Only about one-fifth were open or convertible, two-thirds were five- or seven-passenger sedans or Imperials, the rest coupes or town cars.

More than 50 body styles were offered, but the list consists of only a few basic shells with several variations each: metal or leather quarters, with or without quarter windows, fixed or collapsible (landau) quarters, with or without Imperial division, straight or coach sill, plain or recessed hood/cowl, etc .

With few exceptions, the "41" styles had plain hood and straight sill, the "42" styles had plain hood and coach sill, and the "43" styles had recessed hood/cowl and straight sill.

Windshield treatment varied from vertical vee to 22 degree sloping, as follows:

Vertical vee swing-out (Pennsylvania): 4130, 4155

7 degree flat swing-out: 4212, 4220, 4225, 4264, 4291

7 degree vee-type swing-out: 4312, 4320, 4325, 4335, 4376, 4380, 4391

7 degree flat crank-up (V-V): 4330, 4355, 4361, 4375, 4381

16 degree flat swing-out, folding: 4302

18 degree flat crank-up (V-V) "Madame X": 4130, 4155, 4161, 4175, 4276, 4476

21 degree flat swing-out: 4235

22 degree flat, divided: 4260

The sobriquet "Madame X" (with an "e") is not prominent, if it appears at all, in Cadillac promotional literature. Perhaps the only place Cadillac printed it is in body style listings found in various parts lists, as early as March 1930. The term is associated with job/style numbers 4130, 4155, 4161, 4175, in plain, -S, -C, or -SC variations. In later parts lists, job number 4476 is listed as having a "Madame X" windshield.

"Madame X" has a Hollywood flavor, but is no more inappropriate than the style designations "Fleetbourne," "Fleetdowns," etc. The term must have arisen from a distinctive styling feature common to the four basic body styles. Further, the term more likely came from Detroit than from Pennsylvania Dutch country. The most distinctive styling feature of the "41" series bodies built in Detroit is the 18 degree flat, crank-up (V-V) windshield. It is unlikely that the Pennsylvania versions with vertical vee swingout windshields were thought of as "Madame X" bodies. Job/style number 4276, being style 4476 with coach sill, also has a "Madame X" windshield.

Chrome-plated window reveals were used on "41" bodies but were not unique to those styles. Although early body specs listed chrome-plated reveals, July 1930 body specs listed painted reveals on "41" bodies. Painted window reveals on "Madame X" bodies are probably as rare as the "standard" rear-mounted spare tire.

In simplest terms, 1930-31 Fleetwood four-door bodies with 18 degree windshield, mounted on Cadillac V-16 chassis are "Madame X", and two coupe body styles have the "Madame X" windshield.

Body details unique to the V-16 or introduced with the V-16 and seen on the full 1931 line include: single bar bumpers, dual horns, concave monogram bar, radiator screen, 13-inch Guide "Tiltray" headlights, dual rear lights matching the headlights, triple molding on dust shield panels of straight sill styles, five doors in the hood, single matching door in the side of the cowl, and none, one, or two rectangular vent doors in the top of the cowl. Most bodies with recessed hood/cowl had one triangular door in the top of the cowl.

1930 Cadillac, V-16, four-door phaeton, JAC

Chassis: Frame similar to 353 except for five-point engine mount on V-16. Brake system had vacuum assist operated on manifold vacuum, not vacuum pump. Brake drums 16-1/2 inch diameter. Specially balanced whitewall tires used.

Driveline: Rear engine support at tail of transmission. Heavier clutch linings (chassis unit 7-2991 and later used thinner lining of V-8). Rear axle shafts same as on 353 except made of special steel. Optional 3.47:1 final drive ratio dropped mid-model.

1931 Cadillac, V-16, two-door coupe, JAC

Engine: Extra effort and expense went into a polished, plated, enameled, uncluttered engine compartment. Wiring was concealed and covers were used on engine and dash to hide plumbing and controls.

Twin coils were mounted in recesses in the radiator top tank. Spark plug wires came out the rear of the double deck distributor cap and disappeared under the cover inside the vee. The narrow (45 degree) vee allowed for outboard mounting of manifolds and dual carburetors. Intake pipes from higher in the engine compartment were added at engine number 702502 to eliminate the problem of road splash entering the carburetors. Fuel feed was by dual vacuum tanks operated by vacuum pump. By May 1930, the chrome-plated vacuum tanks were superseded by painted units. The dual exhaust system ended in fan-shaped tailpipe tips.

To silence the overhead valve system, hydraulically rotated eccentric bushings were used in the rocker arms. The early use of a different head thickness for various compression ratios was replaced by the use of a single head with gaskets of different thicknesses. Right and left heads and blocks were interchangeable. One row of head studs went through the block to the crankcase, the second row seated in the block.

Engine lubrication was full pressure from oil pump on rear main bearing cap. At engine unit number 7-1038, the oil level indicator was moved from rear of right-hand cylinder block to left side of crankcase. The belt-driven fan was mounted on ball bearings, lubricated by grease fitting, not engine oil pressure. Crankshaft thrust was taken by center main. A harmonic balancer was mounted on front end of crankshaft. A single chain to drive camshaft and generator was provided with automatic adjuster incorporated in an idler acting on the outside of the chain. A thermostat was used to close the crankcase ventilation intake at 1931 higher engine temperatures. The double outlet water pump on the right side of the engine was driven by an extension shaft from the rear of the generator. A cooling system condenser tank was used once again.

The engine, transmission assembly was mounted at the four corners of the engine plus a dual mount at the rear of the transmission. The front mounts were supported by diagonal members in the frame.

I.D. DATA: Serial numbers were not used on the 452/452-A series. Engine numbers were stamped on crankcase right-hand side, on the generator drive chain housing. Starting: 700001. Ending: 703251.

Style No.	Body Type & Seating	Price	Weight	Prod. Total
4108-C	4-dr. Imp. Lan. Cabr.-5/7P	—	—	—
4130	4-dr. Imp.-5/7P	7300	5920	—
4130-5	4-dr. Sed.-5P	6950	5850	—
4155	4-dr. Imp. Cabr.-5/7P	7350	5940	—
4155-C	4-dr. Imp. Lan. Cabr.-5/7P	—	—	—
4155-5	4-dr. Sed. Cabr.-5P	7125	5900	—
4155-SC	4-dr. Lan. Sed. Cabr.-5P	—	—	—
4161	4-dr. Imp. Clb. Sed.-5P	—	—	—
4161-C	4-dr. Imp. Lan. Clb. Sed.-5P	—	—	—
4161-5	4-dr. Clb. Sed.-5P	6950	5740	—
4175	4-dr. Imp.-7P	7525	6020	—
4175-C	4-dr. Imp. Lan.-7P	—	—	—
4175-5	4-dr. Sed.-7P	7225	5980	—
4200	4-dr. Sed. Cabr.-7P	—	—	—
4206	2-dr. Cpe.-2/4P	—	—	—
4207	2-dr. Cpe.-2/4P	—	—	—
4208	4-dr. Imp. Cabr.-5/7P	—	—	—
4212	4-dr. Trans. Twn. Cabr.-5/7P	8750	5915	—
4212-C	4-dr. Coll. Trans. Twn. Cabr.-5/7P	—	—	—
4220	4-dr. Trans. Twn. Cabr.-7P	8750	5850	—
4220-B	4-dr. Trans. Twn. Cabr.-7P	—	—	—
4225	4-dr. Trans. Twn. Cabr.-7P	8750	5850	—
4225-C	4-dr. Coll. Trans. Twn.Cabr.-7P	—	—	—
4235	2-dr. Conv. Cpe.-2/4P	6900	5670	—
4243	4-dr. Phae.	—	—	—
4244	4-dr. Phae.	—	—	—
4246	4-dr. Phae.	—	—	—
4257-A	4-dr. Tr.-7P	—	—	—
4257-H	4-dr. Tr.-5P	—	—	—
4260	4-dr. Spt. Phae.-5P	6500	—	—
4260-A	4-dr. Spt. Phae.-5P	—	—	—
4260-B	4-dr. Spt. Phae.-5P	—	—	—
4262	4-dr. Imp. Cabr.-7P	—	—	—
4264	4-dr. Twn. Brgm.-5/7P	9200	5765	—
4264-B	4-dr. Town Brgm.-5/7P	9700	5675	—
4275	4-dr. Imp. Sed.-7P	—	—	—
4275-C	4-dr. Imp. Landau Sed.-7P	—	—	—
4276	2-dr. Cpe.-2/4P	6850	5765	—
4280	4-dr. All Weather Phae.-4P	7350	5675	—
4285	4-dr. All Weather Spt.Cabr.-5P	—	—	—
4291	4-dr. Transformable Limo. Brgm.-7P	8750	6020	—
4302	2-dr. Rds.-2/4P	5350	5325	—
4312	4-dr. Transformable Twn. Cabr.-5/7P	7000	5930	—
4312-C	4-dr. Collapsible Transformable Twn. Cabr.-5/7P	—	—	—
4320	4-dr. Transformable Twn. Cabr.-7P	7150	5850	—
4320-C	4-dr. Collapsible Transformable Twn. Cabr.-7P	—	—	—
4325	4-dr. Transformable Twn. Cabr.-7P	7150	5850	—
4325-C	4-dr. Collapsible Transformable Twn. Cabr.-7P	—	—	—
4330	4-dr. Imp.-5/7P	6300	5920	—
4330-5	4-dr. Sed.-5P	5950	5850	—
4335	2-dr. Conv. Cpe.-2/4P	5900	5655	—
4355	4-dr. Imp. Cabr.-5/7P	6350	5940	—
4355-C	4-dr. Collapsible Imp. Cabr.-5/7P	—	—	—
Style No.	**Body Type & Seating**	**Price**	**Weight**	**Prod. Total**
4355-5	4-dr. Sed. Cabr.-5P	6125	5885	—
4361	4-dr. Imp. Club Sed.-5P	—	—	—
4361-5	4-dr. Club Sed.-5P	5950	5740	—
4375	4-dr. Imp.-7P	6525	6020	—
4375-C	4-dr. Collapsible Imp.-7P	—	—	—
4375-5	4-dr. Sed.-7P	6225	5980	—
4376	2-dr. Cpe.-2/4P	5800	5750	—
4380	4-dr. All Weather Phae.-5P	6650	5690	—
4381	2-dr. Cpe.-5P	5950	—	—
4391	4-dr. Transformable Limo. Brgm.-7P	7150	6020	—
4391-C	4-dr. Collapsible Transformable Limo. Brgm.-7P	—	—	—
4412	4-dr. Transformable Twn. Cabr.-5/7P	—	—	—
4476	2-dr. Cpe.-2/4P	5800	5765	—
3289-A	4-dr. Trans. Twn. Cabr.-7P	—	—	—
3981	4-dr. Sed. Cabr.-5P	—	—	—
3991	4-dr. Trans. Limo. Brgm.-7P	—	—	—

2950-X	4-dr. Sed.-7P	—	—	—
2901-LX	4-dr. Sed.-7P	—	—	—
2951-LX	4-dr. Sed.-7P	—	—	—
30-X	4-dr. Sed.-7P	—	—	—
LX-2905	4-dr. Twn. Sed.-5P	—	—	—
LX-2913	2-dr. Cpe.-5P	—	—	—
30-152	4-dr. Twn. Sed., Fisher-5P	—	—	—
30-158	2-dr. Cpe., Fisher-2/4P	—	—	—
30-159	4-dr. Sed., Fisher-5P	—	—	—
30-168	2-dr. Conv. Cpe., Fisher-2/4P	—	—	—
30-172	2-dr. Cpe., Fisher-5P	—	—	—

ENGINE: 45 degree, overhead valve V-16. Cast nickel iron blocks on silicon/aluminum crankcase. B & S: 3 x 4 in. Disp.: 452 cu. in. C.R.: 5.35:1 early std., 5.11:1 std., 4.98:1 opt. Brake H.P.: 175-185 @ 3400 R.P.M. SAE/Taxable H.P.: 57.5. Main bearings: five. Valve lifters: pushrod/rocker arm with hydraulic rotary eccentric silencer in rocker arm. Carb.: float feed, auxiliary air control; manufactured by Cadillac under C.F. Johnson patents.

CHASSIS: (Series: 452/452-A) W.B.: 148 in. O.L.: approx. 222-1/2 in. Front/Rear Tread: 59/59-1/2 in. Tires: 7.00-19 early, 7.50-19 mid-model.

TECHNICAL: Selective, synchromesh transmission. Speeds: 3F/1R. Left drive, center control, (rhd optional). Twin disc clutch. Shaft drive, (torque tube). 3/4 floating rear axle, spiral bevel drive. Overall ratio: 4.39:1 std., (3.47:1), 4.07:1, 4.75:1 opt. Vacuum assisted mechanical brakes on four wheels. Wood artillery wheels (wire, disc, demountable wood optional). Wheel size: 19 in.

OPTIONS: Mirrors ($10.00-32.00). Sidemount cover(s) (5.00-40.00). Tonneau windshield (185.00). Wind wings (47.50). Radio (200.00). Heater (41.00-55.00). Heron or Goddess ornament (20.00). Auxiliary lights (37.50-75.00). Seat covers (26.75-73.50). Trunks (100.00-119.00). Five wire wheels (70.00). Six wire wheels, fender wells, trunk rack (210.00). Five demountable wood wheels (50.00). Six demountable wood wheels, fender wells, trunk, rack (190.00). Five disc wheels (50.00). Six disc wheels, fender wells, trunk rack (190.00). Fenders other than black (100.00).

HISTORICAL: Introduced January 1930. Model year sales: 3,251. Model year production: 3,251. The president and general manager at Cadillac was Lawrence P. Fisher.

Note: Although a token number (approximately one percent) of the V-16 chassis were sold to domestic and foreign coachbuilders, all body styles advertised by Cadillac were "Catalog Customs" by Fleetwood. The customer was able to order limited variations in the "Catalog Customs," or a full-custom creation.

It is remarkable that Fleetwood was able to turn out 400 to 500 bodies per month at a time when activities at the Pennsylvania shop were being phased out and "production" at a new location in Detroit was being set up.

Through the fall of 1930, dealers were required to furnish the factory with weekly and monthly owner reaction and service reports on each V-16 delivered.

1931 Cadillac, V-16, seven-passenger limousine, JAC

1931 CADILLAC

1931 Cadillac, Series 355-A, town sedan, JAC

CADILLAC — SERIES 355-A — EIGHT: Similar to Series 353 except as follows:

Bodies: New body, longer and lower. Longer hood with five hood ports (doors). Matching doors in cowl. Modified coach sill, no compartments in splash pan. Battery and tool compartments under front seat. Metal floor boards. Oval instrument panel, with same grouping as Series 353. Radiator screen, single bar bumper, dual horns. Headlight diameter reduced one inch.

Chassis and driveline: New frame with divergent side rails. Rear springs mounted directly under frame rails. Metal covers on springs. Radiator mounted lower in frame. Condenser tank for cooling system.

Engine: Displacement same as Series 353. Series designation on V-8s no longer matches displacement. Five point engine suspension, similar to V-16. Intake muffler added. Distributor 1-1/2 inches higher than on 345. Fan lower to match lower radiator.

I.D. DATA: Serial numbers were not used. Engine numbers were stamped on crankcase just below the water inlet on the right hand side. Starting: 800001. Ending: 810717.

Style No.	Body Type & Seating	Price	Weight	Prod. Total
Fisher				
31252	4-dr. Twn. Sed.-5P	2845	4675	—
31258	2-dr. Cpe.-2/4P	2695	4480	—
31259	4-dr. Sed.-5P	2795	4660	—
31262	4-dr. Sed.-7P	2945	4760	—
31263	4-dr. Imp. Sed.-7P	3095	4835	—
31272	2-dr. Cpe.-5P	2795	4500	—
Fleetwood				
4502	2-dr. Rds.-2/4P	2845	4450	—
4503	4-dr. Sed.-7P	—	—	—
4535	2-dr. Conv. Cpe.-2/4P	2945	4450	—
4550	4-dr. Trans. Twn. Cab.-7P	—	—	—
4557	4-dr. Tr.-7P	3195	—	—
4560	4-dr. Phae.-4/5P	2945	4395	—
4580	4-dr. All Wthr. Phae.-5P	3795	4685	—

1931 Cadillac, Series 370-A, V-12, phaeton, OCW

51

ENGINE: 90 degree L-head. Eight. Cast iron on aluminum crankcase. B & S: 3-3/8 x 4-15/16 in. Disp.: 353 cu. in. C.R.: 5.35:1 std., 5.26:1 opt. Brake H.P.: 95 plus @ 3000 R.P.M. SAE/Taxable H.P.: 36.45. Main bearings: three. Valve lifters: mechanical. Carb.: Cadillac/Johnson, with intake silencer,

CHASSIS: (Series 355-A) W.B.: 134 in. O.L.: approx. 203 in. Height: 72-1/2 in. Front/Rear Tread: 57-1/4/59-1/2 in. Tires: 6.50 x 19. (7.00 x 18 on optional wheels). (Series 355-A Commercial Chassis.) W.B.: 152 in.

1931 Cadillac, Series 370-A, V-12, coupe, JAC

TECHNICAL: Selective, synchromesh transmission. Speeds: 3F/1R. Lhd., center controls, rhd optional. Twin disc clutch. Shaft drive, (torque tube). 3/4 floating rear axle, spiral bevel drive. Overall ratio: 4.75:1 std.; 4.07:1, 4.54:1 opt. Mechanical brakes on four wheels. Wood artillery wheels std. (wire, disc, demountable wood opt.). Wheel size: 19 in. std. 18 in. w/opt. wheels.

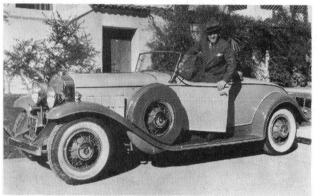

1931 Cadillac, Series 370-A, V-12, roadster, JAC

OPTIONS: Trunks ($100.00-119.00). Tonneau windshield (185.00). Wind wings (25.00-47.50). Tire cover(s) (5.00-40.00). Mirrors (10.00-32.00/pair). Radio (price on application). Heater (41.00-55.00). Auxiliary lights (37.50-75.00). Seat covers (26.75-73.50). Heron or Goddess mascot (20.00). Five wire wheels (70.00). Six wire wheels w/fender wells, trunk rack (240.00). Five demountable wood wheels (50.00). Six demountable wood wheels w/wells and rack (230.00). Four natural wood wheels (10.00).

HISTORICAL: Introduced August 1930. Model year sales: 10,717. Model year production: 10,717. The president and general manager of Cadillac was Lawrence P. Fisher.

1931

Series 355, V-8, 134" wb

Fisher Bodies

	FP	5	4	3	2	1
Rds	2845	15,350	25,600	51,200	89,600	128,000
Phae	2945	14,650	24,400	48,800	85,400	122,000
Cpe-2P	2695	9100	15,200	30,400	53,200	76,000
Cpe-5P	2795	8900	14,800	29,600	51,800	74,000
Sed	2795	5400	9000	18,000	31,500	45,000
Twn Sed	2845	5650	9400	18,800	32,900	47,000
Sed-7P	2945	5900	9800	19,600	34,300	49,000
Imp Limo	3095	6000	10,000	20,000	35,000	50,000

Fleetwood Bodies, V-8

	FP	5	4	3	2	1
Rds	3095	16,300	27,200	54,400	95,200	136,000
Conv	2945	16,300	27,200	54,400	95,200	136,000
Phae	3495	17,400	29,000	58,000	101,500	145,000
A/W Phae	3795	18,000	30,000	60,000	105,000	150,000

CADILLAC — SERIES 370-A — TWELVE: Similar to 30-31 V-16 except as follows:

Bodies: Some bodies by Fisher, but all body interiors by Fleetwood. Modified coach sill with single molding on splash shield. Battery mounted in right front fender. Hood four inches shorter than V-16 five inches longer than V-8. Instrument panel similar to V-8 panel. Headlights one inch smaller diameter than V-16. Dual rear lights ball-shaped like V-8. Dual horns slightly smaller than on V-16.

Chassis and driveline: Frame has divergent side rails like Series 355. Rear springs mounted under frame rails. Front tread same as V-8. Brakes have vacuum assister, operated from left manifold only. Brake drums 15 inch. In addition to 140 and 143 inch wheelbase passenger car chassis, a 152 inch wheelbase chassis was offered for semi-commercial use.

Engine: Dual intake silencers, slightly smaller than the single unit on V-8, positioned at rear where V-16 vacuum tanks were mounted. Carburetors similar to V-16, but reversed so that air inlet is at rear. Single vacuum tank mounted on center of dash where V-16 oil filter was mounted. Oil filter mounted on left side of crankcase. Bore 1/8 inch larger than V-16. Rear center (No. 3) main takes thrust. Exhaust manifolds have two sections rather than three. Spark plug wires come out top of distributor cap rather than rear.

I.D. DATA: Serial numbers were not used on the 1931 Cadillac Series 370-A. Engine numbers were stamped on the right-hand side of the crankcase, on generator drive chain housing. Starting 1000001. Ending 1005733.

Style No.	Body Type & Seating	Price	Weight	Prod. Total
Fisher 140" wb				
31152	4-dr. Twn-5P	3945	5330	—
31158	2-dr. Cpe 2/4P	3795	5135	—
31159	4-dr. Sed.-5P	3895	5315	—
31172	2-dr. Cpe.-5P	3895	5155	—
Fisher 143" wb				
31162	4-dr. Sed-7P	4195	5445	—
31163	4-dr. Imp. Sed-7P	4345	5520	—
Fleetwood 140" wb				
4702	2-dr. Rds-2/4P	3945	5010	—
4735	2-dr. Conv. Cpe-2/4P	4045	5105	—
4760	4-dr. Phae-5P	4045	5050	—
4780	4-dr. All Wthr. Phae.-5P	4895	5340	—

ENGINE: 45 degree overhead value. Twelve. Cast iron on aluminum crankcase. B & S: 3-1/8 x 4 in. Disp.: 368 cu. in. C.R.: (5.38:1) 5.20:1 std., 5.03:1 opt. Brake H.P.: 135 @ 3400 R.P.M. SAE/Taxable H.P.: 46.9. Main bearings: Four. Valve lifters: Mechanical, with hydraulic silencer on rocker bushing. Carb.: dual Cadillac/Johnson, with intake silencer.

CHASSIS: (Series 370-A) W.B.: 140 in. except seven-passenger sedan and Imperial 143 in. O.L.: 210-220 in. Height: 72-1/2 in Front/Rear Tread: 57-1/4/59-1/2 in. (see note). Tires: 7:00 x 19 whitewall. (7.50 x 18 on opt. wheels). (Series 370-A Commercial chassis) W.B.: 152 in.

Note: 60-1/2 in. rear tread on town sedan beginning with chassis unit number 10-2720.

TECHNICAL: Selective, synchromesh transmission. Speeds: 3F/1R. Lhd, center control, rhd optional. Twin disc clutch. Shaft drive (torque tube). 3/4 floating rear axle, spiral bevel drive. Overall ratio: 4.54:1 std.; 4.07:1, 4.91:1 opt. Mechanical brakes on four wheels, w/vacuum assister. 15 in. drums. Wood artillery wheels std. (wire, disc, demountable wood opt.). Wheel size 19 in. std. (18 in. w/opt. wheels).

OPTIONS: Trunks ($100.00-119.00). Tonneau windshield (185.00). Wind wings (24.00-47.50). Tire cover(s) (5.00-40.00). Mirrors (10.00-32.00/pair). Radio (price on application). Heater (41.00-55.00). Auxiliary lights (37.50-75.00). Seat covers (26.75-73.50). Heron or Goddess mascot (20.00). Five wire wheels (70.00). Six wire wheels w/fender wells, trunk rack (240.00). Five demountable wood wheels (50.00). Six demountable wood wheels w/wells and rack (230.00). Four natural wood wheels (10.00).

HISTORICAL: Introduced October 1930. Roadster used as pace car in Indy. Model year sales: 5,733. Model year production: 5,733. The president and general manager of Cadillac was Lawrence P. Fisher.

1932 CADILLAC

1932 Cadillac, Series 355-B, town sedan, JAC

CADILLAC — SERIES 355-B — EIGHT: Series 355-B is representative of changes for 1932. Differences in other 1932 models are noted separately.

Bodies: Longer and lower, with an entirely restyled front assembly. Roof line lowered one to three inches. Longer hood has six ports. New front styling includes a flat grille built into the radiator shell, head and side lights of streamlined bullet shape, and elimination of fender tie-bar and monogram bar. Trumpets of dual horns project through headlight stanchions. Headlight lenses 9-1/2 inch diameter. Dual taillights match headlights. Super-safe lighting features three-filament bulbs and four control positions for degree and angle of illumination. Front license plate mounted on bumper.

Runningboards curved to match sweep of front fenders and blend into rear fenders. The tail of the rear fenders is blended into the fuel tank valance. The trunk on the town coupe, town sedan, and five-passenger convertible coupe is integral with the body.

Driver's vision is increased by 30 percent as a result of elimination of the outside visor and construction of the 12 degree sloping windshield and corner posts. Large ventilator in top of cowl, none in sides of cowl. All separate body moldings eliminated. Three-spoke steering wheel affords easy view of instrument cluster in front of driver. The right side of the panel is occupied by a "locker."

Chassis: Frame redesigned, using more box construction and no front or rear tubular cross member. Brake drums cast molybdenum. "Cardan" shaft replaced by cable control for front brakes. "Full Range Ride Control" by driver adjustment of shock absorber valves. V-threaded spring shackle pins to control side play. Wire wheels standard, with optional full chrome covers to simulate disc wheels. Optional demountable wood wheels fit same hubs as wire wheels.

Driveline: "Triple-Silent Synchro-Mesh" transmission, by use of constant-mesh helical gears with ground and lapped tooth profile for all forward gears. Rear axle redesigned to be lighter and stronger, through use of improved heat treatments. Final drive ratios changed, but smaller tires give same net effect. "Controlled Free Wheeling" used — vacuum assist on clutch, controlled by foot button. Depressing button releases clutch; releasing button or depressing accelerator re-engages clutch.

Engine: Twenty-one percent increase in power achieved mostly from new manifold design plus carburetor revisions. Intake manifold redesigned to give equal length path to each cylinder. Location of inlet and exhaust valves interchanged on middle cylinders of each block, placing inlet valves side by side at the center so that one leg of the inlet manifold can service both middle cylinders. Exhaust manifold placed atop the intake manifold, with single exhaust pipe to the rear. Air filter added to intake muffler. External tuning chamber on tailpipe. Mechanical fuel pump replaces vacuum tank fuel feed. Separate vacuum pump for wipers. Oil filter mounted along left side of crankcase. Increased capacity from battery and air-cooled generator. Manual advance on distributor eliminated. Six-point engine suspension (four corners of engine plus dual mount at rear of transmission).

Fan mounted closer to radiator. Close fitting fan shroud adjustable and must be moved up or down on radiator as fan assembly is moved for adjustment of belt tension. Radiator of full-bonded-fin construction. Thermostat controlled shutters retained.

I.D. DATA: There were no serial numbers used for the Series 355-B Cadillac. Engine numbers were stamped on crankcase near the water inlet on the right-hand side. Starting: 1200001. Ending: 1202700.

Job No.	Body Type & Seating	Price	Weight	Prod. Total
Fisher 134" wb				
32-8-155	2-dr. Rds.-2/4P	2895	4635	—
32-8-178	2-dr. Cpe.-2/4P	2795	4705	—
32-8-168	2-dr. Conv. Cpe.-2/4P	2945	4675	—
32-8-159	4-dr. Std. Sed.-5P	2895	4885	—
Fisher 140" wb				
32-8-256	4-dr. Std. Phaeton-5P	2995	4700	—
32-8-280	4-dr. Spec. Phaeton-5P	3095	4750	—
32-8-273	4-dr. All Wthr. Phae.-5P	3495	5070	—
32-8-279	4-dr. Spt. Phae.-5P	3245	4800	—
32-8-272	2-dr. Cpe.-5P	2995	4715	—
32-8-259	4-dr. Spec. Sed.-5P	3045	4965	—
32-8-252	4-dr. Town Sed.-5P	3095	4980	—
32-8-262	4-dr. Sed.-7P	3145	5110	—
32-8-263	4-dr. Imp. Sed.-7P	3295	5150	—
Fleetwood 140" wb				
4930-5	4-dr. Sed.-5P	3395	4965	—
4975-5	4-dr. Sed.-7P	3545	5110	—
4975	4-dr. Limo.-7P	3745	5150	—
4981	2-dr. Twn. Cpe.-5P	3395	4915	—
4912	4-dr. Twn. Cab.-5/7P	4095	4990	—
4991	4-dr. Limo. Brgm.-7P	4245	5100	—
4925	4-dr. Twn. Cab.-7P	4245	5100	—
4975-H4	4-dr. Limo.-7P	—	—	—
4985	2-dr. Conv. Cpe.-5P	—	—	—

1932 Cadillac, Series 355-B, phaeton, JAC

ENGINE: (Series 355-B) Ninety degree L-head. Eight. Cast iron on aluminum crankcase. B & S: 3-3/8 x 4-15/16 in. Disp.: 353 cu. in. C.R.: 5.38:1 std.; 5.70:1, 5.20:1 optional. Brake H.P.: 115 @ 3000 R.P.M. SAE Taxable/H.P.: 36.45. Main bearings: three. Valve lifters: mechanical. Carb.: Cadillac/Johnson.

CHASSIS: (Series: 355-B) W.B.: 134, 140 in. O.L.: 207, 213 in. Front/Rear Tread: 59-7/8/61 in. Tires: 7.00 x 17. (Series: 355-B Commercial Chassis) W. B.: 156 in.

TECHNICAL: Selective, synchromesh transmission. Speeds: 3F/1R. Lhd. center controls, rhd optional. Twin disc clutch — selective vacuum-activation. Shaft drive, (torque tube). 3/4 floating rear axle, spiral bevel drive. Overall ratio: 4.36:1, 4.60:1. Mechanical brakes on four wheels, (15 in. drums). Wire wheels std. Demountable wood opt. Wheel size: 17 in. drop center.

OPTIONS: Tire cover(s) ($5.00-$20.00 each). Trunks ($100.00-$180.00). Heron or Goddess mascot ($20.00). Radio (price on application). Heater ($37.50-$47.50). Auxiliary lights ($37.50-$57.50).

Wind wings ($25.00-$47.50). Tonneau shield ($185.00). Seat covers ($26.50-$73.50). Mirrors ($8.00-$16.00 each). Full covers for wire wheels ($10.00 each). Six wire wheels w/fender wells and trunk rack ($130.00). Five demountable wood wheels ($30.00). Six demountable wood wheels w/wells and rack ($166.00). Colored fender set ($50.00).

HISTORICAL: Introduced January 1932. Model year sales: 2,700. Model year production: 2,700. The president and general manager of Cadillac was Lawrence P. Fisher.

1932 Cadillac, Series 370-B, V-12, touring, OCW

CADILLAC — SERIES 370-B — TWELVE: Overall styling and appearance identical to V-8, except for emblems.

Mechanical features same as V-8, except for minor differences dictated by increased power and weight (gear ratios, tire size, vacuum assist on brakes, battery/generator capacity). Dual exhaust system has tuning chambers in mufflers rather than attached to tailpipes. Dual ignition coils are mounted in top tank of radiator.

The engine is basically the same as the 370-A. Fuel feed changed from vacuum tank to mechanical pump. New Cuno disc-type self-cleaning oil filter mounted at right-hand side of clutch housing; connected to starter pedal to rotate discs each time pedal is depressed. New Detroit Lubricator dual carburetors are first departure by Cadillac in 20 years from a Cadillac/Johnson carburetor.

I.D. DATA: Serial numbers were not used. Engine numbers were stamped on the right-hand side of the crankcase on the generator drive chain housing. Starting: 1300001. Ending: 1301740.

Job No.	Body Type & Seating	Price	Weight	Prod. Total
Fisher 134" wb				
32-12-155	2-dr. Rds.-2/4P	3595	4870	—
32-12-178	2-dr. Cpe.-2/4P	3495	4085	—
32-12-168	2-dr. Conv. Cpe.-2/4P	3645	5060	—
32-12-159	4-dr. Std. Sed.-5P	3595	5175	—

1932 Cadillac, Series 370-B, V-12, convertible coupe, JAC

Job No.	Body Type & Seating	Price	Weight	Prod. Total
Fisher 140" wb				
32-12-236	4-dr. Std. Phae.-5P	3695	5240	—
32-12-280	4-dr. Spec. Phae.-5P	3795	5290	—
32-12-273	4-dr. All Wthr. Phae.-5P	4195	5385	—
32-12-279	4-dr. Spt. Phae.-5P	3945	5340	—
32-12-272	2-dr. Cpe.-5P	3695	5220	—
32-12-259	4-dr. Spec. Sed.-5P	3745	5345	—
32-12-252	4-dr. Twn. Sed.-5P	3795	5370	—

Job No.	Body Type & Seating	Price	Weight	Prod. Total
32-12-262	4-dr. Sed.-7P	3845	5460	—
32-12-263	4-dr. Imp. Sed.-7P	3995	5500	—
Fleetwood 140" wb				
5030-S	4-dr. Sed.-5P	4095	5345	—
5075-S	4-dr. Sed.-7P	4245	5460	—
5075	4-dr. Limo.-7P	4445	5500	—
5081	2-dr. Twn. Cpe.-5P	4095	5225	—
5012	4-dr. Twn. Cab.-5/7P	4795	5380	—
5091	4-dr. Limo. Brgm.-7P	4945	5580	—
5025	4-dr. Twn. Cab.-7P	4945	5580	—

Job No.	Body Type & Seating	Price	Weight	Prod. Total
Fleetwood 140" wb Special				
5029	Imp.-5P	—	—	—
5030	4-dr. Imp. Sed.-5P	—	—	—
5030-FL	4-dr. Imp. Cab.-5P	—	—	—
5030-SFL	4-dr. Sed. Cab.-5P	—	—	—
5031	Imp. Sed.-5P	—	—	—
5031-5	Sed.-5P	—	—	—
5055	Imp. Sed.-5P	—	—	—
5055-C	Coll. Imp. Sed.-5P	—	—	—
5056	Imp. Cab.-5P	—	—	—
5057	Tr.-7P	4895	5295	—
5065	Imp. Sed.-7P	—	—	—
5075-FL	4-dr. Limo. Cab.-7P	—	—	—
5075-H4	Imp. Sed.-7P	—	—	—
5082	Sed.-5P	—	—	—
5085	2-dr. Conv. Cpe.-5P	4995	5200	—

1932 Cadillac, Series 370-B, V-12, town cabriolet, JAC

ENGINE: 45 degree overhead valve. Twelve. Cast iron on aluminum crankcase. B & S: 3-1/8 x 4 in. Disp.: 368 cu. in. C.R.: 5.30:1 std.; 5.08:1, 4.90:1 opt. Brake H.P.: 135 @ 3400 R.P.M. SAE/Taxable H.P.: 46.9. Main bearings: four. Valve lifters: mechanical w/hydraulic silencer on rocker bushing. Carb.: Detroit Lubricator Type L-13, R-13/Model 51.

CHASSIS: (Series 370-B) W.B.: 134, 140 in. O.L.: 207, 213 in. Front/Rear Tread: 59-7/8/61 in. Tires: 7.50 x 17. (Series 370-B Commercial Chassis) W.B.: 156 in.

TECHNICAL: Selective, synchromesh transmission. Speeds: 3F/1R. Lhd, Center control, rhd optional .Twin disc clutch — selective vacuum-activation. Shaft drive (torque tube). 3/4 floating rear axle, spiral bevel drive. Overall ratio: 4.60:1, 4.80:1. Mechanical brakes on four wheels, with vacuum assist (15 in. drums). Wire wheels std. Demountable wood opt. Wheel size: 17 in. Drop center.

OPTIONS: Tire cover(s) ($5.00-20.00 each). Trunks (100.00-180.00). Heron or Goddess mascot (20.00). Radio (price on application). Heater (37.50-47.50). Auxiliary lights (37.50-57.50). Wind wings (25.00-47.50). Tonneau shield (185.00). Seat covers (26.50-73.50). Mirrors (8.00-16.00 each). Full covers for wire wheels (10.00 each). Six wire wheels w/fender wells and trunk rack (150.00). Five demountable wood wheels (30.00). Six demountable wood wheels w/wells and rack (186.00). Colored fender set (50.00)

HISTORICAL: Introduced January 1932. Model year sales: 1,740. Model year production: 1,740. The president and general manager of Cadillac was Lawrence P. Fisher.

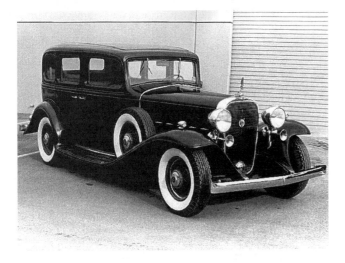

1932 Cadillac, Series 370-B, V-12, town sedan, OCW

CADILLAC — SERIES 452-B — SIXTEEN:
Styling and appearance same as V-8 and V-12, except for emblems and longer hood with seven ports. A few Fleetwood body styles had an 18 degree rather than the typical 12 degree windshield. Some body styles achieved the ultimate proportions — radiator over front axle, windshield midway between the axles, and all seating between the axles.

With the longer wheelbase and more power and weight, some mechanical details were beefed up versions of the V-8, V-12 designs (10 in. deep frame, heavier axles, 18 in. rims, 11 in. clutch, 16 in. brake drums, different gear ratios, greater battery/generator capacity).

The engine remained basically the same as in 1930-31. As on the V-12, carburetors were changed to Detroit Lubricator, and oil filter was changed to Cuno. Fuel feed was by mechanical pump. Intake silencers with filter took the place of the vacuum tanks on the dash. In a departure from the smooth, uncluttered look of the earlier V-16, the spark plug wires sprouted from the top of the distributor cap. A more efficient and dependable design, but a real compromise in appearance.

I.D. DATA: Serial numbers were not used. Engine numbers were stamped on the right-hand side of the crankcase on the generator drive chain housing. Starting: 1400001. Ending: 1400300.

Job No.	Body Type & Seating	Price	Weight	Prod. Total
Fisher 143" wb				
32-16-155	2-dr. Rds.-2/4P	4595	5065	—
32-16-178	2-dr. Cpe.-2/4P	4495	5530	—
32-16-168	2-dr. Conv. Cpe.-2/4P	4645	5505	—
32-16-159	4-dr. Std. Sed.-5P	4595	5625	—
Fisher 149" wb				
32-16-256	4-dr. Std. Phae.-5P	4695	5400	—
32-16-280	4-dr. Spec. Phae.-5P	4795	5450	—
32-16-273	4-dr. All Wthr. Phae.-5P	5195	5525	—
32-16-279	4-dr. Spt. Phae.-5P	4945	5500	—
32-16-252	4-dr. Twn. Sed.-5P	—	—	—
32-16-259	4-dr. Spec. Sed.-5P	—	—	—
32-16-262	4-dr. Sed.-7P	—	—	—
32-16-263	4-dr. Imp. Sed.-7P	—	—	—
32-16-272	2-dr. Cpe.-5P	—	—	—
Fleetwood 149" wb				
5130-S	4-dr. Sed.-5P	5095	5735	—
5175-S	4-dr. Sed.-7P	5245	5865	—
5175	4-dr. Limo.-7P	5445	5905	—
5181	2-dr. Twn. Cpe.-5P	5095	5605	—
5112	4-dr. Twn. Cab.-5/7P	5795	5775	—
5191	4-dr. Limo. Brgm.-7P	5945	5935	—
5125	4-dr. Twn. Cab.-7P	5945	5935	—
Fleetwood 149" wb Special				
5112-C	4-dr. Coll. Twn. Cab.-5/7P	—	—	—
5120	4-dr. Trans. Twn. Cab.-7P	—	—	—
5125	4-dr. Trans. Twn. Cab.-7P	—	—	—
5125-C	4-dr. Coll. Tr. Twn. Cab.-7P	—	—	—
5125-Q	4-dr. Trans. Cab.-7P	—	—	—
5129	4-dr. Imp.-5P	—	—	—
5130-FL	4-dr. Imp. Cab.-5P	—	—	—
5130-SFL	4-dr. Sed. Cab.-5P	—	—	—
5131	4-dr. Imp. Sed.-5P	—	—	—
5131-S	4-dr. Sed.-5P	—	—	—
5140-B	Spec. Sed.-5P	—	—	—
5155	4-dr. Imp. Sed.-5P	—	—	—
5155-C	4-dr. Coll. Imp. Sed.-5P	—	—	—
5156-C	4-dr. Coll. Imp.-5P	—	—	—
5164	4-dr. Trans. Twn. Brgm.-7P	—	—	—
5165	4-dr. Imp. Limo.-7P	—	—	—
5175-C	4-dr. Coll. Limo.-7P	—	—	—
5175-FL	4-dr. Limo. Cab.-7P	—	—	—
5175-H4	4-dr. Imp. Sed.-7P	—	—	—
5185	2-dr. Conv. Cpe.-5P	—	—	—
Fleetwood 165" wb Special				
5177	4-dr. Imp.-8P	—	—	—

ENGINE: (Series 452-B) 45 degree overhead valve. Sixteen cylinders. Cast iron on aluminum crankcase. B & S: 3 x 4 in. Disp.: 452 cu. in. C.R.: 5.36:1 std.; 5-00:1, 4.90:1 opt. Brake H.P.: 165 @ 3400 R.P.M. Taxable H.P.: 57.5. Main bearings: five. Valve lifters: mechanical w/hydraulic silencer on rocker bushing. Carb.: Detroit Lubricator Type L-14, R-14/Model 51.

CHASSIS: (Series 452-B) W.B.: 143, 149 in. O.L.: 216, 222 in. Front/Rear Tread 59-7/8/61 in. Tires: 7.50 x 18.

TECHNICAL: Selective synchromesh transmission. Speeds: 3F/1R. Lhd, center control, rhd optional. Twin disc-clutch — selective vacuum-activation. Shaft drive (torque tube). 3/4 floating rear axle, spiral bevel drive. Overall ratio: 4.31:1, 4.64:1. Mechanical brakes on four wheels with vacuum assist (16 in. drums.) Wire wheels std. Demountable wood opt. Wheel size: 18 in. drop center.

OPTIONS: Tire covers ($5.00-20.00 each). Trunks (100.00-180.00). Heron or Goddess (20.00). Radio (price on application). Heater (37.50-57.50). Wind wings (25.00-47.50). Tonneau shield (185.00). Seat covers (26.50-73.50). Mirrors (8.00-16.00 each). Full covers for wire wheels (10.00 each). Six wire wheels w/fender wells and trunk racks (150.00). Five demountable wood wheels (30.00) Six demountable wood wheels. w/wells and rack (186.00). Colored fender set (50.00).

1932 Cadillac, Series 452-B, V-16, all-weather phaeton, JAC

HISTORICAL: Introduced January 1932. Model year sales: 300. Model year production: 300. The president and general manager of Cadillac was Lawrence P. Fisher.

1933 Cadillac, Series 355-C, Fleetwood sedan, OCW

CADILLAC — SERIES 355-C — EIGHT: In the mid-Twenties, Cadillac broke with functional body design and began a period of "stylish functional." The 1933 "C" cars ushered in the period of styling/streamlining for its own sake. A face lift, simple in execution but startling in effect, transformed th "B" cars and started the concept of selling cars on the basis of styling features and selling replacement cars on the basis of changes in style.

Bumpers were sectioned, with plain ends and a three-bar center. The grille was made vee-shaped and blended into the painted (chrome optional) radiator shell. The radiator filler cap disappeared under the hood on the right side (same side as the oil level gauge). The fender tie-bar, after a year's absence, was sectioned and the center section hidden behind the grille. Six horizontal doors replaced the vertical hood doors. Skirts (valances) were added to front and rear fenders. The most significant change in body detail was the introduction of no-draft Individually Controlled Ventilation (I.C.V.) or pivoting vent windows in the front doors and rear quarter or rear door windows. In early production, the front door window had to be lowered to disengage the channel at its front edge from the vent window to allow the vent window to pivot. In later production, the sealing channel was attached to the door frame rather than the window glass so that the vent window could be operated independently of the window glass. Windshield and rear quarter windows were made stationary. Absence of windshield operating mechanism on closed cars allowed room to conceal the wiper motor behind the headboard. The cowl ventilator was baffled and drained in such a way as to be rainproof. Chassis changes were few and of minor nature. Controlled free wheeling was discontinued. Vacuum assist was added to the V-8 brake system. Changes in shock absorber valves extended the range of the ride control system. At engine unit number 30-3607, the dual point, four lobe distributor was replaced by a single point, eight lobe unit.

I.D. DATA: Serial numbers were not used. Engine numbers were stamped on crankcase near the water inlet on the right-hand side. Starting: 3000001. Ending: 3002100.

Job No.	Body Type & Seating	Price	Weight	Prod. Total
Fisher 134" wb				
33-8-155	2-dr. Rds.-2/4P	2795	—	—
33-8-168	2-dr. Conv. Cpe.-2/4P	2845	4825	—
33-8-178	2-dr. Cpe.-2/4P	2695	4855	—
Fisher 140" wb				
33-8-252	4-dr. Sed.-5P	2995	5060	—
33-8-256	4-dr. Phae.-5P	2895	4865	—
33-8-259	4-dr. Sed.-5P	2895	5000	—
33-8-262	4-dr. Sed.-7P	3045	5105	—
33-8-263	4-dr. Imp. Sed.-7P	3195	5140	—
33-8-272	2-dr. Cpe.-7P	2895	4850	—
33-8-273	4-dr. All Wthr. Phae.-5P	3395	5110	—
Fleetwood 140" wb				
5330-S	4-dr. Sed.-5P	3295	—	—
5375-S	4-dr. Sed.-7P	3445	—	—
5375	4-dr. Limo.-7P	3645	—	—
NA	2-dr. Cpe.-5P	—	—	—
5312	4-dr. Trans. Twn. Cab.-5/7P	3995	—	—
5391	4-dr. Trans. Limo. Brgm.-7P	4145	—	—
5325	4-dr. Trans. Twn. Cab.-7P	4145	—	—
5357	4-dr. Tr.-7P	—	—	—
5381	2-dr. Twn. Cpe.-5P	—	—	—
5312-C	4-dr. Coll. Trans. Twn. Cab.-5/7P	—	—	—
5325-C	4-dr. Coll. Trans. Twn. Cab.-7P	—	—	—
5375-C	4-dr. Coll. Limo.-7P	—	—	—
5375-H4	Limo. w/4" extra headroom-7P	—	—	—
5330-FL	4-dr. Imp. Cabr.-5P	—	—	—
5375-FL	4-dr. Imp. Cabr.-7P	—	—	—
5364	4-dr. Trans. Twn. Brgm.-5p	—	—	—
5320	4-dr. Trans. Twn. Cabr.-7P	—	—	—

ENGINE: (Series 355-C) Ninety degree L-Head. Eight. Cast iron on aluminum crankcase. B & S: 3-5/8 x 4-15/16 in. Disp.: 353 cu. in. C.R.: 5.4:1 std., 5.7:1 opt. Brake H.P.: 115 @ 3000 R.P.M. H.P.: 36.45. Main bearings: three. Valve lifters: mechanical. Carb.: Cadillac/Johnson.

CHASSIS: (Series 355-C) W.B.: 134, 140 in. O.L.: approx. 207-213 in. Front/Rear Tread: 59-7/8/61 in. Tires: 7.00 x 17. (Series Semi-Commercial Chassis) W.B.: 156 in.

TECHNICAL: Selective, synchromesh transmission. Speeds: 3F/1R. Lhd, center control, rhd optional. Twin disc clutch. Shaft drive, (torque tube). 3/4 floating rear axle, spiral bevel drive. Overall ratio: 4.36:1, 4.60:1. Mechanical brakes on four wheels with vacuum assist. (15 in. drums.) Wire wheels std. Demountable wood opt. Wheel size: 17 in. Drop center.

OPTIONS: Sidemount cover(s). Wheel discs (chrome $10.00 each/body color 12.50 ea). Radio (Standard 64.50, Imperial 74.50). Heater Hot air or hot water. Draft deflector for convertible coupe (35.00/pair). Luggage sets (37.00-110.00). Trunks w/luggage (104.00-180.00). Seat covers (10.00/seat). Mirrors. Lorraine spotlight (24.50). Dual Pilot Ray lights (44.50). Heron radiator ornament (20.00). Six wire wheels with fender wells. Five demountable wood wheels. Six demountable wood wheels with fender wells.

HISTORICAL: Introduced January 1933. Innovations: Fisher no-draft individually controlled ventilation (I.C.V.) (vent windows). Model year sales: 2,100. Model year production: 2,100. The president and general manager of Cadillac was Lawrence P. Fisher.

CADILLAC — SERIES 370-C — TWELVE: The only way to tell the difference between the V-8 and V-12 Cadillac for 1933 is to check the emblems or look under the hood. (Lift the left side to check water level in the radiator — the filler cap and oil level gauge are on the left side on V-12 and V-16, on the right side on V-8s.)

I.D. DATA: Serial numbers were not used. Engine numbers were stamped on the right-hand side of the crankcase on the generator drive chain housing. Starting: 4000001. Ending: 4000953.

Job No.	Body Type & Seating	Price	Weight	Prod. Total
Fisher 134" wb				
33-12-155	Rds.-2/4P	3495	—	—
33-12-168	Conv. Cpe.-2/4P	3545	5125	—
33-12-178	Cpe.-2/4P	3395	5165	—
Fisher 140" wb				
33-12-252	Twn. Sed.-5P	3695	5385	—
33-12-256	Phae.-5P	3595	—	—
33-12-259	Sed.-5P	3595	5335	—
33-12-262	Sed.-7P	3745	5440	—
33-12-263	Imp. Sed.-7P	3895	5500	—
33-12-272	Cpe.-5P	3595	—	—
33-12-273	All Wthr. Phae.-5P	4095	5405	—
Fleetwood 140" wb				
5430-S	4-dr. Sed.-5P	3995	5335	—
5475-S	4-dr. Sed.-7P	4145	5440	—
5475	4-dr. Limo.-7P	4345	5500	—
NA	2-dr. Cpe.-5P	—	—	—
5412	4-dr. Trans. Twn. Cab.-5/7P	4695	—	—
5425	4-dr. Trans. Twn. Cab.-7P	4845	—	—
5420	4-dr Trans. Twn. Cab.-7P	—	—	—
5425-C	4-dr. Coll. Trans. Twn. Cab.-7P	—	—	—
5430-FL	4-dr. Imp, Cabr.-5P	—	—	—
5455	4-dr. Imp. Cab. (Madame X)-5/7P	—	—	—

Job No.	Body Type & Seating			
5457-A	4-dr. Tr.-7P	—	—	—
5464	4-dr. Trans. Twn. Brgm.-7P	—	—	—
5475-H4	4-dr. Limo. w/4" extra headroom-7P	—	—	—
5475-FL	Limo. Cabr.-7P	—	—	—
5481	2-dr. Twn. Cpe.-5P	—	—	—
5482	4-dr. Sedanette-5P	—	—	—
5485	2-dr. Conv. Coupe-5P	—	—	—

1933 Cadillac, Series 452-C, V-16, coupe, OCW

ENGINE: 45 degree overhead valve. Twelve cylinder. Cast iron on aluminum crankcase. B & S: 3-1/8 x 4 in. Disp.: 368 cu. in. C.R.: 5.6:1 std.; 5.4:1, 5.1:1 opt. Brake H.P.: 135 @ 3400 R.P.M. H.P.: 46.9. Main bearings: four. Valve lifters: mechanical w/hydraulic silencer on rocker bushing. Carb.: Detroit Lubricator Type L-13, R-13/Model 51.

CHASSIS: (Series: 370-C) W.B.: 134, 140 in. Length: approx. 207-213 in. Front/Rear Tread: 59-7/8/61 in. Tires: 7.50 x 17. (Semi-commercial chassis.) W.B.: 156 in.

TECHNICAL: Selective, synchromesh transmission. 3F/1R. Lhd, center control, rhd optional. Twin disc clutch. Shaft drive (torque tube). 3/4 floating rear axle, spiral bevel drive. Overall ratio: 4.60:1, 4.80:1. Mechanical brakes on four wheels with vacuum assist. (15 in. drums.) Wire wheels standard. Demountable wood optional. Wheel size: 17 in. drop center.

OPTIONS: Sidemount cover(s). Wheel discs (chrome $10.00 each/body color 12.50 each). Radio (Standard 64.50, Imperial 74.50). Heater, hot air or hot water. Draft deflector for convertible coupe (35.00/pair). Luggage sets (37.00-110.00). Trunks w/luggage (104.00-180.00). Seat Covers (10.00/seat). Mirrors. Lorraine spotlight (24.50). Dual Pilot Ray lights (44.50). Heron radiator ornament (20.00). Six wire wheels with fender wells. Five demountable wood wheels. Six demountable wood wheels with fender wells.

HISTORICAL: Introduced January 1933. Innovations: Fisher no-draft individually controlled ventilation (I.C.V.) (vent windows). Model year sales: 953. Model year production: 953. The general manager of Cadillac was Lawrence P. Fisher.

CADILLAC — SERIES 452-C — SIXTEEN: For 1933, Cadillac announced that V-16 production would be limited to 400 cars. These were to be serially numbered — the number and the owner's name to be displayed on a plate inside the car. Nearly 70 body styles were suggested. Only half of these body styles were actually built, and half the total production of 126 cars were in the five most conservative five- or seven-passenger sedan styles.

V-16s had the vee-shaped grille/radiator shell, skirted fenders, and no-draft ventilation common to the full line. Detail distinction was achieved with a new, winged goddess mascot; large, spinner hubcaps; absence of crankhole cover in the grille, and an awkward, four-bar bumper. Hood side panels carried two vertical doors plus three stylized horizontal louvers. Vertical louvers on front fender skirts, shown in promotional literature and used on mockups, were replaced in "production" by three horizontal louvers matching the hood louvers.

Some new styling details were shown on various bodies. Instead of ending at the front of the cowl, some hoods were extended back over the cowl to the windshield. Many four-door bodies sported a rear body panel that swept back over the fuel tank, with a door opening for carrying parcels. At least one open and one closed four-door design offered a built-in trunk. A few styles even retained the "Madame X" look seen on some of the first V16s.

Mechanical changes were few. A higher compression ratio was available to utilize improved gasolines. Except on early production, wheel size was reduced from 18 in. to 17 in. Beginning with engine unit number 50-24, the starter ring gear was moved from the clutch centerplate to the flywheel — same as on the V-8 and V-12.

I.D. DATA: Serial numbers were not used. Engine numbers were stamped on the right-hand side of the crankcase on the generator drive chain housing. Starting: 5000001. Ending: 5000126.

Job No.	Body Type & Seating	Price	Weight	Prod Total
Fisher 143" wb				
33-16-168	2-dr. Conv. Cpe.-2/4P	—	—	—
33-16-272	2-dr. Cpe.-5P	—	—	—
Fleetwood 143" wb				
5508	2-dr. Conv. Cpe.-2/4P	—	—	—
5509	2-dr. Cpe.-2/4P	—	—	—
Fleetwood 149" wb				
5502	2-dr. Rds.-2/4P	—	—	—
5512	4-dr. Twn. Cab.-5/7P	6850	6110	—
5513	4-dr. Twn. Cab.-5/7P	—	—	—
5514	4-dr. Twn. Cab.-5/7P	—	—	—
5520	4-dr. Twn. Cab.-7P	—	—	—
5521	4-dr. Twn. Cab.-7P	—	—	—
5524	4-dr. Twn. Cab.-7P	—	—	—
5525	4-dr. Twn. Cab.-7P	6850	6270	—
5526	4-dr. Twn. Cab.-7P	—	—	—
5530	4-dr. Imp. Sed.-5P	—	—	—
5530-S	4-dr. Sed.-5P	6250	6070	—
5530-FL	4-dr. Imp. Cab.-5/7P	—	—	—
5530-SFL	4-dr. Sed. Cab.-5/7P	—	—	—
5530-H4	4-dr. Imp. Sed.-5P	—	—	—
5531	4-dr. Imp. Sed.-5/7P	—	—	—
5531-5	4-dr. Sed.-5/7P	—	—	—
5532	4-dr. Imp. Sed.-5/7P	—	—	—
5532-5	4-dr. Sed.-5/7P	—	—	—
5533	4-dr. Twn. Imp.-5P	—	—	—
5533-5	4-dr. Twn. Sed.-5P	—	—	—
5535	2-dr. Conv. Cpe.-2/4P	—	—	—
5536	2-dr. Spt. Conv. Cpe.-2/4P	—	—	—
5540	4-dr. Imp. Cab.-5/7P	—	—	—
5540-5	4-dr. Sed. Cab.-5/7P	—	—	—
5545	4-dr. Imp. Cab.-5/7P	—	—	—
5545-5	4-dr. Sed. Cab.-5/7P	—	—	—
5550	4-dr. Full Coll. Twn. Cab.-7P	—	—	—
5555	4-dr. Imp. Cab.-5/7P	—	—	—
5555-C	4-dr. Coll. Imp. Cab.- 5/7P	—	—	—
5557	4-dr. Tr.-7P	—	—	—
5558	4-dr. Phae.-5P	—	—	—
5559	4-dr. Spt. Phae.-5P	—	—	—
5560	4-dr. Spt. Phae.-5P	—	—	—
5561	4-dr. Close Cpld. Imp.-5P	—	—	—
5561-5	4-dr. Close Cpld. Sed.-5P	—	—	—
5563	4-dr. Spt. Imp.-5/7P	—	—	—
5563-5	4-dr. Spt. Sed.-5/7P	—	—	—
5564	4-dr. Twn. Brgm.-5/7P	—	—	—
5564-B	4-dr. Twn. Brgm. w/canework-5/7P	—	—	—
5565	4-dr. Limo.-7P	—	—	—
5565	4-dr. Sed.-7P	—	—	—
5566	4-dr. Limo.-7P	—	—	—
5566-5	4-dr. Sed.-7P	—	—	—
5573	4-dr. Limo.-7P	—	—	—
5573-5	4-dr. Sed.-7P	—	—	—

Job No.	Body Type & Seating	Price	Weight	Prod Total
5574	4-dr. Imp. Cab.-7P	—	—	—
5574-5	4-dr. Sed.-7P	—	—	—
5575	4-dr. Limo.-7P	6600	6270	—
5575-5	4-dr. Sed.-7P	6400	6200	—
5575-FL	4-dr. Imp. Cab.-7P	—	—	—
5575-SFL	4-dr. Sed. Cab.-7P	—	—	—
5576	2-dr. Cpe.-2/4P	—	—	—
5577	2-dr. Spt. Cpe.-2/4P	—	—	—
5578	4-dr. All Wthr. Spt. Phae.-5P	—	—	—
5579	4-dr. All Wthr. Phae.-5P	8000	6110	—
5579-A	4-dr. All Wthr. Phae.-5P	—	—	—
5580	4-dr. Conv. Phae.-5P	—	—	—
5581	2-dr. Twn. Cpe.-5P	6250	6000	—
5583	2-dr. Cpe.-2P	—	—	—
5585	2-dr. Conv. Cpe.-5P	7500	5910	—
5586	2-dr. Conv. Cpe.-4P	—	—	—
5590	4-dr. Limo. Brgm.-7P	—	—	—
5591	4-dr. Limo. Brgm.-7P	6850	6300	—
5592	4-dr. Limo. Brgm.-7P	—	—	—
5599	2-dr. Aerodynamic Cpe.-5P	—	—	—

1933 Cadillac, Series 452-C, V-16, seven-passenger sedan, JAC

ENGINE: (Series 452-C) 45 degree overhead valve. Sixteen. Cast iron on aluminum crankcase. B & S: 3 x 4 in. Disp.: 452 cu. in. C.R.: 5.7:1 std.; 5.4:1, 5.1:1 opt. Brake H.P.: 165 @ 3400 R.P.M. Taxable H.P.: 57.5. Main bearings: five. Valve lifters: mechanical w/hydraulic silencer on rocker bushing. Carb.: Detroit Lubricator Type L-14, R-14/Model 51.

CHASSIS: (Series 452-C) W.B.: 143, 149 in. O.L.: approx. 216-222 in. Front/Rear Tread 59-7/8/61 in. Tires: 7.50 x 17.

TECHNICAL: Selective, synchromesh transmission. Speeds: 3F/1R. Lhd, center controls rhd optional. Twin disc clutch. Shaft drive (torque tube). 3/4 floating rear axle, spiral bevel drive. Overall ratio: 4.31:1, 4.64:1. Mechanical brakes on four wheels with vacuum assist. (15 in. drums.) Wire wheels std. Demountable wood option. Wheel size: 17 in. drop center.

1933 Cadillac, Series 452-C, V-16, seven-passenger limousine, JAC

OPTIONS: Wheel discs. Radio (Standard ($64.50, Imperial 74.50). Heater, hot air or hot water. Luggage sets (37.00-110.06). Trunks w/luggage (104.00-180.00). Mirrors. Lorraine spotlight (24.50). Dual Pilot Ray lights (44.50). Goddess radiator ornament (plated gold 50.00, silver 40.00). Six wire wheels with fender wells. Five demountable wood wheels. Six demountable wood wheels with fender wells.

HISTORICAL: Introduced January 1933. Innovations: Fisher no-draft individually controlled ventilation (I.C.V.) (vent windows). The president and general manager of Cadillac was Lawrence P. Fisher.

1934 CADILLAC

CADILLAC — MODEL 355-D — SERIES 10, 20, FLEETWOOD (30) — EIGHT: 1934 Cadillacs were completely restyled and mounted on an entirely new chassis, but used the same basic engines as in 1933.

1934 Cadillac, Model 355-D, convertible sedan, OCW

Bodies: Bodies on the Series 10 and 20 cars were built by Fisher. Bodies on the V-8 Fleetwood Series were shared with the 12s and 16s. Styling emphasized streamlining, including concealment of all chassis features except the wheels. Body construction was improved for better insulation against engine heat and reduction of engine, road, and wind noise. Bumpers were a stylish but ineffective biplane design, mounted against telescoping springs. The grille was vee-shaped and sloping, set into a painted shell. Although restricted use of chrome was a feature of the overall ornamentation, a chrome-plated radiator shell was available as an option. Horns and radiator filler cap were concealed under the hood. Teardrop Guide Multibeam headlights were mounted on streamlined supports attached to the fenders. Parking lamps were mounted in the headlight supports. Airfoil shaped front fenders were brought low over the chassis. The hood sills were high, with the entire fender shape molded into the radiator shell. A curious horizontal crease broke the nose contour of the fenders. Hoods extending nearly to the windshield carried shutter-type louvers in the side panel. Windshields were fixed and steeply sloping; 18 degrees flat on Fisher bodies, 25 degrees flat or a 29-1/2 degree vee on Fleetwood bodies. Cowl vents opened toward the windshield; one vent on flat windshield bodies, two vents projecting through openings in the hood on vee windshield bodies. Bodies were two inches lower than on previous models. Added passenger space in the front compartment was achieved by moving the hand brake lever to the left of the driver, under the instrument panel. On 12s and 16s, the gearshift lever was moved forward to the clutch housing. Rear fenders were airfoil shaped and carried rear lights that matched the headlights. The gas tank filler on Fisher bodies was on the left side at the rear of the body; on Fleetwood bodies in the left rear fender. All bodies featured a beaver tail rear deck that completely covered the chassis. On Fleetwood bodies, the spare was concealed inside the rear deck, unless optional fender mounts were specified.

Chassis: Significant changes in chassis design resulted in improved riding and handling plus decreased driver fatigue. The new independent "knee action" front suspension with coil springs and center point steering resulted in greatly reduced unsprung weight. Front shocks were now an integral part of the suspension; the shock arm being the upper suspension arm. An inverted steering box, mounted on the outside of the frame, was used on Fleetwood-bodied cars. Hotchkiss drive replaced the torque tube drive. Rear brakes were operated by pull rods and cables. A new frame of X design added to chassis strength and allowed for the reduction in overall vehicle height. A stabilizer bar to control body roll in turns was added at the rear of the chassis. The brake and clutch pedal assembly was relocated from transmission to frame. Mufflers on Fleetwood-bodied cars were relocated to the outside of the frame. In Fisher bodies, the battery was under the front seat, on the right side. In the Fleetwood bodies, the battery was under the right front fender and was removed from underneath.

Engine: Engine changes were few, but horsepower was increased. All engines used Lynite aluminum pistons. Compression ratios were increased. Intake ducting to the carburetor air cleaner was extended to the radiator casing, providing cold, dense air rather than the hot air in the engine compartment. The combination of aluminum pistons, cold intake air, and higher compression with improved fuels resulted in increased horsepower and engine speeds. Detail changes in the V-8 engine included a change to Detroit Lubricator carburetor, use of dual valve springs, discontinuation of the oil filter, and solenoid starter control with starter button on instrument panel. One V-8 engine change to be appreciated by anyone removing a cylinder head was the change from head studs to cap screws. The change was actually made so that the heads could be turned before lifting, so as to clear the hood shelf. Another change, not necessarily appreciated, was the elimination of provision for hand cranking.

I.D. DATA: Serial numbers were on top surface of frame side bar, right side, just ahead of dash. Same as engine number. Starting: 3100001. Ending: 3108318 (with 1935). Engine numbers were stamped on crankcase near the water inlet on the right-hand side. Starting: 3100001. Ending: 3108318 (with 1935).

Style No.	Body Type & Seating	Price	Weight	Prod. Total
Series 10 Fisher 128" wb				
34728	2-dr. Spt. Cpe.-2/3P	2395	4550	—
34718	2-dr. Conv. Cpe.-2/4P	2495	4515	—
34721	4-dr. Conv. Sed.-5P	2695	4750	—
34722	2-dr. Twn. Sed.-5P	2545	4630	—
34709	4-dr. Sed.-5P	2495	4715	—
34702	4-dr. Twn. Sed.-5P	2545	4735	—
Series 20 Fisher 136" wb				
34678	2-dr. Spt. Cpe.-2/3P	2595	4660	—
34668	2-dr. Conv. Cpe.-2/4P	2695	4625	—
34671	4-dr. Conv. Sed.-5P	2895	4860	—
34659	4-dr. Sed.-5P	2695	4825	—
34652	4-dr. Twn. Sed.-5P	2745	4815	—
34662	4-dr. Sed.-7P	2845	4945	—
34663	4-dr. Imp. Sed.-7P	2995	4970	—
Series Fleetwood (30) 146" wb vee windshield				
Some listings show these as 56-styles.				
5702	Rds.-2P	—	—	—
5712-C	Coil. Twn. Cab.-5P	—	—	—
5712-LB	Twn. Cab.-5P	5495	5540	—
5712-MB	Twn.Cab.-5P	—	—	—
5720	Twn. Cab.-7P	—	—	—
5720-C	Coll. Twn. Cab.-7P	—	—	—
5725-B	Twn. Cab.-7P	—	—	—
5725-LB	Twn. Cab.-7P	5595	5650	—
5725-MB	Twn. Cab.-7P	—	—	—
5730	Imp. Sed.-5P	—	—	—
5730-FL	Imp. Cab.-5P	4145	5500	—
5730-FM	Imp. Brgm.-5P	—	—	—
5730-S	Sed.-5P	3745	5465	—
5733	Imp. Twn. Sed.-5P	—	—	—
5733-S	Twn. Sed.-5P	3795	5415	—
5735	Conv. Cpe.-2P	4045	5115	—
5757	Tr.-7P	—	—	—
5759	Spt. Phae.-5P	—	—	—
5775	Imp. Sed. (Limo.)-7P	4095	5580	—
5775-6	Limo.-7P	—	—	—
5775-E	Imp. Sed.-7P	—	—	—
5775-FL	Imp. Cab.-7P	4295	5580	—
5775-FM	Imp. Brgm.-7P	—	—	—
5775-H4	Imp. Sed.-7P	—	—	—
5775-S	Sed.-7P	3895	5545	—
5775-W	Limo.-7P	—	—	—
5776	Coupe-2P	3895	5150	—
5780	Conv. Sed. w/div.-5P	4295	5465	—
Style No.	**Body Type & Seating**	**Price**	**Weight**	**Prod. Total**
5780-B	Conv. Sed.-5P	—	—	—
5780-5	Conv. Sed.-5P	5430	—	—
5785	Coll. Cpe.-5P	4295	5415	—
5788	Stat. Cpe.-5P	—	—	—
5789-A	Vict. Cpe.-4P	—	—	—
5791	Limo. Brgm.-7P	5495	5580	—
5791-B	Limo. Brgm.-7P	—	—	—
5799	Aero. Cpe.-5P	4295	5430	—
Series Fleetwood (30) 146" wb flat windshield				
6030-B	Imp. Sed.-5P	—	—	—
6030-FL	Imp. Cab.-5P	3695	5500	—
6030-FM	Imp. Brgm.-5P	—	—	—
6030-S	Sed.-5P	3295	5465	—
6033-S	Twn. Sed.-5P	3345	5415	—
6035	Conv. Cpe.-2P	—	—	—
6075	Imp. Sed.-7P	3645	5580	—
6075-B	Limo. (spec. back)-7P	—	—	—
6075-D	Limo.-7P	—	—	—
6075-E	Limo.-7P	—	—	—
6075-FL	Imp. Cab.-7P	3845	5580	—
6075-FM	Imp. Brgm.-7P	—	—	—
6075-H3	Limo.-7P	—	—	—
6075-H4	Limo.-7P	—	—	—
6075-0	Imp. Sed.-7P	—	—	—
6075-S	Sed.-7P	3445	5545	—

Some confusion exists regarding style numbers on 1934-35 Fleetwood bodies. Following the previous Fleetwood system, V-8s would be 56- or 60- styles, V-12s would be 57- or 61- styles, and V-16s would be 58- or 62- styles. This system was followed in promotional literature, in the 1934 Master Parts List, and in early factory records. However, since the bodies were identical for all these series, Fleetwood stamped all body plates 57- or 60-. Master Parts Lists after 1934 used only 57- and 60- style numbers for 1934-35 Fleetwood bodies. Starting in 1936, V-8 and V-12 style numbers reflected the new 1936 series designations, but V-16s retained the 57- system. 60- styles were no longer offered.

ENGINE: Ninety degree L-head. Eight. Cast iron block on aluminum crankcase. B & S: 3-3/8 x 4-15/16 in. Disp.: 353 cu. in. C.R.: 6.25:1 std.; 5.75:1 opt. Brake H.P.: 120 @ 3000 R.P.M. SAE/Taxable H.P.: 36.45. Main bearings: three. Valve lifters: mechanical. Carb.: Detroit Lubricator, Model 51.

CHASSIS: (Series 10) W.B.: 128 in. O.L.: 205-3/4, 207-1/2 in. Front/Rear Tread: 59-3/8/62 in. Tires: 7.00 x 17. (Series 20) W.B.: 136 in. O.L.: 213-3/4, 215-1/2 in. Front/Rear Tread: 59-3/8/62 in. Tires: 7.00 x 17. (Series Fleetwood (30)) W.B.: 146 in. O.L.: 227-9/16 in. Front/Rear Tread: 59-3/8/62 in. Tires: 7.00 x 17.

1934 Cadillac, Model 355-D, town coupe, JAC

TECHNICAL: Selective synchromesh transmission. Speeds: 3F/1R. Lhd, center control, emergency brake at left-under panel (rhd optional). Twin disc clutch. Shaft drive, Hotchkiss. 3/4 floating rear axle, spiral bevel drive. Overall ratio: (Series 10, 20) 4.60:1 std.; 4.36, 4.8:1 opt. (Series 30) 4.80:1 std. 4.60:1 opt. Mechanical brakes with vacuum assist on four wheels. Wire wheels. Wheel size: 17 in. drop center.

OPTIONS: Sidemount cover(s) ($20.00 each). Radio (standard/master) (64.50/74.50). Heater (44.50). Seat covers. Spotlight (24.50). Flexible steering wheel.

HISTORICAL: Introduced January 1934. Model year sales: 8,318 (with 1935). Model year production: 8,318 (with 1935). The president and general manager of Cadillac was Lawrence P. Fisher to May 31, 1934. Nicholas Dreystadt became general manager after June 1, 1934.

1934 Cadillac, Model 370-D, V-12, town sedan (with Jean Harlow), JAC

CADILLAC — MODEL 370-D — TWELVE: Except for the engine and various emblems, the V-12 was much the same car as the 146-inch wheelbase V-8.

I.D. DATA: Serial numbers were located on top surface of frame side bar, right side, just ahead of dash. Same as engine number. Starting: 4100001. Ending: 4101098 (with 1935). Engine numbers stamped on the right-hand side of the crank-case, on the generator drive chain housing. Starting: 4100001. Ending: 4101098 (with 1935).

Style No.	Body Type & Seating	Price	Weight	Prod. Total
Fleetwood 146" wb vee windshield				
5702	Rds.-2P	—	—	—
5712-C	Coll. Twn. Cab.-5P	—	—	—
5712-LB	Twn. Cab.-5P	6195	5990	—
5712-MB	Twn.Cab.-5P	—	—	—
5720	Twn. Cab.-7P	—	—	—
5720-C	Coll. Twn. Cab.-7P	—	—	—
5725-B	Twn. Cab.-7P	—	—	—
5725-LB	Twn.Cab.-7P	6295	6040	—
5725-MB	Twn.Cab.-7P	—	—	—
5730	Imp. Sed.-5P	—	—	—
5730-FL	Imp. Cab.-5P	4845	5765	—
5730-FM	Imp. Brgm.-5P	—	—	—
5730-S	Sed.-5P	4445	5735	—
5733	Imp. Twn. Sed.-5P	—	—	—
5733-S	Twn.Sed.-5P	4995	5700	—
5735	Conv. Cpe.-2P	4745	5485	—
5757	Tr.-7P -	—	—	—
5759	Spt. Phae.-5P	—	—	—
5775	Imp. Sed. (Limo.)-7P	4795	5790	—
5775-B	Limo.-7P	—	—	—
5775-E	Imp. Sed.-7P	—	—	—
5775-FL	Imp. Cab.-7P	4995	5790	—
5775-FM	Imp. Brgm.-7P	—	—	—
5775-H4	Imp. Sed.-7P	—	—	—
5775-S	Sedan-7P	4595	5760	—
5775-W	Limo.-7P	—	—	—
5776	Cpe.-2P	4595	5520	—
5780	Conv. Sed. w/div.-5P	4995	5800	—
5780-6	Conv. Sed.-5P	—	—	—
5780-S	Conv. Sed.-5P	—	5770	—
5785	Coll. Cpe.-5P	4995	5685	—
5788	Stat. Cpe.-5P	—	5720	—
5789-A	Vict. Cpe.-4P	—	—	—
5791	Limo. Brgm.-7P	6195	6030	—
5791-B	Limo. Brgm.-7P	—	—	—
5799	Aerodynamic Cpe.-5P	4995	5720	—

Style No.	Body Type & Seating	Price	Weight	Prod. Total
Fleetwood 146" wb flat windshield				
Some listings show these as 61- styles.				
6030-B	Imp. Sed.-5P	—	—	—
6030-FL	Imp. Cab.-5P	4395	5765	—
6030-FM	Imp. Brgm.-5P	—	—	—
6030-S	Sed.-5P	3995	5735	—
6033-S	Twn. Sed.-5P	4045	5700	—
6035	Conv. Cpe.-2P	—	—	—
6075	Imp. Sed.-7P	4345	5790	—
6075-B	Limo. (spec. back)-7P	—	—	—
6075-D	Limo.-7P	—	—	—
6075-E	Limo.-7P	—	—	—
6075-FL	Imp. Cab.-7P	4545	5790	—
6075-FM	Imp. Brgm.-7P	—	—	—
6075-H3	Limo.-7P	—	—	—
6075-H4	Limo.-7P	—	—	—
6075-0	Imp. Sed.-7P	—	—	—
6075-S	Sed.-7P	4145	5760	—

Some confusion exists regarding style numbers on 1934-35 Fleetwood bodies. Following the previous Fleetwood system, V-8s would be 56- or 60- styles, V-12s would be 57- or 61-styles, and V-16s would be 58- or 62- styles. This system was followed in promotional literature, in the 1934 Master Parts List, and in early factory records. However, since the bodies were identical for all these series, Fleetwood stamped all body plates 57- or 60-. Master Parts Lists after 1934 used only 57- and 60- style numbers for 1934-35 Fleetwood bodies. Starting in 1936, V-8 and V-12 style numbers reflected the new 1936 series designations, but V-16s retained the 57- system. 60- styles were no longer offered.

ENGINE: 45 degree, overhead valve. Twelve. cast iron block on aluminum crankcase. B & S: 3-1/8 in. x 4 in. Disp.: 368 cu. in. C.R.: 6.0:1 std.; 5.65:1 opt. Brake H.P.: 133 @ 3400 R.P.M. SAE/Taxable H.P.: 46.9. Main bearings: four. Valve lifters: mechanical w/hydraulic silencer on rocker bushing. Carb.: Dual Detroit Lubricator, Type R-13, L-13, Model 51.

CHASSIS: W.B.: 146 in. O.L.: 227-9/16 in. Front/Rear Tread: 59-3/8/62 in. Tires: 7.50 x 17.

TECHNICAL: Selective, synchromesh transmission. Speeds: 3R/1R. Lhd, center control; emergency at left under panel

(rhd optional). Twin disc clutch. Shaft drive, Hotchkiss. 3/4 floating rear axle, spiral bevel drive. Overall ratio: 4.80:1 std., 4.60:1 opt., 5.11:1 opt. Mechanical brakes with vacuum assist on four wheels. Wire wheels. Wheel size: 17 in. drop center.

OPTIONS: Sidemount cover(s) ($20.00 each). Radio (standard/master) (64.50/74.50). Heater (44.50). Seat covers. Spotlight (24.50). Flexible steering wheel.

HISTORICAL: Introduced January 1934. Model year sales: 1,098 (with 1935). Model year production: 1,098 (with 1935). The president and general manager of Cadillac was Lawrence P. Fisher to May 31, 1934. Nicholas Dreystadt was general manager after June 1, 1934.

1934 Cadillac, Model 452-D, V-16, town sedan, JAC

CADILLAC — MODEL 452-D — SIXTEEN: V-16s shared the Fleetwood bodies with the eights and twelves, but were given a few distinctive styling details. The grille was of eggcrate design. Headlights were mounted on the radiator shell rather than the fenders, and the parking lights were on the fenders rather than in the headlight supports. Three spears were placed on the hood side panels and front fender skirts. There was no crease across the nose of the front fenders.

Chassis changes were the same as on the eights and twelves, with minor differences to accommodate the added weight, power, and tremendous 154-inch wheelbase.

I.D. DATA: Serial numbers were on top surface of frame side bar, right side, just ahead of dash. Same as engine number. Starting: 5100001. Ending: 5100150 (with 1935). Engine numbers were stamped on the right-handside of the crankcase, on the generator drive chain housing. Starting: 5100001. Ending: 5100150 (with 1935).

Style No.	Body Type & Seating	Price	Weight	Prod. Total
Fleetwood 154" wb vee windshield				
Some listings show these as 58- styles.				
5702	Rds.-2P	—	—	—
5712-C	Coll. Twn. Cab.-5P	—	—	—
5712-LB	Twn. Cab.-5P	8850	—	—
5712-MB	Twn. Cab.-5P	—	—	—
5720	Twn. Cab.-7P	—	—	—
5720-C	Coll. Twn. Cab.-7P	—	—	—
5725-B	Twn. Cab.-7P	—	—	—
5725-LB	Twn. Cab.-7P	8950	6390	—
5725-MB	Twn. Cab.-7P	—	—	—
5730	Imp. Sed.-5P	—	—	—
5730-FL	Imp. Cab.-5P	7700	—	—
5730-FM	Imp. Brgm.-5P	—	—	—
5730-S	Sed.-5P	7300	6100	—
5733	Imp. Twn. Sed.-5P	—	—	—
5733-S	Twn. Sed.-5P	7350	6085	—
5735	Conv. Cpe.-2P	7600	5900	—
5757	Tr.-7P	—	—	—
5759	Spt. Phae.-5P	—	—	—
5775	Imp. Sed. (Limo.)-7P	7650	6210	—
5775-B	Limo.-7P	—	—	—
5775-E	Imp. Sed.-7P	—	—	—
5775-FL	Imp. Cab.-7P	7850	—	—
5775-FM	Imp. Brougham-7P	—	—	—
5775-H4	Imp. Sed.-7P	—	—	—
5775-S	Sed.-7P	7450	6190	—
5775-W	Limo.-7P	—	—	—
5776	Cpe.-2P	7450	5840	—
5780	Conv. Sed. w/div.-5P	7850	6100	—
5780-B	Conv. Sed.-5P	—	—	—
5780-S	Conv. Sed.-5P	—	—	—
5785	Coll. Cpe.-5P	7885	—	—
5788	Stat. Cpe.-5P	—	—	—
5789-A	Vict. Cpe.-4P	—	—	—

Style	Body Type & Seating	Price		
5791	Limo. Brgm.-7P	8850	—	—
5791-B	Limo. Brgm.-7P	—	—	—
5799	Aerodynamic Cpe.-5P	7850	—	—

Fleetwood 154" wb flat windshield

Some listings show these as 62- styles.

Style	Body Type & Seating	Price		
6030-B	Imp. Sed.-5P	—	—	—
6030-FL	Imp. Cab.-5P	7050	—	—
6030-FM	Imp. Brgm.-5P	—	—	—
6030-S	Sed.-5P	6650	—	—
6033-S	Twn. Sed.-5P	6700	6085	—
6035	Conv. Cpe.-2P	—	—	—
6075	Imp. Sed.-7P	7000	6210	—
6075-B	Limo. (spec. back)-7P	—	—	—
6075-D	Limo.-7P	—	—	—
6075-E	Limo.-7P	—	—	—
6075-FL	Imp. Cab.-7P	7200	—	—
6075-FM	Imp. Brgm.-7P	—	—	—
6075-H3	Limo.-7P	—	—	—
6075-H4	Limo.-7P	—	—	—
6075-O	Imp. Sed.-7P	—	—	—
6075-S	Sed.-7P	6800	6190	—

Some confusion exists regarding style numbers on 1934-35 Fleetwood bodies. Following the previous Fleetwood system, V-8s would be 56- or 60- styles, V-12s would be 57- or 61- styles, and V-16s would be 58- or 62- styles. This system was followed in promotional literature, in the 1934 Master Parts List, and in early factory records. However, since the bodies were identical for all these series, Fleetwood stamped all body plates 57- or 60-. Master Parts Lists after 1934 used only 57- and 60- style numbers for 1934-35 Fleetwood bodies. Starting in 1936, V-8 and V-12 style numbers reflected the new 1936 series designations, but V-16s retained the 57- system. 60- styles were no longer offered.

ENGINE: 45 degree, overhead valve. Sixteen. Cast iron block on aluminum crankcase. B & S: 3 x 4 in. Disp.: 452 cu. in. C.R.: 6.0:1 std., 5.57:1 opt. Brake H.P.: 169.2 @ 3400 R.P.M. SAE/Taxable H.P.: 57.5. Main bearings: five. Valve lifters: mechanical w/hydraulic silencer on rocker bushing. Carb.: Dual Detroit Lubricator, Type R-14, L-14, Model 51.

CHASSIS: (Series 452-D) W.B.: 154 in. O.L.: 240 in. Front/Rear Tread: 59-3/8/62 in. Tires: 7.50 x 17.

TECHNICAL: Selective synchromesh transmission. Speeds: 3F/1R. Lhd, center control, emergency at left under panel (rhd optional). Twin disc clutch. Shaft drive, Hotchkiss. 3/4 floating rear axle, spiral bevel drive. Overall ratio: 4.64:1 std.; 4.31:1 opt., 4.07:1 opt. Mechanical brakes with vacuum assist on four wheels. Wire wheels. Wheel size: 17 in. Drop center.

OPTIONS: Sidemount cover(s) ($20.00 each). Radio (standard/master) (64.50/74.50). Heater (44.50). Seat covers. Spotlight (24.50). Flexible steering wheel.

HISTORICAL: Introduced January 1934. Model year sales: 150 (with 1935). Model year production: 150 (with 1935). The president and general manager of Cadillac was Lawrence P. Fisher to May 31, 1934. Nicholas Dreystadt was general manager after June 1, 1934.

1935 CADILLAC

CADILLAC — MODEL 355-D — SERIES 10, 20, 30 — EIGHT: V-8 Cadillac for 1935 remained virtually unchanged from 1934. The biplane bumpers of 1934 were replaced by more conventional units. One major change was introduced on Fisher bodies — the all-steel Turret Top. Fleetwood bodies did not have the steel top until 1936. For 1934, Fleetwood bodied V-8s on 146 in. wheelbase were designated Series 30. Fisher bodied cars continued under the designations Series 10 and Series 20.

Having been associated with funeral and ambulance equipment for many years, Cadillac embarked on an extra effort in 1935 to consolidate this business. Three Fleetwood-bodied seven-passenger livery sedans were offered on the V-8 Series 30 chassis. Additionally, a 160 in. wheelbase commercial V-8 chassis was offered for hearse and ambulance adaptation.

1935 Cadillac, Series 10, V-8, town coupe, HAC

I.D. DATA: Serial numbers were on top surface of frame side bar, right side, just ahead of dash. Same as engine number. Starting: 3100001 (with 1934). Ending: 3108318. Engine numbers were stamped on crankcase near the water inlet on the right-hand side. Starting: 3100001 (with 1934). Ending: 3108318.

Style No.	Body Type & Seating	Price	Weight	Prod. Total
Series 10 Fisher 128" wb				
35728	2-dr. Spt. Cpe.-2/3P	2345	4550	—
35718	2-dr. Conv. Cpe.-2/4P	2445	4515	—
35721	4-dr. Conv. Sed.-5P	2755	4750	—
35722	2-dr. Twn. Cpe.-5P	2495	4630	—
35709	4-dr. Sed.-5P	2445	4715	—
35702	4-dr. Twn. Sed.-5P	2495	4735	—
Series 20 Fisher 136" wb				
35678	2-dr. Spt. Cpe.-2/3P	2545	4660	—
35668	2-dr. Conv. Cpe.-2/4P	2645	4625	—
35671	4-dr. Conv. Sed.-5P	2955	4860	—
35659	4-dr. Sed.-5P	2645	4825	—
35652	4-dr. Twn. Sed.-5P	2695	4815	—
35662	4-dr. Sed.-7P	2795	4945	—
35663	4-dr. Imp. Sed.-7P	2945	4970	—

Style No.	Body Type & Seating	Price	Weight	Prod. Total
Series 30 Fleetwood Livery 146" wb				
6075-L	4-dr. Livery Limo.-7P	—	—	—
6075-LL	4-dr. Livery Limo.-7P	—	—	—
6075-SL	4-dr. Livery Sed.-7P	—	—	—

Series 30 Fleetwood 146" wb vee windshield

Some listings show these as 56- styles.

Style No.	Body Type & Seating	Price	Weight	Prod. Total
fs6075-S	Sed.-7P	3445	5545	—

Some confusion exists regarding style numbers on 1934-35 Fleetwood bodies. Following the previous Fleetwood system, V-8s would be 56- or 60- styles, V-12s would be 57- or 61- styles, and V-16s would be 58- or 62- styles. This system was followed in promotional literature, in the 1934 Master Parts List, and in early factory records. However, since the bodies were identical for all these series, Fleetwood stamped all body plates 57- or 60-. Master Parts Lists after 1934 used only 57- or 60- style numbers for 1934-35 Fleetwood bodies. Starting in 1936, V-8 and V-12 style numbers reflected the new 1936 series designations, but V-16s retained the 57-system; 60- styles were no longer offered.

ENGINE: Ninety degree L-head. Eight. Cast iron block on aluminum crankcase. B & S: 3-3/8 x 4-15/16 in. Disp.: 353 cu. in. C.R.: 6.25:1 std. 5.75:1 opt. Brake H.P.: 130 @ 3400 R.P.M. SAE/Taxable H.P.: 36.45. Main bearings: three. Valve lifters: mechanical. Carb.: Detroit Lubricator, Model 51.

CHASSIS: (Series 10) W.B.: 128 in. O.L.: 207-1/2 in. Front/Rear Tread: 59-3/8/62 in. Tires: 7.00 x 17. (Series 20) W.B.: 136 in. O.L.: 215-1/2 in. Front/Rear Tread: 59-3/8/62 in. Tires: 7.00 x 17. (Series 30) W. B.: 146 in. O.L.: 227-9/16 in. Front/Rear Tread: 59-3/8/62 in. Tires: 7.00 x 17. (Commercial chassis) W.B.: 160 in.

TECHNICAL: Selective, synchromesh transmission. Speeds: 3F/1R. Lhd, center control, emergency brake at left under panel (rhd optional). Twin disc clutch. Shaft drive, Hotchkiss. 3/4 floating rear axle, spiral bevel drive. Overall ratio: (Series 10, 20) 4.60:1 std.; 4.36:1, 4.8:1 opt. (Series 30) 4.80:1 std.,

4.60:1 opt. Mechanical brakes with vacuum assist on four wheels. Wire wheels. Wheel size: 17 in. Drop center.

OPTIONS: Sidemount cover(s) ($20.00 ea.). Radio (standard/master) (64.50/74.50). Heater (44.50). Seat covers. Spotlight (24.50). Flexible steering wheel.

HISTORICAL: Introduced January 1935 (continuation of 1934 line). Innovations: All-steel Turret Top — Fisher bodies only. Model year sales: 8,318 (with 1934). Model year production: 8,318 (with 1934). The general manager of Cadillac was Nicholas Dreystadt.

1935 Cadillac, Series 40, V-12, town cabriolet, OCW

CADILLAC — MODEL 370-D — SERIES 40 — TWELVE: Virtually the same as 1934, except for new bumper. Designation changed to Series 40.

I.D. DATA: Serial numbers were on top surface of frame side bar, right side, just ahead of dash. Same as engine number. Starting: 4100001 (with 1934). Ending: 4101098. Engine numbers were stamped on the right-hand side of the crankcase, on the generator drive chain housing. Starting: 4100001 (with 1934). Ending: 4101098.

Style No.	Body Type & Seating	Price	Weight	Prod. Total
Series 40 Fleetwood 146" wb vee Windshield				
5702	Rds.-2P	—	—	—
5712-C	Coll. Twn. Cab.-5P	—	—	—
5712-LB	Twn. Cab.-5P	6195	5990	—
5712-MB	Twn. Cab.-5P	—	—	—
5720	Twn. Cab.-7P	—	—	—
5720-C	Coll. Twn. Cab.-7P	—	—	—
5725 B	Twn. Cab.-7P	—	—	—
5725-LB	Twn. Cab.-7P	6295	6040	—
5725-MB	Twn. Cab.-7P	—	—	—
5730	Imp. Sed.-5P	—	—	—
5730-FL	Imp. Cab.-5P	4845	5765	—
5730-FM	Imp. Brgm.-5P	—	—	—
5730-S	Sed.-5P	4445	5735	—
5733	Imp. Twn. Sed.-5P	—	—	—
5733-S	Twn. Sed.-5P	4995	5700	—
5735	Conv. Cpe.-2P	4745	5485	—
5757	Tr.-7P	—	—	—
5759	Spt. Phae.-5P	—	—	—
5775	Imp. Sed. (Limo.)-7P	4795	5790	—
5775-B	Limo.-7P	—	—	—
5775 E	Imp. Sed.-7P	—	—	—
5775-FL	Imp. Cab.-7P	4995	5790	—
5775-FM	Imp. Brgm.-7P	—	—	—
5775-H4	Imp. Sed.-7P	—	—	—
5775 S	Sed.-7P	4595	5760	—
5775-W	Limo.-7P	—	—	—
5776	Cpe.-2P	4595	5520	—
5780	Conv. Sed. w/div.-5P	4995	5800	—
5780-8	Conv. Sed.-5P	—	—	—
5780-S	Conv. Sed.-5P	—	5770	—
5785	Coll. Cpe.-5P	4995	5685	—
5788	Stat. Cpe.-5P	—	5720	—
5789-A	Vict. Cpe.-4P	—	—	—
5791	Limo. Brgm.-7P	6195	6030	—
5791-B	Limo. Brgm.-7P	—	—	—
5799	Aero. Cpe.-5P	4995	5720	—
Series 40 Fleetwood 146" wb flat windshield				
Some listings show these as 61- styles.				
6030-B	Imp. Sed.-5P	—	—	—
6030-FL	Imp. Cab.-5P	4395	5765	—
6030-FM	Imp. Brgm.-5P	—	—	—
6030-S	Sed.-5P	3995	5735	—
6033-S	Twn. Sed.-5P	4045	5700	—
6035	Conv. Cpe.-2P	—	—	—
6075	Imp. Sed.-7P	4345	5790	—
6075-B	Limo. (spec. back)-7P	—	—	—
6075-D	Limo.-7P	—	—	—
6075-E	Limo.-7P	—	—	—
6075 FL	Imp. Cab.-7P	4545	5790	—
6075-FM	Imp. Brgm.-7P	—	—	—
6075-H3	Limo.-7P	—	—	—
6075-H4	Limo.-7P	—	—	—
6075-0	Imp. Sed.-7P	—	—	—
6075-S	Sed.-7P	4145	5760	—

Some confusion exists regarding style numbers on 1934-35 Fleetwood bodies. Following the previous Fleetwood system, V-8s would be 56- or 60- styles, V-12s would be 57- or 61- styles, and V-16s would be 58- or 62- styles. This system was followed in promotional literature, in the 1934 Master Parts List, and in early factory records. However, since the bodies were identical for all these series, Fleetwood stamped all body plates 57- or 60-. Master Parts Lists after 1934 used only 57- and 60- style numbers for 1934-35 Fleetwood bodies. Starting in 1936, V-8 and V-12 style numbers reflected the new 1936 series designations, but V-16s retained the 57- system; 60- styles were no longer offered.

ENGINE: 45 degree, overhead valve. Twelve. Cast iron block on aluminum crankcase. B & S: 3-1/8 in. x 4 in. Disp.: 368 cu. in. C.R.: 6.0:1 std., 5.65:1 opt. Brake H.P.: 150 @ 3600 R.P.M. SAE/Taxable H.P.: 46.9. Main bearings: four. Valve lifters: mechanical w/hydraulic silencer on rocker bushing. Carb.: Dual Detroit Lubricator, Type R-13, L-13, Model 51.

CHASSIS: W.B. 146 in. Front/Rear Tread: 59-3/8/62 in. Tires: 7.50 x 17.

TECHNICAL: Selective, synchromesh transmission. Speeds: 3F/1R. Lhd, center control; emergency brake at left under panel (rhd optional). Twin disc clutch. Shaft drive, Hotchkiss. 3/4 floating rear axle, spiral bevel drive. Overall ratio: 4.80:1 std.; 4.60:1 opt., 5.11:1 opt. Mechanical brakes with vacuum assist on four wheels. Wire wheels. Wheel size: 17 in. Drop center.

OPTIONS: Sidemount cover(s) ($20.00 each). Radio (standard/master) (64.50/74.50). Heater (44.50). Seat covers. Spotlight (24.50). Flexible steering wheel.

HISTORICAL: Introduced January 1935 (continuation of 1934 line). Model year sales: 1,098 (with 1934). Model year production: 1,098 (with 1934). The general manager of Cadillac was Nicholas Dreystadt.

CADILLAC — MODEL 452-D — SERIES 60 — SIXTEEN: Virtually the same as 1934, except for new bumper. Designation changed to Series 60.

I.D. DATA: Serial numbers were on top surface of frame side bar, right side, just ahead of dash. Same as engine number. Starting: 5100001 (with 1934). Ending: 5100150. Engine numbers were stamped on the right-hand side of the crankcase, on the generator drive chain housing. Starting: 5100001 (with 1934). Ending: 5100150.

Style No.	Body Type & Seating	Price	Weight	Prod. Total
Series 60 Fleetwood 154" wb vee windshield				
Some listings show these as 58- styles.				
5702	Rds.-2P	—	—	—
5712-C	Coll. Twn. Cab.-5P	—	—	—
5712-LB	Twn. Cab.-5P	8950	6100	—
5712-MB	Twn. Cab.-5P	—	—	—
5720	Twn. Cab.-7P	—	—	—
5720-C	Coll. Twn. Cab.-7P	—	—	—
5725-B	Twn. Cab.-7P	—	—	—
5725 LB	Twn. Cab.-7P	9050	6390	—
5725-MB	Twn. Cab.-7P	—	—	—
5730	Imp. Sed.-5P	—	—	—
5730-FL	Imp. Cab.-5P	7800	6150	—
5730-FM	Imp. Brgm.-5P	—	—	—
5730-S	Sed.-5P	7400	6085	—
5733	Imp. Twn. Sed.-5P	—	6140	—
5733-S	Twn. Sed.-5P	7450	6050	—
5735	Conv. Cpe.-2P	7700	5800	—
5757	Tr.-7P	7700	5800	—
5759	Spt. Phae.-5P	—	—	—
5775	Imp. Sed. (Limo.)-7P	7750	6210	—
5775-B	Limo.-7P	—	—	—
5775 E	Imp. Sed.-7P	—	—	—
5775-FL	Imp. Cab.-7P	7950	—	—
5775 FM	Imp. Brgm.-7P	—	—	—
5775-H4	Imp. Sed.-7P	—	—	—
5775-S	Sed.-7P	7550	6190	—
5775-W	Limo.-7P	—	—	—
5776	Cpe.-2P	7550	5840	—
5780	Conv. Sed. w/div.-5P	7950	6100	—

Style No.	Body Type			
5780-B	Conv. Sed.-5P	—	—	—
5780-S	Conv. Sed.-5P	—	6080	—
5785	Coll. Cpe.-5P	—	6000	—
5788	Stat. Cpe.-5P	—	—	—
5789-A	Vict. Cpe.-4P	—	—	—
5791	Limo. Brgm.-7P	8950	6225	—
5791-B	Limo. Brgm.-7P	—	—	—
5799	Aerodynamic Cpe.-5P	8150	6050	—

Series 60 Fleetwood 154" wb flat windshield
Some listings show these as 62- styles.

Style No.	Body Type			
6030-B	Imp. Sed.-5P	—	—	—
6030-FL	Imp. Cab.-5P	7150	—	—
6030-FM	Imp. Brgm.-5P	—	—	—
6030-S	Sed.-5P	6750	6050	—
6033-S	Twn. Sed.-5P	6800	6085	—
6035	Conv. Cpe.-2P	—	—	—
6075	Imp. Sed.-7P	7100	6210	—
6075 B	Limo. (spec. back)-7P	—	—	—
6075-D	Limo.-7P	—	—	—
6075-E	Limo.-7P	—	—	—
6075-FL	Imp. Cab.-7P	7300	—	—
6075-FM	Imp. Brgm.-7P	—	—	—
6075-H3	Limo.-7P	—	—	—
6075 H4	Limo.-7P	—	—	—
6075 0	Imp. Sed.-7P	—	—	—
6075 S	Sed.-7P	6900	6190	—

Some confusion exists regarding style numbers on 1934-35 Fleetwood bodies. Following the previous Fleetwood system, V-8s would be 56- or 60- styles, V-12s would be 57- or 61- styles, and V-16s would be 58- or 62- styles. This system was followed in promotional literature, in the 1934 Master Parts List, and in early factory records. However, since the bodies were identical for all these series, Fleetwood stamped all body plates 57- or 60-. Master Parts Lists after 1934 used only 57- and 60- style numbers for 1934-35 Fleetwood bodies. Starting in 1936, V-8 and V-12 style numbers reflected the new 1936 series designations, but V-16s retained the 57-system; 60- styles were no longer offered.

ENGINE: 45 degree, overhead valve. Sixteen. Cast iron block on aluminum crankcase. B & S: 3 x 4 in. Disp.: 452 cu. in. C.R.: 6.0:1 std. Brake H.P.: 185 @ 3800 R.P.M. SAE/Taxable H.P.: 57.5. Main bearings: five. Valve lifters: mechanical w/hydraulic silencer on rocker bushing. Carb.: Dual Detroit Lubricator, Type R-14, L-14, Model 51.

CHASSIS: W.B. 154 in. O.L.: 240 in. Front/Rear Tread: 59-3/8/62 in. Tires: 7.50 x 17.

TECHNICAL: Selective, synchromesh transmission. Speeds: 3F/1R. Lhd, center control, emergency brake at left under panel (rhd optional). Twin disc clutch. Shaft drive, Hotchkiss. 3/4 floating rear axle, spiral bevel drive. Overall ratio: 4.64:1 std. 4.31:1 opt., 4.07:1 opt. Mechanical brakes with vacuum assist on four wheels. Wire wheels. Wheel size: 17 in. Drop center.

OPTIONS: Sidemount cover(s) ($20.00 each). Radio (standard/master) (64.50/74.50). Heater (44.50). Seat covers. Spotlight (24.50). Flexible steering wheel.

HISTORICAL: Introduced January 1935 (continuation of 1934 line). Model year sales: 150 (with 1934). Model year production: 150 (with 1934). The general manager of Cadillac was Nicholas Dreystadt.

1936 CADILLAC

CADILLAC — SERIES 36-60 — EIGHT: A new model for 1936 — more than a LaSalle, less than a full size Cadillac — the same concept as the LaSalle, but with that name — Cadillac. Smaller, shorter, lighter, less powerful, less expensive, but with full Cadillac quality. Limited to three body styles, by Fisher. The convertible coupe had a rumbleseat, but the closed coupe had only a small folding seat inside for an extra passenger. Both these body styles had a single fenderwell on the side opposite the driver. Vee windshield, grille and fender treatment were the same as on the larger V-8s. The engine was the same new engine as in the Fleetwood bodied V-8s, but with a 3/8 in. smaller bore. The transmission was the smaller unit, similar to that in the LaSalle. Many dimensions were less than on the larger V-8s, to fit the concept of a lower priced, less pretentious, but equally high-quality product.

1936 Cadillac, Series 36-70, coupe, OCW

I.D. DATA: Engine numbers were on top of the crankcase, just behind the fan support. Starting: 6010001. Ending: 6016712.

Model No.	Body Type & Seating	Price	Weight	Prod. Total
36-6077	Cpe.-2P	1645	3830	—
36-6067	Conv. Cpe.-2P	1725	3940	—
36-6019	Tr. Sed.-5P	1695	4010	—

ENGINE: Ninety degree, L-head. Eight. Cast iron block (blocks cast enbloc with crankcase). B & S: 3-3/8 x 4-1/2 in. Disp.: 322 cu. in. C.R.: 6.25:1. Brake H.P.: 125 @ 3400 R.P.M. SAE/Taxable H.P.: 36.45. Main bearings: three. Valve lifters: hydraulic. Carb.: Stromberg EE-25.

CHASSIS: W.B.: 121 in. O.L.: 196 in. Height: 65-3/4/67-1/2 in. Front/Rear Tread: 58/59 in. Tires: 7.00 x 16.

TECHNICAL: Selective, synchromesh transmission. Speeds: 3P/1R. Lhd, center control, emergency brake at left under panel (rhd optional). Single disc clutch. Shaft drive, Hotchkiss. Semi-floating rear axle, spiral bevel drive. Hydraulic brakes on four wheels. Disc wheels. Wheel size: 16 in.

OPTIONS: Sidemount cover(s) ($20.00). Radio (master/standard 89.50/54.50). Heater (18.50). Seat covers. Flexible steering wheel (16.00). Trim rings (1.50 each). Wheel discs (4.00 each).

HISTORICAL: Introduced October 1935. Model year sales: 6,712. Model year production: 6,712. The general manager of Cadillac was Nicholas Dreystadt.

1936 Cadillac, Series 36-70, four-door sedan, JAC

CADILLAC — SERIES 36-70, 36-75 — EIGHT: Though not the best seller in 1936, the Series 36-70 and 36-75 were the basic Cadillacs. Lower priced LaSalles and Series 60s were better sellers; V-12s and V-16s were better cars; but the 346 cu. in. V-8s were the ones that survived to form the main source of Cadillac business for years to come.

BODIES: Bodies were all vee windshield styles by Fleetwood. A narrower radiator shell supported the new louver-style "Convex vee" grille. Headlights were mounted on the radiator shell; parking lights were inside the headlights. Front fenders were new, with a crease along the center line.

The cowl vent was changed back to opening forward. Built in trunks on "touring" styles, town sedans, and convertibles sedans. Stationary and convertible coupes had rumbleseats plus a separate door for the spare tire at the extreme rear of the deck. All bodies now used the all-steel Turret Top.

ENGINE: The Cadillac V-8 for 1915 got detachable cylinder heads for 1918, compensated crankshaft for 1924, side by side rods for 1928, and a complete replacement design for 1936. The new engine, produced in two displacements, featured: Blocks and crankcase cast enbloc. Water jacket full length of the cylinder bore, more rigid crankshaft with six counterweights. New connecting rods with large ends split at an angle to allow for removal from top of engine. Hydraulic valve silencers. New manifolding and downdraft carburetor. Suction type crankcase ventilation (fumes taken out through exhaust system). Simplified lubrication system (only piping was to hydraulic lifters). Combination fuel and vacuum pump on front engine cover. Starter on right-hand side, in front of bell housing. Generator serviced by removing panel under left front fender. Pressure cap on radiator.

CHASSIS: New chassis features: Two mufflers in series. Battery under left side of front seat. Double universal joint in steering shaft. Single plate clutch. Ride control discontinued, but ride stabilizer added at front. First hydraulic brakes on a Cadillac (used on LaSalle two years earlier).

I.D. DATA: Engine numbers were on top of the crankcase, just behind the fan support. Starting: 3110001. Ending: 3115248.

Style No.	Body Type & Seating	Price	Weight	Prod. Total
Series 36-70 Fleetwood 131" wb				
36-7057	Cpe.-2P	2595	4620	—
36-7067	Conv. Cpe.-2P	2695	4690	—
36-7019	Tr. Sed.-5P	2445	4670	—
36-7029	Conv. Sed.-5P	2745	4710	—
Fleetwood Series 36-75 138" wb				
36-7509	Sed.-5P	2645	4805	—
36-7519	Tr. Sed.-5P	2645	4805	—
36-7509F	Formal Sed.-5P	3395	4805	—
36-7529	Conv. Sed.-5P	3395	5040	—
36-7539	Twn. Sed.-5P	3145	4840	—
36-7503	Sed.-7P	2795	4885	—
36-7513	Imp. Sed.-7P	2995	5045	—
36-7523	Tr. Sed.-7P	2795	4885	—
36-7533	Imp. Tr. Sed.-7P	2995	5045	—
36-7543	Twn. Car-7P	4445	5115	—
Fleetwood Commercial Cars				
36-7503L	Comm. Sed.-7P	2695	—	—
36-7513L	Comm. Imp. Sed.-7P	2865	—	—
36-7523L	Comm. Tr. Sed.-7P	2695	—	—
36-7533L	Comm. Imp. Tr. Sed.-7P	2865	—	—

ENGINE: Ninety degree, L-head. Eight. Cast iron block (blocks cast enbloc with crankcase). B & S: 3-1/2 x 4-1/2 in. Disp.: 346 cu. in. C.R.: 6.25:1. Brake H.P.: 135 @ 3400 R.P.M. SAE/Taxable H.P.: 39.20. Main bearings: three. Valve lifters: hydraulic. Carb.: Stromberg EE-25.

CHASSIS: (Series 36-70) W.B.: 131 in. O.L.: 206-1/4 in. Height: 66, 69-1/2 in. Front/Rear Tread: 60-3/16/60-1/2 in. Tires: 7.50 x 16. (Series 36-75) W.B.: 138 in. O.L.: 213-1/2 in. Height: 68-13/16 in. Front/Rear Tread: 60-3/16/62-1/2 in. Tires: 7.50 x 16. (Series 36-75 Commercial Chassis) W.B.: 156 in.

TECHNICAL: Selective, synchromesh transmission. Speeds: 3F/1R. Lhd, center control, emergency brake at left under panel (rhd optional). Single disc clutch. Shaft drive, Hotchkiss. Semi-floating rear axle, spiral bevel drive. Overall ratio: (36-70) 4.55:1 std.; 4.3:1 opt. (36-75) 4.6:1 std.; 4.3:1 opt. Hydraulic brakes on four disc wheels. Wheel size: 16 in.

1936 Cadillac, Series 36-85, touring sedan, OCW

OPTIONS: Sidemount cover(s) ($20.00). Radio (master/standard) (89.50/54.50). Heater (18.50). Seat covers. Flexible steering wheel (16.00). Trim rings (1.50 each). Wheel discs (4.00 each).

HISTORICAL: Introduced October 1935. Model year sales: 5,248. Model year production: 5,248. The general manager of Cadillac was Nicholas Dreystadt.

For the first time since 1914, Cadillacs were designated as a year model — "The 1936 Cadillacs." Annual model changes and introduction in the fall of the year would now become regular practice.

CADILLAC — SERIES 36-80, 36-85 — TWELVE: The 1936 V-12 was essentially a 1936 V-8 with a 12-cylinder engine. Performance was greatly improved over previous V-12s. Identification with the hood closed was only possible by reading emblems. Even dual exhaust pipes would no longer identify the V-12. A crossover pipe from left to right manifold resulted in a single exhaust system (with two mufflers in series). Commercial cars and chassis also shared the V-8 and the V-12 engines.

I.D. DATA: Engine numbers were on the upper left surface of the generator drive chain housing. Starting: 4110001. Ending: 4110901.

Style No.	Body Type & Seating	Price	Weight	Prod Total
Fleetwood Series 36-80 131" wb				
36-7057	Cpe.-2P	3295	4690	—
36-7067	Conv. Cpe.-2P	3395	4800	—
36-7019	Tr. Sed.-5P	3145	4945	—
36-7029	Conv. Sed.-5P	3445	4990	—
Fleetwood Series 36-85 138" wb				
36-7509	Sed.-5P	3345	5115	—
36-7509F	Formal Sed.-5P	4095	5115	—
36-7519	Tr. Sed.-5P	3345	5115	—
36-7529	Conv. Sed.-5P	4095	5230	—
36-7539	Twn. Sed.-5P	3845	5065	—
36-7503	Sed.-7P	3495	5195	—
36-7513	Imp. Sed.-7P	3695	5230	—
36-7523	Tr. Sed.-7P	3495	5195	—
36-7533	Imp. Tr. Sed.-7P	3695	5230	—
36-7543	Twn. Car-7P	5145	5300	—
Fleetwood Commercial Cars				
36-7503L	Comm. Sed.-7P	2695	—	—
36-7513L	Comm. Imp. Sed.-7P	2865	—	—
36-7523L	Comm. Tr. Sed.-7P	2695	—	—
36-7533L	Comm. Imp. Tr. Sed.-7P	2865	—	—

Note that V-12s used same style numbers as V-8s.

ENGINE: 45 degree, overhead valve. Twelve. Cast iron block on aluminum crankcase. B & S: 3-1/8 x 4 in. Disp.: 368 cu. in. C.R.: 6.0:1 std, 5.65:1 opt. Brake H.P.: 150 @ 3600 R.P.M. Main bearings: four. Valve lifters: mechanical with hydraulic silencer on rocker bushing. Carb.: Dual Detroit Lubricator, Type R-13, L-13, Model 51.

CHASSIS: (Series 36-80) W.B.: 131 in. O.L.: 206-1/4 in. Height: 66, 69-1/2 in. Front/Rear Tread: 60-3/16/60-1/2 in. Tires: 7.50 x 16. (Series 36-85) W.B.: 138 in. O.L.: 213-1/2 in. Front/Rear Tread: 60-3/16/62-1/2 in. Tires: 7.50 x 16. (Series 36-85 Commercial Chassis) W.B.: 156 in.

TECHNICAL: Selective, synchromesh transmission. Speeds: 3F/1R. Lhd, center control, emergency brake at left under panel (rhd optional). Single disc clutch. Shaft drive, Hotchkiss. Semi-floating rear axle, spiral bevel drive. Overall ratio: 4.6:1 std., 4.3:1 opt. Hydraulic brakes on four wheels. Disc wheels. Wheel size: 16 in.

OPTIONS: Sidemount cover(s) ($20.00). Radio (master/standard) (89.50/54.50). Heater (18.50). Seat covers. Flexible steering wheel (16.00). Trim rings (1.50 each). Wheel discs (4.00 each).

HISTORICAL: Introduced October 1935. Model year sales: 901. Model year production: 901. The general manager of Cadillac was Nicholas Dreystadt.

CADILLAC — SERIES 36-90 — SIXTEEN: The 1936 V-16 was a continuation of the 1935 cars. Built to order only, nearly half of the 52 units were seven-passenger limousines. As with V-8 and V-12 lines, Fleetwood bodies for the V-16 now used the all-steel Turret Top. All body styles had vee windshields. A minor mechanical change involved the use of the "Peak-load" generator.

I.D. DATA: Engine numbers were on the upper surface of the generator drive chain housing. Starting: 5110201. Ending: 5110252.

Style No.	BodyType & Seating	Price	Weight	Prod. Total

Fleetwood Series 36-90, 154" wb

Some listings show these as 58- styles.

Style No.	BodyType & Seating	Price	Weight	Prod. Total
36-5725LB	Twn. Cab.-7P	8850	6390	—
36-5725C	Twn. Cab.-7P	—	—	—
36-5730FL	Imp. Cab.-5P	—	—	—
36-5730S	Sed.-5P	—	—	—
36-5733S	Twn. Sed.-5P	7250	6085	—
36-5735	Conv. Cpe.-2P	—	—	—
36-577 5	Imp. Sed. (Limo.)-7P	7750	6190	—
36 5775FL	Imp. Cab.-7P	7850	6210	—
36-5775S	Sed.-7P	7555	6190	—
36-5776	Cpe.-2P	—	—	—
36-5780	Conv. Sed. w/Div.-5P	7850	6100	—
36-5791	Limo. Brgm.-7P	—	—	—
36-5799	Aero. Cpe.-5P	—	—	—

Some confusion exists regarding style numbers on 1934-35 Fleetwood bodies. Following the previous Fleetwood system, V-8s would be 56- or 60- styles, V 12s would be 57- or 61-styles, and V-16s would be 58- or 62- styles. This system was followed in promotional literature, in the 1934 Master Parts List, and in early factory records. However, since the bodies were identical for all these series, Fleetwood stamped all body plates 57- or 60-. Master Parts Lists after 1934 used only 57- and 60- style numbers for 1934-35 Fleetwood bodies. Starting in 1936, V-8 and V-12 style numbers reflected the new 1936 series designations, but V-16s retained the 57- system; 60- styles were no longer offered.

ENGINE: 45 degree, overhead valve. Sixteen. Cast iron block on aluminum crankcase. B & S: 3 x 4 in. Disp.: 452 cu. in. C.R.: 6.0:1 std; 5.65:1 opt. Brake H.P.: 185 @ 3800 R.P.M. SAE/Taxable H.P.: 57.5. Main bearings: five. Valve lifters: mechanical with hydraulic silencer on rocker bushing. Carb.: Dual Detroit Lubricator, Type R-14, L 14, Model 51.

CHASSIS: W.B.: 154 in. O.L.: 238 in. Front/Rear Tread: 59-3/8/62 in. Tires: 7.50 x 17.

TECHNICAL: Selective, synchromesh transmission. Speeds: 3F/1R. Lhd, center control, emergency brake at left under panel (rhd optional). Twin disc clutch. Shaft drive, Hotchkiss. 3/4 floating rear axle, spiral bevel drive. Overall ratio: 4.64:1 std; 4.31:1 opt, 4.07:1 opt. Mechanical brakes with vacuum assist on four wheels. Wire wheels. Wheel size: 17 in. Drop center.

OPTIONS: Sidemount covers ($20.00). Radio (master/standard) (89.50/54.50). Heater (18.50). Seat covers. Flexible steering wheel (16.00). Trim rings (1.50 each).

HISTORICAL: Introduced October 1935 (continuation of 1935 series). Model year sales: 52. Model year production: 52. The general manager of Cadillac was Nicholas Dreystadt.

1937 CADILLAC

CADILLAC — SERIES 37-60, 37-65, 37-70, 37-75 — EIGHT: A new body style for the Series 60 line was the convertible sedan. Body changes included: eggcrate grille and hood louvers; higher fenders with lengthwise crease along the top; set of three horizontal bars each side of grille; bumpers carrying the Cadillac emblem; swinging rear quarter windows; all-steel body construction. Series 60 shared many features with the LaSalle, but used the 346 cu. in. V-8 engine. A Series 60 commercial chassis with 160-3/8 in. wheelbase was offered.

Series 37-65

A new series, offered in only one body style — a five-passenger touring sedan built by Fisher on the 131 in. wheelbase used on Series 70 cars. This car offered a longer, heavier car than the Series 60 at a price below that of the Fleetwood-bodied cars.

1937 Cadillac, town cabriolet, OCW

Series 37-70, 75

Bodies same as 1936 except for: drip molding running from the bottom of the front pillar up and over the doors and rear quarter window; new fenders and bumpers; headlights rigidly attached (adjusted by moving reflector); wheel discs incorporated a hubcap; built-in trunk used on most bodies. A die-cast eggcrate grille was used, but the hood louver treatment differed from that used on Fisher-bodied cars. Chrome die-cast strips were used at the rear of the hood side panels. A seven-passenger Fisher-bodied special touring sedan, with or without division, was offered on the 138 in. wheelbase. These two body styles had the eggcrate hood louvers typical of all Fisher-bodied Cadillacs for 1937. The Business car line included eight-passenger versions of these Special sedans plus eight-passenger versions of four Fleetwood body styles. The eighth passenger was seated with two others on the auxiliary seats. A Commercial chassis on a 156 in. wheelbase was offered. Engine changes included: lighter flywheel; generator relocated in the vee; oil filter installed; new carburetor with full-automatic electric choke; oil bath air cleaner; relocated distributor. A new transmission design featured: pin-type synchronizers; shifter rails relocated to side of case; cover on bottom of case; extension integral with transmission mainshaft.

I.D. DATA: Engine numbers were on the crankcase, just behind the left cylinder group, parallel to the dash. Starting: (Series 37-60) 6030001; (Series 37-65) 703001; (Series 37-70, 75) 3130001. Ending: (Series 37-60) 6037003; (Series 37-65) 7032401; (Series 37-70, 75) 3134232.

1937 Cadillac, Series 37-65, touring sedan, JAC

Style No.	Body Type & Seating	Price	Weight	Prod. Total
Series 37-60 Fisher 124" wb				
37-6019	Tr. Sed.-5P	1545	3845	—
37-6049	Conv. Sed.-5P	1885	3885	—
37-6067	Conv. Cpe.-2P	1575	3745	—
37-6027	Spt. Cpe.-2P	1445	3710	—
Series 37-65 Fisher 131" wb				
37-6519	Tr. Sed.-5P	1945	4835	—
Series 37-75 Fisher 138" wb				
37-7523S	Spec. Tr. Sed.-7P	2445	4825	—
37-7533S	Spec. Imp. Tr. Sed.-7P	2645	4985	—
Series 37-70 Fleetwood 131" wb				
37-7019	Tr. Sed.-5P	2445	4420	—
37-7029	Conv. Sed.-5P	2795	4460	—
37-7057	Spt. Cpe.-2P	2645	4285	—
37-7067	Conv. Cpe.-2P	2745	4325	—
Series 37-75 Fleetwood 138" wb				
37-7503	Sed.-7P	—	—	—
37-7509-F	Fml. Sed.-5P	3495	4745	—
37-7513	Imp. Sed.-7P	—	—	—
37-7519	Tr. Sed.-5P	2645	4745	—
37-7523	Tr. Sed.-7P	2795	4825	—
37-7529	Conv. Sed.-5P	3445	4980	—

Style No.	Body Type & Seating	Price	Weight	Prod. Total
37-7533	Imp. Tr. Sed.-7P	2995	4985	—
37-7539	Twn. Sed.-5P	3145	4780	—
37-7543	Twn. Car-7P	4545	5055	—
37-7589-A	Cpe.-5P	—	—	—
37-7592	Limo. Brgm.-7P	—	—	—
Series 37-75 Fisher 138" wb Business Cars				
37-7523-SL	Spec. Bus. Tr. Sed.-8P	2575	4825	—
37-7533-SL	Spec. Bus. Imp. Tr. Sed.-8P	2775	4985	—
Series 37-75 Fleetwood 138" wb Business Cars				
37-7503-L	Bus. Sed.-8P	—	—	—
37-7513-L	Bus. Imp. Sed.-8P	—	—	—
37-7523-L	Bus. Tr. Sed.-8P	—	—	—
37-7533-L	Bus. Imp. Sed.-8P	—	—	—

ENGINE: Ninety degree, L-head. Eight. Cast iron block (blocks cast enbloc with crankcase). B & S: 3-1/2 x 4-1/2 in. Disp.: 346 cu. in. C.R.: 6.25:1 std; 5.75:1 opt. Brake H.P.: 135 @ 3400 R.P.M. SAE/Taxable H.P.: 39.20. Main bearings: three. Valve lifters: hydraulic. Carb.: Stromberg AA-25.

CHASSIS: (Series 37-60) W.B.: 124 in. O.L.: 201-1/4 in. Front/Rear Tread: 58/59 in. Tires: 7.50 x 16. (Series 37-65) W.B.: 131 in. O.L.: 208-3/16 in. Front/Rear Tread: 60-3/16/60-1/2 in. Tires: 7.50 x 16. (Series 37-70) W.B.: 131 in. O.L.: 208-3/16 in. Front/Rear Tread: 60-3/16/60-1/2 in. Tires: 7.50 x 16. (Series 37-75) W.B.: 138 in. O.L.: 215-7/8 in. Front/Rear Tread: 60-3/16/62-1/2 in. Tires: 7.50 x 16. (Series 37-60 Commercial Chassis) W.B.: 160-3/8 in. O.L.: 237-7/8 in. Tires: 7.00 x 16. (Series 37-75 Commercial Chassis) W.B.: 156 in. O.L.: 231-1/4 in. Tires: 7.50 x 16.

TECHNICAL: Selective, synchromesh transmission. Speeds: 3F/1R. Lhd, center control, emergency brake at left under panel (rhd optional). Single disc clutch. Shaft drive, Hotchkiss. Semi-floating rear axle, spiral bevel drive. (Series 37-60 Hypoid). Overall ratio: 4.3:1 (Series 37-60 3.69:1). Hydraulic brakes on four wheels. Disc wheels. Wheel size: 16 in.

OPTIONS: Sidemount cover(s) ($15.00-17.50). Radio (master/standard) (79.50/59.50). Heater (19.50-60.00). Seat cov-

ers (7.50 per seat). Wheel disc (4.00 each). Trim rings (1.50 each). Flexible steering wheel (15.00).

HISTORICAL: Introduced November 1936. Model year sales: (Series 60) 7,003; (Series 65) 2,401; (Series 70, 75) 4,232. Model year production: (Series 60) 7,003; (Series 65) 2,401; (Series 70, 75) 4,232. The general manager of Cadillac was Nicholas Dreystadt.

CADILLAC — SERIES 37-85 — TWELVE: Series 37-85 was, once more, a Series 37-75 with a V-12 engine. 1937 was the final model year for this engine. The Series 80 with 131 in. wheelbase was dropped from the line. Oil bath air cleaner and pressure radiator cap were new to the 1937 V-12.

I.D. DATA: Engine numbers were on the upper surface of the generator drive chain housing. Starting: 4130001. Ending: 4130478.

Style No.	Body Type & Seating	Price	Weight	Prod. Total
Series 37-85 Fleetwood 138" wb				
37-7509F	Formal Sed.-5P	4195	5050	—
37-7513	Imp. Sed.-7P	3695	5165	—
37-7519	Tr. Sed.-5P	3345	5050	—
37-7523	Tr. Sed.-7P	3495	5130	—
37-7529	Conv. Sed.-5P	4145	5165	—
37 7533	Imp. Tr. Sed.-7P	3695	5165	—
37 7539	Twn. Sed.-5P	3845	5000	—
37 7543	Twn. Car-7P	5245	5230	—
37-7511	Tr. Cpe.-5P	—	—	—
37-7518	Sed.-5P	—	—	—
37-7589A	Cpe.-5P	—	—	—
37-7591	Limo. Brgm.-7P	—	—	—
Series 37-85 Fisher 138" wb Business Cars				
37-7523SL	Spec. Bus Tr. Sed.-8P	2575	4825	—
37 7533SL	Spec. Bus Imp. Tr. Sed.-8P	2775	4985	—
Series 37-85 Fleetwood 138" wb Business Cars				
37-7503L	Bus Sed.-8P	—	—	—
37-7513L	Bus Imp. Sed.-8P	—	—	—
37-7523L	Bus Tr. Sed.-8P	—	—	—
37-7533L	Bus Imp. Tr. Sed.-8P	—	—	—

ENGINE: 45 degree, overhead valve. Twelve. Cast iron block on aluminum crankcase. B & S: 3-1/8 x 4 in. Disp.: 368 cu. in. C.R.: 6.0:1 std.; 5.65:1 opt. Brake H.P.: 150 @ 3600 R.P.M. SAE/Taxable H.P.: 46.9. Main bearings: four. Valve lifters: mechanical with hydraulic silencer on rocker bushing. Carb.: Dual Detroit Lubricator, Type R-13, L-13, Model 51.

CHASSIS: (Series 37-85) W.B.: 138 in. O.L.: 215-7/8 in. Front/Rear Tread: 60-3/16/61-1/2 in. Tires: 7.50 x 16.

TECHNICAL: Selective, synchromesh transmission. Speeds: 3F/1R. Lhd, center control, emergency brake at left under panel (rhd optional). Single disc clutch. Shaft drive, Hotchkiss. Semi-floating rear axle, spiral bevel drive. Overall ratio: 4.6:1. Hydraulic brakes on four wheels. Disc wheels. Wheel size: 16 in.

OPTIONS: Sidemount cover(s) ($15.00-17.50). Radio (master/standard) (79.50/59.50). Heater (19.50-60.00). Seat covers (7.50 per seat). Wheel discs (4.00 each). Trim rings (1.50 each). Flexible steering wheel (15.00).

HISTORICAL: Introduced November 1936. Model year sales: 478. Model year production: 478. The general manager of Cadillac was Nicholas Dreystadt.

CADILLAC — SERIES 37-90 — SIXTEEN: The 1937 Series 90 remained essentially the same as the 1934-36 cars. 1937 was the final model year for the overhead valve V-16 engine. For the first time, hydraulic brakes (with a vacuum booster on the pedal) were used on these cars. A stabilizer bar was added to the front suspension. A Handy oil filter replaced the Cuno self-cleaning unit. A pressure cap was used on the radiator.

I.D. DATA: Engine numbers were on the upper surface of the generator drive chain housing. Starting: 5130301. Ending: 5130350.

Style No.	Body Type & Seating	Price	Weight	Prod. Total
Series 37-90 Fleetwood 154" wb				
37-5725LB	Imp Twn Cab-7P	—	—	—
37-5730S	Sed-5P	—	—	—
37-5730FL	Imp Cab-5P	—	—	—
37-5733S	Twn Sed-5P	7350	6085	—
37 5735	Conv Cpe-2P	—	—	—
37-5775	Imp Sed-7P	7550	6190	—
37-5775S	Sed-7P	7350	6190	—
37 5775SF	Sed-7P	—	—	—
37-5775FL	Imp Cab-7P	7950	6210	—
37-5775H4	Limo-7P	—	—	—
37-5776	Cpe-2P	—	—	—
37-5780	Conv Sed-5P	7950	6100	—
37-5785	Coll Cpe-5P	—	—	—
37 5791	Limo Brgm-7P	—	—	—
37-5799	Aero Cpe-5P	7500	—	—

ENGINE: 45 degree, overhead valve. Sixteen. Cast iron block on aluminum crankcase. B & S: 3 x 4 in. Disp.: 452 cu. in. C.R.: 6.0:1 std.; 5.65:1 opt. Brake H.P.: 185 @ 3800 R.P.M. SAE/Taxable H.P.: 57.5. Main bearings: five. Valve lifters: mechanical with hydraulic silencer on rocker bushing. Carb.: Dual Detroit Lubricator, Type R-14, L-14, Model 51.

CHASSIS: W.B.: 154 in. O.L.: 238 in. Front/Rear Tread: 59-3/8/62 in. Tires: 7.50 x 17.

TECHNICAL: Selective, synchromesh transmission. Speeds: 3F/1R. Lhd, center control, emergency brake at left under panel (rhd optional). Twin disc clutch. Shaft drive, Hotchkiss. 3/4 floating rear axle, spiral bevel drive. Overall ratio: 4.64:1 std; 4.31:1 opt., 4.07:1 opt. Hydraulic brakes with vacuum booster on four wheels. Wire wheels with disc cover. Wheel size: 17 in. Drop center.

OPTIONS: Sidemount cover(s) ($15.00-17.50). Radio (master/standard) (79.50/59.50). Heater (19.50-60.00). Seat covers (7.50 per seat). Wheel discs (4.00 each). Trim rings (1.50 each). Flexible steering wheel (15.00).

HISTORICAL: Introduced November 1936. Model year sales: 50. Model year production: 50. The general manager of Cadillac was Nicholas Dreystadt.

1938 CADILLAC

1938 Cadillac, Sixty Special, sedan

CADILLAC — SERIES 38-60, 38-60S, 38-65, 38-75 — EIGHT: For 1938, the Series 70 and Fisher-bodied Series 75 Specials were dropped, but a convertible sedan was added to the Series 65 line. The styling bonanza for 1938 was the sensational new Sixty Special Sedan.

Series 60 was restyled with a squared-off grille made up of horizontal bars extending around front and sides of the nose. Three sets of four chrome bars decorated the side panel louvers. Hood was front opening alligator style and headlights were fixed to the sheet metal between fenders and grille.

Sixty Special had much the same nose as the Sixty, with one less bar in the grille assembly. The body was entirely new

and unique, on a double dropped frame three inches lower than the Sixty. There were no runningboards, the floor being at normal runningboard height. Large side windows in chrome frames were flush with the sides of the body. The convertible-shaped top featured a thin roof section and a notched back.

Series 65 (Custom V-8) and Series 75 (Fleetwood) shared a new front end style featuring a massive vertical cellular grille, three sets of horizontal bars on the hood sides, alligator hood, and headlights on the filler piece between fenders and hood. Optional sidemount covers were hinged to the fenders. Quarter windows were of sliding rather than hinged construction. Rear of bodies had rounder corners and more smoothly blended lines; trunks had more appearance of being an integral part of the body. Bodies were all steel except for wooden main sills.

New chassis details included: column gear shift; horns just behind grille; battery under right-hand side of hood; transverse muffler just behind fuel tank; wheels by different manufacturer (not interchangeable with 1937); "Synchro-Flex" flywheel; hypoid rear axle on all series; deletion of oil filter. Compression ratio on Series 75 was raised to 6.70:1, necessitating use of high octane fuel.

I.D. DATA: Serial numbers were on left frame side bar, at the rear of the left front motor support. Starting: same as engine number. Ending: Same as engine number. Engine numbers were on crankcase, just behind left cylinder block. Starting: (Series 38-60) 8270001; (Series 38-60S) 6270001; (Series 38-65) 7270001; (Series 38-75) 3270001. Ending: (Series 38-60) 8272052; (Series 38-60S) 6273704; (Series 38-65) 7271476; (Series 38-75) 3271911.

Style No.	Body Type & Seating	Price	Weight	Prod. Total
Fisher Series 38-60, 124" wb				
38-6127	Cpe-2P	1695	3855	—
38-6167	Conv Cpe-2P	1810	3845	—
38-6149	Conv Sed-5P	2215	3980	—
38-6119	Sed-5P	1775	3940	—
Fisher Series 38-60S, 127" wb				
38-6019S	Spec Sed-5P	2085	4170	—
Fisher Series 38-65 132" wb				
38-6519	Sed-5P	2285	4540	—
38-6519-F	Imp Sed-5P	2360	4580	—
38-6549	Conv Sed-5P	2600	4580	—
Fleetwood Series 38-75, 141" wb Business Cars				
38-7523-L	Bus Tr Sed-7P	3105	4945	—
38-7533-L	Bus Tr Imp-7P	3255	5105	—
Fleetwood Series 38-75 141" wb				
38-7557	Cpe-2P	3275	4675	—
38-7557-B	Cpe-5P	3380	4775	—
38-7567	Conv Cpe-2P	3380	4665	—
38-7519	Sed-5P	3075	4865	—
38-7519-F	Imp Sed-5P	3155	4925	—
38-7559	Formal Sed-5P	3990	4865	—
38-7539	Town Sed-5P	3635	4900	—
38-7529	Conv Sed-5P	3940	5110	—
38-7523	Sed-7P	3205	4945	—
38-7533	Imp Sed-7P	3360	5105	—
38-7533-F	Formal Sed-7P	3990	5105	—
38-7553	Town Car-7P	5115	5175	—

ENGINE: Ninety degree L-head. Eight. Cast iron block (blocks cast enbloc with crankcase). B & S: 3-1/2 in. x 4-1/2 in. Disp.: 346 cu. in. C.R.: (Series 60, 60S, 65) 6.25:1; (Series 75) 6.7:1. Brake H.P.: 135 (140 on 75) @ 3400 R.P.M. SAE/Taxable H.P.: 39.20. Main bearings: three. Valve lifters: hydraulic. Carb.: Stromberg AAV-25.

1938 Cadillac, Series 65, sedan, OCW

CHASSIS: (Series 38-60) W.B.: 124 in. O.L.: 207-5/8 in. Front/Rear Tread: 58/61 in. Tires: 7.00 x 16. (Series 38-60S) W.B.: 127 in. O.L.: 207-5/8 in. Front/Rear Tread: 58/61 in. Tires: 7.00 x 16. (Series 38-65) W.B.: 132 in. O.L.: 211-3/8 in. Front/Rear Tread: 60-1/2/62-3/8 in. Tires: 7.00 x 16. (Series 38-75) W.B.: 141 in. O.L.: 220-5/8 in. Front/Rear Tread: 60-1/2/62-1/2 in. Tires: 7.50 x 16. (Series 38-60 Commercial Chassis) W.B.: 160 in. (Series 38-65 Commercial Chassis) W.B.: 160 in. (Series 38-75 Commercial Chassis) W.B.: 161 in.

TECHNICAL: Selective synchromesh manual transmission. Speeds: 3F/1R. Lhd; gearshift on column; handbrake at left (rhd optional). Single disc clutch. Shaft drive, Hotchkiss. Semi-floating rear axle. Hypoid gears. Overall ratio: (60, 60S, 65) 3.92:1; (75) 4.58:1. Hydraulic brakes on four wheels. Disc wheels. Wheel size: 16 in.

OPTIONS: Radio for Fleetwood bodies ($95.00). Radio (master/standard) (79.50/65.00). Heater (26.50-42.50). Seat covers (7.50 per seat). Spotlight (18.50). Automatic battery filler (7.50). Flexible steering wheel (15.00). Fog lights (17.50 pair). Wheel discs (4.00 each). Trim rings (1.50 each).

HISTORICAL: Introduced October 1937. Model year sales and production: (Series 60) 2,052; (Series 60S) 3,704; (Series 65) 1,476; (Series 75) 1,911. The general manager of Cadillac was Nicholas Dreystadt.

CADILLAC — SERIES 38-90 — SIXTEEN: The Series 90 for 1938 became essentially a Series 75 with a V-16 engine. Even though the wheelbase was 13 inches shorter, the bodies were equal or larger in all dimensions than previous Cadillac V-16s. This was accomplished by fitting the nearly flat engine low in the frame and partially behind the line of the firewall. V-16s were distinguished from the counterpart V-8s by a coarser pitch eggcrate grille, fender lamps, and streamlined louvers on the hood side panels and all fender skirts.

The new V-16 engine was of L-head, short stroke square design, cast enbloc, with 135 degree vee. With each block in running balance, the engine was basically a twin eight. Dual accessories included carburetors, oil bath air cleaners, manifolds, distributors, coils, fuel pumps, and water pumps. The fuel pumps were interconnected so that either one could supply both carburetors if needed. Only the left-hand distributor contained breaker arms; the two arms being electrically independent but operated by a single eight-lobe cam. The right-hand unit acted only to distribute the high tension voltage to the spark plugs in the right bank. A cross pipe connected both exhaust manifolds and fed into a single down-pipe at the left. The generator was placed low in the vee and was driven by an internal rubber ring in the fan hub acting on a driven wheel on the generator shaft. This arrangement allowed for fan speeds less than engine speed and generator speeds nearly twice engine speed — it lasted only one year.

I.D. DATA: Serial numbers were on frame side bar, just ahead of the steering gear. Starting: same as engine number. Ending: same as engine number. Engine numbers were on upper rear left-hand corner of left cylinder block, parallel with cylinder head. Starting: 5270001. Ending: 5270315.

Style No.	Body Type & Seating	Price	Weight	Prod. Total
Fleetwood Series 38-90 141" wb				
38-9057	Cpe-2P	5335	4915	—
38-9057-B	Cpe-5P	5440	5015	—
38-9067	Conv Cpe-2P	5440	4905	—
38-9019	Sed-5P	5135	5105	—
38-9019 F	Imp Sed-5P	5215	5165	—
38 9059	Formal Sed-5P	6050	5105	—
38-9039	Twn Sed-5P	5695	5140	—
38-9029	Conv Sed-5P	6000	5350	—
38-9023	Sed-7P	5265	5185	—
38-9033	Imp Sed-7P	5420	5345	—
38-9033-F	Formal Sed-7P	6050	5345	—
38-9053	Twn Car-7P	7170	5415	—

ENGINE: 135 degree vee L-Head. Sixteen. Cast iron block. B & S: 3-1/4 x 3-1/4 in. Disp.: 431 cu. in. C.R.: 7:1. Brake H.P.: 185 @ 3600 R.P.M. SAE/Taxable H.P.: 67.6. Main bearings: nine. Valve lifters: hydraulic. Carb.: Carter WDO 407s(L) - 408s(R).

CHASSIS: (Series 38-90) W.B.: 141 in. O.L.: 200-5/8 in. Front/Rear Tread: 60-1/2/62-1/2 in. Tires: 7.50 x 16.

TECHNICAL: Selective synchromesh manual transmission. Speeds: 3F/1R. Lhd; gearshift on column; handbrake at left. Single disc clutch. Shaft drive, Hotchkiss. Semi-floating rear axle. Hypoid gears. Overall ratio: 4.31:1. Hydraulic brakes on four wheels. Disc wheels. Wheel size: 16 in.

OPTIONS: Radio ($95.00). Heater (26.50-42.50). Seat covers (7.50 per seat). Spotlight (18.50). Automatic battery filler (7.50). Flexible steering wheel (15.00). Fog lights (17.50 pair).

HISTORICAL: Introduced October 1937. Model year sales and production: 315. The general manager of Cadillac was Nicholas Dreystadt.

1939 CADILLAC

1939 Cadillac, Sixty Special, touring sedan, JAC

CADILLAC — SERIES 39-60S, 39-61, 39-75 — EIGHT: For 1939, Series 61 replaced Series 60 and 65 of 1938. All V-8s had new grille styling; similar in appearance but different in detail dimensions on each series. The pointed center grille and the functional side grilles were die-cast, with finepitch bars. A single die-cast louver was positioned to the rear of each hood side panel. Headlights were once again attached to the radiator casing.

Sixty Special, now bodied by Fleetwood, was offered with optional Sunshine Turret Top or center division. These options were also available on the Series 61 Sedan. Series 61 was available with or without runningboards, had concealed door hinges except for the lower front hinge, and had chrome reveals on all windows.

Chassis changes included: tube and fin radiator core; sea shell horns under the hood; 10mm spark plugs; cross-link steering on Series 61; slotted disc wheels on Series 60S and 61.

I.D. DATA: Serial numbers were located on the left frame side bar, opposite the steering gear. Starting: same as engine number. Ending: same as engine number. Engine numbers were on the crankcase, just behind the left cylinder block, parallel to the dash. Starting: (Series 39-60S) 6290001; (Series 39-61) 8290001; (Series 39-75) 3290001. Ending: (Series 39-60S) 6295513; (Series 39-61) 8295913; (Series 39-75) 3292069.

Style No.	Body Type & Seating	Price	Weight	Prod. Total
Fleetwood Series 39-60S, 127" wb				
39-6019S	Spec Sed-5P	2195	4110	—
39 6019S-A	Spec Sed (STT)-5P	2245	—	—
39-6019S-F	Spec.Sed (Div)-5P	—	—	—
Fisher Series 39-61, 126" wb				
39-6127	Cpe-2P	1695	3685	—
39-6167	Conv. Cpe-2P	1855	3765	—
39-6129	Conv. Sed-5P	2265	3810	—
39-6119	Tr Sed-5P	1765	3770	—
39-6119 A	Tr Sed (STT)-5P	1805	—	—
39-6119-F	Tr Sed (Div)-5P	—	—	—
Fleetwood Series 39-75, 141" wb Business Cars				
39-7523-L	Bus Tr. Sed-8P	3215	4865	—
39 7533-L	Bus Tr. Imp-8P	3370	5025	—
Fleetwood Series 39-75, 141" wb				
39-7557	Cpe-2P	3395	4595	—
39 7557-B	Cpe-5P	3495	4695	—
39 7567	Conv Cpe-2P	3495	4675	—
39-7519	Sed-5P	3100	4785	—
39-7519-F	Imp Sed-5P	3265	4845	—
39-7559	Formal Sed-5P	4115	4785	—
39-7539	Twn Sed-5P	3750	4820	—
39 7529	Conv Sed-5P	4065	5030	—
39-7523	Sed-7P	3325	4865	—
39-7533	Imp Sed-7P	3475	5025	—
39-7533-F	Formal Sed-7P	4115	5025	—
39-7553	Twn.Car-7P	5245	5095	—

ENGINE: Ninety degree L-Head. Eight. Cast iron block (blocks cast enbloc with crankcase). B & S: 3-1/2 x 4-1/2 in. Disp.: 346 cu. in. C.R.: (60S, 61) 6.25:1, (75) 6.7:1. Brake H.P.: 135 (140 on 75) @ 3400 R.P.M. SAE/Taxable H.P.: 39.20. Main bearings: three. Valve lifters: hydraulic. Carb.: Stromberg AAV-26.

CHASSIS: (Series 39-60S) W.B.: 127 in. O.L.: 214-1/4 in. Front/Rear Tread: 58/61 in. Tires: 7.00 x 16. (Series 39-61) W.B.: 126 in. O.L.: 207-1/4 in. Front/Rear Tread: 58/59 in. Tires: 7.00 x 16. (Series 39-75) W.B.: 141 in. O.L.: 225-1/8 in. Front/Rear Tread: 60-1/2/62-1/2 in. Tires: 7.50 x 16. (Series 39-61 Commercial Chassis) W.B.: 162-1/4 in. O.L.: 243-1/2 in. Tires: 7.00 x 16. (Series 39-75 Commercial Chassis) W.B.: 161-3/8 in. O.L.: 245-3/8 in. Tires: 7.50 x 16.

1939 Cadillac, Sixty Special, touring sedan, OCW

TECHNICAL: Selective synchromesh manual transmission. Speeds: 3F/1R. Lhd; gearshift on column; handbrake at left (rhd optional). Single disc clutch. Shaft drive, Hotchkiss. Semi-floating rear axle. Hypoid gears. Overall ratio: (60S, 61) 3.92:1, (75) 4.58:1. Hydraulic brakes on four wheels. Slotted disc wheels. Wheel size: 16 in.

1939 Cadillac, Series 39-90, V-16, seven-passenger sedan, JAC

OPTIONS: Radio ($69.50). Heater (31.50). Seat covers (8.25 per seat). Spotlight (18.50). Windshield washer (5.75). Automatic battery filler (7.50). Fog lights (14.50 pair).

HISTORICAL: Introduced October 1938. Model year sales and production: (Series 60S) 5,513, (Series 61) 5,913, (Series 75) 2,069. The general manager of Cadillac was Nicholas Dreystadt.

CADILLAC — SERIES 39-90 — SIXTEEN: Same as 1938 except for a few detail changes. Chrome strips used along running-board edges. Spears on hood and fender skirts fully chromed. New instrument panel and minor differences in bumpers and taillights. Generator relocated high in the vee and belt driven.

I.D. DATA: Serial numbers were located on the left frame side bar, opposite the steering gear. Starting: same as engine number. Ending: same as engine number. Engine numbers were on the left rear corner on the flat top of the crankcase, parallel to the dash. Starting: 5290001. Ending: 5290138.

Style No.	Body Type & Seating	Price	Weight	Prod. Total
Fleetwood Series 39-90, 141" wb				
39-9057	Cpe-2P	5440	4915	—
39-9057-B	Cpe-5P	5545	5015	—
39-9067	Conv Cpe-2P	5545	4995	—
39-9019	Sed-5P	5240	5105	—
39-9019-F	Imp Sed-5P	5315	5165	—
39-9059	Formal Sed-5P	6165	5105	—
39-9039	Town Sed-5P	5800	5140	—
39-9029	Conv. Sed-5P	6110	5350	—
39-9023	Sed-7P	5375	5185	—
39-9033	Imp Sed-7P	5525	5345	—
39-9033-F	Formal Sed-7P	6165	5345	—
39-9053	Town Car-7P	7295	5415	—

ENGINE: 135 degree vee L-head. Sixteen. Cast iron block. B & S: 3-1/4 x 3-1/4 in. C.R.: 6.75:1. Brake H.P.: 185 @ 3600 R.P.M. SAE/Taxable H.P.: 67.6. Main bearings: nine. Valve lifters: hydraulic. Carb.: Carter WDO-407s (L) - 408s (R).

CHASSIS: W.B.: 141 in. O.L.: 222 in. Front/Rear Tread: 60-1/2/62-1/2 in. Tires: 7.50 x 16.

TECHNICAL: Selective synchromesh manual transmission. Speeds: 3F/1R. Lhd; gearshift on column; handbrake at left. Single disc clutch. Shaft drive-Hotchkiss. Semi-floating rear axle. Hypoid gears. Overall ratio: 4.31:1. Hydraulic brakes on four wheels. Disc wheels. Wheel size: 16 in.

OPTIONS: Radio ($69.50). Heater (31.50). Seat covers (8.25 per seat). Spotlight (18.50). Windshield washer (5.75). Automatic battery filler (7.50). Fog lights (14.50 pair).

HISTORICAL: Introduced October 1938. Model year sales and production: 138. The general manager of Cadillac was Nicholas Dreystadt.

1940 CADILLAC

1940 Cadillac, Sixty Special, sedan, OCW

CADILLAC — SERIES 40-60S, 40-62, 40-72, 40-75 — EIGHT: For 1940, Series 61 was replaced by Series 62, featuring the "Projectile" or "Torpedo" bodies. The one-year-only Series 72 was introduced as a less expensive companion to the Series 75. 1940 was the final year for optional sidemounts.

The identifying feature for all V-8 Cadillacs was once again the grille. Although the grilles were the same pointed shape as in 1939, the grille bars were heavier and fewer in number. Two sets of louver bars appeared on each hood side panel.

Sixty Special was available as a town car as well as a sedan.

Series 62 featured a low, sleek body with chrome window reveals, more slant to the windshield, and a curved rear window. Runningboards were no-cost options. Convertible coupes and sedans were introduced in midyear.

Series 72 had the general appearance of the Series 75, but was three inches shorter and was set apart by rectangular taillights set high on the sides of the trunk. Recirculating ball steering was tried on Series 72 in 1940, to be adopted on all series in 1941.

Sealed beam headlights and turn indicators were standard equipment. The engine manifold was set at five degrees to the engine to cancel the rearward tilt of the engine and give balanced fuel distribution.

I.D. DATA: Serial numbers were located on the left frame side bar, opposite the steering gear. Starting: same as engine number. Ending: same as engine number. Engine number location: on the crankcase, just behind the left cylinder block, parallel to the dash. Starting: (Series 40-60S) 632001; (Series 40-62) 832001; (Series 40-72) 7320001; (Series 40-75) 3320001. Ending: (Series 40-60S) 6324600; (Series 40-62) 8325903; (Series 40-72) 7321525; (Series 40-75) 3320956.

1940 Cadillac, Series 62, four-door sedan, OCW

Style No.	Body Type & Seating	Price	Weight	Prod. Total
Fleetwood Series 40-60S, 127" wb				
40-6019S	Spec. Sed.-5P	2090	4070	—
40-6019S-A	Spec. Sed. (STT)-5P	—	—	—
40-6019S-F	Spec. Sed. (Div)-5P	2230	4110	—
40-6053S	Town Car-5P	—	—	—
40-6053-LB	Town Car-5P	3820	4365	—
40-6053-MB	Town Car-5P	3465	4365	—
Fisher Series 40-62, 129" wb				
40-6219	Tr. Sed.-5P	1745	4030	—
40-6227C	Cpe.-2P	1685	3940	—
40-6229	Conv. Sed.-5P	2195	4230	—
40-6267	Conv. Cpe.-2P	1795	4045	—
Fleetwood Series 40-72, 138" wb				
40-7219	Tr. Sed.-5P	2670	4670	—
40-7219-F	Tr. Sed. (Div)-5P	2790	4710	—
40-7223	Tr. Sed.-7P	2785	4700	—
40-7233	Imp. Sed.-7P	2915	4740	—
40-7259	Formal Sed.-5P	3695	4670	—
40-7233-F	Formal Sed.-7P	3695	4780	—

Style No.	Body Type & Seating	Price	Weight	Prod. Total
Fleetwood Series 40-72, 138" wb Business Cars				
40-7223-L	Bus. Tr. Sed.-9P	2690	4700	—
40-7233-L	Bus. Tr. Imp.-9P	2824	4740	—
Fleetwood Series 40-75, 141" wb				
40-7557	Cpe.-2P	3280	4785	—
40-7557-B	Cpe.-5P	3380	4810	—
40-7567	Conv. Cpe.-2P	3380	4915	—
40-7519	Sed.-5P	2995	4900	—
40-7519-F	Imp. Sed.-5P	3155	4940	—
40-7559	Formal Sed.-5P	3995	4900	—
40-7539	Town Sed.-5P	3635	4935	—
40-7529	Conv. Sed.-5P	3945	5110	—
40-7523	Sed.-7P	3210	4930	—
40-7533	Imp. Sed.-7P	3360	4970	—
40-7533-F	Formal Sed.-7P	3995	4970	—
40-7553	Town Car-7P	5115	5195	—
Fleetwood Series 40-75, 141" wb Business Cars				
40-7523-L	Bus. Tr. Sed.-8P	—	—	—
40-7533-L	Bus. Tr. Imp.-8P	—	—	—

ENGINE: Ninety degree L-head. Eight. Cast iron block (blocks cast enbloc with crankcase). B & S: 3-1/2 x 4-1/2 in. Disp.: 346 cu. in. C.R.: (Series 60S, 62) 6.25:1; (Series 72, 75) 6.7:1. Brake H.P.: 135 (140 on 72, 75) @ 3400 R.P.M. SAE/Taxable H.P.: 39.20. Main bearings: three. Valve lifters: hydraulic. Carb.: Stromberg AAV-26.

1940 Cadillac, Series 62, convertible coupe, OCW

CHASSIS: (Series 40-60S) W.B.: 127 in. O.L.: 216-7/8 in. Front/Rear Tread: 58/61 in. Tires: 7.00 x 16. (Series 40-62S) W.B.: 129 in. O.L.: 216-1/16 in. Front/Rear Tread: 58/59 in. Tires: 7.00 x 16. (Series 40-72S) W.B.: 138 in. O.L.: 226-11/16 in. Front/Rear Tread: 58/62-1/2 in. Tires: 7.50 x 16. (Series 40-75) W.B.: 141 in. O.L.: 228-3/16 in. Front/Rear Tread: 60-1/2/62-1/2 in. Tires: 7.50 x 16. (Series 40-72 Commercial Chassis) W.B.: 165-1/4 in. O.L.: 253-13/16 in. Tires: 7.50 x 16. (Series 40-75 Commercial Chassis) W.B.: 161-3/8 in. O.L.: 248-11/16 in. Tires: 7.50 x 16.

TECHNICAL: Selective synchromesh manual transmission. Speeds: 3F/1R. Lhd; gearshift on column; handbrake at left (Rhd option). Single disc clutch. Shaft drive, Hotchkiss. Semi-floating rear axle. Hypoid gears. Overall ratio: (60S, 62) 3.92:1; (72) 4.31:1; (75) 4.58:1. Hydraulic brakes on four wheels. Slotted disc wheels. Wheel size: 16 in.

Drivetrain Options: Hill-Holder (No rol) ($13.50).

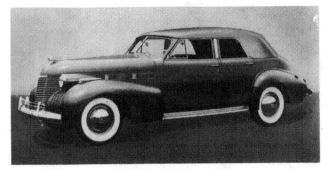

1940 Cadillac, Series 62, convertible sedan, OCW

OPTIONS: Radio ($69.50). Heater (26.50-52.50). Seat covers (8.25 per seat). Spotlight (18.50). Automatic battery filler (7.50). Flexible steering wheel (15.00). Fog lights (14.50 pair). Windshield washer (6.50). Grille guard. Wheel discs (4.00 each). Trim rings (1.50 each).

HISTORICAL: Introduced October 1939. Model year sales and production: (Series 60S) 4,600; (Series 62) 5,903; (Series 72) 1,525; (Series 75) 956. The general manager of Cadillac was Nicholas Dreystadt.

CADILLAC — SERIES 40-90 — SIXTEEN: The last Cadillac with other than a V-8 engine for more than 40 years to come. Only such detail changes as new instrument panel, taillights, and bumpers; plus the introduction of sealed beam head-lights and directional signals distinguished the 1940 from the 1939 V-16.

I.D. DATA: Serial numbers were located on the left frame side bar, opposite the steering gear. Starting: same as engine number. Ending: same as engine number. Engine numbers were on the upper rear corner of the left cylinder block, parallel to the cylinder head. Starting: 5320001. Ending: 5320061.

Style No.	Body Type & Seating	Price	Weight	Prod. Total
Fleetwood Series 40-90, 141" wb				
40-9057	Cpe.-2P	5340	4915	—
40-9057 B	Cpe.-5P	5440	5015	—
40-9067	Conv. Cpe.-2P	5440	4995	—
40-9019	Sed.-5P	5140	5190	—
40 9019-F	Imp. Sed.-5P	5215	5230	—
40-9059	Fml. Sed.-5P	6055	5190	—
40-9039	Twn. Sed.-5P	5695	5140	—
40-9029	Conv. Sed.-5P	6000	5265	—
40 9023	Sed.-7P	5270	5215	—
40 9033	Imp. Sed.-7P	5420	5260	—
40-9033-F	Fml. Sed.-7P	6055	5260	—
40-9053	Twn. Car-7P	7175	5415	—

ENGINE: 135 degree vee L-head. Sixteen. Cast iron block. B & S: 3-1/4 x 3-1/4 in. Disp.: 431 cu. in. C.R.: 6.75:1. Brake H.P.: 185 @ 3600 R.P.M. SAE/Taxable H.P.: 67.6. Main bearings: nine. Valve lifters: hydraulic. Carb : Carter WDO-407s (L) - 408s (R).

CHASSIS: W.B.: 141 in. O.L.: 255-11/16 in. Front/Rear Tread: 60-1/2/62-1/2 in. Tires: 7.50 x 16.

TECHNICAL: Selective synchromesh manual transmission. Speeds: 3F/1R. Lhd; gearshift on column, handbrake at left. Single disc clutch. Shaft drive, Hotchkiss. Semi-floating rear axle. Hypoid gears. Overall ratio: 4.31:1. Hydraulic brakes on four wheels. Disc wheels. Wheel size: 16 in.

OPTIONS: Radio ($69.50). Heater (26.50-52.50). Seat covers (8.25 per seat). Spotlight (18.50). Automatic battery filler (7.50). Flexible steering wheel (15.00). Fog lights (14.50 pair). Windshield washer (6.50).

HISTORICAL: Introduced October 1939. Model year sales and production: 61. The general manager of Cadillac was Nicholas Dreystadt.

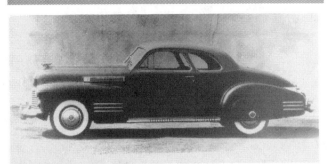

1941 Cadillac, Series 62, coupe, OCW

CADILLAC — SERIES 41-60S, 41-61, 41-62, 41-63, 41-67, 41-75 — EIGHT: For 1941, the Series 61 designation was brought back, replacing LaSalle in the Cadillac price structure. A new Series 63 was offered in one body style. A new Series 67, with Fisher sedan bodies and the longest wheelbase (139 in.), replaced the 1940 Series 72. For the first time since 1926, all Cadillac products used the same engine.

Front end stylists adopted a theme that was to be repeated for years to come. The one-piece hood came down lower in front, included the side panels, and extended sideways to the fenders. A single, rectangular panel of louver trim was used on each side of the hood. Access to the engine compartment was improved, to say the least. The rectangular grille was wide, vertical, and bulged forward in the middle. Rectangular parking lights were built into the top outer corners of the grille. Headlights were built into the nose of the fenders, and provision for built-in accessory fog lights was provided under the headlights. Three chrome spears were on the rear section of all four fenders, except on the Sixty Special. Rear wheel shields (fender skirts) were standard on most bodies.

Sixty Special front fenders extended into the front doors.

Series 61 coupe and sedan were fastback styles reminiscent of the aerodynamic coupes of the Thirties.

Series 62 came in the standard body style lineup, including the only convertible sedan for 1941 and the last such body style offered by Cadillac.

Runningboards were concealed or no-cost options on all but the 60S and 75; the Sixty Special had none and the 75s had nothing but. Power tops, electric divisions, factory-installed air-conditioning, and Hydra-Matic transmissions were available.

1941 Cadillac, Series 60 Special, four-door sedan, OCW

I.D. DATA: Serial numbers were located on the left frame side bar, opposite the steering gear. Starting: same as engine number. Ending: same as engine number. Engine numbers were on the crankcase, just behind the left cylinder block, parallel to the dash. Starting: (Series 41-60S) 6340001; (41-61) 5340001; (41-62) 8340001; (41-63) 7340001; (41-67) 9340001; (41-75) 3340001. Ending: (Series 41-60S) 6344101;

(41-61) 5369258; (41-62) 8364734; (41-63) 7345050; (41-67) 9340922; (41-75) 3342104.

Style No.	Body Type & Seating	Price	Weight	Prod. Total
Fleetwood Series 41-60S, 126" wb				
41-6019S	Sed.-5P	2195	4230	—
41-6019S-A	Sed. (STT)-5P	—	—	—
41-6019S-F	Sed. (Div)-5P	2345	4290	—
Fisher Series 41-61, 126" wb				
41-6127	Cpe.-5P	1345	3985	—
41-6127D	Cpe. Del.-5P	1435	4005	—
41-6109	Tr. Sed.-5P	1445	4065	—
41-6109 D	Tr. Sed. Del.-5P	1535	4085	—
Fisher Series 41-62, 126" wb				
41-6227	Cpe.-2/4P	1420	3950	—
41-6227D	Cpe. Del.-2/4P	1510	3970	—
41-6219	Tr. Sed.-5P	1495	4030	—
41-6219D	Tr. Sed. Deluxe-5P	1535	4050	—
41-6267D	Con. Cpe. Del.-2/4P	1645	4055	—
41-6229D	Con. Sed. Del.-5P	1965	4230	—

Style No.	Body Type & Seating	Price	Weight	Prod. Total
Fisher Series 41-63, 126" wb				
41-6319	Tr. Sed.-5P	1696	4140	—
Fisher Series 41-67, 139" wb				
41-6719	Tr. Sed.-5P	2595	4555	—
41-6719-F	Tr. Sed. (Div)-5P	2745	4615	—
41-6723	Tr. Sed.-7P	2735	4630	—
41-6733	Imp. Tr. Sed.-7P	2890	4705	—
Fleetwood Series 41-75, 136" wb				
41-7519	Tr. Sed.-5P	2995	4750	—
41-7519-F	Tr. Sed. (Div)-5P	3150	4810	—
41-7523	Tr. Sed.-7P	3140	4800	—
41-7533	Tr. Imp.-7P	3295	4860	—
41-7559	Fml. Sed.-5P	3920	4900	—
41-7533-F	Fml. Sed.-7P	4045	4915	—
Business Cars Series 41-75, 136" wb				
41-7523-L	Bus Tr. Sed.-9P	2895	4750	—
41-7533-L	Bus Tr. Imp.-9P	3050	4810	—

ENGINE: Ninety degree L-head. Eight. Cast iron block (blocks cast enbloc with crankcase). B & S: 3-1/2 x 4-1/2 in. Disp.: 346 cu. in. C.R.: 7.25:1. Brake H.P.: 150 @ 3400 R.P.M. SAE/Taxable H.P.: 39.20. Main bearings: three. Valve lifters: hydraulic. Carb.: Stromberg AAV-26, Carter WDO 506s.

1941 Cadillac, Series 62, four-door sedan, JAC

CHASSIS: (Series 41-60S) W.B.: 126 in. O.L.: 217-3/16 in. Front/Rear Tread: 59/63 in. Tires: 7.00 x 15. (Series 41-61) W.B.: 126 in. O.L.: 215 in. Front/Rear Tread: 59/63 in. Tires: 7.00 x 15. (Series 41-62) W.B.: 126 in. O.L.: 216 in. Front/Rear Tread: 59/63 in. Tires: 7.00 x 15. (Series 41-63) W.B.: 126 in. O.L.: 215 in. Front/Rear Tread: 59/63 in. Tires: 7.00 x 15. (Series 41-67) W.B.: 139 in. O.L.: 228 in. Front/Rear Tread: 58-1/2/62-1/2 in. Tires: 7.50 x 16. (Series 41-75) W.B.: 136 in. O.L.: 226-1/8 in. Front/Rear Tread: 58-1/2/62-1/2 in. Tires: 7.50 x 16. (Series 41-62 Commercial Chassis) W.B.: 163 in. O.L.: 252-7/8 in. Tires: 7.00 x 16. (Series 41-75 Commercial Chassis) W.B.: 163 in. O.L.: 252-7/8 in. Tires: 7.50 x 16.

1941 Cadillac, Series 63, four-door sedan, OCW

TECHNICAL: Selective synchromesh manual transmission. Speeds: 3F/1R. Lhd; gearshift on column; handbrake at left (rhd opt. except 60S and 67). Single disc clutch. Shaft drive, Hotchkiss. Semi-floating rear axle. Hypoid gears. Overall ratio: (60S, 61, 62, 63) 3.77:1 (3.36:1 opt.); (67, 75) 4.27:1 (3.77:1 opt.). Hydraulic brakes on four wheels. Slotted disc wheels. Wheel size: 15 in. (16 in. on 67 and 75).

Drivetrain options: Automatic transmission ($125.00), Hillholder (No rol) (11.50).

OPTIONS: Fender skirts ($17.50 pair). Radio (69.50). Heater (59.50-65.00). Seat covers (8.75/seat). Spotlight (18.50). Fog lights (14.50). Backup light (7.50). Windshield washer (7.50). Wheel discs (4.00 each). Trim rings (1.50 each).

HISTORICAL: Introduced September 1940. Model year sales and production: (Series 60S) 4,101; (Series 61) 29,258; (Series 62) 24,734; (Series 63) 5,050; (Series 67) 922; (Series 75) 2,104. The general manager of Cadillac was Nicholas Dreystadt.

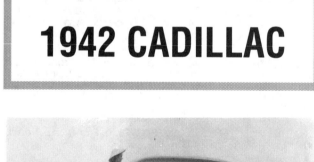

1941 Cadillac, Series 75, Fleetwood limousine, OCW

1942 CADILLAC

1942 Cadillac, Series 61, four-door sedan, OCW

CADILLAC — SERIES 42-60S, 42-61, 42-62, 42-63, 42-67, 42-75 EIGHT: For 1942, the Series lineup remained the same as in 1941. The grille became more massive, with fewer bars.

Parking lights became round and fog light sockets became rectangular and were included within the grille area. A bullet shape appeared on the tops of the bumper guards. Fenders were rounded and longer. Front fenders on all but Series 75 extended into the front doors. Series 62 and 60S rear fenders extended forward into rear doors. The new fenders had heavy moldings along the sides.

Series 75 had the new grille but retained the 1941 fender treatment. A detail trim change on the 75s was a rounded nose on the hood louvers.

The first general styling change on the Sixty Special destroyed the character of the car. Bulbous lines plus superfluous trim in the form of louver bars on the quarters and numerous short vertical bars low on the fenders spoiled its appeal. The only convertible was the Series 62, showing quarter windows for the first time.

A new fresh air ventilating system with air ducts leading from the grille replaced cowl ventilators. Handbrake control was changed from lever to tee-shaped pull handle. Radiator shutter control of engine temperature was replaced by a blocking-type thermostat in the water return fitting on the radiator.

I.D. DATA: Serial numbers were on the right frame side bar, just behind the engine support bracket. Starting: same as engine number. Ending: same as engine number. Engine numbers were on the right-hand side of the crankcase, just above the water pump. Chrome or polished stainless steel brightwork. Starting: (Series 42A-60S) 6380001; (Series 42A-61) 5380001; (Series 42A-62) 8380001; (Series 42A-63) 7380001; (Series 42A-67) 9380001; (Series 42A-75) 3380001. Ending: (Series 42A-60S) 6381500; (Series 42A-61) 5385237; (Series 42A-62) 8384401; (Series 42A-63) 7381500; (Series 42A-67) 9380520; (Series 42A-75) 3381200. Painted "brightwork": (Series 42B-60S) 6386001; 6386375; (Series 42B-61) 5386001; 5386463; (Series 42B-62) 8386001; 8386560; (Series 42B-63) 7386001; 7386250; (Series 42B-67) 9386001; 9386180; (Series 42B-75) 3386001; 3386327.

Style No.	Body Type & Seating	Price	Weight	Prod. Total
Fleetwood Series 42-60S, 133" wb				
42-6069	4-dr. Sed.	2435	4310	—
42-6069-F	4-dr. Sed. (Div)	2589	4365	—
Fisher Series 42-61, 126" wb				
42-6107	Club Cpe.-5P	1560	4035	—
42-6109	4-dr. Sed.	1647	4115	—
Fisher Series 42-62, 129" wb				
42-6207	Club Cpe.-5P	1667	4105	—
42-6207D	Opt. Club Cpe.-5P	1754	4125	—
42-6269	4-dr. Sed.	1754	4185	—
42-6269D	4-dr. Opt. Sed.	1836	4205	—
42-6267D	Opt. Con. Clb. Cpe.-5P	2020	4365	—
Fisher Series 42-63, 126" wb				
42-6319	4-dr. Sed.	1882	4115	—
Fisher Series 42-67, 139" wb				
42-6719	Sed.-5P	2896	4605	—
42-6719-F	Sed. (Div)-5P	3045	4665	—
42-6723	Sed.-7P	3045	4680	—
42-6733	Imp.-7P	3204	4775	—
Fleetwood Series 42-75, 136" wb				
42-7519	Sed.-5P	3306	4750	—
42-7519-F	Sed. (Div)-5P	3459	4810	—
42-7523	Sed.-7P	3459	4800	—
42-7533	Imp.-7P	3613	4860	—
42-7559	Formal Sed.-5P	4330	4900	—
42-7533-F	Formal Sed.-7P	4484	4915	—
Business Cars Series 42-75, 136" wb				
42-7523-L	Bus. Sed.-9P	3152	4750	—
42-7533-L	Bus. Imp.-9P	3306	4810	—

ENGINE: Ninety degree L-head. Eight. Cast iron block (blocks cast enbloc with crankcase). B & S: 3-1/2 x 4-1/2 in. Disp.: 346 cu. in. C.R.: 7.25:1. Brake H.P.: 150 @ 3400 R.P.M. SAE/Taxable H.P.: 39.20. Main bearings: three. Valve lifters: hydraulic. Carb.: Stromberg AAV-26; Carter WDO 486S.

CHASSIS: (Series 42-60S) W.B.: 133 in. O.L.: 224 in. Front/Rear Tread: 59/63 in. Tires: 7.00 x 15. (Series 42-61) W.B.: 126 in. O.L.: 215 in. Front/Rear Tread: 59/63 in. Tires: 7.00 x 15. (Series 42-62) W.B.: 129 in. O.L.: 220 in. Front/Rear Tread: 59/63 in. Tires: 7.00 x 15. (Series 42-63) W.B.: 126 in. O.L.: 215 in. Front/Rear Tread: 59/63 in. Tires: 7.00 x 15. (Series 42-67) W.B.:

139 in. O.L.: 228 in. Front/Rear Tread: 58-1/2/62-1/2 in. Tires: 7.50 x 16. (Series 42-75) W.B.: 136 in. O.L.: 227 in. Front/Rear Tread: 58-1/2/62-1/2 in. Tires: 7.50 x 16. (Series 42-75 Commercial Chassis) W.B.: 163 in. O.L.: 253-1/32 in. Tires: 7.50 x 16.

TECHNICAL: Selective synchromesh manual transmission. Speeds: 3F/1R. Lhd; gearshift on column; handbrake at left (rhd opt. except 60S, 62, 67, 75). Single disc clutch. Shaft drive, Hotchkiss. Semi-floating rear axle. Hypoid gears. Overall ratio: (60S, 61, 62, 63) 3.77:1; (3.36:1 opt.); (67, 75) 4.27:1 (3.77:1 opt.). Hydraulic brakes on four wheels. Slotted disc wheels. Wheel size: 15 in. (16 in. on 67 and 75).

Drivetrain options: Automatic transmission ($135.00). Hillholder (No rol) (12.50).

OPTIONS: Radio ($65.00). Heater (59.50-65.00). Seat covers (9.75/seat). Spotlight (19.50). Fog lights (24.50). Backup light (12.50). Windshield washer (8.25). Wheel discs (4.00 each). Trim rings (1.50 each).

HISTORICAL: Introduced September 1941. Model year sales and production: (Series 60S) 1,875; (Series 61) 5,700; (Series 62) 4,961; (Series 63) 1,750; (Series 67) 700; (Series 75) 1,527. The general manager of Cadillac was Nicholas Dreystadt.

1942 Cadillac, Series 62, four-door sedan, JAC

1946 CADILLAC

SERIES 61 — (V-8) — All 1946 Cadillacs were a continuation of prewar styling and engineering with the unpopular 63 and 67 series being dropped. Features common to each series included dual downdraft carburetors; Torbend disc clutch; directional signals; knee action wheels; double ride stabilizers; permanently lubricated universals; ball bearing steering; mechanical fuel pump; oil bath air cleaner; intake silencer; automatic choke; Synchromesh transmission; sealed beam lighting; front coil springs; Super-Safe hydraulic brakes; wax lubricated rear springs; hypoid rear axle; slotted disc wheels; low pressure tires; large luggage compartments and safety plate glass throughout. Cadillac's lowest-priced Series 61 line was based on the General Motors 'B-Body', also used on cars in the Buick 40, Oldsmobile 70 and Pontiac 26 and 28 series. Fastback styling characterized the two available body styles, which saw a late production startup in May 1946. Standard features included small hubcaps; a wider, more massive grille; bullet-shaped front and rear fenders; skirted rear wheel openings and chrome-plated rear fins. The gas filler cap was located under the rear signal lamp.

SERIES 61 I.D. NUMBERS: Cadillac serial numbers matched the engine numbers and were used for all license, insurance and identification purposes. For 1946, they were located on the right-hand side of the engine crankcase, just above the water pump, and on the right frame side member, behind the engine support. Numbers 5400001 to 5402975 appeared on Series 61 models

SERIES 61

Model Number	Body/Style Number	Body Type & Seating	Factory Price	Shipping Weight	Production Total
46-61	6107	2-dr Clb Cpe-5P	2052	4145	800
46-61	6109	4-dr Sed-5P	2176	4225	2,200
46-61	—	Chassis only			1

1946 Cadillac, Series 62 four-door sedan, (AA)

SERIES 62 — (V-8) — Series 62 Cadillacs were based on the General Motors C-Body, also used on the Cadillac 60S, Buick 50 and 70 and Oldsmobile 90 series. Notchback styling characterized the racy-looking cars in this line except for the Club Coupe, which had fastback styling. The Series 62 four-door sedan was the first Cadillac to enter production after World War II. Styling and technical features were similar to those seen on lower priced models, but on a longer chassis with slightly richer interior appointments.

SERIES 62 I.D. NUMBERS: Engine serial numbers 8400001 to 8418566 appeared on 1946 models.

1946 Cadillac, Series 62 two-door convertible coupe

SERIES 62

Model Number	Body/Style Number	Body Type & Seating	Factory Price	Shipping Weight	Production Total
46-62	6207	2-dr Clb Cpe-5P	2284	4215	2,323
46-62	6267D	2-dr Conv Cpe-5P	2556	4475	1,342
46-62	6269	4-dr Sed-5P	2359	4295	14,900
46-62	—	Chassis only	—	—	1

SERIES 60 SPECIAL FLEETWOOD — (V-8) — The Series 60 Special Fleetwood line included only one model, a four-door sedan also based on the corporate C-Body. However, each door was made two inches wider, amounting to an overall four-inch extension over the standard Series 62 sedan. For easy identification, there were four slanting louvers on the rear roof pillar and a distinctive type of roof drip molding, which was separate for each door opening.

SERIES 60 SPECIAL FLEETWOOD I.D. NUMBERS: Engine serial numbers 6400001 to 6405679 appeared on 1946 models.

SERIES 60 SPECIAL FLEETWOOD

Model Number	Body/Style Number	Body Type & Seating	Factory Price	Shipping Weight	Production Total
46-60S	6069	4-dr Sed-5P	3099	4420	5,700

SERIES 75 FLEETWOOD — (V-8) — Cadillac's Fleetwood long-wheelbase line used totally distinctive bodies that were not shared with other General Motors divisions They were generally characterized by a prewar appearance and came in five different touring sedan configurations: with quarter windows; with auxiliary (jump) seats; business; Imperial seven-passenger and Imperial nine-passenger (the latter two both having jump seats). Standard equipment included large wheel discs, fender skirts, hood, side and lower beltline moldings and stainless steel runningboards.

SERIES 75 FLEETWOOD I.D. NUMBERS: Engine I.D. serial numbers 3400001 to 640579 appeared on 1946 models.

1946 Cadillac, Fleetwood 75 (five-passenger) four-door sedan, (AA)

SERIES 75 FLEETWOOD

Model Number	Body/Style Number	Body Type & Seating	Factory Price	Shipping Weight	Production Total
46-75	7519	4-dr Sed-5P	4298	4860	150
46-75	7523	4-dr Sed-7P	4475	4905	225
46-75	7523L	4-dr Bus Sed-9P	4153	4920	22
46-75	7533L	4-dr Imp Bus Sed-9P	4346	4925	17
46-75	7533	4-dr Imp Sed-7P	4669	4925	221
46-75	—	Commercial Chassis	—	—	1,292

NOTE: Commercial chassis featured a 163-inch wheelbase.

ENGINE: V-8. L-head. Cast iron block. Displacement: 346 cid. Bore and stroke: 3-1/2 x 4-1/2 inches. Compression ratio: 7.25:1. Brake hp: 150 at 3400 rpm. Three main bearings. Hydraulic valve lifters. Carburetor: Carter WCD two-barrel (Models 595S or 595SA) or Stromberg AAV 26 two-barrel (Models 380154 or 380871).

CHASSIS FEATURES: Wheelbase: (Series 61) 126 inches; (Series 62) 129 inches; (Series 60S) 133 inches; (Series 75) 136 inches. Overall length: (Series 61) 215 inches; (Series 62) 220 inches; (Series 60S) 224 inches; (Series 75) 227 inches. Front tread: (All) 59 inches. Rear tread: (All) 63 inches. Tires: (Series 75) 7 50 x 16; (All others) 7 00 x 15.

POWERTRAIN OPTIONS: None available.

CONVENIENCE OPTIONS: Hydra-Matic transmission ($176). Large wheel discs ($19). White sidewall disc. Fog lights. Safety spotlight.

HISTORICAL FOOTNOTES: Division windows between front and rear seats were available on Fleetwood models for limousine use. Commercial chassis were provided for makers of hearses and ambulances. A limited number of dual-cowl phaetons were also constructed on Cadillac chassis this year. The Classic Car Club of America recognizes all 1946 Series 75 models as Classic cars.

1947 CADILLAC

SERIES 61 — (V-8) — A minor styling face lift characterized 1947 Cadillacs, which now had grilles with five massive horizontal blades instead of the six used the previous year. A new identification feature was a striped field for the V-shaped hood crest. Sombrero style wheelcovers were an attractive new option seen on many Cadillacs. In the logo department, a script-type nameplate replaced the block lettering used on the sides of front fenders in 1946. Upholstery and paint combinations were generally revised and steering wheel horn rings were changed to a semi-circular design. The old style rubber stone shields were replaced with a bright metal type and a new winged trunk ornament was used on all models except the Series 60 Fleetwood Special sedan. Other features were basically unchanged over the previous year's cars. The Series 61 models continued to utilize the GM B-Body with fastback styling.

SERIES 61 I.D. NUMBERS: Cadillac serial numbers again matched engine numbers and were used for all license, insurance and identification purposes. They were placed in the same locations as before. Engine serial numbers 5420001 to 5428555 appeared on 1947 Series 61 models.

SERIES 61

Model Number	Body/Style Number	Body Type & Seating	Factory Price	Shipping Weight	Production Total
47-61	6107	2-dr Clb Cpe-5P	2200	4080	3,395
47-61	6109	4-dr Sed-5P	2324	4165	5,160

SERIES 62 — (V-8) — Series 62 Cadillacs were again based on the GM C-Body and had a slightly sleeker appearance than models in the other lines. Notchback styling was seen on all models except the fastback coupe. However it was easy to distinguish this car from a 61 coupe, as the door skins did not flare out above the rocker panels; the side window openings were lower and the reveal moldings circled each window individually instead of looping around all windows, as on the smaller car. The 62 sedan also had door skins that mated flush with the rocker panels, and featured ventipanes on both the front and rear windows. The 62 convertible was the only open-bodied Cadillac available.

1947 Cadillac, Series 62 two-door convertible coupe

SERIES 62 I.D. NUMBERS: Engine serial numbers 8420001 to 8459835 appeared on 1947 Series 62 models.

1947 Cadillac, Series 62 two-door Club Coupe, (AA)

SERIES 62

Model Number	Body/Style Number	Body Type & Seating	Factory Price	Shipping Weight	Production Total
47-62	6207	2-dr Clb Cpe-5P	2446	4145	7,245
47-62	6267	2-dr Conv Cpe-5P	2902	4455	6,755
47-62	6269	4-dr Sed-5P	2523	4235	25,834
47-62	—	Chassis only	—	—	1

1947 Cadillac, Fleetwood 60 Special four-door sedan, (AA)

SERIES 60 SPECIAL FLEETWOOD — (V-8) — Two-inch wider doors were again seen on the Series 60 Special Fleetwood line, giving this car a custom look, as compared to standard Series 62 sedans based on the same GM C-Body shell. A

heavy upper beltline molding, individual window loop moldings and four slanting louvers on the rear roof pillar were identification features as was the new Fleetwood trunk ornament, which varied from that seen on lower models. Bright metal stone guards were adopted this season and skirted rear fenders were used again.

SERIES 60S FLEETWOOD I.D. NUMBERS: Engine serial numbers 6420001 to 6428500 appeared on 1947 Series 60S models.

SERIES 60S FLEETWOOD

Model Number	Body/Style Number	Body Type & Seating	Factory Price	Shipping Weight	Production Total
47-60	6069	4-dr Sed-5P	3195	4370	8,500

1947 Cadillac, Series 75 Fleetwood four-door sedan

SERIES 75 FLEETWOOD — (V-8) — Unchanged in all but minor details for 1947, the big Fleetwood 75 series continued to use the touring sedan body with a stately prewar appearance. It came in the same five configurations marketed the year before and had the same assortment of standard equipment geared to the luxury class buyer.

SERIES 75 FLEETWOOD I.D. NUMBERS: Engine serial numbers 3420001 to 3425036 appeared on 1947 Series 75 models.

SERIES 75 FLEETWOOD

Model Number	Body/Style Number	Body Type & Seating	Factory Price	Shipping Weight	Production Total
47-75	7519	4-dr Sed-5P	4340	4875	300
47-75	7523	4-dr Sed-7P	4517	4895	890
47-75	7523L	4-dr Bus Sed-9P	4195	4790	135
47-75	7533L	4-dr Imp Bus Sed-9P	4388	4800	80
47-75	7533	4-dr Imp Sed-7P	4711	4930	1,005
47-75	—	Chassis only	—	—	3
47-75	—	Commercial Chassis	—	—	2,423
47-75	—	Business Chassis	—	—	200

NOTE: The Commercial Chassis and Business Chassis featured a 163-inch wheelbase.

ENGINE: V-8. L-head. Cast iron block. Displacement: 346 cid. Bore and stroke: 3-1/2 x 4-1/2 inches. Compression ratio: 7.25:1. Brake hp: 150 at 3400 rpm. Three main bearings. Hydraulic valve lifters. Carburetor: Carter WCD two-barrel (Models 595S or 595SA) or Stromberg AAV-26 two-barrel (Models 380154 or 380871).

CHASSIS FEATURES: Wheelbase: (Series 61) 126 inches; (Series 62) 129 inches; (Series 60S) 133 inches; (Series 75) 138 inches. Overall length: (Series 61) 215 inches; (Series 62) 220 inches; (Series 60S) 224 inches; (Series 75) 227 inches. Front tread: (All) 59 inches. Rear tread: (All) 63 inches. Tires: (Series 75) 7 50 x 16; (All others) 7.00 x 15.

POWERTRAIN OPTIONS: None available.

CONVENIENCE OPTIONS: Hydra-Matic transmission ($186). Large wheel discs ($25). White sidewall discs. Fog lights. Safety spotlight. Fender mounted radio antenna.

HISTORICAL FOOTNOTES: Division windows between front and rear windows were available on some Fleetwood models for limousine use. Commercial and business chassis were provided to professional carmakers The Classic Car Club of America recognizes all 1947 Series 75 models as Classic cars.

1948 CADILLAC

SERIES 61 — (V-8) — Major design changes marked the short wheelbase Cadillacs for 1948. They featured General Motors first all-new postwar body with styling advances including tailfins inspired by the Lockheed P-38 fighter plane. There was also an attractive eggcrate grille, which was higher in the middle than on the sides. The front of the car was protected by a heavier and more massive bumper bar that curved around the fenders. The Cadillac crest was centered low in a 'V' above the radiator grille. Chrome headlamp rims were used. Cars in the 61 series lacked bright metal front fender shields and under-taillight trim. A new dashboard with 'rainbow' style instrument cluster and leather grained panels extending to the carpets was seen only this year.

SERIES 61 I.D. NUMBERS: Cadillac serial numbers again matched engine numbers and were used for all license, insurance and identification purposes. They were placed in the same locations as before. Engine serial numbers 481000001 to 486148663 appeared on 1948 Series 61 models.

SERIES 61

Model Number	Body/Style Number	Body Type & Seating	Factory Price	Shipping Weight	Production Total
48-61	6169	4-dr Sed-5P	2833	4150	5,081
48-61	6107	2-dr Clb Cpe-5P	2728	4068	3,521
48-61	—	Chassis only			1

1948 Cadillac, Series 62 two-door Club Coupe

SERIES 62 — (V-8) — The Series 62 was now on the same wheelbase as the lowest priced line, making the club coupe and sedan practically identical to similar models in the Series 61 range except for trim and appointments. Distinguishing features included grooved bright metal front fender gravel guards, rocker panel brightwork, chevron style chrome slashes below taillights and slightly richer interior trim. The convertible coupe was an exclusive offering in this line.

SERIES 62 I.D. NUMBERS: Engine serial numbers 486200001 to 486252704 appeared on 1948 Series 62 models.

SERIES 62

Model Number	Body/Style Number	Body Type & Seating	Factory Price	Shipping Weight	Production Total
48-62	6269	4-dr Sed-5P	2996	4179	23,997
48-62	6207	2-dr Clb Cpe-5P	2912	4125	4,764
48-62	6267	2-dr Conv Cpe-5P	3442	4449	5,450
48-62	—	Chassis only	—	—	2

1948 Cadillac, Fleetwood 60 Special Derham four-door sedan, (M)

SERIES 60 SPECIAL FLEETWOOD — (V-8) — The Series 60 Special Fleetwood sedan was again based on an extended General Motors C-Body shell with two-inch wider front and rear doors. The tailfins, built-in rear bumper design and eggcrate grille seen on the lower-priced lines were used. Appearing again, on the rear roof pillar were four slanting chrome slashes. Instead of the standard wide stone shields, the 60 Special had a thinner type that curved upward along the forward contour of the rear fender and incorporated an attractive ribbed insert panel. At the rear of the car, a band of chrome extended across the bottom of the fender skirts and quarter panels. Standard equipment included cloth and leather upholstery combinations and leather grained doors and instrument panel.

SERIES 60 SPECIAL FLEETWOOD I.D. NUMBERS: Engine serial numbers 486000001 to 486052706 appeared on 1948 Series 60S Fleetwood models.

SERIES 60 SPECIAL FLEETWOOD

Model Number	Body/Style Number	Body Type & Seating	Factory Price	Shipping Weight	Production Total
48-60S	6069	4-dr Sed-5P	3820	4356	6,561

SERIES 75 FLEETWOOD — (V-8) — Consideration was given to the deletion of the long wheelbase line this year, but competitive pressures from Packard in the luxury class market dictated the retention of these models. Again, they featured General Motors old-fashioned 'Turret Top' styling, a throwback to the prewar years. Minor revisions on the outside of the cars included a new background for the V-shaped hood emblem and Cadillac script—replacing block lettering—low on the fenders behind the front wheel opening. Buyers ordering fog lamps got rectangular parking lamps in place of the smaller round style. Stainless steel runningboards were seen once more and the 75s also had the new dashboard treatment, but with burled leather trim.

SERIES 75 FLEETWOOD I.D. NUMBERS: Engine serial numbers 487500001 to 487546088 appeared on 1948 Series 75 Fleetwood models.

SERIES 75 FLEETWOOD

Model Number	Body/Style Number	Body Type & Seating	Factory Price	Shipping Weight	Production Total
48-75	7519X	4-dr Sed-5P	4779	4875	225
48-75	7523X	4-dr Sed-7P	4999	4878	499
48-75	7523L	4-dr Bus Sed-9P	4679	4780	90
48-75	7533X	4-dr Imp Sed-7P	5199	4959	382
48-75	7533L	4-dr Bus Imp-9P	4868	4839	64
48-75	—	Chassis only	—	—	2

NOTE: The commercial chassis featured a 163-inch wheelbase.

ENGINE: V-8. L-head. Cast iron block. Displacement: 346 cid. Bore and stroke: 3-1/2 x 4-1/2 inches. Compression ratio: 7.25:1. Brake hp: 150 at 3400 rpm. Three main bearings. Hydraulic valve lifters. Carburetor: Carter WCD two-barrel (Models 595S or 595SA) or Stromberg AAV26 two-barrel (Models 380154 or 380871).

CHASSIS FEATURES: Wheelbase: (Series 61 and 62) 126 inches; (Series 60S) 133 inches; (Series 75) 136 inches. Overall length: (Series 61 and 62) 214 inches; (Series 60S) 226 inches; (Series 75) 226 inches. Front tread: (All) 59 inches. Rear tread: (All) 63 inches. Tires: (Series 75) 7.50 x 16; (All others) 8.20 x 15.

POWERTRAIN OPTIONS: None available.

CONVENIENCE OPTIONS: Hydra-Matic transmission ($174). Whitewall tires. Radio and antenna. Fog lamps. Safety spotlight. Rear window defroster.

HISTORICAL FOOTNOTES: Division windows between front and rear seats were available on some Fleetwood models for limousine use. Commercial and business chassis were supplied to professional carmakers. The Classic Car Club of America recognizes all 1948 Series 75 models as Classic cars. The following models are recognized as Milestones by the Milestone Car Society: Series 61 coupe (sedanet); Series 62 coupe (sedanet); Series 62 convertible; Series 60S Fleetwood Special sedan.

1949 CADILLAC

SERIES 61 — (V-8) — The big news at Cadillac in 1949 centered on engineering, with the release of a new overhead valve V-8 engine. Only minor appearance changes were seen. They included a more massive grille treatment with grooved extension panels housing the front parking lights and chevron slashes below the taillamps on Series 61 coupes. Once again, the cars in this line lacked front fender gravel shields and rocker panel moldings and had plainer interior trim. A larger luggage compartment lid was seen on all sedans, except early production units. Standard equipment now included twin back-up lamps mounted on the deck lid latch panel.

SERIES 61 I.D. NUMBERS: Cadillac serial numbers again matched engine numbers. They appeared stamped on a boss at the front right-hand face of the engine block and on the right frame side member behind the engine support. Engine serial numbers 496100000 to 496192552 were used on 1949 Series 61 models.

SERIES 61

Model Number	Body/Style Number	Body Type & Seating	Factory Price	Shipping Weight	Production Total
49-61	6169	4-dr Sed-5P	2893	3915	15,738
49-61	6107	2-dr Clb Cpe-5P	2788	3838	6,409
49-61	—	Chassis only	—	—	1

1949 Cadillac, Series 62 two-door Club Coupe, (AA)

SERIES 62 — (V-8) — The major difference between Series 61 and Series 62 models of similar body style was minor trim variations. The higher-priced series again had grooved, front fender stone shields and bright rocker panel moldings. Chevrons below the taillights were no longer seen. The convertible was an exclusive offering, as was a new pillarless two-door 'convertible hardtop' called the Coupe DeVille. A plusher interior was featured and power window lifts were standard on the convertible coupe and Coupe DeVille and optional with other styles.

SERIES 62 I.D. NUMBERS: Engine serial numbers 496200000 to 496292554 appeared on 1949 Series 62 models.

1949 Cadillac, Series 62 Coupe DeVille two-door hardtop

SERIES 62

Model Number	Body/Style Number	Body Type & Seating	Factory Price	Shipping Weight	Production Total
49-62	6269	4-dr Sed-5P	3050	3956	37,617
49-62	6207	2-dr Clb Cpe-5P	2966	3862	7,515
49-62	6237	2-dr Cpe DeV-5P	3496	4033	2,150
49-62	6267X	2-dr Conv Cpe-5P	3497	4218	8,000
49-62	6269	4-dr Export Sed	3050	3956	360
49-62	—	Chassis only	—	—	1

NOTE: The sedan for export was shipped in completely-knocked-down (CKD) form to foreign countries.

1949 Cadillac, Fleetwood 60 Special four-door sedan, (GM)

SERIES 60 SPECIAL FLEETWOOD — (V-8) — The car with the big doors, the 60 Special Fleetwood sedan again had four chrome slashes on the rear roof pillar, thinner rear fender stone guards with front and rear extensions and Cadillac script mounted high on the front fenders, above the crease line. The new grille design with parking lamp extensions was seen along with standard back-up lamps. Hydraulic window lifts were also regular equipment on this car. A more conventional dashboard design appeared on all Cadillacs this year, featuring a horizontal speedometer.

SERIES 60 SPECIAL FLEETWOOD I.D. NUMBERS: Engine serial numbers 496000000 to 496088221 appeared on 1949 Series 60S Fleetwood models.

SERIES 60 SPECIAL FLEETWOOD

Model Number	Body/Style Number	Body Type & Seating	Factory Price	Shipping Weight	Production Total
49-60S	6069X	4-dr Sed-5P	3828	4129	11,399
49-60S	6037X	2-dr Spl Cpe DeV-5P	—	—	1

SERIES 75 FLEETWOOD — (V-8) — To accommodate luxury-class buyers, the long wheelbase Fleetwood models were carried over without any basic changes, except for revisions to the dashboard design that followed those on other models.

SERIES 75 FLEETWOOD I.D. NUMBERS: Engine serial numbers 497500000 to 497577135 appeared on 1949 Series 75 models.

SERIES 75 FLEETWOOD

Model Number	Body/Style Number	Body Type & Seating	Factory Price	Shipping Weight	Production Total
49-75	7519X	4-dr Sed-5P	4750	4579	220
49-75	7523X	4-dr Sed-7P	4970	4626	595
49-75	7523L	4-dr Bus Sed-9P	4650	4522	35
49-75	7533X	4-dr Imp Sed-7P	5170	4648	626
49-75	7533L	4-dr Bus Sed-9P	4839	4573	25
49-75	—	Chassis only	—	—	1
49-75	—	Commercial chassis	—	—	1,861

NOTE: The commercial chassis featured a 163-inch wheelbase and was offered to professional carmakers for the construction of funeral vehicles, ambulances, etc.

ENGINE: V-8. Overhead valves. Cast iron block. Displacement: 331 cid. Bore and stroke: 3-13/16 x 3-5/8 inches. Compression ratio: 7.5:1. Brake hp: 160 at 3800 rpm. Five main bearings. Hydraulic valve lifters. Carburetor: Carter WCD two-barrel Model 742S.

CHASSIS FEATURES: Wheelbase: (Series 61 and 62) 126 inches; (Series 60S) 133 inches; (Series 75) 136 inches. Overall length: (Series 61 and 62) 214 inches; (Series 60S) 226 inches; (Series 75) 226 inches. Front tread: (All) 59 inches. Rear tread: (All) 63 inches. Tires: (Series 75) 7.50 x 16; (All others) 8.20 x 15.

POWERTRAIN OPTIONS: None available.

CONVENIENCE OPTIONS: Hydra-Matic transmission ($174). Whitewall tires. Radio and antenna. Heating and ventilating system. Chrome wheel discs. Fog lights. Safety spotlights. Other standard accessories.

HISTORICAL FOOTNOTES: The one-millionth Cadillac ever produced was a 1949 Coupe DeVille assembled Nov. 25, 1949. The Milestone Car Society recognizes the following 1949 Cadillacs as Milestone Cars: Series 61 coupe (sedanet),

Series 62 coupe (sedanet); Series 62 convertible; Series 60 Special Fleetwood sedan.

1950 CADILLAC

1950 Cadillac, Series 62 Coupe DeVille two-door hardtop, (AA)

SERIES 61 — (V-8) — Cadillacs had extensive styling changes this year. They looked generally heavier and had low, sleek contours with longer rear decks, more sweeping front fenders and a broken rear fender line. The hood protruded out further at the front and was underlined by an even more massive eggcrate grille. Round parking lights were used, but as in the past, when buyers chose fog lamps, an additional bulb and larger housing were used. This setup combined the fog lamps and directional signals. One-piece windshields were introduced and the leading edge of the rear fender, which had a broken-off look, was highlighted by chrome imitation air slots. The rear fenders were longer and ended in a swooping tailfin design. A Cadillac script again appeared on the sides of front fenders, but was now positioned closer to the front door opening gap. As far as Series 61 models went, a big styling change was a return to marketing this line on a shorter wheelbase than used on the 62s. This led to some styling differences. For example, the Series 61 sedan had no rear ventipanes and featured a wraparound backlight. An identifying feature on both models was the absence of rocker panel moldings and rear quarter panel chrome underscores. Cars in Cadillac's lowest price range also had bodies that were four inches shorter than the previous season.

SERIES 61 I.D. NUMBERS: Cadillac serial numbers again matched engine numbers and were used for all license, insurance and identification purposes. They were located on a boss on the right-hand face of the engine block and on the right frame side member behind the engine support. Engine serial numbers 506100000 to 5061103853 appeared on 1950 Series 61 models.

SERIES 61

Model Number	Body/Style Number	Body Type & Seating	Factory Price	Shipping Weight	Production Total
50-61	6169	4-dr Sed-5P	2866	3822	14,619
50-61	6137	2-dr Clb Cpe-5P	2761	3829	11,839
50-61	6169	4-dr Exp Sed-5P	2866	3822	312
50-61	—	Chassis only	—	—	2

NOTE: The sedan for export was shipped in completely-knocked-down (CKD) form to foreign countries.

1950 Cadillac, Series 62 two-door convertible

SERIES 62 — (V-8) — Cars in the Cadillac next-step-up line were identified by slightly richer interior appointments and by chrome underscores running the full length of the body at the bottom. Hydra-Matic drive was now standard in this line. The Series 62 sedan incorporated rear ventipanes. Exclusive models in this range were the convertible coupe and Coupe DeVille, both with standard hydraulic window lifts.

SERIES 62 I.D. NUMBERS: Engine serial numbers 506200000 to 5062103857 appeared on 1950 Series 62 models.

SERIES 62

Model Number	Body/Style Number	Body Type & Seating	Factory Price	Shipping Weight	Production Total
50-62	6219	4-dr Sed-5P	3234	4012	41,890
50-62	6237	2-dr Clb Cpe-5P	3150	3993	6,434
50-62	6237DX	2-dr Cpe DeV-5P	3523	4074	4,507
50-62	6267	2-dr Conv Cpe-5P	3654	4316	6,986
50-62	—	Chassis only	—	—	1

SERIES 60 SPECIAL FLEETWOOD — (V-8) — Eight vertical chrome louvers on the rear fenders characterized the Series 60 sedans. It was built on the same platform as the previous year but had all the new styling features. It looked lower than the 62 because of the extra length and had a different rear deck contour. Hydra-Matic drive and power windows were standard.

SERIES 60 SPECIAL FLEETWOOD I.D. NUMBERS: Engine serial numbers 506000000 to 5060103850 appeared on 1950 Series 60 models.

SERIES 60 SPECIAL FLEETWOOD

Model Number	Body/Style Number	Body Type & Seating	Factory Price	Shipping Weight	Production Total
50-60S	6019X	4-dr Sed-5P	3797	4136	13,755

SERIES 75 FLEETWOOD — (V-8) — An all-new postwar body, which conformed to the other lines for the first time since 1941, was introduced on the luxury-class models this year. It featured six-window styling and a 'high-headroom' limousine-type appearance. Jump seats were used in the seven-passenger sedan and the Imperial limousine. Surprisingly, Hydra-Matic drive was optional, but power windows were standard equipment.

1950 Cadillac, Fleetwood 75 Imperial four-door limousine, (AA)

SERIES 75 FLEETWOOD I.D. NUMBERS: Engine serial numbers 507500000 to 507510387 were used on 1950 Series 75 Fleetwood models.

SERIES 75 FLEETWOOD

Model Number	Body/Style Number	Body Type & Seating	Factory Price	Shipping Weight	Production Total
50-75	7523X	4-dr Sed-7P	4770	4555	716
50-75	7533X	4-dr Imp Sed-7P	4959	4586	743
50-75	7523L	4-dr Bus Sed-7P	—	—	1
50-75	86	Commercial chassis	—	—	2,052

NOTE: The commercial chassis featured a 157-inch wheelbase and was supplied to professional carmakers for the construction of funeral cars, ambulances, etc.

ENGINE: V-8. Overhead valve. Cast iron block. Displacement: 331 cid. Bore and stroke: 3-13/16 x 3-5/8 inches. Compression ratio: 7.5:1. Brake hp: 160 at 3800 rpm. Five main bearings. Hydraulic valve lifters. Carburetor: Carter WCD two-barrel Models 682S or 722S.

CHASSIS FEATURES: Wheelbase: (Series 61) 122 inches; (Series 62) 126 inches; (Series 60S) 130 inches; (Series 75) 146-3/4 inches. Overall length: (Series 61) 211-7/8 inches; (Series 62) 215-7/8 inches; (Series 60S) 224-7/8 inches; (Series 75) 236-5/8 inches. Front tread: (All) 59 inches. Rear tread: (All) 63 inches. Tires: (Series 75) 8.20 x 15; (All others) 8 00 x 15.

POWERTRAIN OPTIONS: None available.

CONVENIENCE OPTIONS: Hydra-Matic drive on Series 61 and 75 ($174). Power windows (on specific models). Heating and ventilating system. Radio and antenna. Chrome wheel discs (Sombrero). Windshield washers. Fog lamps. White sidewall tires. Other standard accessories.

HISTORICAL FOOTNOTES: Stainless steel Sombrero wheelcovers replaced the chrome plated type this year, although the stampings were identical. A hydraulic seat was standard on the Coupe DeVille. An all-time Cadillac production record was set.

1951 CADILLAC

SERIES 61 — (V-8) — A minor face lift and small trim variations were the main Cadillac styling news this year. Miniature egg-crate grilles were set into the outboard grille extension panels below the headlights. Larger, bullet shaped-style bumper guards were used. The features list included handbrake warning lamp; key start ignition; steering column cover; Delco-Remy generator; knee-action front suspension; directionals; mechanical fuel pump; dual downdraft carburetion; slipper-type pistons; rubber engine mountings; oversize brakes; Super Cushion tires; one-piece windshield; intake silencer; 160-hp engine; oil bath air cleaner; equalized manifolding; automatic choke and luxury appointments. On the dashboard, 'idiot lights' were used to monitor oil pressure and electrical charge rate instead of gauges. The smaller body was again used on 61s and again identified by the lack of full-length chrome underscores. However, a new medallion now appeared on the rear roof pillar of these cars, above the upper beltline molding.

1951 Cadillac, Series 61 four-door sedan

SERIES 61 I.D. NUMBERS: Cadillac serial numbers again matched engine numbers and were used for all license, insurance and identification purposes. They were located on a boss at the front right-hand face of the engine block and on the right frame side member behind the engine support. Engine serial numbers for 1951 Series 61 models began at 51610000000. The ending number for all Cadillac series was 110340 (proceeded by applicable model year and series code for final unit).

SERIES 61

Model Number	Body/Style Number	Body Type & Seating	Factory Price	Shipping Weight	Production Total
51-61	6169	4-dr Sed-5P	2917	3827	2300
51-51	6137	2-dr Clb Cpe-5P	2810	3829	2400

1951 Cadillac, Series 62 four-door sedan, (AA)

SERIES 62 — (V-8) — Series 62 models had full-length chrome underscores on the rocker panels, rear fender skirts and lower rear quarters. The sedan had a conventional backlight and featured rear ventipanes. A new Coupe DeVille script was seen on the rear roof pillar of this model that, like the convertible, was an exclusive Series 62 offering. The script clearly distinguished the more luxurious DeVille from the plainer club coupe, a distinction not emphasized in 1950. Hydra-Matic drive was regular equipment on all models (with a new type dial) and power windows were standard on the convertible and Coupe DeVille.

SERIES 62 I.D. NUMBERS: Engine serial numbers 516200000 and up appeared on 1951 Series 62 models.

SERIES 62

Model Number	Body/Style Number	Body Type & Seating	Factory Price	Shipping Weight	Production Total
51-62	6219	4-dr Sed-5P	3528	4102	54,596
51-62	6219	4-dr Exp Sed-5P	—	—	756
51-62	6237	2-dr Clb Cpe-5P	3436	3993	10,132
51-62	6237DX	2-dr Cpe DeV-5P	3843	4074	10,241
51-62	6267	2-dr Conv Cpe-5P	3987	4316	6,117
51-62	126	Chassis only	—	—	2

NOTE: The export sedan was shipped in completely-knocked-down (CKD) form to foreign countries.

1951 Cadillac, Fleetwood 60 Special four-door sedan, (AA)

SERIES 60 SPECIAL FLEETWOOD — (V-8) — The 60 Special Fleetwood sedan was face lifted to conform with the minor changes in other models. Eight vertical chrome louvers on the forward edge of the rear fenders continued to identify this car. All 1951 Cadillacs with full wheel discs featured a new type design lacking the popular Sombrero look. Hydra-Matic and power windows were standard on Sixty Specials.

SERIES 60 SPECIAL FLEETWOOD I.D. NUMBERS: Engine serial numbers 516000000 and up appeared on 1951 Series 60S models.

SERIES 60 SPECIAL FLEETWOOD

Model Number	Body/Style Number	Body Type & Seating	Factory Price	Shipping Weight	Production Total
51-60	6019	4-dr Sed-5P	4142	4136	18,631

SERIES 75 FLEETWOOD — (V-8) — The Series 75 Fleetwood models were also face lifted to conform to the minor changes seen in other lines. Jump seats were used in both the seven-passenger sedan and Imperial limousine. Hydra-Matic drive was optional and hydraulic window lifts were standard. Business sedans were built in limited numbers on a special order basis.

SERIES 75 FLEETWOOD I.D. NUMBERS: Engine serial numbers 517500000 and up appeared on 1951 Series 75 Fleetwood models.

SERIES 75 FLEETWOOD

Model Number	Body/Style Number	Body Type & Seating	Factory Price	Shipping Weight	Production Total
51-75	7523X	4-dr Sed-8P	5200	4555	1,090
51-75	7533X	4-dr Imp Sed-8P	5405	4586	1,085
51-75	7523L	4-dr Bus Sed-8P	—	—	30
51-75	86	Commercial chassis	—	—	2,960

NOTE: The commercial chassis featured a 157-inch wheelbase and was supplied to professional carmakers for construction.

ENGINE: V-8. Overhead valve. Cast iron block. Displacement: 331 cid. Bore and stroke: 3-3/16 x 3-5/8 inches. Compression ratio: 7.5:1. Brake hp: 160 at 3800 rpm. Five main bearings. Hydraulic valve lifters. Carburetor: Carter WCD two-barrel Model 845S, also Rochester BB two-barrel Model 7004200.

CHASSIS FEATURES: Wheelbase: (Series 61) 122 inches; (Series 62) 126 inches; (Series 60S) 130 inches; (Series 75)146-3/4 inches. Overall length: (Series 61) 211-7/8 inches; (Series 62) 215-7/8 inches; (Series 60S) 224-7/8 inches; (Series 75) 238-5/8 inches. Front tread: (All) 59 inches. Rear tread: (All) 63 inches. Tires: (Series 75) 8.20 x 15; (All others) 8.00 x 15.

POWERTRAIN OPTIONS: None available.

CONVENIENCE OPTIONS: Hydra-Matic drive on Series 61 and 75 ($186). Power windows (specific models). Heating and ventilating system. Radio and antenna. Chrome wheel discs. Windshield washers. Fog lamps. White sidewall tires (availability limited).

HISTORICAL FOOTNOTES: The Series 61 line was discontinued in the middle of the year due to lagging sales.

1952 CADILLAC

SERIES 62 — (V-8) — This was Cadillac's 50th anniversary year. Only minor styling and trim changes were seen, but some were specially planned to commemorate the occasion. For example, the V-shaped hood and deck emblems were done as gold castings. The Series 62 sedan was also characterized by a distinct, higher rear deck lid contour. This provided additional luggage space. Back-up lights were standard equipment and were now incorporated in the taillights. The grille wraparound panels were redesigned once again. They now had broad chrome trim below each headlight with side scoop styling and a gold-colored winged emblem mounted in the center. At the rear, all models adopted a new Cadillac trademark, a through-the-bumper dual exhaust system. Deck ornamentation varied by series and, on 62s, took the form of a Cadillac crest over a broad golden 'V'. The Coupe DeVille again had a script nameplate on the rear roof pillar. New standards included self-winding clocks, dual-range Hydra-Matic drive, improved direction signal indicators, glare-proof mirrors, stannate treated pistons, four-barrel carburetion and all other features seen the previous year. Hydraulic window lifts remained as regular equipment on convertibles and Coupe DeVilles.

1952 Cadillac, Series 62 two-door convertible, (AA)

CADILLAC I.D. NUMBERS: Serial numbers and engine numbers were again one and the same. They appeared on the right-hand side of the crankcase above the water pump and on the right frame side bar behind the engine support. The first two symbols were '52' for 1952. The next two symbols indicated the series as follows: '62', '60S' or '75'. The remaining digits represented the con-

secutive unit number and began with 00000 for all series. All series had the same ending number.

1952 Cadillac, Series 62 two-door Club Coupe

SERIES 62

Model Number	Body/Style Number	Body Type & Seating	Factory Price	Shipping Weight	Production Total
52-62	6219	4-dr Sed-5P	3636	4151	42,625
52-62	6237	2-dr Clb Cpe-5P	3542	4174	10,065
52-62	6237DX	2-dr Cpe DeV-5P	3962	4205	11,165
52-62	6267X	2-dr Conv Cpe-5P	4110	4419	6,400

SERIES SIXTY SPECIAL FLEETWOOD — (V-8) — The Sixty Special Fleetwood sedan had the same general styling changes seen in other lines, plus minor trim and appointment variations. For example, the word Fleetwood appeared on the rear deck lid (instead of a Cadillac crest) and the eight vertical fender louvers were seen again. Hydra-Matic drive and hydraulic window lifts were installed at no extra cost to buyers.

SERIES SIXTY SPECIAL FLEETWOOD

Model Number	Body/Style Number	Body Type & Seating	Factory Price	Shipping Weight	Production Total
52-60	6019	4-dr Sed-5P	4720	4258	16,110

1952 Cadillac, Fleetwood 75 Imperial four-door limousine, (GM)

SERIES 75 FLEETWOOD — (V-8) — Styling changes on the long wheelbase series also conformed to the theme for the year with the Golden Anniversary aspect highlighted. Equipment features were the same as before and no business sedans were built.

SERIES 75 FLEETWOOD

Model Number	Body/Style Number	Body Type & Seating	Factory Price	Shipping Weight	Production Total
52-75	7523X	4-dr Sed-8P	5361	4699	1,400
52-75	7533X	4-dr Imp Sed-8P	5572	4734	800
52-76	86	Commercial chassis	—	—	1,694

NOTE: The commercial chassis was built on a 157-inch wheelbase and was provided to makers of professional vehicles for construction of funeral cars, ambulances, etc.

ENGINE: V-8. Overhead valve. Cast iron block. Displacement: 331 cid. Bore and stroke: 3-13/16 x 3-5/8 inches. Compression ratio: 7.5:1. Brake hp: 190 at 4000 rpm. Five main bearings. Hydraulic valve lifters. Carburetor: Carter WFCB four-barrel Model 896S, also Rochester 4GC four-barrel 7004500.

CHASSIS FEATURES: Wheelbase: (Series 62) 126 inches; (Series 60S) 130 inches; (Series 75)147 inches. Overall length: (Series 62 sedan) 215-1/2 inches; (All other 62s) 200-1/2 inches; (Series 60S) 224-1/2 inches; (Series 75) 236-1/4 inches. Front tread: (All) 59 inches. Rear tread: (All) 63 inches. Tires: (Series 75) 8.20 x 15; (Other series) 8.00 x 15. Dual exhaust standard. Rear axle ratio: 3.07:1.

POWERTRAIN OPTIONS: None available.

CONVENIENCE OPTIONS: Hydra-Matic drive on Series 75 ($186). Wheel discs ($28). Windshield washer ($11). Oil filter

($11). Fog lamps ($37). License frames ($4). Outside mirror ($6). Vanity mirror ($2). E-Z-Eye glass ($46). Heater and blower ($114). Push-button radio and rear speaker ($112). Signal-seeking radio and rear speaker ($129). Power steering ($198). Autronic Eye headlight beam control ($53). White sidewall tires Series 62 and 60S ($34). Automatic window regulators ($139). Wheel trim rings ($11).

HISTORICAL FOOTNOTES: Cadillac had the most powerful car in the American industry this year. The 1,300,000th Cadillac of all time was built. Military orders for T41E1 Walker Bulldog tanks and T41 twin 40mm gun motor carriages were secured by the division this year as part of the Korean war buildup. Hydraulically controlled power seats were standard on Coupe DeVille.

1953 CADILLAC

1953 Cadillac, Series 62 Coupe DeVille two-door hardtop, (AA)

SERIES 62 — (V-8) — Changes seen in 1953 included a redesigned grille with heavier integral bumper and bumper guards, the repositioning of parking lamps directly under the headlights, chrome 'eyebrow' type headlamp doors and one-piece rear windows without division bars. Wheel discs were fashioned in an attractive new dished design. Series 62 models were identified by non-louvered rear fenders, the use of thin bright metal underscores on the bottom rear of the cars only and the decoration of both hood and deck lid with Cadillac crests and V-shaped ornaments. As was the practice since 1951, Series 62 sedan bodies measured five inches less than the other styles. A Coupe DeVille roof pillar script was seen again on this luxury hardtop. Standard equipment included all items featured the year before. Late in the production year the limited-edition Eldorado luxury convertible was added to this model range. A full assortment of Deluxe accessories, including wire wheels, were standard on this specialty car, which introduced the wraparound windshield for production models. On August 12, a fire at the Hydra-Matic transmission factory in Livonia, Mich., broke out and would bring a damaging halt to automobile production within a week. It was September 8th before Cadillacs began leaving the factory again.

1953 Cadillac, Series 62 Eldorado two-door convertible, (AA)

CADILLAC I.D. NUMBERS: Serial numbers and engine numbers were again one and the same. They appeared on the right-hand side of the crankcase above the water pump and on the right frame side bar behind the engine support. The first two symbols were '53' for 1953. The next two symbols indicated the series as follows: '62', '60' or '75.' The remaining digits represented the consecutive unit number and began with 00000 for all series. All series had the same ending number, which would be misinterpreted if listed.

SERIES 62

Model Number	Body/Style Number	Body Type & Seating	Factory Price	Shipping Weight	Production Total
53-62	6219(X)	4-dr Sed-5P	3666	4201	47,316
53-62	6219(X)	4-dr Exp Sed-5P	3666	4201	324
53-62	6237(X)	2-dr Cpe-5P	3571	4189	14,353
53-62	6237DX	2-dr Cpe DeV-5P	3995	4252	14,550
53-62	6267X	2-dr Conv Cpe-5P	4144	4476	8,367
53-62	62	Chassis only	—	—	4

ELDORADO SPECIAL

Model Number	Body/Style Number	Body Type & Seating	Factory Price	Shipping Weight	Production Total
53-62	6267SX	2-dr Spt Conv Cpe-5P	7750	4799	532

NOTES: The export sedan was shipped in completely-knocked-down (CKD) form to foreign countries. The symbol X in brackets indicates hydraulic window lifts optional, without brackets indicates this feature standard.

1953 Cadillac, Fleetwood 60 Special four-door sedan, (GM)

SERIES SIXTY SPECIAL FLEETWOOD — (V-8) — Eight vertical louvers on the lower rear fenders directly behind the fender breakline once again characterized the wide door Cadillac sedan. This model was also distinguished by exclusive extra-wide full length chrome underscores and a Fleetwood insignia on the rear deck lid.

SERIES SIXTY SPECIAL FLEETWOOD

Model Number	Body/Style Number	Body Type & Seating	Factory Price	Shipping Weight	Production Total
53-60	6019X	4-dr Sed-5P	4305	4337	20,000

SERIES 75 FLEETWOOD — (V-8) — Styling face lifts on the cars in the 75 Fleetwood line conformed to those seen on other models. Appearance features and equipment were about the same as in previous years. Regular production models included the Imperial eight-passenger limousine with glass partition or eight-passenger sedan, both with jump seats.

SERIES 75 FLEETWOOD

Model Number	Body/Style Number	Body Type & Seating	Factory Price	Shipping Weight	Production Total
53-75	7523X	4-dr Sed-8P	5604	4801	1,435
53-75	7533X	4-dr Imp Sed-8P	5818	4853	765
53-86	8680S	Commercial chassis	—	—	2,005

NOTE: The commercial chassis featured a 157-inch wheelbase and was provided to makers of professional vehicles for construction of funeral cars, ambulances, etc.

ENGINE: V-8. Overhead valve. Cast iron block. Displacement: 331 cid. Bore and stroke: 3-15/16 x 3-5/8 inches. Compression ratio: 8.25:1. Brake hp: 210 at 4150 rpm. Five main bearings. Hydraulic valve lifters. Carburetors: (Hydra-Matic) Carter WCFB four-barrel Model 2005S, also Rochester 4GC four-barrel Model 7005100. (Dynaflow) Carter WCFB four-barrel Models 2088S and 2119S. Also, Rochester 4GC four-barrel Model 7006215.

CHASSIS FEATURES: Wheelbase: (Series 62) 126 inches; (Series 60S) 130 inches; (Series 75) 146-3/4 inches. Overall length: (Series 62 sedan) 215.8 inches; (Other 62s) 220.8 inches; (Series 60S) 224.8 inches; (Series 75) 236.5 inches. Tires: (Series 75) 8.20 x 15; (Others) 8.00 x 15. Dual exhaust system standard. Rear axle ratios: (Series 62 and 60S) 3.07:1; (Series 75) 3.77:1.

POWERTRAIN OPTIONS: None available.

CONVENIENCE OPTIONS: Hydra-Matic drive on Series 75 ($186). Hydraulic window lifts optional on some Series 62 models. Heating and ventilation system ($199). Power steering ($177). Signal-seeking radio with preselector and antenna ($132). Remote control signal-seeking radio with preselector and antenna ($214). Five white sidewall tires ($48 exchange). Tinted E-Z-Eye glass ($46). Autronic Eye Automatic headlamp beam control ($53). Chrome wire wheels ($325). Air conditioning ($620). Other standard GM accessories.

HISTORICAL FOOTNOTES: Standard equipment on the Style Number 6267S Eldorado sport convertible included Hydra-Matic drive, wraparound windshield, special cut-down doors, rich leather-and-cloth upholstery, wire wheels, white sidewall tires, fog lamps. vanity and side mirrors, metal tonneau cover and signal-seeking radio. The Style Number 7533 Series 75 Fleetwood Imperial sedan was fitted with a hydraulically operated glass driver's partition. The Style Number 6267S Eldorado sport convertible is a certified Milestone Car. The futuristic Cadillac LeMans show car convertible was displayed this year and would heavily influence styling of the 1954 Eldorado. It had a special 270-hp V-8 with dual four-barrel carburetion and a fiberglass body. Also, 28,000 Cadillacs were built with Buick Dynaflow transmissions after GM's Hydramatic plant burned to the ground.

1954 CADILLAC

SERIES 62 — (V-8) — Many appearance improvements marked the 1954 Cadillacs. They included a lower, sleeker body, a new cellular grille insert, inverted gull-wing front bumpers and tapered dagmar-style bumper guards. Round, jet-style dual exhaust outlets were incorporated into the vertical bumper extensions and the rear bumper was entirely redesigned. An Eldorado-type wraparound windshield was seen on all models. Sedans used a distinctive type of window reveal molding, which created a built-in sun visor effect. For coupes, a smoothly curved wraparound backlight was referred to as the 'Florentine' style rear window. A wide ventilator intake now stretched across the base of the windshield on all models and the chrome visored headlamp look was emphasized. The Series 62 chassis had a brand new, longer wheelbase. One identifying feature of this line was the lack of rear fender louvers. V-shaped ornaments and crests were used on the hood and deck and there were full-length body underscores in bright metal. Coupe DeVille script was seen on the rear corner pillars of the luxury hardtop, which also had wider sill moldings. The Eldorado had golden identifying crests centered directly behind the air-slot fenderbreaks and wide, fluted beauty panels to decorate the lower rear bodysides. These panels were made of extruded aluminum and also appeared on a unique, one-of-a-kind Eldorado coupe built for the president of the Reynolds Aluminum Co. Also included on the production convertible were monogram plates on the doors, wire wheels and custom interior trimmings with the Cadillac crest embossed on the seat bolsters. Automatic windshield washers, power steering, 12-volt electrical system and aluminum alloy pistons made the long standard equipment list this year. The Series 62 four-door sedan was now seven inches shorter than other models in this range. Another one-off creation was an exclusive Sedan DeVille.

1954 Cadillac, Series 62 two-door convertible

CADILLAC I.D. NUMBERS: Serial numbers and engine numbers were again one and the same. They appeared on the right-hand side of the crankcase above the water pump and on the right frame side bar behind the engine support. The first two symbols were '54' for 1954. The next two symbols indicated series as follows: '62', '60' or '75' The remaining digits represented the consecutive unit number and began with 00000 for each series. All series had the same ending number, which would be misinterpreted if listed.

SERIES 62

Model Number	Body/Style Number	Body Type & Seating	Factory Price	Shipping Weight	Production Total
54-62	6219(X)	4-dr Sed-5P	3933	4330	33,845
54-82	8219(X)	4-dr Exp Sed-5P	3933	4330	408
54-62	6219SX	4-dr Sed DeV-5P	—	—	1
54-62	6237(X)	2-dr Cpe-5P	3838	4347	17,460
54-62	6237DX	2-dr Cpe DeV-5P	4261	4409	17,170
54-62	6267X	2-dr Conv Cpe-5P	4404	4598	6,310
54-62	62	Chassis only	—	—	1

ELDORADO SPECIAL

Model Number	Body/Style Number	Body Type & Seating	Factory Price	Shipping Weight	Production Total
54-62	6267SX	2-dr Spt Conv Cpe-5P	5738	4809	2,150

NOTES: The export sedan was shipped in completely-knocked-down (CKD) form to foreign countries. The symbol X after Body/Style Number with brackets indicates hydraulic window lifts optional equipment; without brackets indicates this feature is standard.

1954 Cadillac, Fleetwood 60 Special four-door sedan, (AA)

SERIES SIXTY SPECIAL FLEETWOOD — (V-8) — The Sixty Special sedan had luxurious Fleetwood style interior appointments. Identifiers included the traditional fender louvers, V-shaped ornaments on the hood and rear deck and a Fleetwood script in the latter location. Wheelbase measurements returned to 133 inches for the first time since 1949. Also seen were a panoramic (wraparound) windshield, new grille, longer more sweeping fenders and all other 1954-style appearance innovations. The newly expanded equipment list appeared on the 60S sedan, too.

SERIES SIXTY SPECIAL FLEETWOOD

Model Number	Body/Style Number	Body Type & Seating	Factory Price	Shipping Weight	Production Total
54-60	6019X	4-dr Sed-5P	4683	4490	16,200

SERIES 75 FLEETWOOD — (V-8) — The big Fleetwood 'high headroom' job came as an eight-passenger limousine with driver's partition or eight-passenger sedan without partition, both having jump seats. V-shaped ornaments appeared on the hood and deck lid with a Fleetwood script in the latter location. Wheelbase increased to 149.8 inches. Styling changes conformed with those seen on other lines.

SERIES 75 FLEETWOOD

Model Number	Body/Style Number	Body Type & Seating	Factory Price	Shipping Weight	Production Total
54-75	7523X	4-dr Sed-8P	5875	5031	889
54-75	7533X	4-dr Imp Sed-8P	6090	5093	611
54-86	8680	Commercial chassis	—	—	1,635

NOTE: The commercial chassis featured a 158-inch wheelbase and was provided to makers of professional vehicles for construction of funeral cars, ambulances, etc.

ENGINE: V-8. Overhead valve. Cast iron block. Displacement: 331 cid. Bore and stroke: 3-13/16 x 3-5/8 inches. Compression ratio: 8.25:1. Brake hp: 230 at 4400 rpm. Five main bearings. Hydraulic valve lifters. Carburetors: Carter WCFB four-barrel Models 2143S, 2109S and 2110S, also Rochester 4GC four-barrel (with air) Model 7006963; (without air) Model 7006962.

CHASSIS FEATURES: Wheelbase: (Series 62) 129 inches; (Series 60S) 133 inches; (Series 75) 149.8 inches. Overall length: (Series 62 sedan) 216.4 inches; (All other 62s) 223.4 inches; (Series 60S) 227.4 inches; (Series 75) 237.1 inches. Front tread: (All) 60 inches. Rear tread: (All) 63.1 inches. Standard tires: (Series 75) 8.20 x 15; (Eldorado) 8.20 x 15 whitewall; (Others) 8.00 x 15. Optional tires (Series 60 and 62 except 6267S) 8.20 x 15 whitewall. Dual exhaust system standard. Rear axle ratios: (standard) 3.07:1; (standard with air conditioning; optional without) 3.36:1.

POWERTRAIN OPTIONS: None available.

1954 Cadillac, Series 62 Coupe DeVille two-door hardtop, (AA)

CONVENIENCE OPTIONS: Hydra-Matic drive on Series 75 ($186). Power brakes ($48). Radio ($120). Heater ($129). Air-conditioning ($620). Power operated window and seat ($124). Chrome wire wheels ($325). White sidewall tires ($49 exchange). E-Z-Eye tinted glass. Autronic Eye automatic headlamp dimmer. Vertical front seat adjuster. Horizontal front seat adjuster (standard on Coupe DeVille, convertible, Eldorado, Series 60S and Series 75). Other standard GM options and accessories.

HISTORICAL FOOTNOTES: Assembly of 1954 models began January 4, 1954, after a 25-day halt for changeover to new production specifications. Fiberglass-bodied Cadillac show cars appearing at the GM Motorama this year included the Park Avenue four-door sedan, El Camino coupe and La Espada convertible.

1955 CADILLAC

SERIES 62 — (V-8) — While no major appearance changes were seen on Cadillacs this year, a number of refinements were apparent. The grille was redesigned with wider spaces between the blades and the parking lamps were repositioned directly below the headlights. On the sides of the body the rub-rail moldings formed a right angle with the vertical trim on the rear doors or fenders of Series 62 and 60S models. This accentuated a character line in the sheet metal. The Florentine curve rear window treatment was adopted for sedans. Three chrome moldings bordered the rear license plate on either side and deck lid decorations consisted of a V-shaped ornament and a Cadillac crest. The Coupe DeVille had a golden script nameplate at the upper body belt just forward of the rear window pillar. The Eldorado sport convertible featured extras such as wide chrome body belt moldings, a distinctive rear fender design with twin round taillights halfway up the fenders and flatter, pointed tailfins. Tubeless tires were a new feature throughout the line.

1955 Cadillac, Series 62 Coupe DeVille two-door hardtop, (AA)

CADILLAC I.D. NUMBERS: Serial numbers and engine numbers were the same again and were found in the same locations. The first two symbols were '55' to designate 1955 model production. The next two symbols indicated the series as follows: '62', '60' or '75'. The remaining digits represented the consecutive unit number and began at 00000 for each series. All series had the same ending number, which would be misinterpreted if listed.

1955 Cadillac, Series 62 Eldorado two-door convertible

SERIES 62

Model Number	Body/Style Number	Body Type & Seating	Factory Price	Shipping Weight	Production Total
55-62	6219(X)	4-dr Sed-6P	3977	4375	44,904
55-62	6219(X)	4-dr Exp Sed-6P	3977	4375	396
55-62	6237(X)	2-dr HT Cpe-6P	3882	4364	27,879
55-62	6237DX	2-dr Cpe DeV-6P	4305	4428	33,300
55-62	6267X	2-dr Conv Cpe-6P	4448	4631	8,150
55-62	62	Chassis only	—	—	7

ELDORADO SPECIAL

55-62	6267SX	2-dr Spt Conv Cpe-5P	6286	4809	3,950

NOTES: The export sedan was shipped in completely-knocked-down (CKD) form to foreign countries. The symbol X in brackets after Body/Style Number indicates hydraulic window lifts optional; without brackets indicates this feature standard.

SERIES SIXTY SPECIAL FLEETWOOD — (V-8) — This model now had 12 vertical louvers at the rear lower side of the back fenders and continued with a Fleetwood script on the rear deck. The special 'glamour' upholstery used in the 60S was similar to the metallic thread fabric with genuine leather trim combination used in the Series 62 Coupe DeVille. Standard equipment included directional signals, back-up lights, oil bath air cleaner, automatic choke, full-pressure lubrication, 12-volt electrical system, knee-action front suspension, hypoid semi-floating rear axle, wheel discs and push-button automatic windshield washers.

SERIES SIXTY SPECIAL FLEETWOOD

Model Number	Body/Style Number	Body Type & Seating	Factory Price	Shipping Weight	Production Total
55-60	6019X	4-dr Sed-6P	4728	4545	18,300

1955 Cadillac, Fleetwood 75 Imperial four-door limousine, (AA)

SERIES 75 FLEETWOOD — (V-8) — The trim on Fleetwood long wheelbase models was distinctive from other lines. A horizontal rub molding ran from the front parking light housings to the trailing edge of the front door and stopped. A full-length vertical air slot-style fenderbreak molding was placed directly behind the rear gap of the back doors. The two moldings did not meet at right angles. Other styling alterations, such as grille design changes, conformed to the new 1955 themes. A Fleetwood script appeared on the deck lid. The high headroom appearance was seen again. Both models continued to feature auxiliary seats for extra passenger carrying capacity and the Imperial sedan limousine had a hydraulically operated glass driver's partition.

SERIES 75 FLEETWOOD

Model Number	Body/Style Number	Body Type & Seating	Factory Price	Shipping Weight	Production Total
55-75	7523X	4-dr Sed-8P	6187	5020	1,075
55-75	7533X	4-dr Imp Sed-8P	6402	5113	841
55-86	8680S	Commercial chassis	—	—	1,975

NOTE: The commercial chassis featured a 158-inch wheelbase and was provided to makers of professional vehicles for construction of funeral cars and ambulances, etc.

ENGINE: V-8. Overhead valve. Cast iron block. Displacement: 331 cid. Bore and stroke: 3.81 x 3.63 inches. Compression ratio: 9.0:1. Brake hp: 250 at 4600 rpm. Five main bearings. Hydraulic valve lifters. Carburetors: Carter WCFB four-barrel Models 2355S, 2354S, 2185S, 2186S, 2266S, 2267S, and 2255, also Rochester 4GC four-barrel (less air conditioning) Model 7007970; (with air conditioning) Model 7007971.

ELDORADO ENGINE: The Eldorado engine had the following changes from the above specifications: Brake hp: 270 at 4800 rpm. Carburetors: Two Rochester 4GC four-barrels (front) Model 7007240; (rear, less air conditioning) Model 7007240; (rear, with air conditioning) Model 7007241.

CHASSIS FEATURES: Wheelbase: (Series 62) 129 inches; (Series 60S) 133 inches; (Series 75) 149.8 inches. Overall length: (Series 62 sedan) 216.3 inches; (Other 62s) 223.2 inches; (Series 60S) 227.3 inches; (Series 75) 237.1 inches. Front tread: (All) 60 inches. Rear tread: (All) 63.1 inches. Tires: (Series 75) 8.20 x 15 six-ply; (Eldorado) 8.20 x 15 four-ply whitewall; (Others) 8.00 x 15. Standard dual exhaust. Rear axle ratios: (standard) 3.36:1; (optional) 3.07:1.

POWERTRAIN OPTIONS: The 270-hp Eldorado engine was available as an optional 'Power Package' in other models for $161 extra.

CONVENIENCE OPTIONS: Radio and antenna ($132). Heating and ventilation system ($129). Power brakes ($48). Four-way adjustable power seat ($70). Vertically adjustable power seat ($54). Power windows ($108). Air conditioning ($620). White sidewall tires. E-Z-Eye safety glass. Autronic Eye automatic headlamp dimmer. Other standard GM options and accessories available.

HISTORICAL FOOTNOTES: Standard equipment on the Eldorado special sport convertible included customized interior and rear body styling; 270-hp dual four-barrel inducted V-8; radio and antenna; heater; power brakes; power seat; power windows; whitewall tires; metal tonneau cover; custom trim and ornamentation; individual circular tail and rear directional lights and saber-spoke wheels. The 1955 Eldorado is a certified Milestone Car. The Park Avenue sedan, a futuristic show car that became the predecessor to the Eldorado Brougham, appeared at the New York Motorama on January 19, 1955. It was built in less than 74 days. Another show car seen this year was the Celebrity hardtop coupe. *Motor Trend* magazine reported fuel consumption figures of 12.9 miles per gallon (stop-and-go) for a Series 62 sedan with the standard 250-hp V-8. Total 1955 model year output reached 140,777 units, a new record high for Cadillac Division.

1956 CADILLAC

1956 Cadillac, Series 62 Sedan DeVille four-door hardtop

SERIES 62 — (V-8) — Although a face lift was the major re-styling news for 1956, there were still many changes in the Series 62 lineup and especially in the Eldorado sub-series. The annual 'beauty treatment' consisted of a new grille with finer textured insert and the repositioning of parking lights in the bumper, below the wing guards. Buyers were given a choice of a standard satin finish grille or optional gold finish, both selections decorated with Cadillac script on the left-hand side. On the rear side fenders of Series 62 models a narrow chrome molding and nine vertical louvers were seen. The Coupe DeVille had a model nameplate and Cadillac crest on the sides of front fenders, while the more standard cars had only the crest. An Eldorado script appeared, with a fender crest on the luxury convertible, which also featured a twin-fin hood ornament. Other extras on this car—now known as the Biarritz—were a ribbed chrome saddle molding extending from the windshield to the rear window pillar along the beltline and flat, pointed rear fender fins Totally new models included a pillarless four-door called the Sedan DeVille and an Eldorado Coupe Seville. The latter represented an especially luxurious hardtop coupe, which was built to Eldorado standards and similarly priced. As usual, the standard four-door 62 sedan was seven inches shorter than the other cars in the same series. Both cars in the Eldorado sub-series were slightly longer this year.

1956 Cadillac, Series 62 Eldorado Seville two-door hardtop, (AA)

CADILLAC I.D. NUMBERS: Serial numbers and engine numbers were the same again and were found in the same locations. The first two symbols were '56' to designate 1956 model production. The next two symbols indicated the series as follows: '62', '60' or '75'. The remaining digits represented the consecutive unit number and began at 00000 for each series. All series had the same ending number, which would be misinterpreted if listed.

1956 Cadillac, Series 62 four-door sedan

SERIES 62

Model Number	Body/Style Number	Body Type & Seating	Factory Price	Shipping Weight	Production Total
56-62	6219(X)	4-dr Sed-6P	4241	4430	26,222
56-62	6219(X)	4-dr Exp Sed-6P	4241	4430	444
56-62	6239DX	4-dr Sed DeV-6P	4698	4550	41,732
56-62	6237(X)	2-dr HT Cpe-6P	4146	4420	26,649
56-62	6237DX	2-dr Cpe DeV-6P	4569	4445	25,086
56-62	6267X	2-dr Conv Cpe-6P	4711	4645	8,300
56-62	62	Chassis only	—	—	19

ELDORADO (SUB-SERIES)

Model Number	Body/Style Number	Body Type & Seating	Factory Price	Shipping Weight	Production Total
56-62	6237DX	2-dr HT Cpe Sev-6P	6501	4665	3,900
56-62	6267SX	2-dr Conv Biarritz-6P	6501	4880	2,150

NOTE: The export sedan was shipped in completely-knocked-down (CKD) form to foreign countries. The symbol X in brackets after Body/Style Number indicates hydraulic window lifts optional; without brackets indicates this feature standard.

SERIES SIXTY SPECIAL FLEETWOOD — (V-8) — Cadillac's non-limousine style Fleetwood model carried the Sixty Special designation in script below the Cadillac crest on the sides of the front fenders. A Fleetwood name also appeared on the rear face of the deck lid. Solid chrome exhaust extension trim moldings were seen on the rear fenders.

SERIES SIXTY SPECIAL FLEETWOOD

Model Number	Body/Style Number	Body Type & Seating	Factory Price	Shipping Weight	Production Total
56-62	6019X	4-dr Sed-6P	6019	4992	17,000

SERIES 75 FLEETWOOD — (V-8) — Side trim on the long wheelbase Fleetwood models was about the same as 1955, except for the addition of exhaust extension moldings on the rear fender. This trim ran along a tapering conical flare from above the wheel housing to the rear bumper. A Fleetwood script appeared on the deck lid and limousine styling was seen again. Changes in grilles and bumpers conformed to those used with other series. Both models had auxiliary seats and the Imperial sedan again featured a glass driver's partition. Standard equipment on all Cadillacs was comparable to that included the previous year.

SERIES 75 FLEETWOOD

Model Number	Body/Style Number	Body Type & Seating	Factory Price	Shipping Weight	Production Total
56-75	7523X	4-dr Sed-8P	6558	5050	1,095
56-75	7533X	4-dr Imp Sed-8P	6773	5130	955
56-86	8680S	Commercial chassis	—	—	2,025

NOTE: The commercial chassis featured a 158-inch wheelbase and was provided to makers of professional vehicles for construction of funeral cars and ambulances, etc.

ENGINES: V-8. Overhead valve. Cast iron block. Displacement: 365 cid. Bore and stroke: 4.00 x 3.63 inches. Compression ratio: 9.75:1. Brake hp: 285 at 4600 rpm. Five main bearings. Hydraulic valve lifters. Carburetor: Carter WCFB four-barrel, Model 2370S.

ELDORADO V-8: The Eldorado engine had the following changes from the above specifications: Brake hp: 305 at 4700 rpm. Carburetors: Two Carter WCFB four-barrel Model 2371.

CHASSIS FEATURES: Wheelbase: (Series 62) 129 inches; (Series 60S) 133 inches; (Series 75) 149.75 inches. Overall length: (Eldorado) 222.2 inches; (Series 62 sedan) 214.9 inches; (Other 62s) 221.9 inches; (Series 60S) 225.9 inches; (Series 75) 235.7 inches. Front tread: (All) 60 inches. Rear tread: (All) 63.1 inches. Tires: (Series 75) 8.20 x 15 black; (Eldorado) 8.20 x 15 whitewall; (Others) 8.00 x 15. Standard dual exhaust.

POWERTRAIN OPTIONS: The 305-hp Eldorado engine was available in other models at extra cost.

CONVENIENCE OPTIONS: Air conditioning. White sidewall tires. E-Z-Eye safety glass. Autronic eye automatic headlamp dimmer. Signal-seeking radio with preselector and antenna. Heating and ventilation system. Power window lifts (specific models). Gold finish grille. Two-way posture power seat ($81). Six-way power seat ($97). Other standard GM accessories available. (Note: Posture power adjustable seat on convertible, DeVilles and Series 60S only. Six-way seat on 62 coupe and sedan and standard for Eldorado).

HISTORICAL FOOTNOTES: The Cadillac Series 62 Sedan DeVille four-door hardtop and Eldorado Seville two-door hardtop were introduced to the public almost a month earlier than other models, on October 24, 1955. The remaining cars in the line were introduced the following month on November 18. The 1956 Hydra-Matic transmission incorporated changes that increased its size and smoothed out shifting characteristics. It was developed by GM at a cost of $35 million. The 1956 line set records in sales and production moving Cadillac from tenth to ninth position in the American sales race. On August 5, 1956, the division announced the purchase of the former Hudson Motor Car plant on Detroit's east end.

1957 CADILLAC

SERIES 62 — (V-8) — For 1957, Cadillac adopted a tubular X-frame, without side rails, on all models. This resulted in greater structural rigidity and provided for lower body lines without loss of useable space. New front end styling was marked by rubber bumper guard tips and dual, circular parking lamps set into the lower bumper section. Side trim was revised and a dual taillight theme was used throughout the line. By utilizing different center frame sections the wheelbases and overall lengths of specific body styles was altered. In the 62 lineup, including the Eldorado sub-series, three different overall measurements appeared on cars with matching wheelbases. The Sedan DeVille was bigger than 'standard' models and the Eldorado Coupe Seville and Biarritz convertible were larger still. Identifying the 'standard' 62 models were vertical bright metal moldings, just forward of the rear wheel openings, highlighted by seven horizontal windsplits. At the upper end this fenderbreak trim joined a horizontal molding that ran along a conical flare extending forward from the taillamps. A crest medallion was seen on the forward angled rear fins. Coupe DeVilles and Sedan DeVilles had special nameplates on the front fenders. Eldorados were further distinguished by the model name above a V-shaped rear deck ornament and on the front fenders. The rear fender and deck contour was sleekly rounded and the wheel housing was trimmed with broad, sculptured stainless steel beauty panels. Also seen were pointed, 'shark' style fins pointing towards the back of the cars. A three-section built-in front bumper was another exclusive trait of the two luxury cars, which came with a long list of standard accessories.

1957 Cadillac, Series 62 two-door convertible, (AA)

CADILLAC I.D. NUMBERS: Serial numbers and engine numbers were again the same. They appeared on a boss on the front right-hand face of the engine block; on the lubrication plate on the left front door pillar (1953-1957) and on the right frame side member behind the engine support. The first pair of symbols were '57' to designate the 1957 model year. The next two symbols indicated series as follows: '62', '60', '70' and '75.' The immediately following numbers, beginning at 00000 for each series, indicated the production sequence in consecutive order. Ending numbers were the same for all series since the engines were installed in mixed production fashion.

1957 Cadillac, Series 62 Eldorado Biarritz two-door convertible, (AA)

SERIES 62

Model Number	Body/Style Number	Body Type & Seating	Factory Price	Shipping Weight	Production Total
57-62	6239(X)	4-dr HT Sed-6P	4713	4595	32,342
57-62	6239(X)	4-dr Exp Sed-6P	4713	4595	384
57-62	6239DX	4-dr DeV HT-6P	5188	4655	23,808
57-62	6237(X)	2-dr HT Cpe-6P	4609	4565	25,120
57-62	6237DX	2-dr Cpe DeV-6P	5048	4620	23,813
57-62	6267X	2-dr Conv Cpe-6P	5225	4730	9,000
57-62	62	Chassis only	—	—	1

SERIES 62 ELDORADO SPECIALS

Model Number	Body/Style Number	Body Type & Seating	Factory Price	Shipping Weight	Production Total
57-62	6237SDX	2-dr HT Cpe Sev-6P	7286	4810	2,100
57-62	6267SX	2-dr Biarritz Conv-6P	7286	4930	1,800
57-62	6239SX	4-dr Sed Sev-6P	—	—	4

NOTES: The export sedan was shipped in completely-knocked-down (CKD) form to foreign countries The Eldorado Sedan Seville was a special order model built in limited quantities. The symbol 'X' after Body Style Number in brackets in-

1957 Cadillac, Fleetwood 60 Special four-door hardtop, (AA)

SERIES SIXTY SPECIAL FLEETWOOD — (V-8) —

The 60S Fleetwood long-deck four-door hardtop sedan featured a wide, ribbed bright metal fairing extending from the lower rear half of the door to the back bumper. A Fleetwood nameplate appeared on the rear deck lid, which also housed the back-up lamps on this car.

SERIES SIXTY SPECIAL FLEETWOOD

Model Number	Body/Style Number	Body Type & Seating	Factory Price	Shipping Weight	Production Total
57-60	6039	4-dr HT Sed-6P	5539	4755	24,000

1957 Cadillac, Eldorado Brougham four-door hardtop, (AA)

SERIES 70 ELDORADO BROUGHAM — (V-8) —

Announced in December of 1956 and released around March of 1957, the Eldorado Brougham was a hand-built, limited-edition four-door hardtop sedan derived from the Park Avenue and Orleans show cars of 1953-1954. Designed by Ed Glowacke, the Brougham featured America's first completely pillarless four-door body styling. Even ventipanes were absent. The Brougham was further distinguished by a brushed stainless steel roof, the first appearance of quad headlights and totally unique trim. The exterior ornamentation included wide, ribbed lower rear quarter beauty panels (extending along the full rocker sills) and a rectangular sculptured side body 'cove' highlighted with five horizontal windsplits on the rear doors. Tail styling treatments followed the Eldorado theme and 'suicide' type mounting was used for the rear doors. Standard equipment included all possible accessories such as a dual four-barrel V-8; air-suspension; low-profile tires with thin whitewalls; automatic trunk lid opener; automatic 'memory' seat; Cruise Control; high-pressure cooling system; polarized sun visors; Signal-Seeking twin speaker radio; electric antenna; automatic-release parking brake; electric door locks; dual heating system; silver magnetized glovebox; drink tumblers; cigarette and tissue dispensers; lipstick and cologne; ladies' compact with powder puff, mirror and matching leather notebook, comb and mirror; Arpege atomizer with Lanvin perfume; automatic starter (with restart function); Autronic-Eye; drum-type electric clock; power windows; forged aluminum wheels and air conditioning. Buyers of Broughams had a choice of 44 full leather interior trim combinations and could select such items as Mouton, Karakul or lambskin carpeting.

SERIES 70 ELDORADO BROUGHAM

Model Number	Body/Style Number	Body Type & Seating	Factory Price	Shipping Weight	Production Total
57-70	7059X	4-dr HT Sed-6P	13,074	5315	400

SERIES 75 FLEETWOOD — (V-8) —

Long wheelbase Cadillacs came in Fleetwood limousine or nine-passenger sedan configurations, both with auxiliary seats. Side trim was the same as on Series 62 models, except that no Cadillac crest was used on the rear fins.

SERIES 75 FLEETWOOD

Model Number	Body/Style Number	Body Type & Seating	Factory Price	Shipping Weight	Production Total
57-75	7523X	4-dr Sed-9P	7348	5340	1,010
57-75	7533X	4-dr Imp Sed-9P	7586	5390	890
57-86	8680S	Commercial chassis	—	—	2,169

NOTE: The commercial chassis featured a 156-inch wheelbase and was provided to professional carmakers for construction of funeral cars and ambulances, etc.

ENGINES: V-8. Overhead valve. Cast iron block. Displacement: 365 cid. Bore and stroke: 4.00 x 3.625 inches. Compression ratio: 10.0:1. Brake hp: 300 at 4800 rpm. Five main bearings. Hydraulic valve lifters. Carburetor: Rochester four-barrel Model 7015701.

ELDORADO V-8: Overhead valve. Cast iron block. Displacement: 365 cid. Bore and stroke: 4.00 x 3.625. Compression ratio: 10.0:1. Brake hp: 325 at 4800 rpm. Five main bearings. Hydraulic valve lifters. Carburetors: Two Carter four-barrel (front) Model 2584S; (rear) Model 2583S.

CHASSIS FEATURES: Wheelbase: (Series 62) 129.5 inches; (Series 60S) 133 inches; (Series 70)126 inches; (Series 75) 149.7 inches. Overall length: (Series 62 sedans) 215.9 inches; (Series 62 coupes and convertibles) 220.9 inches; (Series 62 Eldorado) 222.1 inches; (Series 60S) 224.4 inches; (Series 70) 216.3 inches; (Series 75) 236.2 inches. Front and rear tread: (All models) 61 inches. Tires: (Series 75) 8.20 x 15 six-ply blackwall; (Series 62 Eldorado) 8.20 x 15 whitewall; (Series 70) 8.40 x 15 high-speed type; (Other models) 8.00 x 15 blackwall. Standard dual exhaust.

POWERTRAIN OPTIONS: The 325-hp Eldorado Brougham dual four-barrel V-8 was optional on the Eldorado Seville and Biarritz only. In normal attachments on these models the front carburetor was changed to a Carter four-barrel Model 258S. When air conditioning was also installed the front carburetor was the same model used in the Brougham, which came standard with air conditioning.

CONVENIENCE ACCESSORIES: Hydra-Matic drive, power steering and power brakes were standard in all Cadillacs. Many models (designated by non-bracketed 'X' suffix in charts above) also had standard power window lifts. Fore-and-Aft power seats were standard on the same models. Six-Way power seats were regularly featured on Eldorados and Sixty Specials. Air conditioning, radios, heaters, etc., were optional on most other models (standard in Brougham) along with regular GM factory- and dealer-installed extras.

HISTORICAL FOOTNOTES: The 1957 Eldorado Brougham was designed to compete with the Lincoln-Continental Mark II. The new dual quad headlamps seen on the Brougham were illegal in some states during 1957. The Brougham air suspension system proved unreliable and Cadillac later released a kit to convert cars to rear coil spring-type suspension. This makes Broughams with the feature rarer and more valuable today. The Brougham is a certified Milestone Car. Series 62 sedans were short-deck models with trunks five inches shorter than 60S sedans. Ball joint suspension was a new technical feature adopted this year. Model year sales amounted to 146,841 deliveries earning Cadillac Division ninth industry ranking for two years in-a-row. James M. Roche was appointed general manager of Cadillac January 1, 1957.

1958 CADILLAC

1958 Cadillac, Series 62 Sedan DeVille four-door hardtop, (AA)

SERIES 62 — (V-8) — Cadillacs for 1958 were basically carryover models with a face lift on all but the Brougham. There was a new grille featuring multiple round 'cleats' at the intersection of horizontal and vertical members. The grille insert was wider and the bumper guards were positioned lower to the parking lamps. New dual headlamps were seen throughout all lines and small chrome fins decorated front fenders. Tailfins were less pronounced and trim attachments were revised. The word Cadillac appeared, in block letters, on the fins of Series 62 base models. On the sides of the cars there were five longer horizontal windsplits ahead of the unskirted rear wheel housings; front fender horizontal moldings with crests placed above at the trailing edge and no rocker sill trim. The convertible, Coupe DeVille and Sedan DeVille used solid metal trim on the lower half of the conical projectile flares, while other models had a thin ridge molding in the same location. On Series 62 Eldorados, a V-shaped ornament and model identification script were mounted to the deck lid. The two luxury Cadillacs also had 10 vertical chevron slashes ahead of the open rear wheel housings and crest medallions on the flanks of tailfins. Broad, sculptured beauty panels decorated the lower rear quarters on Eldorados and extended around the wheel opening to stretch along the body sills. Standard equipment was the same as the previous year. All new was an extended deck Series 62 sedan, which was 8.5 inches longer than other models.

CADILLAC I.D. NUMBERS: Serial numbers now used a three symbol prefix. The first pair of numerical symbols '58' designated the 1958 model year. A one-letter alphabetical code (included as part of model number in charts below) indicated model and series. Each prefix was followed by the consecutive unit number, which started at 000001 and up. The serial number was located at the front of the left-hand frame side bar. Engine serial numbers again matched and were found on the center left-hand side of the block above the oil pan.

SERIES 62

Model Number	Body/Style Number	Body Type & Seating	Factory Price	Shipping Weight	Production Total
58K-82	6239(X)	4-dr HT Sed-6P	4891	4675	13,335
58K-62	6239(X)	4-dr Exp Sed-6P	4891	4675	204
58N-62	6239E(X)	4-dr Ext Sed-6P	5079	4770	20,952
58L-62	6239EDX	4-dr Sed DeV-6P	5497	4855	23,989
58G-62	6237(X)	2-dr HT Cpe-6P	4784	4630	18,736
58J-62	6237DX	2-dr Cpe DeV-6P	5231	4705	18,414
58F-62	6267X	2-dr Conv Cpe-6P	5454	4845	7,825
58-62	62	Chassis only	—	—	1

SERIES 62 ELDORADO SPECIAL

Model Number	Body/Style Number	Body Type & Seating	Factory Price	Shipping Weight	Production Total
58H-62	6237SDX	2-dr HT Cpe Sev-6P 7500		4910	855
58E-62	6267SX	2-dr Biarritz Conv-6P7500		5070	815
58-62	6267SSX	2-dr Spl Eldo Cpe-6P	—		1

NOTES: The export sedan was shipped in completely-knocked-down (CKD) form to foreign countries. The Special Eldorado Coupe was a special order model built in limited quantities. Five specially equipped Eldorado Biarritz convertibles were also built (see Historical Footnotes for details). The symbol 'X', in brackets after Body/Style Number, indicates power windows and seat optional; without brackets indicates these features are standard. Style Number 6239E(X) is the new Extended Deck Sedan (Listed above as 4-dr Ext Sed-6P).

SERIES SIXTY SPECIAL FLEETWOOD — (V-8) — The Sixty Special was distinctive and rich-looking this year. Broad ribbed stainless steel fairings decorated the entire rear quarter panel, below the conical flare. Even the fender skirts featured this type of trim, which extended fully forward along the body sills. Sixty Special script appeared on the sides of the tailfins and a Fleetwood script nameplate adorned the rear deck lid. Standard equipment included Hydra-Matic, power brakes, power steering, power windows and fore-and-aft power front seat.

SERIES SIXTY SPECIAL FLEETWOOD

Model Number	Body/Style Number	Body Type & Seating	Factory Price	Shipping Weight	Production Total
58M-60	6039X	4-dr HT Sed-6P	6232	4930	12,900

SERIES 70 FLEETWOOD ELDORADO BROUGHAM — (V-8) — The major change for the Eldorado Brougham was seen inside the car. The interior upper door panels were now finished in leather instead of the metal finish used in 1957. New wheel covers also appeared. Forty-four trim combinations were available, along with 15 special monotone paint colors. This was the last year for domestic production of the handbuilt Brougham at Cadillac's Detroit factory, as future manufacturing of the special bodies was transferred to Pininfarina of Turin, Italy.

SERIES 70 FLEETWOOD ELDORADO BROUGHAM

Model Number	Body/Style Number	Body Type & Seating	Factory Price	Shipping Weight	Production Total
58P-70	7059X	4-dr HT Sed-6P	13,074	5315	304

1958 Cadillac, Fleetwood 75 Imperial four-door limousine, (AA)

SERIES 75 FLEETWOOD — (V-8) — The limousine or nine-passenger long wheelbase sedans were available once again, both with auxiliary seats and the same basic side trim as Series 62 models.

SERIES 75 FLEETWOOD

Model Number	Body/Style Number	Body Type & Seating	Factory Price	Shipping Weight	Production Total
58R-75	7523X	4-dr Sed-9P	8460	5360	802
58S-75	4533X	4-dr Imp Sed-9P	8675	5475	730
58-86	8680S	Commercial chassis	—	—	1,915

NOTE: The commercial chassis features a 156-inch wheelbase and was provided to professional carmakers for construction of funeral cars and ambulances, etc.

ENGINE: V-8. Overhead valve. Cast iron block. Displacement: 365 cid. Bore and stroke: 4.00 x 3.625 inches. Compression ratio: 10.25:1. Brake hp: 310 at 4800 rpm. Five main bearings. Hydraulic valve lifters. Carburetor: Carter AFB four-barrel Model 2862S.

1958 Cadillac, Series 62 Eldorado Biarritz two-door convertible, (AA)

ELDORADO V-8: Same general specifications as above except for following changes: Brake hp: 335 at 4800 rpm. Carburetors: Triple Rochester two-barrel Model 7015801.

CHASSIS FEATURES: Wheelbase: (Series 62) 129.5 inches; (Series 60S) 133 inches; (Series 70) 126 inches; (Series 75) 149.7 inches. Overall length: (58K) 216.8 inches; (58G, 58J and 58F) 221.8 inches; (58N and 58L) 225.3 inches; (58M) 225.3 inches; (58H and 58E) 223.4 inches; (58R and 58S) 237.1 inches. Front and rear tread: (All models) 81 inches. Tires: (Series75) 8.20 x 15 six-ply blackwall; (Series 62 Eldorado) 6.20 x 15 whitewall; (Series 70) 8.40 x 15 high-speed thin whitewall; (Other models) 8.00 x 15 blackwall.

POWERTRAIN OPTIONS: The 335-hp Eldorado engine with triple two-barrel carburetion was used on all Eldorados as standard equipment. This engine was also optional for all other Cadillacs.

1958 Cadillac, Fleetwood 60 Special four-door hardtop, (AA)

CONVENIENCE ACCESSORIES: Radio with antenna and rear speaker ($164). Radio with rear speaker and remote control on Series 75 only ($246). Automatic heating system for Series 75 ($179); for other models ($129). Posture seat adjuster ($81). Six-Way seat adjuster ($103). Power window regulators ($108). E-Z-Eye Glass ($46). Fog lamps ($41). Automatic headlamp beam control ($48). Five sabre spoke wheels ($350). White sidewall 8.20 x 15 four-ply tires ($55). Gold finish grille on Eldorado (no charge); on other models ($27). Four-door door guards ($7). Two-door door guards ($4). Remote control trunk lock ($43). License plate frame ($8). Air conditioning ($474). Series 75 air conditioner ($625). Eldorado engine in lower models ($134). Air suspension ($214). Electric door locks on coupes ($35); on sedans ($57). Local dealer options: Utility kit ($15). Monogram ($12). Blue Coral waxing ($25). Undercoating ($5). Lubrication agreement ($34).

HISTORICAL FOOTNOTES: Five special Eldorado Biarritz convertibles were built with completely automatic top riser mechanisms and metal tonneaus and incorporated humidity sensors, which activated the top riser mechanism in case of rain. These cars had four-place bucket seating and custom leather interior trims including driveshaft tunnel coverings. The 1958 Eldorado Brougham is a certified Milestone Car.

1959 CADILLAC

SERIES 6200 — (V-8) — No single automotive design better characterizes the industry's late-1950s flamboyance than the 1959 Cadillac, which incorporated totally new styling. Large tailfins, twin bullet taillamps, two distinctive rooflines and roof pillar configurations, new jewel-like grille patterns and matching deck latch lid beauty panels personified these cars. The former 62 line was now commonly called the 6200 series and was actually comprised of three sub-series, all with similar wheelbases and lengths. Each will be treated individually here. The five base models were identifiable by their straight body rub moldings, running from front wheel openings to back bumpers, with crest medallions below the tip of the spear. A one-deck jeweled rear grille insert was seen. Standard equipment included power brakes; power steering; automatic transmission; dual back-up lamps; windshield washers and two-speed wipers; wheel discs; outside rearview mirror; vanity mirror and oil filter. The convertible also had power windows and a two-way power seat. Plain fender skirts covered rear wheels and sedans were available in four-window and se-

dans were available in four-window (4W) and six-window (6W) configurations.

CADILLAC I.D. NUMBERS: The engine serial number system adopted in 1958 was used again with numbers in the same locations. The first pair of symbols changed to '59' to designate the 1959 model year. The third symbol (a letter listed as a Body/Style Number suffix in charts below) identified model and series. Consecutive unit numbers began at 000001 and up.

SERIES 6200

Model Number	Body/Style Number	Body Type & Seating	Factory Price	Shipping Weight	Production Total
59-62	6229K	4-dr 6W Sed-6P	5080	4835	23,461
59-62	6229K	4-dr Exp 6W Sed-6P	5080	4835	60
59-62	6239A	4-dr 4W Sed-6P	5080	4770	14,138
59-62	6237G	2-dr HT Cpe-6P	4892	4690	21,947
59-62	6267F	2-dr Conv Cpe-6P	5455	4855	11,130

NOTE: The export sedan was shipped in completely-knocked-down (CKD) form to foreign countries and is indicated by the abbreviation 4-dr Exp 6W Sed.

DEVILLE SUB-SERIES 6300 — (V-8) — The DeVille models, two sedans and a coupe, had script nameplates on the rear fenders, thus eliminating the use of the front fendercrest medallions. They were trimmed like 6200s otherwise. The DeVilles also had all of the same standard equipment listed for 6200s, plus power windows and two-way power seats.

DEVILLE SUB-SERIES 6300

Model Number	Body/Style Number	Body Type & Seating	Factory Price	Shipping Weight	Production Total
59-63	6329L	4-dr 6W Sed-6P	5498	4850	19,158
59-63	6339B	4-dr 4W Sed-6P	5498	4825	12,308
59-63	6337J	2-dr Cpe-6P	5252	4720	21,924

1959 Cadillac, Series 62 six-window, four-door hardtop sedan, (AA)

SERIES 6200 AND 6300 ENGINE

V-8: Overhead valve. Cast iron block. Displacement: 390 cid. Bore and stroke: 4.00 x 3.875 inches. Compression ratio: 10.5:1. Brake hp: 325 at 4800 rpm. Five main bearings. Hydraulic valve lifters. Carburetor: Carter AFB four-barrel Model 2814S.

1959 Cadillac, Series 64 Eldorado Biarritz two-door convertible, (AA)

SUB-SERIES 6400/6900 ELDORADO/BROUGHAM — (V-8) — As if to cause confusion, the 6400 Eldorado sub-series included two 6400 models, the Seville and Biarritz, and one 6900 model, the Brougham. All were characterized by a three-deck, jeweled, rear grille insert, but other trim and equipment features varied. The Seville and Biarritz had the Eldorado model name spelled out behind the front wheel opening and featured broad, full-length body sill highlights that curved over the rear fender profile and back along the upper beltline region. Standard equipment included all items found on DeVilles plus, heater; fog lamps; 345-hp V-8; remote control deck lid; radio with antenna and rear speaker; power vent windows; six-way power seat; air suspension; electric door locks and license frames. The Brougham was now incorporated into the line as an Italian-bodied, limited production car. A vertical crest medallion with Brougham script plate appeared on the front fenders and a single, thin molding ran from front to rear along the mid-sides of the body. Styling on this car was not as radical as in the past and predicted the 1960 themes used on other Cadillacs. The standard equipment list was pared down to match those of other Eldorados, plus Cruise Control, Autronic Eye, air conditioning and E-Z-Eye glass.

1959 Cadillac, Eldorado Brougham four-door hardtop (hand-built by Pininfarina of Turin, Italy), (AA)

SUB-SERIES 6400/6900 ELDORADO/BROUGHAM

Model Number	Body/Style Number	Body Type & Seating	Factory Price	Shipping Weight	Production Total
59-64	6437H	2-dr Sev HT-6P	7401	4855	975
59-64	6467E	2-dr Biarritz Conv-6P	7401	5060	1,320
59-69	6929P	4-dr Brougham HT-6P	13,075	—	99

SERIES SIXTY SPECIAL FLEETWOOD — (V-8) — On this line Fleetwood lettering was used on the front fenders and on the trim strip crossing the bottom of the deck lid. A rear facing, bullet-shaped, scoop-like convex panel was used on the rear doors and fenders and was trimmed by a similarly shaped body rub molding that extended to the front wheel well, at the bottom, and to the headlamps, at the top. Pillared, six-window styling was seen and a three-deck jeweled rear grille was featured. The rear wheels were skirted and wheelbase was now identical to all but the 'Seventy-Five' models. The standard equipment list included all 6200 and 6300 features plus power vent windows and dual outside mirrors.

SERIES SIXTY SPECIAL FLEETWOOD

Model Number	Body/Style Number	Body Type & Seating	Factory Price	Shipping Weight	Production Total
59-60	6029M	4-dr HT Sed-6P	6233	4890	2,250

SERIES 6700 FLEETWOOD 75 — (V-8) — The long wheelbase Fleetwoods were still called Seventy-Fives, although a new numerical series designation was in official use. Production models again were a nine-passenger sedan and Imperial sedan/limousine with auxiliary jump seats. Fleetwood lettering appeared on the rear deck lid trim strip. Single side trim moldings extended from the front wheel housing to the rear of the car. Standard equipment included all items found on the Sixty Special Fleetwood line.

1959 Cadillac, Series 6700 Fleetwood 75 nine-passenger sedan

SERIES 6700 FLEETWOOD 75

Model Number	Body/Style Number	Body Type & Seating	Factory Price	Shipping Weight	Production Total
59-67	6723R	4-dr Sed-9P	9533	5490	710
59-67	6733S	4-dr Imp Sed-9P	9748	5570	690
59-68	6890	Commercial chassis	—	—	2,102

NOTE: The commercial chassis featured a 156-inch wheelbase and was provided to professional carmakers for construction of funeral cars and ambulances, etc.

SERIES 6400/6900 ELDORADO/BROUGHAM ENGINE

V-8: Overhead valve. Cast iron block. Displacement: 390 cid. Bore and stroke: 4.00 x 3.875 inches. Compression ratio: 10.5:1. Brake hp: 345 at 4800 rpm. Five main bearings. Hydraulic valve lifters. Carburetor: Triple Rochester two-barrel Model 7015901.

CHASSIS FEATURES: Wheelbase: (Series 75) 149.75 inches; (All others) 130 inches. Overall length: (Series 75) 244.8 inches; (All others) 225 inches. Tires: (Eldorado and Series 75) 8.20 x 15; (All others) 8.00 x 15. Dual exhaust standard. Rear axle ratios: (Series 75) 3.36:1 standard; 3.77:1 optional; 3.21:1 with air conditioning; (All others) 2.94:1 standard; 3.21:1 optional or mandatory with air conditioning.

POWERTRAIN OPTIONS: The 345-hp Eldorado V-8 was optional on all other Cadillacs at $134.30 extra.

CONVENIENCE OPTIONS: Radio with rear speaker ($165). Radio with rear speaker and remote control ($247). Automatic heating system on Series 75 ($179); on other models ($129). Six-Way power seat on 6200s, except convertible ($188). Six-Way power seat on 6300-6400 and 6200 convertible ($89). Power window regulators ($73). Power vent regulators ($73). Air conditioning, on Series 75 ($624); on other models ($474). Air suspension ($215). Autronic Eye ($55). Cruise Control ($97). Electric door locks on two-doors ($46); on four-doors ($70). E-Z-Eye glass ($52). Fog lamps ($46). White sidewall tires 8.20 x 15 four-ply ($57 exchange), 8.20 x 15 six-ply ($65 exchange). Door guards on four-doors ($7); on two-doors ($4). Remote control trunk lock ($59). License plate frame ($8). Local options: Utility kit ($15); Monogram ($12). Acrylic Lustre finish ($20). Undercoating ($25). Radio foot switch ($10). Gas cap lock ($4). Pair of rugs for front ($8); for rear ($5). Note: Bucket seats were a no-cost option on the Biarritz convertible.

HISTORICAL FOOTNOTES: Assembly of 142,272 units was counted for the 1959 model year. This was the next to last season for selling the Brougham. Flat-top roof styling was used on four-window sedans; six-window models had sloping rooflines with rear ventipanes. Power steering and shock absorbers were improved this year.

1960 CADILLAC

SERIES 6200 — (V-8) — The 1960 Cadillacs exhibited a smoother, more subtle rendition of the styling theme introduced one year earlier. General changes included a full-width grille; the elimination of pointed front bumper guards; increased restraint in the application of chrome trim; lower tailfins with oval shaped nacelles (which enclosed stacked taillights and back-up lamps) and front fender mounted directional indicator lamps. Series 6200 base models had plain fender skirts, thin three-quarter length bodyside spears and Cadillac crests and lettering on short horizontal front fender bars mounted just behind the headlights. Four-window (4W) and six-window (6W) sedans were offered again. The former featured a one-piece wraparound backlight and flat-top roof, while the latter had a sloping rear window and roofline. Standard equipment on 6200 models included power brakes; power steering; automatic transmission; dual back-up lamps; windshield washers and dual speed wipers; wheel discs; outside rearview mirror; and oil filter. Added extras on convertibles included power windows and two-way power seats. Technical highlights were comprised of finned rear drums, a vacuum-operated automatic-releasing floor controlled parking brake and tubular X-frame construction. Interiors were done in Fawn, Blue or Gray Cortina Cord or Turquoise, Green, Persian Sand or Black Caspian cloth with Florentine vinyl bolsters. Convertibles were upholstered in Florentine leather single or two-tone combinations or monochromatic Cardiff leather combinations.

1960 Cadillac, Series 62 two-door convertible, (AA)

CADILLAC I.D. NUMBERS: Engine serial numbers took the same form used in 1959 with the first pair of symbols changed to '60' to indicate the 1960 model year. The applicable codes were stamped in the same locations on cars.

SERIES 6200

Model Number	Body/Style Number	Body Type & Seating	Factory Price	Shipping Weight	Production Total
60-62K	6229K	4-dr 6W Sed-6P	5080	4805	26,824
60-62K	6229K	4-dr Exp 6W Sed-6P	5080	4805	36
60-62A	6239A	4-dr 4W Sed-6P	5080	4775	9,984
60-62G	6237G	2-dr HT Cpe-6P	4892	4670	19,978
60-62F	6267F	2-dr Conv-6P	5455	4850	14,000
60-62( )	62	Chassis only	—	—	2

NOTE: The export (Exp) six-window sedan was shipped in completely-knocked-down (CKD) form to foreign countries. All sedans were pillarless hardtop sedans.

DEVILLE SUB-SERIES 6300 — (V-8) — Models in the DeVille sub-series were trimmed much like 6200s, but there was no bar medallion on the front fenders and special script nameplates appeared on the rear fenders. Standard equipment included all base model features, plus power windows and two-way power seat. Interiors were done in Chadwick cloth or optional Cambray cloth and leather combinations.

DEVILLE SUB-SERIES 6300

Model Number	Body/Style Number	Body Type & Seating	Factory Price	Shipping Weight	Production Total
60-63L	6329L	4-dr 6W Sed-6P	5498	4835	22,579
60-63B	6339B	4-dr 4W Sed-6P	5498	4815	9,225
60-63J	6337J	2-dr HT Cpe-6P	5252	4705	21,585

NOTE: All DeVille sedans were pillarless hardtop sedans.

1960 Cadillac, Eldorado Seville two-door hardtop, (AA)

ELDORADO/BROUGHAM SUB-SERIES 6400/6900 — (V-8) — External variations on the Seville two-door hardtop and Biarritz convertible coupe took the form of bright body sill highlights that extended across the lower edge of fender skirts and Eldorado lettering on the sides of front fenders, just behind the headlamps. Standard equipment was the same as on 6300 models plus heater; fog lamps; Eldorado engine; remote control trunk lock; radio with antenna and rear speaker; power vent windows; six-way power seat; air suspension; electric door locks; license frames; and five whitewall tires. A textured vinyl fabric top was offered on the Eldorado Seville and interior trim choices included cloth and leather combinations. The Brougham continued as an Italian-bodied four-door hardtop with special Brougham nameplates above the grille. It did not sport Eldorado front fender letters or body sill highlights, but had a distinctive squared-off roofline with rear ventipanes—a prediction of 1961 styling motifs for the entire Cadillac line. A fin-like crease, or 'skeg,' ran from behind the front wheel opening to the rear of the car on the extreme lower bodysides and there were special vertical crest medallions on the trailing edge of rear fenders.

Cruise Control, a Guide-Matic headlight dimmer, air conditioning and E-Z-Eye glass were regular equipment.

1960 Cadillac, Eldorado Brougham four-door hardtop

ELDORADO/BROUGHAM SUB-SERIES 6400/6900

Model Number	Body/Style Number	Body Type & Seating	Factory Price	Shipping Weight	Production Total
60-64H	6437H	2-dr Sev HT Cpe-6P	7401	4855	1,075
60-64E	6467E	2-dr Biarritz Conv-6P	7401	5060	1,285
60-69P	6929P	4-dr Brougham-6P	13,075	—	101

SERIES SIXTY SPECIAL FLEETWOOD — (V-8) — The Sixty Special Fleetwood sedan had the same standard equipment as the 6200 convertible and all 6300 models. This car was outwardly distinguished by a Fleetwood script on the rear deck, nine vertical bright metal louvers on rear fenders, vertical crest medallions on front fenders and wide full-length bright metal sill underscores, which extended to the fender skirts and lower rear quarter panels.

SERIES SIXTY SPECIAL FLEETWOOD

Model Number	Body/Style Number	Body Type & Seating	Factory Price	Shipping Weight	Production Total
60-60M	6029M	4-dr HT Sed-6P	6233	4880	11,800

SERIES 6700 FLEETWOOD SEVENTY-FIVE — (V-8) — The long wheelbase sedan and limousine had auxiliary jump seats, high-headroom formal six-window styling, broad ribbed roof edge beauty panels and trim generally similar to 6200 Cadillacs in other regards. The limousine passenger compartment was trimmed in either Bradford cloth or Bedford cloth, both in combinations with wool. Florentine leather upholstery was used in the chauffeur's compartment.

SERIES 6700 FLEETWOOD SEVENTY-FIVE

Model Number	Body/Style Number	Body Type & Seating	Factory Price	Shipping Weight	Production Total
60-67R	6723R	4-dr Sed-9P	9533	5475	718
60-67S	6733S	4-dr Limo-9P	9748	5560	832
60-68	6890	Commercial chassis	—	—	2,160

NOTE: The commercial chassis featured a 156-inch wheelbase and was provided to professional carmakers for construction of funeral cars and ambulances, etc.

ENGINES: V-8. Overhead valve. Cast iron block. Displacement: 390 cid. Bore and stroke: 4.00 x 3.875 inches. Compression ratio: 10.5:1. Brake hp: 325 at 4800 rpm. Five main bearings. Hydraulic valve lifters. Carburetor: Carter two-barrel Model 2814S.

ELDORADO/BROUGHAM ENGINE: V-8. Overhead valve. Cast iron block. Displacement: 390 cid. Bore and stroke: 4.00 x 3.875 inches. Compression ratio: 10.5:1. Brake hp: 345 at 4800 rpm. Five main bearings. Hydraulic valve lifters. Carburetor: Triple Rochester two-barrel Model 7015901.

CHASSIS FEATURES: Wheelbase: (Series 75) 149.75 inches; (All others) 130 inches. Overall length: (Series 75) 244.8 inches; (All others) 225 inches. Tires: (Eldorado and Series 75) 8.20 x 15; (All others) 8.00 x 15. Dual exhaust standard. Rear axle ratios: (Series 75) 3.36:1 standard; 3.77:1 optional; 3.21:1 with air conditioning; (All others) 2.94:1 standard; 3.21:1 optional or mandatory with air conditioning.

POWERTRAIN OPTIONS: The 345-hp Eldorado V-8 with three two-barrel carburetors was $134.40 extra when installed in any Cadillac model.

CONVENIENCE OPTIONS: Air conditioning on Series 62 or 60 ($474); on Series 75 ($624). Air suspension on non-Eldorados ($215); standard on Eldorado Autronic Eye ($46). Cruise Control ($97). Door guards on two-door ($4); on four-door ($7). Electric door locks on two-door ($46); on four-door ($70); standard on Eldorado. E-Z-Eye glass ($52). Fog lamps ($43). Automatic heating system on Series 62 or 60 ($129); on Series 75 ($279). License plate frame ($6). Six-Way power seat ($85-$113) depending on style number. Power window regulators

($118). Power vent windows ($73). Radio with rear speaker ($165); with rear speaker and remote control ($247). Remote control trunk lock ($59). White sidewall tires, size 8.20 x 15 four-ply ($57 exchange); size 8.20 x 15 six-ply ($64). Antifreeze -20 degrees ($8); -40 degrees ($9). Accessory Group 'A' included whitewalls, heater, radio and E-Z-Eye glass for $402 extra and air suspension, Cruise Control and Eldorado engine at regular prices. Accessory Group 'B' included air conditioner, whitewalls, heater, radio and E-Z-Eye glass at $876 extra and six-way power seat, power vent windows and power windows at regular prices. Gas and oil delivery charge was $7 and district warehousing and handling charges averaged $15. Note: Eldorado standard equipment features specified above are those not previously mentioned in text. Consult both sources for complete list.

HISTORICAL FOOTNOTES: *Car Life* magazine selected the 1960 Cadillac as its "Best buy in the luxury field." This was the last year for air suspension and for wraparound windshields, except on the Series 75 Fleetwood models. According to contemporary road tests, gas economy ratings for 1960 Cadillacs were approximately 14 miles per gallon at a steady 60 mph.

1961 CADILLAC

SERIES 6200 — (V-8) — Cadillacs were restyled and re-engineered for 1961. The new grille slanted back towards both the bumper and the hood lip, along the horizontal plane, and sat between dual headlamps. New forward slanting front roof pillars with non-wraparound windshield glass were seen. The revised backlight treatment had crisp, angular lines with thin pillars on some models and heavier, semi-blind-quarter roof posts on others. A new short-deck sedan was situated in the 6300 lineup. It was ostensibly created for rich San Francisco dowagers with small parking stalls in their luxury apartment houses. The DeVille models were retained as the 6300 sub-series (which was technically part of the Sixty-Two line), but the Eldorado Seville and Brougham were dropped. This moved the Eldorado Biarritz convertible into the DeVille sub-series. Standard equipment on base 6200 models included power brakes; power steering; automatic transmission; dual back-up lights; windshield washer and dual speed wipers; wheel discs; plain fender skirts; outside rearview mirror; vanity mirror; and oil filter. Rubberized front and rear coil springs replaced the trouble-prone air suspension system. Wheelbases were decreased on most models. Four-barrel induction systems were now the sole power choice and dual exhaust were no longer available. Series designation trim appeared on the front fenders.

1961 Cadillac, Series 62 two-door convertible, (AA)

CADILLAC I.D. NUMBERS: Engine serial numbers took the same form used in 1960 with the first pair of symbols changed to '61' to indicate the 1961 model year. Applicable codes were stamped in the same locations on the cars. The alphabetical code 'C' identified the new Series 6300 short-deck sedan.

SERIES 6200

Model Number	Body/Style Number	Body Type & Seating	Factory Price	Shipping Weight	Production Total
61-62A	6239A	4-dr 4W Sed-6P	5080	4660	4,700
61-62K	6229K	4-dr 6W Sed-6P	5080	4680	26,216
61-62G	6237G	2-dr HT Cpe-6P	5892	4560	16,005
61-62F	6267F	2-dr Conv-6P	5455	4720	15,500

NOTE: All 6200 sedans were pillarless hardtop sedans.

1961 Cadillac, Series 62 DeVille two-door hardtop

SERIES 62 DEVILLE 6300 SUB-SERIES — (V-8) — DeVille models featured front fender series designation scripts and a lower body 'skeg' trimmed with a thin three-quarter length spear molding running from behind the front wheel opening to the rear of the car. Standard equipment was the same used on 6200 models plus two-way power seat and power windows. The Biarritz convertible also had power vent windows, whitewall tires, six-way power bench seat (or bucket seats) and remote control trunk lock. The new short-deck four-door hardtop appeared in mid-season and is often referred to as the Town Sedan.

SERIES 62 DEVILLE 6300 SUB-SERIES

Model Number	Body/Style Number	Body Type & Seating	Factory Price	Shipping Weight	Production Total
61-63B	6339B	4-dr 4W Sed-6P	5498	4715	4,847
61-63L	6329L	4-dr 6W Sed-6P	5498	4710	26,415
61-63C	6399C	4-dr Twn Sed-6P	5498	4670	3,756
61-63J	6337J	2-dr HT Cpe-6P	5252	4595	20,156

SERIES 62 ELDORADO 6300 MODEL

Model Number	Body/Style Number	Body Type & Seating	Factory Price	Shipping Weight	Production Total
61-63E	6367E	2-dr Biarritz Conv-6P	6477	4805	1,450

NOTE: The Style Number 6399C Town Sedan was the short-deck four-window pillarless hardtop sedan introduced at midyear. The Style Number 6337J was the Coupe DeVille. All 6300 sedans were pillarless hardtop sedans.

1961 Cadillac, Fleetwood 60 Special four-door hardtop, (AA)

SERIES SIXTY SPECIAL FLEETWOOD — (V-8) — The Sixty Special Fleetwood sedan featured semi-blind-quarter four-door hardtop styling with an angular roofline that approximated a raised convertible top. Six chevron slashes appeared on the rear fender sides at the trailing edge. A model nameplate was seen on the front fender. Standard equipment was the same as used on 6300 models including power seats and windows.

SERIES SIXTY SPECIAL FLEETWOOD

Model Number	Body/Style Number	Body Type & Seating	Factory Price	Shipping Weight	Production Total
61-60M	6039M	4-dr HT Sed-6P	6233	4770	15,500

SERIES 6700 FLEETWOOD 75 — (V-8) — The limousine and big sedan for 1961 sported the all-new styling motifs. Standard equipment was the same as used on 6300 models including power seats and windows.

SERIES 6700 FLEETWOOD 75

Model Number	Body/Style Number	Body Type & Seating	Factory Price	Shipping Weight	Production Total
61-67R	6723R	4-dr Sed-9P	9533	5390	699
61-67S	6733S	4-dr Imp Sed-9P	9748	5420	926
61-68	6890	Commercial chassis —	—	—	2,204

NOTE: The commercial chassis featured a 156-inch wheelbase and was provided to professional carmakers for construction of funeral vehicles and ambulances, etc. Series 6700 sedans were full-pillared models with six-window styling. A high-headroom roofline was used on these models.

ENGINE: V-8. Overhead valve. Cast iron block. Displacement: 390 cid. Bore and stroke: 4 x 3-7/8 inches. Compression ratio: 10.5:1. Brake hp: 325 at 4800 rpm. Five main bearings.

Hydraulic valve lifters. Carburetor: Rochester four-barrel Model 701930.

CHASSIS FEATURES: Wheelbase: (Series 75) 149.8 inches; (All others) 129.5 inches. Overall length: (Series 75) 242.3 inches; (Town Sedan) 215 inches; (All others) 222 inches. Single exhaust only. Tires: (Eldorado and Series 75) 8.20 x 15; (All others) 8.00 x 15.

POWERTRAIN OPTIONS: None available.

CONVENIENCE OPTIONS: Air conditioning Series 62 or 60 ($474); Series 75 ($624). Autronic Eye ($46). Cruise Control ($97). Door guards on two-door ($4); on four-door ($7). Electric door locks on two-door ($46); on four-door ($70). E-Z-Eye glass ($52). Pair of fog lamps ($43). Automatic heating system on Series 62 or 60 ($129); on Series 75 ($179). License plate frame ($6). Six-Way power seat ($85-$113). Power windows ($85). Power vent windows ($73). Radio with rear speaker ($16); with remote control ($247). Remote control trunk lock ($59). Five white sidewall tires size 8.20 x 15 four-ply ($58 exchange) standard on Eldorado, size 8.20 x 15 six-ply for Series 75 ($64 exchange). Permanent anti-freeze -20 degrees ($8); -40 degrees ($9). Accessory groups A and B included mostly the same features as 1960 at the combined total of individual prices listed above.

HISTORICAL FOOTNOTES: Total model year output for 1961 amounted to 138,379 units. A limited slip differential was optional at $53.70.

1962 CADILLAC

SERIES 62 — (V-8) — A mild face lift characterized Cadillac styling trends for 1962. A flatter grille with a thicker horizontal center bar and more delicate cross-hatched insert appeared. Ribbed chrome trim panels, seen ahead of the front wheel housings in 1961, were now replaced with cornering lamps and front fender model and series identification badges were eliminated. More massive front bumper end pieces appeared and housed rectangular parking lamps. At the rear, taillamps were now housed in vertical nacelles designed with an angled peak at the center. On Series 6200 models a vertically ribbed rear beauty panel appeared on the deck lid latch panel. Cadillac script also appeared on the lower left side of the radiator grille. The short-deck Town Sedan was switched to the base 6200 lineup, while a similar model was still part of the DeVille sub-series. Standard equipment on 6200 models included power brakes; power steering; automatic transmission; dual back-up lamps; windshield washer and dual speed wipers; wheel discs; fender skirts; remote control outside rearview mirror; left vanity mirror; oil filter; five tubeless blackwall tires; heater and defroster and front cornering lamps.

1962 Cadillac, Series 62 six-window four-door hardtop, (AA)

CADILLAC I.D. NUMBERS: Engine serial numbers took the same form used in 1961 with the first pair of symbols changed to '62' to indicate the 1962 model year. Applicable codes were stamped in the same locations on the cars. The alphabetical code 'C' now identified the Town Sedan in the 6200 series, while the code 'D' was adopted to identify the similar short-deck DeVille sedan added to the lineup this year.

SERIES 6200

Model Number	Body/Style Number	Body Type & Seating	Factory Price	Shipping Weight	Production Total
62-62A	6239A	4-dr 4W Sed-6P	5213	4645	17,314
62-62K	6229K	4-dr 6W Sed-6P	5213	4640	16,730
62-62C	6289C	4-dr Twn Sed-6P	5213	4590	2,600
62-62G	6237G	2-dr HT Cpe-6P	5025	4530	16,833
62-62F	6268F	2-dr Conv-6P	5588	4630	16,800

NOTE: All 6200 sedans were pillarless four-door hardtops. The Town Sedan was of four-window design.

1962 Cadillac, Series 62 two-door convertible

1962 Cadillac, Series 62 Coupe DeVille two-door hardtop, (AA)

SERIES 62 DEVILLE 6300 SUB-SERIES — (V-8) — The DeVille lineup was much more of a separate series this year and some historical sources list it as such. Others list it as a 6200 sub-series. The latter system is utilized here. The new model for 1962 was a variation of Town Sedan, introduced the previous season, with a new Style Number and name. It was now Body Style 6389D and referred to as the Park Avenue four-window sedan. DeVilles were trimmed similar to base 6200 models. They had all of the same standard equipment, plus two-way power seat and power windows. The Style Number 6367E Biarritz convertible also featured power vent windows, white sidewall tires and a six-way power bench seat. Buyers could substitute bucket seats, in place of the last item, at no cost.

SERIES 6200 DEVILLE 6300 SUB-SERIES

Model Number	Body/Style Number	Body Type & Seating	Factory Price	Shipping Weight	Production Total
62-63B	6339B	4-dr 4W Sed-6P	5631	4675	27,378
62-63L	6329L	4-dr 6W Sed-6P	5631	4660	16,230
62-63D	6389D	4-dr Park Ave Sed-6P	5631	4655	2,600
62-63J	6347J	2-dr HT Cpe-6P	5385	4595	25,675

SERIES 62 ELDORADO 6300 MODEL

Model Number	Body/Style Number	Body Type & Seating	Factory Price	Shipping Weight	Production Total
62-63E	6367E	2-dr Biarritz Conv-6P	6610	4620	1,450

NOTES: The Park Avenue sedan was a short-deck DeVille sedan. The Style Number 6347J was the Coupe DeVille. All Sedan DeVilles were pillarless hardtop sedans.

SERIES SIXTY SPECIAL FLEETWOOD — (V-8) — The Sixty Special Fleetwood sedan stood apart in a crowd. It had chevron slash moldings on the rear roof pillar and a distinctly cross-hatched rear deck latch panel grille. Standard equipment comprised all features found on closed cars in the 6300 DeVille sub-series.

SERIES SIXTY SPECIAL FLEETWOOD

Model Number	Body/Style Number	Body Type & Seating	Factory Price	Shipping Weight	Production Total
62-60W	6039	4-dr HT Sed-6P	6366	4710	13,350

1962 Cadillac, Series 6700 Fleetwood 75 four-door limousine

SERIES 6700 FLEETWOOD 75 — (V-8) — The limousine and big sedan for 1962 sported the new styling motifs. Standard equipment was the same used on Sixty Special Fleetwoods. A distinctive high-headroom look was again seen.

SERIES 6700 FLEETWOOD 75

Model Number	Body/Style Number	Body Type & Seating	Factory Price	Shipping Weight	Production Total
62-67R	6723R	4-dr Sed-9P	9722	5325	696
62-67S	6733S	4-dr Limo-9P	9937	5390	904
62-68	8890	Commercial chassis	—	—	2,280

NOTE: The commercial chassis featured a 156-inch wheelbase and was provided to professional carmakers for construction of funeral cars and ambulances, etc. Series 6700 sedans and limousines were full-pillared models with six-window styling.

ENGINE: V-8. Overhead valve. Cast iron block. Displacement: 390 cid. Bore and stroke: 4.00 x 3.875 inches. Compression ratio: 10.5:1. Brake hp: 325 at 4800 rpm. Five main bearings. Hydraulic valve lifters. Carburetor: Carter two-barrel Model 2814S.

CHASSIS FEATURES: Wheelbase: (Series 75) 149.8 inches; (All others) 129.5 inches. Overall length: (Series 75) 242.3 inches; (Town Sedan) 215 inches; (All others) 222 inches. Single exhaust only. Tires: (Eldorado and Series 75) 8.20 x 15; (All others) 8.00 x 15. (Note: The Park Avenue sedan had the same wheelbase and length as the 1961 Town Sedan.)

CONVENIENCE OPTIONS: Air conditioning on Series 62 or 60 ($474); on Series 75 ($624). Air suspension on non-Eldorados ($215); standard on Eldorado. Autronic Eye ($46). Cruise Control ($97). Door guards on two-door ($4); on four-door ($7). Electric door locks on two-door ($46); on four-door ($70); standard on Eldorado. E-Z-Eye glass ($52). Fog lamps ($43). Automatic heating system on Series 62 or 60 ($129); on Series 75 ($279). License plate frame ($6). Six-Way power seat ($85-$113) depending on style number. Power window regulators ($118). Power vent windows ($73). Radio with rear speaker ($165); with rear speaker and remote control ($247). Remote control trunk lock ($59). White sidewall tires size 8.20 x 15 four-ply ($57 exchange); size 8.20 x 15 six-ply ($64). Antifreeze -20 degrees ($8); -40 degrees ($9). Accessory Group 'A' included whitewalls, heater, radio and E-Z-Eye glass for $402 extra and air suspension, cruise control and Eldorado engine at regular prices. Accessory Group 'B' included air conditioner, whitewalls, heater, radio and E-Z-Eye glass at $876 extra and six-way power seat, power vent windows and power windows at regular prices. Gas and oil delivery charge was $7 and district warehousing and handling charges averaged $15. Bucket seats were available for 6267F, 6339B, 6347J or 6389D as an option ($108).

HISTORICAL FOOTNOTES: This was the 60th anniversary year for Cadillac. The automaker produced 160,840 Cadillacs during the year, all equipped with the new dual-safety braking system and 59 percent sold with air conditioning.

1963 CADILLAC

SERIES 62 — (V-8) — In overall terms, 1963 Cadillacs were essentially the same as the previous models. Exterior chang-

es imparted a bolder and longer look. Hoods and deck lids were redesigned. The front fenders projected 4-5/8 inches further forward than in 1962, while the tailfins were trimmed down somewhat to provide a lower profile. Bodyside sculpturing was entirely eliminated. The slightly V-shaped radiator grille was taller and now incorporated outer extensions that swept below the flush-to-fender dual headlamps. Smaller, circular front parking lights were mounted in these extensions. A total of 143 options, including bucket seats with wool, leather or nylon upholstery fabrics and wood veneer facings on dash, doors and seatbacks, set an all-time record for interior appointment choices. Standard equipment for cars in the 62 series (6200 models) included power brakes; power steering; automatic transmission; dual back-up lamps; windshield washers; dual speed wipers; wheel discs; remote control outside rearview mirrors; left-hand vanity mirror; oil filter; five tubeless black tires; heater; defroster and cornering lights. Convertibles were equipped with additional features, also used on all 6300 models.

CADILLAC I.D. NUMBERS: Engine serial numbers took the same form used in 1962, with the first pair of symbols changed to '63' to indicate the 1963 model year. Applicable codes were stamped in the same locations on the cars. The alphabetical body identification code 'C' was no longer used, since the short-deck Town Sedan was dropped from the 62 Series. However, the short-deck 6300 model, called the Sedan DeVille Park Avenue, was retained and used the same 'D' body identification symbol. Rooflines on two-door hardtops were restyled, which brought a change in body style coding, but not in the alphabetical suffix.

SERIES 62 (6200 MODELS)

Model Number	Body/Style Number	Body Type & Seating	Factory Price	Shipping Weight	Production Total
63-62K	6229K	4-dr 6W Sed-6P	5214	4610	12,929
63-62G	6257G	2-dr Cpe-6P	5026	4505	16,786
63-62N	6239N	4-dr 4W Sed-6P	5214	4595	16,980
63-62F	6267F	2-dr Conv-6P	5590	4544	17,600
63-62	6200	Chassis only	—	—	3

NOTE: All 6200 series sedans are pillarless four-door hardtops.

1963 Cadillac, Eldorado Biarritz two-door convertible, (AA)

SERIES 62 — DEVILLE 6300 SUB-SERIES — (V-8) — This line reflected Series 62 styling revisions, but incorporated a DeVille signature script above the lower beltline molding, near the rear of the body. Standard features on DeVilles (and on base 6200 convertibles) were the same as on closed body 6200 models, plus two-way power seats and power windows. Model 6367E, the Eldorado Biarritz convertible, had special styling with untrimmed bodysides, full-length stainless steel underscores and a rectangular grid pattern rear decorative grille. Power vent windows, white sidewall tires and six-way power seats (in bench seat models) were standard in Eldorados.

1963 Cadillac, Series 62 Coupe DeVille two-door hardtop

SERIES 62 DEVILLE 6300 SUB-SERIES

Model Number	Body/Style Number	Body Type & Seating	Factory Price	Shipping Weight	Production Total
63-63L	6329L	4-dr 6W Sed-6P	5633	4650	15,146
63-63J	6357J	2-dr Cpe DeV-6P	5386	4520	31,749
63-63B	6339B	4-dr 4W Sed-6P	5633	4065	30,579
63-63D	6389D	4-dr Park Ave Sed-6P	5633	4590	1,575

SERIES 62 ELDORADO BIARRITZ 6300 MODEL

Model Number	Body/Style Number	Body Type & Seating	Factory Price	Shipping Weight	Production Total
63-63E	6367E	2-dr Spt Conv-6P	6609	4640	1,825

NOTES: The Park Avenue was a short-deck DeVille sedan. The Style Number 6357J was the Coupe DeVille. All Sedan DeVilles were pillaress four-door hardtops.

SERIES SIXTY SPECIAL FLEETWOOD — (V-8) — The Sixty Special Fleetwood sedan was, again, distinguished by chevron slashes of bright metal on the sides of the roof 'C' pillars. Also seen were full-length bright metal underscores, clean side styling, a rear end quadrant pattern grille and Cadillac crest medallions towards the back of the rear fenders. Standard equipment included all normal 6300 sub-series features, plus power ventipanes.

1963 Cadillac, Fleetwood 60 Special four-door hardtop, (AA)

SERIES SIXTY SPECIAL FLEETWOOD

Model Number	Body/Style Number	Body Type & Seating	Factory Price	Shipping Weight	Production Total
63-60M	6039M	4-dr HT Sed-6P	6366	4690	14,000

SERIES 6700 — FLEETWOOD 75 — (V-8) — Cadillac's extra-long nine-passenger cars were the only pillared four-door sedans in the line. Standard equipment was the same as on base 6300 models and Series 62 convertibles. Trimmings included a full-length lower beltline molding of a simple but elegant design. Convertible top-like rooflines and windshields with forward 'dog leg' style pillars were 1962 carryovers seen exclusively on this line.

SERIES 6700 FLEETWOOD 75

Model Number	Body/Style Number	Body Type & Seating	Factory Price	Shipping Weight	Production Total
63-67R	6723R	4-dr Sed-9P	9724	5240	680
63-67S	6733S	4-dr Limo-9P	9939	5300	795
63-68	6890	Commercial chassis	—	—	2,527

NOTE: The commercial chassis featured a 156-inch wheelbase and was provided to professional carmakers for construction of funeral cars, ambulances, etc.

ENGINE: V-8. Overhead valve. Cast iron block. Displacement: 390 cid. Bore and stroke: 4.00 x 3.875 inches. Compression ratio: 10.5:1. Brake hp: 325 at 4800 rpm. Five main bearings. Hydraulic valve lifters. Carburetor: Rochester four-barrel Model 710930.

NOTE: Although neither engine displacement nor output changed, the 1963 Cadillac V-8 was completely redesigned. Quieter, smoother and more efficient, the new engine was one-inch lower, four inches narrower and 1-1/4 inches shorter than the 1962 V-8. It was also some 82 pounds lighter, due to the use of aluminum accessory drives.

CHASSIS FEATURES: Wheelbase: (Series 75) 149.8 inches; (all other series) 129.5 inches. Overall length: (Series 75) 243.3 inches; (Park Ave) 215 inches; (all other models) 223 inches. Tires: (Series 75) 8.20 x 15; (all other series) 8.00 x 15. Rear axle ratio: (Series 75) 3.38:1; (all other series) 2.94:1.

CONVENIENCE OPTIONS: Air conditioner for Series 60-62 ($474). Air conditioner for Series 75 ($624). Automatic headlight control ($45). Bucket seats in styles 6267F, 6339B, 6357J, or 6389D with leather upholstery required ($188). Controlled differential ($54). Cruise Control ($97). Door guards for two-door styles ($4); for four-door styles ($7). Electric door locks

for two-door styles ($46); for four-door styles ($70). E-Z-Eye Glass ($52). Leather upholstery for styles 6339B, 6357J, 6389D, or 6039M ($134). License plate frame ($6). Padded roof for style 6357J ($91); for style 6039M ($134). Six-way power seat ($85-$113 depending on body style). Power window regulators as an option ($118). Power ventipanes as an option ($73). Radio with rear seat speaker ($165). Radio with rear seat speaker and remote control ($247). AM/FM radio ($191). Front seat belts in Series 60-62 models ($22). Rear seat belts in same models ($22). Adjustable steering wheel ($48). Remote control trunk lock ($53). Five white sidewall tires, 8.20 x 15 four-ply on Series 60-62; standard on Eldorado ($57 exchange). Five white sidewall tires, 8.20 x 15 six-ply on Series 75 models ($64 exchange).

HISTORICAL FOOTNOTES: Cadillac's new-for-1963 V-8 was the first major redesign of its V-8 since that powerplant's introduction as a 331-cid engine in 1949. Cadillac production totaled 163,174 for the year.

1964 CADILLAC

SERIES 62 — (V-8) — It was time for another face lift this year and, really, a minor one. New up front was a bi-angular grille that formed a V-shape along both its vertical and horizontal planes. The main horizontal grille bar was now carried around the bodysides. Outer grille extension panels again housed the parking and cornering lamps. It was the 17th consecutive year for Cadillac tailfins, with a new, fine-blade design carrying on this tradition. Performance improvements, including a larger V-8, were the dominant changes for the model run. Equipment features replicated those of 1963 for the most part. Introduced as an industry first was Comfort Control, a completely automatic heating and air conditioning system controlled by a dial thermostat on the instrument panel.

1964 Cadillac, Series 62 Sedan DeVille four-door hardtop, (AA)

CADILLAC I.D. NUMBERS: Engine serial numbers were located on the left side of the engine block and left-hand frame side bar. The first two symbols '64' identified the 1964 model year. The third symbol, a letter, designated body type. The last six numerical symbols indicated unit production sequence. The short-deck Park Avenue sedan, formerly coded with a 'D', was discontinued.

SERIES 62 (6200 MODELS)

Model Number	Body/Style Number	Body Type & Seating	Factory Price	Shipping Weight	Production Total
64-62K	6229K	4-dr 6W Sed-6P	5236	4575	9,243
64-62N	6239N	4-dr 4W Sed-6P	5236	4550	13,670
64-62G	6257G	2-dr Cpe-6P	5048	4475	12,166

NOTE: All 6200 sedans were pillarless four-door hardtops.

SERIES 62 — DEVILLE 6300 SUB-SERIES — (V-8) — Styling changes for new DeVilles followed the Series 62 pattern. Equipment features were about the same as the year before. Performance gains from the new engine showed best in the lower range, at 20 to 50 mph traffic driving speeds. A new technical feature was Turbo-HydraMatic transmission, also used in Eldorado convertibles and Sixty Special sedans. A DeVille script, above the lower belt molding at the rear, was continued as an identifier.

1964 Cadillac, Series 62 DeVille two-door convertible

SERIES 62 DEVILLE 6300 SUB-SERIES

Model Number	Body/Style Number	Body Type & Seating	Factory Price	Shipping Weight	Production Total
64-63L	6329L	4-dr 6W Sed-6P	5655	4600	14,627
64-63B	6339B	4-dr 4W Sed-6P	5655	4575	39,674
64-63J	6357J	2-dr HT Cpe-6P	5408	4495	38,195
64-63F	6267F	2-dr Conv-6P	5612	4545	17,900

SERIES 62 ELDORADO BIARRITZ 6300 MODEL

Model Number	Body/Style Number	Body Type & Seating	Factory Price	Shipping Weight	Production Total
64-63P	6367P	2-dr Spt Conv-6P	6630	4605	1,870

NOTE: Style Number 6357J was the Coupe DeVille. All Sedan DeVilles were pillarless four-door hardtops. The Convertible DeVille was coded similar to 6200 models, but was considered a 6300.

SERIES SIXTY SPECIAL FLEETWOOD — (V-8) — The Sixty Special Fleetwood sedan had the new styling features combined with carryover trim. Standard equipment was the same as the previous year.

SERIES SIXTY SPECIAL FLEETWOOD

Model Number	Body/Style Number	Body Type & Seating	Factory Price	Shipping Weight	Production Total
64-60M	6039M	4-dr HT Sed-6P	6388	4680	14,550

SERIES 6700 — FLEETWOOD 75 — (V-8) — This line featured the same limousine-type styling seen in 1963, combined with a new frontal treatment, angular taillamps and revised rear sheet metal. The back fenders swept rearward in a straighter and higher line, while the fins began with a more pronounced kickup and housed new notch-shaped taillamp lenses.

SERIES 6700 FLEETWOOD 75

Model Number	Body/Style Number	Body Type & Seating	Factory Price	Shipping Weight	Production Total
63-67R	6723R	4-dr Sed-6P	9746	5215	617
63-67S	6733S	4-dr Limo-9P	9960	5300	808
63-67Z	6890Z	Commercial chassis	—	—	2,527

NOTE: The commercial chassis featured a 156-inch wheelbase and was provided to professional carmakers for construction of funeral cars, ambulances, etc.

ENGINE: V-8. Overhead valve. Cast iron block. Displacement: 429 cid. Bore and stroke: 4.13 x 4.00 inches. Compression ratio: 10.5:1. Brake hp: 340 at 4600 rpm. Five main bearings. Hydraulic valve lifters. Carburetor: Carter AFB four-barrel Model 3655S.

CHASSIS FEATURES: Wheelbase: (Series 75) 149.8 inches; (all other series) 129.5 inches. Overall length: (Series 75) 243.8 inches; (all other series) 223.5 inches. Tires: (Series 75 and Eldorado) 8.20 x 15; (all other series) 8.00 x 15. Rear axle ratio: (Series 75) 3.36:1; (all other series) 2.94:1.

CONVENIENCE OPTIONS: Air conditioner for Series 60-62 ($474). Air conditioner for Series 75 ($624). Automatic headlight control ($45). Bucket seats in styles 6267F, 6339B, 6357J, or 6389D with leather upholstery required ($188). Controlled differential ($54). Cruise Control ($97). Door guards for two-door styles ($4); for four-door styles ($7). Electric door locks for two-door styles ($46); for four-door styles ($70). E-Z-Eye Glass ($52). Leather upholstery for styles 6339B, 6357J, 6389D, or 6039M ($134). License plate frame ($6). Padded roof for style 6357J ($91); for style 6039M ($134). Six-way power seat ($85-$113 depending on body style). Power window regulators as an option ($118). Power ventipanes as an option ($73). Radio with rear seat speaker ($165). Radio with rear seat speaker and remote control ($247). AM/FM radio ($191). Front seat belts in Series 60-62 models ($22). Rear seat belts in same models ($22). Adjustable steering wheel ($48).

Remote control trunk lock ($53). Five white sidewall tires, 8.20 x 15 four-ply on Series 60-62; standard on Eldorado ($57 exchange). Five white sidewall tires, 8.20 x 15 six-ply on Series 75 models ($64 exchange).

HISTORICAL FOOTNOTES: For the first time since 1956, the Biarritz name was not used on a Cadillac convertible this year. Cadillac produced a record 165,959 cars during 1964.

1965 CADILLAC

CALAIS SERIES — (V-8) — The Calais series replaced the Sixty-Two line for 1965 as one of numerous Cadillac changes. A broader, more unified grille and vertically mounted headlamps featured the styling improvements. The Cadillac tailfin was said to be gone but symmetrical rear fender forms tapered to thin edges, top and bottom, giving a traditional visual impression. Curved side windows with frameless glass were new and convertibles had tempered glass backlights. Last seen in 1956, the standard wheelbase pillared sedan made a return this year. Perimeter frame construction allowed repositioning of engines six inches forward in the frame, thus lowering the transmission hump and increasing interior room. Standard Calais equipment was comprised of power brakes; power steering; automatic transmission; dual back-up lights; windshield washers and dual speed wipers; full wheel discs; remote controlled outside rearview mirror; visor vanity mirror; oil filter; five tubeless black tires; heater; defroster; lamps for luggage, glove and rear passenger compartments; cornering lights and front and rear seat safety belts.

CADILLAC I.D. NUMBERS: Vehicle numbers were now located on the right- or left-hand side of the forward frame crossmember. The original engine serial number was the same as the vehicle identification number. The first symbol was a letter (see Body/Style Number suffixes) indicating series and body style. The second symbol was a number designating the model year. The following six numbers designated the sequential production code and started with 100001 and up. Body/Style Numbers were revised to reflect a more rational arrangement of models. The new five digit codes began with '68' except in the case of Fleetwood Seventy-Five models and early production Fleetwood Eldorado convertibles, all of which were coded '69'. The third number was a '2' on Calais; '3' on DeVille; '4' on Eldorado; '0' on 60 Specials and '7' on 75 limousines. The final two symbols corresponded to Fisher Body Division Style Number codes. The five digit numbers were found on the vehicle data plate, affixed to engine side of the firewall, and may have been followed by a letter suffix corresponding to those on the charts below.

CALAIS SERIES 682

Model Number	Body/Style Number	Body Type & Seating	Factory Price	Shipping Weight	Production Total
65-682	68257-G	2-dr HT Cpe-6P	5059	4435	12,515
65-682	68239-N	4-dr HT Sed-6P	5247	4500	13,975
65-682	68269-K	4-dr Sed-6P	5247	4490	7,721

1965 Cadillac, DeVille two-door convertible

DEVILLE SERIES — (V-8) — DeVilles kept their rear fender signature scripts for distinctions of trim. One auto writer described this feature as "Tiffany-like." Standard equipment matched that found in Calais models, plus power window lifts.

DEVILLE SERIES 683

Model Number	Body/Style Number	Body Type & Seating	Factory Price	Shipping Weight	Production Total
65-683	68367-F	2-dr Conv-6P	5639	4690	19,200
65-683	68357-J	2-dr HT Cpe-6P	5419	4480	43,345
65-683	68339-B	4-dr HT Sed-6P	5666	4560	45,535
65-683	68369-L	4-dr Sed-6P	5666	4555	15,000

NOTES: Style Number 68357-J was called the Coupe DeVille. Other models were Convertible or Sedan DeVilles. Some sources quote substantially lower factory list prices for 1965 Cadillacs. This may be due to a strike that occurred early in the year, which probably brought $1 price increases after it was settled. The United Auto Workers (UAW) walkout closed Cadillac's newly expanded Clark Avenue (Detroit) factory from September 25, 1964, through the following December and created a decline in production and sales for the 1964 calendar year. The higher retail prices are being used in this book.

FLEETWOOD SIXTY SPECIAL SUB-SERIES — (V-8) — Poised on a new 133-inch wheelbase, the Sixty Special sedan wore Fleetwood crests on the hood and deck. All features found in lower priced Cadillacs were standard, as well as power ventipanes, glare-proof rearview mirror and automatic level control. Like Calais and DeVilles, the Fleetwood Sixty Special had an improved Turbo-HydraMatic transmission with a variable stator. A new Fleetwood Brougham trim option package was introduced at a price of $199. Its main feature was a more richly appointed interior.

FLEETWOOD SIXTY SPECIAL SUB-SERIES 680

Model Number	Body/Style Number	Body Type & Seating	Factory Price	Shipping Weight	Production Total
65-680	68069-M	4-dr Sed-6P	6479	4670	18,100

FLEETWOOD ELDORADO SUB-SERIES — (V-8) — Under a new model arrangement, the Eldorado became a one-car Fleetwood sub-series but was really less distinguished than before. Fleetwood hood and deck lid crests were the main difference in outer trim. Additional standard equipment, over that found in Sixty Specials, included white sidewall tires and a six-way power seat for cars with regular bench seating.

FLEETWOOD ELDORADO SUB-SERIES 684

Model Number	Body/Style Number	Body Type & Seating	Factory Price	Shipping Weight	Production Total
65-684	68467-E	2-dr Eldo Conv-6P	6754	4660	2,125

FLEETWOOD 75 SUB-SERIES — (V-8) — Cadillac's longest, heaviest, richest and highest priced models were, again, more conventionally engineered than the other lines. For example, the new perimeter frame was not in use and neither was the improved automatic transmission. In addition, automatic level control was not featured. Even the annual styling face lift did not affect these tradition-bound luxury cars. They came with all power controls found in Eldorados and added courtesy and map lights to the standard equipment list. Sales of commercial chassis earned an increase of 30 units, while limousine deliveries tapered slightly downward and the popularity of the nine-passenger sedan saw a considerable decline.

FLEETWOOD 75 SUB-SERIES 697

Model Number	Body/Style Number	Body Type & Seating	Factory Price	Shipping Weight	Production Total
65-697	69723-R	4-dr Sed-9P	9746	5190	455
65-697	69733-S	4-dr Limo-9P	9960	5260	795

FLEETWOOD 75 SUB-SERIES 698

Model Number	Body/Style Number	Body Type & Seating	Factory Price	Shipping Weight	Production Total
65-698	69890-Z	Commercial chassis	—	—	2,669

ENGINE: V-8. Overhead valve. Cast iron block. Displacement: 429 cid. Bore and stroke: 4.13 x 4.00 inches. Compression ratio: 10.5:1. Brake hp: 340 at 4600 rpm. Five main bearings. Hydraulic valve lifters. Carburetor: Carter AFB four-barrel Model 3903S.

CHASSIS FEATURES: Wheelbase: (commercial chassis) 156 inches; (Series 75) 149.8 inches; (Series 60 Special) 133 inches; (all other series) 129.5 inches. Overall length: (Series 75) 243.8 inches; (Series 60 Special) 227.5 inches; (all other series) 224 inches. Front tread: (all series) 62.5 inches. Rear tread: (all series) 62.5 inches. Automatic level control standard where indicated in text. A new engine mounting system and patented quiet exhaust were used. Tires: (Series 75) 8.20 x 15; (Eldorado) 9.00 x 15; (all others) 8.00 x 15.

CONVENIENCE OPTIONS: Air conditioner, except 75 series models ($495). Air conditioner, 75 series model ($624). Bucket seats with console in F-J-B models with leather upholstery ($188). Controlled differential ($54). Cruise Control ($97). Door guards on two-door models ($4); on four-door models ($7). Fleetwood Brougham option on M model ($199). Soft Ray tinted glass ($52). Delete-option heater and defroster on 75 series models ($135 credit), on other models ($97 credit). Leather upholstery on J-B-L-M models ($141). License plate frame ($6). Padded roof on J model ($124); on B or L models ($140). Left-hand four-way power bucket seat on F-J-B models ($54). Power door locks on G-F-J-E models ($46); on N-K-B-L-M models ($70). Power headlight control on R-S models ($46); on other models ($51). Six-way power front seat on G-N-K models ($113); on F-J-B-L-M models ($85). Power window regulators on G-N-K models ($119). Power vent window regulator option ($73). Radio with rear speaker ($165). Radio with rear speaker and remote control ($246). AM/FM radio ($191). Rear seat belts ($18). Front seat belt delete option ($17 credit). Adjustable steering wheel, except on R-S models ($91). Remote control trunk lock, except on R-S models ($53). Twilight Sentinel, except on E-R-S models ($57). Five white sidewall tires, 9.00 x 15 size with four-ply construction, except E-R-S models ($57 exchange). Five white sidewall tires, 9.00 x 15 size with six-ply construction on R-S models only ($64 exchange).

HISTORICAL FOOTNOTES: Vinyl roofs for Coupe and Sedan DeVilles came in four different colors. A tilt telescope steering wheel option was highlighted this season. The Cadillac factory closed July 8, 1964, for the changeover to 1965 model production. This was 22 days earlier than usual, as a 471,000-square foot expansion of facilities was planned. The plant reopened August 24, when production of cars to 1965 specifications commenced. It was the longest plant shutdown in Cadillac history and the new manufacturing potential of 800 cars per day was an all-time high. Cadillac's three-millionth car, a 1965 Fleetwood Brougham, was produced on November 4, 1964. Cadillac's new engineering center was dedicated. The Fleetwood Sixty Special Brougham was frequently referred to as a separate model.

1966 CADILLAC

CALAIS — (V-8) — SERIES 682 — For 1966, Cadillac offered 12 models in three series, Calais, DeVille and Fleetwood. Cadillac 'firsts' seen this season included variable ratio steering and optional front seats with carbon cloth heating pads built into cushions and seatbacks. Comfort and convenience innovations were headrests, reclining seats and an AM/FM stereo system. Engineering improvements made to the perimeter frame increased ride and handling ease. Newly designed piston and oil rings were adopted and new engine and body mountings were employed. All models, except the 75 series limousines were mildly face lifted. Changes included a somewhat coarser mesh for the radiator grille insert, which was now divided by a thick, bright metal horizontal center bar housing rectangular parking lamps at its outer ends. A Cadillac crest and V-shaped molding trimmed the hood of Calais. Separate, rectangular side marker lamps replaced the integral grille extension designs. There was generally less chrome on all Cadillac models this year.

1966 Cadillac, Calais four-door hardtop

CADILLAC I.D. NUMBERS: Vehicle identification numbers were found on the left center pillar post. The original engine serial number was the same as the vehicle identification number. The numbering system was the same employed a year earlier with the second symbol changed to a '6' for the 1966 model year. All Eldorados now utilized the first two symbols '68' for their Style Number. The Sixty Special Brougham was now a separate model of the Fleetwood series with a 'P' Style Number suffix applied.

CALAIS SERIES 682

Model Number	Body/Style Number	Body Type & Seating	Factory Price	Shipping Weight	Production Total
66-682	68269-K	4-dr Sed-6P	5171	4460	4,575
66-682	68239-N	4-dr HT Sed-6P	5171	4465	13,025
66-682	68257-G	2-dr HT Cpe-6P	4986	4390	11,080

DEVILLE — (V-8) — SERIES 683 — Following the general styling theme found on Calais models, the DeVille series was again distinguished with Tiffany-like script above the rear tip of the horizontal body rub moldings. Standard equipment additions followed the pattern of previous years. Cadillac crests and V-shaped moldings, front and rear, were identifiers.

1966 Cadillac, DeVille two-door convertible

DEVILLE SERIES 683

Model Number	Body/Style Number	Body Type & Seating	Factory Price	Shipping Weight	Production Total
66-683	68369-L	4-dr Sed-6P	5581	4535	11,860
66-683	68339-B	4-dr HT Sed-6P	5581	4515	60,550
66-683	68357-J	2-dr Cpe DeV-6P	5339	4460	50,580
66-683	68367-F	2-dr Conv Cpe-6P	5555	4445	19,200

1966 Cadillac, Fleetwood 60 Special Brougham four-door sedan

FLEETWOOD SIXTY SPECIAL — (V-8) — SUB-SERIES 680/681 — Models in this range were characterized by traditional standard equipment additions and by emblems containing a Cadillac shield encircled by a laurel wreath, which appeared on the hood and center of the deck. Fleetwood designations, in block letters, were also found at the right-hand side of the deck. The Brougham had the wreath-style medallions on the roof pillar, along with Tiffany script in the same location to identify this extra-rich model.

FLEETWOOD SIXTY SPECIAL SUB-SERIES 680/681

Model Number	Body/Style Number	Body Type & Seating	Factory Price	Shipping Weight	Production Total
66-680	68069-M	4-dr Sed-6P	6378	4615	5,445
66-681	68169-P	4-dr Brghm-6P	6695	4616	13,630

FLEETWOOD ELDORADO — (V-8) — SUB-SERIES 684 — Fleetwood-type trim was seen again on the Eldorado. Equipment additions included white sidewall tires and a six-way power front bench seat. It was to be the last season that conventional engineering characterized this model.

FLEETWOOD ELDORADO SUB-SERIES 684

Model Number	Body/Style Number	Body Type & Seating	Factory Price	Shipping Weight	Production Total
66-684	68567-E	2-dr Eldo Conv-6P	6631	4500	2,250

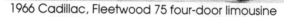

1966 Cadillac, Fleetwood 75 four-door limousine

FLEETWOOD SEVENTY-FIVE — (V-8) — SERIES 697/698 — Fleetwood exterior trim and Fleetwood interior appointments enriched the cars in Cadillac's high-dollar lineup. The first major restyling since 1959 was seen on these models, as well as perimeter-type frames. The new look brought the appearance of the big sedan and the limousine up-to-date so that it matched the visual impression of other Cadillac lines. A big jump in sales for both regular production models, but not the commercial chassis, was the result.

FLEETWOOD 75 SUB-SERIES 697

Model Number	Body/Style Number	Body Type & Seating	Factory Price	Shipping Weight	Production Total
66-697	69723-R	4-dr Sed-9P	10,312	5320	980
66-697	69733-S	4-dr Limo-9P	10,521	5435	1,037

FLEETWOOD 75 SUB-SERIES 698

Model Number	Body/Style Number	Body Type & Seating	Factory Price	Shipping Weight	Production Total
66-698	69890-Z	Commercial chassis	—	—	2,463

ENGINE: V-8. Overhead valve. Cast iron block. Displacement: 429 cid. Bore and stroke: 4.13 x 4.00 inches. Compression ratio: 10.5:1. Brake hp: 340 at 4600 rpm. Five main bearings. Hydraulic valve lifters. Carburetor: Carter AFB four-barrel Model 3903S.

CHASSIS FEATURES: Chassis features for 1966 Cadillacs were the same as the previous year, except overall length of all models increased slightly as follows: (Series 75) 244.5 inches; (Series 60 Special) 227.7 inches; (Eldorado) 224.2 inches; (all other series) 224.2 inches. Fleetwood 75s now had the perimeter frame. See 1965 Cadillac chassis features for other details.

CONVENIENCE OPTIONS: Air conditioner, except 75 series models ($495). Air conditioner, 75 series model ($624). Bucket seats with console in F-J-B models with leather upholstery ($188). Controlled differential ($54). Cruise Control ($97). Door guards on two-door models ($4); on four-door models ($7). Fleetwood Brougham option on M model ($199). Soft Ray tinted glass ($52). Delete option heater and defroster on 75 series models ($135 credit); on other models ($97 credit). Leather upholstery on J-B-L-M models ($141). License plate frame ($6). Padded roof on J model ($124); on B or L models ($140). Left-hand four-way power bucket seat on F-J-B models ($54). Power door locks on G-F-J-E models ($46); on N-K-B-LM models ($70). Power headlight control on R-S models ($46); on other models ($51). Six-way power front seat on G-N-K models ($113); on F-J-B-L-M models ($85). Power window regulators on G-N-K models ($119). Power vent window regulator option ($73). Radio with rear speaker ($165). Radio with rear speaker and remote control ($246). AM/FM radio ($191). Rear seat belts ($18). Front seat belt delete option ($17 credit). Adjustable steering wheel except on R-S models ($91). Remote control trunk lock, except on R-S models ($53). Twilight Sentinel, except on E-R-S models ($57). Five white sidewall tires, 9.00 x 15 size with four-ply construction, except E-R-S models ($57 exchange). Five white sidewall tires, 9.00 x 15 size with six-ply construction on R-S models only ($64 exchange). A new seat warmer sold for $60.20. The recliner seat with headrest was $64.20 extra and was available only in F-J-B-H models with Eldorado bench seats or optional bucket seats. Headrests were a separate $40.15 option for all Cadillacs.

HISTORICAL FOOTNOTES: This was the best ever sales and production year (196,675 cars) in Cadillac history and the second year running for sales increases, despite a downturn in the overall market for U.S. cars. A record of 5,570 one-week builds was marked December 5 and a record one-day output of 1,017 cars was achieved October 27. The 1966 models were introduced October 14, 1965. Towards the end of the summer, in 1966, a new assembly line was set up to manufacture front-wheel-drive Eldorados conforming to 1967 model specifications.

1967 CADILLAC

1967 Cadillac, Coupe DeVille two-door hardtop

CALAIS — (V-8) — SERIES 682 — New at Cadillac for 1967 was a redesigned side panel contour that created a longer look and more sculptured appearance. The coupe roof structure was restyled after the Florentine show car and gave added privacy to rear seat passengers. Technical improvements included a revised engine valve train, different carburetor, Mylar printed circuit instrument panel, re-tuned body mounts and a new engine fan with clutch for quieter operation. A squarer cornered radiator grille insert had a cross-hatch pattern that appeared both above the bumper and through a horizontal slot cut into it. Rear end styling revisions were highlighted by metal divided taillamps and a painted lower bumper section. The new front grille had a forward angle and blades that seemed to emphasize its vertical members. Rectangular parking lamps were housed at the outer ends. Listed as standard equipment for cars in this line were automatic transmission; power brakes; power steering; heater and defroster; reflectors; full wheel discs; three-speed windshield wipers and washers; left-hand remote control outside rearview mirror; inside non-glare rearview mirror; visor vanity mirror; cigarette lighter; electric clock; cornering lights; lamps for the rear compartment, glovebox and luggage compartment; interior courtesy lamps; and all standard GM safety features. Also included at base price were Automatic Climate Controls; rear cigarette lighter (except coupes); padded dashboard; Hazard Warning system; and front and rear seat belts with outboard retractors.

CADILLAC I.D. NUMBERS: The vehicle identification numbers took the same general form and were found in the same locations as in 1966 models. The second symbol was changed to a '7' for the 1967 model year.

CALAIS SERIES 682

Model Number	Body/Style Number	Body Type & Seating	Factory Price	Shipping Weight	Production Total
67-682	68269-K	4-dr Sed-6P	5215	4520	2,865
67-682	68249-N	4-dr HT Sed-6P	5215	4550	9,880
67-682	68247-G	2-dr Cpe-6P	5040	4445	9,085

DEVILLE — (V-8) — SERIES 683 — Minor trim variations and slightly richer interiors separated DeVilles from Calais. For example, Tiffany-style chrome signature script was again found above the bodyside molding on the rear fenders. DeVille equipment lists were comprised of all the same features found on Calais models, plus power-operated window regulators; rear cigarette lighters in all styles; and two-way power front seats. An innovative slide-out fuse box and safety front seatback lock for two-door models were additional Cadillac advances for the 1967 model year.

DEVILLE SERIES 683

Model Number	Body/Style Number	Body Type & Seating	Factory Price	Shipping Weight	Production Total
67-683	68369-L	4-dr Sed-6P	5625	4675	8,800
67-683	68349-B	4-dr HT Sed-6P	5625	4550	59,902
67-683	68347-J	2-dr Cpe DeV-6P	5392	4505	52,905
67-683	68367-F	2-dr Conv-6P	5608	4500	18,200

1967 Cadillac, Fleetwood 60 Special Brougham four-door sedan

FLEETWOOD SIXTY SPECIAL — (V-8) — SUB-SERIES 680/681 — Full-length bright metal body underscores; Fleetwood wreath and crest emblems for the hood, trunk and roof pillars; the lack of horizontal lower body rub moldings and Fleetwood block letters on the lower front fenders and passenger side of the deck lid characterized the new Sixty Special. The Brougham featured a padded Cordova vinyl top with model identification script attached to the roof 'C' pillars. Added to the list of DeVille equipment were Automatic Level Control suspension and power-operated ventipanes. The Brougham also included lighted fold-down trays; adjustable reading lamps; and carpeted fold-down footrests.

FLEETWOOD SIXTY SPECIAL SUB-SERIES 680/681

Model Number	Body/Style Number	Body Type & Seating	Factory Price	Shipping Weight	Production Total
67-680	68069-M	4-dr Sed-6P	6423	4685	3,550
67-681	68169-P	4-dr Brghm-6P	6739	4735	12,750

FLEETWOOD SEVENTY-FIVE — (V-8) — SUB-SERIES 697/698 — The year's new styling was beautifully rendered on the Cadillac long wheelbase models, which had extra-long rear fenders and an extended 'greenhouse' with a formal, high-headroom look. Fleetwood wreath and crest emblems decorated the hood and the trunk and there were Fleetwood block letters at the right side of the deck lid. A simple horizontal body rub molding, lengthened to fit the elongated sheet metal, trimmed the sides of these elegant machines. Standard equipment included all found in DeVilles, plus Automatic Level Control; air conditioning; carpeted fold-down foot rests; and 8.20 x 15, four-ply 8PR blackwall tires.

FLEETWOOD SEVENTY-FIVE SUB-SERIES 697/698

Model Number	Body/Style Number	Body Type & Seating	Factory Price	Shipping Weight	Production Total
67-697	69723-R	4-dr Sed-6P	10,360	5335	835
67-697	69733-S	4-dr Limo-6P	10,571	5450	965
67-698	69890-Z	Commercial chassis —	—	—	2,333

NOTE: The commercial chassis was built on a 156-inch wheelbase and was provided to professional carmakers for the manufacture of hearses and ambulances, etc.

ENGINE: V-8. Overhead valve. Cast iron block. Displacement: 429 cid. Bore and stroke: 4.13 x 4.00 inches. Compression ratio: 10.5:1. Brake hp: 340 at 4600 rpm. Five main bearings. Hydraulic valve lifters. Carburetor: Rochester Quadrajet four-barrel Model 7028230.

FLEETWOOD ELDORADO — (V-8) — SUB-SERIES 693 — The 1967 Cadillac Eldorado was a completely new front-wheel-drive six-passenger coupe. It was described as a "sports-styled" automobile and the first car to combine front-wheel-drive, variable ratio power steering and automatic level control. Built off the Oldsmobile Toronado platform utilizing the same basic body shell, the Eldorado was shorter and lower than even the smallest Cadillacs, but could provide full six-passenger seating because of its drivetrain layout. The Cadillac V-8 was fitted to the platform with changes in the oil pan, exhaust manifolds, accessory and drive belt layout and engine mount system. It had dual exhaust, but a single outlet muffler and tailpipe arrangement. An improved fresh-air system eliminated the need for front ventipanes. The Eldorado shared 1967 Cadillac technical changes such as Mylarbacked circuitry; bigger power brake booster; slide-out fuse box; improved automatic headlamp dimmer and braided rayon brake hoses, but was the only model in the line to offer the front disc brake option. The typical assortment of Fleetwood extra equipment was standard on Eldorados as well.

1967 Cadillac, Fleetwood Eldorado two-door hardtop

FLEETWOOD ELDORADO SUB-SERIES 693

Model Number	Body/Style Number	Body Type & Seating	Factory Price	Shipping Weight	Production Total
67-693	69347-H	2-dr HT Cpe-6P	6277	4590	17,930

CHASSIS FEATURES: Wheelbase: (Series 75) 149.8 inches; (commercial chassis) 156 inches; (Eldorado) 120 inches; (Sixty Special) 133 inches; (all other models) 129.5 inches. Overall length: (Series 75) 244.5 inches; (Eldorado) 221 inches; (Sixty Special) 227.5 inches; (all other models) 224 inches. Rear axle ratio: 2.94:1. Transmission: three-speed Turbo-Hydramatic. Tires: (Series 75) 8.20 x 15; (all other models) 9.00 x 15. Front tread: (Eldorado) 63.5 inches; (all other models) not available. Rear tread: (Eldorado) 63.0 inches; (all other models) not available.

POWERTRAIN OPTIONS: A 3.21:1 rear axle gear ratio was standard on Series Seventy-Five and Eldorado; optional on other models. A controlled differential was $40.15 extra on all models except Eldorados. An air injection reactor was $34.13 extra on all Cadillacs and required on all cars built for California sale. Closed positive crankcase ventilators were $4 extra on all Cadillacs and required on all cars built for California sale.

CONVENIENCE OPTIONS: Auxiliary horn ($12). Automatic level control option on models G-N-K-F-J-B-L ($79). Automatic Climate Control except R and S models ($516). Bucket seats with console on models F-J-B-H with leather upholstery required ($184). Firemist finish ($132). Cruise control ($95). Rear window defogger on models G-N-K-J-B-L-M-P ($27). Front disc brakes on Eldorado only ($105). Door guards on model G-F-J-H ($5); on models N-K-B-L-M-P-R-S ($8). Expanded vinyl upholstery on models G-N-K ($42). Soft Ray glass ($51). Guide-Matic headlamp control ($50). Headrests ($53). Leather upholstery, models J-B-L-M-P ($138); model H ($158). License frame, single ($6); pair ($12). Padded roof, models J-H ($132); models B-L ($137). Power door locks, two-door ($47); four-door ($68). Power door locks for Fleetwood 75 models ($116). Power ventipanes, except models H-M-P, power windows required ($72). Rear quarter power ventipanes on Eldorado only ($63). Power windows on Calais models ($116). AM radio ($162). AM/FM radio ($188). AM/FM stereo, except Fleetwood 75 models ($288). AM radio rear controls on Fleetwood 75 models ($242). Reclining front seat with headrests on models F-J-B-H with bucket seats or Eldorado bench seats required ($84). Four-way left-hand power bucket seat on models F-J-B-H ($53). Six-way power front seat on models G-N-K ($111); models F-J-B-L-H-M-P-R ($83). Rear center seat belt ($11). Front shoulder straps ($32). Tilt-telescope steering wheel ($90). Remote control trunk lock ($52). Twilight Sentinel on Eldorado ($37); other models ($32). White sidewall tires, size 9.00 x 15 four-ply 8PR-5 except nine-passenger models ($56 exchange). White sidewall tires, size 8.20 x 15, four-ply 8PR-5 on nine-passenger models ($64 exchange).

HISTORICAL FOOTNOTES: Dealer introduction date for 1967 Cadillacs and Eldorados was October 6, 1966. The Eldorado featured concealed, horizontally mounted headlamps. A new assembly line was set up at the Detroit factory to build Eldorados. A third successive year of record production and sales was marked by Cadillac Division in 1967. Based on the Eldorado's popularity, Cadillac sales for a single month passed the 20,000 unit level for the first time in the company's history, setting an all-time high of 22,072 cars in October 1966. A year later, 23,408 cars conforming to 1968 specifi-

cations were built in October 1967. Calvin J. Werner was general manager of Cadillac.

1968 CADILLAC

CALAIS — (V-8) — SERIES 682 — Cadillac was not about to alter its popular product in any major way, so the same basic styling and engineering continued into the 1968 model year, with a number of refinements, but no drastic changes. New grilles were added. They had an insert with a finer mesh and step-down outer section, which held the rectangular parking lights just a little higher than before. Rear end styling was modestly altered. An obvious change was a 8-1/2 inch longer hood, designed to accommodate recessed windshield wipers. The deck lid also had more of a rake. An enlarged engine offered more cubic inches and torque than any other American V-8 and put out 375 hp. Of 20 exterior paint color combinations, 14 were totally new. On the inside enriched appointments included molded inner door panels and a selection of 147 upholstery combinations, 76 in cloth, 67 in leather and four in vinyl. The Calais four-door pillared sedan was dropped. Standard features for the two remaining styles included Turbo-Hydramatic; power steering; power brakes; power windows; heater and defroster; center armrests; electric clock; dual back-up lamps; cornering lights; front and rear side marker lamps; Light Group; Mirror Group; padded instrument panel; seat belts; trip odometer; ignition key warning buzzer; recessed three-speed wipers and washers and five 9.00 x 15 blackwall tires.

CADILLAC I.D. NUMBERS: Vehicle identification numbers were stamped on the top of the instrument panel this year and were visible through the windshield. The first symbol was a '6' for Cadillac. The second and third symbols correspond to the same symbols in the series code number. The fourth and fifth symbols correspond to the last two symbols in the standard Fisher Body Division code (Style Number, without letter suffix). The sixth symbol was an '8' for 1968 model year. The seventh symbol was an assembly plant code as follows: 'Q' = Detroit, Michigan; 'E' = Linden, New Jersey. The next group of six numbers was the sequential unit production code. The number sequence began with 100001 at each assembly plant. Body/Style Numbers, on the vehicle data plate (located on firewall) were prefixed with '68' for 1968 and suffixed with a single letter, which also indicated series and model and corresponds to the letter on the charts below.

CALAIS SERIES 682

Model Number	Body/Style Number	Body Type & Seating	Factory Price	Shipping Weight	Production Total
68-682	68247-G	2-dr Cpe-6P	5315	4570	8,165
68-682	68249-N	4-dr HT Sed-6P	5491	4640	10,025

1968 Cadillac, DeVille two-door convertible

DEVILLE — (V-8) — SERIES 683 — On paper, it seemed that the main distinctions of cars in the DeVille lineup were the installation of a power-operated front seat with horizontal adjustment and the addition of illuminated door panel reflectors. There were, however, richer appointments inside and out, including the traditional rear fender Tiffany-like script and plusher upholstery trims. In addition, twice as many body styles were provided in DeVille level finish.

DEVILLE SERIES 683

Model Number	Body/Style Number	Body Type & Seating	Factory Price	Shipping Weight	Production Total
68-683	68369-L	4-dr Sed-6P	5785	4680	9,850
68-683	68349-B	4-dr HT Sed-6P	5785	4675	72,662
68-683	68347-J	2-dr Cpe DeV-6P	5552	4595	63,935
68-683	68367-F	2-dr Conv DeV-6P	5736	4600	18,025

NOTE: Some sources list lower prices for 1968 Cadillacs, indicating a midyear increase. The higher recorded prices are being used in this book.

1968 Cadillac, Fleetwood 60 Special Brougham four-door sedan

FLEETWOOD SIXTY SPECIAL — (V-8) — SUB-SERIES 680/681 — Features distinguishing 1968 Sixty Specials, in addition to a longer wheelbase, were the same exterior and interior appointments used in 1967 models. Extra items of standard equipment included Automatic Level Control; front and rear power operated ventipanes and, on Broughams, adjustable reading lamp; padded roof with special scripts and emblems; and carpeted folding foot rests.

FLEETWOOD SIXTY-SPECIALS SUB-SERIES 680/681

Model Number	Body/Style Number	Body Type & Seating	Factory Price	Shipping Weight	Production Total
68-680	68069-M	4-dr Sed-6P	6583	4795	3,300
68-681	68169-P	4-dr Brghm-6P	6899	4805	15,300

NOTE: See price increase notation under DeVille specifications chart.

FLEETWOOD SEVENTY-FIVE — (V-8) — SUB-SERIES 697/698 — Again marked by simple extra-long body rub moldings, a formal high-headroom look (with doors cut into roof) and Fleetwood-type wreath and crest emblems, the nine-passenger models had the longest Cadillac production car wheelbase, as well as power front ventipanes, Automatic Level Control, right-hand manually operated outside rearview mirrors, 8.20 x 15-8PR blackwall tires and Automatic Climate Control air conditioning as standard equipment.

FLEETWOOD SEVENTY-FIVE SUB-SERIES 697/698

Model Number	Body/Style Number	Body Type & Seating	Factory Price	Shipping Weight	Production Total
68-697	69723-R	4-dr Sed-9P	10,629	5300	805
68-697	69733-S	4-dr Limo-9P	10,768	5385	995
68-698	69890-Z	Commercial chassis	—	—	2,413

NOTE: The commercial chassis was built on a 156-inch wheelbase and was provided to professional carmakers for the manufacture of hearses and ambulances, etc.

FLEETWOOD ELDORADO — (V-8) — SUB-SERIES 693 — The 1968 Eldorado had the front parking lamps located to the leading edge of the fenders, where they were mounted vertically. To accommodate recessed windshield wipers, the hood was lengthened by 4-1/2 inches. On the rear fenders, small round safety lamps were now affixed. The design of the lens for the front cornering lamps (formerly vertically ribbed) was modified. The new 472-cid V-8, with 525 pound-feet of torque, made it possible to spin the front-driven wheels on smooth, dry surfaces. Spring rates were slightly lowered to give a more cushiony ride. Upholstery trim included diamond pattern cloth and vinyl; Deauville cloth with vinyl bolsters in four color choices and genuine leather options. Removed from the rear roof pillar, but not the hood and deck lid, were the familiar wreath and crest-style Fleetwood emblems. Regular equipment on the luxury sports-type car included all Fleetwood standards plus power rear quarter ventipanes; power front disc brakes; retractable headlamp covers; and Rosewood pattern dash panel appliques.

1968 Cadillac, Fleetwood Eldorado two-door hardtop

FLEETWOOD ELDORADO SUB-SERIES 693

Model Number	Body/Style Number	Body Type & Seating	Factory Price	Shipping Weight	Production Total
68-693	69347-H	2-dr HT Cpe-6P	6605	4580	24,528

NOTE: See price increase notation under DeVille specifications chart.

ENGINE: V-8. Overhead valve. Cast iron block. Displacement: 472 cid. Bore and stroke: 4.30 x 4 06 inches. Compression ratio: 10.5:1. Brake hp: 375 at 4400 rpm. Five main bearings. Hydraulic valve lifters. Carburetor: Rochester Quadrajet four-barrel Model 7028230.

NOTE: The new engine featured a metal temperature monitoring device; air injection emissions control system; integral air conditioning system (still optional); cast crankshaft and connecting rods; integral water crossover pipe with thermostatic passages; engine bearings with more surface area and 15-plate battery.

CHASSIS FEATURES: Wheelbase: (Series 75) 149.8 inches; (commercial chassis) 156 inches; (Eldorado) 120 inches; (Sixty Special) 133 inches; (all other models) 129.5 inches. Overall length: (Series 75) 245.2 inches; (Eldorado) 221 inches; (Sixty Special) 228.2 inches; (all other models) 224.7 inches. Rear axle ratio: 2.94:1. Transmission: three-speed Turbo-Hydramatic. Tires: (Series 75) 8.20 x 15; (all other models) 9.00 x 15. Front tread: (Eldorado) 63.5 inches; (all other models) not available. Rear tread: (Eldorado) 63.0 inches; (all other models) not available.

POWERTRAIN OPTIONS: Optional axle ratio data not available. Air injector reactor and closed positive crankcase ventilation standard. Controlled differential was now $52.65 extra on all models except Eldorado.

CONVENIENCE OPTIONS: Auxiliary horn ($16). Automatic level control option on models G-N-K-F-J-B-L ($79). Automatic Climate Control, except R and S models ($516). Bucket seats with console on models F-H with leather upholstery required ($184). Firemist finish ($132). Cruise control ($95). Rear window defogger on models G-N-K-J-B-L-M-P ($27). Front disc brakes on Eldorado only ($105). Door guards on model G-F-J-H ($5); on models N-K-B-L-M-P-R-S ($8). Expanded vinyl upholstery on models G-N-K ($42). Soft Ray glass ($51). GuideMatic headlamp control ($51). Headrests ($53). Leather upholstery, models J-B-L-M-P ($138); model H ($158). License frame, single ($6); pair ($13). Padded roof, models J-H ($132); models B-L ($137). Power door locks, two-door ($47); four-door ($68). Power door locks for Fleetwood 75 models ($116). Power ventipanes, except models H-M-P, power windows required ($72). Rear quarter power ventipanes on Eldorado only ($63). Power windows on Calais models ($116). AM radio ($162). AM/FM radio ($188). AM/FM stereo, except Fleetwood 75 models ($288). AM radio rear controls on Fleetwood 75 models ($242). Reclining front seat with headrests on models F-H with bucket seats or Eldorado bench seats required ($84). Four-way left-hand power bucket seat on models F-J-B-H ($53). Six-way power front seat on models G-N-K ($111); models F-J-B-L-H-M-P-R ($83). Rear center seat belt ($11). Front shoulder straps ($32). Tilt-telescope steering wheel ($90). Remote control trunk lock ($52). Twilight Sentinel on Eldorado ($37); other models ($32). White sidewall tires, size 9.00 x 15, four-ply 8PR-5, except nine-passenger models ($56 exchange). White sidewall tires, size 8.20 x 15, four-ply 8PR-5 on nine-passenger models ($63 exchange). Four new items of optional equipment were: Twin front and rear floor mats for all models except H-R-S ($17). One-piece front and rear floor mats for Eldorado

($20). Twin front floor mats for Fleetwood 75 models ($10) and front seat warmer for all models except Fleetwood 75s, which came instead with rear seat warmer only, both at ($95).

HISTORICAL FOOTNOTES: Dealer introduction for 1968 Cadillacs and Eldorados took place September 21, 1967. A fourth successive yearly sales record was set this year despite 21-day United Auto Workers (UAW) shutdown at Fisher Body Fleetwood plant in Detroit (November 1967). Production was down 1.1 percent, due to the same strike. Four-wheel disc brakes with floating calipers were optionally available. Cadillacs featured an all-new dashboard design.

1969 CADILLAC

CALAIS — (V-8) — SERIES 682 — Although its overall size and character was largely unchanged, the 1969 Cadillac was restyled in the Eldorado image. An Eldorado-like front fender treatment evolved and helped to emphasize a stronger horizontal design line. Rear quarters were extended to give the car a longer look. There was also an all-new grille with dual horizontal headlamps positioned in the outboard step-down areas of the grille. The hood was again extended, a total of 2-1/2 inches, to add to the impression of extra length. Calais models came with all GM safety features: V-8; Turbo-Hydramatic; variable-ratio power steering; dual power brakes; power windows; center front armrest; electric clock; two front cigarette lighters; twin front and rear ashtrays; a complete set of interior and exterior courtesy, safety and warning lights; Mirror Group; concealed three-speed windshield washers and wipers and five 9.00 x 15-4PR black sidewall tires. All regular Cadillac models had a new, squarer roofline and sculptured rear deck and bumper treatments.

CADILLAC I.D. NUMBERS: Serial numbers and engine numbers took the same general form used in 1968. The serial number was in the same location. The sixth symbol was changed to '9' to indicate the 1969 model year.

CALAIS SERIES 682

Model Number	Body/Style Number	Body Type & Seating	Factory Price	Shipping Weight	Production Total
69-682	68249-N	4-dr HT Sed-6P	5660	4630	6,825
69-682	68247-G	2-dr HT Cpe-6P	5484	4555	5,600

NOTE: On January 1, 1969, headrests (restraints) became mandatory on all U.S. cars. Cadillac prices were increased $18, with new prices reflected above.

1969 Cadillac, Coupe DeVille two-door hardtop (with optional vinyl roof)

DEVILLE SERIES — (V-8) — SERIES 683 — DeVilles had all of the features used in Calais, plus rear center armrests; dual rear cigarette lighters and two-way power-operated horizontal front seat adjusters. A model identification signature script still sat above the horizontal bodyside rub molding towards the back of the rear fenders.

DEVILLE SERIES 683

Model Number	Body/Style Number	Body Type & Seating	Factory price	Shipping Weight	Production Total
69-683	68369-L	4-dr Sed DeV-6P	5954	4640	7,890
69-683	68347-J	2-dr Cpe DeV-6P	5721	4595	65,755
69-683	68349-B	4-dr Sed DeV-6P	5954	4660	72,958
69-683	68367-F	2-dr Conv DeV-6P	5905	4590	16,445

NOTE: On January 1, 1969, head restraints became mandatory on all U.S. cars. Cadillac prices increased $18, with new prices reflected above.

1969 Cadillac, Fleetwood 60 Special Brougham four-door sedan

FLEETWOOD SIXTY SPECIAL — (V-8) — SUB-SERIES 680/681 — Fleetwood models had all standard features of DeVilles, except the limousine had no front center armrest. Extra regular equipment included Automatic Level Control. The Brougham included adjustable reading lamps and a Dual Comfort front seat. External identification was provided with bright metal body underscores, Fleetwood emblems and lettering and padded Brougham roof. The wheelbase for Sixty Specials was again 3-1/2 inches longer than on other models. Interior appointments were enriched and new, Eldorado-like front and rear styling was seen.

FLEETWOOD SIXTY SPECIAL SUB-SERIES 680/681

Model Number	Body/Style Number	Body Type & Seating	Factory Price	Shipping Weight	Production Total
69-680	68069-M	4-dr Sed-6P	6779	4765	2,545
69-681	68169-P	4-dr Brghm-6P	7110	4770	17,300

NOTE: On January 1, 1969, head restraints became mandatory on all U.S. cars. Cadillac prices were increased $18, with new prices reflected above.

FLEETWOOD SEVENTY-FIVE — (V-8) — SUB-SERIES 697/698 — Stretched bodies and trim; Fleetwood emblems and embellishments; doors cut into a formal, high headroom roof and generally higher appointment and trim levels continued to mark Cadillac's most luxurious line. All DeVille equipment plus Automatic Level Control; Automatic Climate Control; rear window defogger; four rear ashtrays and 8.20 x 15 four-ply blackwall tires were standard.

FLEETWOOD SEVENTY-FIVE SUB-SERIES 697/698

Model Number	Body/Style Number	Body Type & Seating	Factory Price	Shipping Weight	Production Total
69-697	69723-R	4-dr Sed-6P	10,841	5430	880
69-697	69733-S	4-dr Limo-9P	10,979	5555	1,156
69-698	69890-Z	Commercial chassis	—	—	2,550

NOTE: On January 1, 1969, head restraints became mandatory on all U.S. cars. Cadillac prices were increased $18, with new prices reflected above. Dealer preparation charges were $90 on Calais, DeVille and Eldorado; $115 on Fleetwood Sixty Special and Brougham; $150 on Fleetwood Seventy-Fives. These charges are included in retail prices listed above.

1969 Cadillac, Fleetwood Eldorado two-door hardtop

FLEETWOOD ELDORADO — (V-8) — SUB-SERIES 693 — The front-wheel-drive Eldorado continued to be offered as a single model; a six-passenger, two-door hardtop on a short wheelbase platform. There was a new cross-hatch grille that was separated from the headlights. The dual headlights were now part of the body design and were fully exposed and stationary. Standard equipment included power-operated rear quarter vent windows.

FLEETWOOD ELDORADO SUB-SERIES 693

Model Number	Body/Style Number	Body Type & Seating	Factory Price	Shipping Weight	Production Total
69-693	69347-H	2-dr HT Cpe-6P	6711	4550	23,333

NOTE: On January 1, 1969, head restraints became mandatory on all U.S. cars. Cadillac prices were increased $18, with new prices reflected above.

ENGINE: V-8. Overhead valve. Cast iron block. Displacement: 472 cid. Bore and stroke: 4.30 x 4 06 inches. Compression ratio: 10.5:1. Brake hp: 375 at 4400 rpm. Five main bearings. Hydraulic valve lifters. Carburetor: Rochester Quadrajet four-barrel Model 7028230.

CHASSIS FEATURES: Wheelbase: (commercial chassis) 156 inches; (Seventy-Five) 149.8 inches; (Sixty Special) 133 inches; (Eldorado) 120 inches; (all other models) 129.5 inches. Overall length: (Seventy-Five) 245.5 inches; (Sixty Special) 228.5 inches; (Eldorado) 221 inches; (all other models) 225 inches. Front tread: (Eldorado) 83 inches; (all other models) not available. Rear tread: (Eldorado) 63.5 inches; (all other models) not available. Tires: (Seventy-Five) 8.20 x 15 four-ply blackwall; (all other models) 9.00 x 15 four-ply blackwall.

POWERTRAIN OPTIONS: All cars used the 472 cid/375 hp V-8 with no other powerplants available. Turbo-Hydramatic transmission was standard equipment throughout the line. Controlled differential was $52.65 extra on all models except Eldorado. Standard axle ratios: (Seventy-Five) 3.21:1; (Eldorado) 3.07:1; (all other models) 2.94:1.

CONVENIENCE OPTIONS: Automatic Climate Control option ($516). Automatic level control, models G-N-F-J-B-L ($79). Bucket seats with console, model H with leather upholstery required ($184). Firemist paint ($132). Cruise Control ($95). Rear window defogger, models G-N-H-J-B-L-M-P ($26). Door guards, models G-F-J-H ($5); models N-B-L-M-P-R-S ($8). Dual comfort seat, standard in Brougham, optional models F-J-B-M ($105). Twin front and rear floor mats, all models except H-R-S ($17). One-piece front and rear floor mats, model H ($20). Twin front floor mats, models R-S ($10). Soft Ray tinted glass ($53). Guide-Matic headlamp control ($51). Head restraints ($18). Note: Head restraints mandatory after January 1, 1969. Leather upholstery, models J-B-L-M-P ($138); model H ($158). License frame, single ($6); dual ($13). Power door locks, includes electric seatback release, models G-F-J-H ($68); models N-B-L-M-P ($68); models R-S ($116). AM radio ($162). AM/FM radio ($188). AM/FM stereo radio, except models R-S ($288). AM rear-control radio models R-S ($242). Four-way left-hand bucket seat, model H ($53). Six-way power seat adjuster: front seat, models G-N ($116); front seat models F-J-B-L-H-M-R with bench seat only ($90); models F-J-B-M-P for right-hand Dual Comfort seat, Code Y accessories required, ($116). Front seat warmer, available all models except rear seat only in models R-S ($95). Front shoulder belts ($32). Tilt and telescope steering wheel ($95). Trumpet horn ($16). Remote control trunk lock ($32). Twilight Sentinel, Eldorado ($37); other models ($32). Expanded vinyl roof in standard production colors, models G-N ($42). Vinyl roof, models J-B-L ($153). Padded vinyl roof, model H ($158). Whitewall tires, size 9.00 x 15 four-ply, except models R-S ($57 exchange). Whitewall tires, size 8.20 x 15 four-ply, models R-S only ($63 exchange). Whitewall tires, heavy-duty high mileage type for Eldorado ($83 exchange).

HISTORICAL FOOTNOTES: Dealer introductions for 1969 Cadillacs and Eldorados was held September 26, 1968. Production of the Eldorado body for 1969 was transferred from the Fleetwood plant in Detroit to the Fisher Body plant in Euclid, Ohio. Cadillac enjoyed its fifth consecutive record sales year and built over 250,000 units for the first time in company history (calendar year figures). Strikes again affected the 1969 model run and production of cars built to 1969 specifications peaked at 223,267 units, of which 199,934 were regular Cadillacs. Total production fell 2.9 percent over the 1968 model run.

1970 CADILLAC

CALAIS — (V-8) — SERIES 682 — A relatively minor restyling marked the 1970 Cadillacs. A face lift included a grille with 13 vertical blades set against a delicately cross-hatched rectangular opening. The bright metal headlamp surrounds were bordered with body color to give a more refined look. Narrow, vertical 'vee' taillights were seen again, but no longer had smaller V-shaped bottom lenses pointing downward below the bumper. Wheel discs and winged crest fender tip emblems were new. A Calais signature script was placed above the rear end of the horizontal lower belt molding, just ahead of the chromed taillight dividers. Standard equipment included Turbo-Hydramatic transmission; power steering; front disc brakes; power windows; center front armrest; electric clock; two front cigarette lighters; twin front and rear ashtrays; complete interior and exterior courtesy lamps; safety, warning and convenience lights; outside remote control left-hand mirror; visor vanity mirror and L78-15 bias-belted fiberglass blackwall tires.

CADILLAC I.D. NUMBERS: Serial numbers and engine numbers took the same general form used in 1969. The serial number was in the same location. The sixth symbol was changed to a '0' to indicate the 1970 model year.

CALAIS SERIES 682

Model Number	Body/Style Number	Body Type & Seating	Factory Price	Shipping Weight	Production Total
70-682	68249-N	4-dr HT Sed-6P	5813	4680	5,187
70-682	68247-G	2-dr HT Cpe-6P	5637	4620	4,724

1970 Cadillac, Sedan DeVille four-door hardtop (with optional vinyl roof)

DEVILLE SERIES — (V-8) — SERIES 683 — DeVilles had all of the same features as Calais models, plus dual rear cigarette lighters, two-way horizontal control front seat adjustment and rear center armrest in all models, except convertibles. Exterior distinction came from a DeVille script above the rear end of the belt molding and from the use of long, rectangular back-up light lenses set into the lower rear bumper as opposed to the smaller, square lenses used on the Calais. A new feature seen this year was a body color border around the edge of the vinyl top covering, when this option was ordered. This treatment had first been seen on 1969 Fleetwoods. The Sedan DeVille and DeVille convertible were in their last season.

DEVILLE SERIES 683

Model Number	Body/Style Number	Body Type & Seating	Factory Price	Shipping Weight	Production Total
70-683	68369-L	4-dr Sed-6P	6118	4690	7,230
70-683	68349-B	4-dr HT DeV-6P	6118	4725	83,274
70-683	68347-J	2-dr Cpe DeV-6P	5884	4650	76,043
70-683	68367-F	2-dr Conv DeV-6P	6068	4660	15,172

FLEETWOOD SIXTY SPECIAL — (V-8) — SUB-SERIES 680/681 — The Fleetwood models had all the equipment ordered in DeVilles plus Automatic Level Control. The Brougham also came with adjustable reading lights; Dual Comfort front seat with two-way power adjustment (left side) and a padded vinyl top. Distinguishing Sixty Specials externally were bright metal wheelhouse moldings; wide full-length rocker panels with rear extensions and block lettering, denoting the series, positioned in back of the front wheel opening. At the end of the 1970 model run, the 'standard' Sixty Special sedan was dropped. A noticeable trim change was the use of a thin, horizontal beltline molding on all 1970 Sixty Specials.

1970 Cadillac, Fleetwood 60 Special Brougham four-door sedan

FLEETWOOD SIXTY SPECIAL SUB-SERIES 680/681

Model Number	Body/Style Number	Body Type & Seating	Factory Price	Shipping Weight	Production Total
70-680	68069-M	4-dr Sed-6P	6953	4830	1,738
70-681	68169-P	4-dr Brghm-6P	7284	4835	16,913

FLEETWOOD SEVENTY-FIVE — (V-8) — SUB-SERIES 697/698 — Special equipment found on the big Cadillac sedan and limousine included Automatic Level Control; rear window defogger; four rear ashtrays and a manual right-hand outside rearview mirror. Separate Climate Control systems were provided for front and rear compartments. Fleetwood wreath crests appeared at the extreme edge of the rear fenders, above the belt molding, on both models. As usual, the doors on the limousine were cut into the roof and a fixed driver's partition with adjustable glass compartment divider was inside. The front compartment was trimmed in genuine leather, the rear in one of five combinations. Three of these were the more standard Divan cloth trims, while Decordo cloth or Dumbarton cloth with leather were the richest selections available.

FLEETWOOD SEVENTY-FIVE SUB-SERIES 697/698

Model Number	Body/Style Number	Body Type & Seating	Factory Price	Shipping Weight	Production Total
70-697	69723-R	4-dr Sed-6P	11,039	5530	876
70-697	69733-S	4-dr Limo-9P	11,178	5630	1,240
70-698	69890-Z	Commercial chassis	—	—	2,506

NOTE: The commercial chassis was built on a 156-inch wheelbase and was provided to professional carmakers for the manufacture of hearses and ambulances, etc.

1970 Cadillac, Fleetwood Eldorado two-door hardtop (with optional sunroof), (AA)

FLEETWOOD ELDORADO — (V-8) — SUB-SERIES 693 — A new, 500 cid/400 hp V-8 was the big news for the Eldorado this year. A special '8.2-Litre' badge was placed on the left-hand side of the redesigned grille to announce the industry's biggest powerplant. The grille itself again had a cross-hatched insert, but horizontal blades were set upon it, emphasizing the V-shape of the front. Thinner vertical taillamps were used, giving a more rakish look. The winged-V emblems used at the front of the fenders on other Cadillacs were added to the Eldorado front parking lamp lenses. Bright rocker panel trim, with front and rear extensions, was used. There was also Eldorado block lettering at the lower front fender, behind the wheel housing.

FLEETWOOD ELDORADO SUB-SERIES 693

Model Number	Body/Style Number	Body Type & Seating	Factory Price	Shipping Weight	Production Total
70-693	69347-H	2-dr HT Cpe-6P	6903	4630	23,842

ENGINE: V-8. Overhead valve. Cast iron block. Displacement: 472 cid. Bore and stroke: 4.30 x 4.06 inches. Compression ratio: 10.0:1. Brake hp: 375 at 4400 rpm. Five main bearings. Hydraulic valve lifters. Carburetor: Rochester Quadrajet four-barrel Model 4MV.

ELDORADO ENGINE: V-8. Overhead valve. Cast iron block. Displacement: 500 cid. Bore and stroke: 4 30 x 4.304 inches. Compression ratio: 10.0:1. Brake hp: 400 at 4400 rpm. Five main bearings. Hydraulic valve lifters. Carburetor: Rochester Quadrajet four-barrel Model 4MV.

CHASSIS FEATURES: Wheelbase: (Seventy-Five) 149.8 inches; (Eldorado) 120 inches; (Sixty Special) 133 inches; (all other models) 129.5 inches. Overall length: (Seventy-Five) 245.3 inches; (Sixty Special) 288.5 inches; (Eldorado) 221 inches; (all other models) 225 inches. Tires: L78-15.

POWERTRAIN OPTIONS: Controlled differential, except Eldorado ($53).

CONVENIENCE OPTIONS: Automatic Climate Control ($516). Automatic Level Control on models G-N-F-J-B-L ($79). Bucket seats with console in Eldorado with leather upholstery required ($184). Bucket seats in Eldorado, with cloth upholstery, as SPO ($292). Special carpets with matching instrument carpet panels in all models, except H-R-S, as SPO ($32); in Eldorados, as SPO ($37). Cloth front compartment in limousine, as SPO ($126). Firemist paint, as SPO ($205). Special paint, except Firemist, as SPO ($179). Dual Comfort front seat in model L, as SPO with standard cloth upholstery ($184). Dual Comfort front seat in model L as SPO with production leather upholstery ($316). Vinyl padded roof in models R-S as SPO ($758). Vinyl padded roof with Landau bows in models R-S, as SPO ($2,131). Vinyl padded blind quarter roof in models R-S without Landau bows, as SPO ($2,026). NOTE: The term 'SPO' means "Special Production Option." Cruise control ($95). Rear window defogger ($26-$37). Door edge guards ($6-$10). Dual Comfort seat with-standard Brougham trim in models F-J-B-M ($105). Soft Ray glass ($53). Guide-Matic headlamp control ($51). Leather upholstery ($156-$184). License frame(s) in all models ($6-$13). Floor and trunk mats ($11-$20). Power door locks in standard wheelbase models ($68); in limousines ($116). Signal seeking radio AM/FM with rear control ($289); without rear control ($222); with stereo, except models R-S ($322). AM/FM radio ($188). Power seats, Eldorado left-hand four-way bucket ($53); six-way front ($90-$116); six-way left-hand front with Dual-Comfort ($90-$116). Shoulder belts ($32). Tilt and telescope steering wheel ($95). Electric powered sunroof in models B-H-J-L-P with vinyl top required and six-way seat recommended ($626). Trumpet horn ($15). Remote control trunk lock ($53). Twilight Sentinel ($37). Expanded vinyl upholstery in models G-N ($42). Vinyl roof in models J-B-L ($153); in Eldorado ($158). White sidewall L78-15 tires models R-S ($46); all other models ($40).

HISTORICAL FOOTNOTES: A total of 238,745 Cadillacs, built for the 1970 model run, set an all-time divisional record. Calendar year sales totals were off the mark, however, due to a major GM strike. They peaked at just 152,859 units. George R. Elges became general manager of Cadillac Division this year. Sales of the new Cadillac line began September 18, 1969. The optional Trackmaster skid control system was made available for the Eldorado, subsequent to initial model introductions.

1971 CADILLAC

CALAIS — (V-8) — SERIES 682 — Cadillacs were completely restyled with pairs of individually housed squarish headlamps set wider apart. The V-shaped grille had an eggcrate style insert and was protected by massive vertical guards framing a rectangular license plate indentation. The Calais wheelbase stretched 133 inches long. A wide hood with full-length windsplits, a prominent center crease and hidden windshield wipers was seen. A Cadillac crest decorated the nose and new indicator lamps appeared atop each front fender.

A horizontal beltline molding ran from behind the front wheel housing, almost to the rear stopping where an elliptical bulge in the body came to a point. The rear wheel openings were again enclosed with fender skirts. Calais signature script was on front fenders and the right side of the deck lid. Taillamps were of the same general shape as a year earlier, but were no longer divided by a chrome bar. Long, horizontal back-up lamps were set in the bumper, on either side of a deeply recessed license plate housing. Standard Calais equipment included Turbo-Hydramatic transmission; power steering; dual power brakes with front discs; power windows; center front armrest; electric clock; twin front cigarette lighters; twin front and rear ashtrays; complete interior and exterior courtesy, safety, warning and convenience lights; remote control left-hand outside rearview mirror; visor vanity mirror; L78-15 bias belted tires and the 472-cid four-barrel V-8 engine.

CADILLAC I.D. NUMBERS: Serial numbers and engine numbers took the same general form used in 1970. The serial number was in the same location. The sixth symbol was changed to a '1' to indicate the 1971 model year.

CALAIS SERIES 682

Model Number	Body/Style Number	Body Type & Seating	Factory Price	Shipping Weight	Production Total
71-682	68249-N	4-dr HT Sed-6P	6075	4715	3,569
71-682	68247-G	2-dr HT Cpe-6P	5899	4635	3,360

1971 Cadillac, Coupe DeVille two-door hardtop (with optional vinyl roof)

DEVILLE SERIES — (V-8) — SERIES 683 — DeVilles had all equipment standard on Calais models plus dual rear cigarette lighters, two-way horizontal front seat adjuster and rear center armrests on all styles, except the DeVille. To set them apart visually, DeVilles had thin, bright metal rocker panel steps and signature script on front fenders bearing the series name. The bottoms of the rear fenders were decorated with a bright metal beauty panel that was wider than the rocker strips and blended into the molding running along the bottom of the fender skirt. As on Calais, the lower beltline molding ended on the elliptical rear fender bulge, where thin rectangular side markers were placed above and below the chrome strip. Only two body styles remained in this series.

DEVILLE SERIES 683

Model Number	Body/Style Number	Body Type & Seating	Factory Price	Shipping Weight	Production Total
71-683	68349-B	4-dr HT Sed DeV-6P	6498	4730	69,345
71-683	68347-J	2-dr Cpe DeV-6P	6264	4685	66,081

FLEETWOOD SIXTY SPECIAL — (V-8) — SUB-SERIES 681 — The Sixty Special was now a one model line, including only the Brougham sedan. It came with standard extras such as Automotive Level Control; adjustable reading lights; two-way adjustable Dual Comfort front seat and a padded vinyl roof. New exterior styling was seen along with several new trim features. The windows were cut nearly into the roof in semi-limousine fashion and had softly rounded corners. Vertically angled rectangular coach lamps were a common option incorporated into the rear roof pillar. A broad rocker panel trim plate, with rear extension, was used. The Fleetwood name was block lettered on the front fenders, behind the wheel opening and on the right-hand side of the rear deck lid. The new window styling included a wide pillar separating the front and rear door glass.

1971 Cadillac, Fleetwood 60 Special Brougham four-door sedan

FLEETWOOD SIXTY SPECIAL SUB-SERIES 681

Model Number	Body/Style Number	Body Type & Seating	Factory Price	Shipping Weight	Production Total
71-681	68169-P	4-dr Brghm-6P	7763	4910	15,200

FLEETWOOD SEVENTY-FIVE — (V-8) — SUB-SERIES 697/698 — The long wheelbase Fleetwoods came with everything found on DeVilles (except front center armrest in limousine) plus Automatic Level Control; Automatic Climate Control; rear window defogger; four rear ashtrays and manual right-hand outside rearview mirror. Externally they had the new Cadillac styling and window treatments similar to those described for the Sixty Special. However, the rear roof pillar could be custom finished in several different ways including triangular 'coach' windows or vinyl covered 'blind quarter' looks. Ornamentation included the traditional Fleetwood laurel wreath crests and lettering plus thin horizontal belt moldings. However no rocker sill strips, panels or extension moldings were used. And, of course, the limousine had the doors cut into the roof, special upholstery appointments and a driver's partition with adjustable division window.

FLEETWOOD SEVENTY-FIVE SUB-SERIES 697/698

Model Number	Body/Style Number	Body Type & Seating	Factory Price	Shipping Weight	Production Total
71-697	69723-R	4-dr Sed-6P	11,869	5335	752
71-697	69733-S	4-dr Limo-9P	12,008	5475	848
71-698	69890-Z	Commercial chassis	—	—	2,014

NOTE: The commercial chassis was built off a 157-1/2-inch wheelbase and was provided to professional carmakers for the manufacture of hearses and ambulances, etc.

1971 Cadillac, Fleetwood Eldorado two-door convertible

FLEETWOOD ELDORADO — (V-8) — SUB-SERIES 693 — The second generation of front-wheel-drive Eldorados appeared this year including a new convertible. Used again was the big 500-cid V-8, but with a lower compression ratio and 35 fewer horsepower. Rear coil springs were another new technical feature. The Eldorado wheelbase was stretched more than six inches, too. Body styling was heavily sculptured. A vertically textured, rectangular grille was new. Front fenders had a chiseled cut-off look and a vertical windsplit that harkened back to the early 1950s, appeared just behind the doors. Fender skirts were something new for Eldorados and added to the old-fashioned classical image. So did the revival of convertible styling in this line. Trim features included twin vertical front bumper guards; Fleetwood wreaths on the hood and deck; Eldorado script on the lower front fenders; short horizontal beltline moldings on front fenders and doors; rocker sill beauty panels and a stand-up hood ornament. Narrow 'coach' windows were cut into the rear roof pillars of the Eldorado coupe. Rear end treatments for the new body included a raised and extended trunk lid appearance; extra large backlight and a massive rear bumper with a flat in-and-out look that housed vertical wraparound taillights at each side. Standard fare for the sporty luxury series included all DeVille equipment, less rear armrests, plus Automatic Level Control and front-wheel-drive technology.

FLEETWOOD ELDORADO SUB-SERIES 693

Model Number	Body/Style Number	Body Type & Seating	Factory Price	Shipping Weight	Production Total
71-693	69367-E	2-dr Conv Cpe-6P	7751	4690	6,800
71-693	69347-H	2-dr HT Spt Cpe-6P	7383	4650	20,568

ENGINE: V-8. Overhead valve. Cast iron block. Displacement: 472 cid. Bore and stroke: 4.30 x 4.06 inches. Compression ratio: 10.0:1. Brake hp: 375 at 4400 rpm. Five main bearings. Hydraulic valve lifters. Carburetor: Rochester Quadrajet four-barrel Model 4MV.

ELDORADO ENGINE: V-8. Overhead valve. Cast iron block. Displacement: 500 cid. Bore and stroke: 4.30 x 4.304 inches. Compression ratio: 9.0:1. Brake hp: 365 at 4400 rpm. Five main bearings. Hydraulic valve lifters. Carburetor: Rochester Quadrajet four-barrel Model 4MV.

CHASSIS FEATURES: Wheelbase: (commercial chassis) 157-1/2 inches; (Seventy-Five) 151-1/2 inches; (Sixty Special) 133 inches; (Eldorado) 126.3 inches; (all other models) 130 inches. Overall length: (Seventy-Five) 247.3 inches; (Sixty Special) 228.8 inches; (Eldorado) 221.6 inches; (all other models) 225.8 inches. Tires: L78-15.

POWERTRAIN OPTIONS: Controlled differential, except Eldorado ($58). Trackmaster for Eldorado only ($211).

CONVENIENCE OPTIONS: Automatic Climate Control ($537). Automatic Level Control for Calais and DeVille ($79.) Cruise control ($95). Rear window defogger in Eldorado ($37); in other models ($32). Eldorado grid-type rear window defogger ($63). Door edge guards in two-door ($6); in four-door ($10). Power door locks for 75 ($118); other models ($71). Power door locks with electric seatback release in coupes and convertibles ($71). DeVille, Dual Comfort front seat ($105). Front and rear floor mats; twin type in 75 ($10); one-piece type in Eldorado ($20); twin type in other models ($17). Soft Ray tinted glass ($59). Guide-Matic ($51). Lamp monitors ($50). License frames, one ($6); pair ($12). Remote control right mirror ($26). Brougham and 75 opera lamps ($53). Firemist paint ($132). Radios, AM/FM push-button ($138); AM/FM signal-seeking stereo ($328); AM/FM with tape ($416); AM/FM stereo signal-seeking with rear control in 75 ($421). DeVille vinyl roof ($156). Eldorado padded vinyl roof ($161). DeVille and Brougham six-way seat ($92). Six-way seat in DeVille/Brougham/Calais, with passenger Dual-Comfort in DeVille/Brougham ($118). Shoulder belts in convertible front seat or rear seat all models ($32). Tilt and Telescope steering wheel ($95). DeVille/Eldorado/ Brougham sunroof with vinyl or padded roof mandatory ($626). Trumpet horn in Eldorado coupe ($16). Remote control trunk lock ($58). Trunk mat ($8). Twilight Sentinel ($41). Expanded vinyl Calais upholstery ($42). Expanded leather upholstery, in DeVille/Brougham ($174); in Eldorado coupe ($184). White sidewall L78-15 tires, in 75 ($49); in others ($42).

HISTORICAL FOOTNOTES: Model year production was curtailed by labor disputes and peaked at 188,537 units. The new models were introduced September 29, 1982. For the first time ever, Cadillac built cars outside of Detroit. Some 1971 Coupe and Sedan DeVilles were built at a GM Assembly Division (GMAD) factory in Linden, N.J. Sales, for calendar year 1971, hit a new high of 267,868 units. Hints of a forthcoming downsized Cadillac line were heard in Detroit.

1972 CADILLAC

CALAIS — (V-8) — SERIES C/SERIES 682 — In 1972, General Motors kept busy with the task of re-engineering its cars to conform to new fuel and safety standards established by Federal Government mandate. There was little time to pay attention to altering appearances and few styling changes were seen in the latest Cadillacs. A modest frontal revision placed more emphasis on horizontal grille blades. The parking lamps were moved from the bumper to between the square bezeled headlamps, which were now set wider apart. V-shaped emblems made a return appearance on the hood and deck lid. A number of equipment changes were seen. As usual (since 1967) the list of Calais features started with all regulation safety devices, to which was added variable ratio power steering; dual power brakes with front discs; automatic transmission; power windows; all courtesy and warning lights; a new bumper impact system; three-speed wipers and windshield washers; visor vanity mirror; two front cigar lighters; automatic parking brake release; front center armrest; passenger assist straps; side marker and cornering lights; the 472-cid four-barrel V-8; flow-through ventilation and five L78-15 black sidewall bias belted tires. Externally, the Calais was identified by front fender model script; thin horizontal belt moldings; fender skirts; full wheel covers and a script on the right side of the trunk.

CADILLAC I.D. NUMBERS: The GM serial numbering system changed slightly this year to incorporate an alphabetical series code and a new alphabetical code designating engine type. The serial number was again located on top of the instrument panel, where it was visible through the windshield. The first symbol was a number '6' to indicate production by Cadillac. The second symbol was a letter identifying the series as follows: C = Calais; D = DeVille; B = Brougham; L = Eldorado and F = Fleetwood 75. The third and fourth symbols were numbers identifying the body type and they correspond to the numerical portion of the Body/Style Numbers shown in the charts below. The fifth symbol was a letter identifying the engine, as follows: R = 472-cid V-8; S = 500-cid Eldorado V-8. The sixth symbol was a number identifying model year, such as '2' for 1972. The seventh symbol was a letter designating the manufacturing point as follows: Q = Detroit, Michigan, and E = Linden, New Jersey. The next group of numbers was the sequential production code. Body/Style Numbers were also changed this year on some data plates and factory literature, but not all. The first symbol of the new type of code was the series identifying letter given above. For example, the new system used a 'C' to designate Calais (the old system used the three numbers '682'). The second and third symbols of the new type code were numbers identifying body style. These numbers correspond to the charts below and were the same as the fourth and fifth numbers used in the past. For example, the Body/Style Code for a Calais coupe was 68247 under the old system and C47 under the new system. Of course, despite the new GM system, Cadillac had been using letter codes for different body styles since the mid-1950s and these were used again. They were the same as in the past: G = Calais coupe; N = Calais sedan; etc. Research shows that GM cars built in 1972 used the new system on the serial number tag and the old system on the vehicle data plate below the hood. From 1973 on, the new system was used in both locations. Also, this new system was used through 1975, the last year covered in this edition of the *Standard Catalog of American Cars.*

CALAIS SERIES C/CALAIS SERIES 682

Model Number	Body/Style Number	Body Type & Seating	Factory Price	Shipping Weight	Production Total
682/C	C49-N	4-dr HT Sed-6P	5938	4698	3,875
682/C	C47-G	2-dr HT Cpe-6P	5771	4642	3,900

NOTE: Body/Style Numbers in column two above are the new type used on the serial number tag mounted to top of instrument panel, visable through windshield. Research indicates that the old type Body/Style Number was still found on the vehicle data plate below the hood. With the new system the Calais sedan is Body/Style Number C49; with the old system 68249. This note applies only to 1972 Cadillacs, as the new system was used in both locations from 1973 on.

1972 Cadillac, Sedan Deville four-door hardtop

DEVILLE — (V-8) — SERIES D/SERIES 683 — DeVille standard equipment included all found on Calais plus rocker panel moldings; rear center armrest and twin rear cigarette lighters. Of course, the rocker panel trim helped in identifying the cars, but there was also new DeVille signature script affixed to the sides of the rear roof pillars.

DEVILLE SERIES D/DEVILLE SERIES 683

Model Number	Body/Style Number	Body Type & Seating	Factory Price	Shipping Weight	Production Total
683/D	D49-B	4-dr Sed DeV-6P	6390	4762	99,531
683/D	D47-J	2-dr Cpe DeV-6P	6168	4682	95,280

![1972 Cadillac, Fleetwood 60 Special Brougham four-door sedan]

1972 Cadillac, Fleetwood 60 Special Brougham four-door sedan

FLEETWOOD SIXTY SPECIAL — (V-8) — SUB-SERIES B/681 — Fleetwood models had all DeVille features plus Automatic Level Control and, on the Brougham, Dual Comfort front seat; rear seat reading light; carpeted foot rests and a padded vinyl roof with rear window chrome molding. As the only Cadillacs on the 133-inch wheelbase, Broughams were identified by their large, rounded corner, four window styling, Fleetwood front fender lettering and laurel wreath hood and deck badges. Many were sold equipped with the coach lamp option and bright body underscores, with rear extensions included as well.

FLEETWOOD SIXTY SPECIAL SUB-SERIES B/681

Model Number	Body/Style Number	Body Type & Seating	Factory Price	Shipping Weight	Production Total
681/B	B69-P	4-dr Brghm-6P	7637	4858	20,750

FLEETWOOD SEVENTY-FIVE — (V-8) — SUB-SERIES F/697 — Fleetwood 75s had all DeVille equipment (less front seat armrest on limousine) plus Automatic Level Control; carpeted foot rests; fixed ratio power steering; remote control right-hand outside mirror; rear window defogger and Automatic Climate Control. The sedan included folding auxiliary seats. The limousine had the doors cut into the roof and had the traditional partition and glass divider. Trim included bright body underscores with rear extensions; horizontal thin belt moldings; Fleetwood front fender lettering and laurel wreath badges for the hood and deck lid. Several optional rear roof treatments were available making these models true factory-built semi-custom-type vehicles.

FLEETWOOD SEVENTY-FIVE SUB-SERIES F/697

Model Number	Body/Style Number	Body Type & Seating	Factory Price	Shipping Weight	Production Total
697/F	F23-R	4-dr Sed-6/9P	11,948	5620	995
697/F	F33-S	4-dr Limo-9P	12,080	5742	960
698/Z	69890-Z	Commercial chassis	—	—	2,462

NOTE: The commercial chassis was built on a 157-1/2-inch wheelbase platform and was provided to professional carmakers for the manufacture of hearses and ambulances, etc.

1972 Cadillac, Fleetwood Eldorado two-door coupe

FLEETWOOD ELDORADO — (V-8) — SUB-SERIES L/693 — The 1972 Eldorados had a vertical textured grille. The Cadillac name was engraved on the left side of the upper grille surround and Eldorado script appeared above the cornering lights on the lower front fender tips. The 8.2-Litre badges were moved to the sides of the body, below the belt molding and behind the front wheel openings. New full wheel covers with concentric rings were seen. Eight colors of Sierra grain leather were supplied as convertible upholstery selections. Standard equipment included the detuned 1972 version of the

500-cid V-8; front-wheel-drive chassis layout; Automatic Level Control; front center armrest only and 'coach windows' on the hardtop coupe.

FLEETWOOD ELDORADO SUB-SERIES L/693

Model Number	Body/Style Number	Body Type & Seating	Factory Price	Shipping Weight	Production Total
693/L	L67-E	2-dr Conv-6P	7681	4966	7,975
693/L	L47-H	2-dr HT Cpe-6P	7360	4880	32,099

ENGINE: V-8. Overhead valve. Cast iron block. Displacement: 472 cid. Bore and stroke: 4.30 x 4 06 inches. Compression ratio: 8.5:1. SAE Net hp: 220. NOTE: horsepower ratings are now expressed in SAE net hp. A gross hp rating of 345 at 4400 rpm was also listed. Five main bearings. Hydraulic valve lifters. Carburetor: Rochester Quadrajet four-barrel.

ELDORADO ENGINE: V-8. Overhead valve. Cast iron block. Displacement: 500 cid. Bore and stroke: 4.30 x 4.304 inches. Compression ratio: 8.5:1. Brake hp: 365 at 4400 rpm. SAE net hp: 235. Five main bearings. Hydraulic valve lifters. Carburetor: Rochester Quadrajet four-barrel (Eldorado special).

POWERTRAIN OPTIONS: Cruise Control ($92). Controlled differential ($56). Eighty-amp generator ($41). Heavy-duty cooling system ($56). Exhaust emissions system, required on all cars built for California sale ($15). Trackmaster ($205). Trailer towing package, Eldorado ($62); all others ($92).

CONVENIENCE OPTIONS: Automatic Climate Control ($523). Automatic Level Control ($77). Rear window defoggers; grid type in Eldorado convertible ($62); standard type in Eldorado coupe ($36); standard type in all others, except regular equipment in 75 ($31). Door edge guards, two-door ($6); four-door ($9). Power door locks, in two-doors, includes automatic seatback release ($69); in 75 ($115); in other four-doors ($69). Dual Comfort seat in DeVille and Eldorado ($103). Front and rear twin rubber floor mats ($16). Front and rear one-piece rubber floor mats for Eldorados ($19). Front and rear twin rubber floor mats for 75 ($10). Soft Ray tinted glass ($57). Convertible hard boot ($40). Auxiliary horn ($15). Bumper impact strips ($24). One license frame ($6); two ($11). Remote control right-hand outside rearview mirror, standard on 75 ($26). Roof pillar coach lights on Brougham and 75 ($51). Firemist paint ($128). AM/FM radios, regular ($183); stereo signal-seeking ($320); stereo signal-seeking with rear control in 75 only ($410); stereo with tape player ($406). Full vinyl padded top for DeVilles, including 'halo' on Coupe DeVille ($152). Full vinyl Eldorado padded top ($157). Custom Cabriolet Eldorado Coupe roof ($360). Power seat options ($89-$115 depending on model and use of Dual Comfort seats). Twin front shoulder harness in convertible ($31). Tilt & Telescope steering wheel ($92). DeVille Brougham/Eldorado Coupe sunroof, with vinyl top mandatory ($610). Sunroof with Eldorado Coupe Custom Cabriolet treatment ($1,005). White sidewall tires, on 75 ($47); others ($41). Remote control trunk lock ($56). Trunk mat ($8). Twilight Sentinel ($40). Expanded vinyl Calais upholstery ($41). Expanded leather DeVille/Brougham upholstery ($169). Expanded leather Eldorado Coupe upholstery ($179).

HISTORICAL FOOTNOTES: Introductions of the 1972 line took place in September 1971 with production continuing until July 7, 1972. Calendar year production peaked at 266,780 cars and model year output hit 267,787 units. It was a record breaking year. Cadillac celebrated its 70th anniversary this season.

1973 CADILLAC

CALAIS — (V-8) — SERIES 6C — New energy absorbing bumpers were seen on GM cars this year and it brought Cadillac styling refinements with them. Grilles were widened and had an intricate eggcrate design. Larger, vertical rectangles housed the parking lamps between wide spaced headlamps, which had square bezels, but round lenses. Bumpers ran fully across the front of the cars and wrapped around each end. Vertical guards were spaced much wider apart, at a point outboard of the grille. The rear end had a bumper with a wider, flatter upper section housing an angled license plate recess. Border outline moldings, vertically 'veed', paralleled the fender edge shape at the rear bodysides. Single, rectangular rear side marker lamps, horizontally mounted, were placed over and under the rear tip of the thin beltline trim. Cadillac script was seen on the front fender sides, below the belt molding, behind the wheel opening. Cloth upholstery was standard and equipment features were comparable to 1972.

CADILLAC I.D. NUMBERS: The serial number system and locations were the same as the previous year with the sixth symbol changed to '3' to indicate the 1973 model year. Calais were numbered 6C( )R3Q 100001 to 350000; DeVilles 6D( )R3Q 100001 to 350000 or 6D4( )R3E 3500001 to 400000; Eldorados 6L( )S3Q 400001 to 450000; Broughams 6B69R3Q 100001 to 350000 and Seventy-Fives 6F( )R3Q 100001 to 350000. The new Body/Style Number codes were used on both serial number tags and vehicle data plates.

CALAIS SERIES 6C

Model Number	Body/Style Number	Body Type & Seating	Factory Price	Shipping Weight	Production Total
6C	C47/G	2-dr HT Cpe-6P	5886	4900	4,202
6C	C49/N	4-dr HT Sed-6P	6038	4953	3,798

1973 Cadillac, Coupe DeVille two-door hardtop (with optional vinyl roof)

DEVILLE — (V-8) — SERIES 6D — Bright body underscores with rear extensions distinguished the DeVille externally. There were also DeVille signatures on the rear roof pillars. Equipment specifications were comparable to 1972. The DeVille was actually a Calais with added trim, richer appointments, rear armrest and standard power seat.

DEVILLE SERIES 6D

Model Number	Body/Style Number	Body Type & Seating	Factory Price	Shipping Weight	Production Total
6D	D47/J	2-dr Cpe DeV-6P	6268	4925	112,849
6D	D49/N	4-dr Sed DeV-6P	6500	4985	103,394

FLEETWOOD SIXTY SPECIAL BROUGHAM — (V-8) — SERIES 6B — Standard equipment on the Brougham included DeVille features (with different body underscores); Automatic Level Control; Dual-Comfort front seat; rear reading lights; a new front reading lamp; padded vinyl roof with rear chrome moldings and carpeted, rear compartment foot rests. Four window, rounded corner roof styling, with extra wide center pillars, was seen again. Tires with pencil thin whitewall bands were used.

1973 Cadillac, Fleetwood 60 Special Brougham four-door sedan

FLEETWOOD SIXTY SPECIAL BROUGHAM SERIES 6B

Model Number	Body/Style Number	Body Type & Seating	Factory Price	Shipping Weight	Production Total
6B	B69/P	4-dr Sed-6/9P	7765	5102	24,800

FLEETWOOD SEVENTY-FIVE — (V-8) — SERIES 6F — The long wheelbase, high-dollar Fleetwoods were immense automobiles with low-cut, extra-large rounded corner side window treatments and rather large 'coach windows' cut into the rear roof pillars. Fleetwoods had the annual Cadillac styling changes plus thin, horizontal bodyside molding; front fender nameplates; full-length body underscores with rear extensions; and Fleetwood-style laurel wreath badge ornamen-

tation. Equipment inclusions were carpeted foot rests; fixed ratio power steering; rear seat window defogger; Automatic Climate Control and right-hand outside rearview mirrors operated by remote control. Bumper impact strips were standard on Seventy-Fives, optional on other Cadillacs.

FLEETWOOD SEVENTY-FIVE SERIES 6F

Model Number	Body/Style Number	Body Type & Seating	Factory Price	Shipping Weight	Production Total
6F	F23/R	4-dr Sed-6P	11,948	5620	1,017
6F	F33/S	4-dr Limo-9P	12,080	5742	1,043
6F	F90/Z	Commercial chassis	—	—	2,212

NOTE: The commercial chassis was built off a 157-1/2-inch wheelbase platform and provided to professional carmakers for manufacture of hearses and ambulances.

1973 Cadillac, Fleetwood Eldorado two-door convertible

FLEETWOOD ELDORADO — (V-8) — SERIES 6L — The front-wheel-drive Eldorados were restyled stem to stern. A new eggcrate grille was seen. The front bumper had an angular, in-and-out look with wide spread vertical guards. Parking lamps wrapped around the body corners. On the sides of the cars, a thin rub molding ran from behind the forward wheel housing and stretched nearly to the round, rear side marker lamps, which had wreath and crest ornamentation. Gone were the vertical rear fender breaks (along with the windsplit trim), but fender skirts and bright underscores were used again. Eldorado script was seen behind the front wheel openings. The deck lid still bulged up at the top center, but was flatter along its rear face. The rear bumper was flatter and straighter, too. Vertical taillamps looked somewhat like the previous type, but with the heavy chrome housings deleted. They slanted slightly forward at the same angle as the fender line. Standard Eldorado extras included Automatic Level Control, new energy absorbing bumper system, 'coach' windows for coupes and the 500-cid V-8.

FLEETWOOD ELDORADO SERIES 6L

Model Number	Body/Style Number	Body Type & Seating	Factory Price	Shipping Weight	Production Total
6L	L47/H	2-dr HT Cpe-6P	7360	5094	42,136
6L	L67/E	2-dr Conv-6P	7681	5131	9,315

ENGINE: V-8. Overhead valve. Cast iron block. Displacement: 472 cid. Bore and stroke: 4.30 x 4.06 inches. Compression ratio: 10.0:1. Brake hp: 375 at 4400 rpm. Five main bearings. Hydraulic valve lifters. Carburetor: Rochester Quadrajet four-barrel Model 4MV.

ELDORADO ENGINE: V-8. Overhead valve. Cast iron block. Displacement: 500 cid. Bore and stroke: 4.30 x 4.304 inches. Compression ratio: 9.0:1. Brake hp: 365 at 4400 rpm. Five main bearings. Hydraulic valve lifters. Carburetor: Rochester Quadrajet four-barrel Model 4MV.

CHASSIS FEATURES: Wheelbase: (commercial chassis) 157-1/2 inches; (Seventy-Five) 151-1/2 inches; (Sixty Special) 133 inches; (Eldorado) 126.3 inches; (all other models) 130 inches. Overall length: (Seventy-Five) 251 inches; (Sixty Special) 232 inches; (Eldorado) 222 inches; (all other models) 231 inches. Width: (all models) 80 inches. Tires: L78-15.

POWERTRAIN OPTIONS: Cruise Control ($92). Controlled differential ($56). Eighty-amp generator ($41). Heavy-duty cooling system ($56). Exhaust emissions system, required on all cars built for California sale ($15). Trackmaster ($205). Trailer towing package, Eldorado ($62); all others ($92).

CONVENIENCE OPTIONS: Automatic Climate Control ($523). Automatic Level Control ($77). Rear window defoggers; grid type in Eldorado convertible ($62); standard type in Eldorado coupe ($36); standard type in all others, except regular equipment in 75 ($31). Door edge guards, two-door ($6);

four-door ($9). Power door locks, in two-doors, includes automatic seatback release ($69); in 75 ($115); in other four-doors ($69). Dual Comfort seat in DeVille and Eldorado ($103). Front and rear twin rubber floor mats ($16). Front and rear one-piece rubber floor mats for Eldorados ($19). Front and rear twin rubber floor mats for 75 ($10). Soft Ray tinted glass ($57). Convertible hard boot ($40). Auxiliary horn ($15). Bumper impact strips ($24). One license frame ($6); two ($11). Remote control right-hand outside rearview mirror, standard on 75 ($26). Roof pillar coach lights on Brougham and 75 ($51). Firemist paint ($128). AM/FM radios, regular ($183); stereo signal-seeking ($320); stereo signal-seeking with rear control in 75 only ($410); stereo with tape player ($406). Full vinyl padded top for DeVilles, including 'halo' on Coupe DeVille ($152). Full vinyl Eldorado padded top ($157). Custom Cabriolet Eldorado Coupe roof ($360). Power seat options ($89-$115 depending on model and use of Dual Comfort seats). Twin front shoulder harness in convertible ($31). Tilt & Telescope steering wheel ($92). DeVille Brougham/Eldorado Coupe sunroof, with vinyl top mandatory ($610). Sunroof with Eldorado Coupe Custom Cabriolet treatment ($1,005). White sidewall tires, on 75 ($47); others ($41). Remote control trunk lock ($56). Trunk mat ($8). Twilight Sentinel ($40). Expanded vinyl Calais upholstery ($41). Expanded leather DeVille/Brougham upholstery ($169). Expanded leather Eldorado Coupe upholstery ($179). Steel-belted radial ply tires, size L78-15 with Space Saver spare, for all models except 75 ($156). Lighted right-hand visor vanity mirror ($430). Theft deterrent system ($80), Brougham d'Elegance Group ($750). Deluxe robe and pillow ($85). Left-hand remote control thermometer mirror ($15).

HISTORICAL FOOTNOTES: Dealer introductions were held September 21, 1972. Model year production hit a record 304,839 Cadillacs. The five-millionth Cadillac, a blue Sedan DeVille, was built June 27, 1973. A Cotillion white Eldorado convertible paced the Indianapolis 500 with Jim Rathmann driving. Robert D. Lund became general manager of Cadillac Division, January 1, 1973.

1974 CADILLAC

CALAIS — (V-8) — SERIES 6C — A major restyling marked the 'Gas Crunch' era Cadillacs of 1974. A wide eggcrate grille was used. Dual round headlamps were mounted in close together square bezels. Further outboard were double-deck wraparound parking lamps. Shorter, vertical grille guards appeared in about the same position as before. Rear fendersides were flatter, without the elliptical bulge. The thin beltline molding was positioned lower by several inches. The rear end had vertical bumper ends with the taillights built in. Both bumpers, especially the rear, protruded further from the body. Coupes sported large, wide 'coach' windows giving a thick center pillar look. A new curved instrument panel housed a digital clock. Standard equipment included variable ratio power steering; dual power brakes; front disc brakes; automatic transmission; power windows; all courtesy and warning lights; three-speed wipers and electric washers; visor vanity mirror; two front cigar lighters; front and rear armrests; remote control left-hand outside mirror; assist straps; side and cornering lights; automatic parking brake release; front center armrest; litter container; flow-through ventilation; L78-15/B blackwall bias belted tires and a 472-cid four-barrel V-8.

CADILLAC I.D. NUMBERS: The serial number system and locations were the same as the previous year with the sixth symbol changed to a '4' to indicate the 1974 model year. Calais were numbered 6C4( )R4Q 100001 and up; DeVilles 6D5( )R4( ) 100001 and up; Eldorados 6L( )S4Q( ) 100001 and up; Broughams 6B69R4Q 100001 and up and Seventy-Five 6F( )R4Q 100001 to 350000.

CALAIS SERIES 6C

Model Number	Body/Style Number	Body Type & Seating	Factory Price	Shipping Weight	Production Total
6C	C49/N	4-dr HT Sed-6P	7545	4979	2,324
6C	C47/G	2-dr HT Cpe-6P	7371	4900	4,449

1974 Cadillac, Coupe DeVille two-door hardtop

DEVILLE — (V-8) — SERIES 60 — DeVilles again had all Calais equipment plus rocker moldings; rear center armrests; rear cigar lighters and power front seat adjuster. A DeVille script nameplate replaced the Calais signature above the rear tip of the lower belt molding. New options included a DeVille d'Elegance luxury appointments package and a fully padded vinyl Cabriolet roof treatment. Ingredients of the former package were velour upholstery; Deluxe padded doors; front seatback storage pockets; deep pile carpeting; floor mats; see-through standup hood ornament and vinyl tape accent stripes. The Cabriolet group incorporated a landau style top with bright metal forward divider strip. A Space Saver spare tire was standard when DeVilles were ordered with optional white sidewall steel belted radial tires.

DEVILLE SERIES 6D

Model Number	Body/Style Number	Body Type & Seating	Factory Price	Shipping Weight	Production Total
6D	D49/B	4-dr Sed DeV-6P	8100	5032	60,419
6D	D47/J	2-dr Cpe DeV-6P	7867	4924	112,201

NOTE: At the beginning of the 1974 model year, the following factory retail prices were in effect for Calais and DeVille models: C49/N ($6,327); C47/G ($6,153); D49/B ($6,793); D47/J ($6,560). Midyear price increases, although nothing new to the auto industry, became much more common after the early 1970s.

1974 Cadillac, Fleetwood 60 Special Brougham four-door sedan

FLEETWOOD BROUGHAM — (V-8) — SERIES 6B — The 1974 Fleetwood Sixty Special Brougham came with all DeVille standard equipment plus Automatic Level Control; Dual Comfort front seat; front and rear reading lights; padded vinyl roof with chrome rear window moldings; carpeted foot rests and L78-15/B white sidewall tires of bias belted construction. Fleetwood ornamentation, nameplates and round corner, four window roof styling were seen again. The Brougham d'Elegance option package was available again, including the same type of appointments outlined for the DeVille d'Elegance, but at nearly twice the price on the bigger car. Even more ostentatious was the Talisman group with four-place seating in Medici crushed velour armchair-style seats; full length center consoles with writing set in front and rear vanity; reclining front passenger seat; assist straps; special Turbine wheel discs; seatback pockets; deep-pile carpeting floor mats; stand-up hood ornament and special rear roof pillar Fleetwood Talisman scripts. Even more luxurious was a leather trim Talisman package, an option that cost only $100 less than a brand new 1974 four-cylinder Ford Pinto two-door sedan.

FLEETWOOD BROUGHAM SERIES 6B

Model Number	Body/Style Number	Body Type & Seating	Factory Price	Shipping Weight	Production Total
6B	B69/P	4-dr Sed-6P	9537	5143	18,250

FLEETWOOD SEVENTY-FIVE — (V-8) — SERIES 6F — Standard equipment on 1974 models in the Fleetwood Seventy-Five line began at the DeVille level plus Automatic Level Control;

carpeted foot rests; fixed ratio power steering; rear seat window defogger; Automatic Climate Control; trailering package and remote control right-hand outside rearview mirror. Black sidewall L78-15/D tires (optional on other Cadillacs) were used. Also found on all of the big Fleetwoods were new, gray and white bumper impact strips, which cost extra on other models. Series script appeared on the front fenders, behind the wheelhousings, and 'coach' windows appeared in the rear roof pillar. Twilight Sentinel was now featured on all 75s at regular prices.

FLEETWOOD SEVENTY-FIVE SERIES 6F

Model Number	Body/Style Number	Body Type & Seating	Factory Price	Shipping Weight	Production Total
6F	F23/R	4-dr Sed-6P	13,120	5719	895
6F	F33/S	4-dr Limo-9P	13,254	5883	1,005
6F	F90/2	Commercial chassis	—	—	2,265

NOTE: The commercial chassis was built off a 157-1/2-inch wheelbase platform and supplied to professional carmakers for the manufacture of hearses and ambulances, etc. Introductory factory retail prices for conventional Fleetwood models were as follows: B69/P ($8,083); F23/R ($12,344) and F33/S ($12,478). A midyear price increase resulted in the factory retail prices shown in the chart above.

1974 Cadillac, Fleetwood Eldorado two-door hardtop

FLEETWOOD ELDORADO — (V-8) — SERIES 6L — A new grille for Eldorados had the opposite design change, compared to other Cadillacs. The eggcrate look was gone and a finer cross-hatched insert was used. It also had a wide, brushed aluminum top header bar, providing a neoclassical appearance. A Cadillac signature was engraved on the left side of the header. The rear fender line looked squarer and a bumper/taillight arrangement that telescoped on impact was used. A curved instrument panel was new, too. The equipment list included all DeVille features plus L78-15/B whitewall bias belted tires; 'coach' windows on the coupe and the big 500-cid V-8. Expanded leather interiors were standard in what was now America's only production luxury convertible.

FLEETWOOD ELDORADO SERIES 6L

Model Number	Body/Style Number	Body Type & Seating	Factory Price	Shipping Weight	Production Total
6L	L47/H	2-dr HT Cpe-6P	9110	4960	32,812
6L	L67/E	2-dr Conv-6P	9437	5019	7,600

NOTE: Introductory prices for the 1974 front-wheel-drive Eldorados were $7,656 for the coupe and $7,873 for the convertible. A midyear price increase resulted in the factory retail prices shown in the chart above.

ENGINE: V-8. Overhead valve. Cast iron block. Displacement: 472 cid. Bore and stroke- 4.30 x 4.06 inches. Compression ratio: 8.25:1. SAE net hp: 205 at 4000 rpm. Hydraulic valve lifters. Carburetor: four-barrel.

ELDORADO ENGINE: V-8. Overhead valve. Displacement: 500 cid. Bore and stroke: 4.3 x 4.3 inches. Compression ratio: 8.25:1. SAE net hp: 210 at 3800 rpm. Hydraulic valve lifters. Carburetor: four-barrel.

CHASSIS FEATURES: Wheelbase: (commercial chassis) 157-1/2 inches; (Seventy-Five) 151-1/2 inches; (Brougham) 133 inches; (Eldorado) 126 inches; (other models) 130 inches. Overall length: (Seventy-Five) 252 inches; (Brougham) 234 inches; (Eldorado) 224 inches; (other models) 231 inches. Width: (all models) 80 inches. Tires: (Seventy-Five) L78-15/D blackwall; (Eldorado and Brougham) L78-15/B white sidewall bias belted; (all others) L78-15/B black sidewall bias belted.

POWERTRAIN OPTIONS: Controlled differential, except Eldorado ($56). Emissions test, required in California ($20). High

altitude performance package ($16). High energy electronic ignition ($77). Trackmaster skid control ($214).

CONVENIENCE OPTIONS: Automatic Climate Control, standard in 75 ($523). Airbag restraint system, except 75 and Eldorado convertible ($225). Automatic Level Control on Calais/DeVille ($77). Brougham d'Elegance group ($750). Cruise Control ($95). Coupe DeVille Custom Cabriolet, with sunroof ($640); without sunroof ($220). Eldorado Custom Cabriolet Coupe, with sunroof ($1,005); without sunroof ($385). Rear window defogger, except 75 and convertible ($64). Deluxe robe and pillow ($85). DeVille d'Elegance group, in Sedan DeVille ($355); in Coupe DeVille ($300). Door edge guards, two-door ($6); four-door ($10). Power door locks, two-door including seatback release ($69); four-door, except 75 ($69); 75 sedan and limousine ($115). Dual Comfort front seat in DeVille, Eldorado, 75 sedan ($108). Fleetwood Brougham Talisman group ($1,800). Fleetwood Brougham Talisman group with leather trim ($2,450). Front/rear twin floor mats in all except Eldorado/75 ($17). Eldorado front and rear one-piece floor mats ($20). Twin rubber front floor mats in 75 ($11). Soft Ray tinted glass ($57). Guide-Matic headlamp control ($49). Trumpet horn ($15). Bumper impact strips, standard on 75 ($24). Lamp monitors ($48). License frame ($6). Illuminated vanity mirror ($43). Right-hand remote control outside rearview mirror, standard in 75 ($27). Opera lamps on Brougham 75 ($52). Firemist paint ($132). Special Firemist paint ($200). Special non-Firemist paint ($174). Radios (all with power antenna), AM/FM push-button ($203); AM/FM with tape ($426); AM/FM signal-seeking ($340); AM/FM stereo with rear control in 75 ($430). Fully-padded vinyl roofs, on DeVille/Calais ($152); Eldorado coupe ($157); 75 ($741). Six-way power seat in Calais ($120), in DeVille/Fleetwood, except limousine ($89); passenger seat only, with Dual-Comfort ($120); driver's seat only, with Dual-Comfort ($89). Convertible shoulder harness ($33). Tilt & Telescope steering ($94). Sunroof, DeVille/Brougham/Eldorado coupe ($610). Theft deterrent system ($80). Left-hand remote control thermometer mirror ($15). Tires, L78-15/D whitewall, on 75 ($47); others ($41); LR78-15/B whitewall steel belted radial on 75 ($162); on Calais ($156); on DeVille with Space Saver spare ($156); L78-15/B blackwall bias belted with Space Saver spare ($35); whitewall ($63). Eldorado convertible top boot ($40). Trailering package, standard on 75 ($65). Remote control trunk lock ($60). Trunk mat ($80). Twilight Sentinel, standard in 75 ($42). Expanded vinyl upholstery in DeVille/Brougham ($184). Expanded leather upholstery in Eldorado coupe ($195). Special wheel discs, except Eldorado ($40). Controlled cycle windshield wipers ($25).

HISTORICAL FOOTNOTES: Model introductions took place on September 16, 1973. Model year production hit 242,330 cars. All U.S. auto sales were off this season, as a side effect of the Arab oil embargo. Because of this, Cadillac's lower production level was still sufficient to pull down a greater market share.

1975 CADILLAC

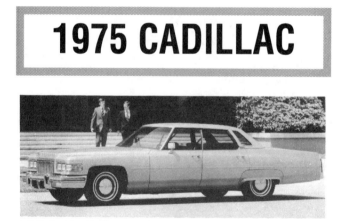

1975 Cadillac, Calais four-door hardtop

CALAIS — (V-8) — SERIES 6C — Styling changes for 1975 brought dual, square headlight lenses flanked by rectangular cornering lights wrapping around the body. A new cross-hatched grille appeared. Calais coupes and sedans had triangular 'coach' windows in their 'C' pillars. Standard equipment was about the same as in 1974, plus front fender lamp monitors; power door locks; high-energy ignition; steel-belted radial tires and catalytic converter. Once again, substantial midyear price increases were seen. Also, all cars offered at the beginning of the model run were equipped with 500-cid V-8s and electronic fuel injection became optional in March 1975.

CADILLAC I.D. NUMBERS: The serial number system and locations were unchanged. The sixth symbol changed to a '5' for the 1975 model year. Calais were numbered 6C4( )S5( )100001 and up; DeVilles 6D4( )S5( )100001 and up; Eldorados 6D4( )S59100001 and up; Broughams 6B69S5( )100001 and up; Seventy-Fives 6F( )S5( )100001 and up and Sevilles 6S69R6Q 4500001 and up (Sevilles sold in 1975 were considered 1976 models and all production of this model was quartered in the Detroit assembly plant, Code 'Q'). Engine code 'R' was now applied to the new 350-cid Seville V-8.

CALAIS SERIES 6C

Model Number	Body/Style Number	Body Type & Seating	Factory Price	Shipping Weight	Production Total
6C	C49/N	4-dr HT Sed-6P	8377	5087	2,500
6C	C47/G	2-dr HT Cpe-6P	8184	5003	5,800

NOTE: Initial 1975 pricing is reflected above. Two rounds of price increases were seen, the sedan going to $8,390 and then $8,806; the coupe going to $8,197 and then $8,613.

1975 Cadillac, Coupe DeVille d'Elegance two-door hardtop

DEVILLE — (V-8) — SERIES 6D — Chrome underscores, DeVille series rear fender nameplates and richer interiors identified Coupe and Sedan DeVille models. They both had slim, triangular rear quarter windows and power front seat adjusters. Luxury level options, including d'Elegance and Cabriolet packages were available again.

DEVILLE SERIES 6D

Model Number	Body/Style Number	Body Type & Seating	Factory Price	Shipping Weight	Production Total
6D	D49/B	4-dr HT Sed-6P	8801	5146	63,352
6D	D47/J	2-dr HT Cpe-6P	8600	5049	110,218

NOTE: At the beginning of the 1975 model year, prices were those seen above. Two rounds of midyear increases were seen, the sedan going to $8,814 and then $9,230; the coupe going to $8,613 and then $9,029.

1975 Cadillac, Fleetwood Brougham four-door sedan

FLEETWOOD BROUGHAM — (V-8) — SERIES 6B — The Sixty Special designation was retired this year. Identification features for Broughams included front fender script, Fleetwood decorative touches and the traditional extra equipment such as padded top; automatic leveling; dual-comfort seats and reading lamps. Talisman and d'Elegance option groups were available again. Size was unchanged from 1974.

FLEETWOOD BROUGHAM SERIES 6B

Model Number	Body/Style Number	Body Type & Seating	Factory Price	Shipping Weight	Production Total
6B	B69/P	4-dr Sed-6P	10,414	5242	18,755

NOTE: Initial 1975 pricing is reflected above. Two rounds of price increases were seen, the Brougham going to $10,427 and then $10,843.

FLEETWOOD SEVENTY-FIVE — (V-8) — SERIES 6F — Both long wheelbase Cadillacs came with two separate climate control systems; automatic leveling air shocks; folding jump seats; rear window defogger; trailering equipment and remote control right-hand outside rearview mirrors. The limousine had a leather front chauffeur's compartment and glass partition window. Script identification nameplates were worn on the front fenders, behind the wheel opening. Fleetwood decorative trim was seen. New triangular rear quarter windows, of much slimmer design than before, were seen.

FLEETWOOD SEVENTY-FIVE SERIES 6F

Model Number	Body/Style Number	Body Type & Seating	Factory Price	Shipping Weight	Production Total
6F	F23/R	4-dr Sed-9P	14,218	5720	876
6F	F23/S	4-dr Limo-9P	14,557	5862	795
6F	F90/Z	Commercial chassis	—	—	1,328

NOTE: Initial 1975 pricing is reflected above. Two rounds of price increases were seen, the 75 sedan going to $14,231 and then $14,647; the 75 limousine going to $14,570 and then $14,986.

1975 Cadillac, Fleetwood Eldorado two-door convertible

FLEETWOOD ELDORADO — (V-8) — SERIES 6L — The Eldorado lost its rear fender skirts this season and saw a major face lift, as well. Square headlamps were new. Wraparound cornering lamps were gone, being replaced by a narrow, rectangular type, housed in the front fender tips. The parking lamps and directionals were placed in the bumper ends. Larger rear quarter windows appeared on the coupe and a new cross-hatch grille was used on both styles. The rear fender wells were enlarged, causing the horizontal belt molding to end just ahead of the wheel opening. On the coupes, Fleetwood ornaments decorated the roof 'C' pillar. Front-wheel-drive technology was retained.

FLEETWOOD ELDORADO SERIES 6L

Model Number	Body/Style Number	Body Type & Seating	Factory Price	Shipping Weight	Production Total
6L	L47/H	2-dr HT Cpe-6P	9935	5108	35,802
6L	L67/E	2-dr Conv-6P	10,354	5167	8,950

NOTE: Introductory prices for 1975 are reflected above. Two rounds of price increases were seen, the Eldorado coupe going to $9,948 and then $10,364; the Eldorado convertible going to $10,367 and then $10,783.

SEVILLE — (V-8) — SERIES 6S — The Seville was introduced as a downsized 1976 Cadillac in April 1975. It appeared in dealer showrooms the first day of May. It was based on the GM front engine/rear drive 'X' car platform used for the Chevrolet Nova and its derivatives such as Oldsmobile Omega, Pontiac Ventura and Buick Apollo. The exterior panels were, however, exclusive to Cadillac and the equipment and trim level was as rich as possible. Included at a base price of $12,479 were padded vinyl roof; air conditioning; Automatic Level Control; power seats; power windows; power door locks; AM/FM stereo; leather or special cloth upholstery; Tilt & Telescope steering wheel; chimes and GR78-15/B steel-belted radial whitewall tires. Sevilles came only as four-door sedans with crisp, angular-curved styling that was purely modern. Square headlamps, wraparound cornering lights and an eggcrate grille with narrow vertical center division bar were seen. The base powerplant was a 350-cid Oldsmobile product, to which electronic fuel injection was added.

SEVILLE SERIES 6S

Model Number	Body/Style Number	Body Type & Seating	Factory Price	Shipping Weight	Production Total
6S	6S69	4-dr Sed-6P	12,479	4232	16,355

ENGINE: V-8. Overhead valve. Cast iron block. Displacement: 500 cid. Compression ratio: 8.5:1. SAE net hp: 190 at 4000 rpm. Hydraulic valve lifters. Carburetor: four-barrel.

SEVILLE ENGINE: V-8. Overhead valve. Cast iron block. Displacement: 350 cid. Bore and stroke: 4.057 x 3.385 inches. Compression ratio: 8.0:1. SAE net hp: 180 at 4400 rpm. Induction system: Electronic fuel injection.

CHASSIS FEATURES: Wheelbase: (commercial chassis) 157-1/2-inches; (Seventy-Five) 151-1/2 inches; (Brougham) 133 inches; (Eldorado) 126.3 inches; (Seville) 114.3 inches; (all others) 130 inches. Overall length: (Seventy-Five) 253 inches; (Brougham) 234 inches; (Eldorado) 225 inches; (Seville) 204 inches; (all others) 231 inches. Width: (Seville) 72 inches; (all others) 80 inches. Tires: (Seville) GR78-15/B; (all others) LR78-15.

POWERTRAIN OPTIONS: Controlled differential ($60). Trackmaster ($250). Fuel injection ($600).

CONVENIENCE OPTIONS: Talisman Brougham ($1,788). Astro roof ($843). Sunroof ($668). Rear window defroster, standard on 75 ($73). Automatic Level Control ($84). Cruise control ($100). Eldorado reclining seat ($188). Air cushion restraints ($300). Coupe DeVille Cabriolet without sunroof ($236). Eldorado Cabriolet Coupe, without sunroof ($413). Brougham d'Elegance Group ($784). DeVille d'Elegance Group ($350). Dual Comfort six-way passenger seat ($125). AM/FM stereo with tape ($229). Padded roof on 75 ($745).

HISTORICAL FOOTNOTES: Dealer introductions took place September 19, 1974. Model year production was 264,731 cars. Lower axle ratios used for fuel mileage improvements, except on limousines. This was the first time prices on production models surpassed price of 1957-1960 Eldorado Broughams.

1976 Cadillac

Even though 1976 was a year of refinement rather than major body or engineering change at Cadillac, it signaled the end of several eras. GM's last convertible was in its final season. This would be the final year for the low-rung Calais (after a dozen years in the lineup), and for the traditional mammoth Cadillac. Full-size Cadillacs retained the same ample dimensions as in 1975, but the new international-size Seville (introduced in mid-year) was 27 in. shorter, 8 in. narrower and a thousand pounds lighter than a Sedan deVille. New grilles on all models carried on the traditional Cadillac crosshatch theme, though with a finer pattern than in 1975 (actually crosshatching within crosshatching). Cornering lamps on Calais, DeVille, Brougham, nine-passenger and limo got new horizontal chrome trim, while taillamps gained a new bold look. Standard wheel discs kept the three-dimensional Cadillac crest on the hub (except Eldorado). Cadillac's ten models came in four size categories: Family (Calais/DeVille), Personal (Eldorado), International (Seville), and Executive (Fleetwood Brougham and Seventy Five). Full size Cadillacs stretched as long in wheelbase as 133 in. and 233.7 in., overall (limos, 151.5 and 252.2 in., respectively). They still carried a monstrous 500 cu. in. V-8. The smaller Seville, however, actually cost more than bigger Cadillacs. It was powered by a more reasonably sized 350 cu. in. V-8 with electronic fuel injection. (Fuel injection was optional in all models except the Fleetwood Seventy-Five.) Eight different color accent stripes were available, and seven convertible top colors for the Eldorado. Vinyl roofs now were integral padded Elk Grain material except on Seville and Seventy Five, which had cross-grain padded vinyl. Interiors were essentially the same as in 1975 with rosewood grain trim, plus bright wreath/crest and script plaques. New trims for full-size models included sporty plaids, plush velours, knits, and 11 distinctive genuine leathers. Calais and DeVille coupes had a new vinyl roof, whose top molding served as continuation of

the door 'belt' molding. All full-size Cadillacs except Eldorado included a Controlled (limited-slip) Differential for extra traction. All had lamp monitors atop each front fender to show status of front and rear lights. All could have optional illuminated entry and theft-deterrent systems. The new Freedom battery never needed water. All but Eldorado offered new-look turbine-vaned and wire wheel covers. A new option locked doors when the lever was shifted to "Drive." Cadillac also offered Track Master, a computerized skid-control system that automatically pumped the back brakes in an emergency situation to shorten stopping distance. Of special note on the option list was the Air Cushion Restraint System, announced for all models except Eldorado convertible and Fleetwood 75. This was a forerunner of the air bags that received so much publicity a few years later. Another option was the Astroroof, introduced in 1975, with sliding sunshade that permitted use as an electrically-operated sunroof or a transparent closed skylight. Both it and the "ordinary" sunroof panels could give safety along with an open-air feeling, now that the convertible was about to disappear. Three full-size special editions with new refinements were offered this year: d'Elegance, Talisman and Cabriolet. New options included a push-button Weather Band (exclusive to Cadillac) built into the AM/FM stereo signal-seeking radio; loose-pillow style seats for d'Elegance packages; plus power passenger and manual driver seatback recliners for 50/50 front seats. Of the 15 standard and six optional Firemist body colors, 13 were new this year. The list included: Cotillion White; Georgian Silver; Academy Gray; Sable Black; Innsbruck Blue; Commodore Blue; Dunbarton Green; Firethorn; Claret; Pueblo Beige; Kingswood Green; Calumet Cream; Phoenician Ivory; Brentwood Brown; and Chesterfield Brown. For extra cost, buyers could order any of six Firemist colors: Crystal Blue, Amberlite, Greenbrier, Galloway Green, Florentine Gold, or Emberglow. Vinyl roofs came in dark blue, silver blue, firethorn, mahogany, silver or dark brown metallic; or in basic white, black, dark blue-green, buckskin, or ivory. All Cadillacs had as standard: automatic climate control; bumper impact strips; digital clock; automatic glove box light; High Energy Ignition; inside hood release; lamp monitors; remote-control left-hand outside mirror; litter receptacle; automatic trunk light; map light; power six-way front-seat adjuster (not on Calais or 75 Series); power front disc brakes (four-wheel on Eldorado); power door locks; power windows; power steering; AM/FM radio including power antenna; Soft-Ray tinted glass; spare tire cover; tamper-resistant odometer; Turbo Hydramatic transmission; washer fluid level indicator; and steel-belted whitewall tires.

1976 Cadillac, Seville sedan. (OCW)

SEVILLE—SERIES 6K—V-8—Described as "among the most fully equipped cars in the world," Seville had debuted in May 1975 and changed little for its first complete model year. Marketed against Mercedes, the international-size, contemporary styled four-door sedan offered near-European ride/handling qualities, along with respectable fuel mileage. Seville could hit 60 MPH in 11 seconds or less, top 110 MPH, and cruise gently on the highway. The computer-designed chassis actually derived from Chevrolet's Nova, but Cadillac did an extensive reworking of the X-body, with exclusive body panels, and mounted a vinyl top. Seville's front end was unmistakably Cadillac. A horizontal crosshatch grille was arranged in three rows, divided into two sections by a vertical center bar. Quad rectangular headlamps sat above twin rectangular parking/signal lamps and alongside large wraparound cornering lamps. A Seville nameplate was fairly low on the front fender, behind the wheel opening. Up front, a stand-up wreath/crest hood ornament. Large wraparound taillamps (far different from full-size models) and full wheel openings complemented the formal profile. Body preparation included two primers, four finish coats, and an additional lacquer coat. New zincrometal was used in key areas to fight rust. All told, Seville was described as having an "uncluttered" look, less glitzy than other luxury cars had become Measuring about two feet shorter than full size domestic luxury cars, the new breed of Cadillac sold well from the start. The standard 350 cu. in. V-8 (from Oldsmobile) with electronic fuel injection was mounted on a steel sub-frame connected to the body sheet metal through damping cushions, to isolate vibration. An impressive standard equipment list included air conditioning; variable-ratio power steering; power brakes, door locks and seat; courtesy lamps; electric trunk lock release; automatic level control; a fuel monitor; cornering lamps; signal-seeking AM/FM stereo radio with power antenna; tilt/telescoping steering wheel; and GR78 x 15-B steel-belted whitewall tires. Seville's dash held an upper "information band" with functional control panels to the driver's left and right. 50/50 front seats were trimmed in seven Mansion Knit cloth colors, or optional genuine Sierra Grain leather in eight colors. A cross-grain padded vinyl roof was standard.

1976 Cadillac, Calais hardtop sedan. (OCW)

CALAIS—SERIES 6C—V-8— For its final outing, Calais displayed the same front-end look as the more expensive DeVille, with a Cadillac 'V' and crest at the hood front. Interiors could be Morgan Plaid in four possible color combinations, or expanded vinyl in antique light buckskin or black. Standard features included an AM/FM radio with automatic power antenna, automatic climate control, digital clock, tinted glass, lamp monitors, and power door locks. Sedans had small coach windows on the rear pillar; coupes much larger, squarish rear quarter windows. Rear fenders held script nameplates. Electronic fuel injection had become optional on the 500 cu. in. V-8 in March 1975, but the carbureted version continued as standard.

1976 Cadillac, Coupe deVille. (OCW)

1976 Cadillac, Sedan deVille. (OCW)

DEVILLE—SERIES 6C—V-8—Coupe deVille, a name that had been around for over two decades, was advertised as "America's favorite luxury car." The mid-1970s edition had a vinyl cabriolet roof with chrome accent strip at the leading edge, and a squarish quarter window (considerably larger than most such windows at this time). Sedan deVille continued the pillarless hardtop that had been part of the GM tradition for years, but would soon be doomed to extinction. Sedans also featured narrow sail shaped fixed windows in the roof quarter panels. DeVille's crosshatch grille was dominated by a framed set of vertical bars, peaking forward slightly at the center. An upper horizontal bar above the

grille mesh held a Cadillac script at the side and swept down alongside the grille, then outward to wrap around the fenders just above the bumpers. Quad rectangular headlamps met wraparound cornering lamps. Set into traditional tall housings at rear fender tips were vertical inward- and outward-facing side lamps. Horizontal taillamps were below the deck lid; backup lamps in toward the license plate housing. Script nameplates were on rear quarter panels, just above the bodyside molding. New Magnan ribbed knit upholstery came in six colors; Merlin Plaid or Manhattan velour each in two. Eleven leather combinations were available. Distinctive simulated rosewood appliqués and laminates highlighted doors and dash. 50/50 seats had individual fold-down center armrests. The standard 500 cu. in. V-8 (whose days were numbered) could have either a four-barrel carburetor or fuel injection. The special-edition Coupe deVille d'Elegance now carried standard opera lamps behind the quarter windows, which were optional on other deVille coupes. d'Elegance hoods omitted the customary 'V' and crest, substituting a distinctive stand-up see-through ornament along the chrome windsplit. Styling highlights included dual accent stripes on front and sides of hood, door surfaces, and rear deck (in choice of eight colors). Interiors contained new loose-pillow style 50/50 seats in two-toned Magnan ribbed knit cloth (four colors). A 'deVille d'Elegance' script was on the instrument panel and sail panels (coupe only). The package also included wide brushed-chrome lower door moldings, and bodyside moldings with colored vinyl inserts to match the vinyl roof color. Coupe deVille's Cabriolet roof option, with Elk Grain vinyl padded vinyl top, added for 1976 a decorative Cadillac crest on the sail panels. Also part of the package: a standup see-through hood ornament, chrome roof moldings, and French seam around the backlight Cabriolet roofs had been available on Coupe deVille since 1974.

FLEETWOOD SIXTY SPECIAL BROUGHAM—SERIES 6C—V-8— For the last time, the luxurious Brougham would carry on the Sixty Special name, riding a lengthy 133 in. wheelbase--three inches longer than a Sedan deVille. New 'Fleetwood' plaques replaced script on both Brougham and the longer-wheelbase Fleetwood Seventy-Fives. A stand-up "jewel-like" wreath-and-crest hood ornament was now standard on both. Basic styling was similar to DeVille, including the large chrome housings at rear fender tips that held inward- and outward-facing red lenses. The decklid held a wreath-and-crest emblem rather than Calais/DeVille's 'V' and crest. Modest Fleetwood nameplates on front fenders (behind the wheel openings, below the bodyside molding) and decklid corner were in block letters, colored to match the body. Brougham standards included a signal seeking radio with power antenna, automatic level control, lamp monitors, six-way power seat, power windows and door locks, individual reading lights, and carpeted footrests. Standard Dual Comfort 60/40 front seats with fold-down center armrest could be upholstered in Minoa ribbed velour with leather bolsters (three colors) or smooth finish Mansion (five colors). Sierra Grain leather came in 11 trim combinations. Broughams could have premium wheel covers with Fleetwood wreath/crest and black centers. Two luxury option packages were offered again. Brougham's d'Elegance option changed for 1976 to include contoured loose-pillow style seats trimmed in soft Mansion brushed-knit fabric (five colors available), with 50/50 Dual Comfort front seats, seatback pockets, extra-dense pile carpeting, 'Brougham d'Elegance' script on instrument panel, and wide brushed-chrome lower door moldings. The roof was thickly padded in Elk Grain vinyl with roller perimeter around the backlight, rich French seam, and bright chrome belt moldings. Also in the package: turbine-vaned wheel discs, opera lamps, and 'Brougham d'Elegance' script on the sail panels. The Fleetwood Talisman option package included 40/40 front seats with six-way power adjuster and power passenger recliner, trimmed in Medici crushed velour (black or dark blue); special interior trim; console with lighted compartment; stand up wreath/crest hood ornament; padded Elk Grain vinyl roof; turbine-vaned wheel discs; and 'Fleetwood Talisman' identification on sail panels

1976 Cadillac, Fleetwood Brougham sedan (OCW)

FLEETWOOD SEVENTY-FIVE LIMOUSINE—SERIES 6D—V-8—This would be the final year for the long Cadillac limo and nine-passenger sedan (151.5 in. wheelbase and 252.3 in., overall), which weighed in at a whopping 5,800 pounds. Their body style had first appeared for 1971. This year, like Fleetwood Brougham, they gained a new grille pattern plus revised cornering lamps with horizontal chrome trim. Base prices were $14,889 for the nine-passenger sedan and $15,239 for the eight-passenger limo. This model year, a total of 1,815 Fleetwood Seventy-Fives were built: 981 sedans and 834 limos. Fleetwood remained the only American-built vehicle that was designed and built strictly as a limousine. Big Fleetwoods had two separate automatic climate control systems. Interior choices were Medici crushed velour fabric in black or dark blue, or light gray Magnan Knit in light gray. Full-width folding seats held three extra passengers. Passengers could use the control panel to raise/lower windows, turn on reading lamps, operate radio, or (in limo) raise/lower the center partition. Fixed quarter windows behind the rear doors were larger than those on Sedan deVille. (Fleetwood Broughams had no such windows at all). Electronic fuel injection was optional on the 500 cu. in. (8.2-liter) V-8 engine. A cross-grain padded vinyl roof was optional. Seventy-Five models had new graphite-treated rear brake linings, reinforced shoes, and Hydro-Boost power-brake booster. They also boasted four cigarette lighters rather than the usual two.

1976 Cadillac, Eldorado coupe. (OCW)

1976 Cadillac, Eldorado convertible. (OCW)

ELDORADO—SERIES 6E—V-8—Cadillac's personal-luxury coupe had lost its rear skirts in a major 1975 restyle. This year brought no drastic changes, but some styling refinements. The 'Cadillac' script signature was now on the hood (driver's side) rather than the grille itself. Though similar to the 1975 version, this year's crosshatch grille was dominated by vertical bars, peaked forward at the center. It also reached a bit higher than the quad rectangular headlamps. New amber-lensed parking lamps rested down in the bumper; horizontal amber-lensed cornering lamps sat back on front fenders. Massive vertical extensions of the outboard bumper protrusions stood at front fender tips. Eldorado script was on rear fenders and decklid. Wide, simple new taillamps were continuous red slots within wide bezel frames, below the decklid and above the bumper. Backup lights were on each side of the license plate. Additional red lenses, facing both side and rear, sat in the massive vertical chrome fender extensions. Distinctively-shaped opera windows sloped down and forward at the base, following the dip in the quarter

panel. Other styling highlights included dual accent stripes next to upper and lower crease lines of the hood's beveled edges. Upper stripes ended at the hood's rear edge; lower stripes extended all the way to rear edge of door. The big 500 cu. in. V-8 powered Eldos once again, but in weakened, detuned state compared to prior years as a result of more rigorous emissions standards. Bendix electronic fuel injection, which had become optional in 1975, was available again; but the basic engine held a four-barrel carb. New wheel covers had a black center hub area with bright metal raised wreath-and-crest. Eldorado's simulated wood dash insert displayed a carved gunstock pattern. Four-wheel power disc brakes were standard, as was a padded vinyl "half" roof. A sunroof was optional. So was the Astroroof that debuted in 1975, with tinted panel for power sunroof, along with sunshade and metal slider. The front-drive Eldo's rear suspension included upper and lower control arms, helical-coil springs, and automatic level control. Up front were torsion bars. A chain drive connected the torque converter section to the gear portion of the automatic transmission. Interiors could be Mansion Knit fabric in any of four colors; Merlin Plaid in two; or 11 Sierra Grain leather possibilities. The Custom Cabriolet option had first appeared in 1972. That roof this year featured padded Elk Grain vinyl in choice of eleven colors with bright chrome molding, plus wreath/crest ornamentation on sail panels. A Custom Biarritz option arrived late in the model year. That one included thick padding on back roof area, a limousine-style backlight, opera lamps, chrome molding along fenderline, and Sierra Grain pillow-soft leather seats. The package came with or without an Astroroof or sunroof. Eldo held the dubious record of being the world's biggest car with front-wheel drive--delivering gas mileage to prove it. Back in '76, though, the coupe got far less attention than the convertible, simply because this was the final year for any GM ragtop. Though hardly rare with 14,000 copies rolling off the line, they gained considerable media coverage and the covetous attention of speculators hoping to profit mightily from the last of a long line of open-topped Cadillacs. Except for the final 200 all white examples, Eldorado's convertible top came in white, black, dark blue, firethorn, dark blue-green, buckskin, or ivory color.

I.D. DATA: Cadillac's 13-symbol Vehicle Identification Number (VIN) was located on the forward edge of the windshield trim molding, visible through the windshield. The first digit is '6', indicating Cadillac division. The second symbol indicates series: 'B' Fleetwood Brougham; 'C' Calais; 'D' DeVille; 'F' Fleetwood 75; 'L' Eldorado; 'S' Seville; 'Z' commercial chassis. Symbols 3-4 show body type: '47' 2-dr. coupe; '49' 4-dr. hardtop sedan; '69' 4-dr. sedan; '23' 4-dr. sedan w/auxiliary seat; '33' 4-dr. limousine w/auxiliary seat and center partition window; '67' 2-dr. convertible; '90' commercial chassis. Symbol five is the engine code: 'R' V8-350 FI; 'S' V8-500 4Bbl. or FI. The sixth symbol indicates model year ('6' 1976). Symbol seven is for assembly plant: 'Q' Detroit, MI; 'E' Linden, NJ. The last six digits show the sequence in which the car was built: 100001 through 400000 for 'C' series made in Detroit and all Eldorados, 600001 through 690000 for 'C' models built in Linden. An engine unit number is on the block behind the left cylinder head; a nine digit VIN derivative that shows model year, plant and sequence number is on the block behind the intake manifold. Engine number of 350 V-8 is stamped on the front left side of the block, below the head. A body identification plate on the top right surface of the shroud under the hood, near the cowl, reveals style number, trim number, body number, paint number and date of assembly (month 01 through 12, week A through E) followed by codes for factory installed options.

SEVILLE

Series No.	Body/Style No.	Body Type & Seating	Factory Price	Shipping Weight	Prod. Total
6K	S69	4-dr Sedan-5P	12479	4232	43,772

CALAIS

Series No.	Body/Style No.	Body Type & Seating	Factory Price	Shipping Weight	Prod. Total
6C	C47	2-dr Coupe-6P	8629	4989	4,500
6C	C49	4-dr HT Sed-6P	8825	5083	1,700

DEVILLE

Series No.	Body/Style No.	Body Type & Seating	Factory Price	Shipping Weight	Prod. Total
6C	D47	2-dr Coupe-6P	9067	5025	114,482
6C	D49	4-dr HT Sed-6P	9265	5127	67,677

FLEETWOOD BROUGHAM

Series No.	Body/Style No.	Body Type & Seating	Factory Price	Shipping Weight	Prod. Total
6C	B69	4-dr Sedan-6P	10935	5213	24,500

FLEETWOOD SEVENTY-FIVE

Series No.	Body/Style No.	Body Type & Seating	Factory Price	Shipping Weight	Prod. Total
6D	F23	4-dr Sedan-9P	14889	5746	981
6D	F33	4-dr Limo-8P	15239	5889	834
6D	Z90	Commercial Chassis	N/A	N/A	1,509

ELDORADO

6E	L47	2-dr Coupe-5P	10586	5085	35,184
6E	L67	2-dr Conv-5P	11049	5153	14,000

ENGINES: BASE V-8 (Seville): 90-degree, overhead valve V-8. Cast iron block and head. Displacement: 350 cu. in. (5.7-liters). Bore & stroke: 4.057 x 3.385 in. Compression ratio: 8.0:1. Brake horsepower: 180 at 4400 R.P.M. Torque: 275 lb.-ft. at 2000 R.P.M. Five main bearings. Hydraulic valve lifters. Fuel injection (speed-density, port-injected). Built by Oldsmobile. VIN Code: R. BASE V-8 (all except Seville): 90-degree, overhead valve V-8. Cast iron block and head. Displacement: 500 cu. in. (8.2-liters). Bore & stroke: 4.300 x 4.304 in. Compression ratio: 8.5:1. Brake horsepower: 190 at 3600 R.P.M. Torque: 360 lb.-ft. at 2000 R.P.M. Five main bearings. Hydraulic valve lifters. Carburetor: 4Bbl. Rochester M4ME. VIN Code: S. OPTIONAL FUEL-INJECTED V-8 (all except Seville): Same as 500 cu. in. V-8 above, except: Horsepower: 215 at 3600 R.P.M. Torque: 400 lb.-ft. at 2000 R.P.M.

CHASSIS DATA: Wheelbase: (Seville) 114.3 in.; (Calais/DeVille) 130.0 in.; (Fleetwood Brougham) 133.0 in. (Fleetwood 75) 151.5 in.; (Eldorado) 126.3 in. Overall length: (Seville) 204.0 in.; (Calais/DeV) 230.7 in.; (Brghm) 233.7 in.; (Fleetwood 75) 252.2 in.; (Eldorado) 224.1 in. Height: (Seville) 54.7 in. (Calais/DeV cpe) 53.8 in.; (Calais/DeV sed) 54.3 in.; (Brghm) 55.3 in.; (Fleetwood 75 sed) 56.8 in.; (Fleetwood 75 limo) 56.6 in.; (Eldo cpe) 54.2 in. Width: (Seville) 71.8 in.; (Eldo) 79.8 in.; (others) 76.4 in. Front Tread: (Seville) 61.3 in.; (Eldo) 63.7 in.; (others) 61.7 in. Rear Tread: (Seville) 59.0 in.; (Eldo) 63.6 in.; (others) 60.7 in. Standard Tires: (Seville/DeV) GR78 x 15-B SBR wide WSW; (Brghm) GR78 x 15-D SBR wide WSW; (Limo) HR78 x 15-D SBR wide WSW.

TECHNICAL: Transmission: Three-speed Turbo Hydra-matic standard on all models; column shift (400 series exc. Eldo, 425 series). Gear ratios: (1st) 2.48:1; (2nd) 1.48:1; (3rd) 1.00:1; (Rev) 2.07:1 or 2.09:1. Standard axle (final drive) ratio: (Seville) 2.56:1; (limo) 3.15:1; (Eldo) 2.73:1. Optional: (Seville) 3.08:1; (Eldo) 3.07:1; (others) 3.15:1. Hypoid rear axle exc. (Seville) Salisbury type. Steering: variable ratio power assisted. Front suspension: (Seville) unequal length upper/lower control arms, coil springs, stabilizer bar; (Eldo) upper/lower control arms, torsion bars; (others) upper/lower control arms, coil springs, rod-and-link stabilizer bar. Rear suspension: (Seville) multiple leaf spring; (others) four-link drive, coil springs; automatic level control on all except Calais and DeVille. Body construction: (full size) separate body and perimeter frame. Wheel size: (Seville) 15 x 6 JJ; (others) 15 x 6 JK. Brakes: front ventilated disc, rear drum exc. Eldorado four-wheel disc; power booster on all. HEI electronic ignition. Fuel tank: (Seville) 21 gal.; (others) 27.5 gal.

DRIVETRAIN OPTIONS: Fuel-injected V-8 engine ($647) exc. limo. Heavy-duty cooling system ($40). 80-amp alternator ($45). California emission equipment ($50). Limited slip differential ($61); N/A on Eldorado. Trailering pkg. ($85) exc. limo/Seville. Automatic level control: Calais/DeV ($92).

OPTION PACKAGES: Brougham d'Elegance ($885). Coupe deVille Cabriolet ($329); w/Astroroof ($1288); w/sunroof ($1104). deVille d'Elegance ($650). Eldorado Cabriolet ($432); w/Astroroof ($1391); w/sunroof ($1207). Fleetwood Talisman: Brougham ($1813).

CONVENIENCE/APPEARANCE OPTIONS: Astroroof for full vinyl roof ($885) exc. Limos. Astroroof (painted): Calais/DeV/Brghm/Eldo ($985). Sunroof for full vinyl roof ($701) exc. limo. Sunroof for painted roof ($800) exc. limo/Sev. Cruise control ($104). Controlled-cycle wipers ($28). Rear defogger, grid-type ($77) exc. limo. Six-way dual comfort power passenger seat: DeV/Brghm/Eldo ($131). Six-way power front lounge seat: Calais ($131); limo ($98). Power passenger 50/50 seat w/recliner: DeV/Brghm/Eldo ($221). Manual driver's 50/50 seatback recliner ($65) exc. Calais/limo. Power passenger seatback recliner: Sev ($90). Tilt/telescope steering wheel ($102). Automatic door locks ($100). Illuminated entry system ($52). Fuel monitor ($26). Theft deterrent system ($114). Track master ($263) exc. Sev/Eldo. Remote trunk lock ($68) exc. Sev. Opera lamps: Calais/DeV cpe, Brghm, limo ($58). Twilight Sentinel ($47). Guidematic headlamp control ($54). Trumpet horn ($19) exc. Sev. Remote-control right mirror ($30). Thermometer on left mirror ($18) exc. Sev. Lighted vanity mirror, passenger ($44-$60). AM/FM stereo radio w/tape player: Calais/DeV/limo ($239); others ($93). Signal-seeking AM/FM stereo radio ($147). Signal-seeking AM/FM stereo radio w/weather band: Calais/DeV/limo ($209); others ($61). Signal-seeking AM/FM stereo radio w/rear control: limo ($275). Firemist paint ($146). Padded vinyl roof: Calais/DeV ($163). Eldo ($170); limo ($819). Hard

boot (two-piece): conv. ($63). Accent stripes: Calais/DeV ($42). Door edge guards ($7-$11). License frame: each ($7). Expanded vinyl upholstery: Calais ($47). Dual comfort 50/50 front seat: DeV/Eldo ($185). Dual comfort 60/40 front seat: DeV ($123). Leather upholstery ($220-$235) exc. Calais/limo. Front shoulder belts: Eldo conv. ($36). Air cushion restraint system: Calais/DeV/Brghm/Eldo cpe (N/A). Carpeted rubber floor mats, front/rear ($38-$47) exc. limo, front ($26). Trunk mat ($10). Turbine-vaned wheel covers ($45); N/A on Eldorado. Wire wheel covers: ($167) exc. Eldo; on d'Elegance/Talisman ($122). Stowaway spare tire (NC) exc. limo.

HISTORY: Introduced: September 12, 1975 (in showrooms Sept. 18). Model year production (U.S.): 309,139, which set a record. Calendar year production (U.S.): 312,845. Calendar year sales by U.S. dealers: 304,485 for a 3.5 percent share of the industry total, down from 267,049 (3.8 percent) in 1975. Model year sales by U.S. dealers: 299,579.

Historical Footnotes: This year beat the all-time record (set in 1973) for sales and production, with 309,139 Cadillacs built. Seville was the shining star of the sales rise. After a brief 1975 model run, production zoomed upward for full year 1976. At $13,000, Seville was the most costly standard domestic production car built by the Big Four automakers. It also offered a foretaste of what was coming soon as GM downsized all its models. Most Cadillacs, including all Sevilles and Eldorados, were built in Detroit; but 42,570 vehicles emerged from the Linden, New Jersey, plant. Full-size 'standard' Cadillacs continued to sell well, defying the market conditions of the mid-1970s. Exactly 14,000 Eldorado convertibles were built in their final season (compared to just 8,950 in 1975). Cadillac promoted them as the "Last of a magnificent breed." The actual "last" American convertible was driven off the line at Cadillac's Clark Avenue plant in Detroit on April 21, 1976, by General Manager Edward C. Kennard and manufacturing Manager Bud Brawner. Passengers for this major media event included several production workers and Detroit Mayor Coleman Young. Just 60 years before, the first Cadillac to use the name "convertible" had appeared. For the past five years, Eldorado had been the only luxury American convertible; and for 1976, the sole survivor of the breed. Reasons cited for the loss of ragtop popularity included widespread use of air conditioners, high-speed cruising, sunroofs and vinyl roofs—even the improved audio qualities of stereo radio/tape systems, which couldn't be appreciated fully in an open vehicle. Actually, Cadillac produced 200 identical "final" convertibles, dubbed "Bicentennial Cadillacs" by Mr. Kennard. The one and only last example was kept for the company's collection. All 200 were white with white top, white wheel covers and white leather upholstery with red piping, dash and carpeting. A dash plaque confirmed the fact that it was one of the last--at least until the ragtop mysteriously re-emerged once again in the early '80s. Speculation sent prices way up. Their original $11,049 sticker price meant little as some "collectors" quickly began to snap up open Eldos at prices approaching $20,000. But before too long, prices fell almost as swiftly. Convertibles never really disappeared. Within months, various conversion manufacturers were slicing metal roofs off Cadillac coupes to create custom convertibles. But the next regular production ragtop would be Chrysler's LeBaron in 1982. In most recent years over 2,000 Fleetwood commercial chassis had been produced annually, for conversion to hearses and ambulances. Most of those conversions were done by three companies: Superior, Miller-Meteor, or Hess & Eisenhardt. In addition, stretch limousines were built on Cadillac chassis by Moloney (in Illinois) and Wisco (in Michigan), among other specialty firms.

1977

Cadillac's 75th anniversary year arrived with a shock to traditionalists, as full-size models endured an eye-opening downsizing. "You must drive it," the ads declared, "to see why we call it the next generation of the luxury car." The new C-bodied DeVille, Brougham and limousine were 8 to 12 in. shorter, 3-1/2 in. narrower, and an average of 950 pounds lighter than their massive predecessors. Still, many models managed to keep the same leg room in front and rear (or even more). Only Eldorado carried on in its mammoth form a while longer, and Seville had entered life in 1975 with contemporary dimensions.

Even the commercial chassis shrunk, from 157.5 down to 144.5 inches in wheelbase, requiring funeral car and ambulance suppliers to create some new bodies. All models except Seville carried a new lighter, smaller 425 cu. in. (7.0-liter) V-8 engine. That powerplant emerged as the result of testing 110 experimental engines. The huge 500 V-8 was gone. Electronic fuel injection was optional in DeVille, Brougham and Eldorado. Standard Turbo Hydra-matic fed power to low-ratio drive axles. Four-wheel disc brakes were standard on Seville, Eldorado and Brougham. Astroroofs and sunroofs were again available. Carryover special editions included Coupe and Sedan deVille d'Elegance and Brougham d'Elegance. One new special edition joined the lineup: the Eldorado Custom Biarritz. All sedans now had pillars and framed door glass. (The "true" four-door hardtop was gone for good.) With Calais departed, deVille took over as the cheapest Cadillac (base price under $10,000). Dash gauges could be pulled out from the front for servicing. All models had a new two-spoke steering wheel--but those were wide spokes. A new door design offered better hold-open qualities. Anti-corrosion treatment on all models included zinc-rich primers, hot melt sealers, wax coating, Plastisol-R, and deadeners. Cadillac also expanded the use of Zincrometal-R and bi-metal (stainless steel on aluminum), corrosion resistant inner front fender panels, and elimination of areas that trapped dirt and water. Wheels and tires were now match-mounted for smoothest ride.

1977 Cadillac, Seville sedan. (OCW)

SEVILLE—SERIES 6K—V-8—Seville had been the first production American car to offer a 350 cu. in. electronic-fuel-injected engine as standard, and it returned for 1977. Sensors fed engine data back to an on-board analog computer under the dash, which in turn signaled the eight injectors how to meter the fuel charge from the constant-supply fuel rail. Added this year were standard four-wheel power disc brakes, a retuned suspension system, and Butyl rubber body mounts. Other standard features included variable ratio power steering (16.4 to 13.8), front and rear stabilizer bars, 15 in. wide-whitewall steel-belted radial tires, and automatic level control. Seville entered the model year wearing a new vertical grille, rectangular quad headlamps, and new amber parking/signal lamps. A total of 21 body colors were offered (15 standard and six extra-cost Firemist), plus 16 color-coordinated Tuxedo Grain padded vinyl tops (including metallic colors). Painted metal tops were also available, but most customers chose vinyl. A new Scan button on the AM/FM signal-seeking stereo radio allowed sampling of each station for six seconds. Seville's front end was similar to full-size Cadillacs, but the grille used only three horizontal divider bars and many vertical bars, forming vertical "holes." That tight grille pattern was repeated between the license plate holder and bumper guards. Four amber-lensed parking/signal lamps sat below the quad rectangular headlamps, with large cornering lamps on fender sides. Cadillac's crest was on the rear pillar; a Seville nameplate on front fenders between door and wheels. Atop the hood was a stand-up wreath/crest ornament. On the option list: wire wheel covers. Standard upholstery was smooth Dover cloth in claret, black, light gray, dark blue, medium sage green, light yellow-gold, light buckskin, or medium saffron. Optional was Sierra Grain leather in ten colors (including white). Standard fittings included power windows and door locks; tilt/telescope steering wheel; individual rear reading lamps; automatic parking brake release; and a new seat/shoulder belt combination. A chime

warned that seat belts weren't buckled. Concealed wipers worked with a Controlled Cycle system. Body finishing used extensive hand work. Large-diameter Pliacell-R shock absorbers were the same as those on the Cadillac limo. Bolts were epoxy-encapsulated to prevent loosening.

1977 Cadillac, Coupe deVille. (OCW)

1977 Cadillac, Sedan deVille. (OCW)

DEVILLE—SERIES 6C—V-8—The new-generation Fleetwood/DeVille was, in Cadillac's words, "engineered from the ground up, to make more efficient use of space." That meant a new body, new chassis, new suspension, and new engine, in an integrated design. Trunk space grew larger. DeVilles gave more rear leg/headroom. Broughams were just as spacious as before. DeVilles (and Fleetwoods) wore a new horizontal cross-hatch grille with four horizontal and nine vertical divider bars, peaking forward at the center, topped by a 'Cadillac' script nameplate at the side of the wide upper bar. The grille pattern of wide holes was repeated down at the bumper, between the license plate and bumper guards. Small vertical parking/signal lamps just outside the grille, quad rectangular headlamps reaching all the way out to fender edges, and large cornering lenses at the side, were all the same height as the grille. That combination gave the whole front end a wide, uniform appearance that flowed into the bodysides. All that was topped off by a stand-up crest hood ornament. In sum, it carried on the traditional Cadillac look. Bodies had full rear wheel openings and vertical taillamps. New bumpers had dual rubber strip protective inserts. The new instrument panel had a "central control area" that allowed both driver and passenger to reach air conditioning, radio and accessory controls. Options included wire wheel discs, opera lamps, and accent stripes. Standard DeVille/Fleetwood equipment included wide-whitewall steel-belted radial tires, variable-ratio power steering (fixed ratio on limos), cornering lights, lamp monitors, power windows and door locks, Soft-Ray tinted glass, three-speed wiper/washers, Freedom battery, digital clock, color keyed litter container, six-way power driver's seat, center armrests, visor vanity mirror, and Turbo Hydra-matic transmission. Automatic climate control was redesigned so it operated only when necessary. Aberdeen cloth upholstery came in light yellow-gold, dark blue, medium saffron and claret. Ribbed Dynasty cloth came in six colors (including claret). Eleven other interior choices featured leather (including white). The standard AM/FM radio included an automatic power antenna. The DeVille d'Elegance special edition added pillow-style 50/50 Dual Comfort seats in Medici crushed velour cloth in claret, medium saffron, dark blue, or light buckskin color). Upper door pads, inserts in door pull straps and front seatback assist straps were also Medici cloth. Bodyside moldings held vinyl inserts that matched the body color. The Coupe deVille Cabriolet roof option came in 13 coordinated colors, with a Cadillac crest on the sail panel and bright roof moldings.

1977 Cadillac, Fleetwood Brougham sedan. (OCW)

FLEETWOOD BROUGHAM—SERIES 6C—V-8—Billed as a car "for very special people" (whatever that meant), the shrunken Brougham had a distinctively tapered center side pillar that leaned slightly backward, as well as a custom-trimmed small back window. Rocker panel moldings were wider, too. 'Fleetwood' block lettering appeared on the front fenders (just ahead of the door) and decklid. Otherwise, it looked much like DeVille's sedan in the new downsized form. New engine was the 425 cu. in. (7.0-liter) V-8, and four-wheel disc brakes were standard. So was automatic level control. Wheelbase was now identical to DeVille (121.5 inches). Broughams displayed a distinctive roof treatment in Tuxedo Grain vinyl, with opera lamps, carpeted rear footrests, and one-piece wall-to-wall carpeting. New Florentine velour upholstery fabric came in medium saffron, light gray, dark blue, medium sage green, light yellow-gold, light buckskin or claret. Smooth-finish Dover fabric was offered in black, dark blue, light buckskin or claret. Standard 50/50 front seats had individual pull down armrests and a six-way power adjustment for the driver (two-way for passenger). The AM/FM stereo radio included a signal-seeking scanner, and was available with 23-channel CB transceiver. Brougham d'Elegance came equipped with special contoured pillow-style seats trimmed in Florentine velour cloth (in light gray, dark blue, light buckskin, or claret). Upper door jambs and inserts in door pull straps and front seatback assist straps were also Florentine cloth. Also included were three roof-mounted assist straps, turbine-vaned wheel discs, 'd'Elegance' script on sail panel, and distinctive accent striping. Fleetwood Talisman was dropped.

FLEETWOOD LIMOUSINE—SERIES 6D—V-8—Newly designed Fleetwood and Fleetwood Formal Limousines continued to serve as "flagships of the Cadillac fleet," but in sharply shrunken form. The contemporary edition was over a foot shorter and 900 pounds lighter. Large door openings allowed easy entry/exit. Automatic Climate Control could be operated from front or rear. A Dual Accessory Panel let passengers operate power windows and radio, or set temperature. Wheel covers could match any color. Both outside mirrors were remote-controlled. Upholstery choices included dark blue Florentine velour; light gray or black Dover cloth. Formal Limousines had black leather up front, plus a glass partition. Opera lamps were standard. Only 1,299 commercial chassis were turned out this year.

ELDORADO—SERIES 6E—V-8—Unlike the other full-size Cadillacs, Eldorado continued in its previous form (and elephantine size). A brushed chrome molding reached across the new coordinated horizontal-style grille and headlamps. This year's grille pattern featured more thin vertical bars than before and stood on a line with the headlamp tops. Individual 'Eldorado' block letters sat on the hood front, above the grille. Rear fenders held new rectangular side marker lamps, while new vertical taillamps formed into the bumper tips. Power four-wheel disc brakes had cooling fins. In the modified automatic climate control, the compressor ran only when needed. The $1,760 Biarritz option (introduced during the 1976 model year) included a special fully-padded Elk Grain cabriolet roof, formal quarter and rear windows with French seams, and opera lamps. A matching vinyl insert accented the aluminum crossover roof molding. Stripes highlighted front fenders, doors and rear quarter panels. A script nameplate stood to the rear of quarter windows. Black-accented moldings ran from the hood front all the way back and around the roof. Sierra Grain leather covered contoured pillow seats.

I.D. DATA: All Cadillacs again had a 13-symbol Vehicle Identification Number (VIN) on the forward lower edge of the windshield frame, visible through the windshield. The first digit ('6') identifies the Cadillac Division. The second symbol denotes car line/series: 'S' Seville; 'D' DeVille; 'B' Fleetwood Brougham; 'F' Fleetwood limousine; 'L' Eldorado; 'Z' commercial chassis. Digits three and four indicate body type: '23' 4-dr. limousine w/auxiliary seat; '33' 4-dr. formal limousine with partition window; '47' 2-dr. coupe; '69' 4-dr. pillared sedan; '90' commercial chassis (number identifies name of body builder). Next comes the engine code: 'R' V8-350 EFI; 'S' V8-425 4Bbl.; 'T' V8-425 EFI. Symbol six indicates model year ('7' 1977). Seventh is an assembly plant code: 'Q' Detroit; 'E' Linden, NJ. At the end is a six-digit sequence number, running from 100001

to 400000 for C-bodies and Eldos built in Detroit; from 450001 to 550000 for Sevilles from Detroit; and 600001 to 690000 for C-bodies built in Linden. A nine-digit derivative of the VIN appears on the engine. A Body Number Plate has codes for model year, model number, trim combination, body number (assembly plant and sequence built), paint color(s), and a number-letter code that shows the date built. That plate is mounted on the upper left cowl between hood rear seal and windshield except Eldorado, on left side of cowl next to hood rear bumper; and Seville, riveted to cowl above evaporator case.

Series No.	Body/Style No.	Body Type & Seating	Factory Price	Shipping Weight	Prod. Total
SEVILLE					
6K	S69	4-dr Sedan-5P	13359	4192	45,060

Note 1: In addition to total shown, 1,152 Sevilles were built in Canada.

Series No.	Body/Style No.	Body Type & Seating	Factory Price	Shipping Weight	Prod. Total
DEVILLE					
6C	D47	2-dr Coupe-6P	9654	4186	138,750
6C	D69	4-dr Sedan-6P	9864	4222	95,421
FLEETWOOD BROUGHAM					
6C	B69	4-dr Sedan-6P	11546	4340	28,000
FLEETWOOD LIMOUSINE					
6D	F23	4-dr Sedan-8P	18193	4738	1,582
6D	F33	4-dr Fml Limo-7P	18858	4806	1,032
6D	Z90	Commercial Chassis	N/A	N/A	1,299
ELDORADO					
6E	L47	2-dr Coupe-6P	11187	4955	47,344

1977 Cadillac, Eldorado coupe. (OCW)

ENGINES: BASE V-8 (Seville): 90-degree, overhead valve V-8. Cast iron block and head. Displacement: 350 cu. in. (5.7-liters). Bore & stroke: 4.057 x 3.385 in. Compression ratio: 8.0:1. Brake horsepower: 180 at 4400 R.P.M. Torque: 275 lb.-ft. at 2000 R.P.M. Five main bearings. Hydraulic valve lifters. Electronic fuel injection (speed-density, port-type). Built by Oldsmobile. VIN Code: R. BASE V-8 (all except Seville): 90-degree, overhead valve V-8. Cast iron block and head. Displacement: 425 cu. in. (7.0-liters). Bore & stroke: 4.082 x 4.06 in. Compression ratio: 8.2:1. Brake horsepower: 180 at 4000 R.P.M. Torque: 320 lb.-ft. at 2000 R.P.M. Five main bearings. Hydraulic valve lifters. Carburetor: 4Bbl. VIN Code: S. OPTIONAL V-8 (DeVille Brougham, Eldorado): Same as 425 cu. in. V-8 above, but with electronic fuel injection. Horsepower: 195 at 3800 R.P.M. Torque: 320 lb.-ft. at 2400 R.P.M. VIN Code: T.

CHASSIS DATA: Wheelbase: (Seville) 114.3 in.; (DeVille/Brougham) 121.5 in.; (Fleetwood limo) 144.5 in.; (Eldorado) 126.3 in. Overall length: (Seville) 204.0 in.; (DeV/Brghm) 221.2 in.; (Fleetwood limo) 244.2 in.; (Eldo) 224.0 in. Height: (Seville) 54.6 in.; (DeV cpe) 54.4 in.; (DeV sed) 55.3 in.; (Brghm) 56.7 in.; (Fleetwood limo) 56.9 in.; (Eldo) 54.2 in. Width: (Seville) 71.8 in.; (Eldo) 79.8 in.; (others) 76.4 in. Front Tread: (Seville) 61.3 in.; (Eldo) 63.7 in.; (others) 61.7 in. Rear Tread: (Seville) 59.0 in.; (Eldo) 63.6 in.; (others) 60.7 in. Standard Tires: (Seville/DeV) GR78 x 15-B SBR wide WSW; (Brghm) GR78 x 15-D SBR wide WSW; (Limo) HR78 x 15-D SBR wide WSW.

TECHNICAL: Transmission: Turbo Hydra-matic transmission standard on all models; column shift. Gear ratios: (1st) 2.48:1; (2nd) 1.48:1; (3rd) 1.00:1; (Rev) 2.07:1. Standard axle (final drive) ratio: (Seville) 2.56:1, with 3.08:1 optional (std. high altitude); (DeV/Brghm) 2.28:1, with 3.08:1 optional; (limo) 3.08:1. Hypoid rear axle exc. (Eldo), Salisbury type. Steering: variable-ratio, power assisted. Front suspension: independent coil spring, link-type stabilizer exc. (Eldo) same as 1976. Rear suspension: (Seville) Hotchkiss leaf spring, link-type stabilizer; (DeVille/Fleetwood) four-link drive, coil springs; (Eldo) same as 1976. Automatic level control (except DeVille). Body construction: (DeVille/Fleetwood) ladder type frame. Brakes: front disc, rear drum exc. Brghm/Eldo/Seville, four-wheel disc. HEI electronic ignition. Fuel tank; (Seville) 21 gal.; (DeV/Fleetwood) 24 gal.; (Eldo) 27.5 gal.

DRIVETRAIN OPTIONS: Fuel-injected V-8 engine: DeVille/Brougham/Eldo ($702). Heavy-duty cooling system ($43). 80-amp alternator ($47). California emission equipment ($70). Limited slip differential ($61); N/A on Eldorado. High altitude pkg. ($22). Trailering pkg.: Sev ($43); others ($90) exc. limo. Automatic level control: DeV ($100).

OPTION PACKAGES: Brougham d'Elegance ($885). Coupe deVille Cabriolet ($348); w/Astroroof ($1365); w/sunroof ($1169). DeVille d'Elegance ($650). Eldorado Cabriolet ($457); w/Astroroof ($1474); w/sunroof ($1278). Eldorado Custom Biarritz ($1760); w/Astroroof ($2777); w/sunroof ($2581).

CONVENIENCE/APPEARANCE OPTIONS: Astroroof for full vinyl roof ($938) exc. limos. Astroroof (painted): DeV/Sev/Eldo ($1043). Sunroof for full vinyl roof ($742) exc. limo. Sunroof (painted roof): DeV/Sev/Eldo ($846). Cruise control ($111). Controlled-cycle wipers ($30). Rear defogger, grid-type ($83). Six-way dual comfort power seat adjuster, passenger ($107-$148) exc. limo. Six-way power driver's seat adjuster: limo ($99). Power passenger 50/50 seat with six-way adjuster ($197-$248) exc. limo. Driver's 50/50 seat recliner ($110) exc. limo. Power passenger seatback recliner, notchback seat: DeV ($110). Tilt/telescope steering wheel ($109). Automatic door locks ($101). Illuminated entry system ($56). Fuel monitor ($28). Theft deterrent system ($123). Trunk lid release and power pull-down ($61-$73). Opera lamps: DeV ($60). Twilight Sentinel ($51). Guidematic headlamp control ($58). Trumpet horn ($20) exc. Sev. Remote-control right mirror ($32). Lighted thermometer on left mirror ($26). Lighted vanity mirror ($47). AM/FM stereo radio w/tape player: DeV/limo ($254); others ($100). AM/FM stereo radio w/digital display: DeV/limo ($254). AM/FM stereo radio w/CB: DeV/limo ($386); others ($230). Signal seeking/scan AM/FM stereo radio ($156). Seek/scan AM/FM stereo radio w/rear control: limo ($326). Firemist paint ($153). Vinyl roof: DeV ($179); Eldo ($186). Bumper: DeV/Brghm/limo ($8). Accent stripes: DeV/Brghm ($45). Door edge guards ($8-$12). License frame: each ($7). Dual Comfort 50/50 front seats: DeV/Eldo ($187). Leather seats ($235-$252). Two-tone 50/50 dual comfort front seats: Eldo ($471). Twin floor mats ($13-$28) exc. Eldo. Floor mats, one-piece: Eldo front ($31); rear ($19). Trunk mat ($10). Turbine-vaned wheel covers ($49); N/A on Eldorado. Wire wheel covers: Brghm ($129); others ($176) exc. Eldo.

HISTORY: Introduced: September 23, 1976. Model year production (U.S.): 358,487 for a 3.9 percent share of the industry total. Calendar year production (U.S.): 369,254. Calendar year sales by U.S. dealers: 335,785 for a 3.7 percent market share. Model year sales by U.S. dealers: 328,129.

Historical Footnotes: Cadillac executives didn't appreciate Ford's advertising claim that an LTD was now as good as a Cadillac. But the new smaller Cadillacs were selling well, at least at the beginning. Sales of 328,129 units scored 9.5 percent over the 1976 record. Model year production also beat the 1976 score, by 16 percent. Rumors early in the year suggested that Cadillacs might be "upsized" within a couple of years; but that didn't seem likely in view of the need to meet stricter Corporate Average Fuel Economy (CAFE) requirements. Now that the Fleetwood Seventy-Five was gone, conversion companies stepped up production of "stretch" limousines. Moloney Coachbuilders (in Illinois) offered a 40-inch stretch of Brougham for under $15,000 (plus the cost of the car, of course). Phaeton Coach Corp. of Dallas, and the California-based American Custom Coachworks, did similar work. The latter also created custom convertibles based on the Coupe deVille chassis, while an Ohio firm (Convertibles, Inc.) turned out ragtop Eldorado conversions.

1978

Subtle exterior changes dominated the year, as wheelbases and dimensions were virtually identical to 1977. DeVille, Brougham, limo and Eldorado had a bolder horizontal cross-

hatch grille. All but Eldorado had new rear bumper ends with vertical taillamps and three-dimensional crest insignia. Most Broughams, all California Cadillacs and the fuel-injected deVille sedan sported aluminum hoods. After the start of production, Elk Grain vinyl tops would be used on all except Seville, which retained a padded Tuxedo Grain vinyl top. Passenger compartments had seven new interior colors and three new body cloths, including Random velour. Of the 21 body colors, 17 were new and all but two of those were exclusive to Cadillac. Signal seeking AM/FM stereo radios were now standard on all Cadillacs. For the first time, chromed wire wheels from the British firm of Dunlop were offered as options on DeVille, Brougham and Seville models. New electronic level control (standard on all except DeVille) used a height sensor to signal a motor-driven compressor that automatically adjusted for changing loads. Transmissions had higher downshift speeds this year. DeVille and Brougham body mounts were retuned for a smoother, quieter ride. Four new special editions were offered: Seville Elegante, Phaeton Coupe (or Sedan) deVille, and revised Eldorado Custom Biarritz. An available diesel V-8 engine (built by Oldsmobile) for Seville was announced during the model year, at the Chicago Auto Show. So was a new electronic trip computer. All Cadillacs except Seville carried a standard 425 cu. in. V-8. Cadillac hardly tried to hide the boast that owning one had always "expressed success." As the full line catalog modestly proclaimed, "calling something 'the Cadillac of its field' is one of the finest compliments you can pay a product."

1978 Cadillac, Seville sedan. (OCW)

1978 Cadillac, Seville Elegante sedan. (OCW)

SEVILLE—SERIES 6K—V-8—At the rear, Seville displayed new bumper guards, an engraved chrome insignia on taillamps, and a painted accent stripe that extended across the deck-lid to give a wider, lower appearance. Lower bumper rub strips were body-colored. Seville's grille had vertical slots in four rows, with the pattern repeated in two openings on the bumper, alongside the license plate. Amber parking/signal lamps sat below the quad rectangular headlamps, with amber/clear cornering lamps on the fender sides. The Seville script was behind the front wheels; a Cadillac script at the back of rear fenders, just ahead of the angled wraparound taillamps, and on the upper grille bar (driver's side). Once

again, the electronically fuel-injected 350 cu. in. V-8 engine was standard, with an on-board analog computer and new Electronic Spark Selection that altered spark advance to meet varying conditions. The intake manifold was lightweight aluminum. Oldsmobile's 350 cu. in. diesel V-8 became available in mid-year, first offered in seven major cities. Electronic load leveling was new this year. Standard equipment included a tilt/telescoping steering wheel, signal-seeking stereo radio, dual remote-control mirrors, fuel monitor system, power seat, power four-wheel disc brakes, controlled-cycle wipers, and many more luxuries. Sierra Grain leather interiors came in ten colors. Dover cloth upholstery (seven colors) was standard. Buyers could choose either a matching metal roof or Tuxedo Grain padded vinyl top. Sevilles came in 15 standard body colors plus six Firemist options; the vinyl roof came in 16 colors including metallics. Options included real wire wheels as well as wire covers, plus opera lamps, a sunroof, 40-channel CB transceiver, plus electronically-tuned radios and tape player combinations. A new trip computer option offered 11 digital displays, including average speed and miles per gallon, miles to destination, estimated arrival time, engine speed, coolant temp, and voltage. Seville Elegante was offered in two duotone body finishes: Platinum and Sable Black, or Western Saddle Firemist and Ruidoso Brown. Both had a painted metal top rather than vinyl. The second color began just above the beltline. Real wire wheels (not covers) had long-laced spokes. Full-length brushed chrome moldings had etched black grooving. An 'Elegante' script and crest were on the pillar behind the rear doors. Seats used perforated leather inserts (Antique Gray or Antique Medium Saddle) and soft, suede-like trim. The steering wheel was leather-wrapped to match. Front seats included storage pockets. A fold-down center armrest and console separated the driver and passenger. Compartments were provided for a telephone, tapes, and personal items. Only 5,000 or so Elegantes were built this year, but the special edition would remain for future seasons.

1978 Cadillac, Coupe deVille. (OCW)

DEVILLE—SERIES 6C—V-8—Several styling refinements hit DeVille (and Fleetwood) for 1978. A new, bolder grille pattern in three-row checkerboard style was repeated to the left and right of the license plate below. The new pattern had fewer (and more square) holes than before. Cadillac's script was above the grille's header bar (mounted on the body), on the driver's side. A new solid-color wreath-and-crest ornament rode the hood. New, extra-slim vertical taillamps in tall chrome bumper tips had thin backup lamps inset in the middle and built-in side marker lamps. Back bumpers were new. DeVille's padded vinyl roof had a custom-trimmed backlight. Rust prevention measures included Zincrometal panels and bi-metal (stainless steel on aluminum) moldings, plus microencapsulated epoxy-coated screws in key areas. Underhood was the 425 cu. in. (7.0-liter) V-8 introduced the year before. Six-way power driver's seat controls were now in the door armrest. New interiors included seatback pockets. Standard on all models: an AM/FM Signal-Seeking stereo radio with scanner and disappearing antenna. Coupe and Sedan deVilles also had automatic climate control, power windows, and much more. Sunroof, wire wheel discs and 50/50 Dual Comfort seats were available. Nine interior color selections were offered in new Random velour or Hampton woven cloth. Up to a

dozen Sierra Grain leather choices came with color-coordinated carpeting. Options included a custom-trimmed padded vinyl top, rear deck accent stripes, color-keyed bodyside moldings, chromed wire wheels, electronic leveling, and chrome accent moldings. Coupe deVille could have the Cabriolet roof package, including a chrome accent strip to highlight the Elk Grain vinyl top, Cadillac crests, and a French seam around the back windows-offered in 16 coordinated colors. A deVille d'Elegance special edition featured pillow-style 50/50 Dual Comfort seats in new Random velour (antique dark green, light beige, light blue, or dark mulberry). Upper doors and front seatback assist straps wore matching Random velour. High-pile carpeting extended part way up the doors. The glove box door held a 'deVille d'Elegance' insignia, as did the pillar behind backside windows. Hood, door and decklid were striped. Side moldings held vinyl inserts that matched the body color. Other extras: opera lamps, three roof-mounted assist straps, and door pull handles. The d'Elegance trim package came in 21 body colors. Arriving later were Phaeton packages that featured a simulated convertible top (down to authentic-looking welts and stitching). Offered in Cotillion White, Platinum or Arizona Beige (with contrasting top colors), these were identified by 'Phaeton' nameplates on back fenders and wire wheels.

1978 Cadillac, Sedan deVille. (OCW)

FLEETWOOD BROUGHAM—SERIES 6C—V-8—The most noticeable difference in appearance between Brougham and the less costly deVille sedan lay in Brougham's distinctively tapered pillar design between front and rear doors. Brougham also stopped itself with four-wheel disc brakes. New this year, were the restyled grille and back bumper, plus a weight-saving aluminum hood. Front seats now had seatback pockets. Brushed chrome moldings held new wreath-and-crest ornamentation. The Elk Grain vinyl roof held opera lamps just behind the back doors. Color-coordinated wheel discs repeated the body color in the center. Door-pull handles were new, and the door armrest held six-way power driver's seat controls. Brougham interiors held individual reading lamps. The Florentine velour interior was offered in mulberry, light gray, black, light blue, dark green, yellow, or light beige. Leather interiors came in 11 colors. Standard engine was the 425 cu. in. (7.0-liter) V-8. Oversized steel-belted radials rode match-mounted wheels. New standard equipment included electronic leveling control. Joining the option list were seven new interior colors, rear deck accent stripes, color-keyed bodyside moldings, and chrome accent moldings. Available chrome wire wheels showed the Cadillac insignia on a hexagonal center hub. An electronic-tuning stereo radio with digital readout was available with 8-track tape player. The familiar Astroroof was available too. Brougham d'Elegance added contoured pillow-styled seats trimmed in Florentine velour (in five Antique colors), with velour trim in doors, pull straps and seatback assist straps. Medium Saddle leather was also available on the 50/50 Dual Comfort front seats. Plush pile carpeting reached up onto the lower doors, and covered front and rear floormats. A 'Brougham d'Elegance' insignia was on the glove box door; another outside. Also included:

three above-door passenger assist grips, accent stripes, and available turbine-vaned wheel discs.

FLEETWOOD LIMOUSINE—SERIES 6D—V-8—The twin posh "Flagships of the Cadillac fleet" carried styling alterations similar to the "lesser" Fleetwoods. New electronic leveling control was standard. Six-way power driver's seat controls were now in the door armrest. Standard limos sat eight. The seven-passenger Formal Limousine had a standard divided 45/45 front seat with black leather seating, plus a sliding glass partition. Both models had two additional fold-down seats. Florentine velour upholstery was offered in light gray, black, or dark blue. The Automatic Climate Control System could be operated by driver or passengers. A Dual Accessory Control Panel also let passengers operate the power windows--a logical decision, to be sure. A padded Elk Grain vinyl roof was standard. Not quite as many Formal limos were built as the standard variety. Chrome landau bars were available by special order. So were a full landau roof or cabriolet roof, both in padded Elk Grain vinyl. The landau option offered closed-in rear quarters and a smaller back window, as well as opera lamps.

1978 Cadillac, Eldorado Biarritz coupe. (OCW)

ELDORADO—SERIES 6E—V-8—While waiting one more year for an all-new downsized body, Eldorado received no major change other than a revised crosshatch grille dominated by heavier horizontal bars. Also noteworthy on the outside was the padded Elk Grain vinyl top. The four-row peaked checkerboard grille was flanked by quad rectangular headlamps. Amber parking lamps sat low on the bumper. The grille pattern was repeated between license plate and bumper guards, below the protruding protective strip. Massive chrome vertical bumper ends extended upward to form housings for auxiliary lamps, forming a huge bright extension of fender tips. Eldorado block letters stood above the upper grille bar, which tapered outward above the headlamps. Standard engine was the 425 cu. in. (7.0-liter) V-8, available with carburetor or fuel injection. Eldorados had four-wheel disc brakes, front-wheel drive, electronic level control, automatic climate control, power windows and door locks, cornering lights, six-way power seat, three-speed wipers, Freedom battery, and lamp monitors. What else? How about a trip odometer, wide-whitewall steel-belted radial tires, Soft-Ray tinted glass, accent striping, remote control left-hand mirror, color-keyed litter container, vanity mirror, lighters, bumper impact strips, and a stowaway spare tire. Interiors might be Halifax knit in four colors, Random velour in choice of three, or a dozen Sierra Grain leather combinations. Dramatic two-tones were also available on Dual Comfort front seats, in three color combinations. Options included a 40-channel CB, 8-track tape player, Astroroof and sun roof. Eldorado Biarritz, which first appeared during the 1976 model year, now sported a convertible-like padded vinyl top, unique script, accent stripes, and distinctive chrome body moldings. Inside the Custom Biarritz were Sierra Grain leather contoured pillow-style seats in antique medium saddle, white, dark carmine, antique yellow, or antique light blue. The Cabriolet roof accented Eldo's distinctively-shaped quarter windows that tapered downward at the front, with a vinyl-insert molding across the fully padded Elk Grain vinyl top. Black-accented brushed stainless steel belt moldings stretched from rear to hood, terminating in a spearlike design at the front. Special stripes accented front fenders, doors and rear quarter panels. Biarritz came in five colors: Mediterranean Blue Firemist, Cotillion White, Carmine Red, Colonial Yellow, and Ruidoso Saddle. All had opera lamps, remote-control passenger-side mirror, and color-coordinated wheel discs. Customers also had the choice of a Custom Biarritz Classic, with a two-tone paint scheme that not everyone found attractive.

I.D. DATA: Cadillac's 13-symbol Vehicle Identification Number (VIN) again was located on the forward edge of the windshield trim molding, visible through the windshield. Coding was similar to 1978. The model year code changed to '8' for 1978. Engine coding was now as follows: 'B' V8-350 EFI; 'S' V8-425 4Bbl.; 'T' V8-425 EFI; 'N' V8-350 diesel.

Series No.	Body/Style No.	Body Type & Seating	Factory Price	Shipping Weight	Prod. Total
SEVILLE					
6K	S69	4-dr Sedan-5P	14267	4179	56,985
DEVILLE					
6C	D47	2-dr Coupe-6P	10444	4163	117,750
6C	D69	4-dr Sedan-6P	10668	4236	88,951
FLEETWOOD BROUGHAM					
6C	B69	4-dr Sedan-6P	12292	4314	36,800
FLEETWOOD LIMOUSINE					
6D	F23	4-dr Sedan-8P	19642	4772	848
6D	F33	4-dr Fml Limo-7P	20363	4858	682
6D	Z90	Commercial Chassis	N/A	N/A	852
ELDORADO					
6E	L47	2-dr Coupe-6P	11921	4906	46,816

ENGINES: BASE V-8 (Seville): 90-degree, overhead valve V-8. Cast iron block and head. Displacement: 350 cu. in. (5.7-liters). Bore & stroke: 4.057 x 3.385 in. Compression ratio: 8.0:1. Brake horsepower: 170 at 4200 R.P.M. Torque: 270 lb.-ft. at 2000 R.P.M. Five main bearings. Hydraulic valve lifters. Electronic fuel injection. Oldsmobile-built. VIN Code: B. BASE V-8 (All except Seville): 90-degree, overhead valve V-8. Cast iron block and head. Displacement: 425 cu. in. (7.0-liters). Bore & stroke: 4.082 x 4.06 in. Compression ratio: 8.2:1. Brake horsepower: 180 at 4000 R.P.M. Torque: 320 lb.-ft. at 2000 R.P.M. Five main bearings. Hydraulic valve lifters. Carburetor: 4Bbl. VIN Code: S. OPTIONAL V-8 (DeVille, Brougham, Eldo): Same as 425 cu. in. V-8 above but with electronic fuel injection. Horsepower: 195 at 3800 R.P.M. Torque: 320 lb.-ft. at 2400 R.P.M. VIN Code: T. OPTIONAL DIESEL V-8: 90-degree, overhead valve V-8. Cast iron block and head. Displacement: 350 cu. in. (5.7-liters). Bore & stroke: 4.057 x 3.385 in. Compression ratio: 22.5:1. Brake horsepower: 120 at 3600 R.P.M. Torque: 220 lb.-ft. at 1600 R.P.M. Five main bearings. Hydraulic valve lifters. Electronic fuel injection. Oldsmobile-built. VIN Code: N.

CHASSIS DATA: Dimensions same as 1977; see 1977 specifications. Standard Tires: (Seville) GR78 x 15-B wide WSW; (DeVille) GR78 x 15-B wide WSW; (Brougham) HR78 x 15-B wide WSW; (limo) HR78 x 15-D wide WSW; (Eldo) LR78 x 15-B.

TECHNICAL: Transmission: Turbo Hydra-matic transmission standard on all models; column shift. Gear ratios: (1st) 2.48:1; (2nd) 1.48:1; (3rd) 1.00:1; (Rev) 2.07:1. Standard axle ratio: (Seville) 2.56:1 except high-alt. 3.08:1; (DeVille/Brougham) 2.28:1, with 3.08:1 available; (Limo) 3.08:1; (Eldo) 2.73:1 except high-alt. 3.07:1. Hypoid rear axle exc. (Seville) Salisbury type; (Eldo) spiral bevel. Steering/Suspension: same as 1977. Brakes: front disc, rear drum exc. Eldo/Seville/Brougham, four-wheel disc. HEI electronic ignition. Fuel tank: (Seville) 21 gal.; (Eldo) 27 gal.; (others) 25.3 gal.

DRIVETRAIN OPTIONS: Fuel-injected V-8 engine: DeVille/Brougham/Seville ($744). Heavy-duty cooling system ($47). 80-amp alternator ($51). Engine block heater ($20). California emission equipment ($75). Limited slip differential ($67); N/A on Eldo. High altitude pkg. ($33). Electronic level control: DeV ($140). OPTION PACKAGES: Brougham d'Elegance: cloth ($938); leather ($1270). DeVille Cabriolet ($369). DeVille Cabriolet w/Astroroof ($1450). DeVille Cabriolet w/sunroof ($1250). DeVille d'Elegance ($689). DeVille Custom Phaeton ($1929). Eldorado Cabriolet ($484). Eldorado Cabriolet w/Astroroof ($1565). Eldorado Cabriolet w/sunroof ($1365). Eldorado Custom Biarritz ($1865); w/Astroroof ($2946); w/sunroof ($2746). Eldorado Custom Biarritz Classic ($2466); w/Astroroof ($3547); w/sunroof ($3347). Seville Elegante ($2600); Elegante w/Astroroof ($3706); Elegante w/sunroof ($3506).

CONVENIENCE/APPEARANCE OPTIONS: Astroroof w/full vinyl roof ($995) exc. limos. Astroroof (painted) ($1106). Sunroof w/full vinyl roof ($795) exc. limo. Sunroof (painted roof): DeV/Sev/Eldo ($906). Cruise control ($122). Trip computer: Seville ($875). Controlled-cycle wipers ($32). Rear defogger, grid-type ($94). Six-way Dual Comfort power passenger seat adjuster ($118-$150). Power 50/50 seat recliner ($116). Power 50/50 passenger seat recliner ($210-$262). Power passenger seatback recliner, notchback seat: DeV ($116). Tilt/telescope steering wheel ($121). Automatic door locks ($114). Illuminated entry system ($59). Fuel monitor ($29). Theft deterrent system ($130). Trunk lid release and power pull-down ($80) exc. Seville. Trunk lid power pull-down: Sev ($67). Opera lamps: DeV/Sev ($63). Twilight Sentinel ($54). Guidematic headlamp control ($62). Trumpet horn ($21) exc.

Seville. Remote-control right mirror ($34). Lighted thermometer on left mirror ($27). Lighted vanity mirror, passenger ($50). AM/FM stereo radio with digital display; ($106); w/tape player ($106); w/CB ($281); w/tape and CB ($427). Seek/scan AM/FM stereo radio with tape player and digital display: Sev/Brghm ($225). Seek/scan AM/FM stereo radio w/rear control: limo ($203). Firemist paint ($163). Padded vinyl roof: DeV/Sev ($215-$222). Front bumper reinforcement ($9) exc. Sev/Eldo. Chrome accent molding: DeV/Brghm ($85-$100). Accent stripes: DeV/Brghm ($53). Door edge guards ($11-$18). License frame: each ($9). Dual Comfort 50/50 front seats: DeV/Eldo ($198). Leather seating area ($295-$315); Eldo w/two tone and 50/50 dual comfort front seats ($556). Carpeted rubber front floor mats ($31-$34); rear ($15-$21). Trunk mat ($12). Turbine-vaned wheel covers ($54); N/A on Eldo. Locking wire wheels ($541-$595). Locking wire wheel covers ($179-$233). Stowaway spare tire: limo (NC).

HISTORY: Introduced: September 29, 1977. Model year production (U.S.): 349,684 for a 3.9 percent share of the industry total and the second highest Cadillac total ever. Calendar year production (U.S.): 350,761. Calendar year sales by U.S. dealers: 350,813 for a 3.8 percent market share. Model year sales by U.S. dealers: 347,221.

Historical Footnotes: Record sales greeted Cadillac for the third year in-a-row. The model year total beat 1977's mark by six percent. The new Seville diesel (engine built by Oldsmobile) sold only about 2,800 copies, barely half the early prediction. But it was introduced late in the model year. Sevilles in general hit a new production high. Eldorado did well also, as buyers snapped up the last of the vast Eldos before the 1979 downsizing. A three-month shutdown of the Linden, New Jersey, plant, to tool up for the new E-body 1979 Eldorado, Toronado and Riviera models, contributed to a loss in calendar year production of DeVilles this year. Cadillac asserted that the company "consistently leads all U.S. luxury car makes in repeat ownership." Once you own a Cadillac," it was suggested, "it is difficult to accept anything less."

1979

"For some," the 1979 catalog proclaimed, a Cadillac was "an integral part of the good life." For some...the fulfillment of a promise they made to themselves long ago." Could be, but apart from a daringly downsized E-body Eldorado, the year brought few stunning announcements. A new electronic-tuning AM/FM stereo radio with signal seeker and scanner included digital display of time and station frequencies. A new convex remote-control right mirror to increase the field of view was standard on Broughams and limos, optional on DeVilles. Lap seatbelts were the new "free-wheeling" style, and chimes now gently warned passengers to buckle up. A new dome light had dual spot map lamps. Seville and Eldorado could have an optional Trip Computer with digital display that showed average speed, miles yet to travel, engine speed arrival time, and elapsed trip time. DeVilles, Fleetwood Broughams and limousines were powered by a 425 cu. in. (7.0-liter) V-8 with four-barrel carburetor; a fuel-injected version again was available. Oldsmobile's diesel V-8, first offered only on Seville and Eldorado, could go under DeVille/Brougham hoods by year's end. Options for the year included dual electric remote mirrors; an automatically-retracting radio antenna; plus 8-track and cassette tape players (with built-in 40-channel CB available).

1979 Cadillac, Seville sedan with metal painted roof. (OCW)

1979 Cadillac, Seville Elegante sedan. (OCW)

SEVILLE—SERIES 6K—V-8—Carried over with only modest trim changes, Sevilles got a retuned suspension to improve their ride, plus new body mounts. Nameplates moved from the upper right of the grille to the upper left, and that grille had a tighter pattern than before. The grille's pattern of vertical crosshatch slots was repeated in twin insets in the front bumper. Standard engine remained the 350 cu. in. (5.7-liter) V-8 with electronic fuel injection, now rated 170 horsepower. The diesel version introduced at mid-year was offered again. Sevilles destined for California received the three-way catalytic converter with closed-loop electronic controls, previously used only on other GM models. Bodies could have 14 standard colors, with seven Firemist colors available. Interiors came with new solid and striped Dante and Roma knit fabrics in six colors, or 11 shades of Sierra Grain leather. Either the Tuxedo Grain padded vinyl roof (in 17 colors, including metallics) or a plain metal top were offered at the same price. Options included the new digital trip computer and signal-seeking radios. Cadillac's catalog claimed that Seville had been chosen "one of the ten most beautifully designed production cars of the last 50 years." The special edition Elegante came in two-tone Slate Firemist and Sable Black, with accent striping and full-length side moldings with etched black grooving, plus a painted metal roof. Elegante was identified by a Cadillac wreath-and-crest as well as script nameplate. Standard were chrome-plated wire wheels with long-laced spokes. Seating areas and door panels had perforated leather inserts with suede-like vinyl trim, with leather-trimmed steering wheel. The Dual Comfort 40/40 seats had storage pockets and an integral fold-down center armrest. New for 1979 was plush fur-like Tangier carpeting. Elegante's price tag was $2,735.

1979 Cadillac, Coupe deVille "Phaeton" (special edition). (OCW)

1979 Cadillac, Sedan deVille. (OCW)

DEVILLE—SERIES 6C—V-8—Appearance changes for DeVille/Fleetwood included restyled taillamps and a revised front-end look, plus new interior trim. This year's grille had many more horizontal and vertical bars in its simple crosshatch pattern, designed to accentuate the traditional Cadillac front end look. 'Cadillac' script returned this year to the wide upper grille bar (driver's side). A thin molding above the grille extended outward, over the headlamps, to wrap around each fender. Quad rectangular headlamps were outboard of twin vertical rectangular parking lamps. The crosshatch grille pattern repeated itself in twin rectangular openings in the bumper, on either side of the license plate, in familiar Cadillac style. Front fenders held large cornering lamps with clear and amber lenses. Seven new two-tone body color combinations were available for DeVille (and Fleetwood Brougham), with color coordinated accent striping. New brushed chrome wheel covers showed the Cadillac crest on a black background. Also new: seatbelt chimes, a standard AM/FM stereo radio with digital display, dome light with dual spot map lamps, and optional electrically-controlled outside mirrors. Interiors were upholstered in Durand knit cloth (six colors) or genuine leather. Standard fittings included power door locks and windows, six-way power seat, and automatic climate control. The standard 425 cu. in. (7.0-liter) V-8 had new EGR riser tubes. A fuel-injected, 195-horsepower version was optional. The Olds-built 350 cu. in. diesel V-8 became optional in mid-year. Special editions for 1979 included a Custom Phaeton Coupe and Custom Phaeton Sedan, both offering styling touches intended to remind observers of the "classic" convertibles. Features included brushed chrome moldings with flush-mounted opera lamps and the Cadillac crest; reduced size quarter windows; a sporty convertible-like roof; 'Phaeton' script on each rear quarter panel; wire wheel discs; accent striping; 45/55 Dual Comfort front seats with leather seating; and leather-trimmed steering wheel. Phaeton editions came in three color combinations: Cotillion White with dark blue roof and white leather inside; Slate Firemist with black roof and antique slate gray leather upholstery; or Western Saddle Firemist with dark brown roof and antique saddle leather seating. Also on the option list was the deVille d'Elegance, with new soft Venetian velour upholstery, (in choice of four colors) on pillow-style 50/50 seats. It also had Tangier carpeting, special door pull handles, and 'deVille d'Elegance' script on the glove box and exterior. Coupe d'Elegance had opera lamps; sedans had three roof mounted assist straps. Both bodies had side moldings and accent stripes. Coupe deVille also came with a Cabriolet roof treatment, including chrome crossover roof molding, in 17 Elk Grain vinyl colors. A French seam surrounded the back window, and a Cadillac script and crest identified the Cabriolet model.

1979 Cadillac, Fleetwood Brougham d'Elegance sedan. (OCW)

FLEETWOOD BROUGHAM—SERIES 6C—V-8—Brougham sedans had the same new front-end look and restyled taillamps as the less costly DeVille, and the same engine choices. New wheel covers of brushed chrome displayed the Cadillac wreath-and-crest on a dark red background. Dual comfort 45/55 front seats held three people. Upholstery was new slate gray Dante knit cloth. Genuine leather in 11 shades was also available. Tire pressure was raised to 32 psi, and engine recalibrated, to improve gas mileage. Brougham's suspension was retuned and body mounts were new. Inside were individual reading lamps and armrests. Broughams came with four-wheel disc brakes rather than DeVille's disc/drum combination. They also had a few distinctive styling touches to separate them from DeVilles. Pillars between front and rear doors tapered inward toward the beltline. Wide rocker panel moldings continued behind the rear wheels, stretching to the back bumper. Brougham d'Elegance carried new pillow-style seats in Dante and Roma knits, plus plush Tangier carpeting. Three roof-mounted assist straps, a choice of standard or turbine-vaned wheel covers, accent striping, and d'Elegance nameplate directly behind the rear side windows completed the package. Leather seating areas were also offered.

FLEETWOOD LIMOUSINE—SERIES 6D—V-8—About 2,000 limos, offered in standard or Formal form, found buyers each year. Both had the same new crosshatch grille as Fleetwood Brougham, along with new simulated woodgrain interior, a lower profile, and revised two-spoke steering wheel. Fleetwood remained the only American-built chassis for use in "professional" cars used by funeral directors and for ambulances. The basic limo seated eight; the Formal edition, seven. Both were powered by the 425 cu. in. (7.0-liter) V-8, which had to haul over 4,800 pounds of car. Standard interior was dark blue Dante cloth, but slate gray and black were available. Front compartment of the Formal limo was black, with black leather in seating areas separated from the passenger compartment by a sliding glass partition. Interiors were also offered in slate gray and black. All limos included two fold-down auxiliary seats. There was a dual accessory control panel for climate control and windows, along with new optional rear seat controls for the radio. An optional 8-track tape player put controls in the back.

1979 Cadillac, Eldorado Biarritz coupe with brushed stainless steel roof cap and cast aluminum wheels. (OCW)

ELDORADO—SERIES 6E—V-8—Two years after other full-size Cadillacs were downsized, the personal-luxury coupe received similar treatment. Eldorado shrunk drastically in its new front-wheel drive form, down some 1,150 pounds in weight and 20 inches in overall length. Wheelbase was over a foot shorter at 114 inches; width narrower by more than 8 inches. Head and leg room managed to grow, though, in both front and rear seats. As before, Eldos included standard four wheel disc brakes, but independent rear suspension was something new. The new space efficient design also featured electronic level control. Eldo's upright rectangular rear side windows also brought back the look of the recently-abandoned pillarless hardtop. Wide, squarish, closed in rear quarters also helped give Eldo a distinctive appearance. Standard luxury touches included Twilight Sentinel headlamp control, automatic climate control, illuminated entry, and side window defoggers. New 50/45 Dual Comfort front seats came in 11 shades of leather, or pillow-style seating in new Dante knit cloth (six colors). The new instrument panel with driver only controls on the left was simulated burl walnut. Steel-belted whitewall radial tires rode match-mounted wheels. A new flush-mounted windshield reduced wind noise. Standard dual outside mirrors were remote controlled (right mirror convex). New permanently-sealed wheel bearings never needed lubrication. Eldorado's boxy-looking crosshatch grille had rectangular openings and extended down into a cutaway portion of the bumper (not in two separate sections as on other full-size Cadillacs). Quad rectangular headlamps sat above horizontal park/signal lamps, with wide cornering lamps on the forward portion of the front fenders. An Eldorado script was on the trailing segment of the front fenders, as well as on the deck-lid. Narrow three-sided vertical taillamps were an Eldorado exclusive. Eldo still sported a familiar long hood and rather stubby trunk, and fender lines were similar to before. Lamp monitors and the instrument panel were restyle. Inside was a new Dual Comfort front seat with fold-down armrest and new seatback pockets, a new dome light with dual spot map lamps, plus a two-spoke steering wheel. New cast aluminum wheels were optional. So were wire wheel covers with locking device and electrically-controlled outside mirrors with lighted thermometer on driver's side. The optional Cabriolet roof was offered with or without padding. Base powerplant was now Seville's fuel-injected

350 cu. in. (5.7-liter) gasoline V-8. For the first time, the Olds-built 5.7-liter diesel V-8 was an Eldorado option. Eldorado Biarritz had a number of exclusive accents, including a Cabriolet roof treatment with new brushed stainless steel front roof cap and padded vinyl at the rear. The wide chrome crossover roof molding continued forward to the front fenders. Also in the package were new cast aluminum wheels, accent stripes, opera lamps, Biarritz script, a tufted pillow-style interior in five shades of leather or in light blue Dante cloth, fur-like Tangier carpeting, individual rear seat reading lamps, and leather-trimmed steering wheel.

I.D. DATA: Cadillac's 13-symbol Vehicle Identification Number (VIN) was again on the upper left surface of the cowl, visible through the windshield. Coding was similar to 1977-78. The model year code changed to '9' for 1979. The body type code for Eldorado coupe changed to '57'. Assembly plant codes were: 'Q' Detroit; 'E' Linden, NJ (Eldorado only); and 'C' South Gate, CA (DeVille only). Sequence numbers began with 100001 at Detroit (except 450001 for Seville); 600001 at Linden and 350001 at South Gate. Eldorado's body identification plate was on the top right side of the cowl. Diesel Seville body plates were on the top left side of the cowl.

1979 Cadillac, Fleetwood Brougham sedan. (OCW)

SEVILLE

Series No.	Body/Style No.	Body Type & Seating	Factory Price	Shipping Weight	Prod. Total
6K	S69	4-dr Sedan-5P	15646	4180	53,487

DEVILLE

6C	D47	2-dr Coupe-6P	11139	4143	121,890
6C	D69	4-dr Sedan-6P	11493	4212	93,211

FLEETWOOD BROUGHAM

6C	B69	4-dr Sedan-6P	13446	4250	42,200

FLEETWOOD LIMOUSINE

6D	F23	4-dr Sedan-8P	20987	4782	Note 1
6D	F33	4-dr Fml Limo-7P	21735	4866	Note 1
6D	Z90	Commercial Chassis	N/A	N/A	864

Note 1: Total limousine production, 2,025.

ELDORADO

6E	L57	2-dr Coupe-4P	14240	3792	67,436

ENGINES: BASE V-8 (Seville, Eldorado): 90-degree, overhead valve V-8. Cast iron block and head. Displacement: 350 cu. in. (5.7-liters). Bore & stroke: 4.057 x 3.385 in. Compression ratio: 8.0:1. Brake horsepower: 170 at 4200 R.P.M. Torque: 270 lb.-ft. at 2000 R.P.M. Five main bearings. Hydraulic valve lifters. Electronic fuel injection. Oldsmobile-built. VIN Code: B. BASE V-8 (DeVille, Brougham, Fleetwood): 90-degree, overhead valve V-8. Cast iron block and head. Displacement: 425 cu. in. (7.0-liters). Bore & stroke: 4.082 x 4.06 in. Compression ratio: 8.2:1. Brake horsepower: 180 at 4000 R.P.M. Torque: 320 lb.-ft. at 2000 R.P.M. Five main bearings. Hydraulic valve lifters. Carburetor: 4Bbl. VIN Code: S. OPTIONAL V-8 (DeVille, Brougham): Same as 425 cu. in. V-8 above, with fuel injection. Horsepower: 195 at 3800 R.P.M. Torque: 320 lb.-ft. at 2400 R.P.M. VIN Code: T. OPTIONAL DIESEL V-8 (Seville, Eldorado, DeVille, Brougham): 90-degree, overhead valve V-8. Cast iron block and head. Displacement: 350 cu. in. (5.7-liters). Bore & stroke: 4.057 x 3.385 in. Compression ratio: 22.5:1. Brake horsepower: 125 at 3600 R.P.M. Torque: 225 lb.-ft. at 1600 R.P.M. Five main bearings. Hydraulic valve lifters. Fuel injection. Oldsmobile-built. VIN Code: N.

CHASSIS DATA: Wheelbase: (Seville) 114.3 in.; (DeVille/Brougham) 121.5 in.; (Limo) 144.5 in.; (Eldorado) 113.9 in. Overall length: (Seville/Eldo) 204.0 in.; (DeV/Brghm) 221.2 in.; (Limo) 244.2 in. Height: (Seville) 54.6 in.; (DeV cpe) 54.4 in.; (DeV sed) 55.3 in.; (Brghm) 56.7 in.; (Limo) 56.9 in.; (Eldo) 54.2 in. Width: (Seville) 71.8 in.; (Eldo) 71.4 in.; (others) 76.5 in. Front Tread: (Seville) 61.3 in.; (Eldo) 59.3 in.; (others) 61.7 in. Rear Tread: (Seville) 59.0 in.; (Eldo) 60.5 in.; (others) 60.7 in. Standard Tires: (Seville) GR78 x 15-B SBR wide WSW; (Eldo) P205/75R15

SBR wide WSW; (DeV) GR78 x 15-B SBR wide WSW; (Brghm) HR78 x 15-B SBR wide WSW; (Limo) HR78 x 15-D SBR wide WSW.

TECHNICAL: Transmission: Three-speed Turbo Hydra-matic transmission standard on all models; column shift. Eldorado/Seville gear ratios: (1st) 2.74:1; (2nd) 1.57:1; (3rd) 1.00:1; (Rev) 2.07:1. Other models: (1st) 2.48:1; (2nd) 1.48:1; (3rd) 1.00:1; (Rev) 2.07:1. Standard axle ratio: (Seville) 2.24:1; (Eldo) 2.19:1; (DeV/Brghm) 2.28:1; (limo) 3.08:1. Steering: recirculating ball. Front suspension: (Eldo) independent transverse torsion bars, link stabilizer bar; (others) independent with ball joints and coil springs, stabilizer bar. Rear suspension: (Eldo) independent trailing arm; (Seville) Hotchkiss 56 in. leaf springs, five leaves, link stabilizer; (others) four link coil springs, link stabilizer. Electronic level control (except DeVille). Brakes: front disc, rear drum except Brougham/Seville/Eldo, four-wheel disc. HEI electronic ignition. Fuel tank: (Seville/Eldo) 19.6 gal.; (others) 25 gal.

DRIVETRAIN OPTIONS: 425 cu. in. V-8 FI engine: DeV/Fleetwood ($783). 5.7-liter diesel V-8 engine: Seville/Eldo ($287); DeV/Brghm, later in model year ($849). Heavy-duty cooling system ($49). 80-amp alternator ($54). Engine block heater ($21). California emission equipment ($83-$150). California fuel economy equipment: DeV/Fleetwood ($65). Limited slip differential ($70); N/A on Eldo. High altitude pkg. ($35). Electronic level control: DeV ($160). Trailering package ($49-$103).

OPTION PACKAGES: Brougham d'Elegance: cloth ($987); leather ($1344). DeVille Cabriolet ($384). DeVille Cabriolet w/Astroroof ($1522). DeVille Cabriolet w/sunroof ($1312). DeVille d'Elegance ($725). DeVille Custom Phaeton ($2029). Eldorado Cabriolet ($350). Eldorado Cabriolet w/Astroroof ($1488). Eldorado Cabriolet w/sunroof ($1278). Eldorado Biarritz: leather seating ($2600); cloth ($2250). Eldorado Biarritz w/Astroroof: leather seating ($3738); cloth ($3388). Seville Elegante ($2735). Seville Elegante w/Astroroof ($3873). Seville Elegante w/sunroof ($3663).

CONVENIENCE/APPEARANCE OPTIONS: Astroroof (w/full vinyl roof): DeV/Fleetwood/Sev ($998). Astroroof (painted): DeV/Sev/Eldo ($1163). Sunroof (full vinyl roof): DeV/Fleetwood/Sev ($798). Sunroof (painted roof): DeV/Sev/Eldo ($953). Cruise control ($137). Controlled-cycle wipers: DeV/limo ($38). Rear defogger, grid-type ($101). Six-way Dual Comfort power passenger seat adjuster ($125-$160). Power driver's seat recliner ($122). Power passenger seat recliner with six-way adjuster ($221-$280). Power passenger seatback recliner, bench seat: DeV ($122). Tilt/telescope steering wheel ($130). Automatic door locks ($121). Illuminated entry system: DeV/limo ($62). Fuel monitor ($31). Trip computer: Seville ($920). Theft deterrent system ($137). Trunk lid release and power pull-down: DeV/limo ($85). Opera lamps: DeV/Sev ($66). Twilight Sentinel: DeV/limo ($56). Guidematic headlamp control ($91). Trumpet horn ($22). Remote-control right mirror: DeV ($40). Electric remote left mirror w/thermometer ($90). Lighted thermometer on left mirror ($28). Lighted vanity mirror, passenger ($52). Electronic tuning seek/scan AM/FM stereo radio with 8-track tape player ($195); w/8-track and CB ($480); w/cassette ($225); w/CB ($380). Electronic tuning seek/scan AM/FM stereo radio with 8-track player, rear control: limo ($398). Two-tone paint, partial Firemist ($361). Firemist paint ($171). Padded vinyl roof: DeV ($225). Front bumper reinforcement ($9). Chrome accent molding: DeV ($90-$105). Accent stripes: DeV/Fleetwood ($56). Door edge guards ($13-$20). License frame: each ($10). Dual comfort front seats: DeV ($208). Leather seating area ($330-$350). Carpeted rubber front floor mats ($33-$36); rear ($16). Trunk mat ($13). Turbine-vaned wheel covers ($59); N/A on Eldo. Aluminum wheels ($350); N/A on Eldo. Locking wire wheels: DeV/Sev/Fleetwood ($569-$628). Locking wire wheel covers ($189-$292).

HISTORY: Introduced: September 28, 1978. Model year production (U.S.): 381,113 for a 4.1 percent share and a new record. Calendar year production (U.S.): 345,794. Calendar year sales by U.S. dealers: 314,034, which amounted to a 3.8 percent market share. Model year sales by U.S. dealers: 328,815.

Historical Footnotes: DeVilles this year were built at South Gate, California. The DeVille Phaeton's simulated convertible top was hardly likely to satisfy real ragtop fans who could afford the price of one of the re-manufactured versions. One such conversion by Hess & Eisenhardt, called "Le Cabriolet," was marketed through Cadillac dealers. Like other GM divisions, Cadillac had high expectations for diesel power, but that phenomenon was destined to evaporate in the next half-dozen years.

1980

"Through the years," boasted the 1980 full-line catalog, "Cadillac has earned for itself an exclusive place...a solitary niche...in the pantheon of the world's truly fine automobiles." Readers were even reminded how Cadillac had twice won the DeWar trophy in the early years of the century, first for its use of interchangeable parts and, later, for pioneering the electric self-starter. This year brought a restyled Brougham and DeVille, with a more formal roofline that gave more space in back. Their new grille was supposed to boost aerodynamic efficiency, too. Flush-mounted windshields on Eldorado and Seville added style and helped cut wind noise. Suspension refinements included low-friction ball joints and larger bushings, plus new low-rolling-resistance tires. New options: a three-channel garage door opener and heated outside mirrors. On the engine roster, the 368 cu. in. (6.0-liter) V-8 with four-barrel carburetor was standard on Fleetwood Brougham, DeVille and limousines. A digital fuel-injected version (with computerized self diagnostic features) was standard on Eldorado, a no-cost option for Seville. The DFI V-8's memory turned on an "Engine Check" light to warn of malfunctions. Meantime, the engine's microprocessor could make substitutions that might allow the car to continue to run. An MPG Sentinel calculated continual average and instantaneous miles-per-gallon readings at the touch of a button. Rounding out the lineup, Seville's standard 5.7-liter diesel V-8, manufactured by Oldsmobile, was also available under the hood of Eldorado, DeVille and Fleetwood Brougham. Late in the model year a Buick 4.1-liter V-6 was added--the first such offering on a Cadillac, and the first engine other than a V-8 in six decades. Body colors for 1980 were: Cotillion White; Platinum; Sable Black; Steel Blue; Superior Blue; Twilight Blue; Canyon Rock; Princess Green; Blackwatch Green; Colonial Yellow; Flax; Sandstone; Columbian Brown; Bordeaux Red; Saxony Red; and Norfolk Gray. At extra cost buyers could have any of five Firemist colors: Azure Blue, Desert Sand, Victoria Plum, Sheffield Gray, or Western Saddle. For rust protection, over 100 areas were specially treated. All lower body exterior panels were made from pre-coated metals. Each point of metal-to-metal contact contained either a gasket or bi-metal molding. All bodies were dipped in electrically charged primer to increase bonding adhesion.

1980 Cadillac, Seville Elegante sedan. (OCW)

SEVILLE—SERIES 6K—V-8—Billed in the full-line catalog as "quite possibly the most distinctive car in the world today...and the most advanced," the all new Seville was nothing if not dramatic. A total redesign gave buyers more interior space and trunk volume, along with the radical body shape. The side view was the most striking, even on the standard Seville with its straight bodyside molding. The humped deck lid began almost horizontal, but hit a distinctive horizontal crease before tapering down to wide taillamps. Small lenses were inset into the new one-piece, high-strength back bumper: two at the rear and two at the sides. The license plate sat in a deeply recessed housing. On the deck lid were Cadillac's wreath-and-crest, plus the Seville script. Both emblems were repeated on the back roof pillar. The Seville script was also on front fenders, just below the thin bodyside molding.

Chrome rocker moldings were tall and strong. Designed by Wayne Cady, the bustleback body and long hood suggested more than a nodding acquaintance with the impressive old razor-edge styling used on Hooper and Vanden Plas Rolls-Royce in the 1950s. Not everyone loved Seville's bustleback shape, with sloping rear end and "boot" trunk, but it drew considerable attention. Wheelbase was 114 inches; length almost 205 inches; overall dimensions not much different than the 1979 edition. Running gear and front-drive chassis were shared with the other luxury E-body coupes: Eldorado, Buick Riviera, and Olds Toronado. But Seville hardly resembled its mechanical mates. Up front, the squared off look was similar to earlier Sevilles. The front end was lower, and the car weighed 300 pounds less than before. The new yet traditional grille consisted of narrow vertical bars and a wide horizontal header bar with 'Cadillac' script at the side, plus a stand up wreath-and-crest at the hood front. The windshield sat at a sharp angle. Rounded, flared wheel openings housed new all-weather radial tires on new cast aluminum wheels with brushed-chrome centers. Bodies came in a choice of 16 acrylic lacquer finishes with accent striping (plus two tone treatments). Dual Comfort 50/45 front seats were offered in six shades of Heather cloth. Going beyond appearance, Seville was also described as an "electronic wonder." The new version was viewed as a "test" for other GM vehicles. Among other details, Seville was the first to offer a diesel as "standard" powerplant (except in California). The optional engine was a 6.0-liter gasoline V-8 with single-point fuel injection (heavy on digital electronics), which gave better cold start performance and lower emissions. Front wheel drive kept the floor flat, to add roominess. Sevilles had a new four-wheel independent suspension and disc brakes all around. All models had electronic level control, new electronic climate control, electrically-controlled outside mirrors (heated, with lighted thermometer), cruise control, and a rear defogger. Also standard: tungsten-halogen high-beam headlamps, Twilight Sentinel, side window defoggers, tilt/telescope steering wheel, Soft-Ray tinted glass, a new high-pressure compact spare tire, cast aluminum wheels, illuminated entry system, new dual spot map lamps/courtesy lights, and much more. Seek/scan radios were improved. Inside was an accessible center-console instrument display with digital MPG readouts. Stepping up a notch, an Elegante option made Seville's profile even sharper and more distinctive, as a sweeping French curve separated the two-tone upper and lower body colors. The full-length beltline molding swept downward aft of the back door, into the bustle-shaped back end, and the upper color tapered to a point at the base of the humped deck lid. Chrome-plated "Elegante" script was on the sail panels. Also included was accent striping and a stand-up wreath/crest on the hood. Elegante came in three color combinations: Sable Black with Sheffield Gray Firemist, Sheffield Gray Firemist with Norfolk Gray, or Canyon Rock with Desert Sand Firemist. Other features were a leather-trimmed steering wheel, 40/40 Dual Comfort front seats, and leather-topped console with space for umbrella. Interiors were tailored in light beige or slate gray leather. The new simulated teak woodgrain instrument panel, with driver only controls on the left was said to have the look of Butterfly Walnut. Ads referred to "The Beauty of Being First" and dubbed Seville the car "that looks like no other car." William L. Mitchell, who retired as GM's design vice-president in 1977, but was responsible for Seville, insisted it was "destined to be tomorrow's style leader."

DEVILLE—SERIES 6C—V-8—Aerodynamic alterations gave DeVilles a more streamlined profile this year. The new, traditional-style "isolated" grille was made up of narrow vertical bars, peaked forward at the center. A Cadillac script was on the side of the heavy upper header. New flush-mount quad rectangular headlamps stood above new amber-lensed horizontal parking/signal lamps. Matching cornering lamps consisted of a large rectangular lens over a small horizontal one; one followed the line of the headlamps, the other wrapped around in line with the signal lamps. Wheel openings showed a squared-off, formal look. The rear roof pillar held a Cadillac 'V' and crest, plus script nameplate. New wheel covers displayed Cadillac's crest on a dark red background. DeVilles came in 21 body colors. Both DeVille and Brougham had a stiffer roof profile this year, with a sharpened crease line running the full length of the side. Deck lids also had a higher profile, with beveled rear surface. The new roofline added two inches of legroom in the back seat. Base engine was the 368 cu. in. (6.0-liter) carbureted V-8, with 5.7-liter diesel available. Standard features included a convex remote-control right-hand mirror, simulated teak on instrument panel, and new dual spot map lamps/courtesy lights. Durand knit cloth upholstery came in six colors, with Renaissance velour inserts. Leather seating areas came in ten colors. Options included heated side mirrors (available with rear defogger). Astroroof, self-sealing tires, six radio choices, and advanced theft-deterrent system. Coupe deVille was also offered with a dramatic Cabriolet roof that featured a chrome crossover roof molding. That came in 15 colors of Elk Grain vinyl, with French seam surrounding the back window. deVille's d'Elegance had textured Venetian velour upholstery in any of four colors, plus Tampico carpeting, special door pull handles, and 'deVille d'Elegance' script on the glove compartment. The body held accent stripes and another nameplate. Opera lamps were standard on the coupe, three roof-mounted assist straps on the sedan.

1980 Cadillac, Fleetwood Brougham sedan. (OCW)

FLEETWOOD BROUGHAM—SERIES 6C—V-8—Noticeable immediately on the "Cadillac of Cadillacs" was an exclusive new limousine-style, closed-in back window. Center pillars held new electroluminiscent opera lamps, just above the beltline. New wheel covers with silver-colored vaned inserts contained the Cadillac wreath-and-crest on a dark red background. New body trim included a distinctive wide rocker molding that continued onto the rear quarter panels. The familiar tall chrome rear fender caps held integral marker lights, around the corner from the vertical taillamps. On the hood: a stand-up wreath-and-crest ornament. Brougham also had chrome belt moldings. Standard equipment included a Twilight Sentinel that turned headlamps on/off, illuminated entry system, six-way power Dual Comfort front seats, adjustable rear reading lamps, large door pull handles, and tilt/telescope steering wheel. Brougham interiors had new biscuit sculptured seats with bolsters, with embroidered Cadillac wreath on front and rear armrests. Upholstery was Heather knit with Raphael inserts, in slate gray, dark blue, dark green, saddle, light beige, or dark claret. Leather seating was optional in ten shades. At mid-year, a Brougham coupe joined the sedan. Its cabriolet-style roof contained a coach window, plus a chrome molding across the top. Opera lamps shined from each sail panel. Brougham d'Elegance emphasized the privacy window treatment, with the rear quarter panel wrapping around to the small limo-like back window. Inside and on the sail panel was a d'Elegance script nameplate. Standard pillow-style 50/50 Dual Comfort seats combined Heather and Raphael knits. Leather was also available at higher cost.

FLEETWOOD LIMOUSINE—SERIES 6D—V-8—Once again, the big Fleetwoods came in Limousine and Formal Limousine form, with dual accessory control panels. Interiors of the basic limo were upholstered in dark blue Heather cloth. Formal limos carried black leather upholstery up front, and either black or slate gray in back. All had two fold-down auxiliary seats. Opera lamps were now on the rear roof panels, behind the quarter windows. Deeply concave wheel covers had red inserts and Cadillac's wreath-and-crest.

1980 Cadillac, Eldorado coupe. (OCW)

ELDORADO—SERIES 6E—V-8—Downsized the year before, Eldorado entered 1980 with few significant changes beyond a bolder crosshatch grille pattern, dominated by vertical bars. Its upper horizontal bar, with Cadillac script peaked forward and upward. Quad rectangular headlamps sat above amber-lensed parking/signal lamps, with wide horizontal cornering lamps on the fenders. An Eldorado script was behind the front wheel openings, just above the bodyside molding. Wide rocker panel moldings stretched all the way front to rear. Atop the

hood was a Cadillac wreath-and-crest. New two-tone paint schemes were offered. Multi-slot style wheel covers were standard. So was Heather knit-cloth pillow-type front upholstery, offered in six colors for the Dual Comfort 50/45 front seats (for two people). Customers could also select from 10 leather possibilities. The instrument panel featured simulated teak woodgrain. Eldorado enjoyed an improved EPA fuel mileage rating as a result of the 6.0-liter V-8 with electronic fuel injection. A new MPG Sentinel was available with the DFI engine, which also offered new on-board computer diagnostics. New Electronic Climate Control offered digital accuracy. An optional Cabriolet roof of textured Elk Grain vinyl came in 15 colors, including matching Firemist shades. The optional theft-deterrent system now disabled the starter motor. Eldorado Biarritz rode cast aluminum wheels and carried a number of unique styling accents, including an exclusive brushed stainless steel front roof section. The wide chrome molding crossing over that roof continued all the way to the front fenders. Biarritz script and opera lamps enhanced the rear roof pillars, and the model also featured accent stripes. Inside, the tufted pillow-style interior came in seven leather choices or slate gray Heather knit fabric. The steering wheel was leather-trimmed. Biarritz carried a price tag of $18,003, compared to $15,509 for a base Eldo.

1980 Cadillac, Sedan deVille. (OCW)

I.D. DATA: For the last time, Cadillacs had a 13-symbol Vehicle Identification Number (VIN) on the upper left surface of the cowl, visible through the windshield. Coding was similar to 1978-79. The code for model year changed to 'A' for 1980. Engine codes changed to the following: '8' V8-350 FI; '6' V8-368 4Bbl.; '9' V8-368 DFI; 'N' V8-350 diesel.

SEVILLE (DIESEL V-8)

Series No.	Body/Style No.	Body Type & Seating	Factory Price	Shipping Weight	Prod. Total
6K	S69	4-dr Sedan-5P	19662	3911	39,344

DEVILLE

6C	D47	2-dr Coupe-6P	12401	4048	55,490
6C	D69	4-dr Sedan-6P	12770	4084	49,188

FLEETWOOD BROUGHAM

6C	B47	2-dr Coupe-6P	14971	4025	2,300
6C	B69	4-dr Sedan-6P	14927	4092	29,659

FLEETWOOD LIMOUSINE

6D	F23	4-dr Sedan-8P	22586	4629	Note 1
6D	F33	4-dr Fml Limo-7P	23388	4718	Note 1
6D	Z90	Commercial Chassis	N/A	N/A	750

Note 1: Total limousine production, 1,612.

ELDORADO

6E	L57	2-dr Coupe-4P	15509	3806	52,683

PRICE NOTE: Cadillac announced a series of price increases during the model year. By summer, Seville cost $20,796; DeVille coupe $13,115; Brougham sedan $15,816; Formal limo $24,714; and Eldorado $16,401.

1980 Cadillac, Eldorado Biarritz coupe. (OCW)

ENGINES: BASE DIESEL V-8 (Seville); OPTIONAL (DeVille, Brougham, Eldorado): 90-degree, overhead valve V-8. Cast iron block and head. Displacement: 350 cu. in. (5.7-liters). Bore & stroke: 4.057 x 3.385 in. Compression ratio: 22.5:1. Brake horsepower: 105 at 3200 R.P.M. Torque: 205 lb.-ft. at 1600 R.P.M. Five main bearings. Hydraulic valve lifters. Fuel injection. Oldsmobile-built. VIN Code: N. BASE V-8 (DeVille, Brougham, Fleetwood): 90-degree, overhead valve V-8. Cast iron block and head. Displacement: 368 cu. in. (6.0-liters). Bore & stroke: 3.80 x 4.06 in. Compression ratio: 8.2:1. Brake horsepower: 150 at 3800 R.P.M. Torque: 265 lb.-ft. at 1600 R.P.M. Five main bearings. Hydraulic valve lifters. Carburetor: 4Bbl. VIN Code: 6. BASE V-8 (Eldorado); OPTIONAL (Seville): Same as 368 cu. in. V-8 above, but with digital fuel injection. Horsepower: 145 at 3600 R.P.M. Torque: 270 lb.-ft. at 2000 R.P.M. VIN Code: 9. BASE V-8 (Eldorado--California): 90-degree, overhead valve V-8. Cast iron block and head. Displacement: 350 cu. in. (5.7-liters). Bore & stroke: 4.057 x 3.385 in. Compression ratio: 8.0:1. Brake horsepower: 160 at 4400 R.P.M. Torque: 265 lb.-ft. at 1600 R.P.M. Five main bearings. Hydraulic valve lifters. Fuel injection. VIN Code: 8.

CHASSIS DATA: Wheelbase: (Seville/Eldo) 114.0 in.; (DeVille/Brougham) 121.4 in.; (Limo) 144.5 in. Overall length: (Seville) 204.8 in.; (DeV/Brghm) 221.0 in.; (Limo) 244.1 in.; (Eldo) 204.5 in. Height: (Seville) 54.3 in.; (DeV cpe) 54.6 in.; (DeV sed) 55.6 in.; (Brghm) 56.7 in.; (Limo) 56.9 in.; (Eldo) 54.2 in. Width: (Seville) 71.4 in.; (Eldo) 71.5 in.; (others) 76.4 in. Front Tread: (Seville/Eldo) 59.3 in.; (others) 61.7 in. Rear Tread: (Seville/Eldo) 60.6 in.; (others) 60.7 in. Standard Tires: (Seville) P205/75R15 SBR wide WSW; (DeV/Brghm) P215/75R15 SBR wide WSW; (Limo) HR78 x 15-D SBR wide WSW; (Eldo) P205/75R15 SBR wide WSW.

TECHNICAL: Transmission: Turbo Hydra-matic transmission standard on all models: column shift. Gear ratios for DeVille/Brghm w/V8-368: (1st) 2.48:1; (2nd) 1.48:1; (3rd) 1.00:1; (Rev) 2.07:1. Other models: (1st) 2.74:1; (2nd) 1.57:1; (3rd) 1.00:1; (Rev) 2.07:1. Standard final drive ratio: (Seville) 2.41:1; (DeV/Brghm) 2.28:1; (limo) 3.08:1; (Eldo) 2.19:1. Hypoid drive axle. Steering: recirculating ball; power assisted. Front suspension: (Seville/Eldo) independent torsion bars, link-type stabilizer bar; (others) coil springs and link-type stabilizer bar. Rear suspension: (Seville/Eldo) independent trailing arm, coil springs, electronic level control; (others) four-link drive coil springs, electronic level control available (except limo). Brakes: front disc, rear drum exc. Seville/Eldo four-wheel disc. Fuel tank: (Seville) 23 gal.; (others) 20.6 gal. exc. limos, 25 gal. (available on DeV/Brghm). Unleaded fuel only.

DRIVETRAIN OPTIONS: 6.0-liter FI V-8 engine: Seville ($266 credit). 5.7-liter diesel V-8 engine: Eldo ($266); DeV/Fleetwood ($924). Heavy-duty cooling system ($59). 100-amp alternator ($41-$59). Engine block heater ($22). California emission equipment ($83-$250). Limited slip differential ($86) exc. Sev/Eldo. Sport handling pkg.: Sev/Eldo ($95). Heavy-duty suspension: DeV/Brghm ($270). Electronic level control: DeV/Brghm ($169). Trailering package ($100-$118).

OPTION PACKAGES: Brougham d'Elegance: cloth ($1062); leather ($1525). Coupe deVille Cabriolet ($350). deVille d'Elegance ($1005). Eldorado Cabriolet ($363). Eldorado Biarritz: leather seating ($2937); cloth ($2494). Seville Elegante ($2934).

CONVENIENCE/APPEARANCE OPTIONS: Astroroof ($1058); N/A on limo. Cruise control ($147). Controlled-cycle wipers: DeV/limo ($43). Rear defogger, grid-type ($170). Six-way Dual Comfort power passenger seat adjuster: DeV ($395); Eldo ($171). Power driver's seat recliner ($130). Power passenger seatback recliner: Brghm ($71). Notchback passenger seatback recliner: DeV ($130). Tilt/telescope steering wheel ($142). Automatic door locks ($129). Illuminated entry system: DeV/limo ($67). Garage door opener ($125). Theft deterrent system ($153). Trunk lid release and power pull-down: DeV ($92). Opera lamps: DeV ($71). Twilight Sentinel: DeV/limo ($62). Guidematic headlamp control ($72). Front light monitor ($35). Trumpet horn ($26). Electric remote-control left mirror w/thermometer ($97). Lighted thermometer on left mirror ($30). Lighted vanity mirrors, pair ($112). Electronic-tuning seek/scan AM/FM stereo radio with 8-track tape player ($195); w/8-track and CB ($480); w/cassette ($225); w/CB ($380); w/cassette and CB ($510). Electronic-tuning seek/scan AM/FM stereo radio with 8-track player rear control: limo ($398). Two-tone paint: DeV/Brghm ($293). Two-tone paint, partial Firemist: DeV/Brghm ($394). Firemist paint ($201). Padded vinyl roof: DeV ($240). Accent stripes: DeV ($61). Door edge guards ($16-$24). License frame: each ($11). Leather seating area ($435-$595). Carpeted rubber front floor mats ($35-$38); rear ($19). Trunk mat ($15). Turbine-vaned wheel covers: DeV ($63). Cast aluminum wheels: Eldo ($376); NC on diesel Seville. Locking wire wheels: DeV/Brghm ($755). Locking wire wheel covers ($262-$320); NC on Seville. Puncture sealing tires ($105).

HISTORY: Introduced: October 11, 1979. Model year production (U.S.): 231,028 for a 3.4 percent share of the industry total. Calendar year production (U.S.): 203,992. Calendar year sales

by U.S. dealers: 213,002 for a 3.2 percent market share. Model year sales by U.S. dealers: 238,999.

Historical Footnotes: This was not a top-notch year for Cadillac, as sales plummeted over 27 percent. Production fell even further for the model year, down 39.4 percent. The reason evidently was a declining eagerness for big cars, with rising interest in compact, fuel-efficient models. In an attempt to meet these changing attitudes, Cadillac had reduced the size of the standard gasoline engine from its prior 425 cu. in. displacement down to a mere 368 cu. in. (6.0-liters). Buick's V-6 became optional late in the year. But the division also speeded up production of the subcompact J-bodied Cimarron, originally intended for introduction in 1985. Cadillac had problems meeting emissions control standards of the California Air Resources Board, whose restrictions had long been considerably stricter than the rest of the country. The "standard" diesel on the new Seville wasn't offered in California. A new assembly plant for production of lightweight V-6 engines was announced at Livonia, Michigan. Convertible conversions continued to be turned out by (among others) Hess & Eisenhardt in Cincinnati, which claimed to be the largest producer of Cadillac ragtops. The company's 1980 brochure displayed a Coupe deVille conversion.

1981

Biggest news for 1981 was actually an '82 model: the new subcompact Cimarron, introduced in the spring (more on that in the 1982 listing). Second biggest was the new variable-displacement gasoline engine, developed by the Eaton Corporation and standard in all but Seville. Depending on driving conditions, the innovative V-8-6-4 engine ran on four, six, or eight cylinders, switching back and forth as needed. The object, of course, was to conserve fuel in the wake of rising gasoline prices. A microprocessor determined which cylinders weren't necessary at the moment. Then it signaled a solenoid-actuated blocker plate, which shifted to permit the rocker arm to pivot at a different point than usual. Therefore, selected intake and exhaust valves would remain closed rather than operate normally. Valve lifters and push rods traveled up-and-down in the normal manner, but unneeded valve pairs stood idle. When running on four, displacement grew back to eight as soon as you stepped on the gas to pass, demanding maximum power--an assurance to those who might wonder if a four-cylinder Cadillac powerplant was good enough. The system had been tested (and "proven") in over a half-million miles of driving. Cadillac claimed that the "perceived sensation" during displacement changes was "slight," because no shifting was involved. Another feature: push a button and an MPG Sentinel showed the number of cylinders in operation: push again to see instantaneous miles-per-gallon. Though the principle was not new, having been experimented with during World War II, the new engine was hailed as a dramatic answer to the economy problem for large passenger cars. Expanded self-diagnostics now displayed 45 separate function codes for mechanics to investigate. Imaginative but complex, the V-8-6-4 brought more trouble than ease to many owners and didn't last long in the overall lineup. On another level, Buick's 252 cu. in. (4.1-liter) V-6 engine, introduced late in the 1980 model year, continued for a full season as an economy option. Cadillacs now carried an on-board digital computer capable of making 300,000 decisions per second. It could even provide continued operation of the car if critical sensors malfunctioned, making an instantaneous substitution--even turning to a built-in analog computer if the digital electronics collapsed. To improve emissions, the new Computer Command Control module used seven sensors to monitor exhaust, engine speed, manifold air pressure and coolant temperature, then adjust the air/fuel mixture. "Answering Today's Needs with Tomorrow's Technology" was the logical theme of the full-line catalog. Though technically impressive, 1981 was not a year of significant change beyond some new grilles and other cosmetic alterations. Oldsmobile's 350 cu. in. diesel V-8 was available in all six models: Fleetwood Brougham coupe and sedan, Coupe and Sedan deVille, Eldorado, and Seville. A new light went under the hood. Rust-prevention measures touched over 100 specially treated areas, including pre-coated metals. Overdrive automatic transmission was now available with the V-6 engine on

Fleetwood Brougham and DeVille. A memory seat option returned the six-way power driver's seat to one of two selected positions.

1981 Cadillac, Seville Elegante sedan. (OCW)

1981 Cadillac, Sedan deVille with optional wire wheel covers and vinyl roof. (OCW)

SEVILLE—SERIES 6K—V-8—Though basically unchanged for 1980, Seville got a few new touches, including restyled (optional) wire wheel covers. Side accent moldings were now standard. An air dam below the front bumper was added, in an attempt to improve aerodynamic characteristics and gas mileage. Base engine was the Olds-built diesel V-8, now with roller cam followers on the valve lifters. That made Seville the only car around with a standard V-8 diesel. Also new: an improved water detection/removal system for the fuel tank. New component labeling procedures were supposed to prevent theft. Seville's long list of standard equipment included cast aluminum wheels, four-wheel disc brakes, cruise control, power windows and door locks, Soft-Ray tinted glass, tilt/telescope steering wheel, lighted vanity mirrors, and illuminated entry system. Standard gear also included low-rolling-resistance tires, low-fuel warning, and improved windshield washers. New options: Several radio and tape systems of advanced design, a memory system for the power driver's seat, and the modulated-displacement V-8-6-4 engine that was standard in other Cadillacs. A Buick-built 252 cu. in. V-6 with four-barrel carburetor was also available this year. Both gasoline engines brought buyers a credit of several hundred dollars. Sevilles came in 13 high-gloss acrylic lacquer finishes, with accent striping and moldings. Optional were 13 two-tone combinations (such as Twilight Blue over Norfolk Gray) and 8 Firemist paints. Dual Comfort 45/45 seats were upholstered in Heather knit cloth; or 11 leather shades in tucked seating areas. Deep-pile Tiffany carpeting decorated the floor. Also standard: map lamps, assist straps, and an improved electronic-tuning AM/FM stereo radio. Hoods displayed a burnished wreath-and-crest ornament over the vertical-style grille with its large header bar, and engine compartments had a new light. Cast aluminum wheels were standard. One-piece bumpers had built-in guards. A Touring Suspension became optional during the 1981 model year. Seville Elegantes had been easy to spot with their bold 'French Curve' molding separating two-tone body colors. This year, base Sevilles gained the full-length accent moldings that had formerly been an Elegante exclusive. The pricey Elegante package included tucked seating areas and steering wheel in Sierra Grain leather; 40/40 Dual Comfort seats; leather-topped console; Tampico carpeting; 'Elegante'

script on glove box and body; cross-laced wire wheel covers; and chrome side moldings. Elegante came in four color combinations: Sheffield Gray Firemist over Sable Black (slate gray interior); Superior Blue Metallic over Twilight Blue (dark blue interior); Desert Sand Firemist over Briarwood Brown (light beige interior); or Mulberry Gray Firemist over Bordeaux Red (mulberry gray interior).

DEVILLE—SERIES 6C—V-8—Standard engine for DeVille and Fleetwood Brougham was the "modulated displacement" 368 cu. in. (6.0-liter) V-8-6-4, with digital fuel injection. Optional a 252 cu. in. (4.1-liter) V-6, provided by Buick. That V-6 had Computer Command Control and a knock sensor to adjust spark advance, as well as diagnostics. The Olds diesel V-8 was also offered. Externally, DeVilles and Fleetwoods carried a new forward-peaked grille with heavy wide upper header bar (Cadillac script again at the side) over an undivided tight crosshatch pattern. Quad headlamps sat above quad amber parking/signal lamps, with wraparound clear/amber cornering lights. Standard wheel covers displayed a Cadillac crest on dark red background. New standard Electronic Climate Control offered digital accuracy. Standard equipment also included a six-way power passenger seat, power windows, and low-fuel warning. New pillow-style seating came in rich Heather cloth (four colors); or leather in ribbed seating areas (ten colors). Sedan deVilles could have automatic lap shoulder belt for driver and front passenger. Other options: a Heavy-Duty Ride package, wire wheel covers, and Elk Grain vinyl roof.

1981 Cadillac, Fleetwood Brougham coupe with optional wire wheel covers. (OCW)

FLEETWOOD BROUGHAM—SERIES 6C—V-8—Billed again as the "Cadillac of Cadillacs," Broughams came in coupe and sedan form with a grille and front-end look the same as DeVille. The coupe had an Elk Grain vinyl Cabriolet roof treatment with flush-look, small size rear quarter windows and broad sail panels. Both coupe and sedan roofs had a chrome crossover roof molding at the front of the vinyl portion, stretching across the top and sides. Back windows were small (limousine-style). Options included an Astroroof and leather-trimmed steering wheel. A stand-up wreath-and-crest ornament adorned each hood. Standard wheel covers were varied chrome with wreath-and-crest on a dark red background. Three powertrains were offered: standard fuel-injected V-8-6-4, Buick V-6 with automatic overdrive transmission, or diesel V-8. Standard were the Twilight Sentinel that automatically turned headlamps on and off, illuminated entry, tilt/telescope steering wheel, six-way driver and passenger seats, and electroluminescent opera lamps. Dual Comfort coupe front seats held three people; rear seats offered adjustable reading lamps. Standard interior upholstery was Heather knit with Raphael inserts, available in six colors. New door panels displayed an embroidered 'Fleetwood' script. Nine varieties of tucked leather in seating areas were also offered. Brougham d'Elegance had chrome wheel covers with body-colored vanes and wreath-and-crest on dark red background, plus d'Elegance script and accent striping on the body. Coupe interiors came in standard dark blue Heather and Raphael knit fabric; or optional Sierra Grain leather for tufted seating areas (dark claret, white, black, light slate gray, dark blue, light beige, doeskin, or light waxberry). Sedans had knit fabric in dark blue, dark claret, light slate gray or light beige, or leather in doeskin. light beige, light slate gray, dark blue, or dark claret.

1981 Cadillac, Fleetwood limousine. (OCW)

FLEETWOOD LIMOUSINE—SERIES 6D—V-8—Differing mainly in dimensions from DeVille and Fleetwood, carrying the new cross-hatch grille, limos could not have the diesel engine option. Both standard and Formal Limousine models included a dual accessory panel so rear passengers could adjust the climate control and power windows. The formal edition held a sliding glass partition, with seating for seven. Standard limos held eight. Interiors came in dark blue Heather cloth, or black in the back. All carried two fold-down auxiliary seats.

1981 Cadillac, Eldorado coupe. (OCW)

ELDORADO—SERIES 6E—V-8—Up front, Eldo's new grille had a tiny crosshatch pattern below the wide, brushed-chrome finished, peaked upper bar. Quad rectangular headlamps sat above amber-lensed quad parking/signal lamps. Horizontal-style clear/amber cornering lamps sat a short distance back on the fenders. Like Seville, Eldorado also added a front air dam below the bumper. Wheel covers showed big red medallions. Inside, Eldos sported a new center console, woodgrain appliqué on door panels, and simulated teakwood dash trim. Standard equipment this year included low-rolling-resistance tires, low-fuel warning, a new underhood light, and new windshield washers. Also standard: dual-spot map lamps/courtesy lights, seat belt chimes, lamp monitors, electric trunk release and power pull-down, compact spare tire, dual remote-control mirrors, six-way power driver's seat, electronic tuning signal-seeking stereo radio, MPG Sentinel, Twilight Sentinel, accent stripes on bodysides and deck lid, and much more. As before, Eldos featured four-wheel independent suspension, four-wheel disc brakes, and electronic level control. On the option list was a Touring Suspension that included larger tires. New Dual Comfort 45/45 front seats held driver and passenger. Leather upholstery in tufted seating areas came in 10 hues including new doeskin, light waxberry, and dark jadestone. New standard Heather and Dundee fabric came in four colors. Door handles were new, too. Standard engine was the new 368 cu. in. V-8-6-4 with on-board computer diagnostics. Two options were offered: Buick's 4.1-liter V-6 with three-speed automatic transmission (four-speed overdrive with the V-8-6-4), or the Oldsmobile diesel V-8. Major body components now carried labels conforming to vehicle identification numbers, in an attempt to prevent thefts. Eldorado Biarritz included tufted pillow-style seating and steering wheel in Sierra Grain leather, in any of five colors; Tampico carpeting; front console; individual rear reading lamps; opera lamps; accent stripes; and Biarritz script insignia. A brushed stainless steel roof section extended from the flush-mount windshield back to an Elk Grain vinyl Cabriolet roof. A wide chrome molding

crossed the roof, turning a square corner and extending forward to the front fenders. Biarritz came in 21 colors. New standard wire wheel covers had red center sections with the Cadillac wreath-and-crest medallion. The opera lamps were optional on the Eldos.

I.D. DATA: All Cadillacs had a new 17-symbol Vehicle Identification Number (VIN), stamped on a metal tag attached to the upper left surface of the cowl, visible through the windshield. The number begins with a '1' to indicate the manufacturing country (U.S.A.), followed by a 'G' for General Motors and a '6' for Cadillac Division. The next letter indicates restraint system: 'A' manual (standard); 'B' automatic. Symbol five is a letter denoting car line and series: 'S' Seville; 'B' Fleetwood Brougham; 'D' DeVille; 'F' Fleetwood limousine; 'Z' commercial chassis; 'L' Eldorado. Digits six and seven indicate body type: '47' 2-dr. coupe; '69' 4-dr. four-window sedan; '23' six window; eight-passenger sedan w/auxiliary seat; '33' six-window formal limousine w/aux. seat and center partition; '90' commercial chassis (no body); '57' Eldorado coupe. Next comes an engine code: '4' V6-252 4Bbl.; 'N' V8-350 diesel; '6' V8-368 4Bbl.; '9' V8-368 DFI. The next symbol is a check digit. Symbol ten indicates model year ('B' 1981). Symbol eleven denotes assembly plant: '9' Detroit; 'E' Linden, New Jersey (Seville/Eldo). The final six-digit production sequence number began with 100001 for Detroit-built models; 600001 (Eldo) or 680001 (Seville) for those built in New Jersey. An identification number for the V-6 engine was on the left rear of the block; on the V8-350, a code label was on top of the left valve cover and a unit number label atop the right valve cover. Other engines had a unit number on the block behind the left cylinder head, and a VIN derivative on the block behind the intake manifold. A body number plate on the upper horizontal surface of the shroud (except Seville, on front vertical shroud surface) showed model year, build date code, car division, series, style, body assembly plant, body number, trim combination, paint code, modular seat code, and roof option.

SEVILLE V-6/DIESEL V-8

Series No.	Body/Style No.	Body Type & Seating	Factory Price	Shipping Weight	Prod. Total
6K	S69	4-dr Sedan-5P	20598/21088	3688/4028	28,631

Note: Prices and weights shown are for optional gas V-6 and standard diesel V-8. A gas V-8 was also available.

DEVILLE (V-6/V-8-6-4)

6C	D47	2-dr Coupe-6P	13285/13450	3801/4016	Note 1
6C	D69	4-dr Sedan-6P	13682/13847	3852/4067	Note 2

FLEETWOOD BROUGHAM (V-6/V-8-6-4)

6C	B47	2-dr Coupe-6P	15777/15942	3854/4069	Note 1
6C	B69	4-dr Sedan-6P	16190/16355	3884/4115	Note 2

Note 1: Total two-door coupe production, 62,724.

Note 2: Total DeVille/Fleetwood four-door sedan production, 86,991.

FLEETWOOD LIMOUSINE (V-8-6-4)

6D	F23	4-dr Sedan-8P	24464	4629	Note 3
6D	F33	4-dr Fml Limo-7P	25323	4717	Note 3
6D	Z90	Commercial Chassis	N/A	N/A	N/A

Note 3: Total limousine production, 1,200.

ELDORADO (V-6/V-8-6-4)

6E	L57	2-dr Coupe-5P	17385/17550	3615/3822	60,643

FACTORY PRICE AND WEIGHT NOTE: Figures before the slash are for V-6 engine, after slash for variable-displacement gas V-8-6-4. A diesel V-8 was also available on DeVille/Brougham/Eldorado. By late spring 1981, prices rose on all except Eldorado: Seville reached $23,000 for the diesel, Coupe deVille $14,345, and Brougham sedan $17,420.

ENGINES: BASE DIESEL V-8 (Seville); OPTIONAL (DeVille, Brougham, Eldorado): 90-degree, overhead valve V-8. Cast iron block and head. Displacement: 350 cu. in. (5.7-liters). Bore & stroke: 4.057 x 3.385 in. Compression ratio: 22.5:1. Brake horsepower: 105 at 3200 R.P.M. Torque: 200 lb.-ft. at 1600 R.P.M. Five main bearings. Hydraulic valve lifters. Fuel injection. Oldsmobile-built. VIN Code: N. OPTIONAL V-6 (all except limousines): 90-degree, overhead valve V-6. Cast iron block and head. Displacement: 252 cu. in. (4.1-liters). Bore & stroke: 3.965 x 3.40 in. Compression ratio: 8.0:1. Brake horsepower: 125 at 3800 R.P.M. Torque: 210 lb.-ft. at 2000 R.P.M. Four main bearings. Hydraulic valve lifters. Carburetor: 4Bbl. Made by Buick. VIN Code: 4. OPTIONAL (Seville): 90-degree, overhead valve variable displacement. Cast iron block and head. Displacement: 368 cu. in. (6.0-liters). Bore & stroke: 3.80 x 4.06 in. Compression ratio: 8.2:1. Brake horsepower: 140 at 3800 R.P.M. Torque: 265 lb.-ft. at 1400 R.P.M. Five main bearings. Hydraulic valve lifters. Digital fuel injection. VIN Code: 9. BASE V-8 (commercial chassis only): Same specifications as 368 cu. in. engine above, but standard V-8 with four-barrel carburetor. Brake H.P.: 150 at 3800 R.P.M. Torque: 265 lb.-ft. at 1600 R.P.M. VIN Code: 6.

CHASSIS DATA: Wheelbase: (Seville/Eldo) 114.0 in.; (DeV/Brghm) 121.4 in.; (limo) 144.5 in. Overall length: (Seville) 204.8 in.; (DeV/Brghm) 221.0 in.; (Limo) 244.1 in.; (Eldo) 204.5 in. Height: (Seville/Eldo) 54.3 in.; (DeV/Brghm cpe) 54.6 in.; (DeV sed) 55.6 in.; (Brghm sed) 56.7 in.; (Limo) 56.9 in. Width (Seville/Eldo) 71.5 in.; (DeV/Brghm) 76.5 in. Front Tread: (Seville/Eldo) 59.3 in.; (others) 61.7 in. Rear Tread: (Seville/Eldo) 60.6 in.; (others) 60.7 in. Standard Tires: (Seville/Eldo) P205/75R15 SBR wide WSW; (DeV/Brghm) P215/75R15 SBR wide WSW; (Limos) HR78 x 15-D.

TECHNICAL: Transmission: Turbo Hydra-matic transmission standard on all models; column shift. Gear ratios for DeV/Brghm/limo V8-368: (1st) 2.48:1; (2nd) 1.48:1; 1.00:1; (Rev) 2.07:1. Other three-speed models: (1st) 2.74:1; (2nd) 1.57:1; (3rd) 1.00:1; (Rev) 2.07:1. Four-speed automatic in DeV/Brghm w/V-6: (1st) 2.74:1; (2nd) 1.57:1; (3rd) 1.00:1; (4th) 0.67:1; (Rev) 2.07:1. Standard final drive ratio: (Seville/Eldo) 2.41:1 except w/V-6, 2.93:1; (DeV/Brghm) 2.41:1 exc. w/V-6, 3.23:1; (limos) 3.08:1. Steering: recirculating ball (power assisted). Suspension: same as 1980. Brakes: front disc, rear drum exc. Sev/Eldo, four-wheel disc. Fuel tank: (Sev/Eldo) 22.8 gal. w/diesel, 20.3 gal. w/V-8-6-4, 21.1 gal. w/V-6; (DeV/Brghm) 24.6 gal. exc. diesel. 27 gal. and V-6, 25 gal.; (limos) 24.6 gal.

DRIVETRAIN OPTIONS: 4.1-liter gas V-6 engine ($165 credit); Seville ($490 credit). V-8-6-4 gas engine: Seville ($325 credit). 5.7-liter diesel V-8 engine ($325-$351); N/A limo. California emission equipment ($46-$182). Engine block heater ($22). 100 amp alternator ($41). Heavy-duty cooling ($59). Limited slip differential: DeV/Brghm/limo ($86). Electronic level control: DeV/Brghm ($173). Heavy-duty ride package: DeV/Brghm sedan ($270). Touring suspension: Eldo/Sev ($95). Trailering pkg. ($59-$100).

OPTION PACKAGES: Brougham d'Elegance: cloth seating ($1066); leather ($1536). deVille d'Elegance ($1005). Coupe deVille Cabriolet ($363). Eldorado Biarritz ($2937). Eldorado Cabriolet ($363). Seville Elegante ($2734). Appearance value pkg.: DeV ($802).

CONVENIENCE/APPEARANCE OPTIONS: Astroroof ($1058); N/A on limo. Controlled-cycle wiper system: DeV/limo ($45). Rear defogger, grid-type ($134-$175). Automatic door locks ($129). Garage door opener ($125). Illuminated entry system ($67). Digital instrument cluster: Sev/Eldo ($200). Dual Comfort front seats w/six-way power passenger seat adjuster: DeV ($395). Memory driver's seat ($169). Six-way power passenger seat: Eldo ($172). Power driver's seat recliner ($130). Power passenger seat recliner: Brghm ($71). Power passenger seat recliner w/six- way power seat: Eldorado ($302). Notchback passenger seat recliner: DeV ($130). Leather trimmed steering wheel ($79). Tilt/telescope steering wheel ($147). Power trunk lid release and pull down: DeV/limo ($96). Theft deterrent system ($157). Twilight Sentinel: DeV/limo ($65). Guidematic headlamp control ($78). Opera lamps: DeV/Eldo ($72). Trumpet horn ($28). Thermometer on left mirror ($35). Electric remote mirrors w/thermometer on left: limo ($99). Twin lighted vanity mirrors ($116). Electronic tuning seek/scan AM/FM stereo radio with 8-track tape player ($195); with 8-track and CB ($480); w/cassette ($281); w/cassette and CB ($547). Rear-control elect.-tuning radio with 8-track: limo ($398). Full padded vinyl roof: DeV ($240). Two-tone paint: Seville Firemist ($520); DeV/Eldo ($293); partial Firemist: DeV/Eldo ($394). Firemist paint ($208). Accent striping: DeV ($61). Door edge guards ($16-$24). License frames, each ($11). Front console: Eldo/Sev ($151). Leather seating area ($439-$595). Automatic lap/shoulder belts: DeV sed ($150). Carpeted rubber floor mats: front ($35-$38); rear ($20). Trunk mat ($16). Cast aluminum wheels: Eldo ($376); Sev (NC). Locking wire wheels: DeV/Brghm ($755). Turbine-vaned wheel covers: DeV ($63). Locking wire wheel covers ($266-$328). Puncture-sealing tires ($106).

HISTORY: Introduced: September 25, 1980. Model year production: 253,591 (including 13,402 1982 Cimarrons built during the 1981 model year). The total included 30,440 cars with V-6 engine and 42,200 diesels. Calendar year production: 259,135. Calendar year sales by U.S. dealers: 230,665 for a 3.7 percent market share. Model year sales by U.S. dealers: 226,427 (including 8,790 Cimarrons built before September 1981).

Historical Footnotes: "Cadillac is class," the full-line catalog declared, echoing a theme that had been used for decades. "Class" seemed to take many forms by the 1980s. In addition to the customary funeral/ambulance adaptations and stretch limos from various manufacturers, two conversions came from Wisco Corporation (in Michigan): a Renaissance Coupe deVille and a Seville Caballero.

1982

"Best of all...it's a Cadillac," declared the 1982 full-line catalog. Perhaps so, but longtime Cadillac fans must have been startled by the company's latest offering: the four-cylinder Cimarron, with manual floor shift yet. Introduced several years earlier than originally planned, this drastically different breed of luxury was intended to give Cadillac a toehold in the rising market for smaller, fuel-efficient designs. On all except Cimarron, a new lightweight Cadillac 249 cu. in. (4.1-liter) HT-4100 V-8 engine with Digital Fuel Injection (DFI) became standard, coupled to an overdrive automatic transmission. The Oldsmobile-built diesel 5.7-liter V-8 was also available. So was a Buick 4.1-liter V-6, offered as a credit option. A new Fuel Data Panel (standard with the HT-4100 engine) displayed instantaneous MPG, average MPG, estimated driving range, and amount of fuel used. Electronic Climate Control had a new outside temperature display, available by touching a button. New reminder chimes used different tone patterns to warn of unbuckled seatbelts, headlamps left on, or key in ignition. Body mounts, springs and shocks were revised to give a softer ride. All Cadillacs except Cimarron had standard cornering lamps, tungsten-halogen high beam headlamps, power windows and door locks, lamp monitors, twin remote-control mirrors, automatic power radio antenna, six-way power driver's seat, electronic-tuned AM/FM stereo radio with signal seeking/scanning, an underhood light, dual spot map lamps/courtesy lights, steel belted wide whitewall radial tires, and gas cap holder on fuel filler door, among their standard equipment. All except Seville with cloth interior had front seatback map pockets. New to the full-size option list was a remote-locking fuel filler door. The HT-4100 V-8 engine had an aluminum block for light weight and chrome-plated valve covers for looks. During manufacture, it received individually balanced components and automatic in-process gauging, and had to pass a 78-step "stress test" before installation. Features added to improve fuel economy included fast-burn compact combustion chambers, digital fuel injection, and bearings designed for low-drag lubricants. Standard with the HT-4100 engine was a four-speed overdrive automatic transmission, helping to further improve mileage. EPA estimates reached 26 highway/17 city for Fleetwood/DeVille models, 27 highway for Seville/Eldorado. A Fuel Data Panel computed average MPG on the road. On-board computer diagnostics warned of engine problems and helped the mechanic locate the trouble quickly. The digital fuel injection included automatic altitude compensation, determined by a microprocessor, plus constant idle speed. The HT-4100 replaced the troublesome V-8-6-4 modular displacement engine, helping to boost both gas mileage and sales. That new engine was installed in some 90 percent of Sevilles, DeVilles and Eldorados. An HT-4100 nameplate went on front fenders of all models with that engine under the hood.

CIMARRON—SERIES 6J—FOUR—After decades of success in manufacturing large luxury cars, Cadillac turned to a small luxury car in an attempt to rival BMW, Audi, Volvo, Saab, small Mercedes, and similar high class imports. Cimarron came with a standard 112 cu. in. (1.8-liter) four-cylinder engine and four-speed overdrive manual shift with floor lever. Three-speed Turbo Hydra-matic was available. This was Cadillac's first four-cylinder engine since 1914, and first manual shift since 1953. Most Cadillac buyers had never driven one without Hydra-matic in some form. Cimarron was billed as "a new kind of Cadillac for a new kind of Cadillac owner." The company first seemed a bit uncomfortable with its new addition, initially branding it Cimarron by Cadillac rather than a straight out Cadillac. Bodies carried a Cadillac emblem in the grille center, and on taillamps, but no script identification. Five people fit into the car's body-contoured leather seats with lumbar support, feet touching deep-pile Trianon carpeting. Even the trunk was carpeted. Dashes displayed a tachometer, oil pressure gauge and voltmeter. Nine hand-buffed body colors were offered, including four exclusive metallics (Superior Blue, Autumn Amber, Garnet, and Columbian Brown). Cimarron rode on an exclusive Cadillac-tuned touring suspension with MacPherson struts up front and a semi-independent rear, plus front/rear stabilizer bars. Aircraft-type aluminum alloy wheels held match-mounted steel-belted radial tires. Sharing the same J-body as Chevrolet's Cavalier and the similarly derivative Pontiac J2000, Cimarron didn't quite manage a truly separate identity but offered a long list of standard features. Luxuries on every subcompact four-door sedan included air conditioning, twin power mirrors, leather-wrapped steering wheel, power rack-and-pinion steering, and AM/FM stereo radio. All this came at a cost, though: over $12,000 base price, which was far higher than its GM relatives, closer to the level of Eurosport sedans. Cimarron's front end carried a finely-meshed crosshatch horizontal chrome grille and quad rectangular tungsten-halogen headlamps. At the rear were horizontal taillamps. Four of the nine Cadillac body colors were intended solely for Cimarron, as were two of the five interior choices. Wheels displayed small slots, and the full-width back seat could hold three passengers. The initially short option list included a Vista Vent roof and vacuum-type cruise control.

1982 Cadillac, Cimarron sedan. (OCW)

SEVILLE—SERIES 6K—V-8—"With styling imitated but never equaled, Seville is an American standard for the world." So claimed Cadillac in its full-line catalog for 1982. Little change was evident this year, but there was a new standard powerplant under the hood: the lightweight HT-4100 aluminum-block V-8. The idea of a standard diesel engine hadn't lasted long. Seville's chassis carried new shock absorbers and rear springs, along with the familiar four-wheel independent suspension and electronic level control. Optional wire wheel covers had a locking device; aluminum alloy wheels were available at no extra cost. Standard interiors used Heather cloth in a choice of five colors, or leather in stitched seating areas (eight colors). A full cabriolet roof became available in black, white or dark blue diamond-grain vinyl. That option gave Seville the look of a convertible sedan--at least from a distance. The available Touring suspension included P225/70R15 steel-belted radial tires, large-diameter front and rear stabilizer bars, altered power steering that gave more feedback, stiffer front torsion bar and rear spring rates, and increased shock absorber valving. Limited-edition El-

egantes, with a package price of $3,095, used a sweeping two-tone French curve to accent the burnished and bright full-length bodyside moldings. Sail panels carried the 'Elegante' script nameplate. Elegante also had accent striping and a stand-up wreath/crest hood ornament. It came in three two-tone color combinations, including Desert Dusk Firemist over Brownstone. Elegante interiors used tucked leather in seating areas, in three Sierra Grain colors. Steering wheels wore matching leather trim, and the console was leather-topped.

1982 Cadillac, Coupe deVille with optional wire wheel covers. (OCW)

1982 Cadillac, Sedan deVille. (OCW)

DEVILLE—SERIES 6C—V-8—Powered by the new HT-4100 Digital Fuel Injection V-8 with automatic overdrive transmission, DeVille's dash contained a new standard Fuel Data Panel to help determine the most fuel-efficient route. Push buttons could display outside temperature or average trip MPG, or amount of fuel used. This year's new grille was made up of thin vertical bars, sectioned by two horizontal bars. The wide upper horizontal header, finished in brushed chrome and running full width, held the customary Cadillac script. Quad rectangular headlamps stood directly above rectangular amber-lensed parking/signal lamps. Cornering lamps with clear and amber lenses wrapped around the fender sides. DeVilles displayed a wreath-and-crest stand-up hood ornament. Standard interiors used Heather knit cloth with matching Dundee ribbed cloth inserts, in five colors. Leather in the ribbed seating areas was optional, in a choice of eight shades. A Cabriolet roof with bright crossover roof molding was available for the Coupe deVille. deVille d'Elegance had pillow-style seats in Venetian velour cloth, in four colors; plus opera lamps and accent striping. Sedan versions added three roof-mounted passenger assist straps. d'Elegance editions were identified by script on the roof sail panels.

FLEETWOOD BROUGHAM—SERIES 6D—V-8—Priced nearly $3,000 higher, Brougham coupes and sedans looked similar to their DeVille brothers from the front, with the same new three-row grille made up of narrow vertical bars. Standard equipment included a stand-up wreath-and-crest hood ornament, Twilight Sentinel, illuminated entry system, controlled-cycle wipers, tilt/telescope steering wheel, and six-way power seat for driver and passenger. Dual Comfort 55/45 front seats held three people and were trimmed in exclusive Fleetwood design, using Heather knit with Raphael cloth inserts. Eight colors of leather were also available. The coupe carried a distinctive Elk Grain vinyl Cabriolet roof with large quarter windows and electroluminiscent opera lamps. A chrome crossover molding highlighted its forward edge. Sedans had a small (limousine-style) back window and full Elk Grain vinyl roof, with Cadillac's wreath-and-crest insignia on the rear roof (sail) panels. A Brougham nameplate stood at the back of rear fenders. Color-keyed, vaned wheel covers were new. Optional: authentic wire wheels. Brougham d'Elegance offered tufted upholstery in cloth or leather, with 50/50 Dual Comfort seats, special trim and identifying scripts, and special wheel covers to match the body color.

1982 Cadillac, Fleetwood Brougham Coupe d'Elegance. (OCW)

FLEETWOOD LIMOUSINE—SERIES 6D—V-8-6-4—While the innovative (but flawed) variable-displacement V-8-6-4 engine no longer powered other Cadillacs, it remained active under limousine hoods for several more years. Fleetwood's standard limo seated eight. For an extra thousand dollars or so, the Formal limo held seven, with a sliding glass partition between compartments. A second control panel let passengers adjust temperature and power windows. Heather cloth interior came in black or dark gray-blue. Front compartment of the Formal limo was black, with black leather in seating areas.

1982 Cadillac, Eldorado Touring Coupe. (OCW)

ELDORADO—SERIES 6E—V-8—While front-end appearance was similar to DeVille/Fleetwood, the personal-luxury Eldorado coupes were most noted for their side profile. That meant a somewhat stubby deck lid portion, upright rectangular quarter window, and bodyside molding that turned upward in a square corner just behind that quarter window. This year's vertical-style grille contained three narrow horizontal bars. Bumpers held new black rub strips with white centers, while revised taillamps displayed Cadillac's crest insignia. Eldo's full cabriolet roof option, appearing during the model year, offered the look (almost) of a convertible top. Base powerplant was the new HT-4100 DFI V-8 with overdrive automatic transmission. Buick's V-6 was also available. Eldos continued with four-wheel independent suspension and four-wheel disc brakes. Dual Comfort 45/50 seats held three people, with six-way power adjustment for the driver. Heather cloth upholstery with Dundee cloth inserts came in five colors; leather in eight trim colors. An optional Touring suspension (introduced the year before) included P225/70R15 steel-belted radial tires, large-diameter front and rear stabilizer bars, altered power steering that gave more feedback, stiffer front torsion bar and rear spring rates, and increased shock absorber valving. Eldorado's new Touring Coupe special-edition came with the Touring suspension but added extra-wide blackwall tires on aluminum alloy wheels with exposed chrome lug nuts, reclining front bucket seats, a front console, cloisonné hood ornament, leather-wrapped steering wheel, plus red-over-black accent striping on a Sterling Silver metallic finish. Headlamp and taillamp bezels were body-colored. Wide ribbed rocker moldings were gray; wipers and window/windshield moldings black. Upholstery was gray leather, and a hood badge replaced the usual stand-up ornament. A Sable Black Touring Coupe arrived in mid-year, similar but wearing blacked-out reveal moldings and headlamp/taillamp bezels, black bumper rub strips, and aluminum wheels with center hubs. Eldorado Biarritz carried a brushed stainless steel roof cap, wire wheel covers, opera lamps, and 'Biarritz' script on the sail panels. Interiors used genuine leath-

er in seating areas, in five colors, plus a leather-trimmed steering wheel, Tampico carpeting, and rear quarter reading lamps.

1982 Cadillac, Eldorado coupe with cabriolet roof option. (OCW)

I.D. DATA: All Cadillacs again had a 17-symbol Vehicle Identification Number (VIN), stamped on a metal tag attached to the upper left surface of the cowl, visible through the windshield. Coding was similar to 1981. Model year code changed to 'C' for 1982. Code 'G' (Cimarron) was added to car line series. Engine coding was as follows: 'G' L4-112 2Bbl.; '4' V6-252 4Bbl.; '8' V8-250 DFI (HT-4100); 'N' V8-350 diesel; '9' V-8-6-4 368 DFI. Code 'C' for an assembly plant in South Gate, California, was added.

CIMARRON (FOUR)

Series No.	Body/Style No.	Body Type & Seating	Factory Price	Shipping Weight	Prod. Total
6J	G69	4-dr Sedan-5P	12181	2524	25,968

SEVILLE (V-6/V-8)

6K	S69	4-dr Sedan-6P	23269/23434	----/3731	19,998

DEVILLE (V-6/V-8)

6C	D47	2-dr Coupe-6P	15084/15249	----/3783	Note 1
6C	D69	4-dr Sedan-6P	15534/15699	----/3839	Note 2

FLEETWOOD BROUGHAM (V-6/V-8)

6C	B47	2-dr Coupe-6P	17931/18096	----/3825	Note 1
6C	B69	4-dr Sedan-6P	18402/18567	----/3866	Note 2

Note 1: Total two-door coupe production, 50,130.

Note 2: Total DeVille/Fleetwood four-door sedan production, 86,020.

FLEETWOOD LIMOUSINE (V-8-6-4)

6D	F23	4-dr Sedan-8P	27961	4628	Note 3
6D	F33	4-dr Fml Limo-7P	28941	4718	Note 3
6D	Z90	Commercial Chassis	N/A	N/A	N/A

Note 3: Total limousine production, 1,450.

ELDORADO (V-6/V-8)

6E	LS7	2-dr Coupe-6P	18551/18716	----/3637	52,018

FACTORY PRICE AND WEIGHT NOTE: Figures before the slash are for V-6 engine, which was actually a $165 credit option; after slash for standard gasoline V-8. Diesel V-8 was also available.

ENGINES: BASE FOUR (Cimarron): Inline. OHV. Four-cylinder. Cast iron block and head. Displacement: 112 cu. in. (1.8-liters). Bore & stroke: 3.50 x 2.91 in. Compression ratio: 9.0:1. Brake horsepower: 88 at 5100 R.P.M. Torque: 100 lb.-ft. at 2800 R.P.M. Five main bearings. Hydraulic valve lifters. Carburetor: 2Bbl. VIN Code: G. BASE V-8 (Seville, Eldorado, DeVille, Brougham): 90-degree, overhead valve V-8. Aluminum block w/cast iron liners; cast iron head. Displacement: 249 cu. in. (4.1-liters). Bore & stroke: 3.465 x 3.307 in. Compression ratio: 8.5:1. Brake horsepower: 125 at 4200 R.P.M. Torque: 190 lb.-ft. at 2000 R.P.M. Five main bearings. Hydraulic valve lifters. Digital fuel injection. HT-4100. VIN Code: 8. OPTIONAL V-6 (Seville Eldorado, DeVille Brougham): 90-degree, overhead-valve V-6. Cast iron block and head. Displacement: 252 cu. in. (4.1-liters). Bore & stroke: 3.9565 x 3.40 in. Compression ratio: 8.0:1. Brake horsepower: 125 at 4000 R.P.M. Torque: 205 lb.-ft. at 2000 R.P.M. Four main bearings. Hydraulic valve lifters. Carburetor: 4Bbl. Made by Buick. VIN Code: 4. OPTIONAL DIESEL V-8 (Seville, Eldorado, DeVille, Brougham): 90-degree, overhead valve V-8. Cast iron block and head. Displacement: 350 cu. in. (5.7-liters). Bore & stroke: 4.057 x 3.345 in. Compression ratio: 21.6:1. Brake horsepower: 105 at 3200 R.P.M. Torque: 200 lb.-ft. at 1600 R.P.M. Five main bearings. Hydraulic valve lifters. Fuel injection. Oldsmobile-built. VIN Code: N. BASE V-8-6-4 VARIABLE DISPLACEMENT (Limousines only): 90-degree, overhead valve. Cast iron block and head. Displacement: 368 cu. in. (6.0-liters). Bore & stroke: 3.80 x 4.06 in.

Compression ratio: 8.2:1. Brake horsepower: 140 at 3800 R.P.M. Torque: 200 lb.-ft. at 1400 R.P.M. Five main bearings. Hydraulic valve lifters. Digital fuel injection. VIN Code: 9. BASE V-8 (Commercial chassis only): Similar to 368 cu. in. V-8-6-4 above but standard V-8 with 4Bbl. carburetor. Brake H.P.: 150 at 3800 R.P.M. Torque: 265 lb.-ft. at 1600 R.P.M.

CHASSIS DATA: Wheelbase: (Cimarron) 101.2 in.; (Seville/Eldo) 114.0 in.; (DeVille/Brghm) 121.4 in.; (Limo) 144.5 in. Overall length: (Cimarron) 173.0 in.; (Seville) 204.8 in.; (DeVille/Brghm) 221.0 in.; (Limo) 244.0 in. Height: (Cimarron) 52.0 in.; (Seville/Eldo) 54.3 in.; (DeVille/Brghm cpe) 54.6 in.; (DeVille sed) 55.6 in.; (Brghm sed) 56.7 in. Width: (Cimarron) 66.3 in.; (Seville/Eldo) 71.5 in.; (others) 76.5 in. Front Tread: (Cimarron) 55.4 in.; (Seville/Eldo) 59.3 in.; (others) 61.7 in. Rear Tread: (Cimarron) 55.2 in.; (Seville) 60.0 in.; (Eldo) 60.6 in.; (others) 60.7 in. Standard Tires: (Cimarron) P195/70R13 SBR; (Seville/Eldo) P205/75R15 SBR wide WSW; (DeVille/Brghm) P215/75R15 SBR wide WSW; (Limo) HR78 x 15-D wide WSW.

TECHNICAL: Transmission: Four-speed, floor shift manual transmission standard on Cimarron. Manual gear ratios: (1st) 3.53:1; (2nd) 1.95:1; (3rd) 1.24:1; (4th) 0.81:1; (Rev) 3.42:1. Turbo Hydra-matic (THM125C) optional on Cimarron w/floor selector: (1st) 2.84:1; (2nd) 1.60:1; (3rd) 1.00:1; (Rev) 2.07:1. Three-speed Turbo Hydra-matic (THM350C) standard on DeVille/Brghm diesel: (1st) 2.52:1; (2nd) 1.52:1; (3rd) 1.00:1; (Rev) 1.94:1. Turbo Hydra-matic (THM400) std. on limos: (1st) 2.48:1; (2nd) 1.48:1; (3rd) 1.00:1; (Rev) 2.07:1. Four-speed overdrive automatic standard on others (THM325-4L on Eldo/Sev, THM200-4R on DeVille/Brghm): (1st) 2.74:1; (2nd) 1.57:1; (3rd) 1.00:1; (4th) 0.67:1; (Rev) 2.07:1. All automatics except limo had torque converter clutch. Standard final drive ratio: (Cimarron) 3.65:1 exc. w/auto. 3.18:1; (Sev/Eldo) 3.15:1 exc. diesel, 2.93:1; (DeV/Brghm) 3.42:1 exc. 2.93:1 w/diesel, 2.41:1 w/diesel and three-speed trans., 3.23:1 w/V-6, (Limos) 3.08:1. Steering: (Cimarron) rack and pinion; (others) recirculating ball; power assist. Front suspension: (Cimarron) MacPherson struts, anti-roll bar; (Sev/Eldo) torsion bar and link stabilizer bar; (others) coil springs and link stabilizer bar. Rear suspension: (Cimarron) semi-independent trailing arm, coil springs, anti-roll bar; (Sev/Eldo) independent trailing arm, coil springs, electronic level control; (others) four-link, coil springs, elect. level control std. on limo and available on DeVille/Brghm. Brakes: front disc, rear drum exc. Sev/Eldo, four-wheel disc. Fuel tank: (Cimarron) 14.0 gal.; (Sev/Eldo) 20.3 gal. exc. 22.8 w/diesel, 21.1 w/V-6; (DeVille/Brghm) 24.5 gal. exc. 26 w/diesel; (limos) 24.5 gal.

DRIVETRAIN OPTIONS: 4.1-liter V-6 engine ($165 credit). 5.7-liter diesel V-8 engine ($179-$351); N/A limo or Cimarron. California emission equipment: Cimarron ($46); others (N/A). Altitude emissions pkg.: diesel or 4.1 V-8 (NC). Engine block heater: limo ($26); Cimarron ($17). Heavy-duty battery: Cimarron ($22). 100-amp alternator ($48). H.D. radiator: Cimarron ($37). Three-speed auto. transmission: Cimarron ($370). Limited slip differential: DeV/Brghm/limo ($106). Electronic level control: DeV/Brghm ($198). Heavy-duty ride package: DeV/Brghm ($310). FE2 touring suspension: Eldo/Sev ($109).

OPTION PACKAGES: Brougham d'Elegance: cloth seating ($1195); leather ($1730). deVille d'Elegance ($1115). deVille Cabriolet ($398). Eldorado Biarritz ($3335). Eldorado Cabriolet ($398). Eldorado Touring Coupe ($1950). Seville Elegante ($3095).

SEVILLE/DEVILLE/FLEETWOOD BROUGHAM/LIMOUSINE/ELDORADO CONVENIENCE/APPEARANCE OPTIONS: Astroroof ($1195); N/A on limo. Electronic cruise control ($175). Controlled-cycle wiper system: DeV/limo ($53). Rear defogger w/heated outside mirrors ($150-$198). Automatic door locks ($145). Remote-locking fuel filler door ($56). Garage door opener ($140). Illuminated entry system ($76). Digital instrument cluster: Sev/Eldo ($229). Dual Comfort front seats w/six-way power passenger seat adjuster ($413). Memory driver's seat ($180). Six-way power passenger seat: Eldo/Sev ($197). Power driver's seat recliner ($150); passenger, DeV ($150). Power passenger seat recliner w/six-way power seat: Eldo ($347); Sev ($282). Leather-trimmed steering wheel rim ($95). Tilt/telescope steering wheel ($169). Power trunk lid release and pull-down: DeV/limo ($112). Theft deterrent system ($179). Twilight Sentinel: DeV/limo ($76). Guidematic headlamp control ($93). Opera lamps: DeV/Eldo ($85). Trumpet horn ($35) exc. Seville. Electric remote-control outside mirrors ($98). Electric remote mirrors w/thermometer on left: limo ($114). Twin lighted vanity mirrors ($136). Electronic-tuning seek/scan AM/FM stereo radio with 8-track tape player ($225); w/8-track and CB ($515); w/cassette and symphony sound system ($290). Elect-tuning radio w/8-track and rear control: limo ($430). Trib-and antenna ($45). Fully padded vinyl roof: DeVille sed ($267).

Two-tone paint: Sev ($590); DeV/Eldo ($335); partial Firemist, DeV/Eldo ($450). Firemist paint ($229). Accent striping: DeV ($74). Bodyside molding ($61). Door edge guards ($18-$27). License frame ($13). Leather seating area ($498-$680). Carpeted rubber floor mats: front ($41-$43); rear ($24). Trunk mat ($20). Aluminum wheels: Eldo ($429); Sev (NC). Locking wire wheels: DeV/Brghm ($860). Turbine-vaned wheel covers: DeV ($75). Wire wheel covers ($298-$375). Puncture-sealing tires ($130-$175).

CIMARRON CONVENIENCE/APPEARANCE OPTIONS: Vista Vent w/rear tilt ($261). Cruise control, vacuum-type ($145-$155). Power windows ($216). Power door locks ($12). Power trunk release ($29). Tilt steering ($88). Six-way power driver's seat ($183); both seats ($366). Twin lighted vanity mirrors ($92). AM/FM stereo radio w/cassette ($153); w/cassette and CB ($560). Delete radio ($151 credit). Door edge guards ($22). License frame ($12). Decklid luggage rack ($98). Carpeted rubber floor mats: front ($38); rear ($22). Trunk mat ($18). Whitewall tires ($55).

HISTORY: Introduced: September 24, 1981, except Cimarron, May 21, 1981. Model year production: 235,584 (including early '82 Cimarrons). That total included 17,650 V-6 Cadillacs and 19,912 diesels. Only 1,017 Sevilles and 3,453 Eldorados had a V-6. Calendar year production: 246,602. Calendar year sales by U.S. dealers: 249,295 for a 4.3 percent share of the market. Model year sales by U.S. dealers: 237,032; also a 4.3 percent market share.

Historical Footnotes: In Cadillac's 80th anniversary year, it was the only GM division to show a sales increase, though not a gigantic one. A depressed economy typically affects luxury-car buyers the least. The new Cimarron, on the other hand, sold only one-third of the predicted output, and Seville also fell below expectations. Heavy dealer orders or the new models in September 1982 caused officials to add a second shift to the Livonia Engine Plant operation. Cadillac had considered selling the new HT-4100 4.1-liter engine to other GM divisions. As Cadillac's engine plant manager said: "There aren't many V-8s left, and ours is a highly efficient, light-weight, high-quality powerplant." Until a lightweight V-6 engine could be developed, Cadillac planned to use Buick's 251 cu. in. (4.1-liter) V-6 in the new Cimarron, which was built in South Gate, California. But that would not happen. Cadillac's Corporate Average Fuel Economy (CAFE) rating zoomed up to 22.1 MPG this year, from only 18.7 in 1981, largely due to the improved efficiency of the new 4.1 V-8. In September 1982, Robert D. Burger replaced Edward C. Kennard as Cadillac's general manager.

1983

1983 Cadillac, Cimarron sedan. (OCW)

Cadillac for 1983 heralded a new line of electronic fuel-injected engines, eliminating the carburetor. The EFI lineup even included the 2.0-liter four that powered Cimarrons. Once again, the HT-4100 V-8 was Cadillac's standard engine (except on Cimarrons and limousines), now with 10 more horsepower. Automatic four-speed overdrive transmission was standard as well. The 5.7-liter diesel was available again. A new Freedom II battery gave better cold-cranking performance. The curious but undependable variable-displacement V-8-6-4 engine was consigned only to limousine applications. Added to the Eldorado and Seville option lists was a Delco-GM/Bose Symphony Sound System with four amplifiers and speakers in separate enclosures billed as the "industry's most advanced stereo." Sound was automatically balanced for all passengers, reflecting off the windows and interior. Acoustics were based on window location and shape, upholstery, carpeting, and position of driver and passengers. The system included an AM/FM stereo radio and integral cassette player with Dolby tape noise reduction and full-time loudness control. Tested with an "acoustically-sensitive" robot, the system was also offered on Buick Riviera and Olds Toronado.

1983 Cadillac, Seville Elegante sedan. (OCW)

CIMARRON—SERIES 6J—FOUR—A newly fuel-injected 2.0-liter engine with five-speed gearbox promised better starting and gas mileage for Cadillac's smallest car. A new front end placed standard tungsten-halogen foglamps alongside the license plate, while a lower valance panel helped to separate Cimarron from its related (and much cheaper) J-body relatives. The grille had a finer mesh pattern than before, made up of thin vertical bars all the way across, divided into three sections by two subdued horizontal bars. Quad rectangular headlamps and amber parking/signal lamps were inset below the bumper rub strips. The hood medallion was new, and new aluminum alloy wheels contained bigger slots. Performance got a boost from the increased displacement and higher compression, along with the bigger engine's "swirl" intake ports and revised camshaft. That extra gear in the transmission didn't hurt either-—especially since it delivered a higher first-gear ratio for quicker takeoffs, plus closer ratios overall for smoother shift transitions. Ratios in the optional three-speed automatic changed too. Cimarron's ample standard equipment list included air conditioning, tinted glass, P195/70R13 steel-belted radial tires on aluminum alloy wheels, controlled-cycle wipers, lighter, digital clock, electric rear and side window defroster, tungsten-halogen high-beam headlamps, leather reclining bucket seats with lumbar support and adjustable headrests, and an AM/FM stereo radio with extended-range speakers. The dash held gauges for temp, oil pressure, voltage, trip odometer and tachometer. Bumpers contained guards, end caps and rub strips. Cimarrons had power rack-and-pinion steering with a leather-trimmed steering wheel. Drivers enjoyed dual electric remote mirrors, while the front passenger had a visor vanity mirror. In the trunk: a compact spare tire. Cimarron came in ten colors, accented by dual color painted stripes. Three were Cimarron exclusives: Antique Saddle, Midnight Sand Gray, and Garnet. Prices began at $12,215 this year.

SEVILLE—SERIES 6K—V-8—With price tags starting at $21,440, Seville came well equipped with—among other niceties—reminder chimes, electronic climate control with outside temperature display, automatic trunk locking (and release), side defoggers, rear reading lamps, overhead assist handles, and an automatic power antenna for the electronic-tuned radio. Also standard: an underhood light, lamp monitors, power windows and door locks, twin remote mirrors, cornering lamps, and four-wheel power disc brakes. Appearance changed little from 1982, except that this year's grille had a bit less vertical look and carried a Cadillac script. The front end held clear park/signal lamp lenses. Seville could be ordered with a full cabriolet roof that simulated a convertible top, available in black, dark blue, white, or dark briar brown. Inside was Heather cloth upholstery with matching Rocaille cloth inserts, in choice of four colors; or optional leather in nine shades. A new premium sound system was available, using Dolby tape noise reduction. The 4.1-liter aluminum-block V-8 received a horsepower and torque boost in its second year, to improve a power-loss problem. Third-gear acceleration rate was also revised. The 5.7-liter diesel included an engine block heater to improve cold-weather startups. Seville Elegante again came in two-tone with French curve side styling using chrome bodyside moldings, plus 'Elegante' script on the side panels and accent striping. Four two-tone combinations were offered. Sierra Grain tucked leather seating areas were color-coordinated to match the body color, and to complement the leather-trimmed steering wheel. The front console was leather-topped. Wire wheel covers were standard.

1983 Cadillac, Coupe deVille. (OCW)

1983 Cadillac, Sedan deVille. (OCW)

DEVILLE—SERIES 6C—V-8—Few changes were evident in the bodies of DeVille or Fleetwood coupe and sedan models, though underneath the exhaust system was modified. The refined new grille was similar to 1982 with narrow vertical bars separated into three rows, but Cadillac script moved from the upper horizontal bar to the side of the grille itself, leaving that upper bar bare. Distinctive taillamps carried on Cadillac's traditional style. On the hood was a stand-up hood ornament; on the decklid, Cadillac's 'V' and crest. Lengths reached as long as 221 inches, while prices began at $15,970. Horsepower rose by 10 on the HT-4100 Digital Fuel Injected 4.1-liter V-8. The miserly (if troublesome) 5.7-liter diesel was available on DeVille and Fleetwood Brougham models. Standard interior was Heather knit cloth with matching Dundee ribbed cloth inserts. Saddle leather was also available. DeVille d'Elegance offered pillow-style seating in Venetian velour, a six-way power passenger seat, special trim, accent striping, and opera lamps. The Cabriolet version of Coupe deVille added an Elk Grain vinyl partial roof, in color to match the car body, with bright crossover roof molding.

1983 Cadillac, Fleetwood Brougham sedan. (OCW)

FLEETWOOD BROUGHAM—SERIES 6C—V-8—Offered in coupe and sedan form, Broughams displayed a front end similar to DeVille's, with stand-up wreath-and-crest hood ornament. Sedans had a limousine-style rear window, while the coupe's standard Cabriolet vinyl roof featured "privacy size" quarter windows (similar to DeVille's Cabriolet option). Standard equipment included illuminated entry, six-way power driver's and passenger's seat, plus a long list of Cadillac luxury touches. Dual Comfort 55/45 seats (for three people) came with standard Heather cloth upholstery, but leather in eight colors could be ordered. Brougham d'Elegance, offered with both coupe and sedan, featured Heather cloth upholstery in four colors or leather in six, plus special trim, deluxe carpeting and floor mats, and wheel covers that matched the body color. The package also included d'Elegance identifying script, both inside and outside the car.

FLEETWOOD LIMOUSINE—SERIES 6D—V-8-6-4—Luxurious as ever, limousines saw no evident change this year. Sole powerplant was again the V-8-6-4 variable displacement engine, offered only in limos. Fleetwood remained the only domestic mass-produced limousine, though production was modest at only a thousand units. Seven or eight passengers rode in comfort and style, enjoying plentiful chrome and such extras as opera lamps.

1983 Cadillac, Eldorado Touring Coupe. (OCW)

ELDORADO—SERIES 6E—V-8—Like other Cadillacs, Eldorado saw no major changes in its body this year, though the automatic transmission and cruise control were recalibrated to boost performance. Standard engine was the HT-4100 4.1-liter V-8 with its complex (yet reliable) fuel-injection system; optional, a 5.7-liter

diesel. Prices began at $19,334 (suggested retail), which included plenty of standard equipment. The grille was similar to DeVille/Fleetwood, with Cadillac script at the driver's side in the center row. Front fender tips held no lights, so the quad rectangular headlamps and horizontal-style parking/signal lamps had a recessed look. Cornering lamps were in horizontal housings back on the front fenders. Heather cloth upholstery with Rocaille cloth inserts came in four colors: or buyers could choose from ten leather choices. Options included a digital instrument cluster with readouts for fuel level, speed and fuel range (English or metric). Eldorado's convertible had been gone for some time, but the optional full Cabriolet roof simulated a convertible top, with canvas-look fabric, roof bows and welted seams. It came in black, dark blue, dark briar brown, and white. Eldos had a new optional premium sound system, as well as available aluminum wheels. Two special editions were offered again: the Touring Coupe and Biarritz. Touring Coupes had (no surprise) a Touring suspension, large-diameter stabilizer bars, larger P225/70R15 steel-belted radial tires and special cloisonné hood medallion. Only two body colors were available: Sonora Saddle Firemist (light brown) and Sable Black. Reclining saddle leather-faced front bucket seats offered lumbar and lateral support, and included a console. Eldo's Biarritz "dream machine" included a brushed stainless steel roof cap, wire wheel covers, opera lamps, and 'Biarritz' script on the sail panels. Tufted pillow-style seats came in Sierra Grain leather in six colors; so did the steering wheel.

I.D. DATA: All Cadillacs again had a 17-symbol Vehicle Identification Number (VIN), stamped on a metal tag attached to the upper left surface of the cowl, visible through the windshield. Coding was similar to 1981-82. Model year code changed to 'D' for 1983. Engine coding was as follows: 'P' L4-121 TBI; '8' V-8-249 DFI; '9' V-8-6-4 368 DFI; 'N' V8-350 diesel; '6' V8-368 4Bbl. See 1981-82 for further details.

CIMARRON (FOUR)

Series No.	Body/Style No.	Body Type & Seating	Factory Price	Shipping Weight	Prod. Total
6J	G69	4-dr Sedan-5P	12215	2639	19,194

SEVILLE (V-8)

6K	S69	4-dr Sedan-6P	21440	3844	30,430

DEVILLE (V-8)

6C	D47	2-dr Coupe-6P	15970	3935	Note 1
6C	D69	4-dr Sedan-6P	16441	3993	Note 2

FLEETWOOD BROUGHAM (V-8)

6C	B47	2-dr Coupe-6P	18688	3986	Note 1
6C	B69	4-dr Sedan-6P	19182	4029	Note 2

Note 1: Total two-door coupe production, 65,670.

Note 2: Total DeVille/Fleetwood four-door sedan production, 109,004.

FLEETWOOD LIMOUSINE (V-8-6-4)

6D	F23	4-dr Sedan-8P	29323	4765	Note 3
6D	F33	4-dr Fml Limo-7P	30349	4852	Note 3
6D	Z90	Commercial Chassis	N/A	N/A	N/A

Note 3: Total limousine production, 1,000.

ELDORADO (V-8)

6E	L57	2-dr Coupe-6P	19334	3748	67,416

ENGINES: BASE FOUR (Cimarron): Inline. OHV. Four cylinder. Cast iron block and head. Displacement: 121 cu. in. (2.0-liters). Bore & stroke: 3.50 x 3.15 in. Compression ratio: 9.3:1. Brake horsepower: 88 at 4000 R.P.M. Torque: 110 lb.-ft. at 2400 R.P.M. Five main bearings. Hydraulic valve lifters. Throttle-body fuel injection. VIN Code: P. **BASE V-8 (Seville, DeVille, Brougham. Eldorado):** 90-degree, overhead valve V-8. Iron/aluminum alloy block; cast iron head. Displacement: 249 cu. in. (4.1-liters). Bore & stroke: 3.47 x 3.31 in. Compression ratio: 8.5:1. Brake horsepower: 135 at 4400 R.P.M. Torque: 200 lb.-ft. at 2200 R.P.M. Five main bearings. Hydraulic valve lifters. Digital fuel injection. .HT-4100. VIN Code: 8. **BASE V-8-6-4 (Limousine):** 90-degree, overhead valve variable displacement. Cast iron block and head. Displacement: 368 cu. in. (6.0-liters). Bore & stroke: 3.80 x 4.06 in. Compression ratio: 8.2:1. Brake horsepower: 140 at 3800 R.P.M. Torque: 265 lb.-ft. at 1400 R.P.M. Five main bearings. Hydraulic valve lifters. Digital fuel injection. VIN Code: 9. **BASE V-8 (Commercial chassis only):** Similar to 368 cu. in. V-8-6-4 above, but standard V-8 with 4Bbl. carburetor. Brake H.P.: 150 at 3800 R.P.M. Torque: 265 lb.-ft. at 1600 R.P.M. VIN Code: 6. **OPTIONAL DIESEL V-8 (Seville, DeVille, Brougham, Eldorado):** 90-degree, overhead valve V-8. Cast iron block and head. Displacement: 350 cu. in. (5.7-liters). Bore & stroke: 4.057 x 3.385 in. Compression ratio: 22.5:1. Brake horsepower: 105 at 3200 R.P.M. Torque: 200 lb.-ft. at 1600 R.P.M. Five main bearings. Hydraulic valve lifters. Fuel injection. Oldsmobile-built. VIN Code: N.

CHASSIS DATA: Wheelbase: (Cimarron) 101.2 in.; (Seville/Eldo) 114.0 in.; (DeV/Brougham) 121.4 in.; (Lim) 144.5 in. Overall length: (Cimarron) 173.1 in.; (Seville) 204.8 in.; (DeV/Brougham) 221.0 in.; (Limo) 244.3 in.; (Eldo) 204.5 in. Height: (Cimarron) 52.0 in.; (Seville/Eldo) 54.3 in.; (DeV/Brougham cpe) 54.6 in.; (DeV sed) 55.5 in.; (Brougham sed) 56.7 in. Width: (Cimarron) 66.5 in.; (Seville/Eldo) 71.5 in.; (DeV/Brougham) 76.4 in.; (Limo) 75.3 in. Front Tread: (Cimarron) 55.4 in.; (Seville/Eldo) 59.3 in.; (others) 61.7 in. Rear Tread: (Cimarron) 55.2 in.; (Seville/Eldo) 60.6 in.; (others) 60.7 in. Standard Tires: (Cimarron) P195/70R13 SBR; (Seville/Eldo) P205/75R15 SBR wide WSW; (DeV/Brougham) P215/75R15 SBR wide WSW; (Limo) HR78 x 15-D SBR wide WSW.

TECHNICAL: Transmission: Five-speed manual transmission standard on Cimarron. Manual gear ratios: (1st) 3.92:1; (2nd) 2.15:1; (3rd) 1.33:1; (4th) 0.92:1; (5th) 0.74:1; (Rev) 3.50:1. Optional Cimarron three-speed Turbo Hydra-matic (THM125C) gear ratios: (1st) 2.84:1; (2nd) 1.80:1; (3rd) 1.00:1; (Rev) 2.07:1. Three-speed (THM400) automatic standard on limousine: (1st) 2.48:1; (2nd) 1.48:1; (3rd) 1.00:1; (Rev) 2.08:1. Four-speed overdrive automatic standard on all others: (1st) 2.74:1; (2nd) 1.57:1; (3rd) 1.00:1; (4th) 0.67:1; (Rev) 2.07:1. Standard final drive ratio: (Cimarron) 3.83:1 w/5-spd. 3.18:1 w/auto; (Sev/Eldo) 3.15:1 exc. w/diesel 2.93:1; (DeVille/Brghm) 3.42:1 except w/diesel 2.93:1; (Limos) 3.08:1. Steering, Suspension and Brakes: same as 1982. Fuel tank: (Cimarron) 13.6 gal.; (Sev/Eldo) 20.3 gal. exc. w/diesel, 22.8 gal.; (DeVille/Brghm/limo) 24.5 gal. exc. w/diesel, 26 gal.

DRIVETRAIN OPTIONS: 5.7-liter diesel V-8 engine (NC); N/A limo or Cimarron. California emission equipment ($75), exc. diesel ($215). Engine block heater: limo ($27); Cimarron ($18). Heavy-duty battery: Cimarron ($25).100-amp alternator ($50) exc. Cimarron. H.D. radiator: Cimarron ($40). Three-speed automatic trans.: Cimarron ($320). Electronic level control: DeV/Brghm ($203). Heavy-duty ride pkg.: DeV/Brghm ($319). FE2 touring suspension: Eldo/Sev ($115).

OPTION PACKAGES: Seville Elegante ($3879). Brougham d'Elegance: cloth seating ($1250); leather ($1800). deVille d'Elegance ($1150). Cabriolet roof: DeV/Eldo cpe ($415). Full cabriolet roof: Eldo/Seville ($995). Eldorado Biarritz ($3395). Eldorado Touring Coupe ($1975).

SEVILLE/DEVILLE/FLEETWOOD BROUGHAM/LIMOUSINE/ELDORADO CONVENIENCE/APPEARANCE OPTIONS: Astroroof ($1225); N/A on limo. Electronic cruise control ($185). Controlled-cycle wiper system: DeV/limo ($60). Rear defogger w/heated outside mirrors ($160-$210). Automatic door locks ($157). Remote-locking fuel filler door ($59). Garage door opener ($140). Illuminated entry system ($76); std on Brougham. Digital instrument cluster: Sev/Eldo ($238). Dual comfort front seats: DeV ($225). Memory driver's seat ($185) exc. limo. Six-way power passenger seat: DeV/Eldo/Sev ($210). Power driver's seat recliner ($155) exc. limo. Power passenger seat recliner: DeV ($155); Brghm ($90). Power passenger seat recliner w/six-way power seat: DeV/Eldo ($365); Sev ($300). Leather-trimmed steering wheel ($99). Tilt/telescope steering wheel ($179); std. on formal limo. Power trunk lid release and pull-down: DeV/limo ($120). Theft deterrent system ($185). Twilight Sentinel ($79). Guidematic headlamp control ($93). Opera lamps: DeV/Eldo ($88). Trumpet horn ($38) exc. Sev. Electric remote mirrors w/thermometer on left: limo ($99). Electric remote-control outside mirrors ($99) exc. limo. Twin lighted vanity mirrors ($140). Electronic-tuning seek/scan AM/FM stereo radio with 8-track or cassette tape player ($299); with cassette and CB ($577) w/cassette and Bose symphony sound system, Eldo/Sev ($895). Elect.-tuning radio w/8-track and rear control limo ($475). Extended-range rear speakers ($25) w/std. Radio. Triband antenna ($50). Full padded vinyl roof: DeVille sed ($280). Two-tone paint: Sev ($600); DeV/Eldo ($345); Firemist, DeV/Eldo ($465); Firemist paint ($235). Accent striping DeV ($77). Bodyside molding: Eldo Touring cpe ($64). Door edge guards ($19-$29). License frames, each ($14) exc. Seville. Leather seating area ($515-$680). Carpeted rubber floor mats: front ($43-$45); rear ($25). Trunk mat ($21). Aluminum wheels: Eldo/Sev ($429). Locking wire wheels: DeV/Brghm ($860). Turbine-vaned wheel covers: DeV ($77); Eldo/Sev ($389). Locking wire wheel covers ($310-$389) exc. Limo. White-letter tires: Eldo touring cpe ($100). Puncture sealing tires ($135-$180).

CIMARRON CONVENIENCE/APPEARANCE OPTIONS: Astroroof ($915). Vista Vent w/rear tilt ($295). Cruise control, vacuum-type ($170). Power windows ($255). Power door locks ($170). Power trunk release ($40). Garage door opener ($165); retainer ($25). Tilt steering wheel ($99). Six-way power driver's seat ($210); both seats ($420). Twilight Sentinel ($79). Twin lighted vanity mirrors ($95). AM/FM stereo radio with cassette ($203). Delete radio ($151 credit). Power antenna ($55). Door edge guards ($25). License frame ($12). Decklid luggage rack ($98). Carpeted rubber floor mats: front ($38); rear ($22). Trunk mat ($18). Whitewall tires ($55).

HISTORY: Introduced: September 23, 1982. Model year production: 292,714, which came to 5.1 percent of the industry total. That total included 5,223 diesels. Calendar year production: 309,811. Calendar year sales by U.S. dealers: 300,337. Model year sales by U.S. dealers: 290,138 for a 4.5 percent market share.

Historical Footnotes: Sales rose by over 22 percent for the 1983 model year, suggesting that Cadillac's appeal to luxury-minded buyers hadn't waned. Before taking over the Chevrolet division, Cadillac General Manager Robert D. Burger told reporters that the company was "confident about the future of the luxury car business" since research by 1982 suggested a "long-term fundamental shift toward luxury cars...that hold their value." On the other hand, research also showed that Cadillac buyers were considerably older (median age about 60) than car buyers in general--a fact that could become a problem in future years. The popularity of the HT-4100 4.1-liter V-8 brought speculation that a transverse-mounted version would be planned for the 1984 Eldorado. That car's engine compartment would have to be widened, however, to accommodate the V-8. So the switch occurred only when Eldo got a new body for 1986. Rear drive Cadillacs were the longest cars on the market, measuring 121 inches in wheelbase. Buyers still liked them, so they expected to remain in the lineup for awhile longer.

1984

This was more a year of waiting than one of major changes. All Cadillac engines were now fuel injected. All but Cimarron and Fleetwood limousines carried the HT-4100 cu. in. (4.1-liter V-8 with aluminum alloy block and digital fuel injection). This year, that 249 cu. in. engine gained a new exhaust system and catalytic converter, plus revised calibration settings, to meet high-altitude emissions standards. New features on DeVille, Fleetwood Brougham and limos included a goldtone horizontally-winged Cadillac crest ornament on front parking and turn signal lenses; new car-colored bodyside moldings; new goldtone vertically-winged Cadillac crest and goldtone accents on taillamp lenses; and new standard electronic level control. Diesel engine identification plaques were now on the left rear of the decklid. Faster-warming glow plugs went into the optional 5.7-liter diesel V-8, for improved cold startups. A modified optional theft-deterrent system could detect any object on the driver's seat that weighed 40 pounds or more.

1984 Cadillac, Cimarron sedan. (OCW)

CIMARRON—SERIES 6J—FOUR—Cimarron's new crosshatch grille had a bolder look, but kept the Cadillac script at lower left corner. The new front end was evidently designed with a V-6 in mind--but that wouldn't be available just yet. The fuel-injected 2.0-liter four remained standard, with five-speed manual gearbox or optional three-speed automatic. Three new stripe insert colors (white, red, orange) were offered for bumper rub strips, end caps and bodyside moldings; plus gold for the Cimarron d'Oro. Foglamps introduced in 1983 continued as standard. A new rear-end lighting arrangement used horizontal upper red stop/taillamps, accented with flush-mounted winged Cadillac crest ornamentation. New amber turn signal lamps and more dominant white backup lamps were below the red tail/stop lamps. Interiors were now available in combinations of leather and cloth. Push-button heat/vent controls now had accent lights. A 24-position click-stop temperature control lever allowed more precise settings. Optional cruise control now included acceleration/deceleration capability. Cimarron prices began at $12,614. The special edition Cimarron d'Oro, introduced during 1983, was available again with distinctive Sable Black body, highlighted by goldtone accents that replaced all the body chrome. d'Oro also sported black bumpers, headlamp bezels, rip rail and window reveal moldings, wheel opening and rocker panel moldings, and door handles. Goldtone touches included the grille; a lay-down 'Cadillac Cimarron' hood ornament; accent stripes on hood center, body beltline, bumper rub strips and bodyside moldings; d'Oro fender plaques; Cimarron trunk lid script; a '2.0-Liter Fuel Injection' plaque on the trunk lid and winged Cadillac crest ornamentation on taillamps. Gold also tinted the steering wheel spokes and horn pad emblem. In an effort to attract younger motorists to the black/gold small Cadillac, radio commercials played an upbeat jingle promoting the "Cimarron touch."

1984 Cadillac, Seville sedan. (OCW)

1984 Cadillac, Seville sedan with cabriolet roof option. (OCW)

SEVILLE—SERIES 6K—V-8—Restyled taillamps and new body-colored side moldings gave the bustleback front-drive Seville a slightly different look for 1984. Horizontal taillamps were modified to include a clear outer lens and red inner lens. This year's grille had fine vertical accents and a bright script Cadillac nameplate in the lower left corner. The traditional Cadillac stand-up wreath-and-crest hood ornament stood on a tapered hood center molding. Seville had new low-gloss black door trim bezels, instrument panel bezels and air conditioning outlets. New tufted multi-button cloth or leather/vinyl trim were the upholstery choices for base models. New options included aluminum alloy wheels with center hubcaps and exposed chrome lug nuts. Sense-around Delco/Bose stereo was again available, and other sound systems were improved. Seville's lengthy standard equipment included rear reading lights, accent moldings, manual seatback recliner, overhead assist handles, door pull straps, four-wheel power disc brakes, air conditioning, power windows, bumper guards and rub strips, and P205/75R15 steel-belted radial whitewall tires. The limited-edition Elegante could now be ordered in a single color instead of two-tone. That $3,879 package included a leather-trimmed steering wheel, leather 40/40 dual comfort front seats (six-way power adjustment with recliners), console, Tampico carpeting, chrome side moldings, wire wheel covers, and deluxe floor mats.

DEVILLE—SERIES 6D—V-8—New front-drive versions of DeVille and Fleetwood were anticipated, but delayed because of quality control questions; so for 1984 the rear-drive coupe and sedan carried on. Bodyside moldings were now color-keyed to the body finish. Taillamp lenses held goldtone Cadillac wing crests. All models now had electronic level control. The standard fuel injected 249 cu. in. (4.1-liter) V-8 engine fed

into a revised exhaust system with monolithic catalytic converter. Electronic controls were modified to meet stricter emissions standards in high-altitude regions. The diesel V-8 remained on the option list, except in California because of its emissions regulations. Standard equipment included power brakes and steering, whitewall steel-belted radials, electronic level control, automatic climate-control air conditioning, signal-seeking stereo radio with power antenna, cornering lights, and light monitors. All that plus power windows and six-way power seat, tinted glass, a remote-control left outside mirror, right visor mirror, automatic parking brake release, P215/75R15 tires and a stowaway spare. The front-wheel drive editions appeared during the '84 model year as early 1985s.

1984 Cadillac, Coupe deVille. (OCW)

FLEETWOOD BROUGHAM—SERIES 6D—V-8—Brougham sedans had a more closed-in back window plus bright belt and hood moldings, large rocker moldings, and wheel covers that were also used on limos. Electroluminescent opera lamps were standard. The coupe had a stylish roof with custom cabriolet vinyl top enclosing a distinctive rear quarter window. Standard equipment was the same as deVille coupe, but adding four-wheel power disc brakes; a remote-control right mirror, and 45/55 dual-comfort front seats.

1984 Cadillac, Fleetwood Brougham Sedan d'Elegance. (OCW)

FLEETWOOD LIMOUSINE—SERIES 6D—V-8—Limousines carried the same standard equipment as DeVille, plus accent striping, opera lamps, and HR78 x 15-D tires. Only the formal limo had the six-way power seat. Fleetwood limos still used the variable-displacement 6.0-liter V-8-6-4 engine.

1984 Cadillac, Eldorado Biarritz convertible. (OCW)

ELDORADO—SERIES 6E—V-8—For the first time since the famed '76 Eldorado ragtop, Cadillac offered a convertible: the new and posh Biarritz. Its rear side windows raised and lowered automatically with the power top and it contained a glass back window. Convertible bodies came in three colors: Cotillion White, Hatteras Blue, and Autumn Maple Firemist. Each had a white diamond grain vinyl top, glass rear window, and color-coordinated headliner. Reinforced frame rails and crossmember braces and a bolstered body structure added the necessary strength and rigidity. Convertibles had specific wide bright door and fender accent moldings; decklid accent striping; Biarritz script nameplate; and wire wheel covers. Also standard: special Biarritz multi-button tufted seat design and leather-wrapped steering wheel rim, plus Cadillac's theft deterrent system. The revived Biarritz convertible carried a hefty opening price tag: $31,286. That was nearly triple the cost of a '76 Eldo ragtop when it was new. Eldorado coupes started at a more modest $20,342. Eldorado's grille this year was vertically accented with a bright Cadillac script nameplate in the lower left corner. Rectangular headlamps sat above clear park/signal lamps. Appearance changes included new car-colored bodyside moldings plus new low gloss black door trim bezels, instrument panel bezels, and air conditioning outlets. Base Eldos had a new leather seat trim design. Other additions: an improved theft prevention system, new dashboard bezels, suspension refinements, improved stereo performance, and a new glow-plug system in the optional diesel V-8 engine. Coupes had a cabriolet vinyl top with glass rear window, brushed stainless steel roof cover, and opera lamps. Extended-range rear speakers became standard, except on the Delco/Bose sound system. The standard 4.1-liter V-8 engine added a new exhaust system, while the Oldsmobile diesel was not offered in convertibles (or in California). The Touring Coupe was again available, with a distinctive 'Eldorado Touring Coupe' cloisonné hood surface and sail panel ornaments. Also included: black finished windshield window reveal moldings, quarter window channel moldings and wipers; plus body-colored headlamp and taillamp bezels and wheel opening moldings; large ribbed rocker panel moldings; and aluminum alloy wheels. Touring Coupes came only in Sable Black or Sonora Saddle Firemist.

I.D. DATA: All Cadillacs again had a 17-symbol Vehicle Identification Number (VIN), stamped on a metal tag attached to the upper left surface of the cowl, visible through the windshield. Some of the coding changed this year. The number begins with a '1' to indicate the manufacturing country (U.S.A.), followed by a 'G' for General Motors and a '6' for Cadillac Division. The next letter indicates restraint system: 'A' manual; 'B' automatic. Symbol five denotes car line and series: 'S' Seville; 'M' DeVille; 'W' Fleetwood Brougham; 'F' Fleetwood limousine; 'L' Eldorado. Digits six and seven indicate body type: '47' 2-dr. coupe; '69' 4-dr. sedan; '23' eight-passenger limousine; '33' formal limousine with center partition; '57' Eldorado coupe; '67' 2-dr. convertible coupe. Next comes the engine code: 'P' L4-121 TBI; '8' V8-250 FI; 'N' V8-350 diesel; '9' V-8-6-4 368 FI. The next symbol is a check digit. Symbol ten indicates model year ('E' 1984). Symbol eleven denotes assembly plant. Last is a six-digit production sequence number. As before, engines carried an identifying number and bodies held a number plate.

CIMARRON (FOUR)

Series No.	Body/Style No.	Body Type & Seating	Factory Price	Shipping Weight	Prod. Total
6J	G69	4-dr Sedan-5P	12614	2639	21,898

SEVILLE (V-8)

6K	S69	4-dr Sedan-6P	22468	3844	39,997

DEVILLE (V-8)

6D	M47	2-dr Coupe-6P	17140	3935	Note 1
6D	M69	4-dr Sedan-6P	17625	3993	Note 2

FLEETWOOD BROUGHAM (V-8)

6D	W47	2-dr Coupe-6P	19942	3986	Note 1
6D	W69	4-dr Sedan-6P	20451	4029	Note 2
6D	F23	4-dr Sedan-8P	30454	4765	Note 3
6D	F33	4-dr Frml Limo-7P	31512	4852	Note 3

Note 1: Total two-door coupe production, 50,840.

Note 2: Total DeVille/Fleetwood four-door sedan production, 107,920.

Note 3: Total limousine production, 1,839.

ELDORADO (V-8)

6E	L57	2-dr Coupe-6P	20342	3748	74,506
6E	L67	2-dr Conv-6P	31286	N/A	3,300

1984 Cadillac, Sedan deVille. (OCW)

ENGINES: BASE FOUR (Cimarron): Inline. OHV. Four-cylinder. Cast iron block and head. Displacement :121 cu. in. (2.0-liters). Bore & stroke: 3.50 x 3.15 in. Compression ratio: 9.3:1. Brake horsepower: 88 at 4800 R.P.M. Torque: 110 lb.-ft. at 2400 R.P.M. Five main bearings. Hydraulic valve lifters. Throttle-body fuel injection. VIN Code: P. BASE V-8 (Seville, DeVille, Brougham, Eldorado): 90-degree, overhead-valve V-8. Iron/aluminum alloy block; cast iron head. Displacement: 249 cu. in. (4.1-liters). Bore & stroke: 3.47 x 3.31 in. Compression ratio: 8.5:1. Brake horsepower: 135 at 4400 R.P.M. Torque: 200 lb.-ft. at 2200 R.P.M. Five main bearings. Hydraulic valve lifters. Digital fuel injection (single-point, dual injectors). VIN Code: 8. BASE V-8-6-4 (Limousine): 90-degree overhead valve variable-displacement. Cast iron block and head. Displacement: 368 cu. in. (6.0-liters). Bore & stroke: 3.80 x 4.06 in. Compression ratio: 8.2:1. Brake horsepower: 140 at 3800 R.P.M. Torque: N/A. Five main bearings. Hydraulic valve lifters. Fuel injection. OPTIONAL DIESEL V-8 (Seville, DeVille, Brougham, Eldorado): 90-degree, overhead valve V-8. Cast iron block and head. Displacement: 350 cu. in. (5.7-liters). Bore & stroke: 4.05 x 3.38 in. Compression ratio: 22.7:1. Brake horsepower: 105 at 3200 R.P.M. Torque: 200 lb.-ft. at 1600 R.P.M. Five main bearings. Hydraulic valve lifters. Fuel injection. Oldsmobile-built. VIN Code: N.

CHASSIS DATA: Wheelbase: (Cimarron) 101.2 in.; (Seville/Eldo) 114.0 in.; (DeV/Brougham) 121.4 in.; (Limo) 144.5 in. Overall length: (Cimarron) 173.1 in.; (Seville) 204.8 in.; (DeV/Brougham) 221.0 in.; (Limo) 244.3 in.; (Eldo) 204.5 in. Height: (Cimarron) 52.0 in.; (Seville/Eldo) 54.3 in.; (DeV/Brghm cpe) 54.6 in.; (DeV sed) 55.5 in.; (Brghm sed) 56.7 in.; (Limo) 56.9 in. Width: (Cimarron) 66.5 in.; (Seville) 70.9 in.; (DeV/Brghm/limo) 75.3-76.4 in.; (Eldo) 70.6 in. Front Tread: (Cimarron) 55.4 in.; (Seville/Eldo) 59.3 in.; (others) 61.7 in. Rear Tread: (Cimarron) 55.2 in.; (Seville/Eldo) 60.6 in.; (others) 60.7 in. Standard Tires: (Clmarron) P195/70R13; (Seville/Eldo) P205/75R15 SBR WSW; (DeV/Brghm) P215/75R15 SBR WSW; (Limo) HR78 x 15-D SBR WSW.

TECHNICAL: Transmission: Five-speed, floor shift manual transmission standard on Cimarron, Turbo Hydra-matic optional; gear ratios same as 1983. Three-speed automatic standard on limo; four-speed overdrive automatic on others; ratios same as 1983. Standard final drive ratio: (Cimarron) 3.83:1 w/5-spd, 3.18:1 w/auto.; (Sev/Eldo) 3.15:1 exc. w/diesel, 2.93:1; (DeV/Brghm) 3.42:1 exc. w/diesel, 2.93:1. Steering: (Cimarron) power rack and pinion; (others) power recirculating ball. Suspension and brakes: same as 1983. Fuel tank: (Cimarron) 13.6 gal.; (Sev/Eldo) 20.3 gal. exc. w/diesel, 22.8; (DeV/Brghm) 24.5 gal. exc. w/diesel, 26.0.

DRIVETRAIN OPTIONS: 5.7-liter diesel V-8 engine (NC); N/A limo or Cimarron. California emission equipment ($99). Engine block heater ($18-$45). Heavy-duty battery: Cimarron ($26); others ($40). 100-amp alternator ($50) exc. Cimarron. H.D. radiator: Cimarron ($40). Three-speed automatic transmission: Cimarron ($320). Limited slip differential (DeV $120). Heavy-duty ride package: DeV/Brghm ($319). FE2 touring suspension: Eldo/Sev ($115).

OPTION PACKAGES: Cimarron d'Oro ($350). Seville Elegante ($3879). Brougham d'Elegance: cloth seating ($1250); leather ($1800). deVille d'Elegance ($1150). Cabriolet roof: DeV/Eldo cpe ($420). Full cabriolet roof: Eldo/Sev ($995). Eldorado Biarritz ($3395). Eldorado Touring Coupe ($1975).

DEVILLE/FLEETWOOD BROUGHAM/LIMOUSINE/ELDORADO/SEVILLE CONVENIENCE/APPEARANCE OPTIONS: Astroroof ($1225); N/A on limo. Electronic cruise control ($185). Controlled-cycle wiper system: DeV/limo ($60). Rear defogger w/heated outside mirrors ($165-$215). Automatic door locks ($162). Remote-locking fuel filler door ($59). Garage door opener ($140) exc. conv. Illuminated entry system ($76); std on Brougham. Digital instrument cluster: Sev/Eldo ($238). Dual comfort front seats: DeV ($225). Memory driver's seat ($205) exc.

limo/conv. Six-way power passenger seat: DeV/Eldo/Sev ($215-$225). Power driver's seat recliner ($155) exc. Limo. Power passenger seat recliner: DeV ($155); Brghm ($90). Power passenger seat recliner w/six-way power seat: DeV/Eldo/Sev ($315-$380). Leather-trimmed steering wheel ($99). Tilt/telescope steering wheel ($184); std. on formal limo. Power trunk lid release and pull-down: DeV/limo ($120). Theft deterrent system ($190). Twilight Sentinel ($79). Guidematic headlamp control ($93). Opera lamps: DeV/Eldo ($88). Trumpet horn ($38) exc. Seville. Electric remote mirrors w/thermometer on left: limo ($101). Electric remote-control outside mirrors ($101) exc. Limo. Twin lighted vanity mirrors ($140). Electronic-tuning seek/scan AM/FM stereo radio with clock and cassette player ($299); with cassette and CB ($577) exc. Eldo/Sev; w/cassette and Delco-GM/Bose sound system, Eldo/Sev ($895). CB radio: Eldo/Sev ($278). Rear-control ET radio w/cassette: limo ($475). Triband antenna ($50). Full padded vinyl roof: DeVille sed ($285). Two-tone paint: Sev ($600); DeV/Eldo ($345). Firemist ($465). Firemist paint ($235). Accent striping: DeV ($77). Bodyside molding: Eldo Touring cpe ($64). Door edge guards ($19-$29). License frames, each ($14). Leather seating area ($515-$680). Carpeted rubber floor mats: front ($43-$45); rear ($25). Trunk mat ($21). Aluminum wheels: Eldo/Sev ($429). Locking wire wheels: DeV/Brghm ($860). Turbine-vaned wheel covers: DeV ($77). Locking wire wheel covers ($315-$394) exc. Limo. White-letter tires: Eldo touring cpe ($100). Puncture-sealing tires ($135-$180) exc. limo.

CIMARRON CONVENIENCE/APPEARANCE OPTIONS: Vista Vent w/rear tilt ($300). Electronic cruise control ($175). Power windows ($260). Power door locks ($175). Power trunk release ($40). Garage door opener ($165); retainer ($25). Tilt steering wheel ($104). Six-way power driver's seat ($215); both seats ($430). Twilight Sentinel ($79). Twin lighted vanity mirrors ($95). Seek/scan AM/FM stereo radio w/cassette ($203). Delete radio ($151 credit). Power antenna ($60). Door edge guards ($25). License frame ($12). Decklid luggage rack ($100). Cloth upholstery ($100 credit). Carpeted rubber floor mats: front ($38); rear ($22). Trunk mat ($18). Whitewall tires ($55).

HISTORY: Introduced: September 22, 1983. Model year production: 300,300 (not including early '85 DeVille/Fleetwoods). The total includes 2,465 diesels. Calendar year production: 328,534. Calendar year sales by U.S. dealers: 320,017 for a 4.0 percent market share. Model year sales by U.S. dealers: 327,587 (including 46,356 early '85 front-drives).

Historical Footnotes: Sales rose 13 percent for the model year, but Cadillac's market share declined. (Figures are a bit distorted because both front- and rear-drive DeVille/Fleetwood models were sold at the same time.) On the other hand, all the GM divisions experienced a drop in market share. Rising demand, though, kept plants working overtime during 1984. Cimarron continued as Cadillac's weakest seller, largely because it offered little more than the related J-car Chevrolet Cavalier gave for far fewer dollars. Best performers in terms of increased sales were the big Cadillacs: DeVille and Fleetwood Brougham. Research had shown, however, that over three-fourths of Cimarron buyers had never bought a Cadillac before; and that many of them had previously owned an import. Late in 1983, a modern new plant at Orion Township in Michigan had begun production of the new front drive DeVille, to be introduced for 1985 after early production delays. Also late in 1983, Cadillac became part of the Buick-Oldsmobile-Cadillac group. In January 1984, John O. Grettenberger became Cadillac's new chief. Cadillac had offered the last American convertible in 1976, but wasn't the first to return with a ragtop in the '80s. Already on the market were Buick Riviera, Chevrolet Cavalier, Pontiac Sunbird, Chrysler LeBaron, Dodge 600, and Ford Mustang. Cadillac's version was, of course, the most costly of the lot for '84. The convertible was actually a conversion done by ASC Corporation in Lansing, Michigan, after the car was assembled in New Jersey. The work included reinforcing inner rockers, radiator support cross rods, and many body braces. Front and rear anti-roll bars and tougher suspension components were added along with the vinyl convertible top. All told, the convertible weighed 179 pounds more than the coupe from which it evolved.

1985

Front-wheel drive now became the rule at Cadillac, as in nearly all other makes. Two grand old names, DeVille and Fleetwood,

made the switch this year. All Cadillacs except the subcompact Cimarron (and carryover rear drive Brougham) now carried a transverse-mounted, fuel-injected 4.1-liter V-8 engine with die-cast aluminum-block. Two safety improvements arrived this year: anti-lacerative windshield glass (with inner layer of two-part plastic) on Seville's Elegante, plus a high-mount stop lamp on all DeVilles and Fleetwoods. That stop lamp would become required on all cars for 1986.

1982 Cadillac, Seville sedan with cabriolet roof option. (OCW)

CIMARRON—SERIES 6J—FOUR—Cadillac's compact received a major revision for 1985, but went on sale a little later than usual. Production of the 1984 models was extended into autumn 1985, to take advantage of the existing Corporate Average Fuel Economy standards, which were to grow more stringent for the coming year. An optional V-6 engine finally arrived for mid-year models, to deliver a much-needed performance boost. The new 173 cu. in. (2.8-liter) high-output V-6 with fuel injection was built by Chevrolet. Cimarron sales continued sluggish, but style and performance alterations were made to try to draw some younger customers. The restyled body also was intended to give Cimarron more of a Cadillac look. Prices began just under $13,000, well under other Cadillacs but a good deal higher than Chevrolet's Cavalier and the other J-bodied GM models. Stabilizer bars grew longer this year, and front springs became stiffer. Outside, Cimarron's front end grew by almost five inches. The new crosshatch grille reached out to black inner surfaces for headlamp bezels, which were positioned differently than before. Styled aluminum wheels were available for the first time, as an option. Standard transmission was a five-speed manual gearbox, with three-speed automatic or four-speed manual optional. Standard equipment included air conditioning, AM/FM stereo radio with power antenna, center armrests, overhead assist handles, power brakes and steering, bumper guards and rub strips, digital clock, power door locks, electric defoggers (rear and side window), halogen headlamps and foglamps, tinted glass, and electric remote mirrors. Inside were leather reclining bucket seats (driver's side six-way power adjustable), a leather-wrapped tilt steering wheel, tachometer, power windows, and power trunk release. All that and more helped to justify Cimarron's hefty price tag. Cimarron d'Oro added fine-line gold accent stripes on beltline, hood center and rub strips; gold accented grille and wheels; foglamp covers; lower bodyside accent moldings; saddle leather seats; plus gold-tinted hood ornament, steering wheel spokes and horn pad emblem. d'Oro bodies were either red or white, with plaques on front fender and dash.

1985 Cadillac, Seville Elegante sedan. (OCW)

SEVILLE—SERIES 6K—V-8—For its final season in this form, the front-drive Seville sedan changed little. Neither did its companion Eldorado, which used the same chassis layout. Standard engine, as before, was the fuel-injected 250 cu. in. (4.1-liter) V-8, with four-speed overdrive automatic transmission. Buyers could also choose a diesel V-8, but not many did. Seville's base price was $23,729. New to the option list: aluminum alloy wheels with a radial fin design and gray accents. Both spoke and non-spoke versions were available. Seville's Elegante had a new "Inner Shield" windshield with a two-section plastic layer intended to prevent cuts from splintered glass in an accident. Elegante's interior featured standard leather seats, color-coordinated with the car body. Late in the model year, a Commemorative Edition package was announced.

1985 Cadillac, Coupe deVille. (OCW)

1985 Cadillac, Sedan deVille. (OCW)

DEVILLE—SERIES 6C—V-8—A dramatically different front-drive, C-body Coupe deVille (and Fleetwood sedan) hit the market late in March of 1984, as early '85 models. The Grand Old Cadillacs lost two feet in length and about 600 pounds. Their front-drive chassis layout was also used by Buick Electra and Oldsmobile Ninety-Eight. Though not exactly small, both were a far cry from the DeVilles and Fleetwoods of prior eras. Arriving in the fall was a new Fleetwood coupe, with formal cabriolet vinyl roof and opera lamps, as well as wire wheel covers. Both coupe and sedan carried a claimed six passengers. A transverse-mounted 249 cu. in. (4.1-liter) V-8 engine with throttle-body fuel injection was standard; 4.3-liter V-6 diesel a no-charge option. Cadillac's was the only transverse-mounted V-8 available in the world. Oldsmobile's diesel V-8 engine also was available. Inside the automatic transmission, the torque converter clutch was computer-controlled and operated by silicone fluid. All models included the Retained Power Accessory System, which permitted use of power windows and trunk release for 10 minutes after shutting off the engine. A third brake light was now mounted on the rear panel shelf. Standard equipment included four-speed overdrive automatic transmission, power steering and brakes, tungsten-halogen headlamps, body-colored protective side moldings, six-way power driver's seat, power windows and door locks, side window defogger, electronic climate control, a Delco 2000 AM/FM stereo radio with electronic tuning and seek/scan, remote-controlled outside mirrors, courtesy/reading lamps in the sail panel, and power decklid release. Tires were P205/75R14 all-season steel-belted radials.

1985 Cadillac, Fleetwood coupe. (OCW)

1985 Cadillac, Fleetwood sedan. (OCW)

FLEETWOOD—SERIES 6C—V-8—Fleetwood coupes and sedans carried the same standard equipment as the DeVille duo, along with wire wheel covers, opera lamps, dual comfort front seats, and a limousine-style back window. Power-trains were the same as DeVille's. This was the final year for Fleetwood as a separate model. In 1986, it would become a DeVille option package. Fleetwood prices began at $21,495, which was more than $3,000 higher than DeVille.

1985 Cadillac, Fleetwood Seventy-Five limousine. (OCW)

FLEETWOOD SEVENTY-FIVE LIMOUSINE—SERIES 6C—V-8—Like the Fleetwood sedan, the Seventy-Five limo switched to front-drive. The rear-drive version was dropped. To create the new limousine, a C-car platform (same as DeVille/Fleetwood) and coupe body were stretched almost two feet. Even so, the modern edition was more than two feet shorter than the old rear-drive, and weighed 1,200 pounds less. Powertrain was the same as DeVille/Fleetwood: a transverse-mounted 4.1-liter V-8 and four speed overdrive automatic. Rear control panels let passengers unlock the back doors, adjust climate, and control the stereo unit. The basic limo still carried eight passengers, and a seven-passenger formal version appeared later in the model year. Fleetwood Seventy-Five limousines had power-operated mirrors, but other standard equipment similar to Fleetwood sedans. A matching formal Cabriolet vinyl roof was available. Aluminum alloy wheels were made standard on limos.

1985 Cadillac, Fleetwood Brougham sedan. (OCW)

FLEETWOOD BROUGHAM—SERIES 6D—V-8—Brougham, the last surviving rear-drive Cadillac, changed little for 1985 and faced potential extinction in spite of increased sales. That didn't happen. The traditional rear-drive lingered on for several more years, even though all other Cadillacs (including limos) switched to front-drive and shrunken size. Vast inside and out, Broughams continued to attract traditional luxury-car buyers. The Brougham coupe was dropped from the lineup in mid-year. Sedans came with a standard full vinyl roof, while the Brougham coupe included a standard Cabriolet vinyl top with unique rear quarter window. Standard engine was the 4.1-liter V-8; diesel V-8 optional at no charge.

1985 Cadillac, Eldorado coupe. (OCW)

ELDORADO—SERIES 6E—V-8—Few changes were evident on the luxury front-drive personal coupe and convertible. The Biarritz convertible, introduced for 1984, could now get an optional electric defogger for its glass back window. New spoked aluminum alloy road wheels joined the option list. Standard engine remained the 4.1-liter V-8, with throttle-body fuel injection, hooked to a four-speed overdrive automatic transmission. A big diesel V-8 also was available (at extra cost) in the coupe. Eldo's Biarritz coupe had a cabriolet vinyl roof with brushed steel cap, accent moldings, and opera lamps. Convertibles were similarly decked out. Touring Coupes had a stiffer suspension as well as blackout and body-color trim. Eldo coupes began at $21,355, but the convertible cost over $11,000 more. This would be the ragtop's final season, as Eldorado switched to a new body for 1986.

I.D. DATA: Cadillacs again had a 17-symbol Vehicle Identification Number (VIN), stamped on a metal tag attached to the upper left surface of the cowl, visible through the windshield. Coding changed to reflect the new front-drive models. The number begins with a '1' to indicate the manufacturing country (U.S.A.), followed by a 'G' for General Motors and a '6' for Cadillac Division. Symbol four is car line (GM body): 'J' Cimarron; 'K' Seville; 'C' DeVille/Fleetwood; 'D' Brougham; 'E' Eldorado. Symbol five indicates series: 'G' Cimarron; 'S' Seville; 'D' DeVille; 'B' Fleetwood; 'H' Fleetwood limousine; 'W' Fleetwood Brougham (rear-drive); 'L' Eldorado. Digits six and seven indicate body type: '47' 2-dr. coupe; '69' 4-dr. sedan; '23' eight-passenger limo; '33' formal limousine; '57' Eldorado coupe; 2-dr. convertible coupe. Next is engine code: 'P' L4-121 TBI; 'W' V6-173 FI; '8' V8-249 DFI; 'T' V6-262 diesel; 'N' V8-350 diesel. The next symbol is a check digit. Symbol ten indicates model year ('F' 1985). Next is a code for assembly plant: '9' Detroit; 'E' Linden, NJ; 'J' Janesville, WI. Finally comes a six-digit production sequence number, starting with 000001 for Detroit; 400001 for Janesville; 600001 for Linden (E-body); or 800001 for Linden (K-body). An identifying number is also on the engine, and a set of codes on a body number plate.

CIMARRON (FOUR)

Series No.	Body/Style No.	Body Type & Seating	Factory Price	Shipping Weight	Prod. Total
6J	G69	4-dr Sedan-5P	12962/13522	2630/----	19,890

Price/Weight Note: Figure before the slash is for a four-cylinder engine, after the slash for the new Cimarron V-6.

SEVILLE (V-8)

Series No.	Body/Style No.	Body Type & Seating	Factory Price	Shipping Weight	Prod. Total
6K	S69	4-dr Sedan-6P	23729	3688	39,755

DEVILLE (FRONT-DRIVE V-8)

6C	D47	2-dr Coupe-6P	18355	3330	Note 1
6C	D69	4-dr Sedan-6P	18947	3327	Note 2

FLEETWOOD (FRONT-DRIVE V-8)

6C	B47	2-dr Coupe-6P	21495	3267	Note 1
6C	B69	4-dr Sedan-6P	21466	3364	Note 2

Note 1: Total two-door DeVille/Fleetwood production, 37,485.

Note 2: Total DeVille/Fleetwood four-door sedan production, 114,278. For the model year, 42,911 Fleetwoods and 108,852 DeVilles were produced. These figures do not include 45,330 DeVille/Fleetwood produced as early 1985 models (9,390 two-doors and 35,940 four-doors).

FLEETWOOD LIMOUSINE (V-8)

6C	H23	4-dr Limo-8P	32640	3543	Note 3
6C	H33	4-dr Fml Limo-7P	N/A	3642	Note 3

Note 3: Total limousine production was 405 units.

FLEETWOOD BROUGHAM (REAR-DRIVE V-8)

6D	W47	2-dr Coupe-6P	21219	3873	8,336
6D	W69	4-dr Sedan-6P	21835	3915	52,960

ELDORADO (V-8)

6E	L57	2-dr Coupe-6P	21355	3623	74,101
6E	L67	2-dr Conv-6P	32105	3804	2,300

Engine Note: Diesel V-6 engines were available for DeVille/Fleetwood models; diesel V-8s on Seville, Fleetwood Brougham and Eldorado, at no extra charge.

ENGINES: BASE FOUR (Cimarron): Inline. OHV. Four-cylinder. Cast iron block and head. Displacement: 121 cu. in. (2.0-liters). Bore & stroke: 3.50 x 3.15 in. Compression ratio: 9.3:1. Brake horsepower: 88 at 4800 R.P.M. Torque: 110 lb.-ft. at 2400 R.P.M. Five main bearings. Hydraulic valve lifters. Fuel injection. OPTIONAL V-6 (Cimarron): 60-degree, overhead-valve V-6. Cast iron block and head. Displacement: 173 cu. in. (2.8-liters). Bore & stroke: 3.50 x 2.99 in. Compression ratio: 8.9:1. Brake horsepower: 125 at 4800 R.P.M. Torque: 155 lb.-ft. at 3600 R.P.M. Four main bearings. Hydraulic valve lifters. Multi-point fuel injection. Chevrolet-built. BASE V-8 (Seville, Brougham, Eldorado): 90-degree, overhead valve V-8. Cast iron block and head. Displacement: 249 cu. in. (4.1-liters). Bore & stroke: 3.47 x 3.31 in. Compression ratio: 8.5:1. Brake horsepower: 135 at 4400 R.P.M. Torque: 200 lb.-ft. at 2200 R.P.M. Five main bearings. Hydraulic valve lifters. Fuel injection. BASE V-8 (DeVille, Fleetwood, Limo): Same as 249 cu. in. V-8 above, except: Brake H.P.: 125 at 4200 R.P.M. Torque: 190 lb.-ft. at 2200 R.P.M. OPTIONAL DIESEL V-6 (DeVille, Fleetwood): 90-degree overhead valve V-8. Cast iron block and head. Displacement: 262 cu. in. (4.3-liters). Bore & stroke: 4.06 x 3.39 in. Compression ratio: 21.6:1. Brake horsepower: 85 at 3600 R.P.M. Torque: 165 lb.-ft. at 1600 R.P.M. Four main bearings. Hydraulic valve lifters. Fuel injection. OPTIONAL DIESEL V-8 (Seville, Brougham, Eldorado): 90-degree, overhead valve V-8. Cast iron block and head. Displacement: 350 cu. in. (5.7-liters). Bore & stroke: 4.06 x 3.39 in. Compression ratio: 22.7:1. Brake horsepower: 105 at 3200 R.P.M. Torque: 200 lb.-ft. at 1600 R.P.M. Five main bearings. Hydraulic valve lifters. Fuel injection. Oldsmobile-built.

CHASSIS DATA: Wheelbase: (Cimarron) 101.2 in.; (Seville/Eldo) 114.0 in.; (DeV/Fleetwood) 110.8 in.; (Brougham) 121.5 in. Overall length: (Cimarron) 177.9 in.; (Seville) 204.8 in.; (DeV/Fleetwood) 195.0 in.; (Brghm) 221.0 in.; (Eldo) 204.5 in. Height: (Cimarron) 52.0 in.; (Seville/Eldo) 54.3 in.; (DeV/Fleetwood) 55.0 in.; (Brghm cpe) 54.6 in.; (Brghm sed) 56.7 in. Width: (Cimarron) 65.1 in.; (Seville) 70.9 in.; (DeV/Fleetwood) 71.7 in.; (Brghm) 76.5 in.; (Eldo) 70.6 in. Front Tread: (Cimarron) 55.4 in.; (Seville/Eldo) 59.3 in.; (DeV/Fleetwood) 60.3 in.; (Brghm) 61.7 in. Rear Tread: (Cimarron) 55.2 in.; (Seville/Eldo) 60.6 in.; (DeV/Fleetwood) 59.8 in.; (Brghm) 60.7 in. Standard Tires: (Cimarron) P195/70R13 SBR; (Sev/Eldo) P205/75R14 SBR WSW; (DeV/Fleetwood) P205/75R14 SBR WSW; (Brghm) P215/75R15 SBR WSW.

TECHNICAL: Transmission: Five-speed, floor shift manual transmission standard on Cimarron four: gear ratios: (1st) 3.92:1; (2nd) 2.15:1; (3rd) 1.33:1; (4th) 0.92:1; (5th) 0.74:1; (Rev) 3.50:1. Four-speed manual standard on Cimarron V-6: (1st) 3.31:1; (2nd) 1.95:1; (3rd) 1.95:1; (4th) 0.90:1; (Rev) 3.42:1. Cimarron three-speed Turbo Hydra-matic (THM125C) ratios: (1st) 2.84:1; (2nd) 1.60:1; (3rd) 1.00:1; (Rev) 2.07:1. Four-speed overdrive automatic (THM440-T4) standard on DeV/Fleetwood: (1st) 2.92:1; (2nd) 1.57:1; (3rd) 1.00:1; (4th) 0.67:1; (Rev) 2.38:1. Four-speed overdrive auto std on Eldo/Sev (THM325-4L) and Brougham (THM200-4R): (1st) 2.74:1; (2nd) 1.57:1; (3rd) 1.00:1; (4th) 0.67:1; (Rev) 2.07:1. Standard final drive ratio: (Cimarron) 3.83:1 w/5-spd, 3.18:1 w/auto., (Sev/Eldo) 3.15:1 exc. w/diesel, 2.93:1; (DeV/Fleetwood) 2.97:1 exc. w/diesel, 3.06:1; (Brghm) 3.42:1 exc. diesel, 2.93:1; (Limo) 2.97:1 in. Steering: (Cimarron/DeV/Eldo) rack-and-pinion; (others) recirculating ball. Front suspension: (Cimarron) Touring, w/MacPherson struts; (DeV/Fleetwood) MacPherson struts, lower control arms, coil springs and stabilizer bar; (Eldo/Sev) torsion bars, upper/lower control arms, stabilizer bar; (Brghm) upper/lower control arms, coil springs, stabilizer bar. Rear suspension: (Cimarron) semi-independent, trailing arms, coil springs, stabilizer bar; (DeV/Fleetwood) independent struts, coil springs, stabilizer bar, electronic level control; (Eldo/Sev) independent with semi-trailing arms, coil springs, stabilizer bar and electronic level control; (Brghm) four-link rigid axle, coil springs, electronic level control. Brakes: front disc, rear drum exc. Eldo/Sev, four-wheel discs. Disc diameter: (Eldo/Sev) 10.4 in.; (DeV/Fleetwood) 10.25 in.; (Brghm) 11.7 in.; Drum diameter: (DeV/Fleetwood) 8.9 in.; (Brghm) 11.0 in. Fuel tank: (Cimarron) 13.6 gal.; (Sev/Eldo) 20.3 gal. exc. diesel, 22.8; (DeV/Fleetwood) 18.0 gal.; (Brghm) 24.5 gal.

DRIVETRAIN OPTIONS: 173 cu. in. (2.8-liter) V-6 engine: Cimarron ($560). 4.3-liter diesel V-6 engine: DeV/Fleetwood (NC). 5.7-liter diesel V-8 engine; Eldo/Sev/Brghm (NC). California emission equipment ($99). Engine block heater ($45) exc. Cimarron ($20). Heavy-duty battery: Cimarron ($26); others ($40). 100-amp alternator: Eldo/Sev/Brghm ($50). H.D. radiator: Cimarron ($45). Four-speed manual trans: Cimarron ($75 credit). Three-speed automatic trans: Cimarron ($350). Heavy-duty ride package; Brghm ($116). FE2 touring suspension: Eldo/Sev ($115). FE2 touring pkg. (alum wheels, P215/65R15 Eagle GT tires, leather-wrapped steering wheel, revised suspension): DeV ($695); Fleetwood ($375). Delco/Bilstein suspension: Cimarron ($100); req'd w/V-6.

OPTION PACKAGES: Cimarron d'Oro ($975). Seville Elegante ($3879). Brougham or Fleetwood d'Elegance: cloth seating ($1250); leather ($1800). Cabriolet roof: DeV cpe ($498); Eldo ($420). Full cabriolet roof: Eldo/Sev ($995). Eldorado Biarritz ($3395). Eldorado Touring Coupe ($1975).

DEVILLE/FLEETWOOD BROUGHAM/ELDORADO/SEVILLE CONVENIENCE/APPEARANCE OPTIONS: Astroroof ($1225); N/A on limo. Electronic cruise control $185. Controlled-cycle wiper system: DeV/Fleetwood ($60). Rear defogger w/heated outside mirrors ($165-$215). Automatic door locks ($162). Remote-locking fuel filler door ($59). Garage door opener ($140); economy illuminated entry system ($76); std on Brougham. Dual comfort 55/45 front seats: DeV ($235). Memory driver's seat ($205-$225) exc. limo/conv. Six-way power passenger seat ($225) exc. Brougham. Power driver's seatback recliner ($155) exc. Fleetwood ($90); N/A limo. Power passenger seatback recliner: DeV ($155); Brghm/Fleetwood ($90). Power passenger seat recliner w/six-way power seat ($315-$380) exc. limo/Brghm. Leather-trimmed steering wheel ($99). Tilt/telescope steering wheel ($184). Power trunk lid release and pull-down: DeV/Fleetwood ($80-$120); release only, DeV/limo ($40). Theft deterrent system ($190). Twilight Sentinel ($79). Dimming Sentinel ($93-$128). Opera lamps: Eldo ($88). Trumpet horn ($38) exc. Seville. Electric remote-control outside mirrors ($101) exc. limo. Twin lighted vanity mirrors ($140). Automatic day/night mirror ($80). Electronic-tuning seek/scan AM/FM stereo radio w/cassette player ($299); w/cassette and Delco-GM/Bose sound system ($895) exc. Brghm. Electronic-tuning AM/FM stereo radio w/cassette and CB: Brghm ($577). CB radio ($278) exc. Brghm. Electronic-tuning radio with cassette and rear control: limo ($475). Triband antenna ($50). Two-tone paint: Sev ($600); Eldo ($345); partial Firemist, Eldo ($465). Firemist or Pearlmist paint ($235). Decklid and bodyside accent striping: DeV ($52). Bodyside molding: Eldo Touring cpe ($64). Door edge guards ($19-$29). License frames, each ($14). Front license bracket (NC) exc. DeVille. Leather seating area ($515-$680). Carpeted rubber floor mats: front ($43-$45); rear ($25). Trunk mat ($26). Alum wheels: Eldo/Sev/DeV ($429). Fleetwood ($114); std on limo. Spoked aluminum alloy wheels Eldo/Sev ($835); Biarritz/Elegante/conv. ($441). Locking wire wheels: Brghm ($860). Locking wire wheel covers ($315-$394) exc. Fleetwood. P225/70R15 white-letter tires: Eldo touring cpe ($100). Puncture-sealing tires ($135-$180) exc. limo.

CIMARRON CONVENIENCE/APPEARANCE OPTIONS: Vista Vent w/rear tilt ($310). Digital instrument cluster ($238). Garage door opener ($165). Six-way power passenger seat ($225). Twilight Sentinel ($85). Twin lighted vanity mirrors ($95). Seek/scan AM/FM stereo radio w/cassette ($223). Delete radio ($151 credit). Lower bodyside accent moldings ($450). Door edge guards ($25). License frame, rear ($15). Decklid luggage rack ($130). Cloth upholstery ($100 credit). Carpeted rubber floor mats: front ($38); rear ($22). Trunk mat ($26). Aluminum wheels, 14 in. ($40). P195/70R13 SBR WSW tires ($55). P205/60R14 SBR Eagle GT ($94). P205/60R14 SBR OWL tires ($171).

HISTORY: Fleetwood and DeVille were introduced April 5, 1984; Eldorado and Seville, October 2, 1984; Cimarron: November 8, 1984. Model year production: 394,840 (including 45,330 early '85 front-drive DeVille/Fleetwoods). That total included 11,968 V-6 engines and 1,088 diesels. Calendar year production: 322,765. Calendar year sales by U.S. dealers: 298,762 for a 3.6 percent market share. Model year sales by U.S. dealers: 310,942 (not including 46,356 front-drive DeVille/Fleetwoods sold as early 1985s).

Historical Footnotes: The delayed arrival of the new front-drive DeVille/Fleetwood was due to shortages of the Type 440 four-speed automatic transaxle produced at GM's Hydra-matic Division. Production had been delayed for six months. For that reason, both rear-drive and front-drive DeVilles were offered to the public at the same time for a while during 1984. A strike at GM of Canada affected supplies to over 30 General Motors plants in the U.S., including Cadillac's.

1986

All-new Eldorado and Seville models entered the lineup for 1986, loaded with a diagnostic system and electronic instruments. Anti-lock braking was a new option on Fleetwood and DeVille. All Cadillacs were now front-wheel drive except the big Brougham, which hung on for another year with a 5.0-liter V-8 under the hood. Luxury touches promoted in the full line catalog ranged from golden ignition keys all the way to elegant option packages, to deliver "the feeling of uncompromising excellence." In keeping with that promise, diesel engines departed from the Cadillac option list, victims of lack of interest and an unimpressive reliability record. The HT-4100 V-8 added stainless steel exhaust manifolds. Door locks had new rocker switches. Floor consoles contained an ashtray that opened at a finger's touch. And to keep up with the times, a cellular telephone ("discreetly" positioned in fold-down armrest) joined the option list. To attract buyers who preferred good handling to a cushy ride, DeVilles could also get a Touring Coupe or Touring Sedan option with stiffer suspension and related extras. Over 40 body colors were available, including nine Firemist shades and two Pearlmist (black cherry or black emerald) that changed character according to the angle and intensity of sunlight striking the car's surface.

CIMARRON—SERIES 6J—FOUR/V-6—Cimarron entered a new year sporting new wraparound taillamps at the restyled rear end, carrying a price tag that began above $13,000. Inside was new leather trim on the shift boot and knob (manual shift), at a redesigned console. A premium Delco-Bose sound system was now optional, and suspension components were revised. Cadillac's smallest had been extensively reworked as a mid-year 1985 entry with new front-end styling (more evidently Cadillac) and new optional electronic instrument cluster. Most important, though, was the V-6 option, giving the car a much needed performance boost. That "second generation" 2.8-liter V-6 with multi-port fuel injection came from Chevrolet. Standard engine continued to be the 2.0-liter four with five-speed (Getrag-designed) manual gearbox. The 2.8 could have four-speed manual or three-speed automatic. Even with the V-6 available, Cimarron still wasn't selling strongly, enjoying only a modest increase for 1985. To improve handling there was an optional Delco/Bilstein suspension with gas-charged front struts and rear shocks, plus stiffer front spring rates and thicker front stabilizer bar. That suspension was required with the V-6 engine. An impressive standard equipment list included Sierra Grain leather seating areas, air conditioning, cruise control, leather-trimmed tilt steering wheel, aluminum alloy wheels, and plenty of power gadgetry from six-way driver's seat to windows to trunk lid release. The standard seek/scan AM/FM stereo radio included a power antenna. Cimarron used a fine-patterned crosshatch grille with 'Cadillac' script at the driver's side, plus recessed quad rectangular headlamps. Wide parking/signal lamps were inset below the bumper rub strips; foglamps below them, flanking the air dam. 'Cimarron' script appeared on front doors. Yellow beige "chamois" was a new Cimarron color. Twenty dual-color accent stripes were available. Also revised this year was the d'Oro version, whose distinctive front end featured aero composite halogen headlamps and wraparound side marker lights. Offered with a white or red body, the package included: gold custom fine line accent stripes on beltline, rub strips and hood center; gold-accented grille; foglamp covers; lower bodyside accent moldings; d'Oro plaques on front fenders and dash; gold-tinted lay-down wheel ornament; and gold-tinted steering wheel spokes and horn pad emblem. P205/60R14 low profile performance steel-belted radial tires rode on gold-accented 14 in. aluminum alloy wheels. d'Oro also had grooved, body colored lower body accent moldings.

1986 Cadillac, Cimarron sedan. (OCW)

1986 Cadillac, Cimarron d'Oro sedan. (OCW)

SEVILLE—SERIES 6K—V-8—A brand new Seville rode the same new platform as Eldorado--7 inches shorter and 375 pounds lighter than before. Gone was the striking razor-edge styling of 1980-85, replaced by a body not much different from Eldorado's, or from other GM vehicles. Standard engine was the Cadillac 4.1-liter V-8, hooked to four-speed overdrive automatic transaxle. Seville's vertical grille had a fine-mesh crosshatch pattern. Clear rear lenses of the horizontal side marker lamps were angled to match wheel openings. Wide, clear parking/signal lamps were inset into the bumper area. The clearcoat finish had a new (standard) two-tone paint treatment. New front bucket seats were upholstered with Royal Prima cloth and Sierra Grain leather seating areas. The front console included a fold down armrest and storage compartments, while American walnut highlighted the instrument panel, console and steering wheel. Optional: a cellular phone with removable handset in locking storage compartment, and hidden mike between the sun visors. A "drivers information center" in the digital instrument cluster displayed electronic readouts of outside temperature, fuel economy and engine data, including a tachometer reading. Retained Accessory Power allowed many accessories to remain operative up to 10 minutes after shutting off the ignition (or until a door was opened). Standard equipment included reclining bucket seats, Twilight Sentinel headlamp control, cruise control, power trunk release, leather-trimmed tilt/telescope steering wheel, body-colored electric remote mirrors, an AM/FM stereo radio with seek/scan and digital display, power antenna, power four wheel

disc brakes, and aluminum alloy wheels. Seville's special-edition Elegante was offered again, carrying wire wheel covers and displaying a unique mid-tone paint scheme. The package included Tampico carpeting, deluxe floor mats, accent moldings, walnut appliqués, front seatback pockets, dual power reclining front bucket seats with power lumber support, memory driver's seat and six-way power passenger seat. American walnut wood plates trimmed the doors. Elegante was upholstered in Mayfair cloth with Sierra Grain leather seating areas, with a package price tag of $3,595 and up.

1986 Cadillac, deVille Touring Coupe. (OCW)

1986 Cadillac, Sedan deVille. (OCW)

DEVILLE—SERIES 6C—V-8—Front-drive Cadillacs came in coupe and sedan form, with prices starting just under $20,000. Standard engine was the transverse-mounted Cadillac 4.1-liter V-8, with four-speed overdrive automatic. The six-passenger interior sported a new seat trim design, while a closed-in, limousine-style back window was standard. DeVille's grille used many thin vertical bars, along with three horizontal bars and a 'Cadillac' script at the lower corner. Wraparound cornering lamps contained a small amber lens and large clear lens. Wide rectangular parking lights were set into the bumper, below the protective gray rub strips. Coupe or Sedan deVille script identification was at the back of the quarter panels. Wide, bright rocker moldings ran the length of the car. Coupe deVille's assist handles moved from front seatbacks to door lock pillars. Door panels and dash sported cherry woodgrain trim. Optional aluminum alloy wheels had new flush hubcaps. Anti-lock braking (ABS) was an important new option that would gradually find its way onto other models in the years ahead. Developed in accord with a German firm (Teves), ABS used sensors at each wheel to determine when one was about to lock. Then, the system would adjust hydraulic pressure to keep it from locking (and possibly skidding). ABS was also offered on Buick Electra and Olds Ninety-Eight this year. The 4.1-liter V-8 gained a little horsepower, while the 4.3-liter diesel departed. DeVille could have an optional touring package with handling components and "more aggressive, no-nonsense" look. It Included gray rocker moldings and front air dam, rear spoiler, recessed foglamps, body color taillamp bezels, tighter steering ratio (18.4:1), improved spring rates, a solid front stabilizer bar (standard one was hollow), stronger front lower control arm bushings, a much thicker rear stabilizer bar (18 vs. 12MM), and 15 in. performance tires on aluminum alloy wheels. Gray bumper rub strips had silver accent stripes. Starting in February 1986, the touring package was upgraded to include bigger exhaust pipe diameter, higher shift point between first and second gear, and five more horsepower in the engine. The new ratings were 135 horsepower, and 205 pound-feet of torque at 2300 R.P.M. Available on either coupe or sedan, the Touring package also included color keyed dual remote-control mirrors, leather-wrapped steering wheel, gray leather seats and interior trim--even removable quarter window louvers (on coupe). A 'Touring Coupe' or 'Touring Sedan' signature went on back windows. Rather than the whole package, buyers could opt for the Touring Suspension alone: Goodyear Eagle GT blackwall tires on 15 in. aluminum alloy wheels, bigger rear stabilizer bar, tighter shock valving, higher spring/bushing rates, faster steering ratio, and leather-trimmed steering wheel. A newly optional cellular telephone had an overhead microphone, and could operate through the front stereo speakers.

FLEETWOOD—SERIES 6C—V-8—Rather than a distinctly separate model, Fleetwood was actually an option package this year. A fine-grain formal cabriolet roof highlighted the closed-in rear window. The package consisted of reclining comfort seats with six-way power passenger adjustment, power trunk lid release, color-keyed power remote mirrors, a digital instrument panel, rear reading lamp, and accent striping on bodyside and decklid. Other styling extras: opera lamps, wire wheel covers, and Fleetwood identification. A Fleetwood d'Elegance option added walnut wood instrument panel and door trim plates along with deluxe carpeted floor mats, a leather trimmed steering wheel, and d'Elegance identification.

1986 Cadillac, Fleetwood Seventy-Five limousine. (OCW)

FLEETWOOD SEVENTY-FIVE LIMOUSINE—SERIES 6C—V-8—Traditionalists may have scoffed, but the modern front-drive, unibody Fleetwood limo still carried eight passengers in the style that appealed to "Seventy-Five" buyers a generation earlier. Under the hood was a transverse-mounted HT-4100 (4.1-liter) V-8 with digital fuel injection at the chassis, independent four-wheel suspension. Interior trim was revised for '86, electronic instruments became standard, and passengers could take advantage of an optional cellular phone with overhead mike to keep busy hands free. Cherry grain replaced the former walnut woodgrain on instrument panel and door trim plates. Automatic door locking prevented the doors from opening with the limo in gear. Oddly, the stretched limos were created from coupes rather than sedans, with extra doors added in the process of stretching the wheelbase from the normal 110.8 inches to 134.4. Limos came in six body colors, plus one Firemist shade and black cherry Pearlmist.

FLEETWOOD BROUGHAM—SERIES 6D—V-8—Cadillac's traditional rear-drive sedan was now powered by Oldsmobile's 5.0-liter V-8 engine and four-speed overdrive automatic. Standard features included a limo-like closed-in back window and standard full-length vinyl roof, plus a long list of Cadillac equipment--all for a price that began at $21,265. The Brougham coupe was dropped soon before the model year began, and the sedan didn't appear until February 1986, so '85 models remained on sale through the end of the year. At 121.5 inches, Brougham's wheelbase was the longest of any production automobile other than the stretched (but limited-production) front drive Fleetwood. Broughams came in a dozen standard colors plus five optional Firemist hues. Bright moldings ran from front fender tips, below the window line and back around the rear quarters. Broughams also carried large full-length rocker moldings and electroluminescent opera lamps. Standard equipment included an illuminated entry system, electronic climate control with outside-temperature display, power windows and door locks, AM/FM stereo seek/scan radio with power antenna, full padded roof, and whitewall all-season tires. Luxury-minded buyers could again step up to a Brougham d'Elegance. That package consisted of 50/50 Dual Comfort seats (six-way

power passenger seat) upholstered in tufted multi-button cloth or optional leather, a leather-trimmed steering wheel, power trunk release, rear reading lights, controlled-cycle wipers, Tampico carpeting, deluxe floor mats, three overhead assist handles, and turbine-vaned wheel covers.

1986 Cadillac, Eldorado America II coupe (special edition to commemorate sailing championship). (OCW)

1986 Cadillac, Eldorado Biarritz coupe. (OCW)

ELDORADO—SERIES 6E—V-8—A downsized E-body Eldo was designed, according to Cadillac, for "sporty elegance and sheer driving pleasure." Buick Riviera and Olds Toronado rode on the same chassis, but neither of them offered what Eldo had; a transverse-mounted V-8 under the hood. Like the similar Seville, the new Eldo was more than 16 in. shorter than its predecessor. On the down side, both of them now looked a little too much alike, lacking the special styling qualities that had set both apart in previous incarnations. Eldorado's side marker lamps were set into the bodyside moldings at front and rear, with 'Eldorado' script just ahead of the front wheel. A wreath-and-crest was on the wide rear pillar. At the rear were vertical taillamps, with vertical rectangular backup lights alongside the license plate. Along with the altered body came the demise of the Eldo convertible (for the second time in a decade). To improve rust resistance, all body panels (except the roof) were two-sided galvanized metal. Flush composite headlamps held both high- and low-beam bulbs. The fully independent suspension used a fiberglass transverse single leaf spring in the back. A new digital instrument cluster included a tachometer and engine gauges in a "driver information center." Standard equipment included a floor shift lever for the four-speed overdrive automatic transaxle, leather-trimmed tilt/telescope steering wheel, four wheel disc brakes, and front bucket seats with lumbar support. Also standard: cruise control, power windows and door locks, power trunk lid release, Twilight Sentinel, body-colored electric outside mirrors, seek/scan stereo radio with power antenna, aluminum alloy wheels and electronic level control. Eldorado's Biarritz package included a formal cabriolet vinyl roof, opera lamps, wide bodyside accent moldings, two-tone paint, and wire wheel covers. Inside luxuries included leather upholstery, Tampico carpeting, deluxe floor mats, walnut wood appliqués, dual power front reclining bucket seats with power lumbar support, a six-way power passenger seat, and front seatback pockets. American walnut wood found a place on the steering wheel, console, door trim and instrument panel. An optional touring suspension package (Goodyear Eagle GT high-performance P215/60R15 tires, rear stabilizer bar, stiffer front stabilizer bar and specially-tuned components) offered a firmer, better controlled ride, but included no special graphics or ornamentation.

I.D. DATA: All Cadillacs again had a 17-symbol Vehicle Identification Number (VIN), stamped on a metal tag attached to the upper left surface of the cowl, visible through the windshield. Coding was similar to 1985. Model year code changed to 'G' for 1986. Code '67' for convertible body was dropped. Engine coding was as follows: 'P' L4-121 TBI; 'W' V6-173 FI; '8' V8-249 DFI; 'Y' V8-307 4Bbl.

CIMARRON (FOUR/V-6)

Series No.	Body/Style No.	Body Type & Seating	Factory Price	Shipping Weight	Prod. Total
6J	G69	4-dr Sedan-5P	13128/13838	2514/2601	24,534

Price/Weight Note: Figure before the slash is for a Cimarron with four-cylinder engine, after slash for V-6.

SEVILLE (V-8)					
6K	S69	4-dr Sedan-5P	26756	3371	19,098

1986 Cadillac, Seville sedan. (OCW)

DEVILLE (FRONT-DRIVE V-8)					
6C	D47	2-dr Coupe-6P	19669	3239	Note 1
6C	D69	4-dr Sedan-6P	19990	3298	Note 2

FLEETWOOD (FRONT-DRIVE V-8)					
6C	B47	2-dr Coupe-6P	23443	N/A	Note 1
6C	B69	4-dr Sedan-6P	23764	N/A	Note 2

Note 1: Total two-door DeVille/Fleetwood production, 36,350.

Note 2: Total DeVille/Fleetwood four-door sedan production, 129,857.

FLEETWOOD SEVENTY-FIVE LIMOUSINE (V-8)					
6C	H23	4-dr Limo-8P	33895	3358	Note 3
6C	H33	4-dr Fml Limo-7P	35895	3657	Note 3

Note 3: Total limousine production, 1,000.

FLEETWOOD BROUGHAM (REAR-DRIVE V-8)					
6D	W69	4-dr Sedan-6P	21265	3945	49,115

ELDORADO (V-8)					
6E	L57	2-dr Coupe-5P	24251	3291	21,342

ENGINES: BASE FOUR (Cimarron) Inline. OHV. Four-cylinder. Cast iron block and head. Displacement: 121 cu. in. (2.0-liters). Bore & stroke: 3.50 x 3.15 in. Compression ratio: 9.3:1. Brake horsepower: 88 at 4800 R.P.M. Torque: 110 lb.-ft. at 2400 R.P.M. Five main bearings. Hydraulic valve lifters. Fuel injection. VIN Code: P. OPTIONAL V-6 (Cimarron): 60-degree overhead-valve V-6. Cast iron block and head. Displacement: 173 cu. in. (2.8-liters). Bore & stroke: 3.50 x 2.99 in. Compression ratio: 8.5:1. Brake horsepower: 125 at 4800 R.P.M. Torque 155 lb.-ft. at 3600 R.P.M. Four main bearings. Hydraulic valve lifters. Fuel injection. Chevrolet built. VIN Code: W. BASE V-8 (Seville, DeVille, Fleetwood, Limo, Eldorado): 90-degree, overhead valve V-8. Cast iron block and head. Displacement: 249 cu. in. (4.1-liters). Bore & stroke: 3.47 x 3.31 in. Compression ratio: 8.5:1. Brake horsepower: 130 at 4200 R.P.M. Torque: 200 lb.-ft. at 2200 R.P.M. Five main bearings. Hydraulic valve lifters. Fuel injection. VIN Code: 8. BASE V-8 (Brougham): 90-degree overhead valve V-8. Cast iron block and head. Displacement: 307 cu. in. (5.0-liters). Bore & stroke: 3.80 x 3.39 in. Compression ratio: 8.5:1. Brake horsepower: 140 at 3200 R.P.M. Torque: N/A. Five main bearings. Hydraulic valve lifters. Carburetor: 4Bbl. VIN Code: Y.

CHASSIS DATA: Wheelbase: (Cimarron) 101.2 in.; (Seville/Eldo) 108.0 in.; (DeV/Fleetwood) 110.8 in.; (Limo) 134.4 in.; (Brougham) 121.5 in. Overall length: (Cimarron) 177.9 in.; (Seville/Eldo) 188.2 in.; (DeV/Fleetwood) 195.0 in.; (Limo) 218.6 in.; (Brghm) 221.0 in. Height: (Cimarron) 52.0 in.; (Seville/Eldo) 53.7 in.; (DeV/Fleetwood/Limo) 55.0 in.; (Brghm) 56.7 in. Width: (Cimarron) 65.0 in.; (Seville) 70.9 in.; (DeV/Fleetwood) 71.7 in.; (Brghm) 75.3 in.; (Eldo) 71.3 in. Front Tread: (Cimarron) 55.4 in.; (Sev/Eldo) 59.9 in.; (Limo) 60.3 in.; (Brghm) 61.7 in. Rear Tread: (Cimarron) 55.2 in.; (Sev/Eldo) 59.9 in.; (Limo) 59.8 in.; (Brghm) 60.7 in. Standard Tires: (Cimarron) P195/70R13; (Sev/Eldo) P205/70R14; (DeV/Fleetwood) P205/75R14.

TECHNICAL: Transmission: Five-speed, floor shift manual transmission standard on Cimarron four; four-speed manual on V-6. Cimarron optional three-speed Turbo Hydra-matic (THM125C) gear ratios: (1st) 2.84:1; (2nd) 1.60:1; (3rd) 1.00:1; (Rev) 2.07:1. Four-speed overdrive automatic (THM200-4R) standard on Brougham: (1st) 2.74:1; (2nd) 1.57:1; (3rd) 1.00:1; (4th) 0.67:1; (Rev) 2.07:1. Five main bearings. Four-speed (THM440-T4) automatic on other models: (1st) 2.92:1; (2nd) 1.57:1; (3rd) 1.00:1; (4th) 0.70:1; (Rev) 2.38:1. Standard final drive ratio: (Cimarron) N/A; (Sev/Eldo) 2.97:1; (DeV/Fleetwood) 2.97:1; (Brghm) 2.73:1. Steering: power rack-and-pinion exc. Brougham, re-

circulating ball. Front suspension: same as 1985 exc. (Eldo/Sev) MacPherson struts with dual path mounts, coil springs and stabilizer bar. Rear suspension: same as 1985 exc. (Eldo/Sev) independent w/transverse leaf spring, struts, electronic level control. Brakes: front disc, rear drum exc. Eldo/Sev, four-wheel disc. Fuel tank: (Cimarron) 13.6 gal.; (Brghm) 20.7 gal.; (others) 18.0 gal.

DRIVETRAIN OPTIONS: 173 cu. in. (2.8-liter) EFI V-6 engine: Cimarron ($610). Four-speed manual transmission: Cimarron ($75 credit). Three-speed automatic trans.: Cimarron ($390). California emission equipment ($99). High altitude emissions pkg.: Cimarron (NC). Engine block heater: Cimarron ($20); others ($45). Heavy-duty battery: Cimarron ($26); others ($40). Heavy-duty radiator: Cimarron ($45). Electronic level control: Brghm ($203). F72 heavy-duty ride suspension pkg. incl. electronic level control: Brghm ($323). FE2 touring suspension pkg.: DeVille ($695); w/Fleetwood pkg. ($375); Eldo ($200). FE2 touring suspension (15 in. alum alloy wheels, P215/60R15 Goodyear Eagle GT hi-perf BSW tires, rear stabilizer bar, stiffer front stabilizer bar): Eldo/Seville ($155). Delco/Bilstein suspension system: Cimarron V-6 ($100).

OPTION PACKAGES: Cimarron d'Oro package ($975). Fleetwood package; cloth seats ($3150); leather ($3700). Fleetwood d'Elegance: cloth seating ($4445); leather ($4995). DeVille Touring Coupe or Touring Sedan package ($2880). Brougham d'Elegance pkg.: cloth seats ($1950); leather ($2500). Eldorado Biarritz: cloth ($3095); leather ($3495). Seville Elegante: cloth ($3595); leather ($3995). Black cambric cloth roof: DeV ($925). Formal cabriolet roof: DeV cpe ($698). Security option package: DeV/limo ($290); Sev/Eldo ($460); Brghm ($380).

DEVILLE/BROUGHAM/SEVENTY-FIVE/ELDORADO/SEVILLE CONVENIENCE/APPEARANCE OPTIONS: Astroroof ($1255); N/A on limo. Electronic cruise control: DeV/Brghm/limo ($195). Controlled-cycle wiper system: DeV/Brghm/limo ($60). Rear defogger w/heated outside mirrors ($170). Automatic door locks ($170) exc. limo. Remote fuel filler door release ($60). Garage door opener ($140-$165). Illuminated entry system ($80). Digital instrument cluster: DeV ($238). Cellular telephone: DeV ($2850); phone provision ($395). Six-way power passenger seat for dual comfort seats: DeV ($235). Two-position memory seat: DeV ($235); Brghm ($215). Six-way power passenger seat: Eldo/Sev/Brghm ($235). Power driver's seat recliner: DeV/Brghm ($95-$160). Power passenger seat recliner: DeV/Brghm ($95-$395). Power passenger seat recliner w/six-way power seat: Eldo/Sev ($330). Leather-trimmed steering wheel: DeV/Brghm/limo ($105). Tilt/telescope steering wheel: DeV/Brghm/limo ($195). Power trunk lid release: DeV/Brghm/limo ($40). Trunk release and pull-down ($80-$120). Theft deterrent system ($200). Twilight Sentinel: DeV/Brghm/limo ($85). Dimming Sentinel headlamp control ($130) exc. Brougham. Guidematic headlamp control: Brghm ($95). Rear reading lights: Brghm ($33). Trumpet horn: DeV/Brghm/limo ($45). Electric remote-control outside mirrors: DeV/Brghm ($101). Twin lighted vanity mirrors ($140). Automatic day/night mirror ($80). Electronic tuning AM/FM stereo radio w/cassette: Brghm ($299); w/cassette and CB ($577). ET AM/FM stereo radio w/cassette and graphic equalizer ($319) exc. Brougham. ET radio with cassette and rear control: limo ($475). ET AM/FM stereo radio w/cassette and Delco-GM/Bose music system ($895) exc. Brghm/limo. CB radio: DeV ($278). Power triband antenna: DeV/Brghm ($55). Firemist or Pearlmist paint ($240). Two-tone Seville paint ($600). Decklid/bodyside accent striping: DeV/Brghm ($55). Accent moldings: Eldo ($75). Color-keyed door edge guards ($19-$29). License frames, each ($15). Front license bracket: Eldo (NC). Dual comfort seats: DeV ($245). Leather seating area ($400-$550) exc. limo ($940). Carpeted floor mats: front ($45); rear ($25). Trunk mat ($26). Wire wheels: Brghm ($860-$940). Aluminum alloy wheels: DeV ($115-$435); Seville Elegante (NC). Wire wheel covers: Eldo/Sev ($190); DeV/Brghm ($320-$400). Turbine-vaned wheel covers: Brghm ($80). Puncture-sealing tires ($145-$190) exc. limo. P215/65R15 WSW tires: DeV ($66). P215/60R15 SBR BSW tires: Seville (NC). P215/60R15 SBR WSW: Sev/Eldo ($66).

CIMARRON CONVENIENCE/APPEARANCE OPTIONS: Vista Vent ($310). Garage door opener transmitter ($165); retainer ($25). Digital instrument cluster ($238). Twilight Sentinel ($85). Twin lighted visor vanity mirrors ($95). Electronic-tuning seek/scan AM/FM stereo radio w/cassette ($223); w/cassette and Delco-GM/Bose music system ($895). Delete radio ($151 credit). Lower bodyside accent moldings ($450). Door edge guards ($25). Rear license frame ($15). Decklid luggage rack ($130). Cloth seat trim ($100 credit). Carpeted rubber floor mats: front ($38); rear ($22). Trunk mat ($26). 14 in. aluminum alloy wheels ($40). P195/70R13 SBR WSW tires ($55). P205/60R14 SBR BSW tires ($94). P205/60R14 SBR RWL ($171): w/d'Oro ($77).

HISTORY: Introduced: September 26, 1985, except Eldorado/Seville, November 14, 1985; Fleetwood Brougham, February 13, 1986. Model year production: 281,296, including 3,628 with four-cylinder engine and 20,906 with V-6, for a 3.6 percent share of the industry total. Calendar year production: 319,031. Calendar year sales by U.S. dealers: 304,057. Model year sales by U.S. dealers: 300,053 for a 3.8 percent market share.

Historical Footnotes: Cadillac sales dropped a bit for the second year in-a-row, barely edging over 300,000, but that was enough to retain dominance among makers of luxury cars. E-body Eldorado production began at the new Hamtramck, Michigan, plant in late 1985, but delays kept output below peak levels. As a result, Eldorado and Seville sales dropped by half. The rear-drive Fleetwood Brougham enjoyed a comeback of sorts, due to low gasoline prices and its upgraded V-8 engine. Front-drive DeVilles and Fleetwoods also gained in sales for the second year. Cimarron rose as well, but not by much. Cadillac clung to hopes that Cimarron would gain strength against new imports such as Acura Legend, despite complaints that it was little more than a fancy Cavalier. At the upper end of the scale, the future held a new ultra-luxurious two-seater Allante, due out for 1987.

1987

The 1987 Cadillacs, energized by what was regarded as "The new spirit of Cadillac," as well as the introduction of the Allante, featured engineering, convenience and styling refinements. A major effort was made to provide the 1987 Cadillacs with enhanced security features. All major body components were now tagged with the car's individual vehicle identification number. Cadillac's door-into-roof design was regarded as "an inherent security feature that helps reduce access through otherwise vulnerable window weatherstripping." Another important security feature was a standard encapsulated door linkage system that enclosed all exterior-to-interior door handle hinges in single castings, thus rendering "slim-jim" devices ineffective. All models except the Cimarron were also offered with a theft-deterrent system using the underhood horn as an alarm, and the front door lock cylinders and electric door locks to activate itself. The historic nature of the Allante's debut was established by John Grettenberger, who called it "General Motors' new passenger car flagship."

CIMARRON - SERIES 6J - V-6 - The 2.8-liter V-6 and MG 582 five-speed manual transmission were standard on the 1987 Cimarron. Design revisions raised the engine's compression ratio to 8.9:1 from 8.5:1. Driving characteristics were enhanced through changes in the Cimarron's front suspension bushings and stabilizer bar. Lower engine mounts were also used as was a lightweight master cylinder. All Cimarrons had composite tungsten headlamps that had previously been included in the d'Oro package, which was no longer offered. New cashmere cloth and leather seating areas were now offered as an option.

1987 Cadillac, deVille Touring Coupe. (OCW)

1987 Cadillac, deVille Touring Sedan. (OCW)

DEVILLE - SERIES 6C - V-8 AND FLEETWOOD D'ELEGANCE - SERIES 6C - V-8 - Both Cadillacs had new deflected disc front strut valving, a new two-piece front strut mount, new shear-type rear strut mounts and new hydro-elastic engine mounts. The result of these changes was a smoother and quieter ride. The rear brake drums and master cylinder was also revised to provide less pedal travel and improved modulation. Exterior changes included a rear quarter and bumper extension and new taillamps that added 1.5 inches to overall length, and dual-stacked red reflex appliqués, centered between the taillights and the license plate opening. Front-end changes for 1987 involved a restyled grille, new composite headlamps and new hood header molding. New front side markers and cornering and reflex lamps were also used. Nine new exterior colors were introduced. Selected models were also offered with a new cabriolet top. The deVille touring coupe and sedan models were equipped with the ride and handling package plus a front air dam, front fog lights, specific rocker panel molding, body side accent molding, deck lid spoiler, leather seating areas, removable vertical louvers for the coupe quarter windows and leather-wrapped steering wheel, lever knobs and gearshift lever.

1987 Cadillac, Fleetwood Sixty Special sedan. (OCW)

FLEETWOOD SIXTY SPECIAL - SERIES 6C - V-8 - The Sixty Special was created by giving a five-inch wheelbase extension and additional amenities to the d'Elegance model. The new Sixty Special had such exclusive features as rear passenger compartment footrests, rear overhead console, anti-lock brakes and a full vinyl top. The Sixty Special's wider sail panels gave it a more formal look.

FLEETWOOD SEVENTY FIVE LIMOUSINE - SERIES 6C - V-8 - Both the front and rear styling of the limousine and formal limousine was revised for 1987. A new grille, header molding and composite headlights with wrap-around bezel and cornering lamps were used. Rear styling now featured elongated quarter extensions against which the taillamps, bumper and bumper trim fascia fit flush. Also new was a grooved six-inch wide rocker molding made of a stainless steel/aluminum composite with a single-rib accent groove. For 1987, new hydro-elastic engine mounts were used to further isolate powertrain vibration.

1987 Cadillac, Brougham sedan. (OCW)

BROUGHAM - SERIES 6D - V-8 - During 1986, sales of the Brougham increased by more than 30 percent. One result was a major effort to further improve its overall interior, exterior

1906 Cadillac Model M Light Touring Car
(Long Island Automotive Museum)

1907 Cadillac Model K Two-Seat Runabout
(Marcella Knight - Peoria, Illinois)

1911 Cadillac Model 30 Touring Car
(Long Island Automotive Museum)

1916 Cadillac Type 53
Seven-Passenger Touring Car
(C. Donald Scharf)

1927 Cadillac 314-A
Custom Sport Phaeton
(Jim Gwaltney photo)

1929 Cadillac 341-B
Convertible Coupe
(Charles J. Noto -
Hauppage, New York)

1931 Cadillac 452 V-16 Convertible Coupe
(Long Island Automotive Museum)

1934 LaSalle
Model 350 Coupe
(Ron Sobran photo)

1936 Cadillac Series 90 V-16 Convertible Sedan
(Frank Nicodemus - Wappingers Falls, New York)

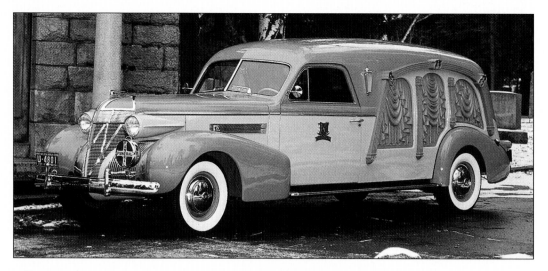

**1939 Cadillac Sayers & Scovill Imperial "Carved Panel" Funeral Coach
(Jerry & Ronda Kayser - Moses Lake, Washington)**

**1939 LaSalle
Series 39-50 Coupe
(Maurice & Jean Hawa -
Miami, Florida)**

**1941 Cadillac Series 61 Five-Passenger Coupe
(Frank L.Nemechek - Batavia, Illinois)**

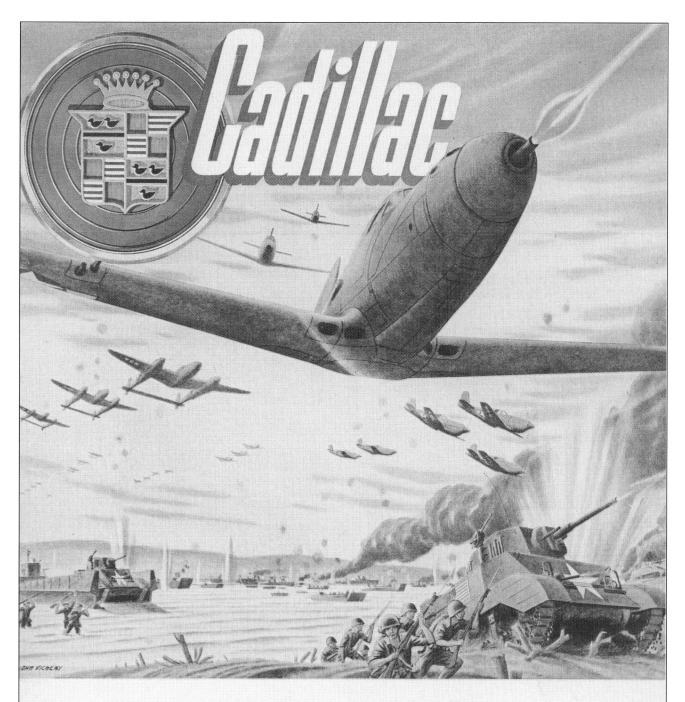

In the Vanguard of Invasion

In every theater of war, wherever American forces are hitting the enemy—by land, by sea or in the air—Cadillac products are usually in the vanguard of invasion.

Such famous fighter planes as the Airacobra, the Lightning, the P-40 and the Mustang—powered by Allison, America's foremost liquid-cooled aircraft engine—all carry Cadillac-built parts. *For Cadillac builds many parts for Allison.*

In land invasions, Cadillac-built tanks are often among the first to "hit the beach" in the desperate business of overcoming enemy defense positions. And these tanks—powered with Cadillac V-type, eight-cylinder engines, equipped with Hydra-Matic transmissions—are equally busy once the beachhead is won, and land fighting is in progress.

"Craftsmanship a Creed . . . Accuracy a Law" has been a Cadillac principle for more than forty years. Thus, all the skills we have acquired throughout this long period of peacetime activity are now being devoted to one single end . . . that the finest soldiers in the world shall not lack for anything that it is within our power to produce.

Every Sunday Afternoon . . . GENERAL MOTORS SYMPHONY OF THE AIR —NBC Network

CADILLAC MOTOR CAR DIVISION — GENERAL MOTORS CORPORATION

LET'S ALL
BACK THE ATTACK
BUY WAR BONDS

1941 Cadillac Sixty Special Four-Door Sedan
(John C. Low - Washington, Pennsylvania)

1947 Cadillac Series 62 Convertible
(Allan A. Rodriguez - San Jose, Costa Rica)

1951 Cadillac Series 62 Convertible
(Ron Sobran photo)

**1955 Cadillac Eldorado Convertible
(Frank Nicodemus - Wappingers Falls, New York)**

**1956 Cadillac Eldorado Seville Two-Door Hardtop
(William J. Boucher - Smithtown, New York)**

**1956 Cadillac Series 62
Four-Door Sedan
(Dan Reed -
Atglen, Pennsylvania)**

**1957 Cadillac Eldorado Biarritz Convertible
(Ed Brandenburg - Huntington Beach, California)**

During the flashy '50s, exterior colors were brought
into the interior also.

The "bat wing" filter body channels air
from the remote air cleaners to the dual
four-barrel carburetors of Ed
Brandenburg's '57 Eldorado.

1957 Cadillac Series 62 Convertible
(Jim Stahley - East Brunswick, New Jersey)

1958 Cadillac Eldorado Biarritz Convertible
(Fred Marsilio - Smithtown, New York)

**1960 Cadillac Eldorado Biarritz Convertible
(Jim Rudnick - Palatine, Illinois)**

1966 Cadillac Series 62 Convertible
(Donald F. Bowser -
Worthington, Pennsylvania)

**1970 Cadillac Eldorado Coupe
(Michael Seaton-Elliott - Hightstown, New Jersey)**

**1973 Cadillac Eldorado Indy Pace Car Convertible
(Tim Pawl - West Bloomfield, Michigan)**

**1975 Cadillac Eldorado Convertible
(Peg Van Luven - Clinton Township, Michigan)**

**1976 Cadillac Seville Four-Door Sedan
(Gary Hauver - Gulf Breeze, Florida)**

1977 Cadillac Sedan deVille Four-Door Sedan
(Gary Hauver - Gulf Breeze, Florida)

1978 Cadillac Seville Custom Convertible
(Ben F. Osborn - Palm Desert, California)

1979 Cadillac Fleetwood Limousine
(James Dougherty - Columbus, Ohio)

1984 Cadillac Eldorado Coupe
(Michael R. Zimmerman -
Wayne, Pennsylvania)

1993 Cadillac Allanté Convertible
(Cadillac Motor Division)

1993 Cadillac Brougham d'Elegance
(Cadillac Motor Division)

The interior of the 1993 Brougham d'Elegance
typified Cadillac luxury.
(Cadillac Motor Division)

Cadillac has long lent the quality and prestige of its products to be modified for use as "professional cars" such as limousines, ambulances, hearses, and flower cars. Shown is a 1952 Cadillac Sayers & Scovill Florentine flower car owned by Eddie Moore, of Orange, Virginia. (photos by Gregg Merksamer)

1961 Cadillac Sayers & Scovill Victoria funeral coach owned by Jonathan Stegura, of Pennsylvania.

1967 Cadillac Miller-Meteor Embassy flower car owned by Carlton Ham, of Franklin, New Hampshire.

First Lady Hillary Rodham Clinton's armor-plated 1995 Cadillac Formal Limousine, by Limousine Werks (photographed in Newburgh, N.Y. July 14, 1998).

1995 Cadillac Eureka Monticello funeral coach with Signature trim package.

1998 Cadillac Eagle Coupe Defleur casket-carrying flower car.

Heralding the cutting edge of Cadillac design for the new millennium, the Evoq concept car is said to have styling cues that will soon be seen throughout the offerings from General Motors' prestige division. (Ron Sobran photo)

The proposed, new Cadillac luxury/sporting two-seater is expected to draw heavily from the Evoq concept vehicle, which began making the rounds of the auto shows during 1999. (Ron Sobran photo) and mechanical features. A new cross-hatch grille, revised header molding and new park and turn signal lamps were introduced. Red reflexes were added to the rear panel and a Cadillac script replaced the Fleetwood script on the deck lid. Brougham script replaced Fleetwood Brougham on the quarter panels. The upgraded d'Elegance version shared the features of the 1986 model along with the changes found in the Brougham. A new tri-color saddle interior combination was used on both models. The Brougham's parking lamp and rear taillights were changed from gold to silver.

1987 Cadillac, Eldorado coupe. (OCW)

ELDORADO - SERIES 6E - V-8 - The 20th anniversary version of the Eldorado featured changes in its suspension and engine damping. The use of deflected disc strut valves on cars with the touring suspension provided a more comfortable ride and better road manners. New hydro-elastic engine mounts were also used. New vehicle-sensitive rear seat belts were used on all Eldorados. A new cashmere cloth and leather interior trim were offered. Twelve new exterior colors, for a total of 19, were introduced. Larger P205/75R14 standard tires was also offered. For the first time, Cadillac offered the cabriolet top as an option for the base Eldorado. The Biarritz had a redesigned cabriolet top.

SEVILLE - SERIES 6K - V-8 - The Seville shared the Eldorado's new features and design changes. New rear electric door locks allowing the driver to lock all doors after opening one rear door without returning to the front door was a welcome feature. The Seville had a standard dual-tone finish; the Elegante had a two-color mid-tone finish. A monotone finish was available for both models. The base Seville was also available in the mid-tone finish.

1987 Cadillac, Allante convertible with detachable hardtop. (OCW)

ALLANTE - SERIES 6V - V-8 - The ultra-luxury Allante's body and interior were built by Pininfarina in Turin, Italy. The finished bodies were flown to GM's Detroit-Hamtramck assembly plant where the powerplant and suspension were installed. Each completed model was driven for 25 miles for an individual evaluation. The front-wheel drive Allante was powered by a specially tuned version of Cadillac's 4.1-liter V-8. It used special magnesium rocker arm covers and an aluminum oil pan. The Allante chassis was intended for use on a convertible. Its all-independent suspension consisting of front MacPherson struts and coil springs in conjunction with rear MacPherson struts and a composite transverse leaf spring provided skidpad readings of 0.82g. Also found on the Allante was a new Bosch II anti-lock braking system and exclusive P225/60VR15 Eagle GT tires. Only two interior options were available for the Allante: a choice of two leather colors and a cellular telephone. The Allante interior was available in either burgundy or natural saddle leather. The Allante seats were manufactured by Recaro and featured a 10-way memory system. The Allante's exterior design, characterized by a wedge-shaped profile and a pronounced forward rake, was aerodynamic with a drag coefficient of 0.34. Cadillac General Manager John Grettenberger remarked that "Allante owners will find that even with the top down they will be able to carry on a conversation in normal tones." Sergio Pininfarina reported that working with Cadillac to produce the Allante was "the realization of a lifelong dream."

I.D. DATA: The 1987 Cadillac had a 17-symbol vehicle identification number (VIN) stamped on a metal tag attached to the upper left surface of the cowl visible through the windshield.

The code was as follows: the first digit, "1," represented the manufacturing country (United States), the second, "G," represented General Motors, the third, "6," represented Cadillac, the fourth was the car line, GM body, as follows: C-deVille and Fleetwood, D-Brougham, E-Eldorado, J-Cimarron, K-Seville, V-Allante. The fifth symbol was the series identification: G-Cimarron, D-deVille, B-Fleetwood, S-Fleetwood Sixty Special, W-Brougham, L-Eldorado, S-Seville, R-Allante. Digits six and seven represent the body style: 47-two-door coupe, 69 four-door sedan, 57-Eldorado coupe, 69-Seville four-door sedan, 67-Allante. The eighth digit identifies the engine: "W"-2.8L V-6; "Y"-5.0L V-8; "1"-2.0L L4; "7"-4.1L V-8; "8"-4.1L V-8; and "9"-5.0L V-8. A check digit follows. The 10th digit represents the model year, "H" for 1987. The next digit represents the assembly plant. The remaining six digits represent the production sequence: Cimarron: 000001 and up; Seville: 000001 and up; deVille, Fleetwood and Sixty Special: 000001 and up; Eldorado: 000001 and up; Brougham: 000001 and up; Allante: 000001 and up.

Cimarron (Four/V-6)

Series No.	Body/Style No.	Body Type & Seating	Factory Price	Shipping Weight	Prod. Total
6J	G69	4-dr. Sed.-5P	15032/N/A	2604/2715	14,561

DeVille (V-8)

Series No.	Body/Style No.	Body Type & Seating	Factory Price	Shipping Weight	Prod. Total
6C	D47	2-dr. Coupe-6P	21316	3312	32,975
6C	D69	4-dr. Sedan-6P	21659	3370	Note 1

Fleetwood D'Elegance (V-8)

Series No.	Body/Style No.	Body Type & Seating	Factory Price	Shipping Weight	Prod. Total
6C	B69	4-dr. Sedan-6P	26104	3421	Note 1

Fleetwood Sixty Special (V-8)

Series No.	Body/Style No.	Body Type & Seating	Factory Price	Shipping Weight	Prod. Total
6C	S69	4-dr. Sedan-6P	34850	3408	Note 1

Fleetwood 75 (V-8)

Series No.	Body/Style No.	Body Type & Seating	Factory Price	Shipping Weight	Prod. Total
6C	H23	4-dr. Limo.-8P	36510	3678	Note 2
6C	H33	4-dr. Fml. Limo.-7P	36580	3798	Note 2

Note 1: Total DeVille/Fleetwood sedan production, 129,521.

Note 2: Total limousine production, 302.

Brougham (V-8)

Series No.	Body/Style No.	Body Type & Seating	Factory Price	Shipping Weight	Prod. Total
6D	W69	4-dr. Sedan-6P	22637	4046	65,504

Eldorado (V-8)

Series No.	Body/Style No.	Body Type & Seating	Factory Price	Shipping Weight	Prod. Total
6E	L57	2-dr. Coupe-6P	23740	3360	17,775

Seville (V-8)

Series No.	Body/Style No.	Body Type & Seating	Factory Price	Shipping Weight	Prod. Total
6K	S69	4-dr. Sedan-6P	26326	3420	18,578

Allante (V-8)

Series No.	Body/Style No.	Body Type & Seating	Factory Price	Shipping Weight	Prod. Total
6V	R67	2-dr. Conv.-2P	54700	3494	3,366

ENGINES: STANDARD (Cimarron): Overhead valve V-6. Cast iron block. Displacement: 173 cu. in. (2.8 liters). Bore & stroke: 3.50 x 2.99 in. Compression ratio: 8.9:1. Brake horsepower: 125 @ 4500 rpm. Torque: 160 lb.-ft. @ 3600 rpm. Hydraulic valve lifters. Multi-port fuel injection. STANDARD (deVille, Fleetwood d'Elegance, Fleetwood Sixty Special, Fleetwood Seventy Five, Seville, Eldorado): 90-degree, overhead valve V-8. Aluminum block and cast iron cylinder liners, cast iron cylinder heads. Displacement: 249 cu. in. (4.1 liters). Bore & stroke: 3.47 x 3.31 in. Compression ratio: 8.5:1. Brake horsepower: 130 @ 4200 rpm. Torque: 200 lb.-ft. @ 2200 rpm. Five main bearings. Hydraulic valve lifters. Digital electronic fuel injection. STANDARD (Allante): 90-degree, overhead valve, V-8. Aluminum block and cast iron cylinder liners, cast iron cylinder heads. Displacement: 250 cu. in. (4.0 liters). Bore & stroke: 3.46 x 3.31 in. Compression ratio: 8.5:1. Brake horsepower: 170 @ 4300 rpm. Torque: 235 lb.-ft. @ 3200 rpm. Five main bearings. Roller hydraulic valve lifters. Sequential multi-port fuel injection. STANDARD (Brougham): 90-degree, overhead valve, V-8. Cast iron block and cast iron cylinder heads. Displacement: 307 cu. in. (5.0 liters). Bore & stroke: 3.8 x 3.39 in. Compression ratio: 8.0:1. Brake horsepower: 140 @ 3200 rpm. Torque: 346 lb.-ft. @ 2000 rpm. Five main bearings. Hydraulic valve lifters. Four-barrel carburetor.

CHASSIS DATA: Wheelbase: (Cimarron) 101.2 in.; (deVille and Fleetwood d'Elegance) 110.8 in.; (Sixty Special) 115.8 in.; (Seville and Eldorado) 108.0 in.; (Allante) 99.4 in.; (Brougham) 121.5 in.; (Fleetwood Seventy Five) 134.4 in. Overall Length: (Cimarron) 177.8 in.; (deVille and Fleetwood d'Elegance) 202.3 in.; (Sixty Special) 201.7 in.; (Seville) 190.8 in.; (Eldorado) 191.2 in.; (Allante) 178.6 in.; (Brougham) 221 in.; (Fleetwood Seventy Five) 218.6 in. Height: (Cimarron) 52.1 in.; (deVille and Fleetwood d'Elegance) 55.0 in.; (Sixty Special) 55.0 in.; (Seville and Eldorado) 53.7 in.; (Allante) 52.2 in.; (Brougham) 56.7 in.; (Fleetwood Seventy Five) 55.0 in. Width: (Cimarron) 65.0 in.; (deVille and Fleetwood d'Elegance) 71.7 in.; (Sixty Special) 71.7 in.; (Seville) 70.9 in.; (Eldorado) 71.3 in.;

(Allante) 73.5 in.; (Brougham) 76.5 in.; (Fleetwood Seventy Five) 71.7 in. Front Tread: (Cimarron) 55.4 in.; (deVille and Fleetwood d'Elegance) 60.3 in.; (Sixty Special) 60.3 in.; (Seville and Eldorado) 59.9 in.; (Allante) 60.4 in.; (Brougham) 61.7 in.; (Fleetwood Seventy Five) 60.3 in. Rear Tread: (Cimarron) 55.2 in.; (deVille and Fleetwood d'Elegance) 59.8 in.; (Sixty Special) 59.8 in.; (Seville and Eldorado) 59.9 in.; (Allante) 60.4 in.; (Brougham) 60.7 in.; (Fleetwood Seventy Five) 59.8 in. Standard Tires: (Cimarron) P195/70R14; (deVille and Fleetwood d'Elegance) Michelin P205/70R14; (Sedan deVille, Fleetwood Sedan and Sixty Special) P205/70R14; (Seville and Eldorado) P205/70R14; (Touring) Goodyear Eagle GT4 P215/65R15; (Allante) Goodyear Eagle VL P225/55VR16; (Brougham) Michelin P225/75R15.

1987 Cadillac, Seville sedan. (OCW)

TECHNICAL: Transmission: (Cimarron) Muncie-Getrag five-spd. manual; (deVille, Fleetwood, Eldorado, Seville) THM 440-T4 automatic four-speed (includes overdrive and viscous converter clutch); (Allante) THM F7 automatic four-speed (includes overdrive, viscous converter clutch and electronic shift control); (Brougham) THM 200-4R TCC automatic four-speed (includes overdrive and torque converter clutch). Steering: All models exc. Brougham: power-assisted rack and pinion. Brougham: power-assisted recirculating ball. Ratios: deVille, Fleetwood: 19.1:1; Seville, Eldorado: 16.5:1; Touring: 15.6:1; Allante: 15.6:1; Brougham: 15-13:1. Front Suspension: (All models exc. Brougham) Independent MacPherson strut with coil springs, strut-type shock absorbers (integral-in strut and electronic variable on Allante) and stabilizer bar; (Brougham) Independent with short/long arms, coil springs, direct acting shock absorbers, and link-type stabilizer bar. Rear suspension: (All models exc. Brougham): fully independent with coil springs. Automatic level control and strut-type superlift shock absorbers on all models exc. Cimarron, Allante and Brougham. Allante: integral-in strut electronic variable shock absorbers with no rear stabilizer; Brougham: four link, coil springs with automatic level control and direct acting shock absorbers. Brakes: Cimarron, Brougham, Fleetwood: power front discs, rear drum; Seville, Allante and Eldorado: power disc, front and rear. Body Construction: (All models exc. Brougham): integral body-frame; Brougham: separate body on frame. Fuel Tank: (Cimarron) 13.6 gal.; (deVille, Fleetwood) 18.0 gal.; (Eldorado, Seville) 18.8 gal.; (Allante) 22 gal.; (Brougham) 25 gal.

DRIVETRAIN OPTIONS: (Seville touring option and Eldorado) Touring Suspension, consists of 15 in. aluminum alloy wheels, Eagle GT P215/60R15 tires, rear stabilizer bar, stiffer front stabilizer bar, turned suspension components, engine block heater; (Brougham sedan) heavy-duty ride package, trailer towing package, wire wheels; (coupe and sedan deVille) ride and handling package, aluminum alloy wheels; (Sixty Special) Ride and handling touring package, aluminum alloy wheels. Option Packages: deVille performance enhancement package (included in touring coupe and sedan, may also be ordered separately), contains retuned suspension, 15 in. aluminum alloy wheels, Eagle GT P215/65R15 blackwall tires, 32mm front and 18mm rear stabilizer bars, faster steering ratio; also available with Eagle GT whitewall tires. Seville Elegante, contains power recliners and power lumbar support adjusters for front bucket seats, six-way power seat adjuster for front bucket seats, front seatback pockets and leather-trimmed headrests. Other features consist of mid-tone paint treatment, wire wheel discs, special interior with Mayfair cloth and Sierra grain leather, and American walnut door trim plates. Eldorado Biarritz, contains power recliners and power lumbar support adjusters for front bucket seats, six-way power seat adjuster for front bucket seats, front seatback pockets and leather-trimmed headrests. Other features include American walnut instrument panel, console and door trim plates, two-tone paint, cabriolet padded roof

with opera lights, closed-in rear window, wire wheel discs, Mayfair cloth and Sierra combination seating areas, accent molding, Biarritz identification, deluxe Tampico carpeting and floor mats. Brougham d'Elegance: six-way front power seat adjuster, trunk lid release, controlled cycle wipers, adjustable rear seat reading lamps, manual passenger front seat recliner, three roof-mounted assist handles, dual comfort 50/50 front seats, multi-button seat trim, accent striping, Brougham d'Elegance turbine vane wheel discs, d'Elegance embroidery on doors, d'Elegance identification, deluxe Tampico floor carpeting and mats.

CIMARRON CONVENIENCE/APPEARANCE OPTIONS: Garage door opener, Vista Vent sunroof, leather and cashmere cloth seating areas, six-way power seat, visor vanity mirrors, Delco-GM Bose symphony sound system, Delco AM stereo/ FM stereo electronically tuned receiver with cassette player, electronic instrument cluster, aluminum alloy wheels, door edge guards, floor mats, deck lid luggage rack, heavy-duty battery, 13 in. narrow strip whitewalls.

DEVILLE CONVENIENCE/APPEARANCE OPTIONS: Cellular telephone, automatic day/night mirror, controlled cycle wiper system, rear window defogger, dimming sentinel, automatic door locks, garage door opener, illuminated entry system, electrically powered mirrors, power driver seat recliner, six-way power seat adjuster, dual comfort 45/55 seats, tilt and telescope steering wheel, trumpet horn, trunk lid release and power pull down, Twilight Sentinel, visor vanity mirrors, Delco-GM Bose symphony sound system, Delco AM stereo/FM stereo electronically tuned receiver with cassette player, universal citizens band transceiver, Cambria cloth texture roof treatment, two-tone paint, formal cabriolet roof, digital instrument cluster, full cabriolet roof, wire wheel discs, aluminum alloy wheels, accent striping, door edge guards, fuel filler door remote release, leather seating areas, firemist paint, pearlmist paint, reversible front and rear floor mats, leather-trimmed steering wheel, theft deterrent system, trunk mat, ride and handling package, anti-lock braking system, heavy-duty battery, engine block heater, puncture sealing tires (not available with ride and handling package).

FLEETWOOD D'ELEGANCE AND SIXTY SPECIAL CONVENIENCE/APPEARANCE OPTIONS: Cellular telephone, memory seat, automatic day/night mirror, controlled cycle wiper system, rear window defogger, dimming sentinel, automatic door locks, garage door opener, illuminated entry system, electrically powered mirrors, power driver seat recliner, six-way power seat adjuster, dual comfort 45/55 seats, tilt and telescope steering wheel, trumpet horn, trunk lid release and power pull down, Twilight Sentinel, visor vanity mirrors, Delco-GM Bose symphony sound system, Delco AM stereo/FM stereo electronically tuned receiver with cassette player, universal citizens band transceiver, Cambria cloth texture roof treatment, two-tone paint, formal cabriolet roof, digital instrument cluster, wire wheel discs, aluminum alloy wheels, accent striping, door edge guards, fuel filler door remote release, leather seating areas, firemist paint, pearlmist paint, reversible front and rear floormats, leather-trimmed steering wheel, theft deterrent system, trunk mat, ride and handling package, anti-lock braking system (standard on Sixty Special), heavy-duty battery, engine block heater, puncture sealing tires (not available with ride and handling package).

ELDORADO CONVENIENCE/APPEARANCE OPTIONS: Cellular telephone, automatic day/night mirror, Astroroof, controlled cycle wiper system, rear window defogger, dimming sentinel, automatic door locks, garage door opener, illuminated entry system, electrically powered mirrors, power driver seat recliner, Delco-GM Bose symphony sound system, Delco AM stereo/FM stereo electronically tuned receiver with cassette player, universal citizens band transceiver, two-tone paint, door edge guards, fuel filler door remote release, firemist paint, pearlmist paint, theft deterrent system, trunk mat, touring suspension, heavy-duty battery, engine block heater, puncture sealing tires (not available with touring suspension), cabriolet roof, wire wheel discs, wide brushed and bright body side accent molding.

SEVILLE CONVENIENCE/APPEARANCE OPTIONS: Cellular telephone, automatic day/night mirror, Astroroof, controlled cycle wiper system, rear window defogger, dimming sentinel, automatic door locks, garage door opener, illuminated entry system, electrically powered mirrors, power driver seat recliner, Delco-GM Bose symphony sound system, Delco AM/FM stereo electronically tuned receiver with cassette player, universal citizens band transceiver, two-tone paint, door edge guards, fuel filler door remote release, firemist paint, pearlmist paint, mid-tone paint treatment, theft deterrent system, trunk mat, touring suspension, heavy-duty battery, engine block heater, puncture seating tires (not available with touring suspension), cabriolet roof, wire wheel discs, wide brushed and bright body side accent molding.

BROUGHAM CONVENIENCE/APPEARANCE OPTIONS: Memory seat, automatic day/night mirror, Twilight Sentinel, Astroroof, automatic door locks, Guidematic headlamp control, six-way power front seat, adjustable rear seat reading lamps, rear window defogger, garage door opener, electrically powered exterior mirrors, power front seat recliner, tilt and telescope steering wheel, visor vanity lighted mirrors, Delco electronically tuned receiver with cassette tape, remote locking fuel filler door, theft deterrent system, security option package, wire wheels, wire wheel discs, accent striping, door edge guards, floor mats, leather seating areas, firemist paint, leather-trimmed steering wheel, electronic level control, trailering package, heavy-duty battery, engine block heater, puncture sealing tires.

HISTORY: Total Cadillac model year output was 282,562. In 1987, Cadillac became the first automobile manufacturer to use multiplexed wiring to control lighting on a production automobile, the Allante. On January 7, 1987, Cadillac became the only General Motors car division with responsibilities for engineering and manufacturing in addition to its marketing and sales activities. As a result, Cadillac had its own staff of engineers, designers, manufacturing personnel and marketing groups. Cadillac General Manager John O. Grettenberger assumed responsibilities for engineering and manufacturing. Robert L. Dorn, previously acting director of the former B-O-C Detroit Product team, became general director of operations for Cadillac.

1988

The 1988 Cadillac line featured a new 4.5-liter V-8 for the Seville, Eldorado, Fleetwood and deVille models. The Eldorado was extensively redesigned and detail changes were evident in the Allante, Brougham and Cimarron. The acceleration of Cadillacs with the new V-8 was better than any comparable Cadillac of the last decade. The Allante offered a new analog instrument option as well as new colors. The Seville was given a new front end look and was available with anti-lock brakes. It also had improved fuel economy. The Eldorado's sheet metal, except for the roof, was all new. Both the Fleetwood Sixty Special and d'Elegance models had added standard equipment features. The best selling of all Cadillac's models, the deVille coupe and sedan also had their standard equipment list extended. The traditional Brougham sedan was changed only in minor details while the Cimarron, in its last year of production, had its list of standard features expanded.

1988 Cadillac, Cimarron sedan. (OCW)

CIMARRON - SERIES 6J - V-6 - In its final year of production, the Cimarron was refined for 1988 by the addition of a speed-density fuel control system, cross-groove drive axles with the standard five-speed transmission, and larger standard all-season and optional high-performance tires. Additional changes for 1988 included a new variable-displacement air conditioning compressor, new standard body-color lower grooved molding, improved corrosion protection and three new exterior and interior colors. Another 1987 option made standard for 1988 in addition to the 14 in. alloy wheels and lower bodyside molding was a heavy-duty battery. Use of the 14 in. alloy wheels in place of the 13 in. wheels of 1987 also resulted in a retuning of the rear shock absorber valving. For 1988, the Cimarron's fuel-injected V-6 was equipped with a speed-density fuel control system. A new V-5 variable displacement air conditioning compressor was also adopted. The use of double-side galvanized steel was expanded to include the doors in 1988.

1988 Cadillac, Sedan deVille. (OCW)

DEVILLE - SERIES 6C - V-8 - The deVille's new V-8 was nearly 20 percent more powerful and 10 percent larger than the unit it replaced. Yet its fuel economy was virtually unchanged from the 1987 level. The larger V-8 also now had roller lifters and low friction pistons. The deVille had a revised suspension and engine mount rates as well as revised heater/air conditioner components and electronic cruise control system. Previous options now standard for the deVille included the tilt and telescope steering wheel, cruise control, dual comfort front seat, controlled cycle wiper system, power trunk release and heavy-duty battery. The deVille's THM 440 automatic transmission now had computer-controlled electronic torque management to prevent over-stressing of driveline components. Six new exterior colors were introduced for the deVille. A 4.5-liter V-8 engine identification plaque was added to the decklid. The armrest switchplate was changed from cherrywood to black for 1988. Among the numerous electronic changes for 1988 found in the deVille were a higher resolution internal speed sensor and a new under-dash relay center.

1988 Cadillac, Fleetwood d'Elegance sedan. (OCW)

FLEETWOOD d'ELEGANCE - SERIES 6C - V-8 - The Fleetwood d'Elegance shared all of the electrical and mechanical refinements of the deVille. It also gained 10 previously optional items as standard equipment. These consisted of tilt and telescope steering wheel, cruise control, controlled cycle wiper system, power trunk pulldown, illuminated entry system, Twilight Sentinel, illuminated vanity mirrors, trunk mat and heavy-duty battery. Only minimal exterior changes took place for 1988. Two new interior colors and six new exterior colors were available.

1988 Cadillac, Fleetwood Sixty Special sedan. (OCW)

FLEETWOOD SIXTY SPECIAL - SERIES 6C - V-8 - The Fleetwood Sixty Special continued to offer a longer wheelbase than the d'Elegance model with which it shared the same refinements and features for 1988.

1988 Cadillac, Brougham sedan. (OCW)

BROUGHAM - SERIES 6D - V-8 - The Brougham's 5.0-liter V-8 received a new electronic spark control system for 1988 as well as a numerically higher axle ratio. Additional improvements included new three-point rear seat belts with integral shoulder belts, revised drip moldings, new light switch lens with ISO-light symbol and the availability of five new exterior and three new interior colors. Previous options made standard for 1988 included a 25 gallon fuel tank (in place of a 20.7 gallon unit), tilt and telescope steering wheel, heavy-duty battery and larger, puncture-sealing tires. Two new valve option packages for the base Brougham were introduced for 1988. A new optional formal vinyl roof was offered with a revised backlight angle, new llama-grained vinyl top material, vinyl top colored drip molding, vinyl top material-covered center pillar appliqué (with opera lamp), rear door quarter window closeout trim and new backlight garnish molding.

1988 Cadillac, Eldorado coupe. (OCW)

ELDORADO - SERIES 6C - V-8 - In response to what Cadillac admitted was a call for "more distinctive styling," the Eldorado was given a major restyling for 1988. Major exterior sheet metal panels including the front fenders, hood, C-pillar, rear quarters and rear deck were all new as were the grille and taillights. The result was a longer, crisper, more tailored appearance. Both the front and rear fenders were subtly bladed. The traditional Eldorado grille had a bolder, more open pattern and the hood was set off by a raised power dome and a new header molding. The side-view was enhanced by the extension of the rear fender line forward into the C-pillar, which was a long time Eldorado trademark. The new rear fender extensions and rear bumper were contoured into a redesigned end panel that, along with a new taillight design, also gave the 1988 model a classic Eldorado appearance. The standard power radio antenna was relocated to the rear fender to provide for improved corrosion protection. As was the case with other Cadillacs powered by the new V-8, the Eldorado had a 4.5-liter V-8 engine identification plaque on the decklid. Six new exterior colors were offered for the 1988 Eldorado, bringing the color choices to 17. Both the Eldorado and Eldorado Biarritz had new design pin stripes. A restyled full vinyl roof was available for the Eldorado. The Biarritz had a revised formal cabriolet roof as standard equipment. Interior changes for 1988 consisted of a redesigned rear seat frame with added cushion suspension system. A new upholstery design featuring horizon-

tal stripes was also used. Two new interior colors, antelope and beechwood, were added to complement the new exterior choices. A total of nine interior colors were offered. New self-storing pull-swing door handles along with new-design wider headrests were also found in the 1988 Eldorado.

1988 Cadillac, Seville Touring Sedan. (OCW)

SEVILLE - SERIES 6K - V-8 - Like the Eldorado, the 1988 Seville had a new look from the windshield forward. It also shared the Eldorado's new choice of colors and interior revisions along with its design and engineering advances. Newly available for the Seville was the electronically controlled Teves anti-lock braking system. The Seville's suspension was refined for 1988 to improve the ride characteristics of the base-suspension models. The touring suspension was also returned for improved roadability. Among the detail changes for 1988 shared by the Seville and Eldorado was a more reliable control unit for the electric engine cooling fan.

1988 Cadillac, Allante convertible. (OCW)

ALLANTE - SERIES 6V - V-8 - The Allante entered its first full year of production after being introduced in March 1987. Its styling, powertrain and features were essentially unchanged for 1988. A number of running changes did take place. These included a reconfiguring of the headrests and the inclusion of a power decklid pulldown as standard equipment. A new option for 1988 was a European-style analog instrument panel that could be ordered in lieu of the standard electronic cluster at no extra charge. Also new for 1988 were two new exterior colors: red and black.

I.D. DATA: The 1988 Cadillac had a 17-symbol vehicle identification number (VIN) stamped on a metal tag attached to the upper left surface of the cowl visible through the windshield. The code was as follows: the first digit, "1," represented the manufacturing country (United States), the second, "G," represented General Motors, the third, "6," represented Cadillac, the fourth was the car line, GM body, as follows: C-deVille and Fleetwood, D-Brougham, E-Eldorado, J-Cimarron, K-Seville, V-Allante. The fifth symbol was the series identification: G-Cimarron, D-deVille, B-Fleetwood, S-Fleetwood Sixty Special, W-Brougham, L-Eldorado, S-Seville, R-Allante. Digits six and seven represent the body style: 47-two-door coupe, 69-four-door sedan, 57-Eldorado coupe, 69-Seville four-door sedan, 67-Allante. The eighth digit identifies the engine: "W"-2.8L V-6; "Y"-5.0L V-8; "5"-4.5L V-8; "7"-4.1L V-8; and "9"-5.0L V-8. A check digit follows. The 10th digit represents the model year, "J" for 1988. The next digit represents the assembly plant. The remaining six digits represent the production sequence: Cimarron: 500001 and up; Seville: 800001 and up; deVille, Fleetwood and Sixty Special: 200001 and up; Eldorado: 600001 and up; Brougham: 700001 and up; Allante: 100001 and up.

Cimarron (V-6)

Series No.	Body/Style No.	Body Type & Seating	Factory Price	Shipping Weight	Prod. Total
6J	G69	4-dr. Sed.-5P	16071	2756	6,454

DeVille (V-8)

Series No.	Body/Style No.	Body Type & Seating	Factory Price	Shipping Weight	Prod. Total
6C	D47	2-dr. Coupe	23049	3437	26,420
6C	D69	4-dr. Sedan	23404	3397	Note 1

Fleetwood d'Elegance (V-8)

Series No.	Body/Style No.	Body Type & Seating	Factory Price	Shipping Weight	Prod. Total
6C	B69	4-dr. Sedan	28024	3463	Note 1

Fleetwood Sixty Special (V-8)

Series No.	Body/Style No.	Body Type & Seating	Factory Price	Shipping Weight	Prod. Total
6C	S69	4-dr. Sedan	34750	3547	Note 1

Brougham (V-8)

Series No.	Body/Style No.	Body Type & Seating	Factory Price	Shipping Weight	Prod. Total
6D	W69	4-dr. Sedan	23846	4156	53,130

Eldorado (V-8)

Series No.	Body/Style No.	Body Type & Seating	Factory Price	Shipping Weight	Prod. Total
6E	L57	2-dr. Coupe	24891	3399	33,210

Seville (V-8)

Series No.	Body/Style No.	Body Type & Seating	Factory Price	Shipping Weight	Prod. Total
6K	S69	4-dr. Sedan	27627	3449	22,968

Allante (V-8)

Series No.	Body/Style No.	Body Type & Seating	Factory Price	Shipping Weight	Prod. Total
6V	R67	2-dr. Conv.	56533	3489	2,569

Note 1: Total DeVille/Fleetwood sedan production, 126,093.

ENGINES: STANDARD: (Cimarron) Overhead valve V-6. Cast iron block. Displacement: 173 cu. in. (2.8 liters). Bore & stroke: 3.50 x 2.99 in. Compression ratio: 8.9:1. Brake horsepower: 125 @ 4500 rpm. Torque: 160 lb.-ft. @ 3600 rpm. Hydraulic valve lifters. Multi-port fuel injection. STANDARD: (deVille, Fleetwood d'Elegance, Fleetwood Sixty Special, Seville, Eldorado) 90-degree, overhead valve, V-8. Aluminum block and cast iron cylinder liners, cast iron cylinder heads. Displacement: 273 cu. in. (4.5 liters). Bore & stroke: 3.62 x 3.31 in. Compression ratio: 9.0:1. Brake horsepower: 155 @ 4000 rpm. Torque: 240 lb.-ft. @ 2800 rpm. Five main bearings. Roller hydraulic valve lifters. Digital electronic fuel injection. STANDARD: (Allante) 90-degree, overhead valve, V-8. Aluminum block and cast iron cylinder heads and liners. Displacement: 250 cu. in. (4.0 liters). Bore & stroke: 3.46 x 3.31 in. Compression ratio: 8.5:1. Brake horsepower: 170 @ 4300 rpm. Torque: 235 lb.-ft. @ 3200 rpm. Five main bearings. Roller hydraulic valve lifters. Sequential multi-port fuel injection. STANDARD: (Brougham) 90-degree, overhead valve, V-8. Cast iron block and cast iron cylinder heads. Displacement: 307 cu. in. (5.0 liters). Bore & stroke: 3.8 x 3.39 in. Compression ratio: 8.0:1. Brake horsepower: 140 @ 3200 rpm. Torque: 346 lb.-ft. @ 2000 rpm. Five main bearings. Hydraulic valve lifters. 4Bbl. carburetor.

CHASSIS DATA: Wheelbase: (Cimarron) 101.2 in.; (deVille, Fleetwood d'Elegance) 110.8 in.; (Sixty Special) 116.0 in.; (Seville and Eldorado) 108.0 in.; (Allante) 99.4 in.; (Brougham) 121.5 in. Overall length: (Cimarron) 177.8 in.; (deVille, Fleetwood d'Elegance) 202.3 in.; (Sixty Special) 201.7 in.; (Seville) 190.8 in.; (Eldorado) 191.2 in.; (Allante) 178.6 in.; (Brougham) 221.0 in. Height: (Cimarron) 52.1 in.; (deVille, Fleetwood d'Elegance) 55.0 in.; (Sixty Special) 55.0 in.; (Seville, Eldorado) 53.7 in.; (Allante) 52.2 in.; (Brougham) 56.7 in. Width: (Cimarron) 65.0 in.; (deVille, Fleetwood d'Elegance) 71.7 in.; (Sixty Special) 71.7 in.; (Seville) 70.9 in.; (Eldorado) 71.3 in.; (Allante) 73.5 in.; (Brougham) 76.5 in. Front Tread: (Cimarron) 55.4 in.; (deVille, Fleetwood d'Elegance) 60.3 in.; (Sixty Special) 60.3 in.; (Seville, Eldorado) 59.9 in.; (Allante) 60.4 in.; (Brougham) 61.7 in. Rear Tread: (Cimarron) 55.2 in.; (deVille, Fleetwood d'Elegance) 59.8 in.; (Sixty Special) 59.8 in.; (Seville, Eldorado) 59.9 in.; (Allante) 60.4 in.; (Brougham) 60.7 in. Standard Tires: (Cimarron) P195/70R14; (deVille, Fleetwood d'Elegance) Michelin P205/70R14; (Sedan deVille, Fleetwood Sedan, Sixty Special) P205/70R14; (Seville, Eldorado) P205/70R14; (Touring) Goodyear Eagle GT4 P215/65R15; (Allante) Goodyear Eagle VL P225/55VR16; (Brougham) Michelin P225/75R15.

TECHNICAL: Transmission: (Cimarron) Muncie-Getrag five-speed manual; (deVille, Fleetwood, Eldorado, Seville) THM 440-T4 automatic four-speed (includes overdrive and viscous converter clutch); (Allante) THM F7 automatic four-speed (includes overdrive, viscous converter clutch and electronic shift control); (Brougham) THM 200-4R TCC automatic four-speed (includes overdrive and torque converter clutch). Steering: (All models exc. Brougham): power-assisted rack and pinion. Brougham: power-assisted recirculating ball. Ratios: deVille, Fleetwood: 19.1:1; Seville, Eldorado: 16.5:1; Touring: 15.6:1; Allante: 15.6:1; Brougham: 15-13:1. Front Suspension: (All models exc. Brougham) Independent MacPherson strut with coil springs, strut-type shock absorbers (integral-in strut and electronic variable on Allante) and stabilizer bar; (Brougham) Independent with short/long arms, coil springs, direct acting shock absorbers, and link-type stabilizer bar. Rear Suspension: (All models exc.

Brougham) Fully independent with coil springs, automatic level control and strut-type superlift shock absorbers on all models exc. Cimarron, Allante and Brougham; (Allante) Integral-in strut electronic variable shock absorbers with no rear stabilizer; (Brougham) Four link, coil springs with automatic level control and direct acting shock absorbers. Brakes: (All models exc. Brougham and Allante) Power front disc and rear drum with Teves anti-lock system; (Allante) Front and rear power disc brakes with Bosch III anti-lock braking system. Body Construction: (All models exc. Brougham) Integral body-frame; (Brougham) Separate body on frame. Fuel Tank: (Cimarron) 13.6 gal.; (deVille, Fleetwood) 18.0 gal.; (Eldorado, Seville) 18.8 gal.; (Allante) 22 gal.; (Brougham) 25 gal.

DRIVETRAIN OPTIONS: Anti-lock braking (not available for Cimarron, Allante and Brougham); Seville Touring option; engine block heater, heavy-duty ride package (Brougham sedan); trailer towing package (Brougham sedan); aluminum alloy wheels (Coupe and Sedan deVille); stylized aluminum wheels (Sixty Special); $115, wire wheels (Brougham sedan). Option Packages: deVille Option Package B, includes door edge guards, front carpeted floor mats, six-way power passenger seat. deVille Option Package C, includes items in Package B plus illuminated entry system, illuminated vanity mirrors, trunk lid power pull down, Twilight Sentinel. deVille Option Package D, includes items in Package C plus remote release fuel filler door, manual driver seat recliner, trumpet horn: $894. Brougham Option Package B, includes door edge guards, carpeted front and rear floor mats, six-way power passenger seat adjuster, trunk mat: $385. Brougham Option Package C, includes items from package B plus illuminated vanity mirrors, rear sail panel reading lamps, power trunk lid pull down, Twilight Sentinel.

CIMARRON CONVENIENCE/APPEARANCE OPTIONS: Garage door opener, Vista Vent sunroof, leather and cashmere cloth seating area, six-way power seat, visor vanity mirrors, Delco-GM Bose symphony sound system, Delco AM stereo/FM stereo electronically tuned receiver with cassette player, electronic instrument cluster, aluminum alloy wheels, door edge guards, floor mats, deck lid luggage rack, heavy-duty battery, 13 in. narrow strip whitewalls.

DEVILLE CONVENIENCE/APPEARANCE OPTIONS: Cellular telephone, automatic day/night mirror, controlled cycle wiper system, rear window defogger, dimming sentinel, automatic door locks, garage door opener, illuminated entry system, electrically powered mirrors, power driver seat recliner, six-way power seat adjuster, dual comfort 45/55 seats, tilt and telescope steering wheel, trumpet horn, trunk lid release and power pull down, Twilight Sentinel, visor vanity mirrors, Delco-GM Bose symphony sound system, Delco AM stereo/FM stereo electronically tuned receiver with cassette player, universal citizens band transceiver, Cambria Cloth texture roof treatment, two-tone paint, formal cabriolet roof, digital instrument cluster, wire wheel discs, aluminum alloy wheels, accent striping, door edge guards, fuel filter door remote release, leather seating areas, firemist paint, pearlmist paint, reversible front and rear floor mats, leather-trimmed steering wheel, theft deterrent system, trunk mat, ride and handling package, anti-lock braking system, heavy-duty battery, engine block heater, puncture sealing tires (not available with ride and handling package).

FLEETWOOD D'ELEGANCE AND SIXTY SPECIAL CONVENIENCE/APPEARANCE OPTIONS: Cellular telephone, memory seat, automatic day/night mirror, controlled cycle wiper system, rear window defogger, dimming sentinel, automatic door locks, garage door opener, illuminated entry system, electrically powered mirrors, power driver seat recliner, six-way power seat adjuster. dual comfort 45/55 seats, tilt and telescope steering wheel, trumpet horn, trunk lid release and power pull down, Twilight Sentinel, visor vanity mirrors, Delco-GM Bose symphony sound system, Delco AM stereo/FM stereo electronically tuned receiver with cassette player, universal citizens band transceiver, Cambria Cloth texture roof treatment, two-tone paint, formal cabriolet roof, digital instrument cluster, wire wheel discs, aluminum alloy wheels, accent striping, door edge guards, fuel filler door remote release, leather seating areas, firemist paint, pearlmist paint, reversible front and rear floor mats, leather trimmed steering wheel, theft deterrent system, trunk mat, ride and handling package, anti-lock braking system (standard on Sixty Special), heavy-duty battery, engine block heater, puncture sealing tires (not available with ride and handling package).

ELDORADO CONVENIENCE/APPEARANCE OPTIONS: Cellular telephone, automatic day/night mirror, Astroroof, controlled cycle wiper system, rear window defogger, dimming sentinel, automatic door locks, garage door opener, illuminated entry system, electrically powered mirrors, power driver seat recliner, Delco-GM Bose symphony sound system, Delco AM stereo/FM stereo electronically tuned receiver with cassette player, universal citizens band transceiver, two-tone paint, door edge guards, fuel filler door remote release, firemist paint, pearlmist paint, theft deterrent system, trunk mat, touring suspension, heavy-duty battery, engine block heater, puncture sealing tires (not available with Touring suspension), cabriolet roof, wire wheel discs, wide brushed and bright body side accent molding.

SEVILLE CONVENIENCE/APPEARANCE OPTIONS: Cellular telephone, automatic day/night mirror, Astroroof, controlled cycle wiper system, rear window defogger, dimming sentinel, automatic door locks, garage door opener, illuminated entry system, electrically powered mirrors, power driver seat recliner, Delco-GM Bose symphony sound system, Delco AM stereo/FM stereo electronically tuned receiver with cassette player, universal citizens band transceiver, two-tone paint, door edge guards, fuel filler door remote release, firemist paint, pearlmist paint, mid-tone paint treatment, theft deterrent system, trunk mat, Touring suspension, heavy-duty battery, engine block heater, puncture sealing tires (not available with Touring suspension), cabriolet roof, wire wheel discs, wide brushed and bright body side accent molding.

BROUGHAM CONVENIENCE/APPEARANCE OPTIONS: Memory seat, automatic day/night mirror, Twilight Sentinel, Astroroof, automatic door locks, Guidematic headlamp control, six-way power front seat, adjustable rear seat reading lamps, rear window defogger, garage door opener, electrically powered exterior mirrors, power front seat recliner, tilt and telescope steering wheel, visor vanity lighted mirrors, Delco electronically tuned receiver with cassette tape, remote locking fuel filler door, theft deterrent system, security option package, wire wheels, wire wheel discs, accent striping, door edge guards, floor mats, leather seating areas, firemist paint, leather-trimmed steering wheel, electronic level control, trailering package, heavy-duty battery, engine block heater, puncture sealing tires.

HISTORY: Production for the model year totaled 270,844 compared with 282,562 the year previous. Cadillac's share of the U.S. car market was 2.52 percent. On the auto show circuit, Cadillac displayed its Voyage concept car. The aerodynamic four-door sedan was designed for fuel efficiency and stability at speeds up to 200 mph. The Voyage also featured a rear-vision video camera that alerted the driver to oncoming vehicles by projecting images on a color monitor located on the instrument panel.

1989

Cadillac for 1989 offered six car lines powered by V-8 engines. The Cimarron was not produced for 1989. New model highlights included longer and restyled deVille and Fleetwood models, a more powerful Allante and refinements in the Seville, Eldorado and Brougham. The Seville was now available in a limited edition Seville Touring Sedan (STS) form. This new model was equipped with a retuned European-feel suspension package for more precise steering control and a firmer feel of the road. The limited production Fleetwood Sixty Sedan had new front leather seats created by Italian designer Giorgelto Giugiaro that featured a split frame design with triple lumbar support . The Allante received a substantial power boost to 200 horsepower that made it capable of 0-60 mph acceleration in less than 8.5 seconds. New comfort and convenience features available in 1989 included an express-down driver's window, electrochromic inside rearview mirror, ElectriClear windshield and an oil life indicator. Cadillac's 4.5-liter, digitally fuel-injected V-8 was the powerplant for the deVille, Fleetwood, Seville and Eldorado models. Cadillac claimed its cars, capable of 0-60 mph in less than 10 seconds, were the fastest domestically produced luxury cars available.

1989 Cadillac, Coupe deVille. (OCW)

1989 Cadillac, Sedan deVille. (OCW)

DEVILLE - SERIES 6C - V-8 - The Cadillac Coupe deVille and Sedan deVille shared a distinctive new interior and exterior appearance as well as a more spacious passenger compartment and increased trunk capacity for 1989. The overall length of the coupe increased 5.8 in. to 202.5 in. while that of the sedan moved up 8.8 in. to 205.2 in. The sedan's wheelbase was also expanded 3.0 in. to 113.8 in. The front overhang of both models increased 2.4 in. to 44.1 in. Their rear overhang was increased 3.4 in. to 47.2 in. New front sheet metal, grille quarter panels and hood were used. A new fascia was used to improve air flow. Both the front and rear bumpers made greater use of chrome and were fitted with an accent-colored rub strip. Bright headlight bezels and cornering lights were also featured along with a rear-mounted power antenna. At the rear a new deck lid, taillamp and fascia were adopted. Highlighting the 1989 model's profile were new rear wheel "eyebrow" openings and lower body side color accent moldings. The sedan, in addition to having new rear doors, had an integrated center high-mounted stop light. If the sedan was ordered with the optional full padded vinyl roof, an electroluminescent wreath-and-crest sail ornament was installed. Beginning with a new seat design with a Primavera cloth trim, numerous interior changes and revisions accompanied the 1989 deVille's larger and restyled exterior. Many changes were noticeable in the front seat. These consisted of wider headrests, a storage-type center armrest with a flip-open lid and a cup holder option, and manual driver and passenger seat recliners. The sedan's rear compartment had raised rack bolsters with integral headrests, increased lower cushion length for improved thigh support and a reduced corner radius for fuller seat appearance and improved passenger comfort. Three-point shoulder belts were installed along with a raised rear package shelf/storage compartment. The sedan's longer wheelbase provided additional interior space. Rear leg room was increased 3.0 in. to 43.3 in. Knee clearance increased 3.1 in. to 6.1 in. Trunk capacity was increased from 16.1 cu. ft. to 18.4 cu. ft. on the sedan and 18.1 cu. ft. on the coupe. The jack was relocated to a position under the trunk floor which now had a flat surface area. A new trunk trim, Tyger, replaced the Teton material used in 1988. A "Tiffany" carpeting was used for the trunk. The deVille models now had new front and rear reversible and washable floor mats with a new retention device. A driver side express-down window was standard as were electrically operated outside car-colored mirrors, front license plate mounting provisions and an AM/FM stereo signal seeking radio with scanner, digital display, cassette player, five-band graphic equalizer and extended range front speakers. A new Delco/Bose II Symphony sound system was optional as was a digital compact disc player integrated with the Bose II radio. Other new options included an electrochromic automatic day/night rearview mirror with three-position sensitivity switch and a heated windshield. Fifteen in. wheels with Michelin P205/70R15 tires were standard. Aluminum touring wheels were now available as an option.

FLEETWOOD - SERIES 6C - V-8 - The Fleetwood Cadillac was available as a coupe model as well as a sedan for 1989. Both versions shared the deVille's new sheet metal and added interior and exterior dimensions. Both Fleetwoods had new rear fender skirts. A fully padded vinyl roof was standard on the sedan. The coupe featured a standard formal cabriolet roof. The electroluminescent wreath-and-crest sail panel ornament were standard for the sedan. The Fleetwood's seats were of a tufted design with elite cloth inserts with Primavera cloth bolsters. The new center armrest offered as an option for the deVille was standard for the Fleetwood interior, which also had the revisions provided for the deVille. Except on those fitted with the Astroroof option, all Fleetwood sedans had new illuminated overhead vanity mirrors. The Fleetwood's revised and enlarged trunk was identical to the deVille's. The Fleetwood also had the deVille's new floor mats, driver's express down window as well as its new mirrors and heated windshield options. The Fleetwood interior now had a real wood nameplate on the glovebox with "Fleetwood" in gold script. The interior trim was in high-gloss American walnut. Joining the standard features found on the 1989 deVilles were the Fleetwood's remote release fuel filler door, trumpet horn and wire wheel covers.

FLEETWOOD SIXTY SPECIAL - SERIES 6C - V-8 - Cadillac described the 1989 Fleetwood Sixty Special as a "luxuriously equipped up-level sedan with all-new styling... (and) a unique and sumptuous seating package trimmed in ultrasoft leather." In line with the deVille and Fleetwood models, the Sixty Special (which was available in five additional colors, or 11 in all for 1989) had numerous new exterior sheet metal and styling components. It also had the larger trunk capacity and new comfort/convenience options. A full-padded vinyl roof was standard, as well as being listed as a delete option. The electroluminescent wreath-and-crest sail panel ornamentation was standard. The Sixty Special interior featured a new exclusive ITAL/Giugiaro seat trim style with "Ultrasoft" leather available in three colors. The front seat now had a unique "Split-Frame" arrangement that allowed independent vertical adjustment of the lower cushion relative to the seat back. Wider headrests were also used. The front seat's electrically powered features now provided for triple-element lumbar supports, thigh supports, side bolsters, heated seat backs and cushions, headrests and slide-out storage drawer. The new center armrest used on the Fleetwood was also found on the Sixty Special as were the revised rear seats. The Sixty Special's front armrest opened to the rear for rear seat access. The rear seat center armrest had a storage compartment. Map pockets were installed in the front seatbacks. Added to the Fleetwood trim was an identification plaque on the quarter panel and glovebox.

1989 Cadillac, Brougham sedan. (OCW)

BROUGHAM - SERIES 6D - V-8 - The traditional rear drive Brougham for 1989 was identified by its restyled grille and front-end panel molding. The header molding no longer had an embedded script. The Cadillac script was now located on the grille. The premier formal padded roof option was offered in five new colors for a total of 12 choices. The Brougham interior included Cadillac's new carpeted and reversible floor mats with a retention device. A 100-amp generator was standard. New standard features consisted of a controlled cycle wiper system, cruise control electronic level control, electrically powered chrome outside mirrors, trumpet horn and a power trunk lid release.

1989 Cadillac, Eldorado coupe. (OCW)

ELDORADO - SERIES 6E - V-8 - The Eldorado continued to be available as the Eldorado coupe and as the Eldorado Biarritz, which was ordered as Option Code YP3. A new white diamond color was introduced, allowing a choice of 18 colors for the Eldorado buyer. The black metallic roof of 1988 was replaced with a sable black version. The Biarritz roof was revised via the elimination of the bright bead adjacent to the roof molding. New options consisted of the electrochromic mirror, Delco/Bose Symphony sound system and digital disc player. New standard features consisted of an accent molding, remote fuel door release, front license plate mounting, the AM/FM stereo radio used on the Sixty Special and aluminum alloy wheels with a snowflake finish. Interior changes for 1989 were headlined by a high-gloss bird's-eye maple wood trim for the instrument panel, front console and door panels that were installed on the Eldorado Biarritz and standard on Eldorados with the B20 Appliqués option. The Eldorado's floor mats were of the new design used on other 1989 Cadillacs. A passive vehicle anti-theft system (VATS) that disengaged the starter, fuel pump and ECM was standard. Also found on all Eldorados was a driver side express-down window with a three-second activation and a tap up/down deactivation. The heater/defroster and bi-level air modes were revised to provide a more gradual and comfortable transition from warm to cool air, as well as an increased bi-level airflow.

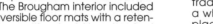

1989 Cadillac, Seville Touring Sedan. (OCW)

SEVILLE - SERIES 6K - V-8 - The Seville offered several interior improvements and new standard features. Cadillac depicted the touring sedan option (Code YP6) as featuring "European styling, exclusive appointments, performance and road manners that make (it) a driver's car in the European tradition." The Seville's color choice was revised to include a white diamond finish for the standard Seville and the replacement of black metallic with sable black. A total of 18 colors were offered. The bird's-eye maple trim also used for the Eldorado was standard for the Seville. The 1998 Elegante seat was now standard. The new Tampico carpets were protected by front and rear mats with the same design as those used on other Cadillacs. The Seville also had the VATS installed on the 1989 Eldorado. New standard equipment included Cadillac's electrochromic day/night mirror, an engine oil life indicator, driver side express-down window and Delco/Bose II Symphony sound system. Except for the Eldorado's accent molding and snowflake wheels, the Seville shared that model's new standard equipment. Power front passenger and driver recliners and 15 in. cast aluminum lace wheels were also standard for the Seville. The Seville touring sedan was available in four exterior colors: white diamond, sable black, black sapphire and carmine red. It featured hand-stitched beechwood ultrasoft leather seating areas, anti-lock braking, touring suspension, a 3.3:1 drive ratio, 15 in. cast aluminum alloy wheels and Goodyear Eagle GT4 blackwall tires. Additional Seville Touring Sedan (STS) features included an STS grille with flush-mounted wreath-and-crest, modified front fender with the cornering light moved to the fascia and headlight monitors removed, car-color front lower airdam and bodyside moldings, matte black export license pocket with bright bead, matte black front bumper impact pads and rear bumper guard vertical insert, car-color outside rearview mirror with black patch, modified Eldorado rear reflexes (moved to bumper), modified export taillamps with three-color European style lenses, STS nameplate on decklid and an STS exclusive cloisonné deck lid lock cover. The STS interior was fitted with a 12-way power front seat, manual articulating front seat headrests, center front armrest with cassette and coin/cup storage console trimmed in ultrasoft leather, net-type map pockets, rear bucket seats with integral headrests, center rear console and rear storage compartment, leather-wrapped front and rear door trim panels, door pull straps and overhead pull straps, high-gloss elm burl wood appliqués on door trim panels and switch plates, horn pad and bar, instrument panel and front and rear consoles, beechwood thaxton floor carpet and a deck lid liner in tara material with STS logo. Other standard STS features consisted of automatic door locks, illuminated driver and passenger side visor vanity mirrors, illuminated entry system, rear window defogger, theft-deterrent system and trunk mat.

1989 Cadillac, Allante convertible. (OCW)

ALLANTE - SERIES 6V - V-8 - The Allante was refined for 1989 by virtue of a larger 4.5-liter port fuel injection engine that provided increased power and improved performance. With 10 percent greater displacement, new low-restriction exhaust manifolds and improved flow air cleaner, the Allante's engine had a 17 percent increase in horsepower and a 13 percent increase in torque. Its 0-60 mph time was improved from 9.5 to 8.3 seconds. Performance from 40 to 80 mph progressed from 12.3 to 10.3 seconds. The Allante's top speed increased from 125 to 135 mph. Exterior changes for 1989 began with a new light blue metallic color choice. Seven colors were available as gold metallic was deleted. Central door unlocking was now available from the trunk. Several improvements took place in the Allante's soft top. The lower well and relocated roller guides prevented fabric wear, a self-folding fabric eliminated the need for tucking and walking around the vehicle, the use of dual springs reduced lifting effort and a major reduction in body squeaks and rattles was achieved. A total of three interior colors, including a new charcoal color, compatible with all exterior colors were offered. Both driver and passenger express-down windows were standard. Cadillac's VATS was also standard. A new seat design was used with a softer foam on cushion and back wings, along with softer wrinkled leather trim and French seams for the wings and head restraints. A softer trim was also used for the instrument panel, doors, armrests and upper door trim. An engine oil life indicator was now standard. The 1989 Allante also had reversible and washable carpeted floor mats with retention features. Significant technical developments were also part of the 1989 Allante package. A new speed-dependent suspension provided for a variety of ride/handling characteristics. At low speed the emphasis was on a greater sense of isolation and smooth road feel. At normal cruising speeds the suspension provided what Cadillac regarded as "traditional Allante ride qualities." For higher speeds the focus was upon stability without a significant loss of ride quality. This system also monitored braking and acceleration to reduce the rate of fore/aft movement. A new variable-assist steering system reduced pump output flow as engine speed increased. It also reduced parking and low speed effort while increasing steering effort and precision at higher speeds. In order to improve ride softness and road isolation, the bushings and cradle mounts were retuned. New 16 x 7 in. wheels and Goodyear P225/55VR16 tires were standard.

I.D. DATA: The 1989 Cadillac had a 17-symbol vehicle identification number (VIN) stamped on a metal tag attached to the upper left surface of the cowl visible through the windshield. The code was as follows: The first digit, "1," represented the manufacturing country (United States), the second, "G," represented General Motors, the third, "6," represented Cadillac, the fourth was the car line, GM body, as follows: C-deVille and Fleetwood, D-Brougham, E-Eldorado, K-Seville, V-Allante. The fifth symbol was the series identification: D-deVille, B-Fleetwood, S-Fleetwood Sixty Special, W-Brougham, L-Eldorado, S-Seville, R-Allante. Digits six and seven represent the body style: 47-two-door coupe, 69-four-door sedan, 57-Eldorado coupe, 69-Seville four-door sedan, 67-Allante. The eighth digit identifies the engine: "Y"-5.0L V-8; "5"-4.5L V-8; "8"-4.5L V-8; and "9"-5.0L V-8. A check digit follows. The 10th digit represents the model year, "K" for 1989. The next digit represents the assembly plant. The remaining six digits represent the production sequence: Seville: 800000 and up; deVille, Fleetwood and Sixty Special: 200000 and up; Eldorado: 600000 and up; Brougham: 700000 and up; Allante: 100000 and up.

DeVille (V-8)

Series No.	Body/Style No.	Body Type & Seating	Factory Price	Shipping Weight	Prod. Total
6C	D47	2-dr. Coupe	25285	3397	4,108
6C	D69	4-dr. Sedan	25760	3470	122,693

Fleetwood (V-8)

6C	B47	2-dr. Coupe	30365	3459	23,294
6C	B69	4-dr. Sedan	30840	3545	26,641

Fleetwood Sixty Special (V-8)

6C	S69	4-dr. Sedan	34840	3598	2,007

Brougham (V-8)

6D	W69	4-dr. Sedan	25699	4190	28,926 (1)

Eldorado (V-8)

6E	L57	2-dr. Coupe	26915	3422	20,633 (2)

Seville (V-8)

6K	S69	4-dr. Sedan	29935	3422	20,422 (3)

Allante (V-8)

6V	R67	2-dr. Conv.	57183	3492	3,296

(1) An additional 12,212 Broughams were produced with the d'Elegance option.

(2) An additional 7,174 Eldorados were produced with the Biarritz option.

(3) An additional 1,893 Sevilles were produced with the Touring Sedan option.

ENGINES: STANDARD: (deVille, Fleetwood, Fleetwood Sixty Special, Seville, Eldorado) 90-degree, overhead valve, V-8. Aluminum block and cast iron cylinder liners, cast iron cylinder heads. Displacement: 273 cu. in. (4.5 liters). Bore & Stroke: 3.62 x 3.31 in. Compression ratio: 9.0:1. Brake horsepower: 155 @ 4000 rpm. Torque: 240 lb.-ft. @ 2800 rpm. Five main bearings. Roller hydraulic valve lifters. Digital electronic fuel injection. STANDARD: (Allante) 90-degree, overhead valve, V-8. Aluminum block and cast iron cylinder liners, cast iron cylinder heads. Displacement: 273 cu. in. (4.5 liters). Bore & Stroke: 3.62 x 3.31 in. Compression ratio: 9.0:1. Brake horsepower: 200 @ 4300 rpm. Torque: 270 lb.-ft. @ 3200 rpm. Five main bearings. Roller hydraulic valve lifters. Sequential multiport fuel injection. STANDARD: (Brougham) 90-degree, overhead valve, V-8. Cast iron block and cast iron cylinder heads. Displacement: 307 cu. in. (5.0 liters). Bore & Stroke: 3.8 x 3.39 in. Compression ratio: 8.0:1. Brake horsepower: 140 @ 3200 rpm. Torque: 346 lb.-ft. @ 2000 rpm. Five main bearings. Hydraulic valve lifters. Four-barrel carburetor.

CHASSIS DATA: Wheelbase: (Coupe deVille, Fleetwood cpe) 110.8 in.; (Sedan deVille, Fleetwood sed, Sixty Special) 113.8 in.; (Seville, Eldorado) 108.0 in.; (Allante) 99.4 in.; (Brougham) 121.5 in. Overall Length: (Coupe deVille, Fleetwood cpe) 202.3 in.; (Sedan deVille, Fleetwood sed, Sixty Special) 205.3 in.; (Seville) 191.4 in.; (Eldorado) 190.8 in.; (Allante) 178.6 in.; (Brougham) 221 in. Height: (Coupe deVille, Fleetwood cpe) 55.0 in.; (Sedan deVille, Fleetwood sed, Sixty Special) 55.0 in.; (Seville, Eldorado) 53.7 in.; (Allante) 52.2 in.; (Brougham) 56.7 in. Width: (Coupe deVille, Fleetwood cpe) 72.5 in.; (Sedan deVille, Fleetwood sed, Sixty Special) 72.5 in.; (Seville) 71.7 in.; (Eldorado) 70.9 in.; (Allante) 73.5 in.; (Brougham) 76.5 in. Front Tread: (Coupe deVille, Fleetwood cpe) 60.3 in.; (Sedan deVille, Fleetwood sed, Sixty Special)

60.3 in.; (Seville, Eldorado) 59.9 in.; (Allante) 60.4 in.; (Brougham) 61.7 in. Rear Tread: (Coupe deVille, Fleetwood cpe) 59.8 in.; (Sedan deVille, Fleetwood sed, Sixty Special) 59.8 in.; (Seville, Eldorado) 59.9 in.; (Allante) 60.4 in.; (Brougham) 60.7 in. Standard Tires: (Coupe deVille, Fleetwood cpe) P205/70R15; (Sedan deVille, Fleetwood sed, Sixty Special) P205/7OR15; (Seville, Eldorado) P205/70R15; (Touring) Goodyear Eagle GT4 P215/65R15; (Allante) Goodyear Eagle VL P225/55VR16; (Brougham) Michelin P225/75R15.

TECHNICAL: Transmission: (deVille, Fleetwood, Eldorado, Seville) THM 440-T4 automatic four-speed (includes overdrive and viscous converter clutch); (Allante) THM F7 automatic four-speed (includes overdrive, viscous converter clutch and electronic shift control); (Brougham) THM 200-4R automatic four-speed (includes overdrive and torque converter clutch). Steering: (All models exc. Brougham): Power-assisted rack and pinion. Brougham: Power-assisted recirculating ball. Ratios: deVille, Fleetwood: 19.1:1; Seville, Eldorado: 16.5:1; Touring: 15.6:1; Allante: 15.6:1; Brougham: 15-13:1. Front Suspension: (All models exc. Brougham) Independent MacPherson strut with coil springs, strut-type shock absorbers (integral-in strut and electronic variable on Allante) and stabilizer bar. (Brougham) Independent with short/long arms, coil springs, direct acting shock absorbers, and link-type stabilizer bar. Rear Suspension: (All models exc. Brougham): fully independent with coil springs. Automatic level control and strut-type superlift shock absorbers on all models exc. Allante and Brougham. Allante: Integral-in strut electronic variable shock absorbers with no rear stabilizer. Brougham: Four link, coil springs with automatic level control and direct acting shock absorbers. Brakes: (All models exc. Brougham and Allante): Power-assisted front disc/rear drum with Teves anti-lock braking system. Allante: Power-assisted front disc/rear disc, Bosch III anti-lock braking system. Brougham: Power-assisted front disc/rear drum. Body Construction: (All models exc. Brougham): Integral body-frame; Brougham: Separate body on frame. Fuel Tank: (deVille, Fleetwood) 18.0 gals.; (Eldorado, Seville) 18.8 gals.; (Allante) 22 gals.; (Brougham) 25 gals.

DRIVETRAIN OPTIONS: Anti-lock braking, $749.25; Seville touring sedan option YP6, $5,754 (includes a touring suspension also available as option FE2, $155, for both the Seville and Eldorado consisting of stiffer front springs, larger diameter front stabilizer bar, a rear stabilizer bar and faster steering. The STS also had a 3.33:1 final drive ratio); engine block heater, $45; heavy-duty ride package (Brougham sedan), $120; Trailer Towing package (Brougham sedan), $299; aluminum alloy wheels (Coupe and Sedan deVille), $480; stylized aluminum wheels (Fleetwood coupe and sedan, Sixty Special), $115; wire wheels (Brougham sedan), $1,000. Option Packages: deVille Option Package B, includes door edge guards, front carpeted floor mats, six-way power passenger seat: $324. deVille Option Package C, includes items in Package B plus illuminated entry system, illuminated vanity mirrors, trunk lid power pull down, Twilight Sentinel: $739. deVille Option Package D, includes items in Package C plus remote release fuel filler door, manual driver seat recliner, trumpet horn: $894. Brougham Option Package B, includes door edge guards, carpeted front and rear floormats, six-way power passenger seat adjuster, trunk mat: $385. Brougham Option Package C, includes items from Package B plus illuminated vanity mirrors, rear sail panel reading lamps, power trunk lid pull down, Twilight Sentinel: $743.

CONVENIENCE/APPEARANCE OPTIONS: Availability of option follows the option price in brackets. The body types are according to this Cadillac code:

Body Type Code	Body Type
J	Coupe deVille
B	Sedan deVille
W	Fleetwood coupe
P	Fleetwood sedan
N	Fleetwood Sixty Special
L	Brougham sedan
H	Eldorado coupe
M	Seville sedan
V	Allante

Accent molding (M, N/A with STS), $150; accent striping (J, B, L, H, std. on W, P, N, M, V4S, YP3), $75; anti-lock braking system (J, B, std. on W, P, N), $925. Anti-lock braking system (H, M, std. on V, YP6), $925; bird's-eye maple appliqués (H, incl. in Eldorado Biarritz), $2435; storage front armrest (J, B, std. on W, P, N), $70; Astroroof (W, P, J, B, H, M, L), $1355.

Biarritz-Eldorado leather (H), $3325; Biarritz-Eldorado cloth (H), $2875; California emissions and testing (W, P, N, J, B, H, M, L), $100; California emissions label (V), $100; cellular mobile telephone (H, M, V), $1975; cellular mobile telephone provision (H, M, V, incl. in analog instrument cluster), $395; coachbuilder delete package (L), $389; rear window defogger (W, P, N, J, B, H, M, L, std. on V and STS), $195; heated windshield defogger (W, P, N, J, B), $250; Brougham d'Elegance cloth (L), $2,286; Brougham d'Elegance leather (L), $2,846; automatic door locks (W, P, N, J, B, H, M, L, incl. in STS), $185; carpeted rear floor mats (J, B, std. on W, P, N), $25; remote release fuel filler door (L, std. on W, P, N, H, M, V), $65; gold ornamentation package (W, P, N, J, B, H, M, L), $395; heavy-duty coachbuilder/livery package (L), $299; heavy-duty ride package (L, incl. with livery package, trailer towing package), $120; digital instrument cluster (J, B, std. on W, P, N), $250; analog instrument cluster (V), no charge; leather seating area (L, without d'Elegance option), $560; leather seating area (W, P, J, B, std. on N), $560; leather seating area (H, M, incl. in STS), $450; two-position driver's side memory seat (W, P, N), $235; automatic day/night mirror (W, P, N, J, B, H, M, L), $80; firemist paint (W, P, N, J, B, H, M, L, not avail. with two-tone paint on H, M), $240; primary firemist paint (H, M with two-tone paint), $190; secondary firemist paint (H, M with two-tone paint), $50; white diamond paint (H. M), $240; monotone lower accent color (W, P, N, J, B, H), no charge; two-tone paint (M, N/A with STS), $225; base radio with cassette tape player (L), $309; Delco-Bose sound system with cassette (W, P, N, J, B), $576; Delco-Bose with compact disc system (W, P, N, J, B, H, M), $872; manual passenger seat recliner (J, B), $45; power driver seat recliner (W, P), $95; power passenger seat recliner (W, P), $95-$410; full padded vinyl roof (H, N/A with STS), $1095; formal cabriolet roof (J, std. on W), $825; full padded vinyl roof (B, std. on P, N, L), $825; full cabriolet roof (J, H, N/A with STS or full padded vinyl roof), $1095; Phaeton roof (N, N/A with STS or full padded vinyl roof), $1195; premier formal vinyl roof (L), $1195; vinyl roof delete (P, N), $374; Seville touring sedan (M), $5754; leather-trimmed steering wheel (J, B, L, std. on W, P, N, H, M, V), $115; theft deterrent system (W, P, N. J, B, H, M, L, incl. in STS), $225; whitewall P215/65R15 tires (H, M with FE2, N/A with STS), $76; touring suspension (H, M, incl. with STS), $115; trunk mat (J, B, std. on W, P, N), $36; wire locking wheel discs (J, B, std. on W, P, N), $365; wire locking wheel discs (L), $445. Wire locking wheel discs (H, M, incl. with Eldorado Biarritz, N/A with STS), $235; aluminum alloy wheels (J, 8), $480; aluminum alloy wheels (M, incl. with FE2, N/A with STS), no charge; stylized aluminum wheels (W, P, N), $115; wire wheels (L), $1000.

1989 Cadillac, Fleetwood coupe. (OCW)

HISTORY: Cadillac had 1,605 dealers at the start of the 1989 calendar year. Compared to the 1988 model year, Cadillac increased its market share from 2.52 percent to 2.70 percent. Model year output totaled 276,138 compared to 270,844 the year previous. As a follow-up to the previous year's Voyage concept car, Cadillac engineers created the Solitaire rear-wheel drive coupe for display on the show circuit. The "dream car" was powered by a dual overhead cam V-12 with port fuel injection, jointly produced by Cadillac and Lotus. The Solitaire featured a memory system that automatically tilted front seats forward for easy exit of back seat occupants. Its aerodynamic front fender skirts opened when the front wheels were turned, and it used two miniature video cameras in place of exterior and interior rearview mirrors. The cameras transmitted color images to video screens on the instrument panel.

1990

Highlights of the 1990 Cadillacs included a new soft top and the world's first front-wheel drive Traction Control system for the Allante. A passive restraint system was installed in every Cadillac. Also for 1990, anti-lock brake systems were available as either standard equipment or as an option on all Cadillac models. Cadillac's 4.5-liter V-8 continued to be a Cadillac exclusive, available only in its full-size, front-wheel drive models. For 1990, the engine benefited from sequential port fuel injection and a higher compression ratio. Horsepower was now 180 with no consequent reduction in fuel economy.

DEVILLE - SERIES 6C - V-8 - The best-selling luxury automobile in America, the 1990 version of the deVille was powered by a more powerful 4.5-liter V-8 engine. Its horsepower was increased from 155 to 190, while torque moved up from 240 to 245 pound-feet. A new windshield wiper system with enhanced overall operation was adopted. Features that were previously optional that were now standard on the deVille consisted of center front seat armrest with a flip-open storage area, door edge guards, manual driver and passenger seat recliners, a leather-trimmed steering wheel rim and a driver's side supplemental inflatable restraint (S.I.R.) system. Five new exterior colors were offered: slate gray, light auburn, dark auburn, medium slate gray and dark slate gray. A total of 15 exterior colors were available. Sable black was now offered as monotone. Replacing the academy gray lower accent molding was medium slate gray. A long list of advances and improvements highlighted the 1990 deVille interior. Two new Primavera cloth colors, slate gray and dark auburn, were introduced. A total of five colors were offered. These two colors were also available in the Sierra grain leather trim, joining six carryover colors from 1989. New standard driver and vanity mirrors with mirror covers were also installed. Also standard was a front seat "clamshell" armrest with a deeper storage area to accommodate both compact discs and cassette tapes. A removable coin holder was located on the driver's side inside area of the armrest. The cup holder now had a new lever feature. The front and rear floor mats were rubber-backed and available with optional retention needles. A new front seatback buckle anchor (on track) was used to provide increased convenience in locating the buckle from any position. The use of the S.I.R. resulted in the elimination of the steering wheel telescoping function. Standard on the deVille was an upgraded acoustics package. A pass-key system that included a passive anti-theft system that disengaged the starter, fuel pump and ECM was also standard. The Express-Open Webasto Astroroof was improved to allow the roof window to open with a single one-second touch on the switch. The roof window could be stopped at any position by tapping the switch a second time. Changes in Cadillac's engine for 1990 consisted of the use of a dual level intake manifold, lightweight pistons, larger valve cylinder heads, new magnesium valve covers and new BCM software. The optional cast aluminum lace wheels offered for the deVille featured either window areas of either silver or gray depending on the car's lower accent molding color. The center cap display had a gray background. A chrome wreath-and-crest were used. The deVille's overall ride characteristics were enhanced by improved vehicle structure. For Sedan deVilles intended for fleet use, a new coachbuilder and heavy-duty livery package was offered.

1990 Cadillac, Fleetwood sedan. (OCW)

FLEETWOOD - SERIES 6C - V-8 - All of the new or improved features introduced for the 1990 deVilles were also found on the Fleetwood Cadillacs. The elite cloth used for the 1989 Fleetwood seats was replaced by a new "Ardmore" material. The Fleetwood's standard aluminum lace wheels differed slightly from the deVille's by having a silver background for the center cap and a chrome wreath in association with a crest in traditional Cadillac colors. Wire wheel discs were optional.

FLEETWOOD SIXTY SPECIAL - SERIES 6C - V-8 - Cadillac's depiction of the 1990 Fleetwood Sixty Special was of a car "for those buyers who seek luxury with power." Added to the Fleetwood's list of 1990 features were a number of items appropriate to the Sixty Special's status. Three new exterior colors, slate gray, medium slate gray and dark slate gray, were available for the Sixty Special. A total of 11 colors were offered. A new ultrasoft leather slate gray color, for a total of three, was also available.

1990 Cadillac, Brougham sedan. (OCW)

BROUGHAM - SERIES 6D - V-8 - The 1990 Brougham featured what Cadillac proclaimed as "contemporary yet classic exterior and interior restyling." This view was justified by a major revamping of the long-lived Brougham package. Three new colors, brownstone, maple red and light antelope, were introduced. A total of 12 colors were offered. A new wide lower bodyside colored accent molding was standard. The moldings were silver frost or light antelope depending on exterior paint color. Three exterior colors could be ordered with matching color accent moldings. Silver frost and light antelope were available only as monotone. The Brougham's front end appearance was revised by the use of halogen composite headlamps, new end caps, rub strip and bumper filler, plus a new windshield pillar pad and drip molding. In profile, a number of restyling efforts were evident. A new combination turn signal/parking/side marker lamp was used. The opera lamp was moved forward and a new bright chrome center pillar was used. New front and rear body-color door edge guards were standard as were new colored wide lower accent moldings. At the rear a new deck lid molding for the license plate opening was found. A new formal padded full vinyl roof was standard. Significant changes took place in the Brougham's interior. Two new colors for the Primavera cloth upholstery, antelope and dark maple red, were introduced. A total of four colors were offered. The same colors were added to the standard Brougham's grain-leather interior, making for a total availability of seven colors. Joining antelope and dark maple red was black for the d'Elegance Brougham's Sierra grain leather interior, which was also available in three other colors. Revisions to the Brougham's seating areas consisted of the replacement of Royal Prima with Primavera cloth, outboard front seat cushions contoured on the standard Brougham for increased lateral support, a new standard front seat center armrest with storage compartment, and a change in the d'Elegance seat to a 55/45 configuration. Carpeted rubber-backed floor mats with retention needles were now used. New standard automatic safety belts for driver and right front passenger were installed. A black walnut burl trim was used for the instrument panel, doors and steering wheel horn pad. Both a power driver seat recliner and an electronic digital instrument panel were now standard. An improved electronic climate control system with three automatic and two manual settings was adopted. The standard AM/FM radio with a preset graphic equalizer, cassette tape player and signal seeking and scanner feature with digital display was also upgraded. Both a new compact disc player and an electrochromic inside rearview mirror were optional. Items previously optional that were made standard for 1990 were as follows: side and deck lid accent striping, rear window defogger and heated outside mirrors, door edge guards, carpeted floor mats, front license mounting provisions and trunk mat. The powerplant and chassis of the Brougham benefited from the use of a new standard anti-lock braking system. A 5.7-liter V-8 with throttle body fuel injection was included with the coachbuilder package (which was also revised for 1990) and trailer towing packages. The 5.7-liter V-8 developed 175 horsepower, 295 pound-feet of torque and came with an 8.5 in. ring gear and 3.08:1 final drive ratio as well as a one-time Level 3 Gas Guzzler tax! In addition to the previously mentioned features of the Brougham d'Elegance, this special edition model, option code V4S, had a specific interior trim design including tufted multi-button seats, three overhead assist handles, six-way power passenger seat adjuster, illuminated driver and passenger visor vanity mirrors, rear sail panel reading lights, Twilight Sentinel, power trunk lid pulldown and exterior/interior identification.

1990 Cadillac, Eldorado coupe. (OCW)

ELDORADO - SERIES 6E - V-8 - Cadillac's personal luxury coupe gained added distinction for 1990 via its exterior and interior restyling. It also enjoyed the added power of the 4.5-liter Cadillac V-8. Five new colors for a total of 17 were available for the Eldorado. The new colors were light auburn, dark auburn, crimson (not available for Biarritz), medium slate gray and dark slate gray. The 1990 Eldorado's front end was revised by the use of new bumper molding, a body-color front valance panel and bumper guards changed to gray from body color. The Eldorado's side body appearance was altered by its new standard body molding and revised accent stripes. At the rear was found a new bumper molding, revised backup lamp lens, new license plate pocket, the relocation of the reflex to the rear-end panel and a new deck lid pulldown molding. A central door unlocking system was added to the optional automatic door lock option. Turning the key in either door unlocked the door. Holding the key in turned position for 1.5 seconds unlocked the other door. Three new Mayfair cloth colors, slate gray, antelope and garnet, for a total of four, were offered. Nine Sierra grain leather colors were available for the standard Eldorado. Among these were two new choices: slate gray and dark auburn. These colors plus black were available for the Sierra grain leather of the Biarritz, for a total of nine colors. Leather seating areas were now standard for the Biarritz. Both versions of the Eldorado had modified seating styles for 1990. The standard model had a seat cushion providing improved lateral and lumbar support. The seat back pockets were removed on the standard model. Both versions had new molded side panels. The optional leather seating area now included the power passenger seat recliner. A revised vinyl center front armrest and new carpeted rubber-backed floor mats with retention needles were also used. The electronic climate control now had five instead of three fan speeds as well as three automatic and two manual settings. The S.I.R. driver's side system was standard. A steering wheel with a smaller diameter and a thicker rim cross-section was installed. The telescoping feature was no longer used. Suspension changes for 1990 involved a new direct-acting front stabilizer shaft for improved ride control and a standard ride and handling structural package. New 15 in. optional (not available on touring suspension) cast aluminum wheels were offered. Eight items that were optional in 1989 that were now standard for the 1990 Eldorado were side and deck lid

accent striping, rear window defogger and heated outside mirrors, door edge guards, front and rear carpeted floor mats, illuminated entry system, leather seating area (Biarritz), illuminated vanity driver and passenger mirrors and a trunk mat. The Eldorado Biarritz, Option Code YP3, was distinguished by its two-tone paint treatment (monotone was also available), formal cabriolet roof, opera lamps, "Biarritz" sail panel identification, wire wheel discs (cast aluminum snowflake available), specific interior design, specific front bucket seats, bird's eye maple appliqués, power driver and passenger seat recliners, power lumbar support adjusters for driver and passenger seats and deluxe front and rear floor carpet mats. Broadening the Eldorado's market appeal was the introduction of the touring coupe model. Its Beechwood leather and bird's-eye maple wood interior provided an ambiance that Cadillac said was "intentionally designed with fewer chrome appointments." Other touring coupe features included an extra wide molding rocker panel, touring suspension, dual exhaust system, anti-lock braking system and forged aluminum wheels.

1990 Cadillac, Seville Touring Sedan. (OCW)

SEVILLE - SERIES 6K - V-8 - With the exception of the following, the 1990 Seville shared the changes made in the Eldorado for 1990. The Seville was offered in four new colors, for a total of 16. The four colors were light auburn, dark auburn, medium slate gray and dark slate gray. New side body reflexes were used. The corner turn signal lamps were relocated from the body to the bumper. A new white crystalline taillamp lens was used. Interior developments consisted of two new Sierra grain leather color choices, slate gray and dark auburn, for a total of nine. The Seville's seat style was revamped to provide for envelope-type seat back pockets and molded side panels. The Seville Touring Sedan was now built entirely at Detroit/Hamtramck. It had new front and rear body-color low fascias with a black bead and a body-color rocker molding, also with a black bead. The rear view appearance was updated by use of a larger cloisonné STS deck lid emblem and dual outlet exhaust. Larger 16 in. diamond-cut finish, forged aluminum wheels with larger Goodyear Eagle GT4 P215/60R16 tires were also introduced for 1990. The STS for 1990 also had a new 6KY69 body style code.

1990 Cadillac, Allanté convertible. (OCW)

ALLANTE - SERIES 6V - V-8 - The Allante was available in two body styles for 1990. The Allante convertible hardtop included both a convertible top and a removable all-aluminum hardtop. The new convertible was offered as a convertible only and did not include the hardtop. The standard and optional content of the two models was identical with the following exceptions: an analog instrument cluster was standard on the convertible and a no-cost option on the convertible hardtop. The digital instrument cluster standard on the convertible hardtop was an extra cost feature for the convertible. A pearl white exterior color was available at no charge on the convertible hardtop and an extra-cost option for the convertible. The only exterior change for 1990 was the addition of a new beige metallic color. This provided a total of eight color choices for the Allante. A new natural beige durosoft leather color was also offered. Other revised or new items for 1990 included a standard S.I.R. driver-side system, a smaller steering wheel with a thicker rim cross-section, new standard Delco-Bose compact digital disc player and an improved cellular telephone option. A Traction Control system providing increased steering ability and improved stability when accelerating as well as increased traction on slippery surfaces was standard. New chassis calibration involving revised strut valving and the use of gas-charged struts. A new direct-acting front stabilizer shaft was also used. Shift points for the Allante's transmission were changed to 40 and 60 mph from 1989's 25 and 60 mph.

I.D. DATA: The 1990 Cadillac had a 17-symbol vehicle identification number (VIN) stamped on a metal tag attached to the upper left surface of the cowl visible through the windshield. The code was as follows: The first digit, "1," represented the manufacturing country (United States), the second, "G," represented General Motors, the third, "6," represented Cadillac, the fourth was the car line, GM body, as follows: C-deVille and Fleetwood, D-Brougham, E-Eldorado, K-Seville, V-Allante. The fifth symbol was the series identification: D-deVille, B-Fleetwood, S-Fleetwood Sixty Special, W-Brougham, L-Eldorado, S-Seville, Y-Seville Touring Sedan, R-Allante w/hardtop, S-Allante conv. Digits six and seven represent the body style: 47-two-door coupe, 69-four-door sedan, 57-Eldorado coupe, 69-Seville four-door sedan, 67-Allante. The eighth digit identifies the engine: "Y"-5.0L V-8; "3"-4.5L V-8; "7"-5.7L V-8; "8"-4.5L V-8; and "9"-5.0L V-8. A check digit follows. The 10th digit represents the model year, "L" for 1990. The next digit represents the assembly plant. The remaining six digits represent the production sequence: Seville: 800000 and up; deVille, Fleetwood and Sixty Special: 200000 and up; Eldorado: 600000 and up; Brougham: 700000 and up; Allante: 100000 and up.

deVille (V-8)

Series No.	Body/Style No.	Body Type & Seating	Factory Price	Shipping Weight	Prod. Total
6C	D47	2-dr. Coupe	26960	3486	2,438
6C	D69	4-dr. Sedan	27540	3466	131,717

Fleetwood (V-8)

Series No.	Body/Style No.	Body Type & Seating	Factory Price	Shipping Weight	Prod. Total
6C	B47	2-dr. Coupe	32400	3538	17,569
6C	B69	4-dr. Sedan	32980	3618	22,889

Fleetwood Sixty Special (V-8)

Series No.	Body/Style No.	Body Type & Seating	Factory Price	Shipping Weight	Prod. Total
6C	S69	4-dr. Sedan	36980	3657	1,824

Brougham (V-8)

Series No.	Body/Style No.	Body Type & Seating	Factory Price	Shipping Weight	Prod. Total
6D	W69	4-dr. Sedan	27400	4283	21,529 (1)

Eldorado (V-8)

Series No.	Body/Style No.	Body Type & Seating	Factory Price	Shipping Weight	Prod. Total
6E	L57	2-dr. Coupe	28855	3426	13,610 (2)

Seville (V-8)

Series No.	Body/Style No.	Body Type & Seating	Factory Price	Shipping Weight	Prod. Total
6K	S69	4-dr. Sedan	31830	3481	31,235
6K	Y69	4-dr. Sedan	36320	3557	1,893

Allante (V-8)

Series No.	Body/Style No.	Body Type & Seating	Factory Price	Shipping Weight	Prod. Total
6V	R67	2-dr. Conv. HT	57183	3522	Note 3
6V	S67	2-dr. Conv.	51550	3470	Note 3

(1) An additional 12,212 Broughams were equipped with the d'Elegance option.

(2) An additional 1,507 Eldorados with the touring coupe option were built. The Biarritz option was found on an additional 7,174 Eldorados.

Note 3: Allante production totaled 3,101 with no further breakout available.

ENGINES: STANDARD: (deVille, Fleetwood, Fleetwood Sixty Special, Seville, Eldorado) 90-degree, overhead valve, V-8. Aluminum block and cast iron cylinder liners, cast iron cylinder heads. Displacement: 273 cu. in. (4.5 liters). Bore & Stroke: 3.62 x 3.31 in. Compression ratio: 9.5:1. Brake horsepower: 180 @ 4300 rpm. Torque: 240 lb.-ft. @ 3000 rpm. Five main bearings. Roller hydraulic valve lifters. Sequential port fuel injection. STANDARD: (Allante) 90-degree, overhead valve, V-8. Aluminum block and cast iron cylinder liners, cast iron cylinder heads. Displacement: 273 cu. in. (4.5 liters). Bore & Stroke: 3.62 x 3.31 in. Compression ratio: 9.0:1. Brake horsepower: 200 @ 4400 rpm. Torque: 270 lb.-ft. @ 3200 rpm. Five main bearings. Roller hydraulic valve lifters. Sequential multiport fuel injection. STANDARD: (Brougham) 90-degree, overhead valve, V-8. Cast iron block and cast iron cylinder heads. Displacement: 307 cu. in. (5.0 liters). Bore & Stroke: 3.8 x 3.39 in. Compression ratio: 8.0:1. Brake horsepower: 140 @ 3200 rpm. Torque: 346 lb.-ft. @ 2000 rpm. Five main bearings. Hydraulic valve lifters. Four-barrel carburetor. Available as part of coachbuilder or trailer towing package: 90-degree, overhead valve, V-8. Cast iron block and cast iron cylinder heads. Displacement: 350 cu. in. (5.7 liters). Bore & Stroke: 3.48 x 4.00 in. Compression ratio: 9.3:1. Brake horsepower: 175 @ 4200 rpm. Torque: 400 lb.-ft. @ 2000 rpm. Five main bearings. Hydraulic valve lifters. Fuel injection.

1990 Cadillac, Sedan deVille. (OCW)

CHASSIS DATA: Wheelbase: (Coupe deVille, Fleetwood cpe) 110.8 in.; (Sedan deVille, Fleetwood sed, Sixty Special) 113.8 in.; (Seville, Eldorado) 108.0 in.; (Allante) 99.4 in.; (Brougham) 121.5 in. Overall Length: (Coupe deVille, Fleetwood cpe) 202.7 in.; (Sedan deVille, Fleetwood sed, Sixty Special) 205.6 in.; (Seville) 190.8 in.; (Eldorado) 190.4 in.; (Allante) 178.6 in.; (Brougham) 221 in. Height: (Coupe deVille, Fleetwood cpe) 54.9 in.; (Sedan deVille, Fleetwood sed, Sixty Special) 55.2 in.; (Seville, Eldorado) 53.7 in.; (Allante) 52.2 in.; (Brougham) 56.7 in. Width: (Coupe deVille, Fleetwood cpe) 71.7 in.; (Sedan deVille, Fleetwood sed, Sixty Special) 71.7 in.; (Seville) 72.0 in.; (Eldorado) 72.4 in.; (Allante) 73.5 in.; (Brougham) 76.5 in. Front Tread: (Coupe deVille, Fleetwood cpe) 60.3 in.; (Sedan deVille, Fleetwood sed, Sixty Special) 60.3 in.; (Seville, Eldorado) 59.9 in.; (Allante) 60.4 in.; (Brougham) 61.7 in. Rear Tread: (Coupe deVille, Fleetwood cpe) 59.8 in.; (Sedan deVille, Fleetwood sed, Sixty Special) 59.8 in.; (Seville, Eldorado) 59.9 in.; (Allante) 60.4 in.; (Brougham) 60.7 in. Standard Tires: (Coupe deVille, Fleetwood cpe) Michelin P205/70R15; (Sedan deVille, Fleetwood sed, Sixty Special) P205/70R15; (Seville, Eldorado) P205/70R15; (Touring) Goodyear Eagle GT4 P215/65R15; (STS with 16 x 7 in. wheels) 215/60R16; (Allante) Goodyear Eagle VL P225/55VR16; (Brougham) Michelin P225/75R15.

TECHNICAL: Transmission: (deVille, Fleetwood, Eldorado, Seville) THM 440T4 automatic four-speed (includes overdrive and viscous converter clutch); (Allante) THM F7 automatic four-speed transaxle (includes overdrive, viscous converter clutch and electronic shift control); (Brougham) THM 200-4R automatic four-speed (includes overdrive and torque converter clutch); (Brougham with Coachbuilder Package or Trailer Towing Package) THM-700-automatic 4R four-speed (includes overdrive and a torque converter clutch). This transmission is also fitted with a modified prop shaft and 8.5 in. rear axle. Steering: (All models exc. Brougham): Power-assisted rack and pinion. Brougham: Power-assisted recirculating ball. Ratios: deVille, Fleetwood: 18.6:1; Seville, Eldorado: 16.5:1; Touring: 15.6:1; Allante: 15.6:1; Brougham: 15-13:1. Front Suspension: (All models exc. Brougham) Independent MacPherson strut with coil springs, strut-type shock absorbers (integral-in strut and electronic variable on Allante) and stabilizer bar; (Brougham) Independent with short/long arms, coil springs, direct acting shock absorbers and link-type stabilizer bar. Rear Suspension: (All models exc. Brougham): fully independent with coil springs. Automatic level control and strut-type superlift shock absorbers on all models except Allante and Brougham. Allante: Integral-in strut electronic variable shock absorbers with no rear stabilizer. Brougham: Four link, coil springs with automatic level control and direct acting shock absorbers. Brakes: (All models exc. Brougham and Allante): Power assisted front disc/rear drum with Teves anti-lock braking system; Allante: Power assisted front disc/rear drum, Bosch III anti-lock braking system; Brougham: Power assisted front disc/rear drum, Bosch ABS. Body Construction: (All models exc. Brougham): Integral body-frame; Brougham: Separate body on frame. Fuel Tank: (deVille, Fleetwood) 18.0 gals.; (Eldorado, Seville) 18.8 gals.; (Allante) 22 gals.; (Brougham) 25 gals.

DRIVETRAIN OPTIONS: Optional 3.23:1 rear axle ratio for Brougham with towing package. Anti-lock braking, $925; touring suspension, $155; engine block heater, $45; heavy-duty ride package (Brougham sedan), $120; trailer towing package (Brougham sedan). $549. Option Packages: deVille Option Package B, includes front and rear carpeted floor mats, six-way power passenger seat, front and rear seat adjuster, trunk mat: $356. deVille Option Package C. includes items in Package B plus illuminated entry system, illuminated vanity mirrors, trunk lid power pull down, Twilight Sentinel: $771. deVille Option Package D, includes items in Package C plus remote release fuel filler door, automatic day/night mirror, electrochromic trumpet horn: $961. deVille Option Package E, includes items in Package D plus automatic door locks: $1146. Fleetwood Option Package B, includes automatic door locks and theft deterrent system: $410. Fleetwood Sixty Special Option Package B, includes automatic door locks and theft deterrent system: $410. Brougham Option Package B, includes illuminated vanity mirrors-driver and passenger, rear sail panel reading lamps, reclining power passenger seat, six-way power passenger seat, power trunk lid pulldown, Twilight Sentinel: $768. Brougham Option Package C, includes items from Package B plus automatic door locks, remote release fuel filler door, theft-deterrent system: $1243. Brougham d'Elegance Option Package C, includes automatic door locks, remote release fuel filler door, theft-deterrent system: $475. Eldorado and Seville Option Package B, includes automatic door locks, theft-deterrent system: $410.

CONVENIENCE/APPEARANCE OPTIONS: Availability of option follows the option price in brackets. The body types are according to this Cadillac code:

Body Type Code	Body Type
J	Coupe deVille
B	Sedan deVille
W	Fleetwood coupe
P	Fleetwood sedan
N	Fleetwood Sixty Special
L	Brougham sedan
H	Eldorado coupe
M	Seville sedan
G	Seville Touring Sedan
V	Allante

Accent striping (J, B. std. on W, P. L. N, H, M), $75; anti-lock braking system (J, B. std. on W, P. N. L), $925; anti-lock braking system (H. M, std. on F, G, V), $925; bird's-eye maple appliqués (H, incl. in YP3, std. on M), $245; Astroroof (W. P, J, B, H, M, L, G), $1355; Biarritz-Eldorado leather (H), $3180; California emissions and testing (W, P, N, J, B, H, M. L, G), $100; California emissions label (F, V, w/L05), $100; cellular mobile telephone (F, V), $1195; cellular mobile telephone provision (F, V, incl. in cellular mobile telephone), $395; coachbuilder delete package (L), $139; rear window defogger (W, P. N, J, B, std. on L, H. M, F, G. V), $195; Brougham d'Elegance cloth (L) $2171; Brougham d'Elegance leather (L), $2731; gold ornamentation package (W, P, N, J. B, H, M, L), $395; livery package (L), $299; digital instrument cluster (J, B, std. on W, P, N, L, H, M, G, V), $250; digital instrument cluster (F), $495; analog instrument cluster (V, std. on F), no charge: leather seating area (L, w/o d'Elegance option), $560; leather seating area (W, P, J, B, std. on N), $560: leather seating area (M, std. on G), $450; leather seating area (H, incl. in YP3), $545; two-position driver's side memory seat (W, P, N). $235; automatic day/night mirror (W, P, N, L, H, M, G), $80; firemist paint (W, P, N, J, B, H, M, L, not avail. with two-tone paint on H, M), $240; primary firemist paint (H, M with two-tone paint), $190; secondary firemist paint (H, M with two-tone paint), $50.

pearl white paint (F), $700; white diamond paint (H, M), $240: two-tone paint (M), $225; monotone lower accent color (W, P, N, J, B, L, H-with YP3), no charge; base radio with Delco/Bose sound system (W, P, N, J, B, M, G), $576; Delco-Bose with compact disc system (L), $296; Delco-Bose sound system with compact disc music system (W, P, N, J, B, H, M, G), $872; power driver seat recliner (W, P), $95; power passenger seat recliner (W, P), $95; power passenger seat (W, P), $95; full padded vinyl roof (H, N/A with YP3), $1095; formal cabriolet roof (J, std. on W), $825; full padded vinyl roof (B, std. on P, N, L), $825; full cabriolet roof (J, H, N/A with YP3 or Astroroof), $1095; phaeton roof (M, N/A with Astroroof), $1195; vinyl roof delete (P, N), $374; leather-trimmed steering wheel (L), $115; theft deterrent system (J, B), $225; whitewall P215/65R15 tires (H, M with FE2). $76; touring suspension (H, M, std on G), $155; trailer towing package (L), $549; wire locking wheel discs (J, B), $365; wire locking wheel discs delete (W, P, N), $115; wire locking wheel discs (L), $445; wire locking wheel discs (H, M, std. in YP3), $235; cast aluminum snowflake wheels (M, incl. with FE2, std. on H), no charge; cast aluminum wheels (H), $115; cast aluminum lace wheels (J, B, std. on W, P, N, M), $480; wire wheels (L), $1000; ElectriClear windshield (W. P, J, B), $250.

HISTORY: Cadillac's model year production totaled 268,698 compared with 276,138 the year previous. Its share of the automotive market moved up to 2.8 percent. John Grettenberger, who had served as Cadillac general manager since January 1984, was credited by many industry observers as having played a major role in improving Cadillac's quality. Cadillac's newest concept car was the Aurora, a name that would later in the decade be adopted by Oldsmobile. Cadillac's version of the Aurora sedan used many features already part of regular-production cars, such as Traction Control, the 4.5-liter V-8 and electronically adjustable struts. Innovative equipment on the car included all-wheel drive, four-passenger inflatable restraints and a sunroof that the driver could adjust automatically to darken, all of which had the potential for inclusion on future Cadillacs. Another new item was the ETAK in-car navigation system that used a CD-ROM to store maps for all the United States. Aurora's ETAK maps were displayed on a working full-color flat screen liquid crystal display.

1991

Anti-lock brakes became standard equipment in all Cadillacs in 1991. The 4.5-liter V-8 formerly used to power most Cadillacs was replaced by a more powerful 4.9-liter V-8 with port fuel injection. This new engine saw service in DeVille/Fleetwood, Eldorado and Seville models. Also new, and coupled to the 4.9-liter V-8, was the 4T60-E electronically controlled four-speed automatic transmission with overdrive. The rear-wheel drive Brougham sedan's standard 5.0-liter V-8 received fuel injection and delivered 21 percent more horsepower (up to 170) over the previous year's carbureted unit. Computer Command Ride was new to Fleetwood, Seville and Eldorado, and automatically adjusted struts to provide increased damping and road control as those vehicles' speed increased.

1991 Cadillac, deVille Touring Sedan. (OCW)

DEVILLE - SERIES 6C - V-8 - Joining the Coupe deVille and Sedan deVille in 1991 was a Touring version of the Sedan deVille. All three were powered by the new 4.9-liter V-8 mated to the 4T60-E electronically controlled four-speed automatic transmission with overdrive. This engine replaced the previously standard 4.5-liter V-8. An improved version of the Teves anti-lock braking system was also now standard equipment. Other new standard features of the deVille series included structural enhancements for improved crashworthiness, 15-inch cast aluminum wheels and a larger, higher capacity front braking system. Computer Command Ride was optional and offered three damping modes to enhance ride and handling characteristics. Formerly optional, but made standard equipment in 1991 were side and decklid accent striping, rear window defogger with heated outside mirrors, Twilight Sentinel and automatic door locks including a new central door unlocking system. Appearance-wise, the deVille featured a new power dome hood, wider grille with grid design and integral Cadillac script, revised front bumper guards and rear bumper rub strip, and a 4.9 Port Fuel Injection V8 decklid emblem. Inside, EZ-Kool solar-control glass for all windows was made standard, Esteem seat cloth replaced the previously used Primavera, and an engine oil life indicator became standard. A Phaeton roof was optional for the Sedan deVille while both a Cold Weather Package and a Security Package were also new options. The former included a heated windshield system and engine block heater while the latter featured remote keyless entry, illuminated entry and a theft-deterrent system.

1991 Cadillac, Fleetwood sedan. (OCW)

FLEETWOOD - SERIES 6C - V-8 - As in previous years, much of what was updated on deVille models also found its way into the Fleetwood coupe and sedan. This included the 4.9-liter V-8, rated at 200 horsepower, and 4T60-E four-speed automatic transmission with overdrive, viscous converter clutch and electronic shift control. Deviating from the updates listed in the deVille listing, Fleetwood models received Computer Command Ride as standard equipment, the previously optional electrochromic automatic day/night mirror as standard, and cast aluminum lace wheels as an option. Inside, again deviating from deVille updates, was a new White Sierra Grain Leather color was added to the seven colors available in sedans and six in coupes. Also new was darker stained American Walnut wood appliqués and the optional Custom Seating Package including driver memory seat and driver/passenger seats power recliners. Outside, again, different from the deVille refinements, was the bodyside inserts with integral Fleetwood lettering replacing the previously seen script on rear quarter panels.

1991 Cadillac, Brougham sedan. (OCW)

FLEETWOOD SIXTY SPECIAL - SERIES 6C - V-8 - Cadillac's limited production, executive class sedan mimicked the updates of the Fleetwood coupe and sedans. Unique to the Sixty Special sedan was its new body style designator: 6CG69, Sixty Special plaque

on the rear quarter panels, Sixty Special nameplate replacing previously used engine plaque at the rear, and the optional Express-Open Astroroof. Updates included a new standard front seat armrest that included a cupholder, coinholder and storage for CDs. The power front floor storage drawer formerly offered was eliminated to accommodate rear climate control outlets. With the new 4.9-liter V-8 and 4T60-E transmission, the Sixty Special's final drive ratio was 2.73:1. Also, the 4.9-liter V-8 featured the improved CS144 Generation II alternator that provided a higher power output. The 140-amp alternator provided increased air flow and could withstand higher-temperature operation. The leather interior of the Sixty Special was styled by famed Italian designer Giugiaro of Milan. The hand-crafted leather was offered in three color choices. A six-position memory feature was added as standard to the front seats, which had 22 power adjustments. Also, the Sixty Special's wiper system was refined to provide a wider clearing pattern with less blade chatter and greater resistance to snow and ice fatigue. Eleven exterior color selections were available in 1991.

BROUGHAM - SERIES 6D - V-8 - Cadillac's Brougham series again consisted of the Brougham sedan and special edition Brougham d'Elegance sedan (option code V4S). Power was supplied by the revised 5.0-liter V-8 with throttle body injection (TBI). The "new" 5.0-liter V-8 was rated at 170 horsepower, and featured roller valve lifters for less friction and cast iron exhaust manifolds contoured for minimal flow resistance. Available previously only with the Coachbuilder Package, the 185-horsepower 5.7-liter V-8 with TBI was now a stand-alone Brougham engine option. Both engines were paired with the 4L60 Hydramatic four-speed automatic transmission with overdrive. Final drive ratio was 3.08:1 (3.73:1 with Coachbuilder and Armor options). Formerly optional, but now standard features of the Brougham were rear sail panel reading lamps, passenger seat power recliner and six-way power seat adjuster, and leather-trimmed steering wheel. New standard features included electronic variable orifice steering system in which steering effort was reduced during low-speed driving and increased during high-speed maneuvers to improve stability, and a new ride package. This package consisted of deflected disc shock absorbers, new body mounts and high-rate front and rear springs. Outside, the Brougham received clearcoat paint as standard, with two new colors added (12 total): Victorian Red and Dark Antelope. Eleven vinyl top color choices were available. Also new was the optional central door unlocking system included with the automatic door lock system. Brougham's stopping power was provided by the Bosch II anti-lock braking system. Standard tires were self-sealing P225/75R15 Uniroyals that had a distinctive gold letter treatment. An available trailer towing package gave the Brougham a towing capacity of 5,000 pounds. The d'Elegance sedan featured a specific trim design with multi-button tufted seats. In addition, the interior package included three overhead assist handles and illuminated driver/passenger vanity mirrors. The d'Elegance again also featured Twilight Sentinel, power trunk pulldown, and specific exterior/interior ornamentation.

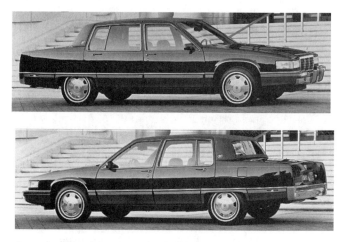

1991 Cadillac, Fleetwood Sixty-Special sedan. (OCW)

SEVILLE - SERIES 6K - V-8 - The Seville sedan and Seville Touring Sedan (STS) again comprised the Series 6K lineup. Updates and revisions mirrored those changes listed for the Eldorado, with the exception of the following: The STS received new, blue-tinted outside rearview mirrors as standard equipment and its seating area was revised. In addition to redesigned seats, new full Beechwood leather front bucket seats included six-way power seat adjusters, power recliners and power lumbar support for driver and passenger. There was also a full-width rear leather seat with integral headrests. The previously seen rear console was eliminated to accommodate a third, center rear seat passenger. Final drive ratio for the Seville sedan was 2.97:1 while the STS's was 3.33:1. The STS was equipped with the firmer ride and handling of a touring suspension package. It included 23mm front and 16mm rear stabilizer bars, special 16-inch forged aluminum wheels with Goodyear Eagle GT4 P215/60R16 tires. A touring package with 15-inch cast aluminum wheels and Goodyear Eagle GT4 P215/65R15 tires was optional on the Seville sedan. High-gloss birdseye maple wood was used to accent the Seville's instrument panel and console, while the STS exclusively featured elm burl high-gloss wood in all door panels, instrument panel and console. The 1991 Sevilles also received a new taillamp treatment and neutral density back-up lamps.

1991 Cadillac, Eldorado coupe. (OCW)

ELDORADO - SERIES 6E - V-8 - In addition to the previously offered Eldorado coupe and special edition Eldorado Biarritz coupe (option code YP3), a special edition Eldorado Touring Coupe (option code YP5) joined the series for 1991. As with other Cadillacs, anti-lock braking became standard on Eldos in 1991. Powering the coupes was the 4.9-liter V-8 mated to the 4T60-E electronically controlled four-speed automatic transmission with overdrive. The 4.9-liter V-8 with port fuel injection improved the Eldo's 0-60 mph time to 8.2 seconds over the previously used 4.5-liter V-8. The transverse-mounted engine was comprised of an aluminum block with wet, cast iron cylinder liners and cast iron cylinder heads. It had a compression ratio of 9.5:1 and needed premium unleaded fuel with a minimum octane rating of 91. Eldorado coupes also received new focused engine mounts that aimed the mounts at the engine/transmission torque axis, which aided in isolating engine noise and reducing vibration. Computer Command Ride became standard equipment. Also new was the exterior color Polo Green, upping the total to 16 colors for Eldos and 15 for Biarritz. New options included a heated windshield system that melted frost and ice five times faster than a conventional defroster and a Security Package that included remote keyless entry, automatic door locks with central door unlocking capability and theft-deterrent system. The 4.9-liter V-8's functions were controlled by Cadillac's GMP4 Powertrain Control Module (PCM). This 64-kilobyte on-board computer sensed vital operating conditions, including engine rpm, intake manifold pressure and air temperature, outside air temperature, coolant temperature, exhaust gas oxygen content, throttle position, vehicle speed, accessory load level and brake operation. The PCM also functioned as a data storage system for service technicians to diagnose malfunctions. The Eldorado's Body Computer Module (BCM)—the heart of the car's sophisticated electronic information system—also provided driver and diagnostic information. The BCM also monitored and controlled functions such as air conditioning, Twilight Sentinel headlamp operation, theft alarm and electric cooling fan. Eldo's exhaust system featured a new wide-oval catalytic converter that provided 38 percent less restriction than the previous year's unit. The Touring Coupe had dual exhaust pipes with a specific rear valance and rocker moldings. The Touring Coupe's final drive ratio was 3.33:1, and its suspension provided a more "international feel" of driving. This suspension package included a 23mm diameter front stabilizer bar, 16mm diameter rear stabilizer bar and 16-inch styled aluminum wheels with Goodyear Eagle GT4 P215/60R16 tires. The steering system was modified to include a quicker ratio (2.97 turns lock-to-lock vs. 3.13) and a higher effort steering gear compared to the standard Eldo. The Touring Coupe's coachwork featured body color front and rear fascias and rocker moldings, all with black bead edging. Side mirrors and door handles were also body color. The Touring Coupe also featured a grille-mounted Cadillac wreath-and-crest emblem. A cloisonné emblem highlighted the rear decklid, while Eldorado script was dropped from the fenders and decklid. The Touring Coupe also received specific taillamp treatment, and offered six exterior colors: white, black, bright red (crimson), polo green, medium slate gray metallic and black sapphire metallic.

1991 Cadillac, Allante convertible with detachable hardtop. (OCW)

ALLANTE - SERIES 6V - V-8 - The Allante, again available as a convertible and as a convertible hardtop that included both a convertible top and a removable all-aluminum hardtop, retained the 4.5-liter V-8 and F-7 four-speed automatic transaxle used previously. For 1991, this engine received a new air intake resonator for quieter performance. It took the edge off the induction "roar" (an example was hill driving), but left the exhaust note unchanged. For improved power output, the aluminum engine's cast iron cylinder heads featured straighter intake ports and were equipped with large, 45mm intake and 38mm exhaust valves. Exhaust was evacuated through thin-wall, cast iron manifolds that were shaped for minimum flow resistance. Also, to help reduce oil aeration, a new gearotor-type oil pump was added to the engine. Final drive ratio was 3.21:1. The Allante's chassis was also upgraded with the second-generation speed-dependent damping system added as standard equipment. With this system, damping-select time was reduced for faster response to road inputs and vehicle speed changes. It also offered enhanced lift and dive control as well as improved diagnostics. The convertible featured an improved, Phase II ergonomically-designed, power-fastening, folding softtop. Inside, the Allante's previous light charcoal interior carpeting and floor mats were replaced with dark charcoal counterparts. Allante continued to offer the Bosch III anti-lock braking system and traction control as standard equipment. The traction control system was refined for 1991 with the addition of rubber isolated plungers that reduced noise when the system was engaged. Allante's variable-assist rack-and-pinion power steering system was also improved with a revised pump and adapter that resulted in quieter operation and enhanced reliability.

I.D. DATA: The 1991 Cadillac had a 17-symbol vehicle identification number (VIN) stamped on a metal tag attached to the upper left surface of the cowl visible through the windshield. The code was as follows: The first digit, "1," represented the manufacturing country (United States), the second, "G," represented General Motors, the third, "6," represented Cadillac, the fourth and fifth represented the car line/series, as follows: C/B-Fleetwood, C/D-deVille, C/G-Fleetwood Sixty Special, C/Z-commercial chassis, D/W-Brougham, E/L-Eldorado, K/S-Seville, K/Y-Seville Touring Sedan, V/R-Allante convertible hardtop, and V/S-Allante convertible. Digit six represents the body style: 1-two-door coupe/sedan, 2-two-door hatchback/liftback, 3-two-door convertible, 4-two-door station wagon, 5-four-door sedan, 6-four-door liftback/hatchback, and 8-four-door station wagon. Digit seven identifies the restraint code: 1-active (manual) belts, 3-active (manual) belts w/driver's side airbag, and 4-passive (automatic) belts. The eighth digit identifies the engine: "B"-L26 4.9L V-8; "E"-L03 5.0L V-8; "7"-LLO 5.7L V-8; and "8"-LQ6 4.5L V-8. A check digit follows. The 10th digit represents the model year, "M" for 1991. The eleventh digit represents the assembly plant. The remaining six digits identify the production sequence number.

deVille (V-8)

Series No.	Body/Style No.	Body Type & Seating	Factory Price	Shipping Weight	Prod. Total
CD1	D47	2-dr. Coupe	30205	3545	Note 1
CD5	D69	4-dr. Sedan	30455	3623	Note 2
CT5	T69	4-dr. Tour Sed.	33455	N/A	Note 2

Fleetwood (V-8)

CB1	B47	2-dr. Coupe	34675	3594	Note 1
CB5	B69	4-dr. Sedan	34925	3676	Note 2

Fleetwood Sixty Special (V-8)

CG5	G69	4-dr. Sedan	38325	3707	Note 2

Note: Cadillac tallied deVille and Fleetwood production together with no series breakout available.

Note 1: deVille/Fleetwood coupe production totaled 12,134 with no further breakout available.

Note 2: deVille/Fleetwood sedan production totaled 135,776 with no further breakout available.

Brougham (V-8)

DW5	W69	4-dr. Sedan	30225	4282	27,231 (*)

(*) Includes Broughams equipped with d'Elegance option.

Eldorado (V-8)

EL1	L57	2-dr. Coupe	31245	3470	16,212 (*)

(*) Includes Eldorados equipped with Touring Coupe and Biarritz options.

Seville (V-8)

KS5	S69	4-dr. Sedan	33935	3513	Note 1
KY5	Y69	4-dr. Tour Sed.	37135	3565	Note 1

Note 1: Seville production totaled 26,431 with no further breakout available.

Allante (V-8)

VR3	R67	2-dr. Conv. HT	60800	3537	Note 1
VS3	S67	2-dr. Conv.	55250	3480	Note 1

Note 1: Allante production totaled 2,500 with no further breakout available.

ENGINES: BASE V-8: (Allante) 90-degree, overhead valve V-8. Aluminum block and cast iron cylinder liners, cast iron cylinder heads. Displacement: 273 cu. in. (4.5 liters). Bore & Stroke: 3.62 x 3.31 in. Compression ratio: 9.0:1. Brake horsepower: 200 @ 4400 rpm. Torque: 270 lb.-ft. @ 3200 rpm. Roller hydraulic valve lifters. Tuned port fuel injection. BASE V-8: (deVille, Fleetwood, Fleetwood Sixty Special, Seville, Eldorado) 90-degree, overhead valve V-8. Aluminum block with cast iron cylinder liners, cast iron cylinder heads. Displacement: 300 cu. in. (4.9 liters). Bore & Stroke: 3.62 x 3.62 in. Compression ratio: 9.5:1. Brake horsepower: 200 @ 4100 rpm. Torque: 275 lb.-ft. @ 3000 rpm. Roller hydraulic valve lifters. Sequential port fuel injection. BASE V-8: (Brougham) 90-degree, overhead valve V-8. Cast iron block and cylinder heads. Displacement: 305 cu. in. (5.0 liters). Bore & Stroke: 3.74 x 3.48 in. Compression ratio: 9.3:1. Brake horsepower: 170 @ 4200 rpm. Torque: 255 lb.-ft. @ 2400 rpm. Throttle body fuel injection. OPTIONAL V-8: (Brougham—standard on Coachbuilders edition or Brougham w/towing package) 90-degree, overhead valve V-8. Cast iron block and cylinder heads. Displacement: 350

cu. in. (5.7 liters). Bore & Stroke: 4.00 x 3.48 in. Compression ratio: 9.8:1. Brake horsepower: 185 @ 3800 rpm. Torque: 300 lb.-ft. @ 2400 rpm. Roller hydraulic valve lifters. Throttle body fuel injection.

CHASSIS DATA: Wheelbase: (Coupe deVille, Fleetwood cpe) 110.8 in.; (Sedan deVille, Fleetwood sed, Sixty Special) 113.8 in.; (Seville, Eldorado) 108.0 in.; (Allante) 99.4 in.; (Brougham) 121.5 in. Overall Length: (Coupe deVille, Fleetwood cpe) 202.6 in.; (Sedan deVille, Fleetwood sed, Sixty Special) 205.6 in.; (Seville) 190.8 in.; (Eldorado) 191.4 in.; (Allante) 178.7 in.; (Brougham) 221 in. Height: (Coupe deVille, Fleetwood cpe) 54.9 in.; (Sedan deVille, Fleetwood sed, Sixty Special) 55.2 in.; (Seville, Eldorado) 53.2 in.; (Allante) 51.2 in.; (Brougham) 57.4 in. Width: (Coupe deVille, Fleetwood cpe) 73.4 in.; (Sedan deVille, Fleetwood sed, Sixty Special) 73.4 in.; (Seville) 72.0 in.; (Eldorado) 72.4 in.; (Allante) 73.5 in.; (Brougham) 76.5 in. Front Tread: (Coupe deVille, Fleetwood cpe) 60.3 in.; (Sedan deVille, Fleetwood sed, Sixty Special) 60.3 in.; (Seville, Eldorado) 59.9 in.; (Allante) 60.4 in.; (Brougham) 61.7 in. Rear Tread: (Coupe deVille, Fleetwood cpe) 59.8 in.; (Sedan deVille, Fleetwood sed, Sixty Special) 59.8 in.; (Seville, Eldorado) 59.9 in.; (Allante) 60.4 in.; (Brougham) 60.7 in. Standard Tires: (Coupe deVille, Fleetwood cpe) Michelin P205/70R15; (Sedan deVille, Fleetwood sed, Sixty Special) P205/70R15; (Seville, Eldorado) P205/70R15; (Touring) Goodyear Eagle GT4 P215/65R15; (STS with 16 in. wheels) 215/60R16; (Allante) Goodyear Eagle VL P225/55VR16; (Brougham) Michelin P225/75R15.

TECHNICAL: Transmission: (deVille, Fleetwood, Eldorado, Seville) 4T60-E electronically controlled four-speed automatic with overdrive (includes viscous converter clutch); (Allante) THM-F7 four-speed automatic (includes viscous converter clutch); (Brougham) THM 4L60 four-speed automatic with overdrive (includes torque converter clutch). Steering: (All exc. Brougham) Power-assisted rack-and-pinion; (Brougham) Power-assisted recirculating ball. Front Suspension: (All exc. Brougham) Independent MacPherson strut with coil springs, strut-type shock absorbers (integral-in strut and electronic variable on Allante and Computer Command Ride on Fleetwood, Seville, Eldorado) and stabilizer bar; (Brougham) Independent with short/long arms, coil springs, direct acting shock absorbers and link-type stabilizer bar. Rear Suspension: (deVille, Fleetwood) fully independent with coil springs, automatic level control and (deVille) strut-type superlift shock absorbers (Fleetwood) Computer Command Ride; (Eldorado, Seville) Fully independent transverse monoleaf w/automatic level control and Computer Command Ride, no rear stabilizer; (Allante) Fully independent transverse monoleaf w/integral-in strut electronic variable shock absorbers, no rear stabilizer; (Brougham) Four link, coil springs w/automatic level control and direct acting shock absorbers and stabilizer bar. Brakes: (All exc. Allante) Power assisted front disc/rear drum w/Teves anti-lock braking system (Eldorado, Seville, Brougham used Bosch II ABS); (Allante) Power assisted front and rear disc w/Bosch III anti-lock braking system. Body Construction: (All exc. Brougham) Integral body-frame; (Brougham) Separate body on frame. Fuel Tank: (deVille, Fleetwood) 18.0 gals.; (Eldorado, Seville) 18.8 gals.; (Allante) 22.0 gals.; (Brougham) 25.0 gals.

DRIVETRAIN OPTIONS: (Brougham) 5.7-liter V-8 $250. (Brougham) V92 Trailer Towing pkg. $550. FE2 Touring Suspension pkg. (Eldorado-stnd STS) $155; (Seville-stnd STS) $155. (deVille) FX3 Computer Command Ride $380.

DEVILLE CONVENIENCE/APPEARANCE OPTIONS: Coupe deVille Spring Edition Pkg. (incl. cast alum whls, f&r carpeted floor mats, illum entry, leather seating, illum vanity mirrors, six-way pwr pass. seat, full cabriolet roof and gold ornamentation) $1,481. Opt. Pkg. B $320. Opt. Pkg. C $586. Opt. Pkg. D $1,045. Security Pkg. $385. Cold Weather Pkg. $369. Digital Instrument Cluster $250. Illuminated Entry Syst. $90. Auto Day/Night Mirror $110. Astroroof $1,550. Coachbuilders Pkg. (Sedan deV) $1,000. Gold Ornamentation Pkg. $395. H.D. Livery Pkg. (Sedan deV) $1,000. Leather Seating $570. Firemist Paint $240. Lower Accent Firemist Paint $50. Two-tone Paint (Sedan deV) $225. Delco-Bose Sound Syst. $575; w/CD $872. Formal Cabriolet Roof (Coupe deV) $925. Full Cabriolet Roof (Coupe deV) $1,095. Phaeton Roof (Sedan deV) $1,095. Locking Wire Whl Discs $235. Lace Cast Alum Whls $235.

FLEETWOOD AND SIXTY SPECIAL CONVENIENCE/APPEARANCE OPTIONS: Security Pkg. $295. Cold Weather Pkg. $369. Custom Seating Pkg. $425. Astroroof $1,550. Gold Ornamentation Pkg. $395. Leather Seating $570. Delco-Bose Sound Syst. $575; w/CD $872.

ELDORADO CONVENIENCE/APPEARANCE OPTIONS: Eldorado Spring Special Pkg. (incl. cast alum whls, full cabriolet roof, leather seating, Delco Bose sound syst., and gold ornamentation) $115. YP3 Biarritz Opt. $3,275. YP5 Touring Coupe Opt. $2,050. Birdseye Maple Wood Appliqué $245. Security Pkg. $480. Heated Windshield Syst. $309. Astroroof $1,550. Gold Ornamentation Pkg. $395. Leather Seating $555. Auto Day/Night Mirror $110. Firemist Paint $240. Lower Accent Firemist Paint $50. White Diamond Paint $240. Delco-Bose Sound Syst. $575; w/CD $872. Full Vinyl Roof $1,095. Full Cabriolet Roof $1,095. P215/65R15 WSW Tires (only w/FE2 Touring Susp.) $76. Locking Wire Whl Discs $235. Cast Alum Whls $115.

SEVILLE CONVENIENCE/APPEARANCE OPTIONS: Heated Windshield Syst. $309. Astroroof $1,550. Gold Ornamentation Pkg. $395. Leather Seating $460. Auto Day/Night Mirror $110. Firemist Paint $240. Lower Accent Firemist Paint $50. White Diamond Paint $240. Delco-Bose Sound Syst. $575; w/CD $872. Phaeton Roof $1,195. P215/65R15 WSW Tires (only w/FE2 Touring Susp.) $76. Locking Wire Whl Discs $235.

BROUGHAM CONVENIENCE/APPEARANCE OPTIONS: Opt. Pkg. B $325. Opt. Pkg. C $685. Opt. Pkg. C (d'Elegance) $360. Astroroof $1,550. Coachbuilder Pkg. ($139 credit). d'Elegance Cloth Int. $1,875. d'Elegance Leather Int. $2,445. Gold Ornamentation Pkg. $395. Leather Seating $570. Livery Pkg. $299. Auto Day/Night Mirror $110. Firemist Paint $240. Lower Accent Firemist Paint $50. CD Music Syst. $396. Full Vinyl Roof $925. Locking Wire Whl Discs $445. Wire Whls $1,000.

ALLANTE CONVENIENCE/APPEARANCE OPTIONS: Digital Instrument Cluster (conv. only) $495. Pearl White Paint (conv. only) $700.

HISTORY: Cadillac's model year production totaled 220,284 compared with 268,698 the year previous. Based on sales of 213,288 automobiles in 1991 (vs. 258,168 the year before), Cadillac's share of the U.S. market was 2.61 percent compared with 2.78 percent in 1990.

1992

The 1992 Seville and Eldorado models were Cadillac's first totally new offerings since the luxury automaker was reorganized in 1987 as an autonomous General Motors division. Fleetwood models received traction control as standard equipment while deVille models offered this function as an option. The Brougham sedan retained its distinction as America's longest production vehicle, but was not subject to "gas guzzler" taxes in 1992.

1992 Cadillac, Coupe deVille. (OCW)

DEVILLE - SERIES 6C - V-8 - The lineup again consisted of a Coupe deVille, Sedan deVille and Touring Sedan (deVille). All were again powered by the 4.9-liter V-8 mated to the 4T60-E electronically controlled four-speed automatic transmission with overdrive. The deVille's V-8 received platinum-tipped spark plugs with a 100,000-mile replacement interval as standard equipment. Other new standard items (formerly offered as optional equipment) were an electrochromic automatic day/night inside rearview mirror, six-way power adjuster for the front passenger seat, and front and rear carpeted floor mats. New options included brake-only traction control (available only with Computer Command Ride), which regulated tire spin during acceleration; driver's side electrochromic outside rearview mirror; and Delco-Bose Gold Series CD sound system. New deVille features included

six exterior colors: Slate Green, Light Beige (monotone only), Taupe, Autumn Brown, Academy Gray and Dark Plum; three new lower accent molding colors: Light Beige, Academy Gray and Dark Plum; and three new interior colors: Light Gray, Neutral and Taupe. Other changes included revised seating in the Touring Sedan consisting of new split-frame Dual Comfort front seats trimmed in Beechwood leather with six-way power adjusters and power recliners and manual headrests. The rear seat was also redesigned and now featured two individual headrests. The deVille's throttle position sensor and throttle body design were upgraded to provide improved throttle feel. Also, deVille's exhaust system featured new 2.5-inch diameter pipe and revised pipe routing. The Touring Sedan featured wide, chrome-plated bodyside molding with "Touring Sedan" identification located on the forward edge of the front doors; body-color front and rear fascia and body-color "sport" door handles. Only monotone color choices were available on the Touring Sedan, including five new colors: Slate Green, Light Beige, Royal Maroon, Academy Gray and Dark Plum, and a vinyl top could not be ordered. A quicker 17:1 steering gear was exclusive to the Touring Sedan as were specific 16-inch aluminum alloy wheels with a distinctive wreath-and-crest center cap. Goodyear GA P215/60R16 tires were standard equipment.

1992 Cadillac, Fleetwood coupe. (OCW)

FLEETWOOD - SERIES 6C - V-8 - The new exterior and interior colors available listed for deVille were also part of the changes for the 1992 Fleetwood. Returning to power the Fleetwood coupe and sedan offered was the 4.9-liter V-8 paired with the 4T60-E electronically controlled four-speed automatic transmission with overdrive. New standard features included the brake-only traction control system; 100,000-mile replacement interval; platinum-tipped spark plugs; and driver's side electrochromic outside rearview mirror. A new option was the Delco-Bose Gold Series CD sound system. Fleetwood models also received upgrades to the exhaust system and throttle body design, as mentioned in the deVille listing. The Fleetwood's power-assisted rack-and-pinion steering system was refined, with its power steering pump, gear assembly and tie-rod ends being upgraded. Suspension modifications were also carried out to the Fleetwood's struts, rear stabilizer bar, rear springs and toe links to improve durability. The Fleetwood's heating/air conditioning system featured a new compressor and temperature valve motor mounted on the A/C control module.

1992 Cadillac, Fleetwood Sixty Special sedan. (OCW)

FLEETWOOD SIXTY SPECIAL - SERIES 6C - V-8 - The Sixty Special's new features mirrored those of the Fleetwood coupe and sedan with the exception of two new interior leather colors: Light Gray and Black. The new, standard brake-only traction control system used the same integral front bearing wheel-speed sensors as the Teves anti-lock braking system. The traction control system applied pulses of brake pressure to a drive wheel if it began to spin. This system was fully functional up to 24 mph, with the traction control operation gradually phased out between 24 and 30 mph.

1992 Cadillac, Brougham sedan. (OCW)

BROUGHAM - SERIES 6D - V-8 - Cadillac's only rear-wheel drive sedan—again also available in d'Elegance trim (option code V4S)—was basically a carry-over from the previous year, except that Brougham's appearance was improved by a new, more durable base coat/clear coat paint process. The 5.0-liter V-8 coupled to the Hydra-matic 4L60 four-speed automatic transmission with overdrive remained as the standard powertrain. The 5.7-liter V-8 was again optional equipment, but required when the trailer towing, Coachbuilder or Armoring options were ordered. The Brougham again also was available with the Funeral Coach Package (option code B9Q) for aftermarket conversion to funeral service. In this configuration, only the 5.0-liter V-8 was offered.

1992 Cadillac, Eldorado Touring Coupe. (OCW)

ELDORADO - SERIES 6E - V-8 - Inside and out, it was an all-new Eldorado coupe and Touring Coupe (option code YP5) for 1992. The Eldo returned to a traditional hardtop configuration with the "door glass into roof" design rather than a full door frame. Overall, compared to the previous year's Eldo, length of the luxury coupe increased 10.8 inches to 202.2 inches, body width increased 3.5 inches to 74.8 inches, and height increased to 54 inches. Structurally, Eldo's unibody construction was improved with the addition of crush zones for enhanced safety and an integrated, solid feel. The front frame was stiffer and featured new engine and transmission mounts for improved stability and road noise isolation. The returning 4.9-liter V-8 received 100,000-mile replacement interval, platinum-tipped spark plugs, and was again coupled to the 4T60-E electronically controlled four-speed automatic transmission with overdrive. Eldorados also received a new brake/transmission shift interlock and featured improved braking via larger front and rear brake rotors and larger front calipers. Eldo's redesigned appearance included a larger flush-glass windshield and flush-glass door and rear-quarter windows; revamped front fenders, rear quarter panels, and hood with stand-up ornament; body-color fascias with rub strips; chrome-plated grille; revised park, signal and cornering lamps; flush door handles; revamped bodyside moldings with bright upper strip and integral "Eldorado" or "Touring Coupe" lettering with gray border; low-gloss black rocker molding; new center high-mounted stoplamp integrated into package shelf; new taillamp assembly and rear fascia, new decklid with revised locking emblem and new "Eldorado" lettering integrated into rear license plate pocket. The trunk was also redesigned to reduce liftover height while offering 15.3 cubic feet of space (an increase of 1.2 cubic feet over the previous year's version). In addition, the trunklid opened to a full upright

position. Inside, interior volume increased two cubic feet (115 cubic feet overall). New Bistro Cloth trim was used and seats were redesigned for enhanced comfort. Other new features included a revamped instrument panel that had Zebrano wood accents, a steering column-mounted transmission shift level, a more compact center front mini console, center front overhead console and modular headliner with ergonomically positioned courtesy/reading lamps and retractable coat hooks. The standard climate control system was improved with an upgraded electronic solar sensor and adjustable outlets with five-speed fan control. Optional equipment included more supple leather seating areas; Sport Interior package that included full floor console with shift lever and analog instrument cluster; heated front seats (available only with leather); and Delco-Bose Gold Series CD sound system. Other new equipment found on the Eldo included 16-inch cast aluminum wheels with Michelin XGT4 P225/60R16 touring tires (blackwall or whitewall could be selected). The redesigned Eldo achieved a 0.33 coefficient of drag compared to the previous year's 0.38. Steering ratio was 16.5:1, which required 2.81 turns lock-to-lock. The Eldo's curb-to-curb turning circle was 40 feet. Weight distribution, front to rear was 62.8 percent to 37.2 percent. The Touring Coupe featured a monochromatic paint scheme, specific chrome-plated grille with wreath-and-crest emblem, a specific, body-color front fascia and integral foglamps. The rear, body-color fascia featured dual cutouts for chrome-plated exhaust tips. The Touring Coupe was offered in 11 colors, including three new ones: Slate Green, Dark Plum and Gold Diamond. Final drive ratio for the Touring Coupe was 3.33:1. Computer Command Ride was standard equipment and featured four electronically controlled struts that were revalved for stiffer suspension qualities. The Touring Coupe rode on specific 16-inch aluminum wheels and Goodyear Eagle GA P225/60HR16 tires.

1992 Cadillac, Seville sedan. (OCW)

SEVILLE - SERIES 6K - V-8 - While the refinements/upgrades of the all-new Seville basically mirrored those of the Eldo, the overall appearance of each was kept distinct. According to Cadillac's exterior design studio, the Seville was nicknamed the "greyhound" because of its rounded, muscular look while the Eldo was nicknamed the "needle" because of its sharp, razor edge styling and angular body lines. The lineup was again comprised of a Seville sedan and Seville Touring Sedan (STS). The all-new Seville's overall length of 203.9 inches was 13.1 inches longer than the previous year's measure. As with the Eldo, the Seville's electronic systems were streamlined. A new simplified main computer, the Instrument Panel Cluster eliminated the Body Control Module offered previously as well as integrating the Powertrain Control Module functions. The Seville's source of power was again the 4.9-liter V-8 mated to the 4T60-E electronically controlled four-speed automatic transmission with overdrive. Appearance-wise, the Seville featured composite headlamps and wraparound parking, signal and cornering lamps. A chrome-plated grille had light gray inserts. In the rear, the center high-mounted stop lamp ran the entire length of the decklid. Inside, interior volume was increased 6.5 cubic feet to 119.5 cubic feet. The STS had a body-color grille that featured a pewter color wreath-and-crest emblem.

1992 Cadillac, Allante convertible. (OCW)

ALLANTE - SERIES 6V - V-8 - The all-new 1993 convertible was launched early in spring 1992, so the 1992 Allante was basically a carry-over from the year previous. It was again offered in convertible and convertible hardtop configurations and was powered by the 4.5-liter V-8 paired with the F-7 four-speed automatic transaxle.

I.D. DATA: The 1992 Cadillac had a 17-symbol vehicle identification number (VIN) stamped on a metal tag attached to the upper left surface of the cowl visible through the windshield. The code was as follows: The first digit, "1," represented the manufacturing country (United States), the second, "G," represented General Motors, the third, "6," represented Cadillac, the fourth and fifth represented the car line/series, as follows: C/B-Fleetwood, C/D-deVille, C/G-Fleetwood Sixty Special, C/T-deVille Touring Sedan, D/W-Brougham, E/L-Eldorado, K/S-Seville, K/Y-Seville Touring Sedan, V/R-Allante convertible hardtop, and V/S-Allante convertible. Digit six represents the body style: 1-two-door coupe/sedan, 2-two-door hatchback/liftback, 3-two-door convertible, 4-two-door station wagon, 5-four-door sedan, 6-four-door liftback/hatchback, and 8-four-door station wagon. Digit seven identifies the restraint code: 1-active (manual) belts, 2-active (manual) belts w/dual airbags, 3-active (manual) belts w/driver's side airbag, 4-passive (automatic) belts, and 5-passive (automatic) belts w/driver's side airbag. The eighth digit identifies the engine: "B"-L26 4.9L V-8; "E"-L03 5.0L V-8; "7"-L05 5.7L V-8; and "8"-LQ6 4.5L V-8. A check digit follows. The 10th digit represents the model year, "N" for 1992. The eleventh digit represents the assembly plant. The remaining six digits identify the production sequence number.

deVille (V-8)

Series No.	Body/Style No.	Body Type & Seating	Factory Price	Shipping Weight	Prod. Total
CD1	D47	2-dr. Coupe	31740	3519	Note 1
CD5	D69	4-dr. Sedan	31740	3591	Note 2
CT5	T69	4-dr. Tour Sed.	35190	3627	Note 2

Fleetwood (V-8)

CB1	B47	2-dr. Coupe	36360	3566	Note 1
CB5	B69	4-dr. Sedan	36360	3642	Note 2

Fleetwood Sixty Special (V-8)

CG5	G69	4-dr. Sedan	39860	3653	Note 2

Note: Cadillac tallied deVille and Fleetwood production together with no series breakout available.

Note 1: deVille/Fleetwood coupe production totaled 8,423 with no further breakout available.

Note 2: deVille/Fleetwood sedan production totaled 133,808 with no further breakout available.

Brougham (V-8)

DW5	W69	4-dr. Sedan	31740	4276	13,761 (*)

(*) Includes Broughams equipped with d'Elegance option.

Eldorado (V-8)

EL1	L57	2-dr. Coupe	32470	3604	31,151 (*)

(*) Includes Eldorados equipped with Touring Coupe option.

Seville (V-8)

KS5	S69	4-dr. Sedan	34975	3648	Note 1
KY5	Y69	4-dr. Tour Sed.	37975	3721	Note 1

Note 1: Seville production totaled 43,953 with no further breakout available.

Allante (V-8)

VR3	R67	2-dr. Conv. HT	62790	3555	Note 1
VS3	S67	2-dr. Conv.	57170	3491	Note 1

Note 1: Allante production totaled 1,931 with no further breakout available. It was an abbreviated model year as the 1993 Allante was launched in spring 1992.

ENGINES: BASE V-8: (Allante) 90-degree, overhead valve V-8. Aluminum block and cast iron cylinder liners, cast iron cylinder heads. Displacement: 273 cu. in. (4.5 liters). Bore & Stroke: 3.62 x 3.31 in. Compression ratio: 9.0:1. Brake horsepower: 200 @ 4400 rpm. Torque: 270 lb.-ft. @ 3200 rpm. Roller hydraulic valve lifters. Tuned port fuel injection. BASE V-8: (deVille, Fleetwood, Fleetwood Sixty Special, Seville, Eldorado) 90-degree, overhead valve V-8. Aluminum block with cast iron cylinder liners, cast iron cylinder heads. Displacement: 300 cu. in. (4.9 liters). Bore & Stroke: 3.62 x 3.62 in. Compression ratio: 9.5:1. Brake horsepower: 200 @ 4100 rpm. Torque: 275 lb.-ft. @ 3000 rpm. Roller hydraulic valve lifters. Sequential port fuel injection. BASE V-8: (Brougham) 90-degree, overhead valve V-8. Cast iron block and cylinder heads. Displacement: 305 cu. in. (5.0 liters). Bore & Stroke: 3.74 x 3.48 in. Compression ratio: 9.3:1. Brake horsepower: 170 @ 4200 rpm. Torque: 255 lb.-ft. @ 2400 rpm. Roller hydraulic valve lifters. Throttle body fuel injection. OPTIONAL V-8: (Brougham—standard on coachbuilders edition or Brougham w/towing package) 90-degree, overhead valve V-8. Cast iron block and cylinder heads. Displacement: 350 cu. in. (5.7 liters). Bore & Stroke: 4.00 x 3.48 in. Compression ratio: 9.8:1. Brake horsepower: 185 @ 3800 rpm. Torque: 300 lb.-ft. @ 2400 rpm. Roller hydraulic valve lifters. Throttle body fuel injection.

CHASSIS DATA: Wheelbase: (Coupe deVille, Fleetwood cpe) 110.8 in.; (Sedan deVille, Fleetwood sed, Sixty Special) 113.8 in.; (Seville) 111.0 in.; (Eldorado) 108.0 in.; (Allante) 99.4 in.; (Brougham) 121.5 in. Overall Length: (Coupe deVille, Fleetwood cpe) 205.1 in.; (Sedan deVille, Fleetwood sed, Sixty Special) 208.0 in.; (Seville) 203.9 in.; (Eldorado) 202.2 in.; (Allante) 178.7 in.; (Brougham) 221.0 in. Height: (Coupe deVille, Fleetwood cpe) 54.4 in.; (Sedan deVille, Fleetwood sed, Sixty Special) 55.0 in.; (Seville, Eldorado) 54.0 in.; (Allante) 51.2 in.; (Brougham) 57.4 in. Width: (Coupe deVille, Fleetwood cpe) 73.4 in.; (Sedan deVille, Fleetwood sed, Sixty Special) 73.4 in.; (Seville) 74.4 in.; (Eldorado) 74.8 in.; (Allante) 73.5 in.; (Brougham) 76.5 in. Front Tread: (Coupe deVille, Fleetwood cpe) 60.2 in.; (Sedan deVille, Fleetwood sed, Sixty Special) 60.2 in.; (Seville, Eldorado) 60.9 in.; (Allante) 60.4 in.; (Brougham) 61.7 in. Rear Tread: (Coupe deVille, Fleetwood cpe) 59.9 in.; (Sedan deVille, Fleetwood sed, Sixty Special) 59.9 in.; (Seville, Eldorado) 60.9 in.; (Allante) 60.4 in.; (Brougham) 60.7 in. Standard Tires: (Coupe deVille, Fleetwood cpe) Michelin P205/70R15; (Sedan deVille, Fleetwood sed, Sixty Special) P205/70R15; (Seville, Eldorado) P225/60R16; (Touring) Goodyear Eagle GA P225/60HR16; (Allante) Goodyear Eagle VL P225/55VR16; (Brougham) Uniroyal P225/75R15.

TECHNICAL: Transmission: (deVille, Fleetwood, Eldorado, Seville) 4T60-E electronically controlled four-speed automatic with overdrive (includes viscous converter clutch); (Allante) THM-F7 four-speed automatic (includes viscous converter clutch); (Brougham) THM 4L60 four-speed automatic with overdrive (includes torque converter clutch). Steering: (All exc. Brougham) Power-assisted rack-and-pinion; (Brougham) Power-assisted recirculating ball. Front Suspension: (All exc. Brougham) Independent MacPherson strut with coil springs, strut-type shock absorbers (integral-in strut and electronic variable on Allante and Computer Command Ride on Fleetwood, Seville, Eldorado) and stabilizer bar; (Brougham) Independent with short/long arms, coil springs, direct acting shock absorbers and link-type stabilizer bar. Rear Suspension: (deVille, Fleetwood) fully independent with coil springs, automatic level control and (deVille) strut-type superlift shock absorbers (Fleetwood) Computer Command Ride; (Eldorado, Seville) Fully independent transverse monoleaf w/automatic level control and Computer Command Ride, no rear stabilizer; (Allante) Fully independent transverse monoleaf w/integral-in strut electronic variable shock absorbers, no rear stabilizer; (Brougham) Four link, coil springs w/automatic level control and direct acting shock absorbers and stabilizer bar. Brakes: (All exc. Eldorado, Seville, Allante) Power assisted front disc/rear drum w/Teves anti-lock braking system (Brougham used Bosch II ABS); (Eldorado, Seville) Power assisted front and rear disc w/Bosch II anti-lock braking system; (Allante) Power assisted front and rear disc w/Bosch III anti-lock braking system. Body Construction: (All exc. Brougham) Integral body-frame; (Brougham) Separate body on frame. Fuel Tank: (deVille, Fleetwood) 18.0 gals.; (Eldorado, Seville) 18.8 gals.; (Allante) 22.0 gals.; (Brougham) 25.0 gals.

DRIVETRAIN OPTIONS: (Brougham) 5.7-liter V-8 $250. (Brougham) V4P Trailer Towing pkg. $550. (deVille) NW9 Traction Control $175. (deVille) FX3 Speed Sensitive Suspension $380.

DEVILLE CONVENIENCE/APPEARANCE OPTIONS: Opt. Pkg. B $356. Opt. Pkg. C $803. Security Pkg. $295. Cold Weather Pkg. $369. Digital Instrument Cluster $495. Astroroof $1,550. Coachbuilders Pkg. (Sedan deV) $1,000. Gold Ornamentation Pkg. $395. H.D. Livery Pkg. (Sedan deV) $1,000. Leather Seating $570. Firemist Paint $190. Delco-Bose Sound Syst. $575; w/CD $872. Formal Cabriolet Roof (Coupe deV) $925. Full Cabriolet Roof (Coupe deV) $1,095. Phaeton Roof (Sedan deV) $1,095. Locking Wire Whl Discs $235. Lace Cast Alum Whls $235.

FLEETWOOD AND SIXTY SPECIAL CONVENIENCE/APPEARANCE OPTIONS: Security Pkg. $295. Cold Weather Pkg. $369. Custom Seating Pkg. $425. Astroroof $1,550. Gold Ornamentation Pkg. $395. Leather Seating $570. Firemist Paint $190. Delco-Bose Sound Syst. $575; w/CD $872. Full Vinyl Roof (N/A cpe) $925.

ELDORADO CONVENIENCE/APPEARANCE OPTIONS: YP5 Touring Coupe Opt. $4,000. Opt. Pkg. B $181. Security Pkg. $480. Seating Pkg. $340. Accent Striping $75. Heated Front Seats $120. Astroroof $1,550. Gold Ornamentation Pkg. $395. Heated Windshield $309. Leather Seating $650. Auto Day/Night Mirror $110. Firemist Paint $240. Gold/White Diamond Paint $240. Delco-Bose Sound Syst. w/CD & Cassette $972. Sport Interior $146. P225/60R16 WSW Tires $76.

SEVILLE CONVENIENCE/APPEARANCE OPTIONS: Opt. Pkg. B $181. Security Pkg. $480. Seating Pkg. $340. Sport Interior $146. Accent Striping $75. Heated Front Seats $120. Heated Windshield Syst. $309. Astroroof $1,550. Leather Seating $650. Auto Day/Night Mirror $110. Firemist Paint $240. Gold/White Diamond Paint $240. Delco-Bose Sound Syst. w/CD & Cassette $972.

BROUGHAM CONVENIENCE/APPEARANCE OPTIONS: Opt. Pkg. B $325. Opt. Pkg. C $685. Opt. Pkg. C (d'Elegance) $360. Astroroof $1,550. Coachbuilder Pkg. $295. Funeral Coach Pkg. ($1,680 credit). d'Elegance Cloth Int. $1,875. d'Elegance Leather Int. $2,445. Gold Ornamentation Pkg. $395. Leather Seating (d'Elegance) $570. Auto Day/Night Mirror $110. Firemist Paint $240. Radio w/CD & Cassette $396. Full Vinyl Roof $925. Locking Wire Whl Discs $445. Wire Whls $1,000.

ALLANTE CONVENIENCE/APPEARANCE OPTIONS: Digital Instrument Cluster (conv. only) $495. Pearl White Paint (conv. only) $700.

HISTORY: Cadillac's model year production totaled 233,027 compared with 220,284 the year previous. Based on sales of 214,176 automobiles in 1992 (vs. 213,288 the year before), Cadillac's share of the U.S. market remained at 2.61 percent. A 1993 Allante convertible was selected as the pace car for the 1992 Indianapolis 500.

1993

It was Cadillac's 90th Anniversary and also a year of "musical chairs" for the names of the automaker's products. The previously offered Brougham sedan was now called the Fleetwood, with the Brougham moniker reserved for an upscale option package available on the Fleetwood sedan. The former Fleetwood series, comprised of a coupe and sedan, was discontinued. The previously available Fleetwood Sixty

Special was now simply called the Sixty Special. The Allante convertible was greatly revamped (launched early in spring 1992), but it was the final year for the luxury two-seater. Eldorado added a Sport Coupe package and Sport Appearance Package to "dress-up" the personal luxury coupe. The Northstar powertrain, with "limp-home" capability (after loss of all engine coolant) also debuted in 1993.

1993 Cadillac, Sedan deVille. (OCW)

1993 Cadillac, Sedan deVille (special edition). (OCW)

DEVILLE - SERIES 6C - V-8 - The deVille series lineup returned intact from the year previous, but "America's best-selling luxury car" received several upgrades, including speed sensitive steering and speed sensitive suspension as standard equipment. Speed sensitive steering varied the amount of steering effort required of the driver in proportion to the vehicle's speed. The deVille's power-assisted rack-and-pinion steering's ratio was 17.6:1 with 2.97 turns required lock-to-lock. Speed sensitive suspension automatically selected from three settings—comfort, normal and firm—to provide optimal ride and handling characteristics at all operating speeds. The 4.9-liter V-8 and 4T60-E electronically controlled four-speed automatic transmission with overdrive again was the deVille's power source. A new feature for 1993 was the Generation II CS144 alternator that delivered 140 amps of power. The CS144 incorporated a self-cooling design for optimal reliability. Final drive ratio for the Coupe deVille and Sedan deVille was 2.73:1. Exterior improvements included a revised grille for a "bolder" appearance, new blacked-out quarter window molding on the Sedan deVille/Touring Sedan, and formal cabriolet roof on the Coupe deVille. Two new exterior colors were offered, Dark Cherry and Bronze, upping the total numbers of clearcoat paint colors available to 14. Two new interior options were available in 1993, Beechwood leather seat color choice and a trunk convenience net. The deVille continued to offer a driver's side airbag, solar control glass all-around, Pass-Key II anti-theft system and Twilight Sentinel headlamp system as standard fare. Remote keyless entry, traction control and Astroroof remained on the optional equipment list. The Touring Sedan (deVille) featured the aforementioned speed sensitive steering and suspension systems as well as traction control as standard items. Outside, the Touring Sedan was distinguished by a grille-mounted wreath-and-crest emblem, front and rear body-color fascia, body-color door handles and chrome-plated bodyside door moldings with "Touring Sedan" identification. Inside, Beechwood color leather was used, and the leather-trimmed steering wheel included a tilt feature and driver's side airbag. The instrument panel and doors were trimmed with American Walnut wood inserts.

1993 Cadillac, Sixty Special sedan. (OCW)

SIXTY SPECIAL - SERIES 6C - V-8 - No longer using the Fleetwood name, the Sixty Special's refinements were in line with those of the deVille series. Already employing speed sensitive suspension and traction control as standard fare, the Sixty Special added speed sensitive steering to the list. Front end styling was revised with a "bolder" appearing grille. Inside, front seating was a 45/55 design for the driver and two front passengers. The new styled seats featured French stitching and included front dual comfort, six-way power seat adjusters, manual recliners, adjustable headrest and seatback pockets. An Ultra Seating Package was optional, and included a split frame design that allowed for adjustment of the lower seat cushion independently of the seatback. A trunk convenience net was a new standard item on the Sixty Special. The net, mounted transversely across the trunk compartment, secured items from rolling or sliding. Pass-Key II anti-theft system was also a standard feature

to aid the driver included: door ajar, oil level, oil change and low engine coolant. Other new features included Power Drain Protection (exclusive to Fleetwood), which protected the battery if lights were left on by automatically shutting off lights after 10 minutes of inactivity. Additionally, Retained Accessory Power allowed operation of window/windshield/entertainment controls for 10 minutes after the ignition was switched off. The Fleetwood Brougham package included a full vinyl top (which could be deleted), sail panel badging, specific seat design with six-way driver's seat memory and heated and three-position lumbar front seats, instrument panel badging and rear seat storage armrest. Other packages available for the Fleetwood included Coachbuilder Limousine with a 7,200 pound capacity, Heavy-Duty Livery, and Funeral Coach.

1993 Cadillac, Eldorado Touring Coupe. (OCW)

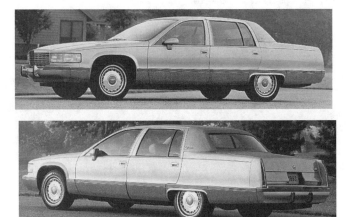

1993 Cadillac, Fleetwood Brougham sedan. (OCW)

FLEETWOOD - SERIES 6D - V-8 - The overall length of America's longest regular production car increased 4.1 inches to 225.1 inches, and with that change Cadillac also renamed the former Brougham sedan, now called the Fleetwood. The wheelbase remained as before, 121.5 inches, and even the Brougham moniker was retained for an upscale option package that could be ordered for the "base" Fleetwood sedan. The formerly standard 5.0-liter V-8 was discontinued, and the previously optional 5.7-liter V-8 was now the powerplant for the Fleetwood series. This V-8 featured a new starter motor that turned the engine more quickly and enhanced reliability. The 5.7-liter V-8 was rated at 185 horsepower and 300 pound-feet of torque. It was paired with the 4L60 Hydra-matic four-speed automatic transmission. The standard axle ratio for the Fleetwood was 2.56:1 while the Brougham's was 3.08:1. Bosch ASRIIU traction control was standard equipment. The 1993 Fleetwood sedan met mandated 1997 federal standards for dynamic side impact testing, and featured dual airbags as standard equipment. The exterior of the Fleetwood featured larger, flush-glass design windshield and back window. The front view was updated with a new grille integrated into the hood. One-piece front and rear bumpers were nickel-chrome-plated to match the new stainless steel bodyside molding, which featured the Fleetwood name in block letters in each front door molding. The rear of the Fleetwood had an all-new bumper system with a gray, grooved rub strip that extended around the entire perimeter of the car. Bright reveal moldings surrounded the side windows with Argent Metallic window trim. Bright wheel opening moldings also featured chrome-plated stainless steel treatment. Snap-in rear wheel opening skirts could be easily removed. New aerodynamic outside rearview mirrors and flush door handles matched the body color. Fleetwood's aerodynamic refinements dramatically lowered its coefficient of drag from a previous reading of 0.49 to 0.36. Both the Fleetwood and Brougham rode on 15-inch cast aluminum wheels fitted with Michelin XW4 P235/70R15 whitewall tires. Goodyear Eagle GA tires were required when the trailer towing package (rated at 7,000 pounds) was ordered. A full-size spare was optional equipment. Standard were a stainless steel exhaust system and plastic, 23-gallon fuel tank. Fleetwood offered 20.8 cubic feet of trunk space (up 1.2 cubic feet over 1992). Interior volume was 125.2 cubic feet. Inside, Fleetwood offered split frame seat construction with power seat recliners as standard items. New indicators

ELDORADO - SERIES 6E - V-8 - All-new in design the year before, the Eldorado gained not only more members in its series, but also the Cadillac-exclusive Northstar engine under the hood of two of those members. An Eldorado Sport Coupe joined the ranks already consisting of the base coupe and Eldo Touring Coupe. The Sport Coupe could be ordered either with a Sport Appearance Package (SAP) or Sport Performance Package (SPP—of which the SAP was included). It was both the Touring Coupe and Sport Coupe with SPP that featured the Northstar 4.6-liter, 32-valve, dual overhead cam V-8 engine. Both the block and cylinder head assembly of the Northstar engine were constructed of cast aluminum. For increased rigidity, iron bore liners were cast into the block. Rather than the traditional five-bearing cap assembly for the crankshaft, the Northstar featured a two-piece block with a large, one-piece girdle assembly. This configuration provided for an extremely rigid carrier for the crankshaft. The aluminum cylinder heads had four distinct camshafts. The Northstar's compression ratio was 10.3:1. Mated to the Northstar was the all-new 4T80-E electronically controlled four-speed automatic transmission with torque converter clutch. Designed specifically for the Northstar engine, the 4T80-E featured equal-length drive axles to help eliminate torque steer. The Eldorado and Eldo Sport Coupe with SAP were powered by the 4.9-liter V-8 paired with the 4T60-E electronically controlled four-speed automatic transmission with overdrive. The Powertrain Control System integrated engine and transmission functions to deliver controlled power to the drive wheels. New standard features for the Eldo included speed sensitive steering, a multi-link short/long arm (SLA) rear suspension, and dual airbags. The SLA suspension system included a short upper control arm, a longer lower control arm, shock absorbers and an additional lateral link. These components were mounted on a subframe that was rubber-isolated from the car's body. This system, introduced on the early-launch 1993 Allante, provided increased ride stability as well as improved steering responsiveness. Another new feature for 1993 was the high-density polyethylene fuel tank, which replaced the previous welded steel tank. The "plastic" tank provided better crashworthiness, corrosion resistance and improved thermal management. Eldo was also fitted with a revised, stainless steel exhaust system featuring a new longitudinal muffler design. Eldorados also received a new waterborne paint process as well as two new exterior colors: Light Beige Metallic and Dark Cherry Red Metallic, for a total of 17 available colors. Included in the eight interior color selections was the new Saddle color. Bistro knit cloth was standard with Nuance leather seating areas optional (with heated front seats part of the package). A new option for Eldos was the express-open sunroof. In addition to the Northstar V-8, the Sport Coupe with SPP also featured traction control, road sensing suspension and low-rolling resistance Michelin XW4 P225/60R16 tires. Road sensing suspension included four specially equipped struts with two damping rates: soft and firm. Under most conditions, the system operated in the soft mode. It shifted to firm mode when more control was needed. Steering ratio for the Sport Coupe was 15.6:1 with 2.65 turns required lock-to-lock. Outside, the Sport Coupe was distinguished by a chrome grille with wreath-and-crest ornament in the center. In the rear, a specific fascia was used to accommodate the dual exhaust. Also, on SPP-equipped models, a Northstar engine identification plaque was located on the decklid. Sport Coupes featured three cloth seat color selections and eight leather choices. Optional was an electrochromic inside rearview mirror. The Touring Coupe also featured SLA rear suspension, road sensing suspension and speed sensitive steering. Standard tires were Goodyear Eagle GA P225/60ZR16 radials mounted on cast aluminum wheels. A new option was chrome wheels. Other standard fare for the Touring Coupe included Pass-Key II anti-theft system, 7000 rpm tachometer and 150 speedometer, electrochromic inside rearview mirror, and leather seating in five color choices including a new Saddle color.

1993 Cadillac, Seville Touring Sedan. (OCW)

SEVILLE - SERIES 6K - V-8 - The Seville sedan and Seville Touring Sedan (STS) again represented the series, with refinements and upgrades aligned with those listed for the Eldorado and Eldo Touring Coupe, respectively. Seville again used the 4.9-liter V-8 and 4T60-E transmission while the STS received the new Northstar 4.6-liter V-8 and 4T80-E transmission. Final drive ratio for the Seville was 2.97:1 while the STS's was 3.71:1. In addition to the Northstar engine, STS featured the new Bosch ASRIIU traction control system. Designed to eliminate wheel spin on slippery road surfaces, the system reduced engine torque by shutting down up to five cylinders simultaneously while applying the brakes. The STS was distinguished by its monochromatic paint scheme, STS badging and Northstar engine identification. The STS also featured a body-color grille with wreath-and-crest emblem, specific rocker molding and bright dual exhaust outlets. New standard features for STS included solar control glass and two new exterior colors: Academy Gray and Dark Cherry Red Metallic.

1993 Cadillac, Allante convertible. (OCW)

ALLANTE - SERIES 6V - V-8 - The redesigned 1993 Allante convertible (no longer offered in convertible hardtop configuration) was an early-1992 launch. This early debut also introduced the world to the Northstar V-8 engine, which now powered the Allante, replacing the 4.5-liter V-8 formerly used. As with all other Northstar applications, the 4.6-liter V-8 was paired with the 4T80-E electronically controlled four-speed automatic transmission. The Northstar debut featured highly efficient compound-geometry valve/port designs and "quiet coil" Direct Ignition System designed to operate at high rpm levels without loss of spark synchronization. The engine's dual stream injector Fluid Induction System was another innovation. This system was isolated from underhood heat sources and cooled the fuel during operation, which enhanced performance. The 4T80-E transmission featured a controlled-flow, dual lubricating system that provided proper lubrication under all operating conditions. Free-wheeling clutches ensured consistent shifting quality. In its final year of production, the Allante was vastly upgraded with the addition of road sensing suspension, speed sensitive steering and the new-generation Bosch ASRIIU traction control system. The convertible also benefited from receiving the short/long arm (SLA) rear suspension that improved steering responsiveness. Other new standard features of the Allante included revised 16-inch cast aluminum wheels fitted with Goodyear Eagle GA

P225/60ZR16 tires and a 23-gallon polyethylene fuel tank. Chrome wheels were a new option. Outside, a new maroon color soft top was offered and the removal aluminum hardtop remained available as an option. A new, three-inch front fascia spoiler enhanced high-speed aerodynamics while new, one-piece side window glass improved weather sealing and acoustics. Three new clearcoat paint colors were offered: Pearl Red, Pearl Flax and Polo Green, upping the total to eight colors available. Allante also featured a headlamp washer system, new outside electric heated rearview mirrors with a foldaway design, and blue tinted glass. New Nuance leather-trimmed bucket seats were orthopedically designed to provide optimal support and comfort. The seats had power eight-way metaphoric adjustments and a new four-way power lumbar control. The console included a transmission shift selector that was slightly offset 20 degrees toward the driver for ease of shifting. Allante also featured the new Pass-Key II anti-theft system as a standard item.

1993 Cadillac, Fleetwood sedan. (OCW)

I.D. DATA: The 1993 Cadillac had a 17-symbol vehicle identification number (VIN) stamped on a metal tag attached to the upper left surface of the cowl visible through the windshield. The code was as follows: The first digit, "1" or "4" represented the manufacturing country (United States), the second, "G," represented General Motors, the third, "6," represented Cadillac, the fourth and fifth represented the car line/series, as follows: C/B-Sixty Special, C/D-deVille, C/T-deVille Touring Sedan, D/W-Fleetwood Brougham, E/L-Eldorado, K/S-Seville, K/Y-Seville Touring Sedan, and V/S-Allante convertible. Digit six represents the body style: 1-two-door coupe, 2-two-door hatchback/liftback, 3-two-door convertible, 4-four-door station wagon, 5-four-door sedan, 6-four-door liftback/hatchback, and 8-four-door station wagon. Digit seven identifies the restraint code: 1-active (manual) belts, 2-active (manual) belts w/dual airbags, 3-active (manual) belts w/driver's side airbag, 4-passive (automatic) belts, and 5-passive (automatic) belts w/driver's side airbag. The eighth digit identifies the engine: "B"-L26 4.9L V-8; "Y"-LD8 4.6L V-8; "7"-L05 5.7L V-8; and "9"-L37 4.6L V-8. A check digit follows. The 10th digit represents the model year, "P" for 1993. The eleventh digit represents the assembly plant. The remaining six digits identify the production sequence number.

deVille (V-8)

Series No.	Body/Style No.	Body Type & Seating	Factory Price	Shipping Weight	Prod. Total
CD1	D47	2-dr. Coupe	33915	3519	4,711
CD5	D69	4-dr. Sedan	32990	3605	Note 1
CT5	T69	4-dr. Tour Sed.	36310	3651	Note 1

Sixty Special (V-8)

Series No.	Body/Style No.	Body Type & Seating	Factory Price	Shipping Weight	Prod. Total
CB5	B69	4-dr. Sedan	37230	3649	Note 1

Note: Cadillac tallied deVille and Sixty Special production together with no series breakout available.

Note 1: deVille/Sixty Special sedan production totaled 125,963 with no further breakout available.

Fleetwood (V-8)

Series No.	Body/Style No.	Body Type & Seating	Factory Price	Shipping Weight	Prod. Total
DW5	W69	4-dr. Sedan	33990	4418	31,774 (*)

(*) Includes Fleetwoods equipped with Brougham option.

Eldorado (V-8)

Series No.	Body/Style No.	Body Type & Seating	Factory Price	Shipping Weight	Prod. Total
EL1	L57	2-dr. Coupe	33990	3604	21,473 (*)

(*) Includes Eldorados equipped with Touring Coupe and Sport Coupe options.

Seville (V-8)

Series No.	Body/Style No.	Body Type & Seating	Factory Price	Shipping Weight	Prod. Total
KS5	S69	4-dr. Sedan	36990	3648	Note 1
KY5	Y69	4-dr. Tour Sed.	41990	3721	Note 1

Note 1: Seville production totaled 37,239 with no further breakout available.

VS3	S67	2-dr. Conv.	59975	3752	4,670

ENGINES: BASE V-8: (Eldorado Touring Coupe, Eldorado Sport Coupe with Sport Performance Package, Seville Touring Sedan, Allante) 90-degree, dual overhead cam Northstar V-8. Aluminum block with cast iron cylinder liners, aluminum cylinder heads. Displacement: 279 cu. in. (4.6 liters). Bore & Stroke: 3.66 x 3.31 in. Compression ratio: 10.3:1. Brake horsepower: (Eldorado Sport Coupe with SPP) 270 @ 5600 rpm; (Eldorado Touring Coupe, Seville Touring Sedan) 295 @ 6000 rpm; (Allante) 295 @ 5600 rpm. Torque: (Eldorado Sport Coupe with SPP) 300 lb.-ft. @ 4000 rpm; (Eldorado Touring Coupe, Seville Touring Sedan, Allante) 290 lb.-ft. @ 4400 rpm. Direct acting hydraulic tappets. Tuned port fuel injection. BASE V-8: (deVille, Sixty Special, Eldorado, Seville) 90-degree, overhead valve V-8. Aluminum block with cast iron cylinder liners, cast iron cylinder heads. Displacement: 300 cu. in. (4.9 liters). Bore & Stroke: 3.62 x 3.62 in. Compression ratio: 9.5:1. Brake horsepower: 200 @ 4100 rpm. Torque: 275 lb.-ft. @ 3000 rpm. Roller hydraulic valve lifters. Sequential port fuel injection. BASE V-8: (Fleetwood) 90-degree, overhead valve V-8. Cast iron block and cylinder heads. Displacement: 350 cu. in. (5.7 liters). Bore & Stroke: 4.00 x 3.48 in. Compression ratio: 9.8:1. Brake horsepower: 185 @ 3800 rpm. Torque: 300 lb.-ft. @ 2400 rpm. Roller hydraulic valve lifters. Throttle body fuel injection.

CHASSIS DATA: Wheelbase: (Coupe deVille) 110.8 in.; (Sedan deVille, Sixty Special) 113.7 in.; (Seville) 111.0 in.; (Eldorado) 108.0 in.; (Allante) 99.4 in.; (Fleetwood) 121.5 in. Overall Length: (Coupe deVille) 203.3 in.; (Sedan deVille, Sixty Special) 206.3 in.; (Seville) 204.4 in.; (Eldorado) 202.2 in.; (Allante) 178.7 in.; (Fleetwood) 225.1 in. Height: (Coupe deVille) 54.8 in.; (Sedan deVille, Sixty Special) 55.1 in.; (Seville, Eldorado) 54.0 in.; (Allante) 51.5 in.; (Fleetwood) 57.1 in. Width: (Coupe deVille) 73.4 in.; (Sedan deVille, Sixty Special) 73.4 in.; (Seville) 74.4 in.; (Eldorado) 75.5 in.; (Allante) 73.7 in.; (Fleetwood) 78.0 in. Front Tread: (Coupe deVille) 60.1 in.; (Sedan deVille, Sixty Special) 60.1 in.; (Seville, Eldorado) 60.9 in.; (Allante) 60.4 in.; (Fleetwood) 61.7 in. Rear Tread: (Coupe deVille) 60.1 in.; (Sedan deVille, Sixty Special) 60.0 in.; (Seville, Eldorado) 60.9 in.; (Allante) 60.4 in.; (Fleetwood) 60.7 in. Standard Tires: (Coupe deVille) Michelin P205/70R15; (Sedan deVille, Sixty Special) P205/70R15; (Touring) Goodyear Eagle P215/60R16; (Seville, Eldorado) Michelin P225/60R16; (Touring) Goodyear Eagle GA P225/60ZR16; (Allante) Goodyear Eagle GA P225/60ZR16; (Fleetwood) Michelin P235/70R15.

TECHNICAL: Transmission: (deVille, Sixty Special, Eldorado, Seville) 4T60-E electronically controlled four-speed automatic with overdrive (includes viscous converter clutch); (Eldorado Touring Coupe, Eldorado Sport Coupe with Sport Performance Package, Seville Touring Sedan, Allante) 4T80-E electronically controlled four-speed automatic (includes torque converter clutch); (Fleetwood) THM 4L60 four-speed automatic with overdrive (includes torque converter clutch). Steering: (All exc. Fleetwood) Power-assisted rack-and-pinion, speed sensitive; (Fleetwood) Power-assisted recirculating ball, speed sensitive, variable assist. Front Suspension: (All exc. Fleetwood) Independent MacPherson strut with coil springs, strut-type shock absorbers (Eldorado Sport Coupe used electronic variable damping shock absorbers w/road sensing suspension) and stabilizer bar; (Fleetwood) Independent with short/long arms, coil springs, direct acting shock absorbers and stabilizer bar. Rear Suspension: (deVille, Sixty Special) Fully independent with coil springs, automatic level control and speed sensitive suspension; (Eldorado, Seville) Fully independent, coil springs, short/long arm w/automatic level control and speed sensitive suspension (Eldorado Sport Coupe used electronic variable damping shock absorbers w/road sensing suspension); (Eldorado Touring Coupe, Seville Touring Sedan) Fully independent, short/long arm w/automatic level control, electronic variable damping shock absorbers w/road sensing suspension; (Allante) Independent, short/long arm w/coil springs, electronic variable damping shock absorbers w/road sensing suspension and stabilizer bar; (Fleetwood) Four link, coil springs w/automatic level control and direct acting shock absorbers and stabilizer bar. Brakes: (All exc. Eldorado, Seville, Allante) Power assisted front disc/rear drum w/Teves anti-lock braking system (Fleetwood used Bosch II ABS); (Eldorado, Seville, Allante) Power assisted front and rear disc w/Bosch II anti-lock braking system. Body Construction: (All exc. Fleetwood) Integral body-frame; (Fleetwood) Separate body on frame. Fuel Tank: (deVille, Sixty Special) 18.0 gals.; (Eldorado, Seville Touring Sedan) 20.0 gals.; (Seville) 18.0 gals.; (Allante) 22.0 gals.; (Fleetwood) 23.0 gals.

DRIVETRAIN OPTIONS: (deVille) NW9 Traction Control $175. (Fleetwood) V4P Trailer Towing Pkg. $70.

DEVILLE CONVENIENCE/APPEARANCE OPTIONS: Opt. Pkg. B: deV $356; Tour Sed $266. Opt. Pkg. C: deV $833; Tour Sed $406. Security Pkg. $295. Cold Weather Pkg. $369. Digital Instrument Cluster $495. Astroroof $1,550. Coachbuilders Pkg. (Sedan deV) $1,000. Gold Ornamentation Pkg. $395. H.D. Livery Pkg. (Sedan deV) $1,000. Leather Seating $570. Firemist Paint $190. Delco-Bose Sound Syst. $575; w/CD $872. Full Vinyl Roof (Sedan deV) $925. Full Cabriolet Roof (Coupe deV) $170. Phaeton Roof (Sedan deV) $1,095. Locking Wire Whl Discs $235. Lace Cast Alum Whls $235. Chrome Whls $1,195.

SIXTY SPECIAL CONVENIENCE/APPEARANCE OPTIONS: Security Pkg. $295. Cold Weather Pkg. $369. Custom Seating Pkg. $425. Ultra Seating Pkg. $3,500. Astroroof $1,550. Gold Ornamentation Pkg. $395. Leather Seating $570. Firemist Paint $190. Delco-Bose Sound Syst. $575; w/CD $872. Chrome Whls $1,195.

ELDORADO CONVENIENCE/APPEARANCE OPTIONS: YP5 Touring Coupe Opt. $5,000. YP7 Sport Appearance Pkg. $875. V4Z Sport Performance Pkg. $3,000. Security Pkg. $480. Accent Striping $75. Heated Front Seats $120. Astroroof $1,550. Heated Windshield $309. Leather Seating $650. Pwr Lumbar Support $292. Auto Day/Night Mirror $110. Firemist Paint $240. Gold/White Diamond Paint $240. Delco-Bose Sound Syst. w/CD & Cassette $972. P225/60R16 WSW Tires $76. Chrome Whls $1,195.

SEVILLE CONVENIENCE/APPEARANCE OPTIONS: Security Pkg. $480. Sport Interior $146. Full Console $146. Accent Striping $75. Heated Front Seats $120. Heated Windshield Syst. $309. Astroroof $1,550. Leather Seating $650. Pwr Lumber Support $292. Auto Day/Night Mirror $110. Firemist Paint $240. Gold/White Diamond Paint $240. Delco-Bose Sound Syst. w/CD & Cassette $972. Chrome Whls $1,195.

FLEETWOOD CONVENIENCE/APPEARANCE OPTIONS: Security Pkg. $545. Astroroof $1,550. Coachbuilder Pkg. (NC). Funeral Coach Pkg. ($1,405 credit). Brougham Cloth Int. $1,680. Brougham Leather Int. $2,250. H.D. Livery Pkg. $150. Leather Seating (Fleetwood) $570. Auto Day/Night Mirror $110. Firemist Paint $190. AM/FM Stereo Radio w/CD & Cassette $396. Full Vinyl Roof $925. Full-size Spare $51.

ALLANTE CONVENIENCE/APPEARANCE OPTIONS: Digital Instrument Cluster (conv. only) $495. Pearlcoat Flax/White Paint $700.

HISTORY: Cadillac's model year production totaled 225,830 compared with 233,027 the year previous. Based on sales of 204,159 automobiles in 1993 (vs. 214,176 the year before), Cadillac's share of the U.S. market was 2.40 percent compared with 2.61 the year previous.

1994

Cadillac thinned its ranks considerably in 1994, dropping both the Allante convertible and Sixty Special sedan as well as eliminating the Coupe deVille. All series except the Fleetwood were "realigned." The DeVille (now identified on the car with a capital "D" series was now comprised of the Sedan DeVille and (Sedan) DeVille Concours. The Eldorado Sport Coupe formerly offered was discontinued, and the Eldo series consisted of the "base" coupe and Eldorado Touring Coupe (ETC). The two trim levels of Seville offered were now distinguished as the Seville Luxury Sedan (SLS) and Seville Touring Sedan (STS). Other than the Sedan DeVille and Fleetwood, powered by 4.9-liter V-8 and 5.7-liter V-8 engines, respectively, the Northstar 4.6-liter V-8 was used in all other Cadillacs. Every Cadillac met 1997 federal mandates for dynamic side impact standards, and all models featured steel safety cage construction, side door beams and front and rear crush zones.

1994 Cadillac, Sedan DeVille. (OCW)

1994 Cadillac, Sedan DeVille Concours. (OCW)

DEVILLE - SERIES 6K - V-8 - The 1994 DeVille (bodyside molding now identified the car as "DeVILLE" instead of the previously used "deVille" quarter panel script) was a completely redesigned automobile, and offered only in sedan form with the discontinuation of the Coupe deVille. The lineup was comprised of the Sedan DeVille and (Sedan) DeVille Concours. The Sedan DeVille was the lone Cadillac to remain powered by the 4.9-liter V-8. This sequential-port fuel-injected engine was refined for 1994, receiving a redesigned intake manifold for quieter operation and a single longitudinal exhaust that lowered exhaust restriction and improved engine performance. The accompanying 4T60-E electronically controlled four-speed automatic transmission was also used exclusively in the Sedan DeVille. It, too, was upgraded, receiving a new third clutch package, premium gear set and rocker pin chain, all of which enhanced wear resistance and reliability. Engine power was applied to the transmission via a viscous converter clutch. The transfer of this power was controlled via a single Powertrain Control Module, which managed engine and transmission functions as a single unit. DeVilles featured speed sensitive steering, speed sensitive suspension, short/long arm rear suspension and Bosch ABSII anti-lock braking system as standard equipment. Full-speed traction control was optional. With the speed sensitive steering, Sedan DeVille's steering ratio was 15.5:1 with 2.97 turns required lock-to-lock. Other new features included a fully-isolated rear sub-frame with urethane upper frame insulators to reduce rough road shake, high-output brake booster, redesigned 15-inch cast aluminum wheels and a high-density polyethylene fuel tank that replaced the previous welded steel unit. The DeVille's interior was also revamped. Dual airbags were standard fare, as was a new HD6 air conditioning compressor (for use with R-134a refrigerant). The standard seating surface was sculptured Saratoga knit cloth available in Light Gray, Dark Blue and Dark Cherry. Nuance leather seating was optional. New leather seat colors were Dark Cherry, Mocha and Dark Blue, upping the total leather color choices to seven. A digital instrument panel included an electronic speedometer, odometer, trip odometer and fuel gauge. Simulated East Indian rosewood accented the panel and upper doors. Also part of the instrument cluster were the Driver Information Center window and automatic Climate Control system settings. A new leather-wrapped four-spoke steering wheel was also included. Interior noise level was reduced via a fiberglass dash mat and noise-absorbing material located in the engine compartment shock towers. A full-perimeter door sealing system that included dual door weatherstrips dampened road noise. The DeVille grew 4.4 inches wider, 3.9 inches longer and 1.3 inches taller over the previous year's model, but its sleeker body lines reduced coefficient of drag from 0.38 to 0.35. Front and rear bumpers featured a chrome-colored molding that flowed into the bodyside molding, which encircled the car. DeVille block lettering was etched into the bodyside molding on the front doors. Also new were body color dual outside rearview mirrors. The rear of the DeVille featured tall, thin taillamps. Thirteen exterior color choices were available including the new White Diamond, Light and Medium Montana Blue, Calypso Green and Mocha. Standard safety

equipment included anti-lockout, automatic door locking with central door unlocking and remote keyless entry. All Cadillacs were equipped with Pass-Key II theft deterrent system. The DeVille Concours was powered by the Northstar 4.6-liter V-8 coupled to the 4T80-E electronically controlled four-speed automatic transmission with viscous converter clutch. In addition to the standard features found on the Sedan DeVille, the Concours added road sensing suspension and Bosch ASRIIU traction control. Inside the Concours had Nuance leather seating, specific instrument panel badging, Zebrano wood trim and a new 11-speaker Delco Electronics active audio system. Outside, the Concours' unique features included a grille-mounted wreath-and-crest emblem, ribbed side molding, specific cast aluminum wheels with Goodyear Eagle GA P225/60HR16 tires, dual exhaust outlets and a "32V Northstar" badge. Chrome wheels were optional. Front and rear bumper assemblies featured an argent color fascia molding that flowed into the bodyside molding. "Cadillac Concours" lettering was etched into the molding on the front doors.

1994 Cadillac, Fleetwood sedan. (OCW)

FLEETWOOD - SERIES 6D - V-8 - The Fleetwood sedan and upscale optional Brougham package for the "base" sedan again comprised the Fleetwood series. Also, the optional coachbuilder limousine package, funeral coach package and trailer towing package were again available. In 1994, all Fleetwoods were powered by the GenII 5.7-liter V-8 with sequential port fuel injection and the new Opti-Spark ignition system. Opti-Spark was an angle-based spark delivery system that ensured precisely timed, high-energy spark needed for optimum fuel efficiency and low emissions. The GenII V-8 was mated to the new 4L60-E electronically controlled four-speed automatic transmission, which replaced the previously used 4L60 unit. The 4L60-E transmission featured altitude compensation and over-rev protection. The transmission shared the same key information with the Powertrain Control Module as the engine to maintain consistent shifting, even in higher altitude, as well as automatically upshifting out of D1 (first gear) to second to protect the engine. New standard features of the Fleetwood included a four-spoke steering wheel, HD6 air conditioning compressor (for use of R-134a refrigerant), turn signal activated "flash-to-pass" feature that allowed the driver to signal the driver in front of intent to pass via bright headlamps (the system worked whether the headlamps were on or not), and a DEFOG feature added to the Climate Control system. The DEFOG function directed 65 percent of the air to the windshield for clearing and 35 percent to the floor heat ducts. Fleetwood's interior carpet was 18-ounce Twilight plush, which gave the appearance of wool with a nylon yarn. Fleetwood was available in 12 exterior colors including the new Light Gray, Light/Medium/Dark Adriatic Blue and Majestic Amethyst. Chrome wheels were a new option for Fleetwood in 1994. The Brougham package again offered a full vinyl top (again a delete option), specific sail panel and instrument panel badging, specific seating (cloth or leather), specific cast aluminum wheels and a 2.93 axle ratio.

ELDORADO - SERIES 6E - V-8 - Missing from the Eldorado lineup was the previously offered Sport Coupe that could be ordered either with a Sport Appearance Package (SAP) or Sport Performance Package (SPP—of which the SAP was included). The Eldo series now consisted of the "base" coupe and Eldorado Touring Coupe (ETC). The Northstar 4.6-

liter V-8 and 4T80-E electronically controlled four-speed automatic transmission with viscous converter clutch remained the power source for the ETC and replaced the 4.9-liter V-8 and 4T60-E transmission previously standard in the Eldo coupe. The short/long arm rear suspension introduced the year before was upgraded with an aluminum alloy lower control arm replacing the previous cast iron unit. This resulted in reduced unsprung mass, which enhanced ride quality. Also new were urethane engine cradle mounts that reduced powertrain vibration. Road sensing suspension was now standard on Eldorado as it was previously on the Touring Coupe. Other new features included a leather-wrapped four-spoke steering wheel, timer and reset buttons that allowed the driver to clock driving time using "stopwatch" functions, the DEFOG feature of the Climate Control system, trunk convenience net and the HD6 air conditioning compressor (for use of R-134a refrigerant). New standard safety equipment included anti-lockout, automatic door locking with central door unlocking and remote keyless entry. Nuance leather seating was optional in the Eldo and four new colors were available: Dark Blue, Mocha, Dark Cherry and Beechwood. Interior noise levels were reduced in 1994 due to the use of thicker front fender closeout panels and cotton sound-absorbing added to door panels and rear package shelf. Windshield thickness was also increased .9mm for enhanced isolation of wind noise. Outside, a "32V Northstar" badge was located on the decklid and dual exhaust outlets were also new. Eldos were available in 13 exterior color choices including the new Calypso Green, Mocha and Light and Medium Montana Blue. ETC models offered 11 exterior color choices including the new Medium Montana Blue, Mocha, Calypso Green, Platinum and Frost Beige.

1994 Cadillac, Seville Luxury Sedan. (OCW)

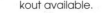

1994 Cadillac, Seville Touring Sedan. (OCW)

SEVILLE - SERIES 6K - V-8 - The Seville series now featured a luxury sedan (SLS) and a touring sedan (STS). Gone from the lineup was the previously available Seville sedan powered by the 4.9-liter V-8 paired with the 4T60-E transmission. For power, both the SLS and STS utilized the Northstar 4.6-liter V-8 and 4T80-E electronically controlled four-speed automatic transmission with viscous converter clutch. Standard equipment common to SLS and STS included speed sensitive steering, road sensing suspension, short/long arm rear suspension, anti-lock brakes and Bosch ASRIIU traction control. New features of the SLS and STS mirrored those listed for the Eldorado and ETC, respectively. The SLS was distinguished by a chrome-plated grille with stand-up wreath-and-crest hood ornament and "SLS" badging. The STS featured a body color

grille with integrated wreath-and-crest emblem, bodyside cladding and STS badged wheels.

I.D. DATA: The 1994 Cadillac had a 17-symbol vehicle identification number (VIN) stamped on a metal tag attached to the upper left surface of the cowl visible through the windshield. The code was as follows: The first digit, "1" or "4" represented the manufacturing country (United States), the second, "G," represented General Motors, the third, "6," represented Cadillac, the fourth and fifth represented the car line/series, as follows: D/H-commercial chassis (rwd), D/W-Fleetwood, E/L-Eldorado, E/T-Eldorado Touring, K/D-DeVille, K/F-Concours, K/S-Seville (SLS), and K/Y-Seville (STS). Digit six represents the body style: 1-two-door coupe, 2-two-door hatchback/liftback, 3-two-door convertible, 4-two-door station wagon, 5-four-door sedan, 6-four-door liftback/hatchback, and 8-four-door station wagon. Digit seven identifies the restraint code: 1-active (manual) belts, 2-active (manual) belts w/dual airbags, 3-active (manual) belts w/driver's side airbag, 4-passive (automatic) belts, 5-passive (automatic) belts w/driver's side airbag, and 6-passive (automatic) belts w/dual airbags. The eighth digit identifies the engine: "B"-L26 4.9L V-8; "P"-LT1 5.7L V-8, "Y"-LD8 4.6L V-8; and "9"-L37 4.6L V-8. A check digit follows. The 10th digit represents the model year, "R" for 1994. The eleventh digit represents the assembly plant. The remaining six digits identify the production sequence number.

DeVille (V-8)

Series No.	Body/Style No.	Body Type & Seating	Factory Price	Shipping Weight	Prod. Total
KD5	D69	4-dr. Sedan	32990	3758	Note 1
KF5	F69	4-dr. Concours Sed.	36590	3985	Note 1

Note 1: DeVille production totaled 120,352 with no further breakout available.

Fleetwood (V-8)

DW5	W69	4-dr. Sedan	33990	4478	27,473 (*)

(*) Includes Fleetwoods equipped with Brougham option.

Eldorado (V-8)

EL1	L57	2-dr. Coupe	37290	3774	Note 1
ET1	T57	2-dr. Tour. Cpe.	40590	3819	Note 1

Note 1: Eldorado production totaled 24,947 with no further breakout available.

Seville (V-8)

KS5	S69	4-dr. SLS Sedan	40990	3831	Note 1
KY5	Y69	4-dr. STS Sedan	44890	3893	Note 1

Note 1: Seville production totaled 46,713 with no further breakout available.

1994 Cadillac, Eldorado Touring Coupe. (OCW)

ENGINES: BASE V-8: (DeVille Concours, Eldorado, Seville) 90-degree, dual overhead cam Northstar V-8. Aluminum block with cast iron cylinder liners, aluminum cylinder heads. Displacement: 279 cu. in. (4.6 liters). Bore & Stroke: 3.66 x 3.31 in. Compression ratio: 10.3:1. Brake horsepower: (DeVille Concours, Eldorado, Seville Luxury Sedan) 270 @ 5600 rpm; (Eldorado Touring Coupe, Seville Touring Sedan) 295 @ 6000 rpm. Torque: (DeVille Concours, Eldorado, Seville Luxury Sedan) 300 lb.-ft. @ 4000 rpm; (Eldorado Touring Coupe, Seville Touring Sedan) 290 lb.-ft. @ 4400 rpm. Direct acting hydraulic tappets. Tuned port fuel injection. BASE V-8: (Sedan DeVille) 90-degree, overhead valve V-8. Aluminum block with cast iron cylinder liners, cast iron cylinder heads. Displacement: 299 cu. in. (4.9 liters). Bore & Stroke: 3.62 x 3.62 in. Compression ratio: 9.5:1.

Brake horsepower: 200 @ 4100 rpm. Torque: 275 lb.-ft. @ 3000 rpm. Roller hydraulic valve lifters. Sequential port fuel injection. BASE V-8: (Fleetwood) 90-degree, overhead valve V-8. Cast iron block and cylinder heads. Displacement: 350 cu. in. (5.7 liters). Bore & Stroke: 4.00 x 3.48 in. Compression ratio: 9.7:1. Brake horsepower: 260 @ 5000 rpm. Torque: 335 lb.-ft. @ 2400 rpm. Roller hydraulic valve lifters. Sequential port fuel injection.

CHASSIS DATA: Wheelbase: (DeVille) 113.7 in.; (Seville) 111.0 in.; (Eldorado) 108.0 in.; (Fleetwood) 121.5 in. Overall Length: (DeVille) 209.7 in.; (Seville) 204.1 in.; (Eldorado) 202.2 in.; (Fleetwood) 225.1 in. Height: (Sedan DeVille) 56.3 in.; (DeVille Concours) 56.0 in.; (Seville) 54.5 in.; (Eldorado) 53.9 in.; (Fleetwood) 57.1 in. Width: (DeVille) 75.5 in.; (Seville) 74.2 in.; (Eldorado) 75.5 in.; (Fleetwood) 78.0 in. Front Tread: (DeVille) 60.9 in.; (Seville, Eldorado) 60.9 in.; (Fleetwood) 61.7 in. Rear Tread: (DeVille) 60.9 in.; (Seville, Eldorado) 60.9 in.; (Fleetwood) 60.7 in. Standard Tires: (Sedan deVille) Michelin P215/70R15; (DeVille Concours) Goodyear Eagle GA P225/60HR16; (Seville, Eldorado) Michelin P225/60R16; (Touring) Goodyear Eagle GA P225/60ZR16; (Fleetwood) Michelin P235/70R15.

TECHNICAL: Transmission: (Sedan DeVille) 4T60-E electronically controlled four-speed automatic with overdrive (includes viscous converter clutch); (DeVille Concours, Eldorado, Seville) 4T80-E electronically controlled four-speed automatic (includes viscous converter clutch); (Fleetwood) 4L60-E electronically controlled four-speed automatic (includes torque converter clutch). Steering: (All exc. Fleetwood) Power-assisted rack-and-pinion, speed sensitive; (Fleetwood) Power-assisted recirculating ball, speed sensitive, variable assist. Front Suspension: (All exc. Fleetwood) Independent MacPherson strut with coil springs, strut-type shock absorbers (DeVille Concours used electronic variable rate dampers) and stabilizer bar; (Fleetwood) Independent with short/long arms, coil springs, direct acting shock absorbers and stabilizer bar. Rear Suspension: (Sedan DeVille) Fully independent, short/long arm w/automatic level control and speed sensitive suspension; (DeVille Concours, Seville, Eldorado) Fully independent, coil springs, short/long arm w/automatic level control and electronic variable dampers w/road sensing suspension; (Fleetwood) Four link, coil springs w/automatic level control, direct acting shock absorbers and stabilizer bar. Brakes: (all exc. Fleetwood) Power assisted front and rear disc w/Bosch II anti-lock braking system; (Fleetwood) Power assisted front disc/rear drum w/Bosch anti-lock braking system; Body Construction: (All exc. Fleetwood) Integral body-frame; (Fleetwood) Separate body on frame. Fuel Tank: (all exc. Fleetwood) 20.0 gals.; (Fleetwood) 23.0 gals.

DRIVETRAIN OPTIONS: (Sedan DeVille) NW9 Traction Control $175. (Fleetwood) V92 Trailer Towing Pkg. $70.

DEVILLE CONVENIENCE/APPEARANCE OPTIONS: Opt. Pkg. 1SB: (Sedan DeV) $428. Astroroof $1,550. Alarm Syst. (Sedan DeV) $295. White Diamond Paint $500. ETR AM/FM Stereo Radio w/Cassette (stnd DeV Concours) $274; w/Cassette & CD: Sedan DeV $670; DeV Concours $396. Heated Windshield (Sedan DeV) $309. Heated Front Seats: Sedan DeV $310; DeV Concours $120. Leather Seats (stnd DeV Concours) $785. Bodyside Stripe $75. Chrome Whls $1,195.

ELDORADO CONVENIENCE/APPEARANCE OPTIONS: V4C Sport Int. Pkg. $146. Alarm Syst. (stnd Touring Coupe) $295. Bodyside Striping (Eldo) $75. Heated Front Seats $120. Astroroof $1,550. Heated Windshield $309. Leather Seating (stnd Touring Coupe) $650. Pwr Lumbar Support (stnd Touring Coupe) $292. Auto Day/Night Mirror (stnd Touring Coupe) $87. White Diamond Paint $500. Delco-Bose Sound Syst. w/CD & Cassette $972. P225/60R16 WSW Tires (Eldo) $76. Chrome Whls $1,195.

SEVILLE CONVENIENCE/APPEARANCE OPTIONS: UY9 Sport Int. Pkg. $146. Alarm Syst. (stnd STS) $295. Bodyside Striping (SLS) $75. Heated Front Seats $120. Heated Windshield $309. Astroroof $1,550. Leather Seating (stnd STS) $650. Pwr Lumbar Support (stnd STS) $292. Auto Day/Night Mirror (stnd STS) $87. White Diamond Paint $500. Delco-Bose Sound Syst. w/CD & Cassette $972. Chrome Whls $1,195.

FLEETWOOD CONVENIENCE/APPEARANCE OPTIONS: Security Pkg. $545. Astroroof $1,550. Coachbuilder Pkg. ($755). Funeral Coach Pkg. ($910 credit). Brougham Cloth Int. $1,680. Brougham Leather Int. $2,250. H.D. Livery Pkg. $150. Leather Seating (Fleetwood) $570. Auto Day/Night Mirror $110. Sungate Windshield $50.

ETR AM/FM Stereo Radio w/CD & Cassette $396. Full Vinyl Roof (Fleetwood) $925. Full-size Spare $95. Chrome Whls $1,195.

HISTORY: Cadillac's model year production totaled 219,485 compared with 225,830 the year previous. Based on sales of 210,686 automobiles in 1994 (vs. 204,159 the year before), Cadillac's share of the U.S. market was 2.3 percent compared with 2.4 the year previous. The Cadillac LSE (Luxury Sedan Euro-Style) show car was exhibited at the major 1994 auto shows. The LSE, a five-passenger sedan finished in Ruby Red, was, according to Cadillac, the "vision for an entry-level luxury sedan for the mid-1990s." It was powered by a 3.0-liter dual overhead cam V-6 rated at 200 horsepower, and its wheelbase measured 107.5 inches. The aim of the LSE was to broaden Cadillac's appeal to young, affluent buyers.

1995

It was the 80th Anniversary of the Cadillac V-8 engine. The 1995 Cadillac lineup mirrored the previous year's offerings. New on all Cadillacs was the PG260 Planetary Gear Starter that featured improved corrosion protection with added lubricants and improved sealing around the driveshaft. The front-wheel drive Cadillacs received structural refinements to improve body stiffness and limit vibration. These revisions included new steering column struts that tied in to the cross-car beam behind the instrument panel, longitudinal braces in the trunk compartment, and a more rigid urethane seal where all stationary glass surfaces mount to the body. All front-drivers also benefited from a newly designed, quieter exhaust system that included a larger muffler and longer tailpipe.

1995 Cadillac, Sedan DeVille. (OCW)

DEVILLE - SERIES 6K - V-8 - Sedan DeVille and DeVille Concours again comprised the lineup, with each retaining the powertrain used the year previous. The Concours sedan's Northstar engine was upgraded by five horsepower (from 270 to 275) due to receiving a new fluid induction system that increased air flow efficiency through smoother intake tuning tubes. Formerly optional features that were made standard on the Sedan DeVille included Bosch ASR5 (Anti-Slip Regulation) traction control, 20-second illuminated entry, airbag electronic sensing and diagnostic module, electronic gear selector display and windshield wiper-activated headlamps. Other new standard features included a trunk lid power pulldown and door edge guards deleted (both 1994 running changes), trunk cargo net, underhood lamp, decklid lock ornamentation in red and black, new accent stripe and three additional exterior waterborne paint colors: Shale, Pearl Red and Amethyst. Inside, Saratoga interior cloth was standard with one new color offered: Neutral Shale. In the optional Nuance leather, Neutral Shale and Cappuccino Cream were new color choices. Other new optional equipment included an electronic compass inside the rearview mirror, programmable garage door opener and sunroof with illuminated driver and front passenger vanity mirrors and rear reading lamps. Changes in the DeVille's suspension included tapered ball studs for stabilizer bar link joints and low friction upper arm bushings. In addition to the upgrades listed for the Sedan DeVille, the DeVille Concours received the Integrated Chassis Control System (ICCS) that improved stopping distance, increased braking stability and reduced unnecessary reaction of the traction control system in low-speed tight turning radius maneuvers. The Concours sedan also featured a traction control disable switch located in the glovebox. Other new, unique-to-Concours features included the programmable garage door opener as standard fare, rear seat storage armrest, 16-inch cast aluminum wheels with diamond-cut finish wreath-and-crest center caps, pre-loaded damper valving suspension components, stiffening brace package for the Northstar V-8 to reduce vibration, and two additional color choices for standard Nuance leather seating: Neutral Shale and Cappuccino Cream.

1995 Cadillac, Fleetwood sedan. (OCW)

FLEETWOOD - SERIES 6D - V-8 - The GenII 5.7-liter V-8 that powered the Fleetwood sedan and its upscale optional Brougham package model was upgraded for 1995. In addition to the aforementioned PG260 starter that all Cadillacs received, the rear-drive Fleetwood's V-8 now also featured Quiet Cam. This revised camshaft design, in conjunction with new sound and vibration reducing composite rocker arm covers, decreased engine mechanical noise and eliminated valve noise on the outside of the car. Again, the 4L60-E electronically controlled four-speed automatic transmission saw service with the GenII V-8. For 1995, the 4L60-E featured a 298mm torque converter clutch assembly that had a higher torque capacity, which enhanced the unit's durability. Formerly optional equipment that was made standard included remote keyless entry, central door unlocking and automatic door locks, and electrochromic inside rearview mirror with new map lights. Other new standard features included ASR5 traction control; larger, foldaway, patch-mounted outside rearview mirrors; quiet door latch system; ignition key anti-lockout feature; revised instrument panel top pad; "SIR Airbag" embossed label for passenger side; and two new exterior color choices: Fawn Gray and Calypso Green. The Brougham sedan added a programmable garage door opener and an upgraded electronic lumbar system for seat adjustments. Also on the Brougham, the optional V4R security package was restructured to include the theft deterrent system and auto lock/unlock fuel filler door. For 1995, Fleetwoods also received increased capacity of the Electronic Control Unit that provided more convenient traction control on/off capability. A toggle switch in the glovebox allowed the traction control to be switched off and on without restarting the engine. As in previous years, the Fleetwood could also be ordered as the V4U Coach-builder Limousine Package, B9Q Funeral Coach Package, or R1P Heavy-Duty Sedan Package with heavy-duty components required for continuous commercial service.

1995 Cadillac, Eldorado coupe. (OCW)

1995 Cadillac, Eldorado Touring Coupe. (OCW)

ELDORADO - SERIES 6E - V-8 - The Eldo coupe and ETC (Eldorado Touring Coupe) again comprised the series, both, again, powered by the Northstar 4.6-liter V-8 mated to the 4T80-E electronically controlled four-speed automatic transmission with viscous converter clutch. Due to the aforementioned new fluid induction system the Northstar received in 1995, the Eldo's and ETC's horsepower ratings each increased by five over the previous year's measure. The Eldo now claimed 275 horsepower (up from 270)

while the ETC had 300 horses (up from 295). Additionally, the ETC also gained torque: 295 pound-feet (up from 290). The appearance of the "base" Eldo was greatly refined with newly designed front and rear fascia and a chrome grille with body color perimeter and new integrated wreath-and-crest emblem (the previous stand-up hood ornament was no longer available. Sail panel badging and wheel opening moldings were also discontinued). Other changes included redesigned 16-inch cast aluminum wheels with diamond cut finish and seven-spoke pattern (common with Seville Luxury Sedan), foglamps integrated into the front fascia, body color rocker and lower door moldings were now one-piece, bodyside molding was body color with chrome stripe and contained "ELDORADO" lettering, body color sill plate was integral, taillight perimeter was now Ruby Red color, front and rear side marker lamps were updated, beveled exhaust tips conformed to lower fascia contour and three new exterior waterborne color choices were offered: Shale, Pearl Red and Amethyst. Inside, the Eldo received windshield wiper-activated headlamps, 20-second illuminated entry, electronic gear selector display, airbag electronic sensing and diagnostic module, and new Charisma cloth replaced the previous Bistro cloth and was available in Neutral Shade (cloth and leather). Powertrain and chassis refinements included the aforementioned PG260 starter motor and fluid induction system as well as the Integrated Chassis Control System that featured steering wheel angle sensor, four-channel anti-lock brake system and ASR5 traction control. The Northstar V-8 received a stiffening brace package to reduce vibration and the Eldo, overall, was stiffened via steering column struts tied in to the cross-car beam behind the instrument panel as well as corner gussets that replaced front shock tower to radiator tie bar braces. Also new were tapered ball studs for the stabilizer bar link joints and lower friction upper control arm bushings. New options included a electronic compass in the inside rearview mirror, programmable garage door opener, chrome wheels (common to Seville Luxury Sedan), rear seat storage armrest, and two Nuance leather seating color choices: Neutral Shale and Cappuccino Cream. Standard features unique to the Touring Coupe included an "ETC" decklid badge (there was no Touring Coupe identification on the doors); body color license plate frame with "ELDORADO" lettering; five new exterior waterborne color choices: Shale, Pearl Red, Amethyst, Cotillion White and Light Montana Blue; and four new Nuance leather seating color choices: Neutral Shale, Cappuccino Cream, Dark Blue and Dark Cherry. Also revised on the ETC was its body color grille with new integrated wreath-and-crest emblem.

1995 Cadillac, Seville Touring Sedan. (OCW)

1995 Cadillac, Seville Luxury Sedan. (OCW)

SEVILLE - SERIES 6K - V-8 - The Seville series again consisted of the luxury sedan (SLS) and touring sedan (STS). Both again used the Northstar 4.6-liter V-8 and 4T80-E electronically controlled four-speed automatic transmission with viscous converter clutch. Engine, chassis and interior upgrades/refinements for the SLS basically mirrored the Eldorado coupe while the STS's mimicked the ETC.

I.D. DATA: The 1995 Cadillac had a 17-symbol vehicle identification number (VIN) stamped on a metal tag attached to the upper left surface of the cowl visible through the windshield. The code was as follows: The first digit, "1" or "4" represented the manufacturing country (United States), the second, "G," represented General Motors, the third, "6," represented Cadillac, the fourth and fifth represented the car line/series, as follows: D/W-Fleetwood, E/L-Eldorado, E/T-Eldorado Touring, K/D-DeVille, K/F-Concours, K/S-Seville (SLS), and K/Y-Seville (STS). Digit six represents the body style: 1-two-door coupe, 2-two-door, 3-two-door convertible, 4-two-door station wagon, 5-four-door sedan, 6-four-door, and 8-four-door station wagon. Digit seven identifies the restraint code: 1-active (manual) belts, 2-active (manual) belts w/dual airbags, 3-active (manual) belts w/driver's side airbag, 4-passive (automatic) belts, 5-passive (automatic) belts w/driver's side airbag, and 6-passive (automatic) belts w/dual airbags. The eighth digit identifies the engine: "B"-L26 4.9L V-8; "P"-LT1 5.7L V-8, "Y"-LD8 4.6L V-8; and "9"-L37 4.6L V-8. A check digit follows. The 10th digit represents the model year, "S" for 1995. The eleventh digit represents the assembly plant. The remaining six digits identify the production sequence number.

1995 Cadillac, Sedan DeVille Concours. (OCW)

DeVille (V-8)

Series No.	Body/Style No.	Body Type & Seating	Factory Price	Shipping Weight	Prod. Total
KD5	D69	4-dr. Sedan	34900	3758	Note 1
KF5	F69	4-dr. Concours Sed.	39400	3985	Note 1

Note 1: DeVille production totaled 109,066 with no further breakout available.

Fleetwood (V-8)

DW5	W69	4-dr. Sedan	35595	4477	27,350 (*)

(*) Includes Fleetwoods equipped with Brougham option.

Eldorado (V-8)

EL1	L57	2-dr. Coupe	38220	3774	Note 1
ET1	T57	2-dr. Tour. Cpe.	41535	3818	Note 1

Note 1: Eldorado production totaled 25,230 with no further breakout available.

Seville (V-8)

KS5	S69	4-dr. SLS Sedan	41935	3892	Note 1
KY5	Y69	4-dr. STS Sedan	45935	3950	Note 1

Note 1: Seville production totaled 38,931 with no further breakout available.

ENGINES: BASE V-8: (DeVille Concours, Eldorado, Seville) 90-degree, dual overhead cam Northstar V-8. Aluminum block with cast iron cylinder liners, aluminum cylinder heads. Displacement: 279 cu. in. (4.6 liters). Bore & Stroke: 3.66 x 3.31 in. Compression ratio: 10.3:1. Brake horsepower: (DeVille Concours, Eldorado, Seville Luxury Sedan) 275 @ 5600 rpm; (Eldorado Touring Coupe, Seville Touring Sedan) 300 @ 6000 rpm. Torque: (DeVille Concours, Eldorado, Seville Luxury Sedan) 300 lb.-ft. @ 4000 rpm; (Eldorado Touring Coupe, Seville Touring Sedan) 295 lb.-ft. @ 4400 rpm. Direct acting hydraulic tappets. Tuned port fuel injection. BASE V-8: (Sedan DeVille) 90-degree, overhead valve V-8. Aluminum block with cast iron cylinder liners, cast iron cylinder heads. Displacement: 299 cu. in. (4.9 liters). Bore & Stroke: 3.62 x 3.62 in. Compression ratio: 9.5:1. Brake horsepower: 200 @ 4100 rpm. Torque: 275 lb.-ft. @ 3000 rpm. Roller hydraulic valve lifters. Sequential port fuel injection. BASE V-8: (Fleetwood) 90-degree, overhead valve V-8. Cast iron block and cylinder heads. Displacement: 350 cu. in. (5.7 liters). Bore & Stroke: 4.00 x 3.48 in. Compression ratio: 10.5:1. Brake horsepower: 260 @ 5000 rpm. Torque: 335 lb.-ft. @ 2400 rpm. Roller hydraulic valve lifters. Sequential port fuel injection.

CHASSIS DATA: Wheelbase: (DeVille) 113.8 in.; (Seville) 111.0 in.; (Eldorado) 108.0 in.; (Fleetwood) 121.5 in. Overall Length: (DeVille) 209.7 in.; (Seville) 204.1 in.; (Eldorado) 202.2 in.; (Fleetwood) 225.1 in. Height: (DeVille) 56.3 in.; (Seville) 54.5 in.; (Eldorado) 53.6 in.; (Fleetwood) 57.1 in. Width: (DeVille) 76.6 in.; (Seville) 74.2 in.; (Eldorado) 75.5 in.; (Fleetwood) 78.0 in. Front Tread: (DeVille) 60.9 in.; (Seville, Eldorado) 60.9 in.; (Fleetwood) 61.7 in. Rear Tread: (DeVille) 60.9 in.; (Seville, Eldorado) 60.9 in.; (Fleetwood) 60.7 in. Standard Tires: (Sedan DeVille) Michelin P215/70R15; (DeVille Concours) Goodyear Eagle RS-A P225/60R16; (Seville, Eldorado) Michelin P225/60R16; (Touring) Goodyear Eagle GA P225/60ZR16; (Fleetwood) Michelin P235/70R15.

TECHNICAL: Transmission: (Sedan DeVille) 4T60-E electronically controlled four-speed automatic with overdrive (includes viscous converter clutch); (DeVille Concours, Eldorado, Seville) 4T80-E electronically controlled four-speed automatic (includes viscous converter clutch); (Fleetwood) 4L60-E electronically controlled four-speed automatic (includes torque converter clutch). Steering: (All exc. Fleetwood) Power-assisted rack-and-pinion, speed sensitive; (Fleetwood) Power-assisted recirculating ball, speed sensitive, variable assist. Front Suspension: (All exc. Fleetwood) Independent MacPherson strut with coil springs, strut-type shock absorbers (DeVille Concours used electronic variable rate dampers) and stabilizer bar; (Fleetwood) Independent with short/long arms, coil springs, direct acting shock absorbers and stabilizer bar. Rear Suspension: (Sedan DeVille) Fully independent, short/long arm w/automatic level control and speed sensitive suspension; (DeVille Concours, Seville, Eldorado) Fully independent, coil springs, short/long arm w/automatic level control and electronic variable dampers w/road sensing suspension; (Fleetwood) Four link, coil springs w/automatic level control, direct acting shock absorbers and stabilizer bar. Brakes: (all exc. Fleetwood) Power assisted front and rear disc w/Bosch anti-lock braking system; (Fleetwood) Power assisted front disc/rear drum w/Bosch anti-lock braking system; Body Construction: (All exc. Fleetwood) Integral body-frame; (Fleetwood) Separate body on frame. Fuel Tank: (all exc. Fleetwood) 20.0 gals.; (Fleetwood) 23.0 gals.

DRIVETRAIN OPTIONS: V92 3,000-Pound Trailer Towing Pkg. (DeV Concours) $110. V4P 7,000-Pound Trailer Towing Pkg. (Fleetwood) $215.

DEVILLE CONVENIENCE/APPEARANCE OPTIONS: Opt. Pkg. 1SB: (Sedan DeV) $428. Astroroof $1,550-$1,700. Elect. Compass $100. Garage Door Opener $107. Theft Deterrent Syst. (Sedan DeV) $295. White Diamond Paint $500. Pearl Red Paint $500. Electrochromic Auto Day/Night Driver's Side Mirror (stnd DeV Concours) $87. ETR AM/FM Stereo Radio w/Cassette (stnd DeV Concours) $274; w/Cassette & CD: Sedan DeV $670; DeV Concours $396. Heated Windshield (Sedan DeV) $309. Heated Front Seats $120. Leather Seats (stnd DeV Concours) $785. Chrome Whls $1,195.

ELDORADO CONVENIENCE/APPEARANCE OPTIONS: UY9 Sport Int. Pkg. $146. Theft Deterrent Syst. (stnd Touring Coupe) $295. Elect. Compass $100. Garage Door Opener $107. Accent Striping (Eldo) $75. Heated Front Seats $120. Astroroof $1,550. Heated Windshield $309. Leather Seating (stnd Touring Coupe) $650. Pwr Lumbar Support (stnd Touring Coupe) $292. Electrochromic Auto Day/Night Driver's Side Mirror (stnd Touring Coupe) $87. White Diamond Paint $500. Pearl Red Paint $500. Delco-Bose Sound Syst. w/CD & Cassette $972. P225/60R16 WSW Tires (Eldo) $76. Chrome Whls $1,195.

SEVILLE CONVENIENCE/APPEARANCE OPTIONS: UY9 Sport Int. Pkg. $146. Theft Deterrent Syst. (stnd STS) $295. Elect. Compass $100. Garage Door Opener $107. Accent Striping (SLS) $75. Heated Front Seats $120. Heated Windshield $309. Astroroof $1,550. Leather Seating (stnd STS) $650. Pwr Lumbar Support (stnd STS) $292. Electrochromic Auto Day/Night Driver's Side Mirror (stnd STS) $87. White Diamond Paint $500. Pearl Red Paint $500. Delco-Bose Sound Syst. w/CD & Cassette $972. Chrome Whls $1,195.

FLEETWOOD CONVENIENCE/APPEARANCE OPTIONS: Security Pkg. $360. Theft Deterrent Syst. $295. Astroroof $1,550. Garage Door Opener $107. Coachbuilder Pkg. ($755). Funeral Coach Pkg. ($910 credit). Brougham Cloth Int. $1,680. Brougham Leather Int. $2,250. H.D. Livery Pkg. $150. Leather Seating (Fleetwood) $570. Heated Front Seats $120. Sungate Windshield $50. ETR AM/FM Stereo Radio w/CD & Cassette $396. Full Vinyl Roof (Fleetwood) $925. Full-size Spare $95. Chrome Whls $1,195.

Cadillac's model year production totaled 200,577 compared with 219,485 the year previous. Based on sales of 180,504 automobiles in 1995 (vs. 210,686 the year before), Cadillac's share of the U.S. market was 2.1 percent compared with 2.3 the year previous.

1996

The Northstar, in either its 275 or 300 horsepower variation, now powered all front-wheel drive Cadillacs. The Arlington, Texas-produced Fleetwood (and optional Fleetwood Brougham package), the lone front-engine, rear-drive Cadillac, was in its final year of production. Introduced in early-1996 as a 1997 model was the all-new rear-drive Catera (see 1997 Catera listing). This midsize luxury sedan was a joint venture between Cadillac and Opel, assembled in Germany, and powered by a 3.0-liter dual overhead cam V-6. All 1996 Cadillacs received daytime running lamps and a new remote keyless entry fob in dark gray with light gray buttons and white icons. The fob functions were: lock, unlock, trunk open and fuel door open. The fobs were identified on back with a "one" or "two" indication, allowing two separate drivers to personalize seat positions that adjusted to the driver when the key was placed in the ignition. Additionally, all front-drive Cadillacs featured an ignition key anti-lockout feature that protected the driver from accidental lockout by disabling the driver's power door lock if the key was left in the ignition. Also, all front-drive Cadillacs received the new communication-based electronics architecture called Class 2, a new designation for an electrical communication protocol on 1996 vehicles that also provided common emissions diagnostic capability in connection with federally mandated On-Board Diagnostic II requirements.

1996 Cadillac, Sedan DeVille. (OCW)

DEVILLE - SERIES 6K - V-8 - It was again the Sedan DeVille and DeVille Concours in the lineup, but both were now powered by the Northstar V-8. Sedan DeVille used the 275-horsepower version of the 4.6-liter engine mated to the 4T80-E electronically controlled four-speed automatic transmission with viscous converter clutch. This combination replaced the formerly standard 4.9-liter V-8 and 4T60-E four-speed transmission. Sedan DeVille's new final drive ratio was 3.11:1. The Concours sedan again featured the 300-horsepower version of the Northstar engine, also coupled to the 4T80-E transmission. Its final drive ratio was revised from 3.11:1 to 3.71:1 for improved acceleration and passing performance. A more powerful Powertrain Control Module (PCM) with microprocessors monitored and directed DeVille engine/transmission operations. Clock speed of the PCM microprocessor was increased from 2.1 megahertz to 3.4 megahertz, which improved processing time 63 percent. Memory size was increased from 64 kilobytes to 96 kilobytes per microprocessor, allowing the PCM to provide more software functionality. For improved throttle response and reduced exhaust emissions, a mass airflow sensor was added. This sensor continually measured the volume of air entering the engine and supplied that information to the PCM. In addition, the PCM was moved from the passenger compartment to the air cleaner housing. This enhanced engine harness reliability by reducing wiring lengths and minimized the number of wires passed through the front of the dash. Improved design precision fuel injectors delivered precise fuel metering, which contributed to more efficient fuel control. Already standard equipment in the Concours, the Sedan DeVille received the Integrated Chassis Control System (ICCS) for 1996. The ICCS featured a steering wheel angle position sensor that read the steering angle of the vehicle and transmitted that position to the brake, traction control and Road Sensing Suspension controller units, which calibrated these systems for improved control and quicker stops.

Optional on the 1996 DeVille was a 3,000-pound trailer towing package that included a wiring harness with oil cooler lines from the oil cooler adapter to the radiator and a radiator end tank to provide extra engine cooling when towing large loads. Other new standard features included dual wall stainless steel exhaust manifolds with single tailpipes and a resonator provided for a quieter interior and more pleasing exhaust note; "Electro-motor" electronic cruise control (which replaced the previous vacuum-operated system), a revised wheel design (in fine grain cast aluminum or chrome finish) that incorporated a wreath-and-crest center cap and Michelin XW4 P225/60R16 whitewall tires. New standard features unique to the Concours sedan included Magnasteer electromagnetic variable-assist power steering (which replaced the previous speed sensitive steering); Rainsense Wiper System that automatically activated in inclement weather; and Continuously Variable Road Sensing Suspension that was a refinement of the previous Road Sensing Suspension, which offered improved damping for a smoother ride. Additionally, the Concours sedan's Delco Electronics Active Audio System could be upgraded to include a factory-installed, trunk-mounted 12-compact disc changer. Also, a Cadillac-exclusive convenience feature offered in the Concours sedan was the Dual-Mode (analog and digital) voice-activated cell phone, available in portable or non-portable package.

1996 Cadillac, Fleetwood sedan. (OCW)

FLEETWOOD - SERIES 6D - V-8 - In its final year of production, the revisions to the Fleetwood sedan and optional Brougham package model were mainly "creature comfort" in nature. Fleetwoods were again powered by the GenII 5.7-liter V-8 paired with the 4L60-E electronically controlled four-speed automatic transmission. Final drive ratio for Fleetwood was 2.56:1 while the Brougham's was 3.42:1. Inside, the Fleetwood received "Electro-motor" electronic cruise control and a new center armrest with dual cupholder, coinholder and CD/cassette storage. Fleetwood models were also pre-wired to accommodate the optional Dual-Mode cell phone. Also new was a six-speaker entertainment system that could be upgraded with the factory-installed, trunk-mounted CD changer. Again, the Fleetwood could also be ordered as the V4U Coachbuilder Limousine Package, B9Q Funeral Coach Package, or R1P Heavy-Duty Sedan Package with heavy-duty components required for continuous commercial service.

1996 Cadillac, Eldorado coupe. (OCW)

ELDORADO - SERIES 6E - V-8 - The Eldorado series models offered and powertrains for those models carried over from the year previous. The Eldo coupe was again powered by the 275-horsepower Northstar 4.6-liter V-8 while the Eldorado Touring Coupe (ETC) again used the 300-horse Northstar engine. Both were mated to the 4T80-E electronically controlled four-speed automatic transmission linked to the engine via a viscous converter clutch. Final drive ratio of the Eldo was 3.11:1 while the ETC's was 3.71:1. Inside the "base" coupe, the seats were redesigned to improve comfort and eight-way memory seats were available as an option (standard on ETC), with adjustability for two different drivers. The seats were designed to reveal a hand-crafted look through French seam stitching. Other new features included the previous dark black trim on seat and window stitches, trimplates, cluster area and radio faceplate being changed to dark gray; the previous speed density air/fuel control system replaced with a mass airflow sensor; the addition of a more powerful Powertrain Control Module (PCM) to help reduce exhaust emissions as well as the PCM being moved from the passenger compartment to the air cleaner housing to enhance its reliability; "Electro-motor" electronic cruise control replacing the previous vacuum-operated system; and Sea Mist Green exterior color choice. New options for the "base" coupe included the Dual-Mode voice-activated cell phone and one leather seating color choice: Sea Mist Green. When leather seating was ordered, a new lamination process was used to bond the leather to the trim pad to reduce wrinkles. Also new for 1996, a computer algorithm in the PCM anticipated air conditioner compressor load cycling to eliminate the driveline disturbances associated with A/C operation while driving; the Road Sensing Suspension module used wheel displacement to calculate body velocities, which eliminated the need for body accelerometers; and customer personalization of four automatic door lock configurations, battery storage and seat position were programmable through the Driver Information Center (DIC). The ETC featured a completely redesigned interior. Entertainment system, climate control system and DIC controls were all integrated into a full center console. Relocating these controls from their previous location on the instrument panel allowed for the widening of the analog gauge cluster making it appear "international" with large speedometer and tachometer dials. New features of the ETC included the Dual-Mode cell phone, Rainsense Wiper System, and a traction control off switch and valet lockout button that deactivated the trunk, fuel door and garage door opener functions, all located in the glovebox. ETC also received Magnasteer variable assist power steering as well as Continuously Variable Road Sensing Suspension for improved ride comfort. In the event of an airbag deployment in the ETC, interior lights were illuminated after one second and remained on for 25 minutes unless manually switched off. Also, automatic door locks unlocked 15 seconds after deployment. Standard rubber for the ETC was Goodyear Eagle RS-A P225/60R16 blackwall tires while Eagle GA P225/60ZR16 blackwalls were optional.

1996 Cadillac, Seville Luxury Sedan. (OCW)

1996 Cadillac, Seville Touring Sedan. (OCW)

SEVILLE - SERIES 6K - V-8 - As in the previous year, the refinements of the "base" Eldo coupe were carried through to the Seville Luxury Sedan (SLS) while those of the Eldorado Touring Coupe were carried through to the Seville Touring Sedan (STS). Again, the SLS was powered by the 275-horsepower Northstar 4.6-liter V-8 and the STS used the 300-horse Northstar engine.

Both versions were paired with the 4T80-E electronically controlled four-speed automatic transmission with viscous converter clutch.

I.D. DATA: The 1996 Cadillac had a 17-symbol vehicle identification number (VIN) stamped on a metal tag attached to the upper left surface of the cowl visible through the windshield. The code was as follows: The first digit, "1" or "4," represented the manufacturing country (United States), the second, "G," represented General Motors, the third, "6," represented Cadillac, the fourth and fifth represented the car line/series, as follows: D/W-Fleetwood, E/L-Eldorado, E/T-Eldorado Touring, K/D-DeVille, K/F-Concours, K/S-Seville (SLS), and K/Y-Seville (STS). Digit six represents the body style: 1-two-door coupe, 2-two-door, 3-convertible, 4-two-door station wagon, 5-four-door sedan, 6-four-door, and 8-four-door station wagon. Digit seven identifies the restraint code: 1-active (manual) belts, 2-active (manual) belts w/dual airbags, 3-active (manual) belts w/driver's side airbag, 4-passive (automatic) belts, 5-passive (automatic) belts w/driver's side airbag, 6-passive (automatic) belts w/dual airbags, and 7-active (manual) belt driver and passive (automatic) belt passenger w/dual airbags. The eighth digit identifies the engine: "P"-LT1 5.7L V-8, "Y"-LD8 4.6L V-8; and "9"-L37 4.6L V-8. A check digit follows. The 10th digit represents the model year, "T" for 1996. The eleventh digit represents the assembly plant. The remaining six digits identify the production sequence number.

DeVille (V-8)

Series No.	Body/Style No.	Body Type & Seating	Factory Price	Shipping Weight	Prod. Total
KD5	D69	4-dr. Sedan	35995	3959	Note 1
KF5	F69	4-dr. Concours Sed.	40495	3981	Note 1

Note 1: DeVille production totaled 100,251 with no further breakout available.

Fleetwood (V-8)

Series No.	Body/Style No.	Body Type & Seating	Factory Price	Shipping Weight	Prod. Total
DW5	W69	4-dr. Sedan	36995	4461	15,101 (*)

(*) Includes Fleetwoods equipped with Brougham option.

Eldorado (V-8)

Series No.	Body/Style No.	Body Type & Seating	Factory Price	Shipping Weight	Prod. Total
EL1	L57	2-dr. Coupe	39595	3765	Note 1
ET1	T57	2-dr. Tour. Cpe.	42995	3801	Note 1

Note 1: Eldorado production totaled 20,816 with no further breakout available.

Seville (V-8)

Series No.	Body/Style No.	Body Type & Seating	Factory Price	Shipping Weight	Prod. Total
KS5	S69	4-dr. SLS Sedan	42995	3832	Note 1
KY5	Y69	4-dr. STS Sedan	47495	3869	Note 1

Note 1: Seville production totaled 38,238 with no further breakout available.

1996 Cadillac, Eldorado Touring Coupe. (OCW)

ENGINES: BASE V-8: (DeVille, Eldorado, Seville) 90-degree, dual overhead cam Northstar V-8. Aluminum block with cast iron cylinder liners, aluminum cylinder heads. Displacement: 279 cu. in. (4.6 liters). Bore & Stroke: 3.66 x 3.31 in. Compression ratio: 10.3:1. Brake horsepower: (Sedan DeVille, Eldorado, Seville Luxury Sedan) 275 @ 5600 rpm; (DeVille Concours, Eldorado Touring Coupe, Seville Touring Sedan) 300 @ 6000 rpm. Torque: (Sedan DeVille, Eldorado, Seville Luxury Sedan) 300 lb.-ft. @ 4000 rpm; (DeVille Concours, Eldorado Touring Coupe, Seville Touring Sedan) 295 lb.-ft. @ 4400 rpm. Direct acting hydraulic tappets. Tuned port fuel injection. BASE V-8: (Fleetwood) 90-degree, overhead valve V-8. Cast iron block and cylinder heads. Displacement: 350 cu. in. (5.7 liters). Bore & Stroke: 4.00 x 3.48 in. Compression ratio: 10.0:1. Brake horsepower: 260 @ 5000 rpm. Torque: 330 lb.-ft. @ 3200 rpm. Roller hydraulic valve lifters. Sequential port fuel injection.

CHASSIS DATA: Wheelbase: (DeVille) 113.8 in.; (Seville) 111.0 in.; (Eldorado) 108.0 in.; (Fleetwood) 121.5 in. Overall Length: (DeVille)

209.7 in.; (Seville) 204.1 in.; (Eldorado) 200.2 in.; (Fleetwood) 225.0 in. Height: (DeVille) 56.4 in.; (Seville) 54.5 in.; (Eldorado) 53.6 in.; (Fleetwood) 57.1 in. Width: (DeVille) 76.5 in.; (Seville) 74.2 in.; (Eldorado) 75.5 in.; (Fleetwood) 78.0 in. Front Tread: (DeVille) 60.9 in.; (Seville, Eldorado) 60.9 in.; (Fleetwood) 61.7 in. Rear Tread: (DeVille) 60.9 in.; (Seville, Eldorado) 60.9 in.; (Fleetwood) 60.7 in. Standard Tires: (Sedan DeVille) Michelin P215/60SR16; (DeVille Concours) Goodyear Eagle RS-A P225/60R16; (Seville, Eldorado) Michelin P225/60SR16; (Touring) Goodyear Eagle RS-A P225/60HR16; (Fleetwood) Michelin P235/70R15.

TECHNICAL: Transmission: (DeVille, Eldorado, Seville) 4T80-E electronically controlled four-speed automatic (includes viscous converter clutch); (Fleetwood) 4L60-E electronically controlled four-speed automatic (includes torque converter clutch). Steering: (All exc. Fleetwood) Power-assisted rack-and-pinion, speed sensitive (Magnasteer on DeVille Concours, Eldorado Touring Coupe and Seville Touring Sedan); (Fleetwood) Power-assisted recirculating ball, speed sensitive, variable assist. Front Suspension: (Sedan DeVille, Eldorado, Seville Luxury Sedan) Independent MacPherson strut with coil springs, strut-type shock absorbers and stabilizer bar and electronic variable road sensing suspension; (DeVille Concours, Eldorado Touring Coupe, Seville Touring Sedan) Independent MacPherson strut with coil springs, strut-type shock absorbers and stabilizer bar and electronic continuously variable road sensing suspension; (Fleetwood) Independent with short/long arms, coil springs, direct acting shock absorbers and stabilizer bar. Rear Suspension: (Sedan DeVille, Eldorado, Seville Luxury Sedan) Fully independent, short/long arm w/automatic level control and electronic variable road sensing suspension; (DeVille Concours, Eldorado Touring Coupe, Seville Touring Sedan) Fully independent, coil springs, short/long arm w/automatic level control and electronic continuously variable road sensing suspension; (Fleetwood) Four link, coil springs w/automatic level control, direct acting shock absorbers and stabilizer bar. Brakes: (all exc. Fleetwood) Power assisted front and rear disc w/Bosch anti-lock braking system; (Fleetwood) Power assisted front disc/rear drum w/Bosch anti-lock braking system; Body Construction: (All exc. Fleetwood) Integral body-frame; (Fleetwood) Separate body on frame. Fuel Tank: (all exc. Fleetwood) 20.0 gals.; (Fleetwood) 23.0 gals.

DRIVETRAIN OPTIONS: V92 3,000-Pound Trailer Towing Pkg. $110. V4P 7,000-Pound Trailer Towing Pkg. (Fleetwood) $215.

1996 Cadillac, Sedan DeVille Concours. (OCW)

DEVILLE CONVENIENCE/APPEARANCE OPTIONS: WA4 Special Edition (Sedan DeV w/gold ornamentation, chrome wheels and simulated convertible top) $1,590. Opt. Pkg. 1SB (Sedan DeV) $530. Astroroof $1,550-$1,700. Elect. Compass $100. Garage Door Opener $107. Theft Deterrent Syst. (Sedan DeV) $295. White Diamond Paint $500. Pearl Red Paint $500. ETR AM/FM Stereo Radio w/Cassette (stnd DeV Concours) $274; w/Cassette & CD: Sedan DeV $869; DeV Concours $595; w/Digital Signal Processing: Sedan DeV $1,064; DeV Concours $790. Heated Windshield (Sedan DeV) $377. Memory Driver's Seat (stnd DeV Concours) $235. Heated Leather Seats $225. Leather Seats (stnd DeV Concours) $785. Chrome Whls $1,195.

ELDORADO CONVENIENCE/APPEARANCE OPTIONS: UY9 Sport Int. Pkg. $146. Theft Deterrent Syst. (stnd Touring Coupe) $295. Elect. Compass $100. Garage Door Opener $107. Accent Striping (Eldo) $75. Heated Front Leather Seats $225. Astroroof $1,550. Heated Windshield $377. Leather Seating (stnd Touring Coupe) $785. Dual Pwr Lumbar Support (stnd Touring Coupe) $292. Memory Driver's Seat (stnd Touring Coupe) $235. Electrochromic Auto Day/Night Driver's Side Mirror (stnd Touring Coupe) $87. White Diamond Paint $500. Pearl Red Paint $500. Bose Sound Syst. w/Cassette $723; w/Cassette & CD Changer $1,318; w/Digital Signal Processing $1,513. P225/60R16 WSW Tires (Eldo) $76. P225/60ZR16 BSW Tires (Touring Coupe) $250. Chrome Whls $1,195.

SEVILLE CONVENIENCE/APPEARANCE OPTIONS: UY9 Sport Int. Pkg. $146. Theft Deterrent Syst. (stnd STS) $295. Elect. Compass $100. Garage Door Opener $107. Accent Striping (SLS) $75. Heated Front Leather Seats $225. Heated Windshield $377. Astroroof $1,550. Leather Seating (stnd STS) $785. Pwr Lumbar Support (stnd STS) $292. Memory Driver's Seat (stnd STS) $225. Electrochromic Auto Day/Night Driver's Side Mirror (stnd STS) $87. White Diamond Paint $500. Pearl Red Paint $500. Bose Sound Syst. w/Cassette $723. w/Cassette & CD Changer $1,318; w/Digital Signal Processing $1,513. P225/60ZR16 BSW Tires (STS) $250. Chrome Whls $1,195.

FLEETWOOD CONVENIENCE/APPEARANCE OPTIONS: Security Pkg. $360. Theft Deterrent Syst. $295. Astroroof $1,550. Garage Door Opener $107. Coachbuilder Pkg. ($755). Funeral Coach Pkg. ($910 credit). Brougham Cloth Int. $1,680. Brougham Leather Int. $2,465. H.D. Livery Pkg. $150. Leather Seating (Fleetwood) $785. Sungate Windshield $50. ETR AM/FM Stereo Radio w/CD & Cassette $200. Full Vinyl Roof (Fleetwood) $925. Full-size Spare $95. Chrome Whls $1,195.

HISTORY: Cadillac's model year production totaled 174,406 compared with 200,577 the year previous. Based on sales of 170,379 automobiles in 1996 (vs. 180,504 the year before), Cadillac's share of the U.S. market was 2.0 percent compared with 2.1 the year previous. The 1996 sales figure listed included 1,676 early launch 1997 Catera sedans sold in the 1996 model year. John F. Smith replaced John O. Grettenberger as general manager of Cadillac. In September 1996, faulty computer chips force the recall of 587,000 Cadillacs.

1997

This marked the first time since 1988 (when the underachieving V-6-powered Cimarron was discontinued) that Cadillac offered something other than a V-8 engine. The all-new Catera used a 200-horsepower dual overhead cam V-6. The DeVille ranks were bolstered with the addition of the d'Elegance sedan joining the existing DeVille and DeVille Concours sedans. All DeVille and Catera models now featured side airbags as standard equipment and the exclusive-to-Cadillac OnStar communication system also debuted as an option on all front-drive models in 1997. All Cadillacs also received improved anti-lockout protection.

CATERA - SERIES 6V - V-6 - Launched during the 1996 model year, the midsize 1997 Catera sports sedan was a joint venture automobile developed by Cadillac and Adam Opel AG and built by Opel in Ruesselsheim, Germany. It was based on the European Opel Omega sedan platform. The five-passenger, rear-drive sedan was imported into the United States, and sold and serviced by more than 765 Cadillac dealers nationwide. The Catera's standard features included dual frontal and side airbags, four wheel disc brakes with anti-lock, speed sensitive power steering, full range traction control, daytime running lamps, Twilight Sentinel headlamp system, foglamps, remote keyless entry, programmable power door locks, Solar-Ray glass, automatic dual zone climate control system, electrochromic inside rearview mirror, four-spoke steering wheel with remote controls for the entertainment system, illuminated entry and 16-inch, seven-spoke alloy wheels with Goodyear Eagle RS-A P225/55R16 tires. Optional items included leather seating with front/rear seat heaters, Bose audio system, automatic power sunroof, garage door opener and five-spoke alloy wheels in either natural or chrome finish. Powertrain consisted of a 3.0-liter dual overhead cam V-6, with Dual-Ram induction and rated at 200 horsepower, paired with a 4L30-E electronically controlled four-speed automatic transmission with overdrive. This transmission featured easy-to-select Sport, Normal and Winter driving modes. Final drive ratio was 3.9:1. To enhance side-impact protection for occupants, the Catera incorporated dual steel beams in each door, reinforced body pillars, a rigid roof and a cross-car beam over the driveline tunnel. The Catera also featured MacPherson strut front suspension designed with advanced hydraulic control arm bushings to enhance stability of the car during hard braking. The rear suspension included automatic load leveling. Turning circle of the Catera was 34.1 feet. Inside, interior volume measured 111.2 cubic feet with an additional 14.5 cubic feet of trunk space. The rear bench seat featured a three-piece fold-down seatback for carrying long objects. The driver's seat had eight-way power adjustment as well as driver and passenger front seats featuring adjustable lumbar support. Catera's instrument panel featured analog gauges, including a tachometer. Outside, the Catera featured a contoured black chrome grille with integrated wreath-and-crest emblem and single-piece front fascia that flowed into the fenders. A thin chrome accent set the grille apart from the hood. Coefficient of drag was 0.33.

1997 Cadillac, DeVille sedan. (OCW)

1997 Cadillac, DeVille d'Elegance sedan. (OCW)

DEVILLE - SERIES 6K - V-8 - The DeVille and DeVille Concours sedans were joined by a new, upscale sedan called the d'Elegance. The Concours was "repositioned" as a sportier sedan for the performance-minded buyers, while the DeVille and d'Elegance offered luxury and high-luxury, respectively. Those two sedans were powered by the 275-horsepower version of the Northstar 4.6-liter V-8 while the Concours again used the 300-horsepower Northstar V-8. Both engine versions were again paired with the 4T80-E electronically controlled four-speed automatic transmission with viscous converter clutch. Key new standard features of the DeVille series included side airbags, Magnasteer electromagnetic variable-assist power steering (already standard on Concours), and a revised seat appearance. The DeVille sedans received revamped hood (with more emphasis on the powerdome), front fascia, fenders and rear upper and lower fascia; new bodyside molding; and refinements to both anti-lock brake and traction control systems. One of the most notable changes to the 1997 DeVille was in profile, with the rear wheel opening being enlarged and the wheels pulled out 10mm per side. This widened rear track improved the wheel-to-body relationship. DeVille and d'Elegance sedans sported a new chrome grille. The d'Elegance and Concours sedans featured both a new personalization programmable package and memory package. The former included remote function activation, activation verification, auto door lock, perimeter lighting and battery storage mode while the latter featured eight-way seat adjustment, outside rearview mirror/lumbar/HVAC settings and radio presets. Unique to the d'Elegance was a gold tone exterior ornamentation package and Rainsense windshield wiper system (already standard on Concours) while Concours exclusives were road texture detection, which increased the effectiveness of anti-lock braking and StabiliTrak, an electronic chassis system that helped the driver control the car on slippery surfaces. Due to a full center console, the Concours sedan's revised interior now accommodated five passengers, while the DeVille and d'Elegance each carried six. Other new DeVille series features included the instrument panel pad, HVAC outlets with chrome finish, and trunk storage dividers. Also, new hydraulic shocks offered damping rates higher than the "firm" setting available with the previous road sensing suspension. A new lower control arm design put the unit's main bushing in line with the wheel center, which allowed the bushing to directly absorb cornering loads. Front brake discs were enlarged one inch (to 11.9 inches in diameter) over the previous units for additional stopping power. The new acoustic headliner and sound-absorbing foam used in the body structure further isolated road and powertrain noise. The aforementioned new optional OnStar communication system used on-board electronics in con-

junction with global positioning system satellite technology to offer around-the-clock driver security in emergency situations.

1997 Cadillac, Eldorado Touring Coupe. (OCW)

ELDORADO - SERIES 6E - V-8 - The Eldorado series returned with the "base" coupe and Eldorado Touring Coupe (ETC), each powered by the Northstar V-8 and 4T80-E combination as in the year previous. New standard features included Magnasteer (already standard on the ETC), hydraulic shocks with higher damping rate, new lower control arm design to better absorb cornering load, one-inch larger front brake discs, trunk storage dividers, improved headliner and acoustic refinements, and more "user friendly" climate control readouts. All 1997 Eldos were manufactured with an analog gauge cluster, full center console and dual zone climate control as standard fare. The Eldo coupe received a new personalization programmable package that included auto door locks, exterior lighting, activation verification and battery storage. The ETC added road texture detection to aid anti-lock braking effectiveness, StabiliTrak system to help the driver maintain control on slippery surfaces, and 11 additional driver information center (DIC) messages, including: headlamps suggested, ice possible (outside temperature of 36 degrees or lower) and check fuel gauge. The ETC also received a new personalization programmable package that included choice of memory recall with remote keyless entry, key in ignition or memory switches; HVAC settings; radio preset settings; battery storage mode; perimeter lighting, activation verification and auto door lock. Also new to the ETC was a memory package that featured eight-way seat adjustments and exit, outside rearview mirror adjustments and lumbar support positions. Eldos offered the OnStar communication system as optional equipment.

1997 Cadillac, Seville Luxury Sedan. (OCW)

1997 Cadillac, Seville Touring Sedan. (OCW)

SEVILLE - SERIES 6K - V-8 - The Seville Luxury Sedan (SLS) and Seville Touring Sedan (STS) again reflected the changes that occurred on the Eldo coupe and ETC, respectively.

I.D. DATA: The 1997 Cadillac had a 17-symbol vehicle identification number (VIN) stamped on a metal tag attached to the upper left surface of the cowl visible through the windshield. The code was as follows: The first digit, "1" or "4," represented the manufacturing country (United States), the second, "G," represented General Motors, the third, "6," represented Cadillac, the fourth and fifth represented the car line/series, as follows: E/L-Eldorado, E/T-Eldorado Touring, K/D-DeVille, K/E-d'Elegance, K/F-Concours, K/S-Seville (SLS), K/Y-Seville (STS), and V/R-Catera. Digit six represents the body style: 1-two-door coupe, 2-two-door, 3-convertible, 5-four-door sedan, 6-four-door, and 8-four-door station wagon. Digit seven identifies the restraint code: 2-active (manual) belts w/dual frontal airbags and 4-active (manual) belts w/dual frontal and side airbags. The eighth digit identifies the engine: "R"-L81 3.0L V-6, "Y"-LD8 4.6L V-8; and "9"-L37 4.6L V-8. A check digit follows. The 10th digit represents the model year, "V" for 1997. The eleventh digit represents the assembly plant. The remaining six digits identify the production sequence number.

Catera (V-6)

Series No.	Body/Style No.	Body Type & Seating	Factory Price	Shipping Weight	Prod. Total
VR5	R69	4-dr. Sedan	29995	3770	25,411 (*)

(*) Production total based on number of cars imported into U.S.

DeVille (V-8)

Series No.	Body/Style No.	Body Type & Seating	Factory Price	Shipping Weight	Prod. Total
KD5	D69	4-dr. Sedan	36995	4015	Note 1
KE5	E69	4-dr. d'Elegance Sed.	39995	4050	Note 1
KF5	F69	4-dr. Concours Sed.	41995	4055	Note 1

Note 1: DeVille production totaled 99,601 with no further breakout available.

Eldorado (V-8)

Series No.	Body/Style No.	Body Type & Seating	Factory Price	Shipping Weight	Prod. Total
EL1	L57	2-dr. Coupe	37995	3843	Note 1
ET1	T57	2-dr. Tour. Cpe.	41395	3876	Note 1

Note 1: Eldorado production totaled 18,102 with no further breakout available.

Seville (V-8)

Series No.	Body/Style No.	Body Type & Seating	Factory Price	Shipping Weight	Prod. Total
KS5	S69	4-dr. SLS Sedan	39995	3901	Note 1
KY5	Y69	4-dr. STS Sedan	44995	3960	Note 1

Note 1: Seville production totaled 42,117 with no further breakout available.

1997 Cadillac, Catera sedan with optional sunroof. (OCW)

ENGINES: BASE V-6 (Catera) 54-degree, dual overhead cam V-6. Cast iron block, aluminum cylinder heads. Displacement: 181 cu. in. (3.0 liters). Bore & Stroke: 3.40 x 3.40 in. Compression ratio: 10.0:1. Brake horsepower: 200 @ 6000 rpm. Torque: 192 lb.-ft. @ 3600 rpm. Variable Dual-Ram induction system. BASE V-8: (DeVille/d'Elegance, Eldorado, Seville) 90-degree, dual overhead cam Northstar V-8. Aluminum block with cast iron cylinder liners, aluminum cylinder heads. Displacement: 279 cu. in. (4.6 liters). Bore & Stroke: 3.66 x 3.31 in. Compression ratio: 10.3:1. Brake horsepower: (DeV-

ille/d'Elegance, Eldorado, Seville Luxury Sedan) 275 @ 5600 rpm; (DeVille Concours, Eldorado Touring Coupe, Seville Touring Sedan) 300 @ 6000 rpm. Torque: (DeVille/d'Elegance, Eldorado, Seville Luxury Sedan) 300 lb.-ft. @ 4000 rpm; (DeVille Concours, Eldorado Touring Coupe, Seville Touring Sedan) 295 lb.-ft. @ 4400 rpm. Direct acting hydraulic tappets. Tuned port fuel injection.

CHASSIS DATA: Wheelbase: (Catera) 107.4 in.; (DeVille) 113.8 in.; (Seville) 111.0 in.; (Eldorado) 108.0 in. Overall Length: (Catera) 194.0 in.; (DeVille) 209.7 in.; (Seville) 204.1 in.; (Eldorado) 200.2 in. Height: (Catera) 56.3 in.; (DeVille) 56.4 in.; (Seville) 54.5 in.; (Eldorado) 53.6 in. Width: (Catera) 70.3 in.; (DeVille) 76.5 in.; (Seville) 74.2 in.; (Eldorado) 75.5 in. Front Tread: (Catera) 59.3 in.; (DeVille) 60.9 in.; (Seville, Eldorado) 60.9 in. Rear Tread: (Catera) 59.8 in.; (DeVille) 60.9 in.; (Seville, Eldorado) 60.9 in. Standard Tires: (Catera) Goodyear Eagle GS-A P225/55HR16; (DeVille/d'Elegance) Michelin P225/60SR16; (DeVille Concours) Goodyear Eagle RS-A P225/60HR16; (Seville, Eldorado) Michelin P225/60SR16; (Touring) Goodyear Eagle RS-A P225/60HR16.

TECHNICAL: Transmission: (Catera) 4L30-E electronically controlled four-speed automatic transmission with overdrive; (DeVille, Eldorado, Seville) 4T80-E electronically controlled four-speed automatic (includes viscous converter clutch); Steering: (Catera) Recirculating ball, speed sensitive; (DeVille, Eldorado, Seville) Power-assisted rack-and-pinion, Magnasteer. Front Suspension: (Catera) MacPherson strut, lower control arms w/hydro bushing, coil spring and stabilizer bar, gas preloaded dampers, continuously variable road sensing suspension; (DeVille/d'Elegance, Eldorado, Seville Luxury Sedan) Independent MacPherson strut with coil springs, strut-type shock absorbers and stabilizer bar and MacPherson strut dampers; (DeVille Concours, Eldorado Touring Coupe, Seville Touring Sedan) Independent MacPherson strut with coil springs, strut-type shock absorbers and stabilizer bar and electronic continuously variable road sensing suspension. Rear Suspension: (Catera) Multilink, coil spring and stabilizer bar, gas preloaded dampers, continuously variable road sensing suspension; (DeVille/d'Elegance, Eldorado, Seville Luxury Sedan) Fully independent, short/long arm and stabilizer bar w/automatic level control and electronic continuously variable road sensing suspension; (DeVille Concours, Eldorado Touring Coupe, Seville Touring Sedan) Fully independent, coil springs, short/long arm and stabilizer bar w/automatic level control and electronic continuously variable road sensing suspension. Brakes: (Catera) dual circuit front and rear disc w/antilock; (DeVille, Eldorado, Seville) Power assisted front and rear disc w/Bosch anti-lock braking system. Body Construction: (all) Integral body-frame. Fuel Tank: (Catera) 18.0 gals.; (DeVille, Eldorado, Seville) 20.0 gals.

DRIVETRAIN OPTIONS: (DeVille) V92 3,000-Pound Trailer Towing Pkg. $110.

CATERA CONVENIENCE/APPEARANCE OPTIONS: Garage Door Opener $107. Heated Seats $400. Bose Sound Syst. $723. Elect. Sunroof $995. Five-Spoke Whls: (Alum) $355; (Chrome) $1,195.

DEVILLE CONVENIENCE/APPEARANCE OPTIONS: WA7 Comfort/Convenience Pkg. (DeV only) $642. WA8 Safety/Security Pkg. $502. Astroroof $1,550. White Diamond Paint $500. Pearl Red Paint $500. H.D. Livery Pkg. (DeV only) $160. Heated Front Seats $225. Leather Seats (DeV only) $785. Active Audio Sound Syst. w/Cassette (DeV) $274; w/Cassette & CD Changer (DeV) $869/(d'Elegance, Concours) $595; w/Digital Signal Processing: (DeV) $1,064; (d'Elegance, Concours) $790. Chrome Whls $1,195.

ELDORADO CONVENIENCE/APPEARANCE OPTIONS: WA7 Memory/Personalization Pkg. $437. WA8 Safety/Security Pkg. $502. WA9 Sport Int. Pkg. $1,223. Elect. Compass $100. Garage Door Opener $107. Accent Striping (Eldo) $75. Heated Front Seats $225. Astroroof $1,550. White Diamond Paint $500. Pearl Red Paint $500. Bose Sound Syst. w/Cassette $723; w/Cassette & CD Changer $1,318; w/Digital Signal Processing $1,513. P225/60SR16 WSW Tires (Eldo) $76. P225/60ZR16 BSW Tires (Touring Coupe) $250. Chrome Whls $1,195.

SEVILLE CONVENIENCE/APPEARANCE OPTIONS: WA7 Memory/Personalization Pkg. $437. WA8 Safety/Security Pkg. $502. WA9 Sport Int. Pkg. $1,223. Elect. Compass $100. Garage Door Opener $107. Accent Striping (SLS) $75. Heated Front Seats $225. Astroroof $1,550. White Diamond Paint $500.

Pearl Red Paint $500. Bose Sound Syst. w/Cassette $723. w/Cassette & CD Changer $1,318; w/Digital Signal Processing $1,513. P225/60ZR16 BSW Tires (STS) $250. Chrome Whls $1,195.

HISTORY: Cadillac's model year production totaled 159,820 compared with 174,406 the year previous (this figure does not include the 25,411 imported Cateras). Based on sales of 182,624 automobiles in 1997 (vs. 170,379 the year before), Cadillac's share of the U.S. market was 2.2 percent compared with 2.0 the year previous. In May 1997, Cadillac announced the Catera would be produced domestically at its next redesign.

1998

All Cadillac models offered the year previous were carried over to 1998. The all-new 1998 Seville, not available until December 1997, was designed to lead Cadillac into the "global" market, with exports to 40 countries (both left- and right-hand drive versions were built at Cadillac's Detroit-Hamtramck assembly facility. StabiliTrak was now offered on all front-drive Cadillacs. The Catera joined the rest of the lineup in offering the OnStar communications system as optional equipment.

1998 Cadillac, Catera sedan with optional chrome wheels. (OCW)

CATERA - SERIES 6V - V-6 - In its sophomore year, the Catera received several upgrades. The entry-luxury sedan continued to be powered by the 3.0-liter dual overhead cam V-6 mated to the 4L30-E electronically controlled four-speed automatic transmission with overdrive. New standard features included an upgrade to the Bosch ABS/ASR 5.3 anti-lock brake and traction control system. The previous system controlled engine output to keep the engine from overpowering the tires on slippery roads. The enhanced system added brake control to the two rear wheels. If one wheel slipped, the system applied the brake to that wheel, transferring drive torque to the wheel that had more traction. Other new features included three additional exterior colors: Sky, Cocoa and Platinum, as well as the radio that now featured Theftlock as a security measure. Power outlets were modified to better accommodate cell phones and other accessories, and the outlets retained power with the key off. Also new, in the event of an accident that activated front airbags the interior lights came on and the doors unlocked automatically 15 seconds after deployment. In addition, a new airbag warning label was applied to the passenger visor. Catera now offered OnStar in-vehicle communications system as optional equipment. Also new on the option list was a Bose entertainment system that included an in-dash, single-slot CD player, radio data system (RDS), weather band, and Theftlock theft deterrent system. The RDS function received digital data in the form of traffic reports or emergency broadcasts that could be monitored any time, even breaking into a CD or cassette in play.

1998 Cadillac, DeVille sedan. (OCW)

1998 Cadillac, DeVille Concours sedan. (OCW)

DEVILLE - SERIES 6K - V-8 - The DeVille, d'Elegance and Concours sedans again comprised the series, and again the first two used the 275-horsepower version of the Northstar 4.6-liter V-8 for power while the Concours featured the 300-horse Northstar. Both versions again were coupled to the 4T80-E electronically controlled four-speed automatic transmission with viscous converter clutch. While StabiliTrak stability control system was already standard equipment on the Concours, it was now offered on the DeVille and d'Elegance as part of a safety/security option package that also included an electronic compass mirror, audible theft deterrent system and programmable garage door opener. The DeVille series offered four new exterior colors for 1998: Baltic Blue, Gold Firemist, Moonstone and Crimson Pearl. Inside, two new interior color choices were available: Camel (available only in leather) and Pewter (available in cloth or leather in the DeVille and leather only in d'Elegance and Concours). Additionally, the series' personalization feature added two new locking modes to the three that already existed: all doors lock when shifting out of park and only the driver's door unlocks when the key is turned off, and all doors lock when shifting out of park and unlock when the key is turned off. Also, the remote keyless entry fob added a feature: when the lock button was pressed, the horn sounded to verify that the doors were locked. All three sedans now came with an airbag warning label affixed to the passenger visor and each received a revised electrochromic day/night inside rearview mirror. The radio installed in DeVille series sedans also received a mute button and Theftlock, while radio data system (RDS) and weather band were offered as part of the optional Active Audio sound system. RDS allowed broadcasters to deliver a 1,200-bits-per-second data stream along with audio content. The Concours' standard radio also received an in-dash, single-slot CD player. Unique new standard features to the Concours included restyled 16-inch cast aluminum wheels as well as the next generation of Magnasteer that reacted to lateral acceleration as well as speed. When the cornering rate was up, as sensed by an on-board lateral accelerometer, steering effort was automatically increased to enhance the driver's feel of the road. Both the d'Elegance and Concours added heated front seats to their list of standard fare. The OnStar in-vehicle communications system was again offered to DeVille/d'Elegance/Concours buyers as a dealer-installed option.

1998 Cadillac, Eldorado coupe. (OCW)

1998 Cadillac, Eldorado Touring Coupe. (OCW)

ELDORADO - SERIES 6E - V-8 - No change occurred in either the Eldorado series lineup from the year previous or in the powertrain combinations used. The new standard features of the Eldo series coupes included four new exterior color choices: Baltic Blue, Gold Firemist, Moonstone and Crimson Pearl, as well as two new interior color selections: Camel (available only in leather) and Pewter (available in cloth or leather in Eldorado and leather only in the Eldorado Touring Coupe). Both the "base" coupe and ETC received an airbag warning label affixed to the passenger visor, new design electrochromic day/night inside rearview mirror, and new radio with Bose speaker system that additionally received a mute button and Theftlock theft-deterrent system. An optional radio selection included radio data system (RDS) and weather band. The series coupes' personalization feature was also upgraded with two new door locking modes as well as the remote keyless entry fob gaining an additional doors-locked verification feature. The OnStar communications system was again a dealer-installed option. StabiliTrak stability control system, while already standard equipment on the ETC, was now optional on the "base" coupe. Unique new standard features found on the ETC were heated front seats and the next-generation of Magnasteer.

1998 Cadillac, Seville SLS sedan. (OCW)

1998 Cadillac, Seville STS sedan. (OCW)

SEVILLE - SERIES 6K - V-8 - In a departure from previous years when the Seville basically mirrored the refinements found on the Eldorado, for 1998, the prestige-luxury sedan was exclusively redesigned as well as being positioned as Cadillac's leading-edge "global market" product. To back up this world-product positioning, the 1998 Seville was introduced at both the Frankfurt (Germany) and Tokyo auto shows in the fall of 1997. Both the Seville Luxury Sedan (SLS) and Seville Touring Sedan (STS) again comprised the lineup. The SLS was again powered by the 275-horsepower version of the Northstar 4.6-liter V-8 while the STS used the more powerful 300-horse Northstar version. Both engines again were paired with the 4T80-E electronically controlled four-speed automatic transmission with viscous converter clutch. Additionally, the STS was programmed for performance shifting via sensors in the vehicle, including the lateral acceleration sensor from StabiliTrak, which was standard equipment on 1998 Sevilles. These sensors evaluated the driver's intentions and programmed the transmission to respond like a manual gearbox during enthusiastic driving. The Seville was computer-designed to meet all world standards for front, side and rear impact, as well as those for roof crush resistance and

offset crashes. A one-piece floor panel extended from the front of the dash to the rear of the trunk, minimizing joints and seams. The interior body side rings were stamped from a single laser-welded blank, saving weight and improving build quality. A pair of hydroformed tubes swept up from the base of the windshield into the roof and back down to the rear wheelwells. These tubes helped form a safety cage around the passenger compartment, while improving torsional and beaming stiffness of the body structure. Compared to the previous year's sedan, the 1998 Seville's overall length decreased from 204.1 inches to 201 inches while its wheelbase increased from 111 inches to 112.2 inches. Track was also increased from 60.9 inches front and rear to 62.7 inches and 62.3 inches, respectively. This wider stance contributed to Seville's 120.4 cubic feet of interior space. Up front, Seville featured projection-beam headlamps that included a rectangular high beam. Parking lights had an optical surface in the middle to focus light in the proper location. The previously used bumper guards were deleted, and the vertical height of the grille was decreased, making it appear wider. The SLS sedan's grille was bright-finished in silver with a chrome edging and contained an integral full color wreath-and-crest emblem. The STS sedan's grille was body color with an argent monochrome integral wreath-and-crest emblem. Foglamps were positioned in the lower grille on the STS while the SLS used extended horizontal bars to cover that area. The Seville's hood featured a power-dome to enhance the image of the Northstar V-8. A high decklid was retained at the rear, which improved both aerodynamics and trunk space. A subtle rocker panel deflector ahead of the rear wheels added functional character as well as eliminating aero drag. The Seville's coefficient of drag was 0.31. The wheels on the SLS had a larger, more aggressive look while those on the STS featured a more open, spoke design to reveal large-capacity brakes. Seville featured Bosch 5.0 four-channel anti-lock braking and all-speed traction control as standard fare. Seville also featured a "smart" electrical system based on 16 electronic control modules linked together into a network capable of transferring data at 10,400 bytes per second. Inside, the SLS featured printed leather inserts for seat and door trim while the STS continued to use fine-perforated leather trim panels for seats and doors. Task-oriented lighting in the Seville reduced glare and maximized visibility. Seville's new instrumentation used a fluorescent light to provide high-definition illumination. The STS sedan's steering wheel (optional on SLS) had a power tilt and telescope feature. The shifter moved through a new serpentine gate for positive selection of the desired gear. The parking brake released automatically when the car was shifted from park. To reduce interior noise, the Seville used 5mm-thick door glass and doors sealed with triple rubber seals. New standard equipment on the Seville included Magnasteer III speed-sensitive power rack-and-pinion steering and Pass-Key III theft deterrent system. The OnStar in-vehicle communications system was optional equipment on both the SLS and STS. Also, a high-performance Bose 4.0 425-watt eight-speaker stereo system (including RDS and weather band) was standard on the STS and optional on the SLS. Additionally, the STS was the first car to offer adaptive seating technology as optional equipment. Adaptive seating, via a network of 10 air cells located in the front bucket seats, automatically recognized occupant position and adjusted the seats' support to custom-fit every individual.

I.D. DATA: The 1998 Cadillac had a 17-symbol vehicle identification number (VIN) stamped on a metal tag attached to the upper left surface of the cowl visible through the windshield. The code was as follows: The first digit, "1" or "4," represented the manufacturing country (United States), the second, "G," represented General Motors, the third, "6," represented Cadillac, the fourth and fifth represented the car line/series, as follows: E/L-Eldorado, E/T-Eldorado Touring, K/D-DeVille, K/E-d'Elegance, K/F-Concours, K/S-Seville (SLS), K/Y-Seville (STS), and V/R-Catera. Digit six represents the body style: 1-two-door coupe, 2-two-door, 3-convertible, 5-four-door sedan, 6-four-door, and 8-four-door station wagon. Digit seven identifies the restraint code: 2-active (manual) belts w/dual frontal airbags and 4-active (manual) belts w/dual frontal and side airbags. The eighth digit identifies the engine: "R"-L81 3.0L V-6, "Y"-LD8 4.6L V-8; and "9"-L37 4.6L V-8. A check digit follows. The 10th digit represents the model year, "W" for 1998. The eleventh digit represents the assembly plant. The remaining six digits identify the production sequence number.

Catera (V-6)

Series No.	Body/Style No.	Body Type & Seating	Factory Price	Shipping Weight	Prod. Total
VR5	R69	4-dr. Sedan	29995	3770	N/A

DeVille (V-8)

Series No.	Body/Style No.	Body Type & Seating	Factory Price	Shipping Weight	Prod. Total
KD5	D69	4-dr. Sedan	37695	4063	Note 1
KE5	E69	4-dr. d'Elegance Sed.	41295	4052	Note 1
KF5	F69	4-dr. Concours Sed.	42295	4012	Note 1

Note 1: DeVille production totaled 111,030 with no further breakout available.

Eldorado (V-8)

Series No.	Body/Style No.	Body Type & Seating	Factory Price	Shipping Weight	Prod. Total
EL1	L57	2-dr. Coupe	38495	3843	Note 1
ET1	T57	2-dr. Tour. Cpe.	42695	3876	Note 1

Note 1: Eldorado production totaled 18,415 with no further breakout available.

Seville (V-8)

Series No.	Body/Style No.	Body Type & Seating	Factory Price	Shipping Weight	Prod. Total
KS5	S69	4-dr. SLS Sedan	42495	3972	Note 1
KY5	Y69	4-dr. STS Sedan	46995	4001	Note 1

Note 1: Seville production totaled 33,270 with no further breakout available.

ENGINES: BASE V-6 (Catera) 54-degree, dual overhead cam V-6. Cast iron block, aluminum cylinder heads. Displacement: 181 cu. in. (3.0 liters). Bore & Stroke: 3.40 x 3.40 in. Compression ratio: 10.0:1. Brake horsepower: 200 @ 6000 rpm. Torque: 192 lb.-ft. @ 3600 rpm. Variable Dual-Ram induction system. BASE V-8: (DeVille/d'Elegance, Eldorado, Seville) 90-degree, dual overhead cam Northstar V-8. Aluminum block with cast iron cylinder liners, aluminum cylinder heads. Displacement: 279 cu. in. (4.6 liters). Bore & Stroke: 3.66 x 3.31 in. Compression ratio: 10.3:1. Brake horsepower: (DeVille/d'Elegance, Eldorado, Seville Luxury Sedan) 275 @ 5600 rpm; (DeVille Concours, Eldorado Touring Coupe, Seville Touring Sedan) 300 @ 6000 rpm. Torque: (DeVille/d'Elegance, Eldorado, Seville Luxury Sedan) 300 lb.-ft. @ 4000 rpm; (DeVille Concours, Eldorado Touring Coupe, Seville Touring Sedan) 295 lb.-ft. @ 4400 rpm. Direct acting hydraulic tappets. Tuned port fuel injection.

CHASSIS DATA: Wheelbase: (Catera) 107.4 in.; (DeVille) 113.8 in.; (Seville) 112.2 in.; (Eldorado) 108.0 in. Overall Length: (Catera) 194.0 in.; (DeVille) 209.8 in.; (Seville) 201.0 in.; (Eldorado) 200.6 in. Height: (Catera) 56.3 in.; (DeVille) 56.0 in.; (Seville) 55.4 in.; (Eldorado) 53.6 in. Width: (Catera) 70.3 in.; (DeVille) 76.5 in.; (Seville) 75.0 in.; (Eldorado) 75.5 in. Front Tread: (Catera) 59.3 in.; (DeVille) 60.9 in.; (Seville) 62.7 in.; (Eldorado) 60.9 in. Rear Tread: (Catera) 59.8 in.; (DeVille) 60.9 in.; (Seville) 62.3 in.; (Eldorado) 60.9 in. Standard Tires: (Catera) Goodyear Eagle RS-A P225/55HR16; (DeVille/d'Elegance) Michelin P225/60SR16; (DeVille Concours) Goodyear Eagle RS-A P225/60HR16; (Seville) Goodyear Eagle LS P235/60HR16; (Eldorado) Michelin P225/60SR16; (Eldorado Touring Coupe) Goodyear Eagle RS-A P225/60HR16.

TECHNICAL: Transmission: (Catera) 4L30-E electronically controlled four-speed automatic transmission with overdrive; (DeVille, Eldorado, Seville) 4T80-E electronically controlled four-speed automatic (includes viscous converter clutch); Steering: (Catera) Recirculating ball, speed sensitive; (DeVille, Eldorado, Seville) Power-assisted rack-and-pinion, Magnasteer. Front Suspension: (Catera) MacPherson strut, lower control arms w/hydro bushing, coil spring and stabilizer bar, gas preloaded dampers; (DeVille/d'Elegance, Eldorado) Independent MacPherson strut with coil springs, strut-type shock absorbers and stabilizer bar and MacPherson strut dampers; (DeVille Concours, Eldorado Touring Coupe, Seville Luxury Sedan, Seville Touring Sedan) Independent MacPherson strut with coil springs, stabilizer bar and electronic continuously variable road sensing suspension. Rear Suspension: (Catera) Multi-link, coil spring and stabilizer bar, gas preloaded dampers; (DeVille/d'Elegance, Eldorado) Fully independent, short/long arm, rear shock w/airlift and stabilizer bar w/automatic level control; (DeVille Concours, Eldorado Touring Coupe) Fully independent, coil springs, short/long arm and stabilizer bar w/automatic level control and electronic continuously variable road sensing suspension; (Seville Luxury Sedan, Seville Touring Sedan) Independent, multi-link, aluminum control arms, lateral toe links, coil springs, stabilizer bar w/automatic level control and electronic continuously variable road sensing suspension. Brakes: (Catera) dual circuit front and rear disc w/Bosch anti-lock braking system; (DeVille, Eldorado) Power assisted front and rear disc w/Bosch anti-lock braking system (Concours had road texture detection); (Seville) power front and rear disc w/four-channel anti-lock braking system and

StabiliTrak. Body Construction: (all) Integral body-frame. Fuel Tank: (Catera) 18.0 gals.; (DeVille, Eldorado) 20.0 gals.; (Seville) 18.5 gals.

DRIVETRAIN OPTIONS: (DeVille) V92 3,000-Pound Trailer Towing Pkg. $110. (Eldorado) StabiliTrak Chassis Control Syst. $495.

CATERA CONVENIENCE/APPEARANCE OPTIONS: Heated Seats $400. Bose Sound Syst. $973. Elect. Sunroof $995. Pwr Rear Sunshade $295. Five-Spoke Chrome Whls $795.

DEVILLE CONVENIENCE/APPEARANCE OPTIONS: R8J Special Ed. Pkg. (DeV only) $2,497. WA7 Comfort/Convenience Pkg. (DeV only) $867. WA8 Safety/Security Pkg.: (DeV, d'Elegance) $995; (Concours) $502. Express Open Sunroof $1,550. White Diamond Paint $500. Crimson Pearl Paint $500. H.D. Livery Pkg. (DeV only) $160. Leather Seats (DeV only) $785. Active Audio Sound Syst. w/Cassette & CD (DeV) $670; w/Cassette & CD & Digital Signal Processing (DeV) $770; (d'Elegance, Concours) $100. Trunk Mounted 12-Disc CD Changer $595. Trunk Storage Syst. $265. Chrome Whls (stnd d'Elegance) $795.

ELDORADO CONVENIENCE/APPEARANCE OPTIONS: R8H Autumn Classic Ed. $2,418. WA7 Comfort/Convenience Pkg. $867. WA8 Safety/Security Pkg.: (Eldo) $502; (Touring Cpe) $207. Accent Striping (Eldo) $75. Astroroof $1,550. White Diamond Paint $500. Crimson Pearl Paint $500. Leather Seats (Eldo) $785. Bose Sound Syst. w/Cassette & CD (Eldo) $1,119; w/Cassette & CD & Digital Signal Processing: (Eldo) $1,219; (Touring Cpe) $100. Trunk Mounted 12-Disc CD Changer $595. P225/60SR16 WSW Tires (Eldo) $76. P225/60ZR16 BSW Tires (Touring Cpe) $250. Trunk Storage Syst. $265. Chrome Whls $795.

SEVILLE CONVENIENCE/APPEARANCE OPTIONS: 1SB Convenience Pkg. $596. 1SC Personalization Pkg. $1,698. Wood Trim Pkg. $495. Accent Striping (SLS) $75. Heated Seats Pkg. (STS) $632. Adaptive Seat Pkg. (STS) $1,202. Express Open Sunroof $1,550. Eng. Block Heater $18. White Diamond Paint $500. Crimson Pearl Paint $500. Console Mounted 6-Disc CD Changer $500. Bose High-Perf. Entertainment Syst.: (SLS) $1,250; (STS) $300. Trunk Storage Syst. $265. P235/60ZR16 BSW Tires (STS) $250. Chrome Whls $795.

HISTORY: Cadillac's model year production totaled 162,715 compared with 159,820 the year previous (this figure does not include imported Cateras).

1999

The Catera gained an optional Sport Package model and an all-new 1999-1/2 Eldorado Touring Coupe debuted mid-model year, otherwise the Cadillac lineup returned intact from the previous year. The big news for Cadillac in 1999 does not fall within the scope of this catalog, that being the debut of the luxury sport utility vehicle named Escalade. It was the first truck-based vehicle in Cadillac's 96-year history. Optional equipment in 1999 included the innovative massaging lumbar seat to provide maximum driver comfort.

1999 Cadillac, Catera sedan. (OCW)

CATERA - SERIES 6V - V-6 - In addition to the sedan that "zigs," the 1999 Catera lineup offered a Sport model option package that allowed the driver, as Cadillac claimed, "to zig with no fear." The Catera Sport sedan featured ZJ1 suspension that was set up for more aggressive handling and response. The ZJ1 package included stiffer front and rear springs, struts and shocks with increased compression and rebound performance; enhanced valving for the rear shocks, automatic leveling system, specific seven-spoke machined aluminum 16-inch wheels and Goodyear Eagle H-rated tires. The Catera Sport sedan's exterior color choices were Ebony, Ivory and Platinum while the interior was Ebony leather. Other Sport model features included next-generation dual front and side airbags, heated front and rear seats, Sport seats with extendable thigh supports, gunmetal interior trim, matte grille, rear spoiler, and specific rocker moldings. Both the Catera and Catera Sport sedans were powered by the 3.0-liter dual overhead cam V-6 mated to the 4L30-E electronically controlled four-speed automatic transmission with overdrive. This V-6 featured sodium-filled valves to help the engine run cooler as well as triple-tipped spark plugs and a high-efficiency oil cooler to help extend engine life. The 1999 Catera was also the first Cadillac to meet low emissions vehicle (LEV) standards, significantly reducing smog-causing exhaust emissions. To meet the standards, Catera featured new powertrain control computers, an electronic throttle control and wide-range heated exhaust oxygen sensors. Catera also received a new fuel tank and evaporative emission system to more efficiently recover vapors during refueling.

1999 Cadillac, DeVille Concours sedan. (OCW)

DEVILLE - SERIES 6K - V-8 - The all-sedan DeVille series again contained the DeVille, d'Elegance and Concours models. The Northstar 4.6-liter V-8 was again the engine for the series, with the 275-horsepower version powering the DeVille and d'Elegance and the 300-horse version powering the Concours. Both engines again were coupled to the 4T80-E electronically controlled four-speed automatic transmission with viscous converter clutch. Both the d'Elegance and Concours sedans offered the new massaging lumbar seats as optional equipment. Built into Cadillac's four-way power lumbar system, a series of 20 independent massage rollers cycled in an up/down motion to massage back muscles. This decreased muscle tension and reduced fatigue for improved comfort.

1999 Cadillac, Eldorado Touring Coupe (OCW)

ELDORADO - SERIES 6E - V-8 - The Eldorado Touring Coupe (ETC) received a mid-model year update (it went into production in January 1999 and was available to customers as a 1999-1/2 model by March). The revised ETC included new body color inserts on side and fascia moldings, which replaced the previous chrome inserts; new seven-spoke wheels with wreath-and-crest center cap; new P235/60HR16 tires and new "ETC" decklid logo with a simplified design. Massaging lumbar seats were optional in the ETC. The "base" coupe again used the 275-horsepower Northstar 4.6-liter V-8 while the ETC used the more powerful 300-horse Northstar. The 4T80-E electronically controlled four-speed automatic transmission with viscous converter clutch was again used with both Northstar versions.

SEVILLE - SERIES 6K - V-8 - The Seville, coming off a major redesign the previous year, returned with its two sedan line-

up: Seville Luxury Sedan (SLS) and Seville Touring Sedan (STS). Powertrain combinations remained unchanged. The STS offered the innovative massaging lumbar seats as optional equipment.

1999 Cadillac, Seville STS sedan. (OCW)

I.D. DATA: The 1999 Cadillac had a 17-symbol vehicle identification number (VIN) stamped on a metal tag attached to the upper left surface of the cowl visible through the windshield. The code was as follows: The first digit, "1" or "4," represented the manufacturing country (United States), the second, "G," represented General Motors, the third, "6," represented Cadillac, the fourth and fifth represented the car line/series, as follows: E/L-Eldorado, E/T-Eldorado Touring, K/D-DeVille, K/E-d'Elegance, K/F-Concours, K/S-Seville (SLS), K/Y-Seville (STS), and V/R-Catera. Digit six represents the body style: 1-two-door coupe, 2-two-door, 3-convertible, 5-four-door sedan, 6-four-door sedan, and 8-four-door station wagon. Digit seven identifies the restraint code: 2-active (manual) belts w/dual frontal airbags and 4-active (manual) belts w/dual frontal and side airbags. The eighth digit identifies the engine: "R"-L81 3.0L V-6, "Y"-LD8 4.6L V-8; and "9"-L37 4.6L V-8. A check digit follows. The 10th digit represents the model year, "X" for 1999. The eleventh digit represents the assembly plant. The remaining six digits identify the production sequence number.

*Note: Production totals not available when this book went to press.

Catera (V-6)

Series Prod. No.	Body/Style No.	Body Type & Seating	Factory Price	Shipping Weight/Total
VR5	R69	4-dr. Sedan	31775	3770*
DeVille (V-8)				
KD5	D69	4-dr. Sedan	38630	3978*
KE5	E69	4-dr. d'Elegance Sed.	42730	4049*
KF5	F69	4-dr. Concours Sed.	43230	4047*
Eldorado (V-8)				
EL1	L57	2-dr. Coupe	39235	3825*
ET1	T57	2-dr. Tour. Cpe.	43495	3856*
Seville (V-8)				
KS5	S69	4-dr. SLS Sedan	43355	3976*
KY5	Y69	4-dr. STS Sedan	47850	4001*

ENGINES: BASE V-6 (Catera) 54-degree, dual overhead cam V-6. Cast iron block, aluminum cylinder heads. Displacement: 181 cu. in. (3.0 liters). Bore & Stroke: 3.40 x 3.40 in. Compression ratio: 10.0:1. Brake horsepower: 200 @ 6000 rpm. Torque: 192 lb.-ft. @ 3600 rpm. Variable Dual-Ram induction system. BASE V-8: (DeVille/d'Elegance, Eldorado, Seville) 90-degree, dual overhead cam Northstar V-8. Aluminum block with cast iron cylinder liners, aluminum cylinder heads. Displacement: 279 cu. in. (4.6 liters). Bore & Stroke: 3.66 x 3.31 in. Compression ratio: 10.3:1. Brake horsepower: (DeVille/d'Elegance, Eldorado, Seville Luxury Sedan) 275 @ 5600 rpm; (DeVille Concours, Eldorado Touring Coupe, Seville Touring Sedan) 300 @ 6000 rpm. Torque: (DeVille/d'Elegance, Eldorado, Seville Luxury Sedan) 300 lb.-ft. @ 4000 rpm; (DeVille Concours, Eldorado Touring Coupe, Seville Touring Sedan) 295 lb.-ft. @ 4400 rpm. Direct acting hydraulic tappets. Tuned port fuel injection.

CHASSIS DATA: Wheelbase: (Catera) 107.4 in.; (DeVille) 113.8 in.; (Seville) 112.2 in.; (Eldorado) 108.0 in. Overall Length: (Catera) 194.0 in.; (DeVille) 209.8 in.; (Seville) 201.0 in.; (Eldorado) 200.6 in. Height: (Catera) 56.3 in.; (DeVille) 56.0 in.; (Seville) 55.4 in.; (Eldorado) 53.6 in. Width: (Catera) 70.3 in.; (DeVille) 76.5 in.; (Seville) 75.0 in.; (Eldorado) 75.5 in. Front Tread: (Catera) 59.3 in.; (DeVille) 60.9 in.; (Seville) 62.7 in.; (Eldorado) 60.9 in. Rear Tread: (Catera) 59.8 in.; (DeVille)

60.9 in.; (Seville) 62.3 in.; (Eldorado) 60.9 in. Standard Tires: (Catera) Goodyear Eagle RS-A P225/55HR16; (DeVille/d'Elegance) Michelin P225/60SR16; (DeVille Concours) Goodyear Eagle RS-A P225/60HR16; (Seville) Goodyear Integrity LS P235/60SR16; (Eldorado) Michelin P225/60SR16; (Eldorado Touring Coupe) Goodyear Eagle RS-A P225/60HR16.

TECHNICAL: Transmission: (Catera) 4L30-E electronically controlled four-speed automatic transmission with overdrive; (DeVille, Eldorado, Seville) 4T80-E electronically controlled four-speed automatic (includes viscous converter clutch); Steering: (Catera) Recirculating ball, speed sensitive; (DeVille, Eldorado, Seville) Power-assisted rack-and-pinion, Magnasteer. Front Suspension: (Catera) MacPherson strut, lower control arms w/hydro bushing, coil spring and stabilizer bar, gas preloaded dampers; (DeVille/d'Elegance, Eldorado) Independent MacPherson strut with coil springs, strut-type shock absorbers and stabilizer bar and MacPherson strut dampers; (DeVille Concours, Eldorado Touring Coupe, Seville Luxury Sedan, Seville Touring Sedan) Independent MacPherson strut with coil springs, stabilizer bar and electronic continuously variable road sensing suspension. Rear Suspension: (Catera) Multi-link, coil spring and stabilizer bar, gas preloaded dampers; (DeVille/d'Elegance, Eldorado) Fully independent, short/long arm, rear shock w/airlift and stabilizer bar w/automatic level control; (DeVille Concours, Eldorado Touring Coupe) Fully independent, coil springs, short/long arm and stabilizer bar w/automatic level control and electronic continuously variable road sensing suspension; (Seville Luxury Sedan, Seville Touring Sedan) Independent, multi-link, aluminum control arms, lateral toe links, coil springs, stabilizer bar w/automatic level control and electronic continuously variable road sensing suspension. Brakes: (Catera) dual circuit front and rear disc w/Bosch anti-lock braking system; (DeVille, Eldorado) Power assisted front and rear disc w/Bosch anti-lock braking system (Concours had road texture detection); (Seville) power front and rear disc w/four-channel anti-lock braking system and StabiliTrak. Body Construction: (all) Integral body-frame. Fuel Tank: (Catera) 16.0 gals.; (DeVille, Eldorado) 20.0 gals.; (Seville) 18.5 gals.

DRIVETRAIN OPTIONS: (DeVille) V92 3,000-Pound Trailer Towing Pkg. $110. StabiliTrak Chassis Control Syst.: (DeV/d'Elegance) $495; (Eldorado) $495.

CATERA CONVENIENCE/APPEARANCE OPTIONS: Sport Pkg. $795. Heated Seats $425. Bose Sound Syst. $973. Elect. Sunroof $995. Pwr Rear Sunshade $295. Five-Spoke Chrome Whls $795.

DEVILLE CONVENIENCE/APPEARANCE OPTIONS: WA7 Comfort/Convenience Pkg. (DeV only) $867. Express Open Sunroof $1,550. White Diamond Paint $500. Crimson Pearl Paint $500. Leather Seats (DeV only) $785. Massaging Lumbar Seats (d'Elegance, Concours) $200. Active Audio Sound Syst. w/Cassette & CD (DeV) $670; w/Cassette & CD & Digital Signal Processing (DeV) $770; (d'Elegance, Concours) $100. Trunk Mounted 12-Disc CD Changer $595. Trunk Storage Syst. $265. Chrome Whls (stnd d'Elegance) $795.

ELDORADO CONVENIENCE/APPEARANCE OPTIONS: WA7 Comfort/Convenience Pkg. (Eldo) $867. Accent Striping (Eldo) $75. Sunroof $1,550. White Diamond Paint $500. Crimson Pearl Paint $500. Leather Seats (Eldo) $785. Massaging Lumbar Seats (Touring Cpe) $200. Bose Sound Syst. w/Cassette & CD & Digital Signal Processing: (Eldo) $1,219. Trunk Mounted 12-Disc CD Changer $595. P225/60ZR16 BSW Tires (Touring Cpe) $250. Trunk Storage Syst. $265. Chrome Whls $795.

SEVILLE CONVENIENCE/APPEARANCE OPTIONS: 1SB SLS Convenience Pkg. $598. 1SC SLS Personalization Pkg. $1,698. 1SE SLS Adaptive Seat Pkg. $2,401. 1SD STS Convenience Pkg. $632. 1SE STS Adaptive Seat Pkg. $1,627. Wood Trim Pkg. $495. Accent Striping (SLS) $75. Massaging Lumbar Seats (STS) $200. Express Open Sunroof $1,550. Eng. Block Heater $18. White Diamond Paint $500. Crimson Pearl Paint $500. Console Mounted 6-Disc CD Changer $500. Bose High-Perf. Entertainment Syst.: (SLS) $1,250; (STS) $300. Trunk Storage Syst. $265. P235/60ZR16 BSW Tires (STS) $250. Chrome Whls $795.

HISTORY: Cadillac, within its future design theme of "The Fusion of Art & Science," debuted its Evoq concept car on the 1999 auto show circuit to rave reviews. The two-seat convertible with detachable hardtop was powered by a 405-horsepower 4.2-liter Northstar V-8 topped by an integrated supercharger/intercooler system. Other features of the Evoq

included an automatic transmission that featured Performance Algorithm Shifting, borrowed from the 1998 Seville Touring Sedan; EyeCue head-up display and the Night Vision System borrowed from the 2000 DeVille. Cadillac also stunned the racing world when the luxury automaker announced it would compete in the 2000 24 Hours of Le Mans endurance race. The racing Cadillac, the prototype was named LMP (for Le Mans Prototype), was based on a Riley & Scott chassis fitted with a twin-turbocharged, intercooled 4.0-liter Northstar V-8 (not a regular production item). With a reported budget of $30 million spread over four years, the reason given for Cadillac to enter the competition arena was "image" and enhancing Cadillac's reputation as a global automobile.

2000

Cadillac's millennium-ending 2000 lineup featured completely restyled full-size DeVille sedans built on a much stiffened platform shared with some other GM marques. The end results were somewhat shorter and slightly narrower than the '99 models, but rode on a 1.5-inch longer wheelbase. Catera received a face-lift and the addition of a Sport version distinguished by 17-inch wheels and other exterior styling fillips. Eldorado and Seville remained largely unchanged in appearance, but received tweaks to their Northstar V-8 engines. While Cadillac's impressive Evoq concept car hinted at future styling for the marque, the year's production models were characterized by technological razzle-dazzle such as a thermal-imaging Night Vision system, updates to StabiliTrak that included automatic shock-absorber dampening adjustment on individual wheels, LED taillights, Ultrasonic Rear Parking Assist, and a system that prevented front-passenger air bags from deploying if the seat was unoccupied or contained a small child.

2000 Cadillac, Catera sedan. (OCW)

CATERA - SERIES 6V - V-6 - For its fourth year in the lineup, the nimble, Opel Omega-based Catera, Cadillac's entry-luxury-level contender, received a freshening up both inside and out as well as enhancements to its Sport model option package. Retaining its overall European look, the Catera featured a new front fascia, headlights, and redesigned hood that contoured around a smaller, matte-black, chrome grille. A new front cowl concealed the wet-arm windshield wipers and washer nozzles. Also revised were the quarter panels, outside rearview mirrors, cornering lights and fog lights. The rear aspect, too, was reworked with new fascia, separated left and right LED (light-emitting diode) taillights, a center brake light, revised Catera badging, and the signature wreath and crest emblem. Catera Sport updates included larger, 17-inch aluminum wheels shod with Goodyear Eagle H-rated all-season tires, high-intensity discharge (HID) Xenon headlights, matte-silver chrome grille, brushed-silver interior trim, and a rear spoiler. Catera interior changes included a reshaped instrument panel and center console—the latter equipped with an additional auxiliary power outlet—and a new center stack for the entertainment system and climate controls. The center armrest was also redesigned and now contained two cupholders. Other interior changes included new door trim panels with integrated door handles, power window switches, and latch-type storage bins front and rear. Side-impact air bags were standard on all 2000 Cateras. New cupholders and upper child seat tethers were added to the rear passenger compartment and optional heated front seats included a new, three-position rheostatic control for a wider comfort range. The new, three-button OnStar system came standard replacing the first-generation OnStar unit.

2000 Cadillac, Catera Sport sedan. (OCW)

2000 Cadillac, DeVille sedan. (OCW)

DEVILLE - SERIES 6K - V-8 - For 2000, the DeVille series again consisted of three four-door sedans. The base model continued to be labelled DeVille, but 1999's opulent d'Elegance became the DeVille High Luxury Sedan (DHS) and the sportier version, formerly Concours, became the DeVille Touring Sedan (DTS). The Northstar 4.6-liter V-8 continued as the engine for the series, with a 275-hp variant powering both DeVille and DHS, while a 300-hp version provided the thrust for the DTS. Both engines again were coupled to the 4T80-E electronically controlled four-speed automatic transmission with overdrive viscous torque converter clutch. "Firsts" that became available on the 2000 DeVilles included Night Vision thermal-imaging technology that permitted drivers to "see" well beyond the range of their headlights at night or under reduced visibilty conditions and Ultrasonic Rear Parking Assist, which used rear-mounted sensors to warn drivers of obstacles during back-up maneuvers.

2000 Cadillac, DeVille DTS sedan. (OCW)

ELDORADO - SERIES 6E - V-8 - With the demise of the Lincoln Mark VIII and the Buick Riviera, by 2000 Cadillac Eldorado was the only luxury coupe being produced in North America. The base Eldorado was rebadged ESC (for Eldorado Sport Coupe) and together with its stablemate, the more powerful and better handling, Eldorado Touring Coupe (ETC) gave buyers a choice between rides that were either cushier or more sporting. Styling for the two coupes was carried over from 1999, although ETC was now largely devoid of chrome trim and sported new, seven-spoke wheels and a new deck lid logo. The big news for both was the extensive redesign of the Northstar 4.6-liter V-8 engines, which allowed them to run smoothly, quietly, and efficiently on regular gasoline. The base Eldorado continued to use the 275-hp Northstar while the ETC's churned out 300 hp. The 4T80-E electronically controlled four-speed automatic transmission with viscous converter clutch was again used with both Northstar versions.

2000 Cadillac, Seville STS sedan. (OCW)

SEVILLE - SERIES 6K - V-8 - Largely unchanged in outward appearance, Seville returned for 2000 with its two-sedan lineup: Seville Luxury Sedan (SLS) and Seville Touring Sedan (STS). Like DeVille and Eldorado, however, their dual-over-head-cam 4.6-liter Northstar V-8s were significantly refined for improved smoothness and quieter operation as well as better mileage using regular fuel. Horsepower ratings were among the highest in their class with 275 for the SLS and 300 for the STS. Targeted by Cadillac to impact the global luxury-sedan market, Sevilles were veritable gadget-laden showcases of American automotive technology. Standard were improved versions of both StabiliTrak and Cadillac's Continuously Variable Road-Sensing Suspension (CVRSS) which, in combination with Magnasteer variable-assist, speed-sensitive power rack and pinion steering and the road-texture detection system, greatly enhanced vehicle performance and passenger safety. New for 2000 was a system to prevent deployment of the front-passenger air bag if the seat was empty or occupied by a small child. Also new was an ultrasonic rear parking assist and GM's advanced three-button OnStar communications service. Performance Algorithm Shifting (PAS) allowed the four-speed automatic transmission to perform more like a manual transmission under spirited driving conditions. Inside, Sevilles were even more luxurious than before with leather, optional Zebrano wood, improved interior storage, an advanced sound system, seats using inflatable air cells to adjust for comfort and support, and even optional massaging lumbar seats in the STS.

I.D. DATA: The 2000 Cadillac had a 17-symbol vehicle identification number (VIN) stamped on a metal tag attached to the upper left surface of the cowl visible through the windshield. The code was as follows: The first digit, "1" or "4," represented the manufacturing country (United States), the second, "G," represented General Motors, the third, "6," represented Cadillac, the fourth and fifth represented the car line/series, as follows: E/L-Eldorado ESC, E/T-Eldorado ETC, K/D-DeVille, K/E-DeVille DHS, K/F-DeVille DTS, K/S-Seville SLS, K/Y-Seville STS, and V/R-Catera. Digit six represents the body style: 1-two-door coupe, 2-two-door, 5-four-door sedan, and 6-four-door sedan. Digit seven identifies the restraint code: 2-active (manual) belts w/dual frontal airbags and 4-active (manual) belts w/dual frontal and side airbags. The eighth digit identifies the engine: "R"-L81 3.0L V-6, "Y"-LD8 4.6L V-8; and "9"-L37 4.6L V-8. A check digit follows. The 10th digit represents the model year, "Y" for 2000. The eleventh digit represents the assembly plant. The remaining six digits identify the production sequence number.

Catera (V-6)

Model No.	Body Style No.	Body Type & Seating	Factory Price	Shipping Weight	Prod. Total
VR5	R69	4-dr. Sed.	31010	3770	*

*Production total not available when this book went to press.

DeVille (V-8)

KD5	D69	4-dr. Sed.	39895	3978	*
KE5	E69	4-dr. DHS Sed.	45595	4049	*
KF5	F69	4-dr. DTS Sed.	45595	4047	*

*Production totals not available when this book went to press.

Eldorado (V-8)

EL1	L57	2-dr. ESC Cpe.	39665	3825	*
ET1	T57	2-dr. ETC Cpe.	43240	3856	*

*Production totals not available when this book went to press.

Seville (V-8)

KS5	S69	4-dr. SLS Sed.	44475	3970	*
KY5	Y69	4-dr. STS Sed.	49075	4001	*

*Production totals not available when this book went to press.

ENGINES: BASE V-6 (Catera) 54-degree, dual overhead cam V-6. Cast iron block, aluminum cylinder heads. Displacement: 181 cu. in. (3.0 liters). Bore & Stroke: 3.40 x 3.40 in. Compression ratio: 10.0:1. Brake horsepower: 200 @ 6000 rpm. Torque: 192 lb.-ft. @ 3600 rpm. Variable Dual-Ram induction system. BASE V-8: (DeVille, Eldorado, Seville) 90-degree, dual overhead cam Northstar V-8. Aluminum block with cast iron cylinder liners, aluminum cylinder heads. Displacement: 279 cu. in. (4.6 liters). Bore & Stroke: 3.66 x 3.31 in. Compression ratio: 10.0:1. Brake horsepower: (DeVille/DHS, Eldorado ESC, Seville SLS) 275 @ 5600 rpm; (DeVille DTS, Eldorado ETC, Seville STS) 300 @ 6000 rpm. Torque: (DeVille/DHS, Eldorado ESC, Seville SLS) 300 lb.-ft. @ 4000 rpm; (DeVille DTS, Eldorado ETC, Seville STS) 295 lb.-ft. @ 4400 rpm. Direct acting hydraulic tappets. Tuned port fuel injection.

CHASSIS DATA: Wheelbase: (Catera) 107.4 in.; (DeVille) 115.3 in.; (Seville) 112.2 in.; (Eldorado) 108.0 in. Overall Length: (Catera) 192.2 in.; (DeVille) 207.2 in.; (Seville) 201.0 in.; (Eldorado) 200.6 in. Height: (Catera) 56.4 in.; (DeVille) 56.7 in.; (Seville SLS) 55.7 in.; (STS) 55.4 in.; (Eldorado) 53.6 in. Width: (Catera) 70.3 in.; (DeVille) 74.5 in.; (Seville) 75.0 in.; (Eldorado) 75.5 in. Front Tread: (Catera) 59.3 in.; (DeVille) 62.7 in.; (Seville) 62.7 in.; (Eldorado) 60.9 in. Rear Tread: (Catera) 59.8 in.; (DeVille) 62.2 in.; (Seville) 62.3 in.; (Eldorado) 60.9 in. Standard Tires: (Catera) Goodyear Eagle RS-A P225/55HR16; (DeVille/DHS) Michelin P225/60SR16; (DeVille DTS) Goodyear P235/55HR17 BSW; (Seville SLS) Goodyear Integrity P235/60R16; (Seville STS) Goodyear Eagle LS P235/60R16; (Eldorado ESC) Michelin XW4 P225/60R16; (Eldorado ETC) Goodyear Eagle RS-A P235/60R16.

TECHNICAL: Transmission: (Catera) 4L30-E electronically controlled four-speed automatic transmission with overdrive; (DeVille, Eldorado, Seville) 4T80-E electronically controlled four-speed automatic overdrive (includes viscous torque converter clutch); Steering: (Catera) Recirculating ball, speed sensitive; (DeVille, Eldorado, Seville) Power-assisted rack-and-pinion, Magnasteer. Front Suspension: (Catera) MacPherson strut, lower control arms w/hydro bushing, coil spring and stabilizer bar, gas preloaded dampers; (DeVille/DHS, Eldorado ESC) Independent MacPherson strut-type with coil springs and stabilizer bar; (DeVille Concours, Eldorado ETC, Seville SLS, Seville STS) Independent MacPherson strut-type with coil springs, stabilizer bar, and electronic continuously variable road sensing suspension. Rear Suspension: (Catera) Multi-link, coil spring and stabilizer bar, gas preloaded dampers; (DeVille/DHS, Eldorado ESC) Fully independent, short/long arm, rear shock w/airlift and stabilizer bar w/automatic level control; (DeVille DTS, Eldorado ETC) Fully independent, coil springs, short/long arm and stabilizer bar w/automatic level control and electronic continuously

variable road sensing suspension; (Seville SLS, Seville STS) Independent, multi-link, aluminum control arms, lateral toe links, coil springs, stabilizer bar w/automatic level control, StabiliTrak and electronic continuously variable road sensing suspension. Brakes: (Catera) dual circuit front and rear disc w/Bosch anti-lock braking system; (DeVille, Eldorado) Power assisted front and rear disc w/Delco-Bosch anti-lock braking system; (Seville) power front and rear disc w/four-channel anti-lock braking system and road texture detection. Body Construction: (all) Integral body-frame. Fuel Tank: (Catera) 16.0 gals.; (DeVille) 18.5 gals.; (Eldorado) 19.0 gals.; (Seville) 18.5 gals.

DRIVETRAIN OPTIONS: V92 3,000-Pound Trailer Towing Pkg. (DTS) $110. WA8 Safety/Security Pkg. (incldg. StabiliTrak, ultrasonic rear parking assist, & three-channel garage door opener, DeV/DHS) $895; WA8 Safety/Security Pkg. (incldg. ultrasonic rear parking assist & three-channel garage door opener, DTS) $400. StabiliTrak (ESC) $495.

CATERA CONVENIENCE/APPEARANCE OPTIONS: Sport Pkg. $2,510. Luxury Pkg. $995. Heated Front Seats $425. Bose Sound Syst. $973. Elect. Sunroof $995. Pwr Rear Sunshade $295. Five-Spoke Chrome Whls $795. Trunk Storage System $265.

DEVILLE CONVENIENCE/APPEARANCE OPTIONS: WA7 Comfort/Convenience Pkg. (DeV) $1,095. WA9 Comfort/Convenience Pkg. (DTS) $695. Express Open Sunroof $1,550. White Diamond Paint $650. Crimson Pearl Paint $650. Leather Seats (DeV only) $785. Front Adaptive Seats (DHS/DTS) $995. Rear Seat Side Airbags $295. Wood Trim Pkg. (DTS) $595. Livery Pkg. (DeV) $160. Active Audio Sound Syst. w/Cassette & CD (DeV) $300; w/Cassette & CD & Digital Signal Processing (DHS/DTS) $300. Glove Box Mounted 6-Disc CD Changer $595. Night Vision (DHS/DTS) $1,995. On Board Navigation (DHS/DTS) $1,995. Integrated Hands-Free Cellular Phone $675. Trunk Storage Syst. $265. Chrome Whls (stnd DHS) $795.

ELDORADO CONVENIENCE/APPEARANCE OPTIONS: WA7 Comfort/Convenience Pkg. (ESC) $867. Expres Open Sunroof (ESC) $1,550. White Diamond Paint (ESC) $650. Crimson Pearl Paint (ESC) $650. Wood Strg. Whl. $395. Programmable Garage Door Opener $107. Bose Sound Syst. w/Cassette & CD & Digital Signal Processing: (ESC) $1,219. Trunk Mounted 12-Disc CD Changer $595. Goodyear Eagle LS P235/60ZR16 BSW Tires (ETC) $250. Trunk Storage Syst. $265. Chrome Whls $795.

SEVILLE CONVENIENCE/APPEARANCE OPTIONS: 1SB SLS Convenience Pkg. $598. 1SC SLS Personalization Pkg. $1,698. 1SE SLS Adaptive Seat Pkg. $2,401. 1SD STS Heated Seats Pkg. $632. 1SE STS Adaptive Seat Pkg. $1,627. Wood Trim Pkg. $595. Accent Striping (SLS) $75. Express Open Sunroof $1,550. Eng. Block Heater $18. White Diamond Paint $650. Crimson Pearl Paint $650. Console Mounted 6-Disc CD Changer $595. Bose AM/FM Stereo w/CD Player (SLS) $950. Bose High-Perf. Entertainment Syst.: (SLS) $1,250; (STS) $300. Ultrasonic Rear Parking Assist $295. Integrated Hands-Free Cellular Phone $675. On Board Navigation (SLS) $2,945; (STS) $1,995. P235/60ZR16 Goodyear Eagle LS Tires (STS) $250. Chrome Whls $795.

HISTORY: As announced during 1999, Cadillac did field an effort to compete in the 2000 24 Hours of Le Mans endurance race. The four racing Cadillacs, named LMP (for Le Mans Prototype), were based on Riley & Scott chassis fitted with a twin-turbocharged, intercooled 4.0-liter Northstar V-8s (not a regular production item). While not ultimately victorious, valuable lessons were learned by the Cadillac contingent and optimism prevailed for a better showing in 2001. One bright spot in Cadillac's Le Mans experience was the flawless performance of the Night Vision systems on its race cars. Derived from thermal-imaging technology developed for the military and proven during the Gulf War, Night Vision was but one element of the technological wizardry that typified production Cadillacs for 2000. Standard and optional features such as Night Vision, StabiliTrak, CVRSS, PAS, Ultrasonic Rear Parking Assist, OnStar, selective air bag deployment and hands-free cellular phone operation—to name a few—brought world attention to Cadillac's state-of-the-art engineering and commitment to excellence.

In 1977, each Cadillac was tested at the end of the assembly line. New Cadillacs were placed on a special roll test apparatus where 161 specific inspections were made under simulated road conditions and speeds up to 70 mph. (OCW)

1979 Cadillac Seville sedan Gucci model with matching luggage. (OCW)

Cadillac...
Standard of the World

THERE is nothing in engineering so distinctive and different as the principle of the 90-degree Cadillac engine. It makes the Cadillac one of the fastest and most powerful of motor cars. It is undoubtedly true, too, that this most successful of all engines is the keystone of Cadillac's dominance of the really fine car field. It is true that Cadillac alone can produce such an engine without the penalty of excessive cost. To anyone but Cadillac, with its wonderful volume—fully one-half of all the fine cars sold in America—the 90-degree engine is prohibitive. It is only in the sense of first cost that it is costly. In the service it commands, it is the costliest of eight cylinder principles. *Priced from $2995 upward, f. o. b. Detroit*

C A D I L L A C

DIVISION OF GENERAL MOTORS CORPORATION

Cadillac and LaSalle Motor Cars

1902 Cadillac.

Cadillac milestones

During its history, Cadillac has introduced many techniques and styling breakthroughs that have helped shape the automotive industry.

Some of the milestones established by Cadillac in this century include:

1902

The Detroit Automobile Co. is reorganized and renamed the Cadillac Autombile Co., launching a new era in fine transportation.

1905

Cadillac is the pioneer of multi-cylinder motorcars, introducing the first four-cylinder engine.

1908

Cadillac is the first American car to be awarded the Dewar Trophy by the Royal Automobile Club of London for being the first car to achieve interchangeability through standardization of parts.

1909

Cadillac is purchased by General Motors Corp.

1912

Cadillac is the first company to equip cars with electric starting, lighting and ignition. For this achievement, the Royal Automobile Club of London awards Cadillac the Dewar Trophy for the second time and bestows the title of "Standard of the World" upon Cadillac for all time. Cadillac is the first and only car company to win the Dewar Trophy twice and the only car company to receive such a title from the RAC.

1915

Cadillac is the first to offer a production car with a V-type, water-cooled, eight-cylinder engine.

1926

Cadillac is the first automaker to develop a comprehensive service policy and place it on a nationwide basis.

1928

Cadillac is the first to install security plate glass as standard equipment, and the first to use the clashless synchromesh transmission.

1912 Cadillac touring.

1928 Cadillac five-passenger four-door.

1930

Cadillac is the first company to build a 16-cylinder automobile engine.

1937

A Cadillac-built V-8 breaks all previous stock car records at the Indianapolis Motor Speedway.

1943

Cadillac is presented with the Army-Navy "E" award for excellence in production of war equipment.

1944

Cadillac produces the M-24, the fastest and most maneuverable combat light tank, serving the country on all battlefronts.

1948

Cadillac's designer, Harley Earl, changes the profile of automobiles with the styling introduction of the tailfin.

1949

Cadillac's one-millionth car is produced on Nov. 25.

1954

Cadillac is the first car manufacturer to provide power steering as standard equipment on its entire line of automobiles.

1964

Cadillac is the first to develop automatic temperature control heating and air conditioning for automobiles.

1965

Cadillac is the first car company to introduce tilt and telescope steering wheels.

1966

Cadillac is the first to introduce variable ratio steering on an American car.

1948 Cadillac 60 Special Derham custom.

1970

Cadillac offers the largest production passenger car engine in the world, introducing a 500-cubic-inch (8.2-liter) V-8 on the Eldorado that delivers 400 horsepower.

1975

Cadillac offers the first U.S. production cars with electronically fuel-injected engine, using analog computer technology to analyze vehicle operating data to determine precise fuel needs on 1975 Eldorado, Fleetwood and deVille models.

1978

Cadillac is the first to test the capability of digital computerization in automotive applications by installing a microprocessor—the "Trip Computer"—on the 1978 Seville.

1980

Cadillac advances fuel delivery technology with the introduction of digital electronic fuel injection, including self-diagnostics and microprocessor controls.

1984

Cadillac introduces the Gold Key Delivery System, a set of standardized procedures for new car delivery, in all Cadillac dealerships. This extra attention to customers and their new automobiles during the delivery process—two vehicle inspections, explanation of features in a ride and drive and product walk-around, two sets of gold keys and more - helped lead to Cadillac earning in 1987 the #1 postion in the annual Sales Satisfaction Index, published in the *Power Report* by J.D. Power & Associates, which evaluates the quality of the customer buying experience.

1985

Cadillac is the first production car manufacturer in the world to transverse-mount V-8 engines in a front-wheel drive configuration for improved space utilization and fuel efficiency in its full-size, six-passenger deVille models.

1987

Cadillac is the first automaker to use multiplexed wiring to control external lighting on a production automobile—the Allante. America's first automobile to compete in the European-dominated ultra-luxury segment of the market, the Cadillac Allante is designed in Italy by Pininfarina. The two-seat roadster bodies and interiors are built by Pininfarina in Italy and shipped by 747 cargo plane to Detroit for installation of suspensions, powertrains and other components, utilizing a number of new production, assembly and transportation techniques.

1970 Cadillac Fleetwood Eldorado.

1978 Cadillac Seville.

1990

Cadillac introduces full-time traction control on the Allante—a first for a domestic manufacturer, anti-lock brakes, and driver-side supplemental inflatable restraints (air bags) on all models except for Brougham.

1993

In observance of its 90th anniversary, Cadillac introduces its revolutionary Northstar V-8 engine, with limp-home capability.

1997

Catera, the Cadillac that "zigs", debuts in early 1996 as a 1997 model. The all-new, V-6-powered, rear-drive sports sedan—a joint venture product of Cadillac and Adam Opel AG—is built in Ruesselsheim, Germany.

1999

Cadillac stuns the motorsports world by announcing that it will return to sports car competition with a factory-backed effort to compete in the 24 Hours of Le Mans.

2000

Cadillac's impressive Evoq concept car hints at future styling for the marque, while the millennium-ending 2000 production models are characterized by technological razzle-dazzle like a thermal-imaging Night Vision system, updates to StabiliTrak including automatic shock-absorber dampening adjustment on individual wheels, LED taillights, Ultrasonic Rear Parking Assist, and a system that prevents front and side passenger air bags from deploying if the seat is unoccupied or contains a small child.

Cadillac led V-8 development

By Maurice Hendry

All this was, however, over-shadowed by the advent of the V-8 in 1914. In retrospect, this car probably ranks as the most important of all luxury cars, and one of the great automobiles in history. Regardless of the claims of contemporaries, they were followers. The Cadillac V-8 was the leader. True, it had its predecessor—the De Dion Hewett, and Rolls-Royce V-8s, but, like the self-starter and earlier claimants, it was Cadillac that made a success of it.

Apart from detachable cylinder heads in 1917 (already established practice) there were few significant changes in the V-8 for many years, because as one English authority remarks, "a design so advanced was able to carry Cadillac through the decade with little alteration."

Important additions came in the 1920s with thermostatic carburetion, four-wheel brakes, and the inherently balanced V-8 engine, and a striking development of the period was the great public acceptance of a closed body which, in the early 1920s actually surpassed in popularity the open type (and forced the development of a smoother engine).

The pioneer V-8 layout was so extensively redesigned in the mid twenties, into the "314", that it became virtually a new engine, although in the factory engineering tables it is lumped in with the first series for convenience. It had a short production life of two years.

The watershed came with the new plain rod V-8s of 1928, introduced in 1927 in the LaSalle first, followed by the 341 Cadillac series. Actually, although the fork-and-blade rods are a fetish in certain quarters, Cadillac engineers couldn't get rid of them fast enough. The immense care in manufacture they required, and the problems they presented in servicing, were simply not worth it all. The plain rods were not only better, they were cheaper to make. I may be accused of the *lese-majeste* to Leland in this, but I think H.M., had he still been at Cadillac in 1927, would have approved the move because he was first and foremost a practical engineer.

Ernest Seaholm agrees that the 341 series and their successors up to the 346 are the "happiest" engines Cadillac

1929 Cadillac V-8 Phaeton.

Exclusive Features of Safety and Ease
Make Your Fine Car Ideals Come True

If you were to name the features of your ideal fine car you could not very well avoid an accurate description of the new Cadillac.

You would, of course, picture your ideal as beautiful beyond compare. Cadillac more than fits this picture. Its compelling beauty, its aristocratic elegance, its individuality of style have established a vogue.

You would certainly demand the utmost safety for yourself and your family. With its new brakes, the quickest and easiest to operate and the most effective ever devised, with

its new transmission that forever eliminates effort, hesitancy and awkwardness from gear-shifting, with its crystal-clear, non-shatterable Security-Plate glass Cadillac offers vital safety features found only in Cadillac-built cars.

Your ideal car must steer with superlative ease. There is no car that men and women find so easy to drive, to master completely, as a Cadillac-built car. You would require also a brilliance, zest and smoothness of performance never known before and that is precisely what you can

expect from the more powerful, more flexible 90-degree, V-type, 8-cylinder Cadillac power plant. Check these requirements, point for point, against the New Cadillac. Any Cadillac-La Salle dealer will gladly provide a car for this purpose.

✢   ✢   ✢

Cadillac dealers welcome business on the General Motors Deferred Payment Plan. Cadillac prices range from $3295 to $7000. Exquisite and exclusive Fleetwood custom models to express your individuality. All prices f. o. b. Detroit.

CADILLAC MOTOR CAR COMPANY
Division of General Motors
Detroit, Michigan   Oshawa, Canada

C A D I L L A C

This ad for the 1929 Cadillac proclaimed "Make Your Fine Car Ideals Come True."

1932 Cadillac V-8 Phaeton.

produced prewar—meaning by "happiest," the most reliable, trouble-free, rugged and successful.

Cadillac had never shown in elegance and style up then, but the advent of Harley Earl and the LaSalle altered all that. Lawrence Fisher had got Earl over from California to do the LaSalle, because Fred Fisher (L.P.'s brother) and Lynn McNaughton (Cadillac general sales manager) had been telling Alfred Sloan it was "high time Cadillac had a designer department." Cadillac president R.A. Collins used to winter at the Huntington Hotel in Pasadena, while visiting Cadillac's California distributor, Don Lee. Earl was chief designer and director of Lee's custom body shop which employed about a hundred men. Collins asked Lee for a golf partner and Earl played golf with Collins several times a week. Impressed by Lee's work for people like Cecil B. DeMille, Wallace Reid, May and Lottie Pickford, and Fatty Arbuckle, Collins told Earl in 1921 "Design me six little sports sedans; and I'll see how they go with my pet dealers."

However, it was several years later before L.P. Fisher brought him to Detroit. The gruff "L.P.," a hard man to convince, did not take long to make up his mind about Earl's potential. Earl treated the car not as an outgrowth of the wagon, but as a vehicle with it's own character and purpose.

When his design for the LaSalle was accepted, Earl said he felt like a new quarterback who had just thrown a pass for a touchdown. In the wake of the LaSalle's sensational reception by the public in March 1927, Alfred Sloan set up a design department (Art and Color) with ten designers and forty shop and office staff under Earl. Not at first welcomed by the various car divisions, it was nicknamed "the beauty parlor." Sloan had to move carefully and insinuate rather than introduce the new section. Earl did not enter in clouds of glory. His office was a little cubbyhole in the General Motors Annex, and Sloan had said "Harley, I think you had better work just for me for a while until I see how they take you."

Earl built up a team and spelled out the ground rules for one that could carry on, having "a good split between the esthetics and advanced engineering design."

This was not the first Art Department ever set up by an American company (as has often been stated). Nor was Earl the first professional stylist. These distinctions probably belong to Pierce-Arrow and Herbert M. Dawley who worked on these lines from 1907. But Dawley (a remarkable man whom the writer was privileged to know) was concerned only with a custom clientele. Earl and his Art and Color Section were undoubtedly the pioneer styling group for the big corporations and have exerted immense influence on the production car. Earl is to modern stylists what D.W. Griffith is to movie producers—the "founder of the profession." Some of the men who trained under Earl: Gordon Buehrig, Phil Wright, Jon Tjaarda, Bill Mitchell, Elwood P. Engel, Gene Bordinat and Dick Teague.

Now American Motors Director of Styling, Teague told me: "There is no question about it, and history will record far beyond my words, that Harley Earl was the head and father of the profession. He had a tough fight and many bloody battles with the engineers and divisional heads. So he had to become an administrator and a guy that got things done. Thus, he was a coach and an orchestra leader and many things were done by others than Earl personally. But there is no doubt he started it and made it a profession. He made plenty of enemies. But Harley had some things going for him from the beginning. For one thing he was six feet four, a tremendous guy, with steel blue eyes and a very imposing figure. He sort of overpowered you with his bigness and grilled you with those eyes of his. He was a good showman and agitator on top of that too, though strangely he was in personal relations a quiet guy and not a good speaker. Stuttered sometimes when excited, and was a master of the malaprop—although that may have been intentional. I remember once he said one day he'd get out of the business, get away from it all, and go and live in the Marihuana Islands!"

"There were men before Earl who knew what a car should look like and had the feel of shape and form line and style—such as Finley Robertson Porter of the Mercer—but they were tied in with coachwork and carriage trade. Earl was definitely the daddy of modern stylists—even those who didn't like him have to admit. He was a terrific guy and I'm a tremendous admirer of his work."

While Earl's "new look" took theme from Hispano-Suiza, the debt was soon repaid. His interpretation was a substantial advance on the original and two years later, Hispano-Suiza, was looking like Cadillac-LaSalle! This typified American versus European styling. The former usually showed more original ideas, but the latter excelled in execution. Whereas the European car was often gaunt, angular—even stark—the American was nicely rounded and more unified in design.

Earl himself had anticipated certain features of the Cadillac of this era in a strictly custom design for Fatty Arbuckle. This car built in 1919-1920 utilized a used Pierce-Arrow '66' chassis with a Cadillac V-8 engine. Even before Earl took over, Cadillacs were gradually moving toward the high, square hood and radiator line. In 1923, the '63' radiator had been given fuller shoulders and the model 314 had carried this further with more height, more depth in side view, and nickel plating standard. When this radiator was given a squared front edge in 1926-27, it was already a prototype for the 341 models. This radiator outline, incidentally, was not exclusive to Hispano-Suiza, being used by Delage and others. The principle was actually hundreds of years old. As many draftsmen will recognize, it is based on the "four-point arch" well known in medieval architecture.

Cadillac themselves were in no doubts about the improvement in appearance, describing the car as "low, long, fleet and beautifully balanced, gracefully prepositioned."

1938 Series 65 V-8 seven-passenger sedan.

This fresh style meant that for the first time the Marque had elegance to match its engineering. Previous Cadillacs had a severely utilitarian look, mainly because road conditions in the USA demanded adequate ground clearance, easily cleaned road wheels, and a minimum of brightwork. The Cadillac had inherited the early American pioneer tradition, where survival counted first and foremost, dictating all other considerations. Leland judged things by their inherent worth, and detested ostentation. This concept applied to the machine came out as "functionalism before elegance" and "serviceability under all conditions." Cadillac had a powerful following amongst commercial concerns who required the best class of vehicle but who also insisted on maximum work and value per dollar spent. Service car lines preferred Cadillacs for these reasons, because it was generally regarded as the tougher car and under severe conditions would cover greater mileage more reliably at less cost.

But times were changing. Roads were getting better in America and improved conditions allowed more elegance to be designed into a car without sacrificing practicality. Packard had foreshadowed this trend with their superbly aristocratic lines. This refined appearance engendered a feeling of engineering superiority, which although not an engineering fact, definitely put Packard at an advantage with wealthy buyers. Their preferences were molded in this area rather than in durability or cost of running, since they hardly ever pressed their cars to the limit in service.

The Earl-designed Cadillacs, in style and feel, stripped Packard of this superiority without abandoning their frontier virtues, and the pioneer American stylist had made his mark.

Engineering-wise, there was soon a matching mechanical advancement in the syncromesh transmission, which must have been as envied by rival salesmen as much as Earl's styling—and remained exclusively Cadillacs for three years.

The same salesman must have felt more than a little groggy a year later when Cadillac announced two straight eights—side by side in one car.

1938 Cadillac Model 75 Fleetwood V-8.

Cadillac had no equals in quality

By Maurice Hendry

Since the epochal V-8 of 1914, Cadillac has known many illustrious rivals in the quality-car field, both in the USA and abroad. In the long-term, none-but-none has been able to duplicate the success of the "Standard of the World." Only one rival has ever been able to displace Cadillac as sales leader, and we all know what eventually happened to Packard.

Since that time, Cadillac can no longer be said to have real "competition." Rivals yes, competitive threats, no. Even Henry Leland himself was unable to duplicate the success of his legendary creation. For all its efforts, Lincoln for many years stood in the Cadillac's shadow as much as Wilfred Leland did in relation to his father. As for Chrysler Imperial, Mercedes-Benz and Rolls-Royce, Cadillac is only aware of them as "low and dim on the horizon." This latter statement might upset fans for "little three" but apart from Lincoln, whose sales are just over a third of the Cadillac total, how do they stand? Nowhere from in front. Imperial? Always an also-ran. Mercedes? A total of 40,000 sales per annum sounds impressive—until you break it into a proliferation of models and realize that only one or two of them are in the Cadillac class and that their sales are only a fraction of

the overall total. As my friend (and *Motor Trend* contributor) Ed Schampel commented recently, when I told him I had offered to debate Cadillac versus Mercedes with *Motor Trend* and found they were unwilling to accept the challenge: "Your points are well taken. Place a Cadillac and a Mercedes side by side and it is easy to see why a Cadillac at $8,000 in America, outsells a Mercedes at $12,000, ten to one. The buying public is not so dumb as some 'experts' would like everyone to believe." As for Rolls-Royce, it would take a logarithmic graph to even indicate its presence in sales charts.

Cadillac was originally a modest little one-lunger, admittedly the best in its class, but priced in three figures instead of four, at a time when Pierce's mainstay, the celebrated Great Arrow, was advertised at figures ranging from $3,000 to $5,000 and its maker bluntly stated "We build the best car possible, then price accordingly." (Take it or leave it.)

Yet Cadillac had a range of four-cylinder models at that time which equalled anything for quality and sold approximately as well as any of, say, the "Three Ps." The answer here is that the marque image in Cadillac's case was set by its most popular model. Up to 1908, this was the single, from then on, the excellent "Thirty" and its succesors of 1912-1914. A deservedly popular car for

1915 Cadillac V-8 engine at the 1990 Chicago Auto Show.

touring, the famous fours gained a fine reputation for their top speed of more than 50 mph, their easy running and smooth ride even on indifferent roads. But it still wasn't regarded as the elite automobile—even with two Dewar Trophies to its credit.

The car that really put Cadillac over (even allowing for the lengthy period of Packard dominance in the twenties and thirties) was the V-type eight cylinder introduced in 1914 for the 1915 model year. It was a new concept in fine cars that obsoleted the engineering leaders in the field virtually overnight and set a pattern that is still being followed today. Almost every Cadillac model series has marked a major advance and been historically important, but it is the V-8 upon which the company's fortunes and foundations have unshakably rested for nearly six decades. Even company publicity (usually cagey about committing themselves too irrevocably to anything), stated in an advertisement of 1927:

"Cadillac's entire reputation as a master builder was based upon the Cadillac V-8."

Masterstroke though the V-8 was, however, it could not have been produced successfully without the steady, step-by-step progress that its predecessors had achieved.

The Thirty boosted that to five figures, almost all its years running at 10,000 cars or more. This success formed a solid base for the advent of the V-8, which although a much more sophisticated, complicated and advanced automobile, maintained the Thirty's market penetration without effort in its initial years. It then more or less continued to improve its position until that memorable day fifteen years later when, as Ernest Seaholm recalled, "I walked into L.P. Fisher's office and found him standing at the window with a far away look in his eyes." (That was in October 1929). L.P. had not only lost a lot of money—he had just launched a sixteen-cylinder car at the wrong moment. "L.P. was fine in a bull market but lost in the Depression" Ernie Seaholm remarked. However, he had plenty of company, and unlike some of his contemporaries, L.P. merely looked out of the window instead of jumping. He stayed with the ship and saw no doubt to his relief, that the V-16 sold exceptionally well in its introduction year—far better than had been planned for, actually. But the V-8 figures told another story. From an

annual average of around 48,000 units for the 1927-29 period, Cadillac-LaSalle figures fell to a mere 26,000 in 1930. In 1931 the V-8 total dropped to 21,000 and in 1932-33 the annual output reached an unbelievable low—between 5,000 and 6,000 cars. That had only happened once before, in 1921 when there were the combined factors of depression and Cadillac's move into a new plant. Even that, however, had been followed by an immediate recovery in 1922 to some 26,000 cars.

But there was no such recovery in 1934. The V-8s remained around the 3,000 mark, V-12 production was limited to three figures and the 16 was down to approximately one car per week! The sometimes-derided straight-eight LaSalle was the company saviour saleswise, with production at 7,000 for 1934, rising to 8,600 in 1935 and 13,000 in 1936. The latter was more than a thousand units above the whole V-8 line for 1936, but 1937 saw the straight-eight LaSalle dropped altogether and an entirely new range of V-8s that, at 46,000 units that year, demonstrated that Cadillac was making a comeback once and for all.

Even though there was a dip to 25,000 in 1938, a bad year for many throughout the industry, there was little question from then on that Cadillac was on top and once again the strong man of the fine car field. Packard lost ground in the thirties at the top of the line, its 12 being well and truly outsold by the Cadillac V-12/16 lineup more than two to one. The V-8s also regained their sales leadership over Packard from 1936. Based on a minimum price limit of $1,500, Cadillac claimed 48% of that market.

While it is true that combined Cadillac V-12/16 sales far surpassed the Packard 12, the late flathead Cadillac 16 on its own did not equal the Packard 12 sales during 1938-40. Also if we take as a basis, engine displacement, car size, and price, the Packard 12 should be restricted to comparison with the V-16 only, which it outsold by about 1,400 units (or over 30%). The only trouble with this is that Packard had no straight equivalent to the Cadillac V-12.

What were the engineering and styling highlights of all those years? Undoubtedly the singles and fours can be summed up in a phrase common to both—"Dewar Trophy." The double award epitomizes in each case a major technical advance, first in manufacture, secondly, in systems. The former is well understood, the latter has unfortunately been completely distorted by the prominence given one of its major functions—the self starter. Because of the convenience benefit of the self starter, even knowledgeable historians mention it alone both in connection with the Dewar Trophy, and as a technical advancement. Rightfully, it was part of a system that had never before been successfully applied in a production automobile, and which was the basis for development in that area from then on. The Dewar Trophy was not awarded for "the self starter." It was awarded for "the Delco System" electric starting, lighting and ignition. The other outstanding Cadillac contribution of this period was to popularize the closed body—a development for which the Fisher Brothers share credit with Henry Leland. Since this took place between the two Trophy awards and at a time when Cadillac was, along with Buick, largely instrumental in providing stability for the none-too-secure General Motors, these were obviously busy and exciting years for Cadillac.

Often overlooked, the Series 314 Cadillac still had its place in the story of the "Standard of the World" and was Cadillac's first "Classic." Labeled by some as "antique" it was outmoded and of stubby design by comparison with the recently introduced, lithe, handsome Packard Eight. Yet it easily outsold the Packard Eight, and was one of the most successful of Cadillac's classic models.

The 314 began in August 1925 for the 1926 model year. The engine was a redesigned V-63, which was the final development of the original 1914 Leland V-8. The crankshaft was shortened slightly and rod length reduced to a narrower engine. This, and other modifications, reduced engine weight by 130 pounds to 714 pounds. Direct acting roller tappets replaced rockers. Valves were angled to bore axis. There was a six-bearing camshaft instead of five, and one timing chain only.

Generator and fan were now V-belt driven, with the distributor at rear skew driven off the camshaft. The redesigned intake and exhaust manifolding gave smoother gas flows. Dual exhausting continued. The famous two-plane crankshaft was a notable engine feature. Introduced on the type 63, it gave inherent dynamic balance and was a major V-8 engine breakthrough. Although it had already been in production for two years, Cadillac advertistments for the 314 continued to emphasize the "new ninety-degree Cadillac."

The main chassis change was the introduction of longitudinal semielliptic springs at the rear in place of the

Cadillac's forgotten classic — Series 314

By Maurice Hendry

1927 Cadilac Series 314 Fleetwood Imperial seven-passenger sedan.

old platform suspensions. This lowered the car and, in comparison with earlier models, the "314" was "sleeker, well-groomed, low-crouching."

The frontal appearance was distinguished by a rounded radiator shell of attractive design. New also were radiator shutters which give it a "classic look."

The 314 gave the illusion of greater length only because the overall height was lowered—wheelbase remained at 132 inches. Nevertheless, it was the first really Classic Cadillac. The V-63 styling was the vintage lovers cup of tea and definitely non-classic as evidenced from its extreme overall height, severely rounded fender lines, etc.

Up to this time, as chief engineer, Ernie Seaholm told me with a laugh. "the Fishers had been absolute dictators of body design and jealously guarded their prerogative. Theirs was a simple approach—full-size line drawing on a blackboard—take it or leave it." While Cadillac was building full-size clay and wood mock-ups or sample bodies back as far as the Type 57 of 1918, they were all designed by body engineers. There were no designers (stylists) in the shops at all, although Cadillac body engineer Fred Keller was one of the best body engineers in the industry.

Fisher made all the closed jobs and Cadillac made all the open cars. About 1922-23, Cadillac, disliking what Fisher was building, made some sample bodies of sedans. Decisions as to the body styles were made by Fred Keeler, chief body engineer, D. McCall White and (earlier) Leland and Durant. In 1925, Harley Earl came.

Larry Fisher was a playboy really, and his brothers sent him over to Cadillac to keep him out of mischief. Fisher had some good ideas and boosted sales, but the guy who made Cadillac style tops was Harley Earl. He really "woke things up." Not until Harley Earl got there did Cadillac concentrate on esthetics.

The 314 style—formulated before Harley Earl arrived in Detroit—was the basis of the epochal 1927 La-Salle...similar body panels, similar molding treatments from cowl back, same position hood louvers, cowl band, cowl lamp position, landau bar deployment, similar tops, similar windshield posts, windshield visor. Earl just took brand new 314 Cadillacs out of final assembly and brought them upstairs. There he proceeded to re-arrange things with cutting and welding torches, screwdrivers and hammers, and clay and fists.

Fleetwood Body of Fleetwood, Pennsylvania, had been purchased for General Motors by Fisher Body on Sept. 1, 1925 to give Cadillac its own "in-house" custom body nameplate. At a Fleetwood stockholders meeting at the time, a GM representative said:

"You know gentlemen, that small oval Fleetwood nameplate means $1,000 per body more to us."

After the acquisition, few chassis other than Cadillac were seen at Fleetwood, Pennsylvania, and in January 1931, all operations were concentrated in Detroit. Similarly, few Cadillacs were thereafter seen with custom bodies other than Fleetwood. But there are some sporadic examples, ranging from Brunn and Le Baron at home, as far afield as Elkington in England.

At the 1925 New York Salon, Ralph Roberts of Le Baron exhibited a 314 sport Phaeton with special radiator, hood and fenders. The 1926 Salon saw a Brunn individual custom convertible coupe 314 "executed much in the Lincoln tradition." There was also a Brunn Cadillac featuring a manganese bronze windshield frame. One Cadillac executive, examining the windshield at Clark Avenue before shipment to the New York show, quipped, "It looks like gold." Inglis M. Uppercu, New York Metropolitan distributor, retorted:

"Judging from the price they charge, it is gold!" Herman Brunn was standing nearby, so Lawrence Fisher asked: "Well, Brunn, what do you say to that?" Brunn replied that others would have to ask the same price for a similar product, and after some examination, "L.P." gruffly conceded the point.

Factory charts were eye-opening. A coupe could be had, for example, in "black, Arizona gray and Naples yellow," or a Phaeton in "Kenilworth gray, sumac red, striped in Hobart red and cream, with basket work at extra cost." Upholstery materials were selected to harmonize with Duco colors. Leathers came in black, blue, gray, brown or green.

The advent of the 314 saw improved Fisher bodies in Standard and Custom lines listed, with prices lowered as much as $500. Closed bodies all featured Fisher one-piece ventilating windshield, adjustable rear-view mirror and automatic windshield wiper. A variety of accessories—robe rails, smoking and leather-covered vanity sets were included. Standard line cars had mohair double-tufted velvet upholstery with Marshall springs. Custom cars were trimmed to the buyers' orders.

Windows in standard cars were operated by segment and pinion mechanism; in the custom line, by cable lifts. The two-door Brougham had specially wide doors (37 inches). To prevent drumming, all closed car tops had two-inch wide wooden slats covered with padding and leather fabric. Custom cars had bumpers at the front, bumperettes at the rear, spring gaiters and Motometer, Duco finish in three color schemes—blue, Waverly gray and Arizona gray— were used on the standard line. The Custom line had six standard Duco color schemes in regular production, and any color scheme to the buyer's order on sixty days notice. Drum lamps and dual filament bulbs replaced tilt-beam headlamps.

For the 314-A the following year, 50 body styles and 500 color combinations were advertised. These were made up as follows: five new Fisher bodies added to the 13 of the previous year, making 18 total Fisher bodies in standard and custom production. There were 32 bodies by outside custom builders, known as the "special custom line," comprising 18 bodies by Fleerwood (five of them new), four new bodies by Brunn and ten by various other coachbuilders. All 500 color combinations were available on the three groups.

The five new Fisher models were: a five-passenger sport Landau sedan and custom two-passenger convertible coupe (both on a 132-inch wheelbase), the Imperial sedan seven-passenger Victoria coupe.

In quality, the 314 upheld Cadillac traditions. According to Charles Lamm Markman and Mark Sherwin, "Cadillac built more quality into a volume-produced automobile than any other maker in any country" in that period. "Less glamorous in appearance than Packard, less startling in appearance than Lincoln, it was nevertheless the epitome of American fine-car achievement under $10,000...the symbol of excellence...it merited the slogan 'Standard of the World.' Even on the mass-produced Fisher bodies, all mating surfaces met snugly. Paint was known for its long lasting originality. Quality showed in the fine, close-fitting doors and hood, the beautifully executed pin-striping, the soft light reflecting from the nickel plating."

Extensively re-engineered, featuring a bewildering variety of body styles and color combinations, the 314 showed a new hand at Cadillac's helm—Lawrence P. Fisher—a personality both playboy and powerful, perfectly fitted for the bull market of the Roaring '20s. The 314 saw only two years' production, but that totalled 50,000 cars—more than the eight cylinder models of Lincoln, Packard, Peerless and Stutz combined.

TWELVE CYLINDERS

Cadillac now rounds out complete coverage of the fine car field with the new V-Type 12 ... a car of exquisite beauty and surpassed in performance by the Cadillac V-16 only

Coachwork by Fisher and Fleetwood — Prices range from $3,795 to $4,995, f. o. b. Detroit

CADILLAC MOTOR CAR COMPANY · DIVISION OF GENERAL MOTORS

Cadillac V-16: Worth its weight in prestige

1931 Cadillac V-16 dual-cowl Phaeton.

By Robert C. Ackerson

In 1926 work began on a new Cadillac engine which has intended to give General Motors premier division the wherewithal to wrest leadership in the American fine car field from Packard. This engine was of course the V-16 which Cadillac introduced in December 1929 just a few short weeks after the stock market crash.

At the time work on the V-16 commenced, the economic indicators most people put their faith in forecasted a bright sales future for the quality automobiles that were beyond the means of all but a few Americans. In the mid '20s Cadillac was only one of a number of top drawer competitors that Packard had to deal with. Pierce-Arrow, Lincoln, Franklin, Marmon and the rather outdated Cunningham were just some of the marques catering to the motoring whims of America's monied aristocracy. In addition to these home grown varieties, by 1927 such foreign manufacturers as Hispano-Suiza and Isotta-Fraschini had through the pages of such prestige periodicals as *Vanity Fair* managed to make a modest sales impact upon the American fine car market.

Yet in spite of this hot bed of competition, Cadillac was already recognized by both its sales adversaries and customers as one of the best of the lot. A good deal of the basis for Cadillac's respected status was due to its famous V-63 model which had been introduced in 1923. With its dynamically balanced V-8 it had quickly established an outstanding reputation for smooth and trouble-free operation.

Ironically, it was the inordinate disparity of wealth in America, which later was to be partly responsible for the Great Depression that created the economic climate in which the Golden Age of the American quality automobile flourished. At the top of the American economic pyr-

amid stood 1 percent of the population into whose bank accounts flowed nearly 19 percent of the nation's annual income. With such tremendous economic resources at their disposal, this select group of Americans could afford the finest automobiles without regard to cost. At the same time, this difference between the rich and the rest of us meant that at the other end of the economic spectrum there were millions of Americans who could not afford one of Henry Ford's Model T's or one of the stylish new Chevrolets. In fact, only one family in five in 1927 even owned an automobile, and it was this basic economic cleavage that was a major cause of the Great Depression. Ironically, when the crash came, the market for high-priced automobiles suffered a severe shock; a victim in effect, of the factors behind its origin.

But the severity of the nation's economic calamity had not yet been realized, when Cadillac unveiled its V-16 in January 1930. From its very first public showing, this 452-cid engine was treated with a high degree of regard both by the motoring press and the general public. Cadillac's rationale for investing in such an engine was outlined by its Chief Engineer, William R. Strickland, in a paper he presented to the Society of Automotive Engineers Detroit section in April 1930. In his presentation he alluded to the fact that while the values and attitudes of the purchasers of quality automobiles had fluctuated over the years, one key consideration had remained paramount; the smooth operation of an automobile in its top gear from speeds as low as 5 mph up to its maximum performance capability. A second performance measure applied to cars of Cadillac's cut of cloth was the five to 25 mph run in high gear. It goes without saying of course, that the customer assumed this would be accomplished without any undue inconvenience to the

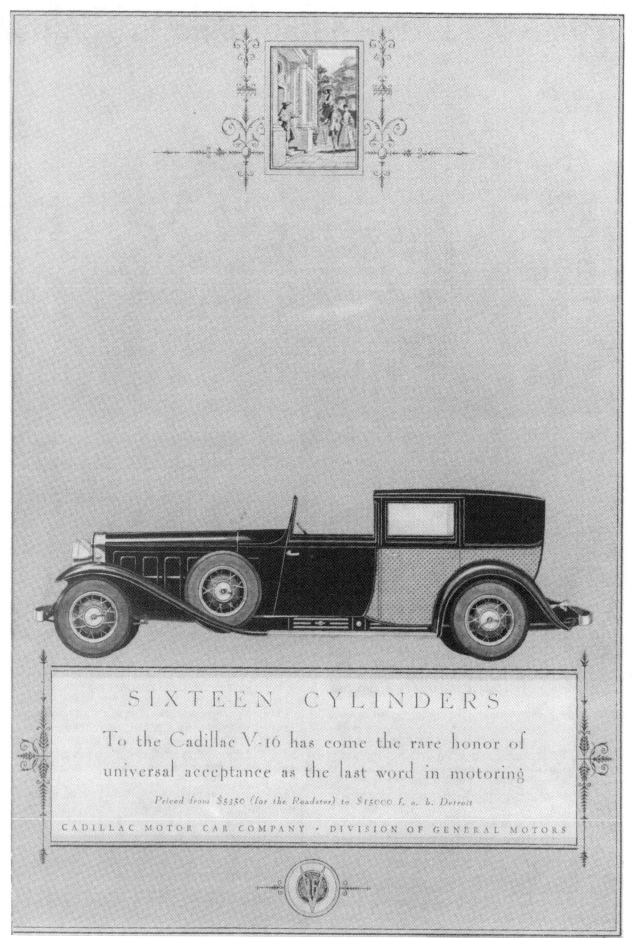

Sixteen Cylinders were advertised in this 1930 Cadillac ad.

1930 Cadillac ad touted "This High Esteem Seems Universal."

automobile's passengers. In addition to this ghost-like performance, the ride of the prestige automobile was expected to be equally unobstrusive. While exterior appearance was a matter of individual taste, the overall effect was usually a combination of restraint and a certain degree of flamboyance that served to manifest what the maverick American writer Thorstein Veblen was referring to when he coined the phrase "conspicuous consumption."

Besides these characteristics of the luxury car market there were other elements Cadillac took into consideration when it decided to produce the V-16. Automobiles of this class had grown in size and weight, thus if Cadillac had chosen to stay with its existing V-8 engine, an increase in displacement of at least 40 percent would be required to cope with the performance standards Cadillac had set for its new creation. While such an expansion was possible it would have seriously compromised the achievement of the remaining criteria by which a top flight American car was judged.

In Strickland's words (which appeared in the *SAE Journal* for Aug. 1930) "at present increasing the displacement of the eight meant going back to larger bores, with the mechanical and dynamical difficulties that were present in the old '48's and which are inherent with large bores." Similarly, the use of a supercharger with its attendant noise was rejected. Thus, whereas Duesenberg, with its great racing heritage would go to a supercharger in 1932 in order to maintain its image as "America's Mightiest Motorcar," Cadillac chose to go the multi-cylinder route to establish its claim as the "Standard of the World." Besides the technical benefits of a 16-cylinder engine (given the knowledge of combustion chamber design which prevailed at the time) an automobile with such a powerplant was certain to possess a certain aura of grandeur that even a supercharged competitor did not enjoy. In this context, the V-16 was a classic example of one-upmanship.

For both its visual and technical attributes the V-16, itself a thing of beauty, delivered 175 bhp. Even more impressive was its all important low speed torque: 320 pound-feet at 1500 rpm, which assured velvet-like low speed operation. Thanks to a hydraulic-valve-silencing device created by General Motors Research Division, the V-16s overhead valves were well-mannered and quiet as they went about performing their tasks.

The sum total of the V-16s features was so impressive that even the Europeans found it impossible to describe its super silent operation without using terms such as "magnificent" and "outstanding."

Identical words could also be used to sum up the V-16s performance capability. The *SAE Journal* for August 1930 contained a detailed evaluation of the V-16 which included some performance figures of a V-16 carrying a five-passenger sedan body and running a 4.39 rear axle. Even with such a heavy non-sporting coachwork, the V-16 was capable of an 87 mph top speed. In 1961 *Car Life* magazine published a "test" in its March issue of a V-16 based upon composite data gleaned from articles published during the V-16s production life. *Car Life* credited a V-16 weighing 6,500 pounds with a zero to 60 mph time of 20 seconds. Thus its not off base to conclude that a V-16 with a lighter weight body and the "high-speed" 3.47 rear axle was capable of a top speed in excess of 100 mph.

A comparison with some of the V-16s contemporaries makes for some interesting reading. The Duesenberg J, although its true horsepower output was closer to 208 than its claimed 265 at 3,600 rpm could still accelerate from rest to 60 mph in less than 13 seconds and exceed

113 mph. But the "Big D" is generally regarded as noisier and rougher riding than the V-16 Cadillac.

Rolls-Royce's mammoth V-12-powered Phantom III, which measured in at a hefty 440 cubic inches, was a faster accelerator than the Cadillac, although inferior in top speed to the American car. However, the Phantom III was in reality a rather complex monster which gave Rolls-Royce a considerable amount of grief. More than likely it stands in history as the model Rolls-Royce would be most happy to forget.

Although it never reached anything even closely resembling a modest level of production, the Marmon V-16 deserves recognition as the automobile which most closely duplicated the Cadillac's overall standards of excellence. Work on this all-aluminum 45-degree V-16 had, like the V-16 Cadillac, commenced in 1926. With 200 bhp it was somewhat more powerful than the Cadillac. This power advantage plus a lighter overall weight gave the Marmon on a top speed, in the vicinity of 105 to 107 mph and a highly respectable zero to 60 mph time of 14 seconds. An outstanding automobile in all respects, the demise of the Marmon 16 was a sad event in automotive history.

A point of some dispute among Cadillac historians concerns the gas consumption of the V-16. Maurice Hendry credits the V-16 with an average miles per gallon figure of 8.5. Yet David Scott-Moncrieff in his book, *The Thoroughbred Motor Car 1930-40* noted the V-16s "fantastic thirst for petrol. To go from Cannes to Nice, about twenty miles, it used to burn five gallons." John R. Bond, writing in the February, 1963 issue of *Car Life* noted that "some owners reported 9-10 miles per gallon under favorable conditions but 6-7mpg was a more usual average." Actually all of this mattered little to the individual who possessed the financial means 45 years ago to purchase an automobile whose price was approximately $10,000.

At times somewhat over-shadowed by the V-16 engine's sensational physical appearance and performance prowess, the V-16's coachwork was masterfully executed. Virtually all 16-cylinder Cadillacs carried Fleetwood bodies; a situation not terribly surprising since Fleetwood had been part of the Fisher body works since 1925. According to Hugo Pfau's fine book, *The Custom Body Era*, "no other custom body builder was encouraged to build on a Cadillac. In fact, it was almost impossible to buy a separate Cadillac chassis for this purpose." Jack E. Triplett, who probably knows more about V-16 coachwork than anyone else believes that only one V-16 chassis of the first series (452-A) was equipped with a body prepared by an American builder besides Fleetwood.

This situation should not be construed to mean that a prospective V-16 customer had to choose from a skimpy selection of body designs. On the contrary, in the 1930-31 V-16 catalog, Fleetwood offered over 30 different body styles. This super-piece of automobile literature also includes the statement that "special custom creations may be had in any mode the purchaser specifies." Certainly it is not a case of excessive enthusiasm for the V-16 to concur with David Holls' statement in *Cadillac: The Complete Seventy-five Year History* that the Fleetwood designers were capable of producing "a car every bit as attractive as what custom body builders across the country were doing at the time."

Initial sales of the 452-A series reflected its impact upon the fine car market. By early April 1930, 1,000 V-16s had been built and certainly the total production figure for 1930 of 2,887 cars was nothing short of remarkable, considering the rapidly deteriorating economic situation in the United States. After 1931 production dropped to a trickle and beyond 1933 the V-16 was built on an "order only" basis. Yet Cadillac's President Lawrence P. Fisher, by using the limited market for the V-16 as a means to endow it with an aura of extreme exclusiveness, was making the best of what was obviously a very poor marketing situation. An ad placed in *Fortune* during 1934 for a V-16 with a very handsome town-car body fairly dripped with this philosophy. Headed by the phrase "This one alone" its text reminded the reader that "the gentleman who owns this car can drive from one end of the earth to the other—and not once will he see another car precisely like his own...Only 400 of these magnificient cars will be produced within the year and early reservations are sincerely advised." As a matter of record only 56 V-16s were built in 1934. In 1936 Cadillac introduced a new V-8 engine which in its 346-cid, 135-bhp form could perform the same tasks as the V-16 and its V-12 running mate without their complexity and expense. Thus the appearance of a totally new V-16 for 1938 necessitates some explanation. E.W. Seaholm, Cadillac's Chief Engineer, writing in the Nov. 27, 1937 issue of *Automotive Industries* implied that the major reason was that in light of the limited sales potential of cars in Cadillac's price class the need to reduce Cadillac's stable of V-8, V-12 and V-16 engines was desirable. While this might have some validity, the minuscule production of the V-16 in 1937 of only 49 units, would seem to suggest that the best way to simplify the Cadillac engine line-up would be to just drop both the V-12 and V-16 and concentrate on the new V-8 with its proven ability to match both of those engines in most critical areas of performance. Given this set of circumstances, why did Cadillac go through the expensive process of designing and building a new V-16? The most plausible explanation centers around that magic word, Prestige. Cadillac was clearly on the move and the announcement of a new V-16, more advanced and powerful than its predecessor, was bound to pay handsome dividends in this area.

In his *Automotive Industries* article, Seaholm referred to a number of criteria the new engine was designed to meet. These included having more than 8 cylinders, producing at least as much power as the current V-16, being lighter in weight and shorter in length than either the V-12 or V-16, being designed in such a way that it would cost less to produce and be easier to service than the original V-16. Perhaps, most importantly, Seaholm noted

that it would also have to "meet the high standard of performance and serviceability required of high-priced automobiles." On every point the V-16 matched or exceeded the mark set for it. With a displacement of 430 cubic inches and its cylinders set in a 130-degree vee, the new V-16 with clutch and all accessories weighed 1,050 pounds, which compared favorably with the older versions weight of 1,165 pounds. In length it was 5 3/4 inches shorter (45 7/8-inches vs. 51-5/8 inches) and with only 1,627 components it was a far simpler piece of equipment than the old V-16 which contained 2,810 parts. In terms of power, it was rated at 185 bhp at 3,600 rpm or in Seaholm's words, "almost precisely the same as that of the former sixteen."

Only 508 of these flathead V-16s were built between 1938 and 1940, which seems to support the thesis that they were developed primarily for prestige reasons.

The importance of the V-16s role in Cadillac's rise to pre-eminence among American automobiles as well as its ascension as one of the world's finest automobiles regardless of price cannot be overemphasized. Although Cadillac didn't surpass Packard in total sales until after World War II, a quick look at their relative corporate behavior during the Depression (as well as an appreciation of where they are today) illustrates just how valuable a merchandising item the V-16 was. Whereas Cadillac's stature as a super-luxury car grew by leaps and bounds during the 1930's, Packard's image and perhaps even its self-image suffered what proved to be irreparable damage as the result of producing a six-cylinder automobile carrying the Packard crest. The divergent paths followed by Cadillac and Packard during those difficult years serve to show that the phrase "as you sow so shall you reap" has meaning beyond its original context. Indeed it is fair to say the Cadillac alone, of all the great American luxury cars of the 1930's, emerged from the economic horror of the Great Depression with its reputation for integrity and quality untarnished. Thus after the end of the Second World War Cadillac was in the strongest position to push forward towards dominance of the American fine car field.

In 1954 a Cadillac advertisement appeared entitled "Cadillac: Worth Its Price in Prestige." As far as its role in Cadillac history is concerned the same can be said of the V-16.

1931 Cadillac 452A V-16 Landau Town Car.

The 16-cylinder Cadillac:

This 1930 Cadillac featured the automobile industry's first V-16 engine. This seven-passenger sedan was the ultimate in luxury and power. Later engineering developments made the V-16 principle outmoded.

Smoothness, silence, acceleration and hill-climbing ability

By Bill Artzberger

The "Roaring '20s." We've heard the term many times. Why was that particular decade remembered above others in American history?

It was a decade of prosperity, economic boom, stock market speculation, prohibition, gangsters and racketeering.

The stock market began a craze that touched nearly everyone from the lowliest wage earner to the most respected banker. There were more millionaires recorded per capita during the '20s than any other period.

Riches, installment buying and new highways, along with the advancing automobile technology, swelled the number of automobiles from 7.3 million to 19.7 million from 1920 to 1929. Automaking became our center of attention employing more than two million workers and trickling down to the point where one in every five Americans was directly or indirectly associated with the auto industry.

The wealthiest of Americans could afford and demand the finest of luxury automobiles. Europe, hoping to prosper from American wealth, sent its most impressive and lavish cars to America, including the Rolls-Royce, Mercedes-Benz, Hispano-Suiza, Isotta-Fraschini and Minerva.

While the Cadillac had gained recognition as a prestigious luxury automobile, it fell to second place in production behind the Packard in 1925. Packard, a luxury automobile of the highest standards, had introduced its Twin-Six (V-12) engine as early as 1916. While Cadillac continued production of its very formidable V-8, it no longer remained first in luxury car sales on its past reputation alone.

Then, in 1921, Packard surprised the auto world by introducing a six-cylinder engine and an automobile that sold for 20 percent less than the Cadillac. It accounted for 70 percent of Packard sales during 1925 and 1926. The Cadillac V-8 still outsold the Packard in-line eight by five to one, but Larry Fisher, the newly appointed general manager at Cadillac, had other plans!

He recalled the clamor and sensationalism that was generated when the Packard Motor Car Co. introduced its Twin-Six. Now, it was Cadillac's turn ... but with a V-16!

But why 16 cylinders? Was it a question of just more numbers than any other automobile? Not exactly.

Engineers then, as now, were always trying to reach the same goals when designing a new engine. The criteria were smoothness, silence, acceleration and hill-climbing ability.

The smoothness could only be acquired with multi-cylinders. Sixteen was chosen as ideal because this number would provide one power impulse for every one-eighth of a turn of the crankshaft. It is also common knowledge that the shock of explosion increased with cylinder volume. Smaller cylinders reduce both audible noise and the vibration of shock. Smaller, therefore lighter, pistons and connecting rods also reduce reciprocating weight. Without going into a dissertation of automotive engineering principles, it should suffice to say that all that is relative to the V-16 engine, to a degree, accomplishes most of the goals of building a smooth, quiet and high-performance engine.

No one had ever built a production V-16 engine up to this point. Ettore Bugatti had designed a "U-16" in 1915 that combined two straight-eight-cylinder engines mounted side-by-side. Each had its own crankshaft, and power was delivered to a single shaft through a series of transfer gears. He made an agreement with the U.S. Air Corps to allow it to be refined and used in a proposed World War I airplane. Two thousand were to be built by the Duesenberg Co. in the United States. Charles B. King, a Duesenberg engineer, was appointed to oversee the development of the U-16. He spent so much time refining it that the war was near its end when production of the engine began. Only 11 of the Bugatti-King engines were ever made.

Perhaps it was the 16-cylinder engine that inspired Larry Fisher and created the spark that brought the Cadillac V-16 to birth.

The new V-16 design was also borrowed from the knowledge of Howard C. Marmon, who also worked on the Bugatti U-16. Owen Nacker was another brainy engineer who was assigned to the V-16 program. Both were friends who were intrigued with the concept and discussed it frequently.

As it developed, the engine had a separate aluminum crankcase. Two eight-cylinder nickel-cast iron blocks were bolted to it at a 45-degree angle. The crankshaft had five main bearings and four balancing counterweights. The bore and stroke was three inches by four inches displacing 452 cubic inches. It was rated between 175 and 195 hp.

The engine was the overhead-valve type. As could be expected from this adroit combination of engineers, a very clever automatic valve adjustment system was developed. This was accomplished by using an eccentric cam on the valve rocker-arm shaft. This cam automatically adjusted the valve lash to zero from a cold to a hot engine. It also accounted for wear when and if it would occur.

The 16-cylinder Cadillac was to make its first public appearance in the fall of 1929. The timing could not have been worse. The stock market crash of '29 washed away millions of dollars of common stock. The audience that the V-16 was aimed at nearly disappeared overnight.

Although the future appeared gloomy, the V-16 was introduced on Dec. 10, 1929. It immediately became the world's no. 1 automotive status symbol.

While 2,887 V-16s were sold in 1930, the Great Depression continued to take its toll. Even the relatively few who could afford the V-16 elected to choose a less conspicuous automobile. Production fell to 750 units in 1931 and continued on the downslide until 1937. Depending on which history reference is used, only 3,878 V-16s were sold in seven years.

One would think that this sordid experience would be enough for the Cadillac Division of GM. But while the ohv V-16 sales were dropping, a new flathead "en-bloc" V-16 was being developed. The new V-16 contained only 1,627 parts compared to the 3,273 parts for the first series V-16. Even though the same high quality was maintained, as well as improved performance, it was more economical to build.

The new V-16 used the most modern technology available in casting the engine block to make it both stronger and lighter. It was a 135-degree "square" engine with a 3 1/4-inch bore and stroke, displacing 431 cid. It weighed 1,050 pounds ... 250 pounds less than the ohv 452.

Again, the new V-16 was introduced at a most inopportune time. While the Depression was showing some signs of improvement, it took another disastrous downturn in the fall of 1937. Nevertheless, the new V-16 was launched.

Only the remaining wealthy were able to afford the revived V-16 Cadillac. These were limited to movie stars, a few remaining Depression "survivors" and some foreign dignitaries. Three hundred and eleven were sold in 1938; 136 in 1939; and 51 in 1940.

While Cadillac V-16 production faced many adversities in its difficult years, it remains one of the world's top-ranking automobiles. It was never rated as the "fastest" automobile made nor was it meant to be. (Tested in proper trim, it could match the very best!) If any of the V-16's attributes are to be acclaimed, they are exactly those the designers set out to accomplish: smoothness, silence, acceleration and hill-climbing ability.

A 1930 Cadillac roadster powered by a V-16 engine.

Cadillac's last V-16

By Robert C. Ackerson

Most automotive historians agree that the seeds of Cadillac's tremendous postwar popularity were sown during the waning years of the '30s.

By 1941 the LaSalle was discontinued, Hydra-Matic was available, the styling elements that would be part of the Cadillac "look" for a decade were well established and a single engine policy that reduced costs without adversely affecting Cadillac's image had been put in place. That latter development sounded the death knell for one of the '30s most exotic engine designs, the V-16. Cadillac had introduced its first V-16 in early 1930, not the most propitious time for a very expensive automobile to begin its career!

Initially, however, demand for the V-16 was strong; 3,250 were produced in 1930. This popularity was a reflection of the appreciation discriminating motorists had for this engine's capability. It not merely delivered 165 hp at 3,400 rpm and 320 lb./ft. of torque at 1,200 rpm but did it with an ease that earned both the admiration and envy of Cadillac's competitors, both foreign and domestic.

The next year Cadillac unveiled a V-12 running mate to the V-16 that displaced 370 cubic inches and was rated a 135 hp at 3,400 rpm and 284 lb./ft. of torque at 1,200 rpm. This meant that Cadillac was producing five different engines, since in addition it also offered V-8 powered Cadillacs and LaSalles.

When Nicholas Dreystadt became Cadillac's general manager in 1934 with the goal of cutting Cadillac's costs without a sacrifice in quality, this proliferation of power plants had its days numbered. After a new V-8 was introduced in 1936 came the elimination of the V-12 following the 1937 model year and the debuting of the less costly V-16 in 1938. This engine had an almost unbelievably low production run; only 514 were built from 1938 through 1940.

Such a limited output makes it tempting to regard the second of Cadillac's V-16s as little more than an aberration, stimulated by the golden glow of a dying era of motoring glory. Yet, in many ways it represented Cadillac's grasp of sound engineering and manufacturing principles, qualities that it carried over into the fabulous '40s and '50s.

In discussing the details of the V-16's development in *Automotive Industries* for Nov. 27, 1937 Cadillac's chief engineer, Ernest W. Seaholm, outlined the design goals pursued by his staff in its creation. It was to have more than eight cylinders and as much power as the existing V-16, be shorter in length than both the V-16 and V-12, be lighter than both, be less expensive to produce, and most certainly perform to Cadillac's very high standards.

For a time, a V-12 was considered but the V-16 overwhelmed the V-12 in its ability to provide both a smoother performance and, with a shorter piston stroke, greater durability. This still left Cadillac's engineers to contend with the higher manufacturing costs associated with a V-16 engine. Seaholm was unperturbed writing: "We believed, however, that we could develop a simplified design in which 16-cylinder advantages would be realized in an engine having actually fewer parts than either the Cadillac 16 or Cadillac 12 then in production."

Seaholm achieved not only this objective but all the others on Cadillac's dream list. The new V-16 had 1,627 numbered parts, the old V-16, 3,273 and the V-12, 810. A similar advantage was enjoyed by the new V-16 when its weight was compared to those of the superseded V-12 and V-16. Whereas their respective weights were 1,165 and 1,300 pounds, the new V-16s was 1,050 pounds.

Admittedly, Seaholm's engine, with 135 degrees between cylinder banks and side valves, lacked the elegant appearance of the previous V-16 with its slender 45 degree V and overhead valves. But the 135-degree design retained the equal firing intervals of the first V-16 while lowering engine height at a minor cost of greater width. As a result, the L-head V-16 was more compact than either the old V-12 and V-16. In terms of absolute power output, the second generation V-16 developed 185 hp at 3,600 rpm, which Seaholm noted was "almost precisely the same as that of the former 16."

The 16-cylinder engine was, of course, a victim of progress. Its L-head design possessed a limited ability to co-exist with high compression ratios, and a year before it was even in production, work was underway leading to Cadillac's overhead-valve V-8 of 1949. Not surprisingly, its guiding light was Ed Cole, who back in the '30s, had been closely involved in the 135-degree V-16's development. In this case, at least, a glorious past was very much a prelude to an even grander future.

1940 Cadillac V-16 Series 90 Fleetwood convertible sedan

WHETHER of the early inverted kettle type or the modern casting en bloc, the function of cylinders is the same. Cylinders are miniature · power houses. In automobile engine building it has been found that power from a group of small cylinders may be applied with greater nicety than from a single large one. The motor car began with one cylinder; continued with two, then four, and six. But from four and six no advance was made until Cadillac introduced the first eight-cylinder engine in America. Here, the industry was given a new standard.

Public interest was aroused by this seemingly great increase in number of cylinders over that of all previous Cadillacs, and particularly of the six-cylinder engines of other makers.

Here was a genuinely new engine, eight-cylinder, and so designed that the cylinders were logically arranged in banks of four, placed side by side in the form of a V, for economy of space, rugged construction, precise assembly.

Although the motor car had previously attained a high state of development, the time had arrived when the public was urging new ideals in power, silence, and smoothness in engine performance.

The Cadillac V-type eight-cylinder engine raised performance standards as no other automotive power plant ever did, and there is even now no pressing need for finer, more capable, or more luxurious cars than the present Cadillacs and La Salles. Yet there are sold in this country every year fairly considerable numbers of automobiles, foreign and domestic, at prices two or three times those of Cadillac and La Salle.

Cadillac, with its vast resources, its magnificent plants and equipment would fail of its high purpose were it to ignore the appeal which has come from a very limited clientele for even finer cars than Cadillac or La Salle, other American custom-built cars, or the worthy creations from abroad. Therefore, Cadillac now presents a V-type 16-cylinder engine mounted in a super chassis carrying Fleetwood custom bodies.

This new car has been named Cadillac V-16 and is an addition to the Cadillac and La Salle eight-cylinder lines.

In designing and building the V-16, Cadillac and Fleetwood organizations have been most lavish in the choice and use of materials.

Elaborate and beautiful as are these new creations, it is the V-type 16-cylinder engine which sets them apart from all other cars. To those who wonder at this new array of cylinders in the Cadillac V-16, it may suffice to say that Cadillac excelled in the building of an eight-cylinder engine because Cadillac first learned to build a one-cylinder engine well.

In designing an engine which might contribute materially more in performance and satisfaction than the eight, there could be no middle ground. The possibilities of eight-cylinder engines attain their maximum in the Cadillac and La Salle power plants. Cadillac engineers might have added two or even four more cylinders and have been certain of some accomplishment, but that would have been only a step toward the goal which has been reached in this new V-type 16-cylinder engine.

Where did all the 16s go?

A documentary study of the 1930-'31 Cadillac V-16s

By Alan Merkel

With the announcement quoted at left, the Cadillac Motor Car Co. set in motion the distribution and sale of the 1930-31 Cadillac V-16s. Where did all the 16s go? I suspect that many of us would hope that the answer to this question would lead us to the discovery of a lifetime by revealing where they all are now. Such is not the case, however. My purpose in assembling this information is to tell you where they all went originally—back when a trip to the Cadillac showroom was all that it took to find and see one.

It should come as no surprise that some of these fine cars did not sell immediately. The Great Depression, of course, was no doubt the biggest factor causing slowness in sales. Out of the nearly 3,250 cars assembled,[1] as many as 558, or 17 percent, were eventually sold in a city different from that to which they were originally ordered to be shipped. The cars were apparently readily diverted to another dealer in another city in order to facilitate or ensure a sale.

In one instance, a special two-passenger Fisher-bodied coupe built in May 1930 went to six locations in Michigan and Ohio before reaching its final destination in Detroit in November 1931. (This car was a Fisher model 2904—a body style that I have not seen listed in previous articles on these cars.)

Other examples are even more extreme when the distances involved are considered. On at least a dozen occasions, V-16s were initially shipped to Los Angeles or San Francisco and were later sent to New York City to be sold. In one instance, a convertible coupe, body style 4335, went to San Francisco in June 1930 and stayed there until April 1932 when it was sent to New York City. Wouldn't we like to go back in time for just one day in late 1931 for a chance to negotiate with the dealer on that new V-16 convertible standing unsold on his lot?

Another well-traveled new V-16 was a seven-passenger Imperial, style 4375, which went to Detroit in February 1930. It was returned to the factory in April and sent to Los Angeles in June. Its travels were only beginning, however. In February 1931 the car went back East to New York City, and two months later it was shipped to its final destination: Stockholm, Sweden.

New York City was the final destination for more 1930-31 V-16s than any other city. Seventeen-and-a-half percent, or a total of 571 '30-31 V-16s, went to four of New York's boroughs. The V-16 shipments to Brooklyn were recorded separately. When the total sent there is added to the Manhattan and other borough figures, the result becomes even more impressive. A total of 23

---

[1]Cadillac began V-16 engine numbers with 700001 and continued this series through 1930 and 1931. The last engine number in 1931 was 703251, but two engines were used on display chassis, and one number was not used.

percent, or practically one-fourth of all V-16s for '30 and '31, went to New York City.

The first car delivered to New York (other than to the Automobile Show) was a seven-passenger sedan, style 4375-S, with engine #700012 (the 12th engine in this series). It was shipped there in February 1930. The last car to go to New York was also the last 1931 V-16 Model 452-A to be built. It was a five-passenger Imperial Cabriolet, style 4355, with engine #703251. It was shipped in February 1932.

Several other metropolitan areas, in addition to New York, received relatively large numbers of the early V-16s. Following is a list of the top 10 cities, ranked in descending order, according to the number of 1930-31 V-16s shipped there as their final destination:

New York City	571
Chicago	247
Los Angeles	208
Brooklyn	192
Philadelphia	185
Detroit	164
San Francisco	118
Newark	105
Boston	92
Cleveland	64

In spite of the fact that 60 percent of the Model 452-A V-16s went to the aforementioned 10 cities, there were sufficient numbers to spread the remainder of the cars to many metropolises in the United States, Canada and other foreign countries.

Final destinations in the United States, including the 10 listed above, totaled 108 different cities across the country. The following cities were at the low end of the list in terms of the number of V-16s shipped there as their final destination:

Akron	1
Albuquerque	3
Ashville	2
Atlantic City	2
Aurora	2
Bay City	1
Bridgeport	1
Charleston, S.C.	1
Denver	3
El Paso	2
Evansville	2
Hammond	1
Huntington	3
Keokuk	1
Lexington	1
Lima	3
Mobile	1
New Bedford	1
Norfolk	1
Norwich	3
Ogdensburg	2
Oshkosh	2
Paterson	1
Phoenix	3
Raleigh	1
Reno	1
Richmond	3
Roanoke	2
Salt Lake City	3
Shreveport	1
South Bend	1
Tulsa	2
Union City	2
Wichita	2
Wilkes Barre	3
Williamsport	3

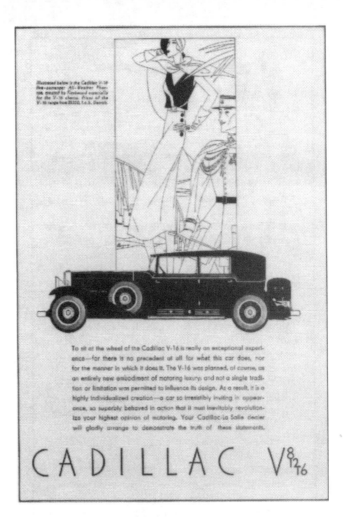

A total of 156 V-16s were shipped out of this country in 1930 and 1931, including chassis which were being shipped to custom coachbuilders.

Fifty-three of these 156 were shipped to Oshawa, home of General Motors of Canada, and went on from there to their final destinations. The remaining 103 cars shipped out of the country went to 16 different locations. Included among these were five V-16s that were shipped to Copenhagen, Denmark in mid-1930 for the European tour.

The numbers of cars and chassis sent out of the country and their destination cities are shown in the table below:

Oshawa, Canada	53
Berlin	18
Antwerp	16
Madrid	13
Paris	11
Stockholm	9
London	9
Copenhagen	7
Mexico City	7
Buenos Aires	3
Bombay	3
Havana	2
San Juan	2
Manila	1
Moscow	1
Port Elizabeth	1
Honolulu	1

Out of the 103 cars and chassis shipped to countries other than Canada, 23 were chassis being sent to custom coachbuilders. These 23 chassis represent 65 percent of the total number of V-16 chassis which Cadillac

Fourteen among the 41 body styles offered on the 1930 V-16 chassis. Illustrations from the collection of Henry Austin Clark Jr. All other photos and illustrations are from the collection of the author.

permitted to be shipped from the factory without bodies, leaving only about a dozen for use by domestic coachbuilders.

It is interesting to note that a good percentage of these exported cars survive today. Aside from V-16s that went to Canada and still exist, I know of surviving V-16s which have returned to this country from London (two returned via South Africa), Berlin, Bombay, Stockholm, Copenhagen and Mexico City.

As would be expected, several Cadillac and General Motors executives received V-16s for their own personal use. The first of these went to L.P. Fisher, president of Cadillac, in February 1930. The car provided to him was a five-passenger Imperial sedan, with engine #700100, the one-hundredth V-16 engine.

Indeed, all of the Fisher brothers at GM received V-16s. Two additional cars were provided to L.P. Fisher and a total of two were provided to W.A. Fisher and C.T. Fisher as shown in the list below:

L.P. Fisher
Five-Passenger Sedan, Eng. #700100
C.T. Fisher
Convertible Coupe, Eng. #700335
W.A. Fisher
All-Weather Phaeton, Eng. #700556
L.P. Fisher
Five-Passenger Sedan, Eng. #701160
A.J. Fisher
Seven-Passenger Sedan, Eng. #701175
E.F. Fisher
All-Weather Phaeton, Eng. #701325
L.P. Fisher
Seven-Passenger Sedan, Eng. #701550
C.T. Fisher
Five-Passenger Imperial, Eng. #701755
F.J. Fisher
Five-Passenger Sedan, Eng. #702236
W.A. Fisher
Custom-Bodied, Eng. #702270

Other GM executives who received V-16s included:

John Jacob Raskob, chairman of the GM finance committee, who alienated the GM board of directors by serving as the Democratic national chairman for Al Smith. (He is also noted for having built the Empire State Building.) He received the first V-16 all-weather Phaeton for his use.

Top: 1930 V-16 No. 4376 two-passenger coupe ($5,800). Bottom: No. 4375-S seven-passenger sedan ($6,225).

Top: 1930 Cadillac V-16 style no. 4302 two-door roadster, which sold for $5,350. Bottom: 1930 V-16 body style no. 4175 (Madame X) Imperial seven-passenger sedan, Fleetwood, $7,525.

Standard Catalog of Cadillac

SIXTEEN CYLINDERS

The Cadillac sixteen-cylinder engine goes far beyond the contemporary conception of brilliant performance. It multiplies power and subdivides it into a continuous flow... constantly at full-volume efficiency... flexible... instantly responsive. This, plus complete individuality in styling, is—in brief—the story of the "V-16"

CADILLAC MOTOR CAR COMPANY · DIVISION OF GENERAL MOTORS

Engine Drawing from catalog: advertisement from March 1930.

Two V-16s were sent to C.S. Mott who served on the GM board for 60 years until his death at age 97, and who was a GM vice president from 1916 to 1937. He received a Madame X seven-passenger Imperial and an all-weather Phaeton. In later years he reportedly drove a Corvair to work and was an advocate of small cars.

H.M. Stephens, who was Cadillac's general sales manager from 1925 to 1930, received a custom-bodied V-16 for his own use. His successor, J.C. Click, made use of two cars. One was a Madame X five-passenger sedan and the other an all-weather Phaeton.

At least 60 V-16s remained at the factory for individuals' use. A few more were sent to the Proving Ground, the Engineering Department, the Experimental Department, and Sales and Service. Of the cars that stayed at the factory for personal or technical use, I know only a couple that survive today.

The dramatic reduction in numbers of V-16s produced from 1930 to 1931 has been well-documented in previous articles on these cars. Of the 3,251 engine numbers used on Model 452-A V-16s, only 364 were used on cars from Jan. 1, 1931 through the end of shipments in early 1932. Actually, four cars with engine numbers below 702887 (the highest engine number shipped in 1930) were not shipped until 1931. Strictly speaking, it could be said that 367 452-As were shipped in 1931 and the rest in 1930. The figure for 1930 is about 2,880 since it was in 1930 that one number was not used and two display chassis were produced.

The following table shows how rapidly the shipments of V-16s began, and how severely they dropped off as the Great Depression's effects were felt. The figures indicate the month/year and the number of cars shipped.

12/29	3
1/30	5
2/30	367
3/30	436
4/30	576
5/30	442
6/30	384
7/30	297
8/30	166
9/30	82
10/30	54
11/30	33
12/30	38
1/31	25
2/31	47
3/31	37
4/31	47
5/31	50
6/31	46
7/31	17
8/31	7
9/31	12
10/31	14
11/31	6
12/31	0
2/32	59

Figures on numbers of V-16s shipped daily can be misleading because days with large shipments were often followed by relatively low numbers. There were, however, a few days when the cars shipped totalled 40 or more. The highest number was 48 on Friday, April 25, 1930. The total (131) for this week in April, however, was not the highest for a single week. The highest total for a single week occurred at the end of March when 155 V-16s were shipped. This week included a daily high of 40 on Thursday and a low of 21 on Saturday.

I estimate the total number of surviving 1930-'31 V-16s with original bodies to be over 150. At one time the survival figure was thought to be less than 100, but I have collected data on well over that number of surviving original cars, with still others known to exist. This figure does not include V-16 chassis without bodies, or V-16 chassis with V-8 roadster, reproduction roadster or reproduction sport phaeton bodies. Including the latter in the count would bring the total number of surviving cars and chassis to over 200.

If anyone wishes to know more about the original destination or body style of a specific car, feel free to write to me at 174 Fawn Valley Drive, McMurray, PA 15317. Give me the engine and body numbers, and I will send you whatever information I have about it. I can provide information on the later years as well as the early V-16s.

(Reprinted with permission from the December 1987 issue of *The Classic Car*, the official publication of the Classic Car Club of America.)

A Classic Cadillac saga

in two acts

By Terry Wenger

Terry Wenger's 1932 Cadillac town sedan.

Act I: The cars of Cadillac, vintage 1932:
A long look at the lineup

On Dec. 17 and 18, 1931, at the Cadillac National Convention in Detroit, the 1932 line of Cadillacs and LaSalles was introduced. Fifty-five cars were on display: 13 V-16s, 19 V-12s, 16 V-8s and seven LaSalles. The majority of available body styles was represented, well-equipped with accessories and painted in many color combinations.

A general description of these 1932 Cadillac and La-Salle models follows.

The various models were designated by the following series numbers: LaSalle, 345-B; Cadillac V-8, 335-B; Cadillac V-12, 370-B; and Cadillac V-16, 452-B. List prices ranged from $2,395 for the LaSalle two-passenger coupe to $5,945 for the V-16 Fleetwood Limousine-Brougham. The addition of accessories, options or custom Fleetwood bodies could boost the prices considerably.

LaSalles used Fisher bodies on 130-inch and 136-inch wheelbases. The Cadillac V-8 and V-12 cars used Fisher bodies on a 134-inch wheelbase, and both Fisher and Fleetwood bodies on a 140-inch wheelbase. The V-16 cars used body configurations similar to the V-8s and V-12s but their respective wheelbases were nine inches longer, at 143 and 149 inches. For the same body style, the base price of the V-8 was $400 more than LaSalle. The V-12 and V-16 options added another $700 and $1,700, respectively, to the V-8 cost.

The 1932 Cadillac was visibly different from its predecessor. Harley Earl's styling was more graceful with long, flowing fenders, radiused window corners and a new front ensemble. The last named incorporated the first true grille used by Cadillac. Thermostatic shutters were no longer visible, and a stoneguard was not necessary. There was no support bar crossing the grille between the headlights, only a grille-mounted medallion proclaiming the powerplant option and the name of the manufacturer. This medallion used a black background for the V-8, blue for the V-12, and red for the V-16—this color theme was also carried out on the hubcap emblems. A winged Cadillac crest graced the top of the radiator shell.

The LaSalle retained the traditional support bar with an "LaS" medallion mounted on it, across a similar grille.

The Cadillac headlights were smaller in diameter than previously and were bullet-shaped with a windsplit running along the top. To improve the lighting, three-filament bulbs were used to obtain four lighting positions, two driving and two passing. The windsplit theme was carried out on the parking lights, taillights, hood doors, and the radiator and gas filler caps. LaSalles used a larger diameter headlight with more conventional two-filament bulbs. All models had plain bar-type bumpers and topped the radiator cap with optional goddess or heron ornaments. Horns were placed under each headlight.

The gracefully curved fenders were joined by curved running boards to continue the fender line. Cadillac fenders were edged in a double bead which ran completely around the car, across the grille pan and the gas tank cover. To enhance the fender lines, the upper bead could be striped or the lower one could be painted a contrasting color.

The windshield was slightly slanted and was the last one which could be raised for ventilation. A new cowl vent was incorporated for additional comfort. The hood retained the vertical vent doors or "ports" as used on previous models. LaSalles featured five ports on each side, Cadillac eights and 12s used six ports per side, and the 16 had seven per side. These doors could be optionally chrome plated. The body sills on all models were curved similar to the coach sill used on the '30-31 V-16 4200 body styles.

In the rear, the taillights were shaped similar to those used on the earlier V-16 and used a small blue lens in the center of the red lens which called attention to the stop-

lights and doubled as the back-up light lens. California state law dictated that all California cars use a small red lens in place of the blue one.

Town sedans, town coupes and five-passenger convertibles used trunks contoured and attached to the body in contrast to the separate trunks used on earlier town sedans. The trunk rack, on cars equipped with side-mounted spares, featured a center medallion which denoted the power plant option on the Cadillac and an "LaS" on the LaSalle. The rack was framed in stainless steel and could be completely chromed as an option.

All models could be ordered with wood or wire wheels. The LaSalle and Cadillac V-8s used 7:00 x 17 tires; V-12s used 7:50 x 17 and the V-16 7:50 x 18. Whitewalls were standard on the Cadillacs, optional on the LaSalles. The wheels were of the new drop center variety, eliminating snap rings. Wire wheels came with a stainless trim ring on the Cadillac and could be decorated further with stainless spokes, chrome wheel covers or two-tone paint schemes. The specifications state that all-chrome or all-stainless steel wire wheels would not be supplied.

The 1932 models had standard recommended color schemes, but almost any color was available. Deviations from the standard carried additional costs; for example, fenders and chassis could be had in colors other than black for $50. Body striping was included at no charge in any color except gold or silver leaf which was $25 extra.

Interiors were available in mohairs, whipcords, broadcloths or leathers, depending on the body style or the owner's desires. Door panel and seat designs varied by series and body style. The dash positioned the instruments directly in front of the driver rather than in the center, as was previous practice; a storage compartment was placed on the right side. The dash was finished in black and capped with walnut moldings. Window frames and vanities were likewise fabricated of walnut and varied in design from model to model.

Mechanically, the 1932 models were similar to the 1931 cars. The major new features were a mechanical fuel pump to replace the vacuum tanks, free wheeling, and adjustable shock absorbers.

The 353 cubic-inch V-8 engine was increased 20 percent in output via redesigned manifolding and valve arrangement. Appearance was heightened by liberal use of chrome acorn nuts and other trim. Cylinder heads were smooth-surfaced, finished in black enamel or porcelain, fastened by chrome acorn nuts. The spark plug covers previously used were eliminated.

The 368 cubic-inch V-12 and the 452 cubic-inch V-16 were basically the same as the previous year's. The distributor cap now had the secondary wires exiting vertically; the wires were no longer hidden.

All Cadillac models used a firewall cover, as used on the 1931 V-12s and V-16s, to hide the normal bolts, nuts and stiffening ribs. This provided the compartment with a neater appearance. Plated lines and fittings were used liberally. Ignition coils were mounted on the firewall inside the car on the V-8 and in the radiator top tank on the V-12 and V-16.

Free-wheeling was incorporated into the clutch mechanism, controlled by a small pedal positioned below the clutch pedal. In addition to releasing the clutch through a vacuum cylinder for free-wheeling, it provided clutchless shifting, if desired, through vacuum valving controlled by the accelerator pedal. In many of the surviving 1932 cars, this mechanism has been removed and discarded.

The suspension system featured adjustable ride control through adjustable shock absorbers. The quality of the ride was controlled by a dash lever with a gauge to designate the ride chosen. The springs were metal-covered leaf type. The front was fitted with adjustable king pins.

Options available on the 1932 models were numerous and were featured in a booklet. Among the more notable ones were all-metal trunks, fitted luggage for both separate and built-in trunks, hot water and hot air (exhaust system) heaters, radio, six-wheel equipment, Fleetwood lap robes and pillows, Pilot Ray driving lamps, spotlights, wind wings and wheel covers.

The 1932 Cadillacs were virtually identical externally for all three series in the same body style; for example, a V-16 Fisher touring sedan looked identical to its V-12 and V-8 counterparts. The subtle differences were in the emblems and tire sizes. The V-16 had one obvious difference, a nine-inch longer hood. In 1931, all three series had been distinctive from one another; and from 1933 onward, the V-16 was styled differently from the V-8 and V-12.

Fleetwood could provide many body styles or modifications not listed in the 1932 price list. Examples of this would be the five-passenger convertible Victoria of which at least three were built, or the "Madame X" body styles, similar to the 1930-31 V-16 Madame X style, of which at least two are still in existence. Both of these styles appeared on the V-12 and V-16 series.

In 1932 the company produced the following cars:

LaSalle	345-B	V-8	3,386
Cadillac	355-B	V-8	2,693
	370-B	V-12	1,709
	452-B	V-16	296

After 1932, the classic styling would be abandoned, starting with the fender skirting of 1933 and progressing to the pontoon fenders and biplane bumpers of the 1934 models.

Beautiful hood ornament

Act II: From the state of Maryland to the Spirit of St. Louis: The tale of a town sedan

My first recollection of the use of the term "Classic Car" was in Robert Gottlieb's column, "Classic Comments," in *Motor Trend* magazine in 1953. His column and the "Sell and Swap" ads in the same publication sparked my enthusiasm for Classic cars.

Unfortunately, as a 10-year-old, it was impractical for me to purchase a Classic at that time. In fact, it would be some 14 years later that I purchased my first "Classic-to-be," a 1940 Cadillac 60 Special.

Over the years, I have developed a preference for the close-coupled sedan body style, known as a town sedan or a club sedan. This body style has a balanced look about it, especially if equipped with a trunk, and can be described as "semi-formal" with its blind-quarter roof styling.

While stationed in the service in Dover, N.J. in the late '60s, I developed an additional preference, following the opportunity to visit the late Paul Marut at his Parkside Motors restoration shop on several occasions. Paul had '32 and '33 Cadillacs in all conditions on the premises. I decided I would one day restore a similar car. Twelve years and several restorations later, that day would come.

In 1982, after selling a recently restored Packard, I began my search for a 1932 Cadillac town sedan. A short time later, I was fortunate to find a V-8 model and purchased it in "kit" form from Bill Coleman of Baltimore.

One June weekend in 1982, Spirit of St. Louis Region members Marc Ohm, Don Hoelscher and I went to get the car. My wife occasionally still reminds me how I left her, our two small boys and our newborn son for all of two days to get that "disaster" of a car. It was a body shell on the frame, accompanied by boxes and piles of parts.

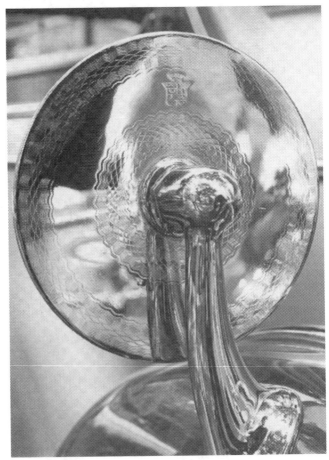
Rear of mirror.

Various stages of restoration.

The car had been disassembled for restoration nine years earlier. Some items had been purchased, some chrome and engine work had been done and then the restoration stopped. Prior to disassembly, the car had endured long outdoor storage. This had collapsed the top, causing complete destruction of the interior and rotting of the wood body frame.

After an inventory, the restoration commenced, to be completed four years later. I handled all phases of the car's restoration with the exceptions of chrome plating, striping and upholstery. The greatest challenge was the woodwork which was an all-new experience for me.

One of the most interesting aspects of the restoration was in the research and parts-locating phase. Over the four-year period, I amassed a three-inch stack of correspondence, diagrams, photos, etc. I am greatly indebted to Ted Raines of the Northern California Region, whom I bombarded with letters on such subjects as disassembly, assembly, and the correct colors of various pieces. He always found time to answer my numerous questions.

In the time that I owned the car, I have put together the following history. This 1932 Cadillac series 355-B town sedan no. 1200547, Body No. 101 was assembled in mid-January 1932, being first registered in Maryland on Feb. 1 of that year. It was originally black with Tokyo Ivory striping and wheels, and a taupe whipcord interior.

From the name written on the preliminary shop manual, which reportedly had always been with the Cadillac, I determined that the car was originally owned by Ray Pritchard, an employee of Chesapeake Cadillac Co. in Baltimore. A relative wrote that he drove it for four years.

Using Maryland registration cards accompanying the car, I learned that William Lockard purchased the vehicle in 1936 from Chesapeake Cadillac and kept it until 1956, when it was sold to Ephraim Vernon Young, Jr.

I could not determine the car's fate from 1957 to 1970, but in 1973 it was purchased by Bill Coleman from Neil Van Dyke of Glen Burnie, Md., who owned it for about three years. It would be interesting to know the whereabouts of the car from 1957 until 1970.

At some time, the car had been repainted the original black and had later sustained damage on both sides in the rear. The free-wheeling vacuum clutch mechanism was removed, probably in the '30s. I have found this typical on most '32s.

During the restoration, the spring coupling between the drive gear and the water pump was found to be broken. It is probable this is what removed the car from regular service.

In its restored condition, the car is painted original '32 colors of Grissette brown on the top, fenders and chassis, with the body lacquered in Stanford brown. The wheels

Rear view.

and striping are in medium cream. The interior is upholstered in taupe whipcord, as originally equipped.

The original cost with options is as follows.

1932 Cadillac V-8 Town Sedan, Model 32-8-252
. . . . $3,095.00
Colored fenders and chassis, Grissette Brown. . . . 50.00
Chrome hood parts. 21.00
6 wire wheels, fender wells, 2 spares and
    trunk rack 130.00
Two metal tire covers 37.00
2 tire cover mirrors 22.00
Goddess 20.00
Hot water heater. 37.50
Fender striping 10.00
Fleetwood lap robe. 45.00
Delivery est 70.00
Tax est 135.00
                                        $3,672.50

As of this writing, I have driven the car only a few hundred miles. It is a very nice driving and riding Cadillac, a joy to drive. Concerning the looks and styling of the car, I have read that the '32 Cadillac was Harley Earl's favorite: I fully agree.

(Reprinted with permission from the June 1987 issue of *The Classic Car*, the official publication of the Classic Car Club of America.)

Standard Catalog of Cadillac

Two giants were saved

1936 Cadillac Series 60 convertible coupe.

By Albert Dunkel

The early 1930s were an unforgettable period in the history of this country. The Great Depression was running rampant. Sales of expensive automobiles had hit new lows. Ford, Chevrolet and Plymouth were the biggest sellers, but poor sales records for Cadillac, Packard, Lincoln and Pierce-Arrow threatened the very existence of these venerable giants.

But, the concept of an ailing luxury car manufacturer being saved from an impending doom was soon to be demonstrated in some notable instances. In 1934, Packard was ready to throw in the towel. The company's line of senior cars was far too expensive to survive in those years. Their early attempt at building a moderately priced car, the Packard 900 in 1932, had not been met with much enthusiasm. During this time, however, Packard had on its drawing boards the plans for a car that had been conceived as early as 1933. It was a car that could give the company a much needed boost: the Packard 120.

The 120 was first introduced as a 1935 model, and the 110-hp straight eight with a 257.2-cubic-inch engine and 120-inch wheelbase was an overnight sensation. Sales of the 120 skyrocked in 1936 and 1937. Its success kept the company afloat at a crucial time when other carmakers were either going out of business or were sustaining losses from which they would never fully recover.

Then, along came the scoffers. Many people at that time, and even to this day, lament the introduction of the Packard 120. They complained that it wasn't a "real Packard." They forget that without the early 120s, the now highly coveted senior Packards made from 1935 through

the early 1940s, including the rare Darrin sports cars, would have never seen the light of day. And today, the junior Packards that saved the company in the '30s are themselves much sought after by car enthusiasts.

There was no attempt by the Packard Motor Car Co. to represent the 120 as a miniature Packard Super Eight or Twelve, or anything close to it. It was, however, an excellent car in the medium price field. *Consumers Research*, in its September 1935 Bulletin, rated it as first choice in the Group 6 Price Range ($1,045 to $1,245). It was the only car in that group to receive an A rating. In the March 1936 Bulletin, it rated Packard 120 as first choice in the Group 5 Price Range ($995 to $1095); and it was given an A rating for the second time.

Packard's eventual end was to come in 1958, but it would have come over 20 years earlier had it not been for the 120.

Just as Packard did an unexpected turnabout in 1935, Cadillac had some surprises coming up for 1936. Sales of the heavy, long wheelbased and traditionally costly Cadillacs were suffering, as were those of the pre-1935 Packards. There were reports that General Motors was considering phasing out Cadillac. Then, late in 1935 an all-new 121-inch wheelbase 125-hp Cadillac made its appearance. Known as the 1936 Series 60, it was the lowest-priced Cadillac since its four-cylinder days. The four-door sedan was priced at $1,695 at the factory, and was widely acknowledged to be a true Cadillac in quality and style—but on a smaller scale and with a much lower price. Advertising claimed it to be capable of 100 mph, with brilliant performance in the usual driving ranges.

CADILLAC
Series 60 Coupe

TRUST THE INSTINCT WHICH IMPELS YOU TO CHOOSE FROM

the Royal Family of Motordom

The natural impulse and instinct of most progressive and ambitious Americans is to own and drive a car by Cadillac. • • They usually have the feeling that the stamp of Cadillac means the removal of the last motoring doubt—the purchase of endless hours and miles of the most flawless travel attainable. • • It is wise and safe to follow an instinct so strong and deep-rooted, so natural and impulsive. Such judgments on the part of great groups of people are to be trusted. • • This is especially true now that the privilege and pride of Cadillac ownership are possible at the lowest prices in more than two decades. • • The satisfaction of rising above the rank and file of the best of motor cars is yours now, at figures which make the Royal Family of Motordom the paramount value of the time and the year.

Prices list at Detroit, and subject to change without notice. Special equipment extra. Available on G. M. A. C.'s new 6% Time Payments.

La Salle $1175

Cadillac $1645

CADILLAC
Fleetwood $2445

1936 Cadillac Series 60 coupe is showcased here.

It has long been my opinion that the 1936 Cadillac Series 60, with its all new 322-cubic-inch engine, was the early opening wedge in a spirited revival for Cadillac although the sale of 6,711 Series 60s was a far cry from the incredible sales record of 55,042 cars enjoyed by the 1936 Packard 120. The success of its high-performance V-8 engine was reflected by the adoption of the same engine by LaSalle in 1937, replacing the lower-powered straight eight used by LaSalle from 1934 through 1936.

Cadillac spent the next several years increasing and perfecting production of high-quality smaller cars. A period that culminated just a year before World War II with the all new 1941 models. Although Cadillac was still in the high-priced luxury car business with its Models 67 and 75, the smaller and popular-priced 346-cid 1941 car was the catalyst that finally sent Cadillac into orbit—a phenomenon that has prevailed through the years that followed. They were a 150-hp "hot rod" of the times. Their body design was one of understated beauty and elegance, and the performance of the smaller series cars equipped with a conventional 3-speed transmission was nothing short of superb. The same engine was used on all 1941 Cadillacs, including the massive Models 67 and 75. There were a few cosmetic changes for 1942 before assembly lines stopped because of the war. The popular acceptance of the 1941s motivated car-hungry buyers to wait in line for Cadillac when it resumed production of passenger cars in 1946.

Paralleling Packard's achievement with the 120, the introduction of a smaller and moderately priced car saved the Cadillac Division of General Motors from probable extinction in the 1930s. And their Model 61 five-passenger coupe cost only $1,345 at the factory in 1941! Cadillac sales for that year hit a record-breaking 66,103. The same basic engine was used through 1948.

One day in 1950, as I strolled through the Don Lee Cadillac agency used car lot in Los Angeles, I observed a '41 Model 62 sedan with a standard column shift transmission. It had been parked there by a Los Angeles surgeon, Dr. Roy Shipley. He was about to trade it in on a new Cadillac, and when I offered him the same amount that the agency would, he agreed to sell the car to me.

He invited me to go on a demonstration ride, boasting that the car would zoom up to 45 in low gear within a half block or so. Before I could dissuade him from exhibiting a driving practice which I regard as destructive to a car—the 50-year-old physician slammed his foot to the floor and made good his boast. I sat there gritting my teeth in anticipation of the rods flying right through the block. Apparently he either didn't do this too often, or the Cad engine and transmission were built to take it without harmful results—for during all of my ensuing years of ownership, the '41 performed flawlessly.

Today all 1941 Cadillacs continue to generate much interest. The 60 Special and Models 67 and 75 have attained status as Classics; and the smaller Models 61, 62 and 63 remain consistently popular with vintage car collectors. Compared to some of the current makes and models of cars coming out of Detroit and overseas, the 1941 Cadillac looks better to me than ever.

A lady & her car

By Dick & Roberta BeGuhn

This is the story of May Luchsinger, a civic leader of Monroe, Wis., and her unusual automobile. It is important to understand the unique experiences which caused May's strong character to develop, which, in turn, may have resulted in her decision to order a special-bodied one-of-a-kind automobile.

No trip to the state of Wisconsin is complete without a stop at the Idle Hour Mansion in Monroe, which has stood through six major wars and as many panics and depressions. This 17-room mansion is one of the finest examples of Wisconsin's century-old architecture. Of even greater interest to readers of this article, it was the home of May Luchsinger until she died in 1955.

May was the granddaughter of Arabut Ludlow, a Vermont orphan, a peddler of hardware and, ultimately, the first president of the First National Bank in Monroe. He built the mansion which was to be May's home in 1857. That it be able to withstand all extremes of weather was his specific directive to the architects, and obviously it was heeded. In 1965 the mansion stood directly in the line of the Palm Sunday tornado, but only three windows were blown out with resulting rain damage. This minimal damage was probably due to the strength of the walls. No expense had been spared to build this lovely home. The walls were constructed five bricks deep, the brick hauled 100 miles from Madison by ox cart. Today, visitors may view the original home, complete with May's original furnishings. The Idle Hour Mansion has been converted into a fine restaurant, which is now a historic attraction for southern Wisconsin connoisseurs.

Arabut Ludlow died in 1897, leaving his widow and five children. His wife died in 1913, and the mansion stood empty for a period of 24 years until May and her husband, who were living in New York at the time, took an interest in the house and spent $75,000 to rejuvenate and modernize it in 1935. Two years later, May's husband died. His widow would remain in Monroe and in this mansion until her death in 1955 at the age of 78.

May Luchsinger was a woman of boundless energy and diverse interests. She loved animals; the headstone of her favorite racing horse, Peter McKinley, can still be seen in the pet graveyard near Idle Hour Mansion. Among her many activities, May served in major offices of the National Woman's Relief Corps. She also served as a director of the bank for which both her father and husband had been president, directed the State Historical Society, was a member of the Board of Education of Monroe, and was honored by the Red Cross for her many contributions. As a widow, May continued to be an active member of her community. She most definitely was an unusual woman for her time. This is the point where the other major participant in our story emerges.

In 1937, the year her widowhood began, May ordered a Cadillac V-12 Fleetwood-bodied limousine coupe. Probably she needed a special car and chauffeur to continue her many community activities as well as those new obligations incurred as a result of her husband's death. The story is told that she desired Fleetwood coachwork, but did not want the long sedan typically associated with Fleetwood bodies. Monroe, a small Wisconsin town, was probably better suited to a coupe than the lengthier sedans or town cars.

Another unusual feature of May's special car was the seating arrangement, which clearly distinguishes it as a limousine coupe. The front passenger seat is not fully padded and hinges to fold up under the dash as a "jump

May Luchsinger's 1937 Cadillac V-12 limousine coupe looks good from any angle.

Below: May Luchsinger.
Right: Idle Hour Mansion.

seat." The seat was designed to be quite comfortable, however, for use by passengers. In the folded position, access to the large rear seat is very easy. In ordering her unusual car, May perhaps insisted upon the quality features provided by a Fleetwood body, but was bothered by the large size of limousines and preferred a less ostentatious model, at least in size. Another theory is that she needed to be seated nearer to her driver for conversation and instruction concerning the complicated daily scheduling of meetings and visitations. One can easily visualize May leaning toward the folded-down front seat to discuss the details of her daily civic rounds with her chauffeur. It is obvious that communication was immensely simplified when the seat was not in place. This would, of course, make last-minute changes easy to affect and save her the time of having to write everything out for her driver ahead of time.

How many women of the 1930s would have ordered a car to fit their needs or even have conceived of the idea? The average female of May's era would not have tried to change the accepted pattern of an automobile or anything else! May must have had very definite ideas about her role as a woman.

In 1956, when Tom Barrett purchased the Cadillac from May's estate, the odometer read 18,000 miles. It now registers 23,000. At some point, the car was repainted. The interior is original and in excellent condition, the cloth used by Fleetwood during this era being of a very good quality. The car has a factory-installed radio which works well. There is a large (12-inch diameter) speaker in the headliner between the visors, with the antenna mounted under the runningboard on the left side. The car has what looks to be a factory heater. There is a small fan mounted close to the engine fan to pull air through a chamber surrounding the exhaust manifold. Any car delivered in Monroe had to have some type of heater for the cold winters. The model number 37-7589 is not described in any manual or reference book. The body number is 1. The engine number is 4130468. The factory made 470 V-12s during 1937, the last model year for the 12. A new flathead V-16 followed in '38, and was produced for three years.

Interior of 1937 limousine coupe.

In studying Cadillacs of the mid-'30s, we find several interesting body styles. Our car in some ways resembles the aerodynamic coupes which followed the '33 World's Fair show car. These coupes were clearly a separate model. There were several 12s, several 16s and, we believe, one V-8. The aerodynamic coupes had such distinguishing features as rain gutters and front opening doors.

Close inspection of the metal work on our car indicates where the factory cut and welded the top section to make a coupe instead of a sedan. There must have been many hours of handwork involved to form the trunk section, rear quarter panels and interior. Apparently there were no parts of the standard coupe that could be used on this body. The wheelbase is 138 inches.

The V-12 engine runs very smoothly and cruises easily at interstate speeds. Its torque allows for extremely low speeds in third gear. We have read several articles attesting that the V-12 outperformed the early V-16 in dependability and smoothness. The 12 does take a back seat to the 16 in the matter of esthetics, however. The V-16 engine does not have exposed air cleaners or horn assemblies. (The air cleaners are smaller and on the carburetors.) The 16 also used a cleaner-looking exhaust system, each eight-cylinder bank exhausting individually. The 12-cylinder in this era directed the left bank over the top rear of the engine to join the right and exhaust together. Earlier 12s had used a dual exhaust system, and it remains a puzzle why such a system was not continued on the V-12. The V-16 was definitely less cluttered and is much easier to restore. We personally regard the Cadillac V-16 as second only to Duesenberg in engine compartment esthetics.

But a V-12 was the engine May Luchsinger requested in her Cadillac, and we will not quarrel with her decision. She was a lady who knew what she wanted. And we're proud of the thoroughbred history of the car she chose. At the 1986 Grand Classic in Indianapolis, May's car scored 98 points in the Primary Custom class. We like to think she would have enjoyed that.

(Reprinted with permission from the December 1986 issue of *The Classic Car*, the official publication of the Classic Car Club of America.)

Engine of 1937 limousine coupe.

May Luchsinger's unusual Cadillac V-12 limousine coupe.

"Magnificent" 1937 Cadillac advertisement.

1938 Cadillac Sixty Special five-passenger sedan.

Revolutionary car

By Ned Comstock

1938 Cadillac Sixty Special was a revolutionary car, a postwar car three years before Pearl Harbor, a car so different that it set auto styles for the next generation, and on top of new Cadillac engineering developed since 1935, Sixty Special style was the magic that turned General Motors into the King of the Castle.

The Sixty Special revolution was the right revolution. The ditches of the past were littered with the bones of earlier innovators, pioneers ahead of their time who died because they were. You could name them as well as I—Stutz, Marmon, Mercer, Wills St Claire, Cord—leaders nobody followed. But Sixty Special ran out in front like Man O' War, and the herd came thundering after.

Some artists who drew Cadillacs for the 1938 annual auto show magazines unwittingly predicted the success of the Special. They pictured the car as a larger edition of the standard Model 60s—rounded lines, slightly bulbous you might say, tiny windows and an all-over look something like a submarine. Maybe they were sketching a car they'd never seen (there were careful write-ups of 1941 LaSalles that never appeared) but more likely they didn't realize how different the car really was.

In this way Sixty Special fulfilled Phase One of its Destiny—it didn't ask the public to accept a new concept, the way for instance Lincoln-Zephyr did. The Special never broke continuity—it looked advanced but not different. It was traditional design but deftly modified, made more graceful by subtle changes that added up to a new car without the jolt of new departures. Conservatives could be comfortable (Many Sixty Specials were chauffeur driven), yet no other maker (except racy Graham) took such a bold styling step that year.

There had been only two cycles of Cadillac style before 1938—the matronly V-51 of 1914 gradually updated to 1925, and the high handsome 341's in 1928. In between came the swing years 1926-1927 which didn't fit either style school. Three forty-one carried on into the 1930s as well as any luxury car could in the Great Depression, but gradually it assumed the tear-drop trend started in 1932 by Reo and Graham. The logical conclusion of this tear-drop concept was a fat and homely vehicle as some of Cadillac's competition discovered too late. It was Cadillac's style triumph that called a halt at this point, and after another interim (Model 60, 1936 and 1937) began a new style cycle in 1938. This was Sixty Special. It was the fork in the road where Cadillac bore right.

Handsome did as handsome was. In 1935 Series 10, the last of the old school was basically 1927 engineering continued, which in turn had used the same bore and stroke since 1915. After an in-between year, Cadillac settled on the performance package that powered Sixty Special in 1938. With more bore and less stroke Cadillac did for the rich man what Henry Ford had done for the poor—introduced him to performance motoring.

The U.S. auto fleet was old and worn in 1937 after the long Depression. The new fast Fords were on the road in numbers, but most of what was going on was slow, with engine design rooted in the 1920s. When 1937 Cadillac, the standard Model 60 priced at $1,660 brought out the new 346-inch short-stroke engine in a car a thousand pounds lighter than its predecessor, it re-stated road performance in America.

Not only was the power multiplied but new gear ratios used it in new ways. Instead of slow slogging, second gear was designed for taking off. Instead of running out of revs after 50 miles an hour, 1937 Cadillac started to breathe deeply, then moved into a whole new performance cycle and set a new standard of the world. This performance was the other half of the Sixty Special revolution of 1938.

I remember to this day the first time I saw the Special in the parking lot at the Gold Club at home. The top half of the car looked light and fleet, the body long and heavy. Instead of round, everything looked square. The roof was flatter, the fenders jutted almost straight back. The windows and the windshield seemed enormous. The running boards were gone, the car was wide. The bulk of it had moved down closer to the road, in contrast to the old top-heavy stage coach sedans. The trunk seemed a natural part of the body. There was no belt moulding along the side, and this seemed strange, but restrained use of chrome trim added a touch of elegance to the black paint work. I spent a half hour inspecting it carefully. People left their cars unlocked in those days. I got in and tried the spacious seats, front and back. The view through the wide windshield seemed panoramic. The quality of fit and trim conveyed a delicious feeling of luxury, and the low-lying bulk meant to me power and security. I sat there a long time.

When I finally got out of the Sixty Special and faced the reality of the parking lot, a funny thing happened. All the other cars seemed strange—dowdy and out of date.

That was the real Sixty Special revolution.

Sixty Special was a '30s superstar

By Robert C. Ackerson

As applied to the automobile, that mode of expression known as styling derives its characteristics from the three basic sources. The first could be identified as the Archetypal Factor. This dictates that the shape of an automobile conform to certain mandates. For example, the stylist must provide space for an engine and if it is an automobile intended for mass use that he is dealing with, accomodations for some type of storage area must be provided. The automobile obviously cannot exceed certain limits of length, width and height. Thus, the stylist is not totally free to run rampant with designs but instead must to a degree operate within certain confines. In effect, it is the reality of that old truism; that form follows function that the automotive stylist must contend with.

Cultural consciousness is the second origin of the stylist's reservoir of inspiration. This influence explains why automobiles from various countries approach the identical problem, namely providing a vehicle capable of transporting humans from point A to point B and arrive at radically different solutions. The Gallic Mind provides the Citroen CX, that of the German Volkswagen Rabbit and the American mentality, an Oldsmobile Cutlass Supreme. All three are classic examples of their society's preference for particular shapes and spatial relationships.

The final element of the stylist's craft is by far the rarest. It is perhaps best described as an ability to transcend the ordinary and create a new form of expression that in the case of an automobile rearranges the relationship of its components but yet does not abandon certain crucial elements of proportion and principle that past masters have perfected.

Men with this type of extraordinary talent are the creators of automobiles with styling that passes the severest test of all time. They stand with the firmness of granite against the vicissitudes of fads, and cultural whims to eventually assume the status of a classic design. The importance of technical excellence in Cadillac's 75-year history cannot, of course, be understated. Yet certainly as influential in the creation and maintenance of Cadillac's position as one of the world's outstanding automobiles has been its styling. It is common knowledge that Cadillac styling of the past 50 years has borne the influence primarily of two men, Harley Earl and William Mitchell.

Not surprisingly, the results of both men's first major assignment at General Motors established styling trends for General Motors and for the entire industry. It was Harley Earl's design for the 1927 LaSalle that literally brought General Motors out of styling's Dark Ages and into industry leadership, a position that withstanding a few slips along the way it has never relinquished. Eleven years later it was Bill Mitchell's turn to break the bonds of tradition and the status quo with the 1938 Cadillac 60 Special. To place this car in its proper historical perspective without doing it dishonor is no easy task, so great was its styling influence upon the American automobile.

In the late 1930s the economic and social changes of the Great Depression and the New Deal had created an egalitarian attitude in the United States that tended to reduce the social acceptability of such forms of conspicuous consumption as the chauffeur-driven automobile. There was still a market for such items of course and in fact in 1938 Cadillac introduced a new version of its V-16 engine for use in the traditionally sized luxury automobile. (It's interesting to ponder if President Carter's de-

1938 Cadillac Sixty Special four-door.

cision to walk to his inaugural parade instead of riding in the Presidential limousine along with his energy program signals the start of its final demise). While Cadillacs for 1936 reflected the trend toward a less ostentatious display of wealth, it was with the 60 Special that Cadillac introduced a wholly new concept of the American luxury automobile. Like Earl's 1927 LaSalle, the 60 Special appealed not only to male drivers but to women who also appreciated a trim, lean and responsive automobile. Unlike the LaSalle which carried overtones of the Hispano-Suiza the 60 Special borrowed nothing from any other automobile. Mitchell's master touch imparted unto the 60S a sense of virtually perfect proportions. Nothing seemed out of place. There were no mishappen forms or unneccessary trim to mar its unencumbered shape.

Mitchell relied upon several key elements to produce what he knew was going to be a winner. The use of chrome trim around the side windows gave the 60 Special a light, quasi-convertible appearance without conveying to the observer (and potential customer) an impression of fragility. This sporting image was accentuated by the 60 Special's bullet-shaped fenders, which at the time were referred to as "suitcase" fenders. The lack of a chrome belt molding and the addition of a ribbed chrome strip where the running board had formerly been added to the 60 Special's outstanding appearance.

Where the 60 Special shone as a major link in the automobile's styling evolution was in its treatment of that necessary but troublesome appendage to its body, the trunk. Prior to the 60 Special, the trunk was treated at best as an addition to the automobile's overall design; at worst it was viewed as a necessary nuisance. Mitchell perceived it as part of the body itself, a fully integrated element of an automobile's styling, of no less significance to the stylist than fenders, roof line or grille work. This solution to the trunk problem plus Mitchell's separation of the body into distinct upper and lower forms resulted in the 60 Special being the first manifestation of what has been called notchback styling, which in modified form has been adopted by every American automotive manufacturer. These features plus a three-inch drop in height from the 1937 models (made possible by a new "double drop" frame), larger windshield and narrow window pillars gave the 60 Special an appearance not only extremely attractive but one distinctive among its contemporaries as well.

Historians have often divided along partisan lines on the question of how much influence the 60 Special exerted upon the Lincoln-Continental and Packard Clipper. When asked his opinion on this subject David Holls of General Motors Styling felt that the 60 Special's role in the Lincoln-Continental's design has been greatly overrated. Noting that they were "just two different kinds of automobiles" Holls added that "there isn't a great deal that's really similar between the two except their side window arrangement and mutual lack of running boards." In contrast, Maurice D. Hendry concludes in his *Cadillac The Complete Seventy-Five Year History* that the 60 Special styling innovations had a "doubtless" influence upon the Lincoln-Continental.

The impact of the 60 Special's styling upon the Packard Clipper is fairly well substantiated by a memo that was prepared by Packard's engineering department. Entitled "Notes on Packard's Styling Problem" this document includes the thought that while Packard had been successful in styling the Clipper it was General Motors that had to be given credit for initiating the basic design concept. The conclusion that they are referring to the 60 Special seems safe to make.

With production reaching 3,703 for the 1938 model run, the 60 Special was Cadillac's best-selling model. By comparison only 2,051 Series 60 Cadillacs on a 124-inch wheelbase (3 inches shorter than the 50s) were built. LaSalle, which has been unjustly labeled "Cadillac's only failure", reached a production figure exceeding 15,000.

The 1939 and 1940 versions of the 60s remained substantially unchanged except for new grille work which featured a main grille of thin horizontal chrome bars flanked by vertical "catwalks."

In 1941 all Cadillacs with the exception of the 60s received all-new bodies featuring the low, wide egg crate grille work that was destined to become a mainstay of Cadillac's postwar styling motif. The 60 Special received a major styling updating that included new front fenders extending into the front door area, and the new front grille work common to all models in the Cadillac line. The end result was the ultimate refinement of Mitchell's original design, a car certainly qualifying as one of the most attractive automobiles ever manufactured in the United States.

Contrasting sharply with this masterpiece was the 1942 60 Special, which was in effect nothing more than a production Series 62 sedan with several regiments of meaningless vertical chrome bars encamped on its front and rear fenders. As a member of GM styling has noted, "the designers lamented that car";—enough said about the 1942 60 Special. There was a beautiful all-new proposal for the 60 Special that was unfortunately shelved.

The Dark Ages for the 60S came to an end in 1948 when its proper status as a Cadillac with its own individualistic personality was restored. Indeed 1948 represents the Renaissance of the 60 Special. After this date there were still some sad moments for the 60 Special, such as its 1958 version with its monstrous rear end of chrome and finny excess. Yet with the passage of time, the concept of the 60 Special has remained a key point in Cadillac's marketing philosophy. In 1957 the Eldorado Brougham, while not having the same visual impact of the original 60S, was still cast in its mold as a quality automobile designed for the individual who enjoys driving a responsive motor car. Similarly the Seville, which has too often been described as European in origin, is really both in style and concept the heir apparent to the 60 Special.

The story of the 60 Special contains a certain degree of irony in that the car that became the 60 Special began as a LaSalle. It was not until the prototype stage was reached that the decision was made to have it wear the Cadillac coat of arms. Naturally, one wonders what would have been this fine design's fate if that change had not been made. Would it have given the LaSalle a new lease on life or would it have been cast into oblivion by the LaSalle's demise? But these questions really represent only the makings of casual conversation between car buffs on a cold mid-February evening. The 60 Special was built, to paraphrase one of Cadillac's great ads, because it deserved to be built. As David Holls told this writer, "nobody can see the 60 Special and not be interested in its styling."

1939 Sixty Special touring sedan

Chrome-plated front parking lights are a trademark of the 1940 Cadillac V-16s. The Derham five-passenger coupe was the only full-custom style offered that season. (Photo courtesy Merle Norman Classic Beauty Collection.)

One-of-a-kind Cadillac

There has always existed a certain group of auto buyers willing to pay a premium to have a car with extra cylinders under its hood. In the early days of automobile history, it took two cylinders to accomplish this end, while Jaguar buyers of current times can achieve their goal with twelve. In the golden era of the 1930s, 16 was the magic number.

Cadillac Motors' first V-16 appeared in 1930; rather poor timing in light of the stock market crash of '29. But, of course, O.M. Nacker started the V-16 development program years earlier, when it seemed there might be many customers interested in these fabulous machines.

As things turned out, by 1934, fewer than 60 Cadillac V-16s were being produced each model year and sales for 1935 through 1937 were 50, 52 and 49 units, respectively. More than a few observers predicted the line would soon disappear due to the small number of deliveries.

But, the Cadillac 16 meant more than just sales. It was an image maker—a symbol of superiority among prestige cars. And weighing cost effectiveness against public perceptions of greatness, Cadillac paid the "penalty of leadership" by introducing a completely new, 16-cylinder power plant for 1938.

This motor came to be known as the "square" V-16 because of its 3 1/4-inch bore and stroke measurements. It weighed 250 pounds less than the earlier power plant and was one-half foot shorter and over a foot lower. A low deck angle of 135-degrees separated the cylinder banks. Displacement was given as 431 cubic inches, compared to 452 in the first V-16. However, the horsepower rating, at 185 bhp, was the same.

It was of monobloc construction, meaning that the design incorporated what were really two straight-eight motors sharing a common crankshaft. Each "block" had its own distributor, fuel line, carburetor, intake and exhaust manifold and ignition system.

Cadillac's V-16 powered "Ninety" series offered 12 different semi-custom models, all of which were built on a 141 1/4-inch wheelbase chassis. Features included synchromesh transmission, hydraulic brakes and 7.50 x 17-inch tires. Gearshifting was accomplished via a lever that entered the steering post and connected with a rod that ran through the column, down to the gearbox.

The bodies provided with the V-16 were the same as on other Cadillacs from the cowl back but front end sheet metal and trim were exclusive to the big-engined cars. The treatment included a verticle, egg-crate grille, new goddess hood ornament, fender mount parking lamps and horizontal "speedline" beading on the sides of the hood and fenders.

Our feature car is a 1940 Series 90 five-passenger coupe with an unusual, streamlined body built by Derham of Rosemont, Pa. It is an example of the only full-custom model offered by Cadillac on the 1940 Series 90 V-16 chassis. Most cars used the semi-custom coachwork created by Fleetwood.

The car is painted shimmering Ruby Red and has a tan padded roof fitted by Derham. The interior is upholstered in an elegant patterned French mohair fabric. Options include white sidewall tires, covered dual sidemount spares with accessory rear view mirrors, front bumper guard and overdrive transmission. It is a senior Classic, having won first in class at the Classic Car Club's mid-winter meet in Buck Hill Falls, Pa.

The car is part of a collection formed by J.B. Nethercutt, chief executive officer of Merle Norman Cosmetics and is regularly on display at the Merle Norman "Tower of Beauty," a corporate collection of functional fine art located in San Sylmar, Calif. It was driven from southern California to the mid-winter meet and continued from there to Kenora, Ontario, Canada. During the trip, the V-16 ran as smooth as a watch and was said to perform "even better than present-day cars."

A tale of two Cadillacs

By Bill Siuru

Dwight D. Eisenhower and George S. Patton Jr. are probably the most well-known personalities of World War II. Besides being famous Army generals, they had something else in common. They left behind Cadillacs with interesting stories.

While Patton is usually depicted as riding across France and into Germany in a Jeep, he also had a 1938 Cadillac at his disposal. Story has it that the car had been shipped to France prior to the war and was taken captive by German occupation forces when they over-ran France. It was left behind as the Germans retreated and was subsequently commandeered by Patton. The Cadillac was a Series 75 Fleetwood Model 7533 seven-passenger Imperial sedan with a sliding glass partition. Records show that some 479 of this model were produced in 1938.

Patton was the ultimate soldier, and faced the prospects of a postwar career in civilian life with great uncertainty. Indeed, he often said "the proper end for the professional soldier is a quick death inflicted by the last bullet of the last battle." However, Patton met his fate not by that last bullet, but while riding in the 1938 Cadillac.

Patton's view of his postwar future took on an almost death wish aura, which on several occasions in 1945 was almost fulfilled. These brushes with death included near misses when his Piper Cub was mistakenly attacked by an inexperienced Free-Polish pilot flying a RAF Spitfire, his speeding Jeep nearly collided with an ox cart, and a minor car accident from which he escaped with minor injuries.

On Dec. 9, 1945, Patton was riding in his Cadillac on his way to do some pheasant hunting in the German countryside. His driver momentarily took his eyes off the road to look at some demolished vehicles that Patton was pointing out to another general riding in the car. In that instance, the truck the Cadillac was following slowed down to make a turn. General Patton's driver, seeing the truck, slammed on the brakes and swerved to miss the truck. But it was too late and the Cadillac collided with the truck. While it was a rather minor accident with only the front end of the Cadillac suffering

Gen. Eisenhower's 1942 Cadillac was presented to him after restoration while he was President of the United States. (Photo courtesy of Eisenhower Library.)

damage, Patton did not fare so well. He was severely injured with a broken neck that left him paralyzed from the neck down. On Dec. 21, Patton died from his injuries.

After the accident, the car was repaired and was used by Army VIPs until 1951. The repairs were quite interesting. While the Cadillac was a 1938 model, the front end was restored using parts from another 1939 Series 75 car that was found in France. Thus the car that now is displayed at the Patton Museum of Cavalry and Armor at Fort Knox, Ky. is deceiving. It looks like a 1939 model; however, the Cadillac buffs will quickly see that it is really a 1938 model. And even the repairs did not duplicate those found on 1939 Cadillacs.

When Eisenhower was running the show in Europe, he used a 1942 Cadillac 75 sedan. The car was painted the typical Army olive drab for camouflage purposes, and accessories included a siren and a red warning light on the left side. The siren was seldom used because of Eisenhower's dislike of sirens.

After the war, the car served Eisenhower when he was chief of staff of the Army. When he was president of Columbia, it was still at Ike's disposal for, as five-star general, he was still on active duty but without a specific assignment. When Eisenhower later became the Supreme Commander of Allied Forces in Europe, that car was shipped to his Paris headquarters after its O.D. paint was replaced by a shiny black paint job. Finally, in 1956, the car was retired and put up for auction. By now the car had 200,000 miles on the odometer, and there was 67,000 miles on its third flathead V-8 engine.

Knowing Ike's endearment to the car, it was purchased anonymously at the auction by some of his friends. It was then shipped back to the Cadillac plant in Detroit and restored to its original condition, including the O.D. paint scheme. On March 13, 1957, the car was presented to Eisenhower on the steps of the White House. On seeing the car, Ike remarked that the car looked like it was ready for a 50,000-mile journey, and the scratches he had remembered on last seeing the car were gone. The car was then shipped to its new home at the Dwight D. Eisenhower Library in Abilene, Kan.

Gen. Patton's 1938 Cadillac 75 as it now appears after being repaired from the accident that took his life. The car now looks like a 1939 model. (Photo courtesy of Patton Museum.)

'41 Cadillac convertible: streamlined beauty!

With its advanced, torpedo type body styling, the '41 Cadillac convertible was a streamlined beauty. It had a highly sophisticated, modern appearance with a great deal of genuine eye appeal.

New design details included a rounded, "coffin-nose" hood, flush mounted "horizontal" headlamps and a wide, chrome radiator grille. Heavier bumpers with curved ends incorporated a streamlined grille guard that extended between the front bumperettes. A valance panel was used between the bumper and front end sheet metal for the first time.

The doors of all Cadillacs opened from the rear on fully concealed hinges. The gas filler tube was also concealed behind a "trap door" on the rear fender. Fender skirts were standard equipment on all Deluxe models.

Cadillac's only convertible coupe came exclusively in Deluxe trim. It was part of the 62 series. This was the last Cadillac ragtop to feature a blind quarter top design. Subsequent convertibles would come with rear quarter windows.

Designated body style 41-6267D, the convertible carried its serial number and engine number (both the same) on the right-hand side of the chain case, in front of the generator. Numbers 8340001 to 8364734 were used on cars in the 62 series. Total series production included 3,100 convertibles.

That indicates strong sales for this body style. 1941 may have been the year that the company discontinued both the V-16 and the LaSalle, but handsome new models—like the 62 convertible—kept Cadillac in first place among America's luxury car builders.

1941 Cadillac convertible.

Anniversary time at Cadillac

By Robert C. Ackerson

Forty-three years ago, on Oct. 22, 1948, Cadillac introduced the modern overhead-valve V-8 engine to American motorists.

In announcing the new V-8 as the "greatest automobile engine ever built," Cadillac clearly recognized that this was a pivotal event, one marking the onset of a new era of performance and motoring excitement.

Like so many other automobile projects, it's probable that Cadillac's ohv V-8 would have reached the production stage far sooner than 1949 if not for World War II. In the mid-'30s, Cadillac was investigating alternatives to its existing line of V-8, V-12 and V-16 engines that would be both less expensive to produce and able to take advantage of the knowledge amassed by Boss Kettering's research into high-octane fuel development.

In describing this time span to prospective customers, Cadillac, in 1949, explained: "As far back as 1936 Cadillac engineers foresaw the direction automotive power should take toward lighter, more powerful, high-compression engines. Their own experience indicated that these engines should be of V-type ... From 1936 to late 1941, experiments were made with virtually all types of design. By Pearl Harbor, certain basic facts had been learned; several experimental models had been made. During the war the project had to be shelved but was revived immediately after V-J Day. In late 1945, first test engines were undergoing block tests—meanwhile basic research, in the typical Cadillac tradition, was going forward. Out of 12 years of effort, America's finest automotive engine was developed and is now presented in the 1949 Cadillac."

Cadillac took every possible measure to make certain that customers would be satisfied with the new engine. Before the first 1949 models were produced, the V-8s accumulated over one million miles of road use. In one test a production model V-8 was pitted against an experimental model in a 100-hour endurance run at 4250 rpm at wide open throttle. At the test's conclusion, there was no appreciable wear on any engine parts nor had there been any mechanical failures. On four different occasions Cadillac V-8s were subjected to a 25,000 mile test cycle at the GM proving ground that exposed them to every conceivable strain and hazard including sustained high-speed runs, pulling tests on grades as steep as 27 percent, runs over muddy roads and water baths.

At the conclusion, Cadillac reported: "Those who know best—test drivers and experimental engine specialists—say without reservation that the new Cadillac engine is more powerful, more durable, more economical than any stock engine ever built, including the great previous Cadillac engines."

At one point, prototype models had displaced just 309 cubic inches. If adopted for production, this would have been uncomfortably close in size to Oldsmobile's new 303 cubic-inch V-8. Instead, Cadillac went to 331 cubic inches, a size that would remain unchanged until 1956 when displacement was increased to 365 cubic inches.

Compared to the old 346-cubic-inch V-8, the new V-8 was superior in virtually every category. In terms of weight it was, at 699 pounds, almost 190 pounds lighter. Its far smaller physical size released designers from many of the constraints imposed upon them by the bulk of older engines. Although the ohv V-8 would eventually have a compression ratio of 10.5:1 (as well as a displacement of 429 cubic inches in 1967, its final year of production), it began with a mild ratio of 7.5:1. This was only marginally higher than the L-head's 7.25:1. While there wasn't a dramatic distinction in the power ratings of the two engines, their specifications differed in many respects:

	1948 Engine	1949 Engine
Bore x Stroke:	3.50 in x 4.50 in.	3.8125 in. x 3.65 in.
Displacement:	346 cu. in.	331 cu. in.
No. of main bearings:	3	5
Horsepower:	150 @ 3400 rpm	160 @ 3800 rpm
Torque: (al.-ft.)	283 @ 1600 rpm	312 @ 1800 rpm

1949 Cadillac Coupe deVille and 1989 Coupe deVille.

1949 Cadillac Coupe deVille.

Cadillac's initial performance claims for its 1949 models were modest. The new model, it reported, would reach 80 mph from rest in 30 seconds. In contrast a typical low-priced American sedan, such as the 1949 Ford 6, needed 36.8 seconds. Compared to the 1948 model's 16.3-second time, the 160-hp Cadillac accelerated from zero to 60 mph in 13.4 seconds. This performance wasn't quite matched by the test of a 1949 Series 62 sedan by England's *The Motor*, which reported the following acceleration times in its March 2, 1950 issue:

0-30mph	5.1 sec.
0-40mph	7.8 sec.
0-50mph	11.6 sec.
0-60mph	15.8 sec.
0-70mph	20.7 sec.
0-80mph	31.7 sec.
Standing start 1/4 mile	20.0 sec.
Top Speed	99.7 mph.

Nonetheless *The Motor* was extremely impressed with the Cadillac, describing it as "a vehicle manifestly intended to cover long distances at a high speed..." Recognizing the Series 62 sedan as one of the less expensive Cadillac models, *The Motor* concluded its analysis by noting: "Viewed in this light the car offers astonishing value for money. It has a performance which few makes can rival, even fewer surpass, a general silence of running (incuding low wind noise), which many will consider unbeaten, and an ease in driving which must be a great asset when very long mileages are attempted."

In recent times, Cadillac's image has suffered some self-inflicted wounds such as the ill-fated V-4-6-8 engine and the less-than-spectacular Cimarron. But in 1989, with the demise of the Cimarron, Cadillac commemorated the 40th anniversary of its revolutionary ohv V-8 by once again becoming an all V-8 car company.

Cadillac also recognized 1989 as the 40th anniversary of the first Coupe deVille, of which just 2,150 were built in 1949. Seven years later, the first four-door Cadillac hardtop, the Sedan deVille, was introduced. With sales of over 41,000 units, it became Cadillac's best selling model.

To date, more than 4.6 million Coupe deVille and Sedan deVille models have been sold making them the best selling nameplate of Cadillac's history.

Postwar pace-setting '49 Cadillac

By R. Perry Zavitz

The 1949 Cadillac was the first car to embody the significant elements to be found in the typical postwar family car. In 1948 Cadillac along with Oldsmobile 98 became the first of the Big Three to offer postwar restyling. However, the 1949 model went further in Cadillac's postwar reconstruction program. It introduced the modern V-8 engine.

All Cadillacs for 1949 were powered by a newly designed V-8 motor. Cadillac had been in the V-8 business since their 1915 models—much longer than anyone else. Except for its V-8 configuration, the new power plant was hardly similar to its predecessors.

The previous engine was of L-head design. The new one had overhead valves with hydraulic valve lifters. Compression ratio was 7.5 to 1. The former engine had a rather orthodox 3 1/2-inch bore and 4 1/2-inch stroke. The cylinders of the 1949 engine were over-square—the bore greater than the stroke. The bore was 3-13/16 inches. (Seldom in countries not using metric measure are increments of less than 1/8th inch used in bore or stroke dimensions.)

Although Oldsmobile introduced a similar V-8 in some models at about the same time, it was smaller and about 6% less efficient on a horsepower-per-cubic-inch basis, than Cadillac. The famous Charles Kettering headed the research on the Olds engine. However, it is said that Cadillac developed its engine independently of Oldsmobile.

These were the first mass-produced high-speed, highcompression, overhead-valve, over-square engines; now common place in North American cars whether V-8 or six.

The ad men who prepared the 1949 Cadillac catalog made strong statements in describing the new engine. "Cadillac presents its greatest engineering achievement in 45 years" they said, and concluded prophetically...... "Cadillac has given the world a new standard for automotive engines."

That engine served Cadillac extremely well. It underwent only minor changes, mostly to increase size and raise compression. After it had grown to 390 cubic inches with a compression ratio of 10.5 to 1, it was honorably discharged at the end of the 1963 model year. During its fourteen years of service, its horsepower doubled to 325. It powered more than 1,800,000 Cadillacs—about twice the number of all Cadillacs built before it appeared!

The 7.5:1 compression ratio was the highest in the industry in 1949. It was high for the around 88 octane gasoline then. One way in which Cadillac's engine reacted to the fuel of the day was clearly demonstrated in the Mobil Gas Economy Run of 1950.

In that contest, Mercury captured most of the publicity with the best showing of ton miles per gallon (a formula taking into consideration the weight of the car and its load, as well as distance travelled). Three of the four Cadillacs in the run finished second, third and fourth best ton miles per gallon in the 751-mile course. In actual miles per gallon, the same three Cadillacs gave the sec-

1949 Cadillac Coupe deVille.

Jewels by Cartier

Cadillac

White Sidewall Tires available at extra cost.

In the illustration shown above, the famous Alexander II Emerald Necklace is photographed with the Cadillac crest, in a position to resemble the renowned Cadillac "V." This matchless jewel—from the vaults of Cartier—is symbolic in its rarity with Cadillac's unique standing among the world's motor cars. For almost half a century, Cadillac has had but a single manufacturing purpose: to build as fine a motor car as it is practical to produce. The fruits of this unparalleled policy have never been so golden as they are today. The new Cadillac is not only the world's most beautiful and distinguished motor car—but its performance is a challenge to the imagination. For it is powered by Cadillac's creative masterpiece— a wholly new, V-type, eight-cylinder engine. From silken start to silken stop—the car performs almost as if it had automatic propulsion. Regardless of the price class from which you expect your next car to come, you owe it to yourself to see and inspect the new Cadillac. A study of its virtues will give you a better yardstick for measuring the value of all motor cars.

★ CADILLAC MOTOR CAR DIVISION ★ GENERAL MOTORS CORPORATION ★

Cadillac often used jewels in its advertisement, as illustrated by this 1949 ad.

1949 Cadillac Series 62 fastback

ond, third and fourth best results of the eight-cylinder cars between 22 and 23 mpg.

Of course, Cadillac owners are usually not penny pinchers at the petrol pumps. For them, the new engines showed its performance in other ways. The 1949 Cadillac could go from 0 to 80 within 30 seconds. Top speed nudged 100 mph.

Cadillac offered four lines in 1949. In the Series 61 line was a club coupe and a four-door sedan. Incidentally, that sedan coupe with a fastback had a factory list price of $2,788. The Series 62 included a convertible as well as a club coupe and a four-door sedan. Wheelbase on the Series 61 and 62 was 126 inches. Overall length at 215 inches was one to four inches less than today's full size Chevrolet, Ford, and Plymouth.

As was customary for so many years, the Fleetwood 60 Special was a one car series—a four-door sedan. It was distinguishable from the lesser models by a more restrained and tasteful use of chrome. Its wheelbase was 133 inches, and overall length 226 inches was the longest in 1949.

The Fleetwood Series 75 surprisingly offered five models on its 136-inch wheelbase. These limousines included a five-passenger sedan, seven-passenger sedan,

seven-passenger Imperial sedan, nine-passenger sedan and nine-passenger Imperial sedan. Because of its short trunk, the 75 was one inch shorter than the 60 Special, despite its long wheelbase.

The styling of the Fleetwood 75 models remained practically unchanged from 1947 through the '48 and '49 seasons.

The 1949 Coupe deVille offered a choice of grey-blue or brown interiors of cloth and leather to harmonize with the many exterior color choices. The front seat was hydraulically adjustable and the windows were hydraulically operated, as with the Series 62 convertible. The Coupe deVille top for 1949 was different from subsequent models.

The style, which featured full height front fenders blending into the sides and rear fenders, the fins, the curved windshield; the overhead-valve, over-square, high-compression, high-speed, V-8 engine; the hardtop; the automatic transmission all combined to make the 1949 Cadillac a unique car. It was the first car to package all these features throughout its entire line (Series 75 styling excepted). In so doing, Cadillac became the standard of the postwar world.

When Eldorado began

1953 Cadillac Eldorado convertible.

By R. Perry Zavitz

Some years go down in the automotive history books as very important because they brought us outstanding cars. One of those years was 1953. Several new car lines were introduced that model year. While small automaker Packard introduced its Caribbean model, giant General Motors fielded no less than four new models—Corvette, Fiesta, Skylark and Eldorado.

While car models come and go, two of those 1953 cars have survived the ups and downs of the last 36 years in the tough automotive world. Of course, they are the Corvette and Eldorado. Let's look at those earliest Eldorados.

When the 1953 Cadillac Eldorado was introduced, it could have slipped unnoticed by some not-so-hip people. They might have thought it was the 1953 edition of the Series 62 convertible. Actually, it was based on the 62 convertible, but there were subtle differences that made this car quite outstanding.

The first Eldorado had a wraparound windshield, unlike the other 1953 Cadillacs. The belt line made a dip near the door handle, like the door tops of the British sports cars, but not as extreme. On other Cadillacs the door line was straight. When the Eldorado's top was down, there was a metal cover that hid the top. That gave it a much cleaner, sleeker look than the other convertibles, even with a top cover in place.

Wire wheels were a popular option in 1953, but on the Eldorado they came as standard equipment. On other Cadillac models, a set of these wheels raised the price $325. This was just one feature on the long list of

items that normally cost extra on other cars, but came standard on Eldorado.

Leather upholstery, radio, heater, windshield washer, Hydra-Matic transmission, power steering, oil filter, white-wall tires and chrome license plate frames were some of the items that came at no extra cost. Of course, the buyer paid for all this in the car's base price.

Here is perhaps the biggest Eldorado difference. Its price was $7,750. Today that would hardly cover the down payment on a new Cadillac, but in 1953 it was almost enough to buy two Series 62 convertibles. With that hefty tariff, it is no surprise that only 532 Eldorados were made in its initial year.

Despite that, Eldorado returned in Cadillac's 1954 lineup. Some changes occurred, however. It was little more than a fancy Series 62 convertible. The door line dipped very slightly, but so did the other 1954 two-door Cadillac hardtops and convertible. The wraparound windshield was now found on all the other Cadillacs. But the still had the metal cover (or boot) for the lowered convertible top.

Standard equipment now included power brakes and two-way power seat. The short list of options included tinted glass, headlight dimmer and four-way power seat. The base price dropped considerably, but at $5,875 it was still quite steep. However, it was now within the reach of more buyers. Consequently, production increased to 2,150.

Production rose to 3,950 Eldorados for 1955. While the car got most of the styling changes applied to the other Cadillacs for the year, its rear styling was totally different. The taillights were no longer stuck in the top of the fins. Instead, a simple round taillight was set on the outside of the fins. On the inner sides, round backup lights matched the taillights, giving a double barrel appearance. The fins themselves were unlike those on the other Cadillacs. They were thinner and straight on top—not having the kickup at the end.

The wire wheels were no longer used. Instead, so-called "sabre spoke wheels" appeared on the Eldorado. The rear fenders had larger openings to better show off these lovely wheels.

Another Eldorado difference was the engine. Cadillac's remarkable ohv, short-stroke V-8 engine had grown in potency from 160 hp in 1949 to 250 in 1955. For the first time in the postwar period, Cadillac offered two versions of its engine. By attaching a second four-barrel carburetor, 20 additional horsepower were obtained. This 270-hp engine was standard in the Eldorado, but available in the other Cadillacs.

For 1956, power was increased again. Another postwar first was a displacement increase. By extending the bore to a full four inches, the displacement rose to 365 cubic inches. Thus, power for the Eldorado became 305 hp—still 20 more than the other Cadillacs.

The price rose from $6,296 in 1955 to $6,556. The Eldorado now offered a two-door hardtop as well, and oddly enough, its price was the same as the convertible. Convertible production of the 1956 model dropped to 2,150. That was the bad news. The good news was that there were 3,900 hardtop Eldorados built, just 50 less than 1955's convertible-only production.

To help distinguish them (though perhaps it caused confusion), the two Eldorados were given different additional names. The convertible was dubbed Biarritz and the hardtops were called Seville—a name Cadillac has been using on other models in recent years.

New styling was introduced on the 1957 Cadillacs. The regular models received a back end appearance which was somewhat like the 1955-56 Eldorados. So, to keep an exclusive appearance, the 1957 Eldorado got a different looking backside. It was quite rounded, but topped with thin fins. Single, round and rather small taillights were located in the body directly below each fin. Back-up lights were situated beside the exhaust outlets in the bumper, which was quite distinctive. It appeared to be in two parts. The license plate was mounted in a chrome trimmed insert in the wide space separating the two visible bumper sections.

At the front end, the grille could be ordered in a gold color. A brief fad was at its height in 1957, whereby buyers could order gold anodized grilles on several cars. The Eldorado was one such car.

Biarritz convertible and Seville hardtop coupe body styles continued, although there were four Seville hardtop sedans that somehow managed to come off the assembly line. Another 1957 Eldorado model was the luxurious Brougham sedan, but that deserves full attention in a future article.

The 1957 Cadillac had the usual horsepower increase. The standard engine grew to an even 300 hp. A change in previous practice put the same engine in the Eldorado. However, an Eldorado-only option was a 325-hp version of the engine. For 1958, horsepower was increased to 310 but there was no optional engine for the Eldorado.

Styling was basically the same for the '58 Eldorado, except for the annual grille and trim revisions. Production took a tumble from 1,800 to 815 Biarritz and 2,100 to 855 Seville models. (Remember that 1958 was a recession year.)

After that year, the Eldorado Seville and Biarritz lost their distinction—looking almost the same as comparable Series 62 models. The Seville was dropped after the 1961 models and the Biarritz name fell by the wayside in 1964. The Eldorado convertible remained through the 1966 models. A new era was introduced for 1967 when the front-wheel-drive coupes were introduced.

All the 1953 through 1958 Eldorados are acknowledged by the Milestone Car Society, which focuses its attention on the great postwar cars.

The LeMans design was radical and predicted the '54 Eldorado's styling and finned wheel covers of later years.

Cadillac's dreams come true in 1953

By Tom LaMarre

The show traveled to New York, Los Angeles, San Francisco, Dallas and Kansas City, drawing more than a million visitors. Vocal groups, orchestras and dancers performed on a mechanized two-level stage. Exotic cars provided a glimpse of the future. After a two-year absence, the Motorama was back.

The General Motors Sales Section, under the direction of Spencer D. Hopkins, was responsible for the 1953 Motorama. T. H. Roberts managed the show with the assistance of H. R. Wilber.

Not to be outdone by rival divisions, Cadillac exhibited two dream cars at the 1953 Motorama—the Orleans and LeMans. The two-tone Orleans was a four-door hardtop with center-opening rear doors. It shared the styling of the production '53 Coupe Deville but had a wraparound windshield and lacked the metal reinforcements on the "C" pillars.

Cadillac's more radical show car was the LeMans, a fiberglass-bodied two-seat convertible with wraparound windshield, push-button doors and a sectioned body. The stylized double-wing hood ornament resembled a Voisin design of the 1930s. Powering the sporty Cadillac was a 270-hp V-8 with dual four-barrel carburetors.

The LeMans influenced the design of the 1954 Eldorado and inspired the finned wheel covers that were used on Eldorados through 1958. Pontiac borrowed the LeMans name in 1961.

The Orleans made its mark, too. The 1957 Eldorado Brougham, which evolved from the Orleans, was a pillarless sedan with center-opening doors and a $13,074 price tag. But Lincoln had much greater success with the concept beginning in 1961 with its new Continentals.

That was the year the last Motorama was held. Like the 1953 Motorama, the 1961 show drew more than a million people, but it had become too expensive to sponsor and GM was tired of competitors lifting ideas from its dream cars.

Though similar to the '53 Coupe DeVille, the Orleans was a four-door hardtop with a wraparound windshield.

Mexican Road Race Cadillacs

Much has been written about the winning performance of Lincolns in the 1952, 1953 and 1954 Carrera Panamericana (Mexican Road Race) events. While the accomplishments are lengendary and worthy of accolades, it's important to note that Cadillacs driven by Keith Andrews and Ed Stringer, in the 1954 Carrera, proved that GM's luxury car gave buyers more than just a "million dollar grin."

By the time the five-day-long race ended on Nov. 23, 1954, Andrews' number 127 Cadillac and Stringer's number 110 Cadillac had fought their way to third and fourth overall positions in the large stock car class. This was considered a remarkable achievement because of the large number of Lincolns competing and because the Cadillacs lacked the massive factory support that Ford Motor Co. gave to most of the Lincoln drivers.

There were 14 Lincolns entered in the large stock car class. Seven of these cars, plus two light stock car class Fords, crossed into Mexico Nov. 1 on a convoy of five trucks that brought them from Long Beach, Calif. Long Beach was the home of race car builder Bill Stroppe, who had expertly prepped the Lincolns for the contest.

Motor Trend magazine (January 1955) detailed the dyno and chassis work done on the cars, pointing out that even one of the transport trucks had a dynoed Lincoln engine. Stroppe had beefed up the cars to the point of adding driver and co-pilot foot rests, seat belts, roll bars and extra gauges. He also prepared the race-winning Lincoln owned by Ray Crawford. Crawford was a grocer who entered the race under his own sponsorship but with indirect Ford help.

Two of the trucks in the Ford-backed convoy held the nine race cars. The others were support vehicles filled with spare parts and tires and an exotic array of "portable" tools and equipment including vehicle lifts, pneumatic power jacks, electric lug wrenches and bottled drinking water. Accompanying the trucks were several cars including a Lincoln sedan with two-way radio communications, which were used for a "dry run" through the nearly 2,000-mile long course. The Lincoln team even had movies of the 1953 race taken from inside a competing car.

In contrast to the Ford commitment, direct support from other U.S. automakers was minimal at best. "To be sure, other U.S. factories helped the entrants whose cars bore their names," noted the *Motor Trend* story, "test and research facilities were at the disposal of loyal drivers in a sort of lend-lease arrangement, almost as though the factories would rather not win". (Some bitter would-be winners preferred to call it "too little and too late.")

Considering how little help the drivers of non-Ford products received, their survival rate was amazing. Twenty-nine heavier domestic stocks were entered, including the Lincolns. The 15 other cars included nine Buicks, two Packards, the pair of Cadillacs, one Chrysler and a sole Oldsmobile. Of these, the 13 finishers were driving four Lincolns, four Buicks, both Packards, both Cadillacs and the Oldsmobile. In addition, the Cadillacs were actually running the strongest at the end, with Andrews' car winning the last two legs.

Speed Age magazine (March 1955) described Andrews' efforts to catch the Lincolns near the end as "a strong threat by a mountain boy in a Cadillac against Lincoln's winning monopoly." The Colorado Springs driver had won the Pike's Peak Hill Climb earlier in the year. By coming in ahead of Crawford and factory driver Walt Faulkner on the 186.47-mile Parral to Chihauhau leg and

222.51-mile Chihuahua to Juarez leg, Andrews became the first driver to beat the Lincolns since 1952.

The performance of the two Cadillacs was a surprise from the start of the first leg, which began in Tuxtla on Nov. 19 and ended 329.4 miles down the rough roads in Oaxaca. The heavy stocks were the third group of cars to leave the starting line and several did not survive the crashes and breakdowns that marred the leg.

Three of the Lincolns failed to make it through the first 100 miles and four of the official factory entries could not complete the leg. The engine in Jack McGrath's Lincoln froze at 33 miles, and Jack Stevenson's car burned a piston at the 72-mile mark. Also out with mechanical failures was the only Chrysler, which was probably the second biggest "factory-backed" entry. (Chrysler chief engineer Bob Rodger—father of the 300 letter cars—actually provided most of the support on an "under-the-table" basis.) Other dropouts included a fifth Lincoln and one Buick.

Andrews' Cadillac finished the leg in third place, clocking a four-hour, two-minute and 20-second run at an average speed of 131.224 mph. Coming in around five mph slower was Stringer's car, which wound up in sixth in the class. *Speed Age* pointed out that observers were quite impressed that both had finished the leg at all, never mind placing within the top 10.

A 252.95-mile run from Oaxaca to Puebla was the route for leg two on Nov. 20. It found the Cadillacs and eight of the nine surviving Buicks pressuring the Lincolns again. The factory Lincoln team lost another contender when Bill Vukovich's car skidded over a 50-foot drop and narrowly missed falling 30 feet over a ledge where it stopped precariously.

Crawford topped the class again with his not officially factory-backed Lincoln. Faulkner was second, but his directly supported car came in only 53 seconds in front of Andrews' Cadillac. Stringer held on to sixth place. On a two-leg basis, Andrews was in second position, with a 24-second advantage over Faulkner, while Stringer was sixth overall behind a pair of Buicks.

A quicker leg was planned for Nov. 21, this being a 75.13-mile trek to Mexico City. The shorter distance over better roads allowed higher speeds and basically trouble-free driving. Andrews again dogged the Lincolns, with a third place finish. "The determined Cadillac chauffeur trailed Faulkner by one minute and 22 seconds—which was close," said *Speed Age*. However, the widening of the gap by almost one minute put Faulkner in second overall for the class. Stringer's Cadillac finished 10th.

For the first time, a fourth marque—Packard—made it into the top 10 (which included 11 cars due to the daily/overall time variances). This car was 11th for the leg, but ninth overall. The Oldsmobile, the other Packard, four additional Lincolns and seven Buicks were still running in addition to the pair of Cadillacs.

Leg four took the action to Leon, a distance of 261.03 miles from Mexico City, with 11 cars biting the dust. A wicked turn along the way wiped out a Borgward, a Pegaso and a Dodge without fatalities. The late Mickey Thompson, driving a Ford, also crashed, as did a Chevrolet. The Lincolns continued to lead the large stock car class, pulling further ahead (temporarily) of Andrews' Cadillac, which came in fourth for the leg. A Buick was third into Leon, although Andrews still held the ranking for all four legs. Stringer's car wound up with a fifth for the leg and the class.

Continuing leg five the same day, the cars did another 329.4 miles before they flashed into Durango. Faulkner and Crawford were back-to-back again, but now in reverse order. Then came Andrews and Stringer, who were third and fourth on the leg (third and fifth overall). One of the non-factory-backed Lincolns dropped out of the running.

A Studebaker, a Ford and two Chevrolets crashed early on the sixth leg, a 251.09-mile journey to Parral. One Buick driver cut a hole in his floorboard to funnel in transmission fluid, but the Dynaflow eventually stopped doing its job. (It's been said that the same driver added transmission fluid to his fuel to make it to the end of an earlier leg!) Both Cadillacs started to gain strength or at least lost less of it than the other cars. Andrews rolled into second place only 47 seconds behind Faulkner, while Stringer came in fifth again. That put them third and fourth in the class for the entire race, with a pair of Buicks right in back of them.

From Parral, it was 186.47 miles to Chihuahua and the end of the seventh and next-to-last leg. The Lincolns came roaring across the finish line first and rather dramatically. With Crawford just inches behind his bumper, Faulkner reached the line in a brakeless car and had to use a controlled skid to bring it to a halt. However, Andrews' Cadillac was the winner of the leg, based on his elapsed time of one hour, 38 minutes and 34 seconds (1:38:34). Faulkner had 1:40:36, Crawford had 1:40:42 and Stringer, in fourth place for the leg, also registered 1:40:42. Their rankings in class, for the overall race, were Crawford, Faulkner, Andrews and Stringer, in respective order.

Not since 1951 had a marque other than Lincolns taken a first in the Carrera Panamericana's heavy stock class. Andrews—who had started nearly nine minutes behind Crawford in Durango—was now less than seven minutes down on him. Only three minutes separated Andrews and Faulkner. Still left in the heavy stock class

at this point were three more Lincolns, five Buicks, two Packards and the Oldsmobile.

Andrews wound up with another win on the 222.51-mile-long leg from Chihuahua to Juarez, which climaxed the race on Nov. 23. Close behind were the Faulkner and Crawford Lincolns. Stringer was fourth. The five-day results placed Crawford first in class with a total time of 20:40:19 for 1,908 miles. Next came Faulkner with 20:42:07. Andrews, with 20:43:14, was next. Then came Stringer with 21:15:13. That was over eight minutes faster than the fifth-place Buick.

Motor Trend's January 1955 article—which was about the Lincoln preparations rather than the race itself emphasized that the company *had* to support a Lincoln victory. Since 1952, many cars had been sold because of the wins in Mexico. If another brand came in first in 1954, sales would swing to that manufacturer. The magazine urged other automakers to follow Lincoln's lead.

Of course, the factory backing did not take anything away from the outstanding nature of Lincoln's products. They were high-quality, well-engineered, powerful automobiles that were fully up to the challenge of Mexican victories. Ford's support was essentially "insurance" that the promotional advantages of winning the race would not evaporate.

Nevertheless, Crawford and Faulkner's one-two finish did tend to eclipse the fact that two Cadillacs performed almost equally as well in the 1954 Carrera. That reality, combined with the strength of the Cadillac team late in the race and the absence of Detroit involvement, would tend to suggest that writers of automotive history have generally overlooked the significance of the "Mexican Road Race Cadillacs."

*The fortunate woman who enjoys posses-
sion of a 1954 Cadillac would find it
difficult, indeed, to single out the one
quality of the car which she finds most
rewarding. Cadillac's new performance,
for instance, is a constant joy through
every mile . . . its great beauty is a source
of unending pride and satisfaction . . . its
marvelous luxury delights her every time
she glances about the car's interior . . . and
its renarkable economy is a continuing
compliment to her practical wisdom. For,
truly, this magnificent motoring creation
is superlative in every respect. If you have
not as yet discovered this for yourself, you
should visit your Cadillac dealer without
delay. You'll be welcome at any time.*

* * *

*Dress designed by Hattie Carnegie expressly
for the Cadillac Convertible.*

CADILLAC MOTOR CAR DIVISION • GENERAL MOTORS CORPORATION

1954 Cadillac Series 62 convertible coupe ad.

Thought went into the 1955 Cadillac

By Gerald Perschbacher

"This year Cadillac designers and engineers present to the motoring public a line of automobiles blending new functional designs with important engineering advancements."

Those were the words of Don E. Ahrens, general manager of the Cadillac Motor Car Division and Vice President of General Motors. Newspaper and magazine reporters first read his words and saw Cadillac's new models on the morning of Nov. 18, 1954.

Ahrens said, "The 1955 Cadillac is immediately identified by its distinctive front end blending refinement of a finely etched cellular grille design with strength through the massive line of bumper, grille guards and rounded lowness of the hood. There is a whole new body side panel treatment carrying the eye to the sweeping and sharply defined fenders that are an intergral part of the car and characteristically Cadillac. Lending a new touch to the distinctive Cadillac rear end, our designers have added a small chrome louver with studied placement to the body panel just below the rear deck lid." To say it another way, a good measure of thought and planning went into the new Cadillac for '55.

Cadillac, as all American car manufacturers, is best remembered in its previous model years for those offerings of uncommon features placed as a sacrifice on the altar of the buying public. But what about the cars that formed the backbone for general sales?

Among eight body styles available in the United States, the Cadillac Sixty-Two Series four-door sedan brought nearly 45,000 sales to the company, followed in second place by the Sixty-Two Coupe De Ville with 33,300. Those are substantial chunks out of the total sales picture of 140, 777 units or chassis produced by Cadillac for '55.

Though the 1955 Sixty-Two sedan was no Eldorado, it was made flashier for '55 according to Ahrens.

"To present a sleeker over-all appearance in our Series Sixty-Two sedan, from Florentine curve rear window design has been adapted from the Cadillac Coupe De Ville. Complementing 1955 Cadillac styling are 19 new colors; innumberable two-tone effects can be derived from this selection."

New releases on Cadillac's new baby mentioned these toys in the playpen: power steering, dual range Hydra-Matic transmission, wheel discs, automatic windshield washer and "coordinator." Tubeless tires were included to reduce the danger of blowouts. "Tubeless" was standard on all models, including the Sixty-Two sedan.

The factory downplayed the overall statistics of the Cadillac, such as a 129-inch wheelbase on the Sixty-Two sedan, 331-cid V-8 engine which generated 250 horsepower at 4600 rpm and maximum torque of 345

Cadillac's bread-and-butter car for 1955 was the Sixty-Two four-door sedan.

at 2800 rpm or that it took 43.3 feet to make a full turn. It wasn't that Cadillac was not proud of its engineering. C.F. Arnold, Chief Engineer of the division, said, "Through these refinements in our 1955 automobile we feel that we have taken another long step toward our goal...that of providing the ultimate in driving satisfaction to Cadillac owners." But in an increasingly harsh sales climate against cutthroat competition, Cadillac needed to present news and views that put the product on its own pedestal of perfection.

That pedestal partially was built through factory hoopla which underlined creature comforts. Ahrens said, "At customer request, optional equipment items installed on particular models at the factory are: redesigned power brakes for more positive action, air conditioning, signal seeking pre-selecting radio, heater and defroster, E-Z eye-glass with an unnoticable gray tint gradation. Autronic Eye, white sidewall tires, power window lifts and horizontal power seat adjustment, vertical front seat adjustable, fog lamps, saber spoke wheels, and specially styled license plate frames."

In whatever combination the buyer preferred, options like this coupled with color selections and interior cloth options, became a steel-encased signature of the owner himself.

The Sixty-Two four-door sedan was "designed to create a mood of stateliness." The familiar speed goddess was flying high atop the new hood, but for '55 that hood was a bit lower and wider than the previous year. Interiors for the Sixty-Two sedan ranged from gabardine fabric in two-tone shades of gray, blue, tan and green to diamond pattern nylon trimmed in gabardine both in dark and light shades of gray, blue and green.

Not spectacular, but definitely conservative, which is what most buyers of Cadillacs were in 1955.

Most auto manufacturers discovered 1955 as a great sales year. Cadillac realized its best year to date back then, with 153,334 units produced for the calendar year and just a hair over 141,000 new car registrations. It wouldn't be until 1960 that those figures were topped.

Cadillac's good sales on the 1955 Sixty-Two sedan resounded a loud "amen" to the words of Cadillac's general manager: "It is our sincere intention to give the motoring public the greatest driving pleasure possible, combining smoothness of operation and instantaneous performance."

World's Best Reason for Ordering a Cadillac !

As almost any Cadillac owner can tell you, his family represents the finest of all reasons for making the move to the "car of cars."

How wonderful it is, for instance, to be able to surround your loved ones with Cadillac's superlative comfort and safety. Every luxury and convenience and motoring safeguard known to automotive science rides with them through every mile.

And how much the car adds to a family's daily

happiness! As a source of family pride and pleasure . . . it is, truly, a thing apart.

And a Cadillac is even friendly to the family exchequer. In fact, the car is surprisingly economical in every phase of cost and operation and upkeep.

If you think the time has come for *your* family to enjoy the countless benefits of Cadillac ownership, visit your Cadillac dealer today. He'll be happy to see you—and your family—at any time.

CADILLAC MOTOR CAR DIVISION • GENERAL MOTORS CORPORATION

1955 Cadillac Series 62 two-door hardtop was spotlighted here.

The huge 1959 Cadillac convertible is one of the most sought-after postwar collectibles.

1959 Cadillac...

Was bigger better?

By Bill Siuru

Cadillac invented the tailfin, and by 1959, most American cars had them in one form or another.

The size and predominance of the tailfins on General Motors cars reached their peak with the 1959 models, and the Cadillac had its version with their twin bullet-like taillights.

1959 was the year all GM products received a complete redesign. This was to allow greater commonality between the GM full-sized cars. For example, one basic set of body panels served Chevrolet, Pontiac, Oldsmobile, and Buick. Even though Cadillac still retained its own body panels, it has more than a passing resemblence to its lesser sisters, such as in roof lines and glass.

Cadillac reshuffled its models for 1959. The base series was the 6200 that included two four-door hardtops, a two-door hardtop, and a convertible. One of the four-doors was called a "six-window" sedan and featured a sloping rear window and rear ventipanes. The less popular "four-window" sedan had a flat roof and a wrap-around rear window. This model, available on all five GM lines, would appear only in 1959 and 1960. Even

on the basic Cadillac, such items as power brakes and Hydramatic were standard.

The DeVille was the Series 6300 and included two four-door hardtop versions and a two-door hardtop. There was no convertible in this series. The standard equipment list was augmented by power windows and power seats.

Finally, the Series 6400 Eldorado Seville hardtop and Biarritz convertible shared their bodies with the 6200 and 6300 series, but the chrome trim was significantly different. The list of standard equipment was quite extensive in keeping with the almost $2,000 price increase compared to models in the 6200 and 6300 series.

Rounding out the Eldorado series was the 6900 Eldorado Brougham now handbuilt in Italy. Only 99 were built in its last year and they had styling features that would appear on regular Cadillacs in future years.

Cadillac still offered its Series Sixty Special Fleetwood model. However, for 1959, this model shared the same wheelbase and overall length as the 6200 / 6300 / 6400 cars. Only a four-door "six-window" hardtop was offered and differed only from the other Cadillacs in trim and standard equipment. Two long wheelbase limousines were offered in the Series 6700 Fleetwood 75 models, and there was a commercial chassis available.

The new 1959 Cadillac car speaks so eloquently—in so many ways—of the man who sits at its wheel. Simply because it *is* a Cadillac, for instance, it indicates his high level of personal achievement. Because it is so beautiful and so majestic, it bespeaks his fine sense of taste and his uncompromising standards. Because it is so luxurious and so regally appointed, it reveals his consideration for the comfort of his fellow passengers. And because it is so economical to own and to operate, it testifies to his great practical wisdom. The magnificent 1959 Cadillac will tell this wonderful story about *you.* So delay no longer. Make the decision now and visit your Cadillac dealer. In fact, the car's extraordinary reception has made it imperative that you place your order soon. Why not stop in tomorrow and make the arrangements?

CADILLAC MOTOR CAR DIVISION • GENERAL MOTORS CORPORATION
EVERY WINDOW OF EVERY CADILLAC IS SAFETY PLATE GLASS

Cadillac...universal symbol of achievement

The 1959 Cadillac four-door hardtop was called the "universal symbol of achievement."

Aircraft styling and advanced engineering for 1959 characterized the Cadillac Cyclone show car.

Cadillac Cyclone —
Unique in the world

By Tom LaMarre

Five years before Lincoln-Mercury introduced its Cyclone, Cadillac used the name for an experimental sports car. There will never be another Cadillac like it.

Unit body construction was used, with all of the body inner panels welded directly to the basic structure.

A one-piece canopy of clear plastic, coated from within to deflect the sun's rays, fits snugly against the panoramic windshield to give the driver true 360-degree vision. The canopy is hinged at the rear and power operated. It lifts to afford easy entrance for the passenger when either door is opened and disappears automatically beneath the rear deck for storage when not in use.

An unusual sliding action results when the door is opened. At a touch of a button on either side, the door moves outward from the car three inches. The person entering the car then slides the door back along the side of the car for easy entrance.

The headlamps are retractable, "much the same as landing lights on an aircraft," Cadillac Division said. When not in use they are stored behind the fine mesh grille. Powering the retraction or lowering of the headlamps is air from the air suspension system.

A special proximity warning device system is located in the large nose cones that project forward from the front of the fuselage-like fenders. They electronically alert the driver with both an audible signal and a warning light of any automobile or other object that is approaching. The pitch of the signal increases as the object draws closer.

Heating and air conditioning are combined in a comfort control system. You dial the temperature you desire and the system calls on warm or cool air to maintain that temperature. These two units, gas heater and air conditioner, are housed in the cowl sections on either side of the passenger compartment doors. That compartment has bucket seats and advanced passenger comforts. The instruments are clustered like an aircraft dashboard, before and between the seats.

A two-way intercom allows passengers to converse with persons outside the car without removing the canopy.

The Cyclone's engine is a standard 1959 Cadillac 325-hp power plant with a low-profile carburetor, special distributor, aluminum cross-flow radiator and twin fan blades.

All auxiliary units such as the power steering pump, air compressor and generator are separate from the engine and are driven by a system of belts. These belts get their power from a shaft which attaches to the front of the drive shaft.

The experimental three-speed transmission and final drive assembly are mounted behind the passenger compartment. The Cyclone has two-speed axle shafts. The exhaust outlets are located ahead of the front wheels, and the muffler lies alongside the engine.

The front suspension is the standard '59 Cadillac air suspension. The rear suspension consists of a modified swing axle with trailing arms.

The front wheels and brake drums are integral aluminum castings with a steel liner for each brake drum. The rear brakes are mounted inboard and are of conventional cast iron. The power brake system uses an air servo instead of the conventional vacuum servo, with the air supplied from the air suspension system. The steering system uses the Saginaw rotary valve with variable ratio added.

Today the Cyclone resides in the collection of the Sloan Museum in Flint, Mich.

Cadillacs of the swingin' '60s

By Charles Webb

From 1960 to 1969, Cadillac made some very attractive automobiles. Styling excesses of the late '50s were replaced with clean lines and more thoughtful, conservative designs. Buyers responded by purchasing Cadillacs in record breaking numbers, from a very respectable 142,184 at the start of the decade to over 223,000 annually by the end. This left no doubt as to what was America's favorite luxury car.

Cadillac didn't take its superiority in the market place for granted. A lot of care went into making "the stan-

The smallest model was the new, short deck Series 62 four-door hardtop. It was seven inches shorter than standard Cadillacs. It was intended for people who had to fit their cars in tight parking spaces. But it wasn't very popular. Only 3,756 were produced. (Late introduction may have helped account for the low sales.)

For the first time since 1954, there were no optional engines. All new Cadillacs came with a 335-hp 390-cubic-inch V-8. The make kept its identity. There is no mistaking a Cadillac regardless of the year it was made.

1960 Cadillac Eldorado Seville.

dard of the world," as the 1962 promotional film "*Pride in the Possession*" showed. It revealed Cadillac engines met government standards for aircraft precision. Each engine block received 14 inspections and every car had to pass 1,400 tests. But perhaps the most important reason for the make's success was stated at the end of the film: "Excellence, if it is to be maintained, must have within it the golden thread of continuity."

Cadillacs underwent several changes during the '60s, yet the automotive styling trends, the wrap-around windshield and air suspension were eliminated. Its lines were crisper and although large, it didn't look bloated. In fact, the '61 Cadillac was a bit smaller.

1961 Cadillac Series 62 convertible.

1963 Cadillac Eldorado convertible

Like many other full-size cars of the era, 1960s Cadillacs aren't especially popular at the moment. Their battleship proportions and poor gas mileage tend to give them low priority on most collectors' want lists. Yet these cars have a great deal going for them in style, comfort and performance. At the rather reasonable prices at which they can be currently purchased, 1960s Cadillacs are definitely worth a second look.

1960

"We have always held that any time is a good time to buy a new Cadillac car. And yet, we do believe that 1960 has become the best of all years to make it yours." Despite these encouraging words from a magazine ad, Cadillac sales were virtually the same as 1959.

Although only face-lifted, enough changes were made to make the 1960 easily distinguishable from the previous model, particularly from the back. The spectacular fins were replaced with lower ones. The overall effect was one of refinement. Ironically, while it may have been better looking, the flashier '59 is more sought after than the 1960 model.

1961

One might say this was the "first" 1960s Cadillac. It seemed more in tune with the decade. It also had improved steering and suspension. The Eldorado was now only available as a convertible.

1962

Cadillac tailfins were a couple inches lower in 1962. Cornering lights, which came on with the turn signal, were placed on the lower front fenders between the wheels and front bumper. Other less obvious changes were a three-phase rear lights setup and a new dual braking system. The latter consisted of a separate piston and brake fluid reservoir for the front and rear. If one of the hydraulic lines broke, only one set of brakes wouldn't operate. If both lines were cut, you could still pull the improved parking brake.

On the inside was a new instrument panel and the availability of bucket seats in the four-window Sedan deVille, Coupe deVille, and Park Avenue. The 60 Special had African Makori wood panels in its doors. Most 1962 Cadillacs, 92.8 percent, had power windows and 59.4 percent came with an air conditioner.

1963

"Cadillac for 1963 has surpassed its own great reputation." That's what the sales catalog claimed and for good reason. A subtle yet noticeable face-lift further refined the make's styling. While the front end treatment was reminiscent of the '59, the tailfins were even smaller than those on the previous year's model. And the lower rear quarter panel "fins" were eliminated.

Perhaps the most significant change was under the hood. Although displacement and horsepower rating remained the same, Cadillacs were powered by a new, smaller, lighter-weight V-8 engine.

The 2,000,000th postwar Cadillac was built this year.

1964 Cadillac Series 62 Sedan deVille.

HOW TO FIT A CADILLAC INTO ANY BUDGET

No matter what you plan to spend on your next car, you need look no further than your authorized Cadillac dealer. Consider the four Cadillacs shown here. All these splendid motor cars, regardless of age or previous service, are automobiles you can own with pride and drive with pleasure. All bear the unmistakable distinction of Cadillac styling. All give you Cadillac's famed engineering and craftsmanship. All give you Hydra-Matic Drive, power steering, power brakes and many other items of equipment that are extra even today on most new cars. Whether you buy one new or used, next time invest in a Cadillac. There never was a better time to match Cadillac luxury to any motor car budget.

Cadillac Motor Car Division • General Motors Corporation

1. 1964 de Ville Convertible   2. 1962 Coupe de Ville
3. 1963 Sedan de Ville   4. 1960 Six-window Sedan

This advertisement shows (clockwise from front): 1964 Cadillac deVille convertible, 1963 Cadillac Sedan deVille, 1960 Cadillac six-window sedan and 1962 Cadillac Coupe deVille.

1964

This may well be the most attractive Cadillac of the 1960s. It only had a minor face lift. But the changes added greatly to its appeal. Especially becoming were the tail- fins. If ever a car looked good in fins, it was the '64 Cadillac. They seemed "just right." The new Caddy was also more powerful than the '63. Engine displacement was increased to 429 cubic inches and horsepower rating was upped to 340. This gave Cadillac a 0 to 60 time of under 10 seconds. Not bad for a make whose lightest model weighed 4,475 pounds. Speaking of models, Cadillac buyers had 11 to chose from. That was more than Lincoln and Imperial combined. One model no longer available was the short deck four- door hardtop. A couple new features offered in '64 were comfort control" and "twilight sentinel." The former operated from a single thermostatic setting that warmed or cooled air as needed. It even adjusted the humidity. The latter automatically turned headlights on at dusk or under poor light conditions (such as going through a tunnel), and turned them off when there was sufficient light. There was even a switch that allowed the owners to leave headlights on for up to a minute and a half after they left their car.

1965 Cadillac Calais four-door.

1965

Cadillacs were restyled in 1965. Vertical stacked headlights and a less fin-like rear deck design were the most striking changes. But they weren't the only ones. Underneath, the tubular X frame used for the last eight years was replaced by a perimeter one. This enabled the make to place the engine several inches forward. That in turn increased interior leg room a bit because the transmission hump shrank. In addition to new looks, Cadillacs were named differently. Rather than previously used series numbers, they were divided into three series: Calais, deVille and Fleetwood. Even though it cost nearly $500 extra, 83 percent of all 1965 Cadillacs came equipped with an air conditioner.

1966

After 1965's big changes, 1966 models received a modest face-lift. A horizontal band divided the grille in its center and the side marker lights were not separate from the grille. There was also a bit less chrome used. A built-in front seat warmer (optional) and new variable ratio power steering were a couple items introduced this year. The powerplant was the same as in 1965, but a Rochester four-barrel carburetor was used instead of a Carter.

1967

Modest side body sculpturing made the '67 Cadillac appear "sleeker." The slightly forward slanting new grille and fenders also added to this illusion. Big news this year was introduction of the front-wheel-drive Eldorado two-door hardtop. While some just view it as a fancier version of Oldsmobile's Toronado, it wasn't. Cadillac began work on it in 1959. A V-12 engine was said to have been considered for use in it but that idea was dropped. The Eldorado's styling was harmonious with the standard Cadillac line, yet distinctive. This personal luxury car was the most popular model in the Fleetwoood series. Nearly 18,000 were made. Total model year sales for the make reached the 200,000 mark for the first time in 1967.

1968

A finer grille and longer hood were the most noticeable styling changes in '68. Other new features included concealed windshield wipers, a different instrument panel, breakaway rearview mirror, more safety padding, and a 375-hp 472-cubic-inch V-8. The sporty Eldorado also had a slightly longer hood (to make room for the hidden wipers), small circular safety lights on the rear fenders, and driving lights integrated into the front fenders. But the basic styling remained.

1969 Cadillac Fleetwood Brougham.

1969

Cadillac received an extensive face-lift in 1969. The headlights were once again horizontal, the roof line and rear deck treatment were changed, and there was a new grille. Styling was clearly influenced by the Eldorado. Cadillac sales literature described it as "traditional dignity with a youthful new look." The make's new "control center dash" added a bit of flair to the interior. The Eldorado was the least altered Cadillac. Outside of a different grille and exposed headlights, it looked much the same as the previous year's model. However, because of the make's face-lift, it no longer seemed quite as distinctive.

THERE'S A NEW CELEBRITY IN TOWN!

It's just now beginning to be seen at the most important events . . . on the nation's roadways . . . and in the driveways of America's fine homes. It's Cadillac for 1965—the newest and most exciting automotive personality of the decade. Its totally new styling attracts attention wherever it goes—and its brilliant new performance is the talk of the highways. Cadillac's great Turbo Hydra-Matic is now standard on all eleven models. An exclusive new accessory, the tilt and telescope steering wheel, adds a new dimension to driving comfort. And the car's quietness and levelness of ride are a revelation. See and drive this great car soon. It is, without any question, the new Standard of the World.

So new! So right! So obviously Cadillac

The 1965 Cadillac was "definned," as this advertisement shows.

By Tom LaMarre

Ads called it the "last of a magnificent breed. The Eldorado convertible. Today an extraordinary luxury car ... Tomorrow a classic. For this is more than one of the finest convertibles ever built. It is the only convertible now built in America. And it will be our last. The very last. Because the Eldorado convertible will not be offered in 1977. We suggest you visit your Cadillac dealer soon. Very soon."

Cadillac claimed to have been the first company to use the word "convertible," a term that it applied to its 1916 Type 53 five-passenger model. And at 10:12 a.m. on April 21, 1976, Cadillac built what was supposed to have been the last American convertible.

In anticipation of increased demand for the instant collectible, a production boost was planned for the 1976 Eldorado convertible. It still wasn't enough. Early in April, the division announced it was to build 200 special edition convertibles, identical white Eldorados with commemorative dash plaques. At the same time, Detroit's Bob Giles hurriedly prepared 200 commemorative envelopes to mark the occasion. They were cancelled in Detroit on April 21, and later a cachet was applied. Beneath the illustration of a 1976 Fleetwood Eldorado convertible was printed, "The end of an era! The Cadillac Motor Car Division of General Motors built the last domestic convertible today at its Detroit plant ... The very last American convertible is a white Fleetwood Eldorado. It will be retained by Cadillac for historical purposes." A couple of stamp collectors bought most of the 200 envelopes.

The real cars were in demand, too, and were soon selling for twice their factory price of $11,049. However, there was little to distinguish the 1976 Eldorado from previous models. It had a new cross-hatch grille and different taillights than those used on the 1975 Eldorado. Otherwise, it was basically the same car. The largest production American passenger car engine, a 500 cubic-inch V-8, was still standard.

The last American convertible that wasn't!

Fourteen thousand 1976 Eldorado convertibles were built, including the special edition cars. Cadillac could have built more had it not been for a shortage of parts.

As it turned out, magazine ads for the Eldo should have had the disclaimer "subject to change without notice," since convertibles made a comeback. That was after the bottom fell out of the market for the 1976 Eldorado convertible—the last American convertible that wasn't.

Sunroofs and air conditioning were blamed for the demise of the convertible. Nostalgia brought it back. Pictured is a 1976 Eldorado.

LASALLE
1927-1940

LaSalle was named for the French adventurer who explored the Mississippi River valley in 1682, and it was a companion to the car named for the French explorer who founded Detroit about 20 years later.

That the LaSalle built by Cadillac was a commercial failure is a reality, but that reality pales in the light of the LaSalle's historic significance. Because of the LaSalle, automobile styling at General Motors moved out of engineering and into a department of its own—Art and Colour, as it was called then, "a sissy name" according to Harley Earl who headed it, though that was perhaps the only negative in this very positive move by GM.

The LaSalle's genesis dated back to the early '20s, as Alfred P. Sloan, Jr. noticed a price gap that needed filling between the Buick and the Cadillac. When Lawrence P. Fisher took over Cadillac's presidency in 1924, a massive expansion program was inaugurated to raise Cadillac's production capability, and Harley Earl, whose work as chief designer for Don Lee Corporation in California had attracted Fisher's attention, was invited to submit design proposals, as he later related, "not quite as conservative as the Cadillac."

Inspired by one of the most sensational-looking cars on the Continent, the Hispano-Suiza, Earl came up with the LaSalle, which was introduced on March 5, 1927 to a reception equally sensational. Art and Colour almost immediately followed. Though built by Cadillac to Cadillac standards, the LaSalle initially was its own car and even a pacesetter for Cadillac. Its 303-cid, 75-hp V-8 engine and its overall look were adapted to the new 341 Series Cadillac introduced for 1928.

That the new LaSalle could hold its own in a performance vein, too, was demonstrated in mid-1927 when Bill Rader drove a stripped stock model at the GM Proving Ground a total of 951.0 miles for a 95.3 mph average, which was only a couple of miles per hour less than a Duesenberg had required the month before to win the famous Memorial Day race of 500 miles at Indianapolis.

In 1928, with LaSalle's help, Cadillac production climbed above 40,000 cars for the first time in history. By the end of 1929 nearly 50,000 LaSalles had been sold. With Cadillac as doting parent, the LaSalle received synchromesh (on second and high gears), safety glass, and chrome in '29.

1930 LaSalle Series 340 Coupe (OCW)

But then the stock market crashed, and the Great Depression began. Fewer than 3,500 LaSalles were sold in each of the 1932 and 1933 model years. By 1934 the LaSalle no longer enjoyed favorite-child status, but instead received hand-me-downs from the parts bins of other GM cars, the Olds straight-eight engine among them.

1935 LaSalle Series 35-50 Four-Door Touring Sedan (OCW)

The new styling was superb, a tall and narrow "V" radiator, artfully designed porthole louvers, pontoon fenders, and the chassis was fine—with independent front suspension and hydraulic brakes. But as the economy began to recover, the LaSalle did not, at least commensurately. Production grew to 7195 cars in 1934, 8651 in 1935, and 13,004 in 1936.

Meanwhile the Packard One-Twenty had been introduced for 1935, and had taken off like a rocket. For 1937 Cadillac made the LaSalle its own again, giving it the L-head V-8 of the Series 60, nice new styling, a lower price range, and a heavy promotion campaign emphasizing that the car was completely Cadillac built. But it was too late.

1937 LaSalle Series 37-50 Convertible Coupe (OCW)

Model year production of 32,000 LaSalles was a terrific leap forward, but the LaSalle remained leagues behind the Junior Packards. Interestingly, in Packard circles, the fact that the marque's lower-priced cars were designated Packard is thought by many to have ultimately resulted in the ruination of the company.

In LaSalle's case, that it wasn't a Cadillac was probably the ruinous factor. People do tend to buy prestige, and a Cadillac was prestige; LaSalle did not have the time to develop a prestigious name before the onset of the Depression, and did not have the opportunity after.

Competition from the Lincoln-Zephyr in the later '30s didn't help either. The LaSalle was discontinued following the 1940 model after a total of 205,000 cars had been built in 13 largely unlucky years. In 1941 the spot filled by the LaSalle in the Cadillac lineup was taken by a new Series 61 model called a Cadillac. That year GM's premier division sold more cars than ever before in its history.

1940 LaSalle Series 40-50 Four-Door Touring Sedan (OCW)

1927 LASALLE

1927 LaSalle, roadster, AA

LASALLE — SERIES 303 — EIGHT: LaSalle — a new line to fill the gap between Buick and Cadillac in the General Motors lineup of prices. Billed as a "Companion Car to Cadillac," the LaSalle boasted Cadillac quality and dependability in a smaller package, at a lower price. Styling stood equal alongside function in the design.

Bodies: The initial offering in March 1927 consisted of roadster, phaeton, coupe, convertible coupe, victoria, and five-passenger sedan by Fisher plus coupe, sedan, and town cabriolet by Fleetwood. A dual cowl sport phaeton was soon available, followed by midyear offerings of town sedan, seven-passenger sedan, and five- and seven-passenger Imperials by Fisher plus a transformable town cabriolet by Fleetwood ("transformable" indicates that the front compartment can be totally enclosed, with windows in the doors, not that the rear quarter can be lowered). Body features included: high, slim radiator set low in the frame. Twelve louvers, centered in hood panels. Twin cowl vents on roadster and phaeton. Bullet-shaped head and cowl lights. Posts under headlights to conduct wiring. Monogram rod between headlights. On roadster and phaetons the cut-down effect of the belt line was accentuated by double molding curving upward onto the cowl. Rear window in coupe and rear curtain in convertible coupe could be opened for communication with rumbleseat passengers. The four-door town sedan was close-coupled, with no rear quarter windows.

Chassis: Similar to Cadillac; scaled to LaSalle size and power. Differences as follows: Fuel feed by manifold vacuum, assisted by engine driven vacuum pump. Mechanical brakes with 14-inch drums on all wheels. Rear semi-elliptic springs shackled at both ends, rear shackle with ball and socket joint. Front wheels run on ball bearings. Watson stabilators.

Driveline: Multiple (11) disc clutch, three-speed selective transmission, torque tube drive, 3/4-floating rear axle with helical bevel gear and pinion.

Engine: The compensated two-plane crankshaft in the V-63 engine and the separate starter and generator on the 314 engine had been major changes, but the basic engine remained the Type 51 design. The 303 engine was a new basic design, with offset blocks and side-by-side connecting rods (babbitted). The outward appearance was the same as the final version of the 314 engine except that the 303 starter was horizontal, mounted behind the flywheel on the right side. The oil filter was mounted on the engine rather than the firewall. The carburetor was similar to Cadillac but reversed. The oil level indicator was mounted behind the right-hand block. A common manifold, connecting the two exhaust manifolds at the front of the engine, fed to a single muffler at the left side of the chassis.

I.D. DATA: Serial numbers were not used. Engine numbers were stamped on plate on front face of dash and on crankcase just below the water inlet on the right side. Starting: 200001. Ending: 212000.

1927 LaSalle, phaeton, JAC

Style No.	Body Type & Seating	Price	Weight	Prod. Total
Fisher — 125" wb				
1168	4-dr. Phae.-4P	2495	3770	NA
1168-B	4-dr. Spt. Phae.-4P	2975	4190	NA
1169	2-dr. Rds.-2/4P	2525	3755	NA
7410	2-dr. Cpe.-2/4P	2585	3770	NA
7400	2-dr. Conv. Cpe.-2/4P	2635	3770	NA
7390	2-dr. Vic.-4P	2635	3985	NA
7380	4-dr. Sed.-5P	2685	4090	NA
7420	4-dr. Twn. Sed.-5P	2495	4065	NA
Fisher — 134" wb				
8090	4-dr. Imp.-5P	2775	4315	NA
8060	4-dr. Sed.-7P	2775	4345	NA
8070	4-dr. Imp.-7P	2875	4570	NA
Fleetwood — 125" wb				
3110	2-dr. Cpe.-2P	4275	5000	NA
3120	4-dr. Sed.-5P	4475	5100	NA
3130	4-dr. Twn. Cab.-5/7P	4500	5100	NA
3051	4-dr. Trans. Twn. Cab.-5/7P	4700	5100	NA

Note: Weight of the four Fleetwood models is approximate.

ENGINE: Ninety Degree V-8, L-head. Eight. Cast iron block of four, offset on copper/aluminum crankcase. B & S: 3-1/8 x 4-15/16 in. Disp.: 303 cu. in. C.R.: 4.8:1 std., 5.3:1 opt. H.P. 75 plus advertised. SAE/N.A.C.C. H.P.: 31.25. Main bearings: three. Valve lifters: mechanical, with rollers riding on cam. Carb.: manufactured by Cadillac under C.F. Johnson patents. Compression: 90-92 PSI at 1000 R.P.M.; 105-107 PSI at 1000 R.P.M. with high-compression heads.

CHASSIS: (Series 303) W.B.: 125 in. O.L.: 185 in. Frt/Rear Tread: 56 in. Tires: 32 x 6.00 (6.00-20). (Series 303) W.B.: 134 in. O.L.: 196-5/8 in. Frt/Rear Tread: 56 in. Tires: 32 x 6.20 (6.50-20).

TECHNICAL: Selective sliding gear transmission, in unit with engine. Speeds: 3F/1R. Left drive, center controls (rhd opt.). Multiple disc clutch, 11 discs. Shaft drive (torque tube). 3/4-floating rear axle, helical bevel drive. Overall ratio: 4.54:1 std. 4.07:1, 4.91:1 opt. Mechanical brakes, 14 in. drums on four wheels. Artillery wheels (wire and disc opt.). Wheel size: 20.

OPTIONS: Wire wheels, fender wells, two spare tires ($250.00). Disc wheels, fender wells, two spare tires (150.00). Wood wheels, fender wells, two spare tires (140.00). Folding trunk rack (35.00). Five wire wheels without spare tire (95.00).

HISTORICAL: Introduced March 1927. Calendar year sales: 16,850. Calendar year production: 16,850. Model year sales: 12,000. Model year production: 12,000. President & general manager was Lawrence P. Fisher.

On June 20, 1927, at the General Motors Proving Ground, Milford, Michigan, Willard Rader and Gus Bell drove a LaSalle roadster on a remarkable endurance test run. In 10 hours, the car covered 951 miles at an average speed of 95.2 miles per hour, the fastest of 252 laps having been run at an average speed of 98.8 miles per hour (the winner at the Indy 500 in 1927 averaged 97.5 miles per hour for 500 miles). The test was terminated when an oil suction line fractured.

The LaSalle was a production roadster with windshield, lamps, fenders, runningboards, and muffler removed. The camshaft had been altered, and a 3.5:1 rear axle and high

Style No.	Body Type & Seating	Price	Weight	Prod. Total
8130	2-dr. Vic.-4P	2550	3985	NA
8120	4-dr. Std. Sed.-5P	2495	4090	NA
8110	4-dr. Sed.-5P	(2450)	(4070)	NA
7420	4-dr. Twn. Sed.-5P	2495	4065	NA
8140-A	2-dr. Bus. Cpe.-2/4P	2350	3935	NA
8110-A	4-dr. Family Sed.-5P	2350	4060	NA
Fisher 134" wb				
8090	4-dr. Imp.-5P	2775	4315	NA
8060	4-dr. Std. Sed.-7P	2775	4345	NA
8070	4-dr. Imp.-7P	2875	4570	NA
8050	2-dr. Cpe.-5P	2625	4050	NA
8080	4-dr. Cabr. Sed.-5P	2675	4060	NA
8060-A	4-dr. Family Sed.-7P	2575	4300	NA
Fleetwood — 125" wb				
3051	4-dr. Trans. Twn. Cab.-5/7P	4700	5100 app	NA
3130	4-dr. Twn. Cabr.-5/7P	4500	5100 app	NA
Fleetwood — 134" wb				
3751	4-dr. Trans. Twn. Cab.5/7P	4900	5100 app	NA

compression heads had been installed. No mechanical adjustments were required during the entire run. The nine stops, taking a total of 7 minutes, 24.7 seconds, were for tire changes, water, oil, and gasoline.

1927 LaSalle, sedan, JAC

1928 LASALLE

1928 LaSalle, sedan, AA

LASALLE — SERIES 303 — EIGHT: The bodies were a continuation of the 1927 LaSalle line. Fisher business coupe, five-passenger family sedan on 125-inch wheelbase, five-passenger coupe, five-passenger cabriolet sedan, seven-passenger family sedan on 134-inch wheelbase added. Fleetwood coupe and sedan dropped, transformable town cabriolet on 134-inch wheelbase added in midyear. The five-passenger standard sedan came with leather or metal back. The five- and seven-passenger family sedans were "economy" versions of the standard sedans. The five-passenger family sedan and the business coupe were offered at the new low price of $2,350. Details remained the same except for added side ventilators in the cowl on closed cars and 28 louvers toward the rear of the hood panels on all body styles. The number of louvers might have signified the year, but Cadillac for 1928 had 30 louvers.

Chassis, driveline, and engine: Similar to 1927 LaSalle except — shock absorbers changed to Lovejoy hydraulic. Clutch changed to twin disc. Many detail changes made to brakes and brake linkage, including 16 in. drums on front wheels only.

I.D. DATA: There were no serial numbers used. Engine numbers were stamped on plate on front face of dash and on crankcase just below the water inlet on the right side. Starting: 212001. Ending: 226806.

Style No.	Body Type & Seating	Price	Weight	Prod. Total
Fisher — 125" wb				
1168	4-dr. Phae.-4P	2485	3770	NA
1168-B	4-dr. Spt. Phae.-4P	2975	4190	NA
1169	2-dr. Rds.-2/4P	2485	3755	NA
8140	2-dr. Cpe.-2/4P	2450	3770	NA
7400	2-dr. Conv. Cpe.-2/4P	2550	3770	NA

1928 LaSalle, two-passenger coupe, JAC

ENGINE: Ninety Degree V-8, L-Head. Eight. Cast iron blocks of four, offset on copper/aluminum crankcase. B & S: 3-1/8 x 4-15/16 in. Disp.: 303 cu. in. C.R.: 4.8:1 std., 5.3:1 opt. Taxable/N.A.C.C. H.P.: 31.25. Main bearings: three. Valve lifters: mechanical, with rollers riding on cams. Carb.: manufactured by Cadillac under C.F. Johnson patents. (Compression) 90-92 PSI @ 1000 R.P.M., 105-107 PSI @ 1000 R.P.M. with high-compression heads.

CHASSIS: (Series: 303) W.B.: 125 in. O.L.: 185 in. Frt/Rear Tread: 56 in. Tires: 32 x 6.00 (6.00-20) (Series: 303) W.B.: 134 in. O.L.: 196-5/8 in. Frt/Rear Tread: 56 in. Tires: 32 x 6.20 (6.50-20).

TECHNICAL: Selective sliding gear transmission, in unit with engine. Speeds: 3F/1R. Left drive, center controls (rhd opt). Twin disc clutch. Shaft drive (torque tube). 3/4-floating rear axle, helical bevel drive. Overall ratio: 4.54:1 std., 4.07:1, 4.91:1 opt.* Mechanical brakes on four wheels, 14-in. rear drums, 16-in. front drums. Artillery wheels (wire and disc opt.). Wheel size: 20 in.

*: 4.91:1 may have been used on some 134-in. wheelbase cars.

1928 LaSalle, phaeton, JAC

OPTIONS: Natural wood wheels ($10.00). Five disc wheels (20.00). Six disc wheels, fender wells, two spare tires (175.00). Five wire wheels (95.00). Six wire wheels, fender wells, two spare tires (250.00). Fender wells for wood wheels (140.00). Folding trunk rack (25.00).

HISTORICAL: Introduced as a continuation of 1927 line. (Minor changes September 1927.) Calendar year sales: 9,956.

Calendar year production: 9,956. Model year sales: 14,806. Model year production: 14,806. President and general manager of LaSalle was Lawrence P. Fisher.

1929 LASALLE

1929 LaSalle, roadster, OCW

LASALLE — SERIES 328 — EIGHT: Similar to 1928 LaSalle Series 303 except:

Bodies: Victoria and business coupe dropped. Landau cabriolet added. Fleetwood 134-inch wheelbase. Transformable town cabriolet available with collapsible quarter. Convertible Imperial sedan (all weather phaeton) available on order. All Fisher bodies except roadster and phaetons on 134-inch wheelbase. Parking lights moved to fenders. Brightwork chrome plated. Security Plate glass in all windows and windshields. Closed body interiors 2-1/2 in. wider, 1 in. higher. Adjustable front seat on closed bodies with no division. Electric tandem windshield wipers. Oval panel on rear of body, formed by quarter molding.

Chassis: Duplex-mechanical brakes — all shoes inside drums.

Driveline: Synchromesh transmission.

Engine: Piston pins pressure lubricated. Midyear change to metric spark plugs.

I.D. DATA: Serial numbers were not used. Engine numbers were stamped on plate on front of dash and on crankcase just below the water inlet on the right side. Starting: 400001. Ending: 422961.

Style No.	Body Type & Seating	Price	Weight	Prod. Total
Fisher — 125" wb				
1186	2-dr. Rds.-2/4P	2345	3990	NA
1185	4-dr. Phae.-4P	2295	4140	NA
1185-B	4-dr. Spt. Phae.-4P	2875	4405	NA
Fisher — 134" wb				
8590	2-dr. Cpe.-2/4P	2495	4310	NA
8580	2-dr. Conv. Cpe.-2/4P	2595	4135	NA
8555	4-dr. Family Sed.-5P	2450	4550	NA
8550	4-dr. Sed.-5P	2595	4490	NA
8610	4-dr. Twn. Sed.-5P	2675	—	NA
8615	4-dr, Imp. Twn. Sed.-5P	—	—	NA
8530	4-dr. Sed.-7P	2775	4615	NA
8540	4-dr. Imp.-7P	2875	4760	NA
8570	2-dr. Cpe.-5P	2625	4335	NA
8600	4-dr. Lan. Cab.-5P	2725	4635	NA
8605	4-dr. Imp. Land. Cab.-5P	—	—	NA
Style No.	**Body Type & Seating**	**Price**	**Weight**	**Prod. Total**

Style No.	Body Type & Seating	Price	Weight	Prod. Total
Fleetwood — 125" wb				
3051	4-dr. Trans. Twn. Cab.-5/7P	4800	5100 app	NA
3130	4-dr. Twn. Cab.-5/7P	4500	—	NA
Fleetwood — 134" wb				
3751	4-dr. Trans. Twn. Cab.- 5/7P	4900	5125 app	NA
3751-C	4-dr. Tr. Coll. Twn. Cab.- 5/7P	—	—	NA
3780	4-dr. Conv. Imp. Sed.-5P	—	—	NA

1929 LaSalle, sedan, JAC

ENGINE: Ninety Degree V-8, L-head. Cast iron blocks of four, offset on copper/aluminum crankcase. B & S: 3 1/4 x 4-15/16 in. Disp.: 328 cu. in. C.R.: 5.3:1 std., 4.8:1 opt. SAE/Taxable/N.A.C.C. H.P.: 33.8. Main bearings: three. Valve lifters: mechanical, with rollers riding on cams. Carb.: manufactured by Cadillac under C.F. Johnson patents. Torque (compression): 105-107 P.S.I. @ 1000 R.P.M., 90-92 P.S.I. @ 1000 R.P.M. with low compression heads.

CHASSIS: (Series 328) W.B.: 125 in. O.L.: 185 in. Frt/Rear Tread: 56/58 in. Tires: 6.50-19 (31 x 6.20). (Series 328) W.B.: 134 in. O.L.: 196-5/8 in. Frt/Rear Tread: 56/58 in. Tires: 6.50-19 (31 x 6.20).

TECHNICAL: Selective transmission with synchromesh. Speeds: 3F/1R. Left drive, center control (rhd opt.). Twin disc clutch. Shaft drive (torque tube). 3/4 floating rear axle, helical bevel drive. Overall ratio: 4.54:1 std.; 4.91:1, 4.07:1 opt. Duplex-mechanical brakes on four wheels, all shoes internal, 15-in. drums on all wheels. Artillery wheels (wire and disc optional). Wheel size: 19 in.

OPTIONS: Tire cover(s) ($5.00-12.00). "LaSalle" radiator ornament (12.00). Heater (40.00). Tonneau windshield (185.00). Seat covers (30.00-230.00). Trunks (60.00-100.00). Fender wells. Colored fenders. Wire wheels. Disc wheels.

HISTORICAL: Introduced August 1928. Innovations: Synchromesh transmission. Safety glass. Model year sales: 22,961. Model year production: 22,961. President and general manager of LaSalle was Lawrence P. Fisher.

1930 LASALLE

LASALLE — SERIES 340 — EIGHT: Slight changes from Series 328 LaSalle. Becoming more like Cadillac (Series 353); differences being mainly in size, weight, and power.

Bodies: Fisher line decreased to seven closed bodies, including convertible coupe. Fleetwood line increased to six. Styling same as Cadillac, with size scaled to six inch shorter wheelbase. Fleetwood line includes Fleetwood seven-passenger touring and four-passenger phaeton, not included in Cadillac line. These two, plus roadster, are distinguished by louvers in side of cowl. With battery under front seat, LaSalle has no hatches in splash pans. Headlights have 10-1/2-in.

lens, are 11-in. overall. Single rear light is mounted on left rear fender.

1930 LaSalle, five-passenger coupe, AA

Chassis, driveline: All bodies on 134-in. wheelbase. Front tread increased from 56 to 57-1/2 in. Rear tread increased from 58 to 59-1/2 in. Rear springs are underslung. Brake system same as Cadillac Series 353, but drums are still 15 in. Exhaust ends in straight pipe. Standard final drive ratio remains at 4.54:1.

Engine: Bore increased by 1/16 in., making displacement same as Series 341-B Cadillac. No cover over spark plugs or intake header. Cover plate on intake header changed in midyear from aluminum to cast iron to eliminate problem with leaking cover plate gaskets.

1930 LaSalle, convertible coupe, JAC

I.D. DATA: Serial numbers were not used. Engine numbers were stamped on crankcase just below the water inlet on the right-hand side. Starting: 600001. Ending: 614995.

Style No.	Body Type & Seating	Price	Weight	Prod. Total
Fisher				
30252	4 dr. Twn. Sed.-5P	2590	4705	NA
30258	2-dr. Cpe.-2/4P	2490	4510	NA
30259	4-dr. Sed.-5P	2565	4690	NA
30262	4-dr. Sed.-7P	2775	4790	NA
30263	4-dr. Imp.-7P	2925	4865	NA
30268	2-dr. Conv. Cpe.-2/4P	2590	4480	NA
30272	2-dr. Cpe.-5P	2590	4530	NA
Fleetwood				
4002	2-dr. Rds.-2/4P	2450	4385	NA
4057	4-dr. Tr.-7P	2525	4480	NA
4060	4 dr. Phae.-4P	2385	4425	NA
4080	4-dr. All-Weath Phae.-5P	3995	4715	NA
4081	4-dr. Sednet. Cab.-5P	3725	4645	NA
4082	4-dr. Sedanette-5P	3825	4645	NA
4151	4-dr. Stat. Trans. Twn. Cab.			Built to order
3351	Trans. Cab.-5P	—	—	NA
3364	Brougham-5P	—	—	NA

ENGINE: Ninety degree V-8, L-head. Cast iron block on silicon/aluminum crankcase. B & S: 3-5/16 x 4-15/16 in. Disp.: 340 cu. in. C.R.: 5.05:1 std., 4.92:1 opt. Brake H.P.: 90 @ 3000 R.P.M. SAE/Taxable H.P.: 35.1. Main bearings: three. Valve lifters: mechanical, with rollers riding on cams. Carb.: manufactured by Cadillac under C.F. Johnson patents.

CHASSIS: (Series 328) W.B.: 134 in. O.L.: app. 201-3/4 in. Frt/Rear Tread: 57-1/2/59-1/2 in. Tires: 6.50-19 w/wood artillery, 7.00-18 w/all others.

TECHNICAL: Selective, synchromesh transmission. Speeds: 3F/1R. Left drive, center controls (rhd opt.). Twin disc clutch. Shaft drive (torque tube). 3/4-floating rear axle, spiral bevel gears. Overall ratio: 4.54:1 std.; 4.07:1, 4.91:1 opt. Safety-mechanical brakes on four wheels (15 in. drums). Wood ar-

tillery wheels (disc, wire, wood demountable opt.). Wheel size: 19 in. w/wood artillery, 18 in. all others.

OPTIONS: Tire cover(s) ($5.50-30.00). Wind wings (25.00-55.00). Tonneau shield (185.00). Radio (175.00). Heater (42.50). Radiator ornament (25.00). Trunks (80.00-115.00). Seat covers (26.75-30.25). Spotlight/driving lights (15.50-80.00). Tire mirrors (32.00/pair). Five wire wheels (60.00). Six wire wheels w/fender wells, trunk rack (190.00). Five demountable wood wheels (50.00). Six demountable wood wheels w/fender wells, trunk rack (190.00). Five disc wheels (50.00). Six disc wheels w/fender wells, trunk rack (190.00).

HISTORICAL: Introduced September 1929. Innovations: radio available; most bodies prewired for radio, with aerial built into top. Model year sales: 11,005. Model year production: 11,005. President and general manager of LaSalle was Lawrence P. Fisher. Since 1926, Cadillac Series designation had been based on cubic inches of engine displacement. For 1930, the dimensions of the LaSalle engine were identical to the 1928/1929, 341-A, -B Cadillac engine. To avoid confusion, the 1930 LaSalle was designated Series 340.

1930 LaSalle, all-weather phaeton, JAC

1931 LASALLE

1931 LaSalle, Fleetwood roadster, OCW

LASALLE — SERIES 345-A — EIGHT: Similar to Series 340 except as follows:

Bodies: No basic changes as with Series 355. Straight sill retained. Hood louvers retained until mid-model. When louvers were replaced by doors, cowl doors did not match hood doors. Radiator screen optional extra. New oval instrument panel, with different grouping than 355. Single bar bumper becomes only fast way to differentiate between 340 and early 345 from a distance.

Chassis and driveline: Metal covers on springs. Radiator positioned vertical instead of sloping to rear.

Engine: Displacement now same as 353 and 355. Series designation on V-8s no longer matches displacement. Intake muffler used. Three point engine mounting retained. Distributor 1-1/2 inches lower than on 355.

I.D. DATA: There were no serial numbers used. Engine numbers were stamped on crankcase just below the water inlet on the right-hand side. Starting: 900001. Ending: 910103.

Style No.	Body Type & Seating	Price	Weight	Prod. Total
Fisher				
31652	4-dr. Twn. Sed.-5P	2345	4665	NA
31658	2-dr. Cpe.-2/4P	2195	4470	NA
31659	4-dr. Sed.-5P	2295	4650	NA
31662	4-dr. Sed.-7P	2475	4750	NA
31663	4-dr. Imp. Sed.-7P	2595	4825	NA
31668	2-dr. Conv. Cpe.-2/4P	2295	4440	NA
31672	2 dr. Cpe.-5P	2295	4490	NA

Style No.	Body Type & Seating	Price	Weight	Prod. Total
Fleetwood				
4602	2-dr. Rds.-2/4P	2245	4345	NA
4657	4-dr. Tr.-7P	2345	4440	NA
4680	4-dr. All. Wthr. Phae.-5P	3245	4675	NA
NA	Sedanette-5P	3245	4650	NA
NA	Sednet. Cab.-5P	3245	4675	NA

ENGINE: Ninety degree L-head. Eight. Cast iron block on aluminum crankcase. B & S: 3-3/8 x 4-15/16 in. Disp.: 353 cu. in. C.R.: 5.35:1 std., 5.26:1 opt. Brake H.P.: 95 plus @ 3000 R.P.M. SAE/Taxable H.P.: 36.45. Main bearings: three. Valve lifters: mechanical. Carb.: Cadillac/Johnson, with intake silencer.

CHASSIS: (Series: 345-A) W.B.: 134 in. O.L.: 202 in. Height: 72-1/2 in. Frt/Rear Tread: 57-1/4/59-1/2 in. Tires: 6.50 x 19 (7.00 x 18 opt. on seven-passenger sedan).

1931 LaSalle, sedan, JAC

TECHNICAL: Selective, synchromesh transmission. Speeds: 3F/1R. LHD center control, RHD opt. Twin disc clutch. Shaft drive, torque tube. 3/4-floating rear axle, spiral bevel drive. Overall ratio: 4.75:1 std., 4.07:1, 4.54:1 opt. Mechanical brakes on four wheels (15 in. drums). Wood artillery wheels. Wheel size: 19 in.

OPTIONS: Trunks ($100.00-119.00). Tonneau windshield (185.00). Wind wings (25.00-47.50). Tire cover(s) (5.00-40.00). Mirrors (10.00-32.00/pair). Radio (price on application). Heater (41.00-55.00). Auxiliary lights (37.50-75.00). Seat covers (26.75-73.50). Heron or Goddess (20.00). Radiator screen (33.00).

HISTORICAL: Introduced August 1930. Model year sales: 10,103. Model year production: 10,103. President and general manager of LaSalle was Lawrence P. Fisher.

1932 LASALLE

LASALLE — SERIES 345-B — EIGHT: Engine and mechanical features same as V-8 Cadillac except for shorter wheelbase (130, 136 in. vs 134, 140 in.). Overall styling and appearance identical to V-8 Cadillac except for: seven body styles, all by Fisher. LaSalle emblems. Five hood ports on shorter hood. Continued use of 1931 (-A) lights. No fender tie-bar used, but monogram bar retained. Dual horns, projecting through headlight stanchions, have right angle trumpets. Dual rear lights used.

1932 LaSalle, coupe, JAC

I.D. DATA: Serial numbers were not used. Engine numbers were stamped on crankcase near the water inlet on the right-hand side. Starting: 1100001. Ending: 1103290.

Style No.	Body Type & Seating	Price	Weight	Prod. Total
Fisher — 130" wb				
32-678	2-dr. Cpe.-2/4P	2395	4660	NA
32-668	2-dr. Conv. Cpe.-2/4P	2545	4630	NA
32-672	2-dr. Twn. Cpe.-5P	2545	4695	NA
32-659	4-dr. Sed.-5P	2495	4840	NA
Fisher — 136" wb				
32-652	4-dr. Twn. Sed.-5P	2645	4895	NA
32-662	4-dr. Sed.-7P	2645	5025	NA
32-663	4-dr. Imp. Sed.-7P	2795	5065	NA

ENGINE: Ninety degree L-head. Eight. Cast iron block on aluminum crankcase. B & S: 3-3/8 x 4-15/16 in. Disp.: 353 cu. in. C.R.: 5.38:1 std.; 5.70:1, 5.20:1 opt. Brake H.P.: 115 @ 3000 R.P.M. SAE/Taxable H.P.: 36.45. Main bearings: three. Valve lifters: mechanical. Carb.: Cadillac/Johnson.

1932 LaSalle, sedan, JAC

CHASSIS: (Series 345-B) W.B.: 130, 136 in. O.L.: 204, 210 in. Frt/Rear Tread: 59-7/8/61 in. Tires: 7.00 x 17.

TECHNICAL: Selective, synchromesh transmission. Speeds: 3F/1R. LHD center controls, RHD opt. Twin disc clutch selective vacuum-activation. Shaft drive, torque tube. 3/4-floating rear axle, spiral bevel drive. Overall ratio: 4.36:1, 4.60:1. Mechanical brakes on four wheels (15-in. drums). Wire wheels std., demountable wood opt. Wheel size: 17 in. drop center.

OPTIONS: Tire cover(s) ($5.00-20.00 each). Trunks (100.00-180.00). Heron or Goddess (20.00). Radio (price on application). Heater (37.50-47.50). Auxiliary lights (37.50-57.50). Wind wings (25.00-47.50). Tonneau shield (185.00). Seat covers (26.50-73.50). Mirrors (8.00-16.00 each). Full covers for wire wheels (10.00 each). Six wire wheels w/fender wells and trunk rack (130.00). Five demountable wood wheels (30.00). Six demountable wood wheels w/wells and rack (166.00). Colored fender set (50.00).

HISTORICAL: Introduced January 1932. Model year sales: 3,290. Model year production: 3,290. President and general manager of LaSalle was Lawrence P. Fisher

1932 LaSalle, convertible coupe, JAC

1932

Series 345-B, V-8, 130" wb

	FP	5	4	3	2	1
Conv	2540	10,550	17,600	35,200	61,600	88,000
RS Cpe	2395	5900	9800	19,600	34,300	49,000
Twn Cpe	2545	5300	8800	17,600	30,800	44,000
Sed	2495	4100	6800	13,600	23,800	34,000

Series 345-B, V-8, 136" wb

	FP	5	4	3	2	1
Sed-7P	2645	4100	6800	13,600	23,800	34,000
Imp Sed-7P	2645	5300	8800	17,600	30,800	44,000
Twn Sed-7P	2645	5400	9000	18,000	31,500	45,000

1933 LASALLE

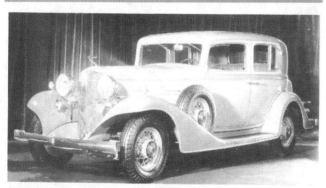

1933 LaSalle, town sedan, OCW

LASALLE — SERIES 345-C — EIGHT: The 1933 LaSalle had most of the new features of the Cadillac line, including new radiator grille/shell, skirted fenders, no draft ventilation, and vacuum-assisted brakes. To provide distinction, the LaSalle had four hood doors and retained the bumper and light system of the "B" Series. The new, hidden fender tie-bar was used but the monogram bar was dropped. Respective body styles had four-inch shorter wheelbase and an average $500 lower price.

I.D. DATA: There were no serial numbers used. Engine numbers were stamped on crankcase near the water inlet on the right-hand side. Starting: 2000001. Ending: 2003381.

Style No.	Body Type & Seating	Price	Weight	Prod. Total
Fisher — 130" wb				
33-659	4-dr. Sed.-5P	2245	4805	NA
33-668	2-dr. Conv. Cpe.-2/4P	2395	4675	NA
33-672	2-dr. Twn. Cpe.-5P	2395	4695	NA
33-678	2-dr. Cpe.-2/4P	2245	4730	NA
Fisher — 136" wb				
33-652	4-dr. Twn. Sed.-5P	2495	4915	NA
33-662	4-dr. Sed.-7P	2495	4990	NA
33-663	4-dr. Imp. Sed.-7P	2645	5020	NA
Fleetwood — 136" wb				
5281	2-dr. Twn. Cpe.-5P	—	—	NA

ENGINE: Ninety degree L-head. Eight. Cast iron block on aluminum crankcase. B & S: 3-3/8 x 4-15/16 in. Disp.: 353 cu. in. C.R.: 5.4:1 std., 5.7:1 opt. Brake H.P.: 115 @ 3000 R.P.M. SAE/Taxable H.P.: 36-45. Main bearings: three. Valve lifters: mechanical. Carb.: Cadillac/Johnson.

CHASSIS: (Series 345-C) W.B.: 130, 136 in. O.L.: app. 204-210 in. Frt/Rear Tread: 59-7/8/61 in. Tires: 7.00 x 17.

TECHNICAL: Selective synchromesh transmission. Speeds: 3F/1R. Lhd center control, Rhd optional. Twin disc clutch. Shaft drive, torque tube. 3/4-floating rear axle, spiral bevel drive. Overall ratio: 4.36:1, 4.60:1. Mechanical brakes on four wheels with vacuum assist (15-in. drums). Wire wheels std., demountable wood opt. Wheel size: 17 in. drop center.

OPTIONS: Sidemount covers. Wheel discs (chrome $10.00 each/body color 12.50 each). Radio (Standard 64.50, Imperial 74.50). Heater: hot air or hot water. Draft deflector for convertible coupe (35.00/pair). Luggage sets (37.00-110.00). Trunks w/luggage (104.00-180.00). Seat covers (10.00/seat). Mirrors. Spotlight (Lorraine 24.50). Dual pilot ray lights (44.50). "Torpedo" ornament (20.00). Six wire wheels with fender wells. Five demountable wood wheels. Six demountable wood wheels with fender wells.

HISTORICAL: Introduced January 1933. Innovations: Fisher no-draft individually controlled ventilation (I.C.V.) (vent windows). Model year sales: 3,381. Model year production: 3,381. President and general manager of LaSalle was Lawrence P. Fisher.

Imp Sed-7P	2495	4200	7000	14,000	24,500	35,000

See page 5 for body style abbreviation explanation

1934 LASALLE

1934 LaSalle, convertible coupe, DW

LASALLE — SERIES 50 — MODEL 350 — EIGHT: By 1933, LaSalle had become a Cadillac, discounted $500; and Cadillac had become a highly individualized luxury product. The early Thirties economy would not support this combination. The General Motors alternative to dropping the Cadillac Division was to produce the 1934 LaSalle, with the hope that LaSalle sales would bring the division out of the red. The 1934 LaSalle was presented as an entirely new car, backed by the prestige of Cadillac/Fleetwood, but not a Cadillac, and priced $1,000 less than the least expensive Cadillac, to compete for buyers in the upper medium price range. Cost was reduced by using off-the-shelf components from other GM divisions and outside suppliers.

Bodies: Body style selection reduced to four, all by Fleetwood. "Bodies by Fleetwood" may have sounded incongruous, but it was a selling point and likely filled a gap in the workload at Fleetwood. Styling emphasized streamlining and concealment of the chassis. Slender vee radiator grille sloped steeply to the rear. Teardrop lamps filleted to radiator housing. Hood, with circular ports, extended nearly to the

25 degree sloping windshield. Cowl vent door opened at the rear. All doors hinged at the rear. Beavertail rear deck completely covered the chassis and concealed luggage and spare-wheel compartment. Air-foil type front fenders arched low in the front to cover the chassis and blended into the radiator housing to eliminate splash shields. Biplane bumpers mounted on concealed coil springs.

Chassis: Entirely new X-type frame designed so as to reduce the overall height of the car by four inches. Entirely new A-frame type independent front suspension with coil springs and center point steering. Semi-elliptic rear springs to accommodate the Hotchkiss drive. Double acting shock absorbers, rear shocks being combined with a ride stabilizer bar. Bendix hydraulic brakes were Cadillac's first departure from mechanicals and were used only on LaSalle in 1934.

Driveline: Single plate dry disc clutch. Three-speed synchromesh transmission with helical cut spline shaft and gears. Rear axle semi-floating, with spiral bevel gears. Hotchkiss drive was a departure from Cadillac's long use of torque tube drive.

Engine: Eight-cylinder inline L-head of conventional design. B & S: 3 x 4-1/4 in., developing 95 hp @ 3700 R.P.M. Main bearings: five. Aluminum pistons, dual downdraft carburetor.

I.D. DATA: Serial numbers were on top surface of frame side bar, left side, just ahead of dash. Starting: 2100001. Serial number same as engine number. Ending: 2107218 (includes January, February, March 1935). Engine numbers were on left side of cylinder block, at front, just below cylinder head. Starting: 2100001. Ending: 2107218 (includes January, February, March 1935).

1934 LaSalle, four-door sedan, HAC

Style No.	Body Type & Seating	Price	Weight	Prod. Total
34159	4-dr. Sed.-5P	1695	3960	—
34182	4-dr. Club Sed.-5P	1695	3960	—
34168	2-dr. Conv. Cpe.-2/4P	1695	3780	—
34178	2-dr. Cpe.-2P	1595	3815	—
	4 dr. Conv. Sed.-5P (probably none built)	—	—	—

ENGINE: Inline. L-head. Eight. Cast iron block (block integral with upper crankcase). B & S: 3 x 4-1/4 in. Disp.: 240.3 cu. in. C.R.: 6.5:1 std., 5.5:1 opt. Brake H.P.: 95 @ 3700 R.P.M. Taxable H.P.: 28.8. Main bearings: five. Valve lifters: mechanical. Carb.: Stromberg EE-23 Duplex downdraft.

CHASSIS: (Series 50) W.B.: 119 in. O.L.: 202-1/4 in. Frt/Rear Tread: 58-15/16/60-1/2 in. Tires: 7.00 x 16.

TECHNICAL: Selective synchromesh transmission. Speeds: 3F/1R. Left-hand drive, center control (rhd opt.). Single plate clutch. Shaft drive, Hotchkiss. Semi-floating rear axle, spiral bevel drive. Overall ratio: 4.78:1. Hydraulic brakes on four wheels (emergency mechanical on rear wheels). Steel wheels with disc cover. Wheel size: 16 in. drop center.

OPTIONS: Dual sidemount. Sidemount cover(s) ($20.00 ea.). Fender skirts (wheel shields) (25.00 pair). Radio (standard 64.50, master 74.50). Heater (hot air, hot water, steam) (steam heater 44.50). Mirrors (8.00-10.00 each). Luggage racks, trunks (85.00-195.00). Seat covers. Spotlight (24.50). Torpedo ornament (20.00). Four spoke flexible steering wheel.

HISTORICAL: Introduced January 1934. Calendar year production: 6,169. Model year sales: 7,218. Model year production: 7,218. The president and general manager of LaSalle was Lawrence P. Fisher to May 31, 1934; Nicholas Dreystadt general manager after June 1, 1934.

A 1934 LaSalle convertible coupe was the Indy pace car in 1934.

Much has been written to the effect that the straight-eight LaSalle engine was in fact an Oldsmobile engine or was built by Oldsmobile for Cadillac. Contemporary factory information to Cadillac/LaSalle salesmen stated that the car was designed and developed by Cadillac engineers and the engine was built in the Cadillac factory. The suggestion was made that salesmen invite prospects to visit the Cadillac factory to see the LaSalle being built. The carefully chosen wording used by the factory leaves open the possibility that Cadillac started with raw or semi-finished Oldsmobile parts and finished/assembled the parts to special Cadillac tolerances. The similarities between Oldsmobile and LaSalle engines, transmissions, rear ends, brakes, etc. are too obvious to go unnoticed. The salesmens' information sheets list the following LaSalle parts sources: A.C. fuel pump, air cleaner, ammeter, Delco battery, Delco-Remy ignition, horn; Guide lights; Harrison radiator, thermostat, New Departure and Hyatt bearings; Stromberg carburetor; Lynite (Alcoa) pistons; Whitney timing chain and sprockets; Thompson valves; Oldberg muffler; Alemite-Zerk chassis lubrication, Automotive Fan & Bearing Co. fan; Borg & Beck clutch; Spicer universal joints; Brown-Lipe differential; Motor Wheel wheels; Saginaw steering gear, Bendix brakes; and A.O. Smith frame.

1935 LASALLE

1935 LaSalle, two-door sedan, AA

LASALLE — SERIES 35-50 — EIGHT: No major changes from 1934, but many detail improvements and a price reduction of approximately $400. Performance improved through detail changes in the engine and a nine percent weight reduction.

Bodies: Now made by Fisher, featuring new all-steel turret roof. Four-door town sedan replaced by two-door sedan. New vee windshield and two-division moldings in rear window. Wipers below windshield. Cowl ventilator opens forward. Gasoline filler neck moved to right rear fender. Built-in trunk on sedans. New, bar-type bumpers. Controls moved from steering wheel to instrument panel.

Chassis: Wheelbase increased to 120 in. Bore increased to 4-3/8 in. New carburetor with electric choke. New generator with charging rate controlled by electrical load and battery condition.

I.D. DATA: Serial numbers were located on top surface of frame side bar, left side, just ahead of dash. Starting: 2200001. Serial number same as engine number. Ending: 2208653. Engine numbers were located on left side of cylinder block, at front, just below cylinder head. Starting: 2200001. Ending: 2208653.

Style No.	Body Type & Seating	Price	Weight	Prod. Total
Fisher 120" wb				
35-5077	2-dr. Cpe.-2P	1225	3475	—
35-5067	2-dr. Conv. Cpe.-2/4P	1325	3510	—
35-5019	4-dr. Sed.-5P	1295	3650	—
35-5011	2-dr. Sed.-5P	1255	3620	—

ENGINE: Inline. L-head. Eight. Cast iron block (block integral with upper crankcase). B & S: 3 x 4-3/8 in. Disp.: 248 cu. in. C.R.: 6.25:1 std.; 5.75:1 opt. Brake H.P.: 105 @ 3600 R.P.M. SAE/Taxable H.P.: 28.8. Main bearings: five. Valve lifters: mechanical. Carb.: Stromberg EE-15 Duplex downdraft.

1935 LaSalle, four-door sedan, JAC

CHASSIS: (Series 50) W.B.: 120 in. O.L.: 200 in. Height: 64-1/2-67-1/2 in. Frt/Rear Tread: 58-1/8/59-1/16 in. Tires: 7.00 x 16.

TECHNICAL: Selective, synchromesh transmission. Speeds: 3F/1R. Left-hand drive, central control (rhd opt.). Single plate dry disc clutch. Shaft drive, Hotchkiss. Semi-floating rear axle, spiral bevel drive. Overall ratio: 4.55:1. Hydraulic brakes on four wheels (emergency mechanical on rear wheels). Disc wheels. Wheel size: 16 in. drop center.

OPTIONS: Dual sidemounts. Sidemount cover(s) ($35.00/pair). Radio (master/standard) (89.50/54.50). Heater (35.00). Clock (14.50). Seat covers. Flexible steering wheel (16.00). Wheel shields (25.00/pair).

HISTORICAL: Introduced March 1935. Innovations: All-steel turret tops. Model year sales: 8,653. Model year production: 8,653. The general manager of LaSalle was Nicholas Dreystadt.

1936 LASALLE

1936 LaSalle, convertible coupe, OCW

LASALLE — SERIES 36-50 — EIGHT: Changed little from the 1935 LaSalle. The new "Convex-Vee" grille retains the shape but has less slope than the old. New hood port treatment partially conceals the ports under a rounded canopy. The handbrake lever is moved to the left of the driver, under instrument panel. The exhaust system has two mufflers, in series. Vacuum advance has been added to the distributor.

I.D. DATA: Engine numbers were on the left side of the engine block at the forward end, just below the cylinder head. Starting: 2210001. Ending: 2223004.

Style No.	Body Type & Seating	Price	Weight	Prod. Total
36-5077	Cpe.-2P	1175	3460	—
36-5067	Conv. Cpe.-2P	1255	3540	—
36-5011	2-dr. Tr. Sed.-5P	1185	3605	—
36-5019	4-dr. Tr. Sed.-5P	1225	3635	—

ENGINE: Inline, L-head. Eight. Cast iron (block integral with upper half of crankcase). B & S: 3 x 4-3/8 in. Disp.: 248 cu. in. C.R.: 6.25:1 std.; 5.75:1 opt. Brake H.P.: 105 @ 3600 R.P.M. SAE/Taxable H.P.: 28.8. Main bearings: five. Valve lifters: mechanical. Carb.: Stromberg EE-15.

CHASSIS: (Series 36-50) W.B.: 120 in. O.L.: 200 in. Height: 65-1/2, 67-1/2 in. Frt/Rear Tread: 58-1/2/59-1/16 in. Tires: 7.00 x 16.

1936 LaSalle, four-door sedan, JAC

TECHNICAL: Selective synchromesh transmission. Speeds: 3F/1R. Left-hand drive, center control (rhd opt.) Handbrake at left, under panel. Single plate clutch. Shaft drive, Hotchkiss. Semi-floating rear axle, spiral bevel drive. Overall ratio: 4.55:1. Hydraulic brakes on four wheels. (Emergency mechanical on rear wheels). Disc wheels. Wheel size: 16 in. drop center.

OPTIONS: Sidemount cover(s) ($17.50). Radio (master/standard 89.50/54.50). Heater (18.50). Clock (14.50). Seat covers. Flexible steering wheel (16.00). Trim rings (1.50 each).

HISTORICAL: Introduced October 1935. Model year sales: 13,004. Model year production: 13,004. The general manager of LaSalle was Nicholas Dreystadt.

1937 LASALLE

1937 LaSalle, four-door sedan, HAC

LASALLE — SERIES 37-50 — EIGHT: Body styling changes were minor: Die-cast eggcrate grille; hood louver treatment featuring rectangular lines; headlights attached lower on the radiator casing; new front fenders with higher rear halves and a lengthwise crease along the top surface; bumpers carrying the LaSalle insignia; entire rear quarter window pivoted and windshields with a 39 degree slope and a deeper vee. 1937 LaSalle bodies were constructed entirely of steel. The line now included a convertible sedan. The big change for 1937 was the return to a V-8 engine — the 322-cubic inch unit as used in the 1936 Cadillac Series 60. This engine shared all the changes made in other 1937 V-8s. Unique to the LaSalle and the Cadillac Series 60 was the relocation of the exhaust down-pipe to the front of the right-hand cylinder block and the use of a single muffler. Chassis changes, common to LaSalle and Cadillac Series 60 included use of hypoid rear axle, addition of front stabilizer bar, new steering box with shaft out of bottom. A LaSalle commercial chassis with 160-3/8 in. wheelbase was offered. This, and all Cadillac commercial chassis, featured one-piece side rails in the frame.

I.D. DATA: Engine numbers were on the crankcase, just behind the left cylinder group, parallel to the dash. Starting: 2230001. Ending: 2262005.

Style No.	Body Type & Seating	Price	Weight	Prod. Total
37-5011	2-dr. Tr. Sed.-5P	1105	3780	—
37-5019	4-dr. Tr. Sed.-5P	1145	3810	—
37-5049	Conv. Sed.-5P	1485	3850	—
37 5067	Conv. Cpe.-2P	1175	3715	—
37 5027	Spt. Cpe.-2P	995	3675	—

ENGINE: Ninety degree, L-head. Eight. Cast iron block (blocks cast enbloc with crankcase). B & S: 3-3/8 x 4-1/2 in. Disp.: 322 cu. in. C.R.: 6.25:1 std.; 5.75:1 opt. Brake H.P.: 125 @ 3400 R.P.M. SAE/Taxable H.P.: 36.45. Main bearings: three. Valve lifters: hydraulic. Carb.: Stromberg AA-25, Carter WDO-374S.

1937 LaSalle, convertible sedan, OCW

CHASSIS: (Series 37-50) W.B.: 124 in. O.L.: 201-1/4 in. Frt/Rear Tread: 58/59 in. Tires: 7.00 x 16. (Series 37-50 commercial chassis) W.B.: 160-3/8 in. O.L.: 237-7/8 in. Tires: 7.00 x 16.

TECHNICAL: Selective, synchromesh transmission. Speeds: 3F/1R. Lhd, center control, emergency brake at left under panel (rhd opt.). Single disc clutch. Shaft drive, Hotchkiss. Semi-floating rear axle. Hypoid gearing. Overall ratio: 3.92:1. Hydraulic brakes on four wheels. Disc wheels. Wheel size: 16 in.

OPTIONS: Sidemount cover(s) ($15.00-17.50). Radio (master/standard 79.50/59.50). Heater (19.50-60.00). Seat covers (7.50 per seat). Wheel discs (4.00 each). Trim rings (1.50 each). Flexible steering wheel (15.00).

HISTORICAL: Introduced November 1936. Model year sales: 32,005. Model year production: 32,005. The general manager of LaSalle was Nicholas Dreystadt.

1938 LASALLE

1938 LaSalle, coupe, OCW

LASALLE — SERIES 38-50 — EIGHT: The 1938 LaSalle remained much the same as the 1937 models. Along with many refine-

ments, there were a few notable changes. LaSalle used the front-opening "alligator" hood and the column gearshift common to the full Cadillac line. The grille remained eggcrate style but was two inches wider. Hood louvers were longer and more visible, due to the fact that the headlights were mounted low, on the sheet metal between the fenders and the grille. Chevrons were deleted from the nose of the front fenders. If used, sidemount covers were hinged on the fenders. Horns were mounted just behind the grille. The battery was under the hood on the right-hand side but was removed from under the fender.

I.D. DATA: Serial numbers were located on left frame side bar, at the rear of the left front motor support. Starting: Same as engine number. Ending: Same as engine number. Engine numbers were on crankcase, just behind left cylinder block. Starting: 2270001. Ending: 2285501.

1938 LaSalle, four-door sedan, OCW

Style No.	Body Type & Seating	Price	Weight	Prod. Total
38-5027	Cpe.-2P	1295	3745	—
38-5067	Conv. Cpe.-2P	1415	3735	—
38-5049	Conv. Sed.-5P	1820	3870	—
38-5011	2-dr. Tr. Sed.-5P	1340	3800	—
38-5019	4-dr. Tr. Sed.-5P	1380	3830	—

ENGINE: Ninety degree, L-Head. Eight. Cast iron block (blocks cast enbloc with crankcase). B & S: 3-3/8 x 4-1/2 in. Disp.: 322 cu. in. C.R.: 6.25:1. Brake H.P.: 125 @ 3400 R.P.M. SAE/Taxable H.P.: 36.45. Main bearings: three. Valve lifters: hydraulic. Carb.: Stromberg AAV-25, Carter WDO 392s.

CHASSIS: (Series 38-50) W.B.: 124 in. O.L.: 201 in. Frt/Rear Tread: 58/59 in. Tires: 7.00 x 16. (Series 38-50 commercial chassis) W.B.: 160 in.

TECHNICAL: Selective synchromesh manual transmission. Speeds: 3F/1R. Lhd "gearshift on column." Handbrake at left (rhd opt.). Single disc clutch. Shaft drive, Hotchkiss. Semi-floating rear axle. Hypoid gears. Overall ratio: 3.92:1. Hydraulic brakes on four wheels. Disc wheels. Wheel size: 16 in.

OPTIONS: Radio (master/standard) ($79.50/65.00). Heater (26.50-42.50). Clock (12.50). Seat cover(s) (7.50 per seat). Spotlight (18.50). Automatic battery filler (7.50). Flexible steering wheel (15.00). Foglights (17.50 pair). Wheel discs (4.00 each). Trim rings (1.50 each).

HISTORICAL: Introduced October 1937. Model year sales and production: 15,501. The general manager of LaSalle was Nicholas Dreystadt.

1939 LASALLE

LASALLE — SERIES 39-50 — EIGHT: The 1939 LaSalle was characterized by a new tall, narrow grille plus side grilles; all fine-pitch die-cast units. A new louver panel was set to the rear of the hood side panels. Headlights were once more fixed to the sides of the radiator casing. Glass area was increased by more than 25 percent. Closed sedans were available with "Sunshine Turret Top." Chrome reveals appeared on all windows and the windshield. All but the lower front door hinge were concealed. Runningboards had become a no cost option. Chassis changes included: tube and fin in place of cellular radiator core; vacuum for crankcase ventilation generated by motion of the car rather than by engine intake system; new cross-link steering hookup.

1939 LaSalle, coupe, OCW

I.D. DATA: Serial numbers were on the left frame side bar, opposite the steering gear. Starting: Same as engine number. Ending: Same as engine number. Engine numbers were on the crankcase, just behind the left cylinder block, parallel to the dash. Starting: 2290001. Ending: 2313028.

Style No.	Body Type & Seating	Price	Weight	Prod. Total
Fisher Series 39-50, 120" wb				
39-5027	Cpe.-2P	1323	3635	—
39-5067	Conv. Cpe.-2P	1475	3715	—
39-5011	2-dr. Tr. Sed.-5P	1358	3710	—
39-5011-A	2-dr. Tr. Sed. (STT)-5P	1398	—	—
39 5029	Conv. Sed.-5P	1895	3780	—
39-5019	4-dr. Tr. Sed.-5P	1398	3740	—
39-5019-A	4-dr. Tr. Sed. (STT)-5P	1438	—	—
39-5019-F	4-dr. Tr. Sed. (Div)-5P	—	—	—

Note: (STT) Sunshine Turret Top.

ENGINE: Ninety degree, L-head. Eight. Cast iron block (blocks cast enbloc with crankcase). B & S: 3-3/8 x 4-1/2 in. Disp.: 322 cu. in. C.R.: 6.25:1. Brake H.P.: 125 @ 3400 R.P.M. SAE/Taxable H.P.: 36.45. Main bearings: three. Valve lifters: hydraulic. Carb.: Carter WDO 423s.

CHASSIS: (Series 39-50) W.B.: 120 in. O.L.: 202-112 in. Frt/Rear Tread: 58/59 in. Tires: 7.00 x 16. (Series 39-50 Commercial Chassis) W.B.: 156-1/2 in. O.L.: 239 in. Tires: 7.00 x 16.

1939 LaSalle, convertible sedan, JAC

TECHNICAL: Selective synchromesh manual transmission. Speeds: 3F/1R. Lhd; gearshift on column, handbrake at left. Single disc clutch. Shaft drive, Hotchkiss. Semi-floating rear axle. Hypoid gears. Overall ratio: 3.92:1. Hydraulic brakes on four wheels. Slotted disc wheels. Wheel size: 16 in.

OPTIONS: Radio ($69.50). Heater (31.50). Seat cover(s) (8.25 per seat). Spotlight (18.50). Windshield washer (5.75). Automatic battery filler (7.50). Foglights (14.50 pair).

HISTORICAL: Introduced October 1938. Model year sales and production: 23,028. The general manager of LaSalle was Nicholas Dreystadt.

1940 LASALLE

1940 LaSalle, Special convertible coupe, OCW

LASALLE — SERIES 40-50, 40-52 — EIGHT: LaSalle ended, as it began, with distinctive body styles; the Series 52 "Torpedo" or "Projectile" bodied "Specials." Introduced as coupe and sedan, the 52 line was expanded in mid-year with convertible coupe and convertible sedan. The "Torpedo" styles featured 45 degree sloping windshield, curved rear window, no belt molding, and rounder, smoother line down rear of body and trunk. A vacuum-powered top was used on the Series 52 convertible coupe.

Body changes on Series 50 and 52 included: wider spacing of center and side grille bars; triple vents on hood side panels, fenders flowing without a valley into the hood; sealed beam headlights built into the fenders, and parking lights on top of the headlights.

I.D. DATA: Serial numbers were on the left frame side bar, opposite the steering gear. Starting: Same as engine number. Ending: Same as engine number. Engine numbers were on the crankcase, just behind the left cylinder block, parallel to the dash. Starting: (Series 40-50) 2320001; (Series 40-52) 4320001. Ending: (Series 40-50) 2330382; (Series 40-52) 4333751.

Style No.	Body Type & Seating	Price	Weight	Prod. Total
Fisher Series 40-50 123 in. w.b.				
40-5027	Cpe.-2P	1240	3700	—
40-5067	Conv. Cpe.-2P	1395	3805	—
40-5011	2-dr. Tr. Sed.-5P	1280	3760	—
40-5011-A	2-dr. Tr. Sed. (STT)-5P	—	—	—
40-5029	Conv. Sed.-5P	1800	4000	—
40-5019	4-dr. Tr. Sed.-5P	1320	3790	—
40-5019-A	4-dr. Tr. Sed. (STT)-5P	—	—	—
40-5019-F	4-dr. Tr. Sed. (Div)-5P	—	—	—

Note: (STT) Sunshine Turret Top

Style No.	Body Type & Seating	Price	Weight	Prod. Total
Fisher Series 40-52 123 in. w.b.				
40-5227C	Cpe. 2P	1380	3810	—
40-5219	Tr. Sed.-5P	1440	3900	—
40-5229	Conv. Sed.-5P	1895	4110	—
40-5267	Conv. Cpe.-2P	1535	3915	—

ENGINE: Ninety degree, L Head. Eight. Cast iron block (blocks case enbloc with crankcase). B & S: 3-3/8 x 4-1/2 in. Disp.: 322 cu. in. C.R.: 6.25:1. Brake H.P.: 130 @ 3400 R.P.M. SAE/Taxable H.P.: 36.45. Main bearings: three. Valve lifters: hydraulic. Carb.: Carter WDO 460s.

CHASSIS: (Series 40-50) W.B.: 123 in. O.L.: 206-3/4 in. Frt/Rear Tread: 58/59 in. Tires: 7.00 x 16. (Series 40-52) W.B.: 123 in. O.L.: 210-1/2 in. Frt/Rear Tread: 58/59 in. Tires: 7.00 x 16. (Series 40-50 Commercial Chassis) W.B.: 159 in. O.L.: 244-7/8 in. Tires: 7.00 x 16.

1940 LaSalle, four-door sedan, JAC

TECHNICAL: Selective synchromesh manual transmission. Speeds: 3F/1R. Lhd; gearshift on column; handbrake at left (rhd opt.). Single disc clutch. Shaft drive, Hotchkiss. Semi-floating rear axle. Hypoid gears. Overall ratio: 3.92:1. Hydraulic brakes on four wheels. Slotted disc wheels. Wheel size: 16 in.

OPTIONS: Radio ($69.50). Heater (26.50-52.50). Seat covers (8.25 per seat). Spotlight (18.50). Automatic battery filler (7.50). Flexible steering wheel (15.00). Foglights (14.50 pair). Windshield washer (6.50). Grille guard. Wheel discs (4.00 each). Trim rings (1.50 each).

HISTORICAL: Introduced October 1939. Model year sales and production: (Series 40-50) 10,382; (Series 40-52) 13,751. The general manager of LaSalle was Nicholas Dreystadt.

"Gee, Our Old LaSalle Ran Great"

1930 Cadillac Fleetway all-weather four-passenger phaeton.

LaSalle led GM styling for years

By Robert C. Ackerson

Even today, 51 years after the last LaSalle was built the mention of its name elicits a certain amount of nostalgia about the not too distant past when the romance of the open road was an irresistable temptation. Even Archie and Edith Bunker, when they sang the praises of those days when life seemed simpler, recalled that, "Gee, our old LaSalle ran great."

In 1925 when the idea for the LaSalle was first proposed by Alfred Sloan, president of General Motors, the economic outlook for the nation looked bright and the horizon of prosperity was free of the dark clouds of the Great Depression four years in the future. The automobile industry had put the disastrous post-WWI sales collapse behind and was leading the nation's economy to new levels of output.

Its undisputed leader was Henry Ford who ranked high on the list of America's most admired men. Ford was the very epitome of the American Captain of Industry. His newly constructed plant at River Rouge, turning out Model Ts at a dizzy pace, was a dramatic symbol of Ford's domination of the industry. It seemed to many that as long as he continued to pass on the benefits of mass production and the vertical consolidation of his corporation his opponents were destined to an inferior competitive position.

In sharp contrast to Ford's apparently impregnable position General Motors was emerging from the most critical period of its history. When the automobile market crashed in 1921 GM had found itself burdened not only with a huge inventory of unsold cars but with extremely high fixed costs. In addition the rather haphazard lines of responsibility set up by William Durant, provided virtually no control over how the company was spending its rapidly dwindling cash reserves. To make matters even more serious Durant had, in a sincere attempt to keep the price of GM common stock from collapsing, been purchasing GM stock on the market with his personal funds.

Durant's efforts were futile. He ended up owing more than $30 million to his stockbrokers and it is virtually a certainty that without the financial intervention of Pierre duPont and the J.P. Morgan interests, General Motors would have been forced into bankruptcy. But four years later, after duPont had briefly served as GM president (1920-23) the corporation, now under the leadership of the brilliant Alfred Sloan was preparing to challenge Ford's position of supremacy. General Motors was about to rise out of the midst of near-ruin and through new innovations in management and a revolutionary marketing concept, emerge the undisputed leader of the automotive industry in America.

While the LaSalle was produced only from 1927 to 1940 the philosophy which inspired its development was basic to General Motors' success. Shortly after assuming control, Sloan and his associates took a long, hard look at the GM lineup of automobiles. Much of what they saw they didn't like. But to follow the Ford lead and attempt to produce a competitor to the Model T seemed pointless. Ford had an iron clad hold on the field of basic transportation and any attempt to do battle with the Dearborn forces on their own terms would be futile.

Instead, Sloan proposed a bold new plan of action. Why not offer, he argued, automobiles beginning at a price just above the Model T and continuing up to the highest level? In each case the General Motors car would be more advanced and more attractive than its competition, thus justifying a slightly higher price tag. As part of this new marketing program work began on the new LaSalle, which was to fill the price gap between the lowest-priced Cadillac and the most expensive Buick. But the LaSalle was not intended to be a watered down version of the rather staid Cadillac. Instead, Sloan intended it to be an automobile with a vibrant, dynamic personality of its own that would compare favorably with the custom-bodied cars of the time.

L'Opéra

LA SALLE—CAR OF THOSE WHO LEAD

Wherever the admired and the notable are gathering, observe the frequency with which a LaSalle rolls to the entrance. The famous, the beautiful, the social arbiters—the roster of LaSalle ownership is studded with their sparkling names. Sophisticated judges, these, of what is best. In a motor car they demand much—so much that all the beauty and out-standing luxury of the LaSalle would fail to satisfy were it not coupled with the incom-

parable character of LaSalle performance. It is the instinctive appreciation of such men and women for all that is finest which leads them to select LaSalle. They are enthused by its Fisher coachwork, its comfort and its impressive, original beauty. They are won even more, however, by the fact that the La Salle chassis, with its magnificently efficient 90-degree, V-type, 8-cylinder engine is to-day's highest expression of the automotive art

You may possess a La Salle on the liberal term-payment plan of the General Motors Acceptance Corporation — the appraisal value of your used car acceptable as cash — priced from $2495 to $2895 f. o. b. Detroit

CADILLAC MOTOR CAR COMPANY
DIVISION OF GENERAL MOTORS CORPORATION
DETROIT, MICHIGAN   OSHAWA, CANADA

LASALLE

MANUFACTURED · COMPLETELY · BY · THE · CADILLAC · MOTOR · CAR · COMPANY · WITHIN · ITS · OWN · PLANTS.

This advertisement for LaSalle appeared in the December 1927 issue of *Country Life* magazine.

Lawrence P. Fisher, Cadillac's general manager, believed that styling was the most effective way to convey this personality to the motoring public, in the mid-1920s G.M. styling, especially as applied to the Buicks and Cadillacs was rather pedestrian and uninspired. Not surprisingly, many Cadillac customers turned to independent coach builders for their body designs. On the west coast the firm of Don Lee had developed a good reputation in this field with personalities such as "Fatty" Arbuckle and Tom Mix included in their list of clients. It was natural therefore that Fisher would call on businesses like Don Lee for possible new talent for the LaSalle project.

On one such visit a young designer named Harley Earl came to his attention. Earl's father had started the Earl Carriage Works prior to World War I and as an adolescent, Earl had worked in his father's business, quickly acquiring the skills of a master stylist. Soon after the senior Earl sold his business to Don Lee he was put in charge of their customizing and coach-building operation. Fisher was quick to recognize Earl's extraordinary ability and brought him back to Detroit to begin work on the styling of the new LaSalle. While this was originally a temporary position it quickly evolved into a permanent relationship. Alfred Sloan, who possessed an uncanny ability to delegate authority and encourage individual initiative and yet retain clear cut lines of authority and accountability, created the General Motors Art and Color Section with Harley Earl in charge. Thus began a long and distinguished career at General Motors for Harley Earl. When Earl retired in 1958 as vice president in charge of styling he was replaced by the equally talented William Mitchell, perhaps best known for the original Corvette Sting Ray.

Historians have been quick to point out the influence of the Hispano-Suiza upon Earl's design for the LaSalle. Since Earl, himself, described the Hispano as a car he greatly admired, the relationship is quite clear. Perhaps symbolic of the European influence was the LaSalle emblem which was based upon the coat-of-arms of Sieur Rene Robert de LaSalle. This design, with the addition of a pair of wings bore a less than coincidental similarity to that of the Hispano-Suiza.

The new LaSalle was an immediate sensation. No effort was made to create a profile that suggested a long smooth flowing line. Instead, Earl deliberately broke up and separated the lines of the car. At the same time, however, his design blended all the elements of the car into a single dominant theme; that of a short, compact automobile with plenty of power. This was just the type of car the sophisticated, relatively affluent buyer of the late twenties was looking for.

The sharp, angular LaSalle side view was further dramatized by the use of 12 large vertical engine louvers, which Earl made no attempt to conceal. As could be expected, in its front view the LaSalle's European flavor was very much in evidence. The two large headlights were connected by a short tie rod carrying a "LaS" monogram in the center. The lights themselves were supported by two very solid appearing vertical tubular posts. When a LaSalle, particularly a roadster, was equipped with optional twin spot lights, also with verti-

cal mounts, the head-on view was very impressive. The mixture of vertical and horizontal lines, reinforced by the high, narrow radiator with its vertical shutters created an impression of speed and grace never before seen on a mass-produced American automobile.

The original LaSalle was a watershed in U.S. automotive design. Being the first production American car to really have been thoroughly styled, it symbolized the growing maturity of the American automotive market. No longer were Americans content with basic transportation. The automobile had become an expression of one's good taste and lifestyle, and the owner of a LaSalle was recognized as a person of discriminating judgment in the choice of his automobile.

During its short 13-year life span the LaSalle served as pace car for the Indianapolis 500 three times (1927, 1934 and 1937). While LaSalle never attempted to establish a reputation based solely on performance it was still known as a good going automobile. In June 1927 a roadster, sans fenders, running boards, lights and windshield averaged 95.2 mph for ten hours at the General Motors Proving Grounds at Milford, Michigan. To this day the Proving Grounds logo carries a representation of this LaSalle.

In 1934, when the LaSalle was thoroughly restyled, Harley Earl's styling team once again broke new ground, setting the styling theme that characterized General Motors cars for the rest of the decade.

While proposed LaSalle models for 1941 reached the clay and wood mock-up stage, 1940 was the final year of production. The reasons for the LaSalle's demise are several. Some historians see LaSalle as a victim of the negative impact created by the 1934-1936 models using some Oldsmobile components. This practice, contrary to legends, did not extend to the engines since the only Olds component was the block casting. The public assumed, and many still believe, the entire straight-eight engine was identical to contemporary Oldsmobiles. Although the 1937 LaSalle returned to the V-8 Cadillac engine, perhaps damage had been done.

Finally the Great Depression had altered the automobile market in such a way as to make the LaSalle's continuation rather redundant as the series 61 Cadillac was competing in the same price field.

In 1955 the LaSalle name was revived for use on two handsome GM "dream cars," a roadster and a pillarless hardtop sedan. Both attracted a great deal of interest but the roadster was especially alluring. True to its heritage it reflected a very strong European influence. Among its innovative features were a 2.5-liter, fuel-injected V-6 engine and a deDion rear axle.

In 1967 when Cadillac introduced its front-wheel-drive Eldorado, and recently with the unveiling of the Seville hopes were high that perhaps the LaSalle name would be resurrected. However, in too many people's minds LaSalle meant a lower-priced Cadillac which was not the impression Cadillac wanted its new cars to convey. It might just be that GM missed a golden opportunity in 1955. Just imagine a LaSalle two-seater, based on Corvette running gear. Given the evolution of the Corvette a slightly higher-priced, more refined roadster would have been just the perfect car to be called a LaSalle.

La Salle $1175   Cadillac $1645

CADILLAC
Fleetwood $2445

THE ROYAL FAMILY OF MOTORDOM

La Salle
CONVERTIBLE COUPE

THE *Difference* IS MORE MARKED THAN EVER

Those who are not able to avail themselves of the rare privileges which Cadillac and La Salle owners enjoy, can still be better served than ever before by a number of excellent cars of lower price. ✧ ✧ ✧ The whole industry has moved forward—mostly in the direction of massed demand and sprightly appearance and performance; but, of course, Cadillac has been, as always, in the forefront of that forward movement. ✧ ✧ ✧ In fact, the difference and the distinction in Cadillac and La Salle have become more marked than ever, for Cadillac has deliberately planned its 1936 creations to widen the gap between the Royal Family of Motordom and all other cars in the world. ✧ ✧ ✧ Those who revel in the special ease and elegance and the pronounced distinction which Cadillac and La Salle provide for their owners, simply cannot satisfy themselves with anything else. ✧ ✧ ✧ The briefest of experiences, either at the wheel or as a chauffeured passenger, will prove this to your entire satisfaction.

Model illustrated $1255. Monthly payments to suit your purse. Prices list at Detroit, Michigan, subject to change without notice. Special equipment extra.

The 1936 LaSalle was part of "the royal family of motordom."

LaSalle: Harley Earl's first assignment

By Richard Kelley

Cadillac's sister car, the LaSalle, lead a checkered career in its 13 years of existence.

The car originally was visualized by Alfred Sloan in 1924 when he asked the Cadillac division to produce a new model to bridge the gap between its lowest priced ($2,995) Cad and the top of the Buick line, which sold for $1,995.

As is now history, LaSalle was Harley Earl's first assignment at General Motors, and his sporty creation caused a sensation when it was unveiled at the 1927 Boston auto show. This was the first major production automobile ever planned by a stylist instead of an engineer, and it heralded a new era for Detroit.

After a first year production of over 10,000, LaSalle continued to advance until the Depression caused sagging sales. Only a new and dynamic design by Earl and thrifty use of parts from other GM divisions (like a re-worked Oldsmobile straight eight in place of LaSalle's V-8) saved the marque from extinction in 1934. Sales began inching upward, and by 1937 LaSalle was boasting the highest sales for the year in its history.

Prices for the all-new 1937 LaSalle started at only $995 and ranged to $1,495. The factory advertised that this was the lowest-priced LaSalle ever, and without mentioning the 1934-36 Olds-engined cars, emphasized that LaSalle was completely Cadillac division-built.

Available at the showrooms was a full line of body styles including two- and four-door sedans, a coupe, a convertible coupe and convertible sedan. The new look followed the GM trend for the year: lush, bulbous bodies with skirted pontoon fenders. New, for 1937, was a narrow checkerboard grille similar to Cadillac's, and a return to a V-8 engine was subtly hinted at by the three chevrons which graced the leading edge of the fenders. The hood was still center hinged and lifted from the sides, but featured six horizontal strips down the hood sides. Another 11 short chrome bars pointed up the bulge where the hood met the radiator shell on each side. Free-standing bullet headlights were mounted on the catwalks, and the bumpers carried the La-Salle logo at the center.

Behind the steering wheel (a banjo-spoked affair that looked like the contemporary Ford wheel) the driver had a 110-mph speedometer and matching clock flanking the central radio controls with two oblong gauges at the right end of the dash to tell him of gas level, oil pressure and amps. The shift lever was still on the floor; it would be moved to the steering column the next year.

Interiors were plush with firm but comfortable seats front and back. With the new and softer suspension, the LaSalle's ride was smooth and easy. A torsion bar at the front and stabilizer bar at the back kept the car level on everything but an all-out road course.

1937 was perhaps LaSalle's finest hour. The car was good-looking, powerful, and a Cadillac in all but name. Sales were the best they ever would be and the top General Motors officials were pleased. But not for long because the minor recession of 1938 hit LaSalle hard.

Sales dropped to half (so did Ford's and Chevrolet's, but they were dealing in hundreds of thousands of units), inched back up the next year and sagged to just over 10,000 cars sold in 1940. At General Motors, a decision was made. There would be no more LaSalle. Although work was done on a prototype for 1941, the production line was closed down in the autumn of 1940. The final car, a torpedo sedan, and LaSalle were dead.

1937 LaSalle convertible.

A WORD ABOUT OLD CADILLACS . . .

The market for cars more than 15 years old may be stronger now than ever. Some buyers of pre-1985 cars are collectors who purchase vehicles that they particularly enjoy, or feel are likely to increase in value the older they get. Other buyers prefer the looks, size, performance, and reliability of what they perceive as yesterday's better-built automobiles.

With a typical year 2000 model selling for around $20,000, many Americans find themselves priced out of the new-car market. Late-model used cars can be pricey too, although often short on distinctive looks and roominess. The older cars may use more fuel, but their purchase prices are typically a whole lot lower.

New cars and late-model used cars tend to depreciate rapidly in value. Many can't tow large trailers or mobile homes and their high-tech engineering is often expensive to maintain or repair. In contrast, well-kept older cars are mechanically simpler, but often very powerful. In addition, they generally appreciate in value as they grow scarce and collectable. Even insuring them can be cheaper.

Selecting a car and paying the right price for it are two considerations old-Cadillac buyers face. What year did Cadillac introduce its first V-8 engine? When did LaSalle enter the new-car marketplace, and why? How did Cadillac distinguish itself in the Dewar Trophy competition of 1908? Which models of both Cadillac and LaSalle are most valuable today? How did the distinguishing features of these fine automobiles change from year to year?

Standard Catalog of Cadillac 1903-2000 answers these questions and many more. The Price Guide section lists all models built for the ninety-one-year period from 1903 through 1993 and points out what they sell for today in six different, graded conditions. Essentially, vehicles built since 1993 are generally considered "used cars" of which few, as yet, have excited the interest of collectors.

The price estimates contained in this book are current as of the publication date, August 2000. After that date, more current pricing may be obtained by referring to *Old Cars Price Guide*, which is available at many book stores, newsstands, and supermarket magazine departments or directly from Krause Publications, 700 E. State St., Iola, WI 54990-0001, telephone 1-800-258-0929.

HOW TO USE THE CADILLAC PRICE GUIDE

On the following pages is a **CADILLAC PRICE GUIDE**. The worth of an old car is a "ballpark" estimate at best. The estimates contained in this book are based upon national and regional data compiled by the editors of *Old Cars News & Marketplace* and *Old Cars Price Guide*. These data include actual bids and prices at collector car auctions and sales, classified and display advertising of such vehicles, verified reports of private sales and input from experts.

Price estimates are listed for cars in six different states of condition. These conditions (1-6) are illustrated and explained) in the **VEHICLE CONDITION SCALE** on the following pages. Values are for complete vehicles — not parts cars — except as noted. Modified car values are not included, but can be estimated by figuring the cost of restoring the subject vehicle to original condition and

adjusting the figures shown here accordingly.

Appearing below is a section of chart takes from the **CADILLAC PRICE GUIDE** to illustrate the following elements:

A. MAKE The make of car, or marque name, appears in large, boldface type at the beginning of each value section.

B. DESCRIPTION The extreme left-hand column indicates vehicle year, model name, body type, engine configuration, and, in some cases, wheelbase.

C. CONDITION CODE The six columns to the right are headed by the numbers one through six (1-6), which correspond to the conditions described in the **VEHICLE CONDITION SCALE** on the following pages.

D. PRICE The price estimates, in dollars, appear below their respective condition code headings and across from the vehicle descriptions.

A. MAKE ———— **CADILLAC**

Description	6	5	4	3	2	1
1958						
Series 62, V-8						
4dr HdT Sh Dk	450	1075	3000	5500	7700	11,000
6W Sed	450	1150	3600	6000	8400	12,000
4 dr Sed DeV	500	1400	4200	7000	9800	14,000
Cpe	800	3400	6900	11,500	16,100	23,000
Cpe DeV	800	3750	7500	12,500	17,500	25,000
Conv	1200	5850	11,700	19,500	27,300	39,000
Eldorado, V-8						
Sev (2 dr Hd Tp)	800	4350	8700	14,500	20,300	29,000
Biarritz Conv	1500	6750	13,500	22,500	31,500	45,000
Fleetwood 60 Special, V-8V-8						
4 dr HdTp	800	3000	6000	10,000	14,000	20,000
Eldorado Brougham, V-8						
4 dr HdTp	1200	4800	9600	16,000	22,400	32,000
Series 75						
8P Sed	650	2800	5700	9500	13,300	19,000
8P Imp Sed	800	3150	6300	10,500	14,700	21,000

C. CONDITION CODE (heads the six columns)

D. PRICE

VEHICLE CONDITION SCALE

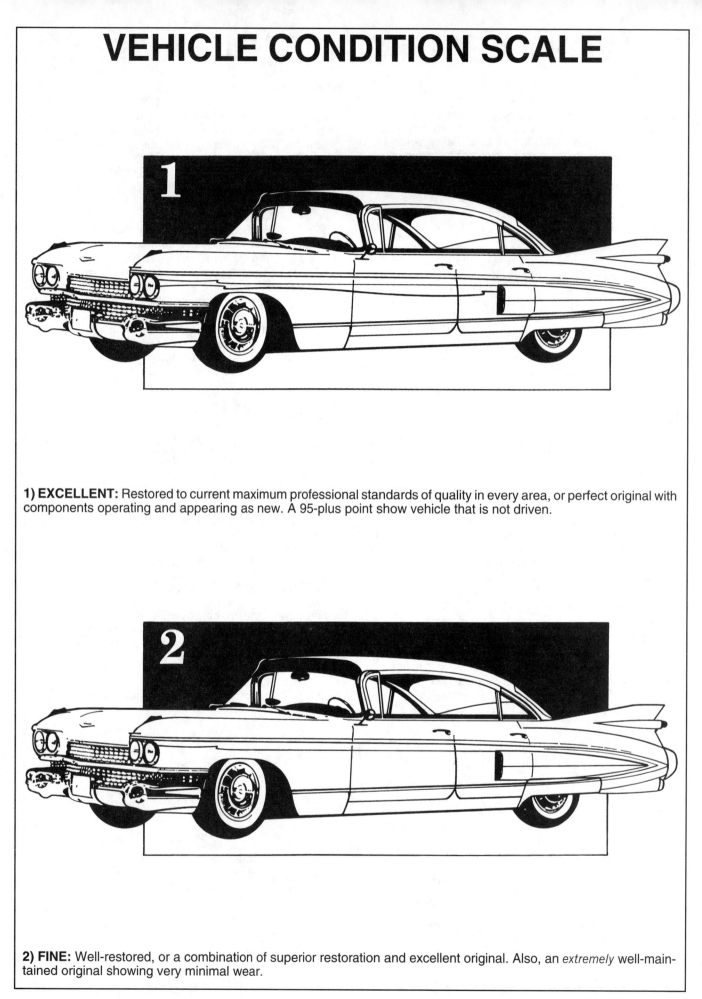

1) EXCELLENT: Restored to current maximum professional standards of quality in every area, or perfect original with components operating and appearing as new. A 95-plus point show vehicle that is not driven.

2) FINE: Well-restored, or a combination of superior restoration and excellent original. Also, an *extremely* well-maintained original showing very minimal wear.

3) VERY GOOD: Completely operable original or "older restoration" showing wear. Also, a good amateur restoration, all presentable and serviceable inside and out. Plus, combinations of well-done restoration and good operable components or a partially restored vehicle with all parts necessary to complete and/or valuable NOS parts.

4) GOOD: A drivable vehicle needing no or only minor work to be functional. Also, a deteriorated restoration or a very poor amateur restoration. All components may need restoration to be "excellent," but the vehicle is mostly usable "as is."

5) RESTORABLE: Needs *complete* restoration of body, chassis and interior. May or may not be running, but isn't weathered, wrecked or stripped to the point of being useful only for parts.

6) PARTS VEHICLE: May or may not be running, but is weathered, wrecked and/or stripped to the point of being useful primarily for parts.

CADILLAC PRICING

	6	5	4	3	2	1
1903 Model A, 1-cyl.						
Rbt	1,500	4,550	7,600	15,200	26,600	38,000
1903 Model A, 1-cyl.						
Tonn Rbt	1,550	4,700	7,800	15,600	27,300	39,000
1904 Model A, 1-cyl.						
Rbt	1,500	4,500	7,500	15,000	26,300	37,500
Tonn Rbt	1,500	4,550	7,600	15,200	26,600	38,000
1904 Model B, 1-cyl.						
Rbt	1,500	4,550	7,600	15,200	26,600	38,000
Tr	1,550	4,700	7,800	15,600	27,300	39,000
1905 Models B-E						
Rbt	1,500	4,450	7,400	14,800	25,900	37,000
Tonn Rbt	1,500	4,550	7,600	15,200	26,600	38,000
1905 Model D, 4-cyl.						
Rbt	1,550	4,700	7,800	15,600	27,300	39,000
Tonn Rbt	1,600	4,800	8,000	16,000	28,000	40,000
1905 Model F, 1-cyl.						
Tr	1,400	4,200	7,000	14,000	24,500	35,000
1906 Model K-M, 1-cyl.						
Rbt	1,400	4,200	7,000	14,000	24,500	35,000
Tr	1,450	4,300	7,200	14,400	25,200	36,000
1906 Model H, 4-cyl.						
Rbt	1,450	4,300	7,200	14,400	25,200	36,000
Tr	1,500	4,450	7,400	14,800	25,900	37,000
1906 Model L, 4-cyl.						
7P Tr	1,550	4,700	7,800	15,600	27,300	39,000
Limo	1,500	4,450	7,400	14,800	25,900	37,000
1907 Model G, 4-cyl. 20 hp.						
Rbt	1,400	4,200	7,000	14,000	24,500	35,000
Tr	1,450	4,300	7,200	14,400	25,200	36,000
Limo	1,350	4,100	6,800	13,600	23,800	34,000
1907 Model H, 4-cyl. 30 hp.						
Tr	1,500	4,450	7,400	14,800	25,900	37,000
Limo	1,450	4,300	7,200	14,400	25,200	36,000
1907 Model K-M, 1-cyl.						
Rbt	1,300	3,950	6,600	13,200	23,100	33,000
Tr	1,350	4,100	6,800	13,600	23,800	34,000
1908 Model G, 4-cyl. 25 hp.						
Rbt	1,400	4,200	7,000	14,000	24,500	35,000
Tr	1,450	4,300	7,200	14,400	25,200	36,000
1908 Model H, 4-cyl. 30 hp.						
Rbt	1,500	4,450	7,400	14,800	25,900	37,000
Tr	1,500	4,550	7,600	15,200	26,600	38,000
Cpe	1,400	4,200	7,000	14,000	24,500	35,000
Limo	1,350	4,100	6,800	13,600	23,800	34,000
1908 Model S-T, 1-cyl.						
Rbt	1,350	4,100	6,800	13,600	23,800	34,000
Tr	1,400	4,200	7,000	14,000	24,500	35,000
Cpe	1,300	3,850	6,400	12,800	22,400	32,000
1909 Model 30, 4-cyl.						
Rds	1,400	4,200	7,000	14,000	24,500	35,000
demi T&C	1,450	4,300	7,200	14,400	25,200	36,000
Tr	1,500	4,450	7,400	14,800	25,900	37,000
1909 Model T, 1-cyl.						
Tr	1,300	3,950	6,600	13,200	23,100	33,000
1910 Model 30, 4-cyl.						
Rds	1,500	4,550	7,600	15,200	26,600	38,000
demi T&C	1,550	4,700	7,800	15,600	27,300	39,000
Tr	1,500	4,450	7,400	14,800	25,900	37,000
Limo	1,400	4,200	7,000	14,000	24,500	35,000
1911 Model 30, 4-cyl.						
Rds	1,500	4,550	7,600	15,200	26,600	38,000
demi T&C	1,550	4,700	7,800	15,600	27,300	39,000
Tr	1,600	4,800	8,000	16,000	28,000	40,000
Cpe	1,450	4,300	7,200	14,400	25,200	36,000
Limo	1,500	4,450	7,400	14,800	25,900	37,000
1912 Model 30, 4-cyl.						
Rds	1,700	5,150	8,600	17,200	30,100	43,000
4P Phae	1,750	5,300	8,800	17,600	30,800	44,000
5P Tr	1,800	5,400	9,000	18,000	31,500	45,000
Cpe	1,500	4,450	7,400	14,800	25,900	37,000
Limo	1,550	4,700	7,800	15,600	27,300	39,000
1913 Model 30, 4-cyl.						
Rds	1,700	5,150	8,600	17,200	30,100	43,000
Phae	1,750	5,300	8,800	17,600	30,800	44,000
Torp	1,800	5,400	9,000	18,000	31,500	45,000
5P Tr	1,850	5,500	9,200	18,400	32,200	46,000
6P Tr	1,900	5,650	9,400	18,800	32,900	47,000
Cpe	1,450	4,300	7,200	14,400	25,200	36,000
Limo	1,550	4,700	7,800	15,600	27,300	39,000
1914 Model 30, 4-cyl.						
Rds	1,750	5,300	8,800	17,600	30,800	44,000
Phae	1,800	5,400	9,000	18,000	31,500	45,000
5P Tr	1,850	5,500	9,200	18,400	32,200	46,000
7P Tr	1,900	5,650	9,400	18,800	32,900	47,000
Lan Cpe	1,500	4,450	7,400	14,800	25,900	37,000
Encl dr Limo	1,550	4,700	7,800	15,600	27,300	39,000
Limo	1,600	4,800	8,000	16,000	28,000	40,000
1915 Model 51, V-8						
Rds	1,850	5,500	9,200	18,400	32,200	46,000
Sal Tr	1,900	5,650	9,400	18,800	32,900	47,000
7P Tr	1,900	5,750	9,600	19,200	33,600	48,000
3P Cpe	1,450	4,300	7,200	14,400	25,200	36,000
Sed Brgm	1,400	4,200	7,000	14,000	24,500	35,000
7P Limo	1,600	4,800	8,000	16,000	28,000	40,000
Berl Limo	1,700	5,050	8,400	16,800	29,400	42,000
1916 Model 53, V-8						
Rds	1,800	5,400	9,000	18,000	31,500	45,000
5P Tr	1,850	5,500	9,200	18,400	32,200	46,000
7P Tr	1,900	5,650	9,400	18,800	32,900	47,000
3P Cpe	1,450	4,300	7,200	14,400	25,200	36,000
Sed Brgm	1,400	4,200	7,000	14,000	24,500	35,000
7P Limo	1,600	4,800	8,000	16,000	28,000	40,000
Berl Limo	1,700	5,050	8,400	16,800	29,400	42,000
1917 Model 55, V-8						
Rds	1,800	5,400	9,000	18,000	31,500	45,000
Clb Rds	1,850	5,500	9,200	18,400	32,200	46,000
Conv	1,750	5,300	8,800	17,600	30,800	44,000
Cpe	1,400	4,200	7,000	14,000	24,500	35,000
Vic	1,450	4,300	7,200	14,400	25,200	36,000
Brgm	1,400	4,200	7,000	14,000	24,500	35,000
Limo	1,500	4,550	7,600	15,200	26,600	38,000
Imp Limo	1,600	4,800	8,000	16,000	28,000	40,000
7P Lan'let	1,700	5,050	8,400	16,800	29,400	42,000
1918-19 Type 57, V-8						
Rds	1,750	5,300	8,800	17,600	30,800	44,000
Phae	1,800	5,400	9,000	18,000	31,500	45,000
Tr	1,700	5,150	8,600	17,200	30,100	43,000
Conv Vic	1,700	5,050	8,400	16,800	29,400	42,000
Brgm	1,350	4,100	6,800	13,600	23,800	34,000
Limo	1,400	4,200	7,000	14,000	24,500	35,000
Twn Limo	1,450	4,300	7,200	14,400	25,200	36,000
Lan'let	1,500	4,550	7,600	15,200	26,600	38,000
Twn Lan'let	1,600	4,800	8,000	16,000	28,000	40,000
Imp Limo	1,550	4,700	7,800	15,600	27,300	39,000
1920-1921 Type 59, V-8						
Rds	1,650	4,900	8,200	16,400	28,700	41,000
Phae	1,700	5,050	8,400	16,800	29,400	42,000
Tr	1,600	4,800	8,000	16,000	28,000	40,000
Vic	1,300	3,850	6,400	12,800	22,400	32,000
Sed	1,250	3,700	6,200	12,400	21,700	31,000
Cpe	1,300	3,850	6,400	12,800	22,400	32,000
Sub	1,250	3,700	6,200	12,400	21,700	31,000
Limo	1,400	4,200	7,000	14,000	24,500	35,000
Twn Brgm	1,450	4,300	7,200	14,400	25,200	36,000
Imp Limo	1,500	4,450	7,400	14,800	25,900	37,000

NOTE: Coupe and Town Brougham dropped for 1921.

1922-1923 Type 61, V-8						
Rds	1,500	4,550	7,600	15,200	26,600	38,000
Phae	1,550	4,700	7,800	15,600	27,300	39,000
Tr	1,500	4,550	7,600	15,200	26,600	38,000
Cpe	1,250	3,700	6,200	12,400	21,700	31,000
Vic	1,300	3,850	6,400	12,800	22,400	32,000
5P Cpe	1,150	3,500	5,800	11,600	20,300	29,000
Sed	1,100	3,350	5,600	11,200	19,600	28,000
Sub	1,300	3,950	6,600	13,200	23,100	33,000
7P Limo	1,350	4,100	6,800	13,600	23,800	34,000
Imp Limo	1,400	4,200	7,000	14,000	24,500	35,000
Lan'let Sed	1,450	4,300	7,200	14,400	25,200	36,000
1924-1925 V-63, V-8						
Rds	1,550	4,700	7,800	15,600	27,300	39,000
Phae	1,700	5,050	8,400	16,800	29,400	42,000
Tr	1,500	4,550	7,600	15,200	26,600	38,000
Vic	1,250	3,700	6,200	12,400	21,700	31,000
Cpe	1,200	3,600	6,000	12,000	21,000	30,000
Limo	1,150	3,400	5,700	11,400	19,950	28,500
Twn Brgm	1,150	3,500	5,800	11,600	20,300	29,000
Imp Sed	1,100	3,350	5,600	11,200	19,600	28,000

Custom models, (V-8 introduced Oct., 1924).

	6	5	4	3	2	1
Cpe	1,150	3,500	5,800	11,600	20,300	29,000
5P Cpe	1,200	3,600	6,000	12,000	21,000	30,000
5P Sed	1,200	3,550	5,900	11,800	20,650	29,500
Sub	1,150	3,500	5,800	11,600	20,300	29,000
Imp Sub	1,200	3,550	5,900	11,800	20,650	29,500

Other models, V-8.

	6	5	4	3	2	1
7P Sed	1,150	3,500	5,800	11,600	20,300	29,000
Vic	1,200	3,550	5,900	11,800	20,650	29,500
Lan Sed	1,200	3,600	6,000	12,000	21,000	30,000
2d Sed	1,050	3,100	5,200	10,400	18,200	26,000
8P Imp Sed	1,100	3,250	5,400	10,800	18,900	27,000

(All Custom and post-Dec. 1924 models have scrolled radiators).

1926-1927 Series 314, V-8						
Cpe	1,450	4,300	7,200	14,400	25,200	36,000
Vic	1,500	4,450	7,400	14,800	25,900	37,000
5P Brgm	1,450	4,300	7,200	14,400	25,200	36,000
5P Sed	1,100	3,350	5,600	11,200	19,600	28,000
7P Sed	1,150	3,500	5,800	11,600	20,300	29,000
Imp Sed	1,100	3,350	5,600	11,200	19,600	28,000
1926-1927 Custom Line, V-8						
Rds	3,450	10,300	17,200	34,400	60,000	86,000
Tr	3,450	10,300	17,200	34,400	60,000	86,000
Phae	3,500	10,600	17,600	35,200	62,100	88,000
Cpe	1,850	5,500	9,200	18,400	32,200	46,000

	6	5	4	3	2	1
Sed	1,550	4,700	7,800	15,600	27,300	39,000
Sub	1,600	4,800	8,000	16,000	28,000	40,000
Imp Sed	1,750	5,300	8,800	17,600	30,800	44,000

1927 Series 314 Std., V-8, 132" wb

Spt Cpe	1,600	4,800	8,000	16,000	28,000	40,000
Cpe	1,500	4,450	7,400	14,800	25,900	37,000
Sed 5P	1,150	3,500	5,800	11,600	20,300	29,000
Sed 7P	1,200	3,600	6,000	12,000	21,000	30,000
Victoria 4P	1,500	4,550	7,600	15,200	26,600	38,000
Spt Sed	1,250	3,700	6,200	12,400	21,700	31,000
Brgm	1,150	3,500	5,800	11,600	20,300	29,000
Imp	1,250	3,700	6,200	12,400	21,700	31,000

1927 Std. Series, V-8, 132" wb

7P Sed	1,200	3,600	6,000	12,000	21,000	30,000

1927 Custom, 138" wb

RS Rds	3,050	9,100	15,200	30,400	53,200	76,000
RS Conv	2,500	7,450	12,400	24,800	43,400	62,000
Phae	3,300	9,850	16,400	32,800	57,400	82,000
Spt Phae	3,450	10,300	17,200	34,400	60,000	86,000
Tr	3,200	9,600	16,000	32,000	56,000	80,000
Conv	2,300	6,950	11,600	23,200	40,600	58,000
Cpe	1,700	5,050	8,400	16,800	29,400	42,000
5P Sed	1,300	3,850	6,400	12,800	22,400	32,000
Sub	1,300	3,950	6,600	13,200	23,100	33,000
Imp Sed	1,350	4,100	6,800	13,600	23,800	34,000
Brn Twn Cabr	1,350	4,100	6,800	13,600	23,800	34,000
Wilby Twn Cabr	1,500	4,550	7,600	15,200	26,600	38,000

1927 Fleetwood Bodies

Limo Brgm	1,700	5,150	8,600	17,200	30,100	43,000
Twn Cabr	1,800	5,400	9,000	18,000	31,500	45,000
Trans Twn Cabr	1,950	5,900	9,800	19,600	34,300	49,000
Coll Twn Cabr	2,000	6,000	10,000	20,000	35,000	50,000
Vic	1,700	5,050	8,400	16,800	29,400	42,000

1928 Fisher Custom Line, V-8, 140" wb

Rds	4,250	12,700	21,200	42,400	74,000	106,000
Tr	4,300	13,000	21,600	43,200	76,100	108,000
Phae	4,400	13,200	22,000	44,000	77,000	110,000
Spt Phae	4,650	13,900	23,200	46,400	81,000	116,000
Conv RS	3,850	11,500	19,200	38,400	67,000	96,000
2P Cpe	1,600	4,800	8,000	16,000	28,000	40,000
5P Cpe	1,500	4,450	7,400	14,800	25,900	37,000
Twn Sed	1,400	4,200	7,000	14,000	24,500	35,000
Sed	1,350	4,100	6,800	13,600	23,800	34,000
7P Sed	1,400	4,200	7,000	14,000	24,500	35,000
5P Imp Sed	1,450	4,300	7,200	14,400	25,200	36,000
Imp Cabr	4,000	12,000	20,000	40,000	70,000	100,000
7P Imp Sed	2,400	7,200	12,000	24,000	42,000	60,000
7P Imp Cabr	4,400	13,200	22,000	44,000	77,000	110,000

1928 Fisher Fleetwood Line, V-8, 140" wb

Sed	1,500	4,550	7,600	15,200	26,600	38,000
5P Cabr	4,250	12,700	21,200	42,400	74,000	106,000
5P Imp Cabr	4,400	13,200	22,000	44,000	77,000	110,000
7P Sed	1,600	4,800	8,000	16,000	28,000	40,000
7P Cabr	4,300	13,000	21,600	43,200	76,100	108,000
7P Imp Cabr	4,500	13,400	22,400	44,800	78,500	112,000
Trans Twn Cabr	4,400	13,200	22,000	44,000	77,000	110,000
Trans Limo Brgm	3,050	9,100	15,200	30,400	53,200	76,000

1929 Series 341-B, V-8, 140" wb

Rds	4,400	13,200	22,000	44,000	77,000	110,000
Phae	4,550	13,700	22,800	45,600	80,000	114,000
Spt Phae	4,950	14,900	24,800	49,600	87,000	124,000
Tr	4,000	12,000	20,000	40,000	70,000	100,000
Conv	4,000	12,000	20,000	40,000	70,000	100,000
2P Cpe	2,800	8,400	14,000	28,000	49,000	70,000
5P Cpe	2,100	6,350	10,600	21,200	37,100	53,000
5P Sed	1,700	5,150	8,600	17,200	30,100	43,000
7P Sed	1,700	5,050	8,400	16,800	29,400	42,000
Twn Sed	1,750	5,300	8,800	17,600	30,800	44,000
7P Imp Sed	1,800	5,400	9,000	18,000	31,500	45,000

1929 Fleetwood Custom Line, V-8, 140" wb

Sed	1,700	5,150	8,600	17,200	30,100	43,000
Sed Cabr	4,650	13,900	23,200	46,400	81,000	116,000
5P Imp Sed	2,000	6,000	10,000	20,000	35,000	50,000
7P Imp Sed	2,050	6,100	10,200	20,400	35,700	51,000
Trans Twn Cabr	4,000	12,000	20,000	40,000	70,000	100,000
Trans Limo Brgm	3,050	9,100	15,200	30,400	53,200	76,000
Clb Cabr	4,250	12,700	21,200	42,400	74,000	106,000
A/W Phae	5,050	15,100	25,200	50,400	88,000	126,000
A/W State Imp	5,050	15,100	25,200	50,400	88,000	126,000

1930 Series 353, V-8, 140" wb Fisher Custom Line

Conv	4,400	13,200	22,000	44,000	77,000	110,000
2P Cpe	2,900	8,650	14,400	28,800	50,400	72,000
Twn Sed	1,700	5,150	8,600	17,200	30,100	43,000
Sed	1,700	5,050	8,400	16,800	29,400	42,000
7P Sed	1,750	5,300	8,800	17,600	30,800	44,000
7P Imp Sed	2,000	6,000	10,000	20,000	35,000	50,000
5P Cpe	2,100	6,250	10,400	20,800	36,400	52,000

1930 Fleetwood Line, V-8

Rds	5,050	15,100	25,200	50,400	88,000	126,000
5P Sed	1,800	5,400	9,000	18,000	31,500	45,000
Sed Cabr	4,400	13,200	22,000	44,000	77,000	110,000
5P Imp	2,000	6,000	10,000	20,000	35,000	50,000
7P Sed	1,800	5,400	9,000	18,000	31,500	45,000
7P Imp	2,000	6,000	10,000	20,000	35,000	50,000
Trans Cabr	5,100	15,400	25,600	51,200	90,100	128,000
Trans Limo Brgm	4,900	14,600	24,400	48,800	85,500	122,000
Clb Cabr	5,050	15,100	25,200	50,400	88,000	126,000
A/W Phae	5,450	16,300	27,200	54,400	95,000	136,000

	6	5	4	3	2	1
A/W State Imp	5,600	16,800	28,000	56,000	98,000	140,000

1930 Fleetwood Custom Line, V-16, 148" wb

Rds	13,200	39,600	66,000	132,000	231,000	330,000
Phae	14,000	42,000	70,000	140,000	245,000	350,000

1930 "Flat Windshield" Models

A/W Phae	14,200	42,600	71,000	142,000	249,000	355,000
Conv	13,200	39,600	66,000	132,000	231,000	330,000
Cpe	5,050	15,100	25,200	50,400	88,000	126,000
Clb Sed	4,800	14,400	24,000	48,000	84,000	120,000
5P OS Sed	4,800	14,400	24,000	48,000	84,000	120,000
5P Sed Cabr	11,200	33,600	56,000	112,000	196,000	280,000
Imp Cabr	11,200	33,600	56,000	112,000	196,000	280,000
7P Sed	5,050	15,100	25,200	50,400	88,000	126,000
7P Imp Sed	5,200	15,600	26,000	52,000	91,000	130,000
Twn Cabr 4212	11,400	34,200	57,000	114,000	200,000	285,000
Twn Cabr 4220	11,400	34,200	57,000	114,000	200,000	285,000
Twn Cabr 4225	11,400	34,200	57,000	114,000	200,000	285,000
Limo Brgm	8,200	24,600	41,000	82,000	144,000	205,000
Twn Brgm 05	8,200	24,600	41,000	82,000	144,000	205,000

1930 "Cane-bodied" Model

Twn Brgm	8,200	24,600	41,000	82,000	144,000	205,000

1930 Madame X Models

A/W Phae	15,000	45,000	75,000	150,000	263,000	375,000
Conv	14,400	43,200	72,000	144,000	252,000	360,000
Cpe	7,400	22,200	37,000	74,000	130,000	185,000
5P OS Imp	7,000	21,000	35,000	70,000	123,000	175,000
5P Imp	6,800	20,400	34,000	68,000	119,000	170,000
Twn Cabr 4312	12,800	38,400	64,000	128,000	224,000	320,000
Twn Cabr 4320	12,800	38,400	64,000	128,000	224,000	320,000
Twn Cabr 4325	12,800	38,400	64,000	128,000	224,000	320,000
Limo Brgm	9,600	28,800	48,000	96,000	168,000	240,000

1931 Series 355, V-8, 134" wb Fisher Bodies

Rds	5,100	15,400	25,600	51,200	90,100	128,000
Phae	4,900	14,600	24,400	48,800	85,500	122,000
2P Cpe	3,050	9,100	15,200	30,400	53,200	76,000
5P Cpe	2,950	8,900	14,800	29,600	51,800	74,000
Sed	1,800	5,400	9,000	18,000	31,500	45,000
Twn Sed	1,900	5,650	9,400	18,800	32,900	47,000
7P Sed	1,950	5,900	9,800	19,600	34,300	49,000
Imp Limo	2,000	6,000	10,000	20,000	35,000	50,000

1931 Fleetwood Bodies, V-8

Rds	5,450	16,300	27,200	54,400	95,000	136,000
Conv	5,450	16,300	27,200	54,400	95,000	136,000
Phae	5,800	17,400	29,000	58,000	102,000	145,000
A/W Phae	6,000	18,000	30,000	60,000	105,000	150,000

1931 Series 370, V-12, 140" wb

Rds	9,000	27,000	45,000	90,000	158,000	225,000
Phae	9,000	27,000	45,000	90,000	158,000	225,000
Conv	8,400	25,200	42,000	84,000	147,000	210,000
A/W Phae	9,200	27,600	46,000	92,000	161,000	230,000
2P Cpe	5,800	17,400	29,000	58,000	102,000	145,000
5P Cpe	5,600	16,800	28,000	56,000	98,000	140,000
Sed	4,800	14,400	24,000	48,000	84,000	120,000
Twn Sed	5,050	15,100	25,200	50,400	88,000	126,000

1931 Series 370, V-12, 143" wb

7P Sed	5,450	16,300	27,200	54,400	95,000	136,000
Imp Sed	5,600	16,800	28,000	56,000	98,000	140,000

1931 Series V-16, 148" wb

2P Rds	14,400	43,200	72,000	144,000	252,000	360,000
Phae	14,600	43,800	73,000	146,000	256,000	365,000
A/W Phae	5,050	15,100	25,200	50,400	88,000	126,000
4476 Cpe	6,000	18,000	30,000	60,000	105,000	150,000
4276 Cpe	6,000	18,000	30,000	60,000	105,000	150,000
5P Cpe	5,800	17,400	29,000	58,000	102,000	145,000
Conv	14,600	43,800	73,000	146,000	256,000	365,000
4361 Clb Sed	6,800	20,400	34,000	68,000	119,000	170,000
4161 Clb Sed	6,800	20,400	34,000	68,000	119,000	170,000
4330 Imp	7,000	21,000	35,000	70,000	123,000	175,000
4330 Sed	3,850	11,500	19,200	38,400	67,000	96,000
4130 Sed	4,000	12,000	20,000	40,000	70,000	100,000
4130 Imp	4,000	12,000	20,000	40,000	70,000	100,000
4335 Sed Cabr	12,200	36,600	61,000	122,000	214,000	305,000
4355 Imp Cabr	12,400	37,200	62,000	124,000	217,000	310,000
4155 Sed Cabr	12,400	37,200	62,000	124,000	217,000	310,000
4155 Imp Cabr	13,000	39,000	65,000	130,000	228,000	325,000
4375 Sed	3,850	11,500	19,200	38,400	67,000	96,000
4175 Sed	4,000	12,000	20,000	40,000	70,000	100,000
4375 Imp	4,250	12,700	21,200	42,400	74,000	106,000
4175 Imp	4,400	13,200	22,000	44,000	77,000	110,000
4312 Twn Cabr	12,400	37,200	62,000	124,000	217,000	310,000
4320 Twn Cabr	12,400	37,200	62,000	124,000	217,000	310,000
4220 Twn Cabr	12,400	37,200	62,000	124,000	217,000	310,000
4325 Twn Cabr	12,200	36,600	61,000	122,000	214,000	305,000
4225 Twn Cabr	12,200	36,600	61,000	122,000	214,000	305,000
4391 Limo Brgm	8,800	26,400	44,000	88,000	154,000	220,000
4291 Limo Brgm	9,200	27,600	46,000	92,000	161,000	230,000
4264 Twn Brgm	9,400	28,200	47,000	94,000	165,000	235,000
4264B Twn Brgm C/N	9,600	28,800	48,000	96,000	168,000	240,000

1932 Series 355B, V-8, 134" wb

Rds	4,700	14,200	23,600	47,200	83,100	118,000
Conv	4,100	12,200	20,400	40,800	71,500	102,000
2P Cpe	2,000	6,000	10,000	20,000	35,000	50,000
Sed	1,650	4,900	8,200	16,400	28,700	41,000

1932 Fisher Line, 140" wb

Std Phae	4,250	12,700	21,200	42,400	74,000	106,000
DW Phae	4,250	12,700	21,200	42,400	74,000	106,000
DC Spt Phae	4,400	13,200	22,000	44,000	77,000	110,000
A/W Phae	4,400	13,200	22,000	44,000	77,000	110,000

	6	5	4	3	2	1
Cpe	2,200	6,600	11,000	22,000	38,500	55,000
Spec Sed	1,700	5,050	8,400	16,800	29,400	42,000
Twn Sed	1,700	5,150	8,600	17,200	30,100	43,000
Imp Sed	1,800	5,400	9,000	18,000	31,500	45,000

1932 Fleetwood Bodies, 140" wb

	6	5	4	3	2	1
Sed	1,800	5,400	9,000	18,000	31,500	45,000
Twn Cpe	2,300	6,850	11,400	22,800	39,900	57,000
7P Sed	2,000	6,000	10,000	20,000	35,000	50,000
7P Limo	2,300	6,850	11,400	22,800	39,900	57,000
5P Twn Car	4,250	12,700	21,200	42,400	74,000	106,000
Twn Cabr	4,400	13,200	22,000	44,000	77,000	110,000
Limo Brgm	2,650	7,900	13,200	26,400	46,200	66,000

1932 Series 370B, V-12, 134" wb

	6	5	4	3	2	1
Rds	7,600	22,800	38,000	76,000	133,000	190,000
Conv	7,200	21,600	36,000	72,000	126,000	180,000
2P Cpe	2,800	8,400	14,000	28,000	49,000	70,000
Std Sed	2,000	6,000	10,000	20,000	35,000	50,000

1932 Series 370B, V-12, 140" wb Fisher Bodies

	6	5	4	3	2	1
Std Phae	7,400	22,200	37,000	74,000	129,000	185,000
Spl Phae	7,600	22,800	38,000	76,000	133,000	190,000
Spt Phae	8,000	24,000	40,000	80,000	140,000	200,000
A/W Phae	7,800	23,400	39,000	78,000	137,000	195,000
5P Cpe	3,200	9,600	16,000	32,000	56,000	80,000
Spl Sed	3,050	9,100	15,200	30,400	53,200	76,000
Twn Sed	2,650	7,900	13,200	26,400	46,200	66,000
7P Sed	2,700	8,150	13,600	27,200	47,600	68,000
7P Imp	2,800	8,400	14,000	28,000	49,000	70,000

1932 Series 370B, V-12, 140" wb Fleetwood Bodies

	6	5	4	3	2	1
Tr	8,800	26,400	44,000	88,000	154,000	220,000
Conv	9,000	27,000	45,000	90,000	158,000	225,000
Sed	3,450	10,300	17,200	34,400	60,000	86,000
Twn Cpe	3,500	10,600	17,600	35,200	61,500	88,000
7P Sed	3,100	9,350	15,600	31,200	54,600	78,000
Limo	3,450	10,300	17,200	34,400	60,000	86,000
5P Twn Cabr	8,600	25,800	43,000	86,000	151,000	215,000
7P Twn Cabr	8,800	26,400	44,000	88,000	154,000	220,000
Limo Brgm	7,200	21,600	36,000	72,000	126,000	180,000

1932 Series 452B, V-16, 143" wb Fisher Bodies

	6	5	4	3	2	1
Rds	12,000	36,000	60,000	120,000	210,000	300,000
Conv	10,800	32,400	54,000	108,000	189,000	270,000
Cpe	8,200	24,600	41,000	82,000	144,000	205,000
Std Sed	7,200	21,600	36,000	72,000	126,000	180,000

1932 Series 452B, V-16, 149" wb Fisher Bodies

	6	5	4	3	2	1
Std Phae	13,800	41,400	69,000	138,000	241,000	345,000
Spl Phae	14,000	42,000	70,000	140,000	245,000	350,000
Spt Phae	13,800	41,400	69,000	138,000	241,000	345,000
A/W Phae	14,000	42,000	70,000	140,000	245,000	350,000

1932 Fleetwood Bodies, V-16

	6	5	4	3	2	1
5P Sed	8,600	25,800	43,000	86,000	151,000	215,000
Imp Limo	9,400	28,200	47,000	94,000	165,000	235,000
Twn Cpe	9,600	28,800	48,000	96,000	168,000	240,000
7P Sed	9,400	28,200	47,000	94,000	165,000	235,000
7P Twn Cabr	13,600	40,800	68,000	136,000	238,000	340,000
5P Twn Cabr	13,400	40,200	67,000	134,000	235,000	335,000
Limo Brgm	8,800	26,400	44,000	88,000	154,000	220,000

1933 Series 355C, V-8, 134" wb Fisher Bodies

	6	5	4	3	2	1
Rds	4,400	13,200	22,000	44,000	77,000	110,000
Conv	3,850	11,500	19,200	38,400	67,000	96,000
Cpe	1,800	5,400	9,000	18,000	31,500	45,000

1933 Series 355C, V-8, 140" wb Fisher Bodies

	6	5	4	3	2	1
Phae	4,100	12,200	20,400	40,800	71,500	102,000
A/W Phae	4,250	12,700	21,200	42,400	74,000	106,000
5P Cpe	1,850	5,500	9,200	18,400	32,200	46,000
Sed	1,750	5,300	8,800	17,600	30,800	44,000
Twn Sed	1,800	5,400	9,000	18,000	31,500	45,000
7P Sed	1,850	5,500	9,200	18,400	32,200	46,000
Imp Sed	1,950	5,900	9,800	19,600	34,300	49,000

1933 Series 355C, V-8, 140" wb Fleetwood Line

	6	5	4	3	2	1
5P Sed	1,800	5,400	9,000	18,000	31,500	45,000
7P Sed	1,850	5,500	9,200	18,400	32,200	46,000
Limo	1,950	5,900	9,800	19,600	34,300	49,000
5P Twn Cabr	4,100	12,200	20,400	40,800	71,500	102,000
7P Twn Cabr	4,250	12,700	21,200	42,400	74,000	106,000
Limo Brgm	2,500	7,450	12,400	24,800	43,400	62,000

1933 Series 370C, V-12, 134" wb Fisher Bodies

	6	5	4	3	2	1
Rds	4,800	14,400	24,000	48,000	84,000	120,000
Conv	4,650	13,900	23,200	46,400	81,000	116,000
Cpe	2,950	8,900	14,800	29,600	51,800	74,000

1933 Series, 370C, V-12, 140" wb Fisher Bodies

	6	5	4	3	2	1
Phae	4,700	14,200	23,600	47,200	83,100	118,000
A/W Phae	4,800	14,400	24,000	48,000	84,000	120,000
5P Cpe	3,100	9,350	15,600	31,200	54,600	78,000
Sed	2,650	7,900	13,200	26,400	46,200	66,000
Twn Sed	2,650	7,900	13,200	26,400	46,200	66,000
7P Sed	2,500	7,450	12,400	24,800	43,400	62,000
Imp Sed	2,700	8,150	13,600	27,200	47,600	68,000

1933 Series 370C, V-12, 140" wb Fleetwood Line

	6	5	4	3	2	1
Sed	2,700	8,150	13,600	27,200	47,600	68,000
7P Sed	2,700	8,150	13,600	27,200	47,600	68,000
Limo	2,800	8,400	14,000	28,000	49,000	70,000
5P Twn Cabr	4,800	14,400	24,000	48,000	84,000	120,000
7P Twn Cabr	4,900	14,600	24,400	48,800	85,500	122,000
7P Limo Brgm	3,200	9,600	16,000	32,000	56,000	80,000

1933 Series 452C, V-16, 154" wb

	6	5	4	3	2	1
DC Spt Phae	10,400	31,200	52,000	104,000	182,000	260,000

1933 Fleetwood Bodies, 149" wb

	6	5	4	3	2	1
Conv	10,200	30,600	51,000	102,000	179,000	255,000
A/W Phae	10,400	31,200	52,000	104,000	182,000	260,000
Sed	7,200	21,600	36,000	72,000	126,000	180,000
7P Sed	7,200	21,600	36,000	72,000	126,000	180,000
Twn Cab	9,000	27,000	45,000	90,000	158,000	225,000
7P Twn Cab	8,800	26,400	44,000	88,000	154,000	220,000
7P Limo	7,400	22,200	37,000	74,000	130,000	185,000
Limo Brgm	7,400	22,200	37,000	74,000	130,000	185,000
5P Twn Cpe	7,000	21,000	35,000	70,000	123,000	175,000
Imp Cab	9,200	27,600	46,000	92,000	161,000	230,000

1934 Series 355D, V-8, 128" wb Fisher Bodies

	6	5	4	3	2	1
Conv	3,050	9,100	15,200	30,400	53,200	76,000
Conv Sed	3,100	9,350	15,600	31,200	54,600	78,000
2P Cpe	1,800	5,400	9,000	18,000	31,500	45,000
Twn Cpe	1,600	4,800	8,000	16,000	28,000	40,000
Sed	1,500	4,550	7,600	15,200	26,600	38,000
Twn Sed	1,550	4,700	7,800	15,600	27,300	39,000

1934 Series 355D, V-8, 136" wb Fisher Bodies

	6	5	4	3	2	1
Conv	3,200	9,600	16,000	32,000	56,000	80,000
Conv Sed	3,300	9,850	16,400	32,800	57,400	82,000
Cpe	1,900	5,650	9,400	18,800	32,900	47,000
Sed	1,500	4,550	7,600	15,200	26,600	38,000
Twn Sed	1,550	4,700	7,800	15,600	27,300	39,000
7P Sed	1,800	5,400	9,000	18,000	31,500	45,000
Imp Sed	2,000	6,000	10,000	20,000	35,000	50,000

1934 Series 355D, V-8, 146" wb Fleetwood bodies with straight windshield

	6	5	4	3	2	1
Sed	1,600	4,800	8,000	16,000	28,000	40,000
Twn Sed	1,650	4,900	8,200	16,400	28,700	41,000
7P Sed	1,700	5,050	8,400	16,800	29,400	42,000
7P Limo	1,750	5,300	8,800	17,600	30,800	44,000
Imp Cab	3,750	11,300	18,800	37,600	66,000	94,000
7P Imp Cab	3,850	11,500	19,200	38,400	67,000	96,000

1934 Series 355D, V-8, 146" wb Fleetwood bodies with modified "V" windshield

	6	5	4	3	2	1
Conv	3,450	10,300	17,200	34,400	60,000	86,000
Aero Cpe	3,200	9,600	16,000	32,000	56,000	80,000
Cpe	2,200	6,600	11,000	22,000	38,500	55,000
Spl Sed	1,800	5,400	9,000	18,000	31,500	45,000
Spl Twn Sed	1,850	5,500	9,200	18,400	32,200	46,000
Conv Sed Div	3,850	11,500	19,200	38,400	67,000	96,000
7P Spl Sed	1,900	5,650	9,400	18,800	32,900	47,000
Spl Limo	1,950	5,900	9,800	19,600	34,300	49,000
Sp Twn Cab	3,850	11,500	19,200	38,400	67,000	96,000
7P Twn Cab	3,900	11,800	19,600	39,200	69,100	98,000
5P Spl Imp Cab	3,900	11,800	19,600	39,200	69,100	98,000
7P Spl Imp Cab	4,000	12,000	20,000	40,000	70,000	100,000
Limo Brgm	3,050	9,100	15,200	30,400	53,200	76,000

1934 Series 370D, V-12, 146" wb Fleetwood bodies with straight windshield

	6	5	4	3	2	1
Sed	2,200	6,600	11,000	22,000	38,500	55,000
Twn Sed	2,250	6,700	11,200	22,400	39,200	56,000
7P Sed	2,300	6,850	11,400	22,800	39,900	57,000
7P Limo	2,400	7,200	12,000	24,000	42,000	60,000
5P Imp Cab	4,250	12,700	21,200	42,400	74,000	106,000
7P Imp Cab	4,300	13,000	21,600	43,200	76,100	108,000

1934 Series 370D, V-12, 146" wb Fleetwood bodies with modified "V" windshield

	6	5	4	3	2	1
Conv	3,900	11,800	19,600	39,200	69,100	98,000
Aero Cpe	3,600	10,800	18,000	36,000	63,000	90,000
RS Cpe	2,550	7,700	12,800	25,600	44,800	64,000
Spl Sed	2,250	6,700	11,200	22,400	39,200	56,000
Spl Twn Sed	2,300	6,950	11,600	23,200	40,600	58,000
Conv Sed	4,400	13,200	22,000	44,000	77,000	110,000
7P Spl Sed	2,400	7,200	12,000	24,000	42,000	60,000
Spec Limo	2,650	7,900	13,200	26,400	46,200	66,000
5P Twn Cab	4,250	12,700	21,200	42,400	74,000	106,000
7P Twn Cab	4,300	13,000	21,600	43,200	76,100	108,000
5P Spl Imp Cab	4,400	13,200	22,000	44,000	77,000	110,000
7P Spl Imp Cab	4,700	14,200	23,600	47,200	83,100	118,000

1934 Series 452D, V-16, 154" wb Fleetwood bodies with straight windshield

	6	5	4	3	2	1
Sed	5,800	17,400	29,000	58,000	102,000	145,000
Twn Sed	6,000	18,000	30,000	60,000	105,000	150,000
7P Sed	6,000	18,000	30,000	60,000	105,000	150,000
Limo	6,200	18,600	31,000	62,000	109,000	155,000
5P Imp Cab	7,600	22,800	38,000	76,000	133,000	190,000

1934 Series 452D, V-16, 154" wb Fleetwood bodies with modified "V" windshield

	6	5	4	3	2	1
4P Conv	8,000	24,000	40,000	80,000	140,000	200,000
Aero Cpe	7,600	22,800	38,000	76,000	133,000	190,000
RS Cpe	9,200	27,600	46,000	92,000	161,000	230,000
Spl Sed	8,800	26,400	44,000	88,000	154,000	220,000
Spl Twn Sed	6,200	18,600	31,000	62,000	109,000	155,000
Conv Sed	9,000	27,000	45,000	90,000	158,000	225,000
7P Spl Sed	6,000	18,000	30,000	60,000	105,000	150,000
Spl Limo	6,400	19,200	32,000	64,000	112,000	160,000
5P Twn Cab	7,400	22,200	37,000	74,000	130,000	185,000
7P Twn Cab	7,600	22,800	38,000	76,000	133,000	190,000
5P Spl Imp Cab	7,800	23,400	39,000	78,000	137,000	195,000
7P Spl Imp Cab	8,000	24,000	40,000	80,000	140,000	200,000
Limo Brgm	6,800	20,400	34,000	68,000	119,000	170,000

1935 Series 355E, V-8, 128" wb Fisher Bodies

	6	5	4	3	2	1
RS Conv	3,050	9,100	15,200	30,400	53,200	76,000
Conv Sed	3,100	9,350	15,600	31,200	54,600	78,000
RS Cpe	1,800	5,400	9,000	18,000	31,500	45,000
5P Twn Cpe	1,600	4,800	8,000	16,000	28,000	40,000
Sed	1,500	4,550	7,600	15,200	26,600	38,000
Twn Sed	1,550	4,700	7,800	15,600	27,300	39,000

	6	5	4	3	2	1
1935 Series 355E, V-8, 136" wb Fisher Bodies						
RS Conv	2,800	8,400	14,000	28,000	49,000	70,000
Conv Sed	2,700	8,150	13,600	27,200	47,600	68,000
RS Cpe	2,100	6,350	10,600	21,200	37,100	53,000
Sed	1,700	5,050	8,400	16,800	29,400	42,000
Twn Sed	1,700	5,150	8,600	17,200	30,100	43,000
7P Sed	1,800	5,400	9,000	18,000	31,500	45,000
Imp Sed	2,000	6,000	10,000	20,000	35,000	50,000
1935 Series 355E, V-8, 146" wb Fleetwood bodies with straight windshield						
Sed	1,600	4,800	8,000	16,000	28,000	40,000
Twn Sed	1,650	4,900	8,200	16,400	28,700	41,000
7P Sed	1,700	5,050	8,400	16,800	29,400	42,000
Limo	1,750	5,300	8,800	17,600	30,800	44,000
5P Imp Cabr	3,750	11,300	18,800	37,600	66,000	94,000
7P Imp Cabr	3,850	11,500	19,200	38,400	67,000	96,000
1935 Series 355E, V-8, 146" wb Fleetwood bodies with modified "V" windshield						
4P Conv	3,450	10,300	17,200	34,400	60,000	86,000
4P Cpe	2,200	6,600	11,000	22,000	38,500	55,000
Spl Sed	1,800	5,400	9,000	18,000	31,500	45,000
Spl Twn Sed	1,850	5,500	9,200	18,400	32,200	46,000
Conv Sed	3,850	11,500	19,200	38,400	67,000	96,000
7P Spl Sed	1,900	5,650	9,400	18,800	32,900	47,000
Spl Limo	1,950	5,900	9,800	19,600	34,300	49,000
5P Twn Cabr	3,850	11,500	19,200	38,400	67,000	96,000
7P Twn Cabr	3,900	11,800	19,600	39,200	69,100	98,000
5P Imp Cabr	3,900	11,800	19,600	39,200	69,100	98,000
7P Imp Cabr	4,000	12,000	20,000	40,000	70,000	100,000
Limo Brgm	3,050	9,100	15,200	30,400	53,200	76,000
1935 Series 370E, V-12, 146" wb Fleetwood bodies with straight windshield						
Sed	2,200	6,600	11,000	22,000	38,500	55,000
Twn Sed	2,250	6,700	11,200	22,400	39,200	56,000
7P Sed	2,300	6,850	11,400	22,800	39,900	57,000
Limo	2,400	7,200	12,000	24,000	42,000	60,000
5P Imp Cabr	4,250	12,700	21,200	42,400	74,000	106,000
7P Imp Cabr	4,300	13,000	21,600	43,200	76,100	108,000
1935 Series 370E, V-12, 146" wb Fleetwood bodies with modified "V" windshield						
Conv	3,900	11,800	19,600	39,200	69,100	98,000
4P Cpe	2,550	7,700	12,800	25,600	44,800	64,000
Spl Sed	2,250	6,700	11,200	22,400	39,200	56,000
Spl Twn Sed	2,300	6,950	11,600	23,200	40,600	58,000
Conv Sed	4,400	13,200	22,000	44,000	77,000	110,000
7P Spl Sed	2,400	7,200	12,000	24,000	42,000	60,000
7P Spl Limo	2,650	7,900	13,200	26,400	46,200	66,000
5P Twn Cabr	4,250	12,700	21,200	42,400	74,000	106,000
7P Twn Cabr	4,300	13,000	21,600	43,200	76,100	108,000
5P Spl Imp Cabr	4,400	13,200	22,000	44,000	77,000	110,000
7P Spl Imp Cabr	4,700	14,200	23,600	47,200	83,100	118,000
Limo Brgm	3,850	11,500	19,200	38,400	67,000	96,000
1935 Series 452E, V-16, 154" wb Fleetwood bodies with straight windshield						
Sed	5,800	17,400	29,000	58,000	102,000	145,000
Twn Sed	6,000	18,000	30,000	60,000	105,000	150,000
7P Sed	6,000	18,000	30,000	60,000	105,000	150,000
7P Limo	6,200	18,600	31,000	62,000	109,000	155,000
5P Imp Cabr	7,600	22,800	38,000	76,000	133,000	190,000
7P Imp Cabr	7,800	23,400	39,000	78,000	137,000	195,000
1935 Series 452D, V-16, 154" wb Fleetwood bodies with modified "V" windshield						
2-4P Cpe	8,800	26,400	44,000	88,000	154,000	220,000
4P Cpe	9,000	27,000	45,000	90,000	158,000	225,000
Spl Sed	8,800	26,400	44,000	88,000	154,000	220,000
Spl Twn Sed	6,200	18,600	31,000	62,000	109,000	155,000
7P Spl Sed	6,000	18,000	30,000	60,000	105,000	150,000
Spl Limo	6,400	19,200	32,000	64,000	112,000	160,000
5P Twn Cabr	7,400	22,200	37,000	74,000	130,000	185,000
7P Twn Cab	7,600	22,800	38,000	76,000	133,000	190,000
5P Spl Imp Cabr	7,800	23,400	39,000	78,000	137,000	195,000
7P Spl Imp Cabr	8,000	24,000	40,000	80,000	140,000	200,000
Limo Brgm	6,800	20,400	34,000	68,000	119,000	170,000
5P Conv	8,400	25,200	42,000	84,000	147,000	210,000
Conv Sed	8,600	25,800	43,000	86,000	151,000	215,000
1936 Series 60, V-8, 121" wb						
2d Conv	2,400	7,200	12,000	24,000	42,000	60,000
2d 2P Cpe	1,200	3,600	6,000	12,000	21,000	30,000
4d Tr Sed	950	2,900	4,800	9,600	16,800	24,000
1936 Series 70, V-8, 131" wb, Fleetwood bodies						
2d Conv	2,800	8,400	14,000	28,000	49,000	70,000
2d 2P Cpe	1,250	3,700	6,200	12,400	21,700	31,000
4d Conv Sed	2,900	8,650	14,400	28,800	50,400	72,000
4d Tr Sed	1,100	3,350	5,600	11,200	19,600	28,000
1936 Series 75, V-8, 138" wb, Fleetwood bodies						
4d Sed	1,500	4,550	7,600	15,200	26,600	38,000
4d Tr Sed	1,550	4,700	7,800	15,600	27,300	39,000
4d Conv Sed	3,050	9,100	15,200	30,400	53,200	76,000
4d Fml Sed	1,500	4,550	7,600	15,200	26,600	38,000
4d Twn Sed	1,550	4,700	7,800	15,600	27,300	39,000
4d 7P Sed	1,600	4,800	8,000	16,000	28,000	40,000
4d 7P Tr Sed	1,700	5,150	8,600	17,200	30,100	43,000
4d Imp Sed	1,750	5,300	8,800	17,600	30,800	44,000
4d Imp Tr Sed	1,800	5,400	9,000	18,000	31,500	45,000
4d Twn Car	2,000	6,000	10,000	20,000	35,000	50,000
1936 Series 80, V-12, 131" wb, Fleetwood bodies						
2d Conv	3,200	9,600	16,000	32,000	56,000	80,000
4d Conv Sed	3,300	9,850	16,400	32,800	57,400	82,000

	6	5	4	3	2	1
2d Cpe	1,800	5,400	9,000	18,000	31,500	45,000
4d Tr Sed	1,700	5,050	8,400	16,800	29,400	42,000
1936 Series 85, V-12, 138" wb, Fleetwood bodies						
4d Sed	1,700	5,150	8,600	17,200	30,100	43,000
4d Tr Sed	1,750	5,300	8,800	17,600	30,800	44,000
4d Conv Sed	3,050	9,100	15,200	30,400	53,200	76,000
4d Fml Sed	1,900	5,650	9,400	18,800	32,900	47,000
4d Twn Sed	1,900	5,750	9,600	19,200	33,600	48,000
4d 7P Sed	1,900	5,650	9,400	18,800	32,900	47,000
4d 7P Tr Sed	1,900	5,750	9,600	19,200	33,600	48,000
4d Imp Sed	2,000	6,000	10,000	20,000	35,000	50,000
4d Imp Tr Sed	2,100	6,250	10,400	20,800	36,400	52,000
4d Twn Car	2,400	7,200	12,000	24,000	42,000	60,000
1936 Series 90, V-16, 154" wb, Fleetwood bodies						
2d 2P Conv	5,200	15,600	26,000	52,000	91,000	130,000
4d Conv Sed	5,450	16,300	27,200	54,400	95,000	136,000
2d 2P Cpe	4,000	12,000	20,000	40,000	70,000	100,000
2d Aero Cpe	4,550	13,700	22,800	45,600	80,000	114,000
4d Sed	3,850	11,500	19,200	38,400	67,000	96,000
4d Twn Sed	3,850	11,500	19,200	38,400	67,000	96,000
4d 7P Sed	3,900	11,800	19,600	39,200	69,100	98,000
4d 5P Imp Cabr	5,600	16,800	28,000	56,000	98,000	140,000
4d 7P Imp Cabr	5,600	16,800	28,000	56,000	98,000	140,000
4d Imp Sed	5,800	17,400	29,000	58,000	102,000	145,000
4d Twn Cabr	6,000	18,000	30,000	60,000	105,000	150,000
4d Twn Lan	5,450	16,300	27,200	54,400	95,000	136,000
4d 5P Conv	5,600	16,800	28,000	56,000	98,000	140,000
1937 Series 60, V-8, 124" wb						
2d Conv	2,200	6,600	11,000	22,000	38,500	55,000
4d Conv Sed	2,300	6,850	11,400	22,800	39,900	57,000
2d 2P Cpe	1,200	3,600	6,000	12,000	21,000	30,000
4d Tr Sed	1,000	3,000	5,000	10,000	17,500	25,000
1937 Series 65, V-8, 131" wb						
4d Tr Sed	1,100	3,250	5,400	10,800	18,900	27,000
1937 Series 70, V-8, 131" wb, Fleetwood bodies						
2d Conv	2,400	7,200	12,000	24,000	42,000	60,000
4d Conv Sed	2,500	7,450	12,400	24,800	43,400	62,000
2d Spt Cpe	1,300	3,950	6,600	13,200	23,100	33,000
4d Tr Sed	1,150	3,500	5,800	11,600	20,300	29,000
1937 Series 75, V-8, 138" wb, Fleetwood bodies						
4d Tr Sed	1,300	3,850	6,400	12,800	22,400	32,000
4d Twn Sed	1,300	3,950	6,600	13,200	23,100	33,000
4d Conv Sed	2,800	8,400	14,000	28,000	49,000	70,000
4d Fml Sed	1,400	4,200	7,000	14,000	24,500	35,000
4d Spl Tr Sed	1,450	4,300	7,200	14,400	25,200	36,000
4d Spl Imp Tr Sed	1,500	4,450	7,400	14,800	25,900	37,000
4d 7P Tr Sed	1,500	4,550	7,600	15,200	26,600	38,000
4d 7P Imp	1,500	4,450	7,400	14,800	25,900	37,000
4d Bus Tr Sed	1,450	4,300	7,200	14,400	25,200	36,000
4d Bus Imp	1,800	5,400	9,000	18,000	31,500	45,000
4d Twn Car	2,650	7,900	13,200	26,400	46,200	66,000
1937 4d Series 85, V-12, 138" wb, Fleetwood bodies						
4d Tr Sed	1,800	5,400	9,000	18,000	31,500	45,000
4d Twn Sed	1,850	5,500	9,200	18,400	32,200	46,000
4d Conv Sed	3,200	9,600	16,000	32,000	56,000	80,000
4d 7P Tr Sed	1,900	5,750	9,600	19,200	33,600	48,000
4d Imp Tr Sed	2,100	6,350	10,600	21,200	37,100	53,000
4d Twn Car	2,950	8,900	14,800	29,600	51,800	74,000
1937 Series 90, V-16, 154" wb, Fleetwood bodies						
2d 2P Conv	6,200	18,600	31,000	62,000	109,000	155,000
2d 5P Conv	6,200	18,600	31,000	62,000	109,000	155,000
4d Conv Sed	6,200	18,600	31,000	62,000	109,000	155,000
2d Cpe	4,400	13,200	22,000	44,000	77,000	110,000
4d Twn Sed	4,000	12,000	20,000	40,000	70,000	100,000
4d 7P Sed	4,100	12,200	20,400	40,800	71,500	102,000
4d Limo	4,300	13,000	21,600	43,200	76,100	108,000
4d 5P Imp Cabr	6,000	18,000	30,000	60,000	105,000	150,000
4d 5P Twn Cabr	6,200	18,600	31,000	62,000	109,000	155,000
4d 7P Imp Cabr	6,200	18,600	31,000	62,000	109,000	155,000
4d 7P Twn Cabr	6,400	19,200	32,000	64,000	112,000	160,000
2d Aero Cpe	4,700	14,200	23,600	47,200	83,100	118,000
4d Limo Brgm	4,400	13,200	22,000	44,000	77,000	110,000
4d Fml Sed	4,650	13,900	23,200	46,400	81,000	116,000
1938 Series 60, V-8, 124" wb						
2d Conv	2,300	6,950	11,600	23,200	40,600	58,000
4d Conv Sed	2,350	7,100	11,800	23,600	41,300	59,000
2d 2P Cpe	1,200	3,600	6,000	12,000	21,000	30,000
4d Tr Sed	1,150	3,500	5,800	11,600	20,300	29,000
1938 Series 60 Special, V-8, 127" wb						
4d Tr Sed	1,400	4,200	7,000	14,000	24,500	35,000
1938 Series 65, V-8, 132" wb						
4d Tr Sed	1,200	3,600	6,000	12,000	21,000	30,000
4d Div Tr Sed	1,400	4,200	7,000	14,000	24,500	35,000
4d Conv Sed	2,800	8,400	14,000	28,000	49,000	70,000
1938 Series 75, V-8, 141" wb, Fleetwood bodies						
2d Conv	2,900	8,650	14,400	28,800	50,400	72,000
4d Conv Sed	2,950	8,900	14,800	29,600	51,800	74,000
2d 2P Cpe	1,800	5,400	9,000	18,000	31,500	45,000
2d 5P Cpe	1,700	5,150	8,600	17,200	30,100	43,000
4d Tr Sed	1,400	4,200	7,000	14,000	24,500	35,000
4d Div Tr Sed	1,500	4,450	7,400	14,800	25,900	37,000
4d Twn Sed	1,450	4,300	7,200	14,400	25,200	36,000
4d Fml Sed	1,450	4,300	7,200	14,400	25,200	36,000
4d 7P Fml Sed	1,600	4,800	8,000	16,000	28,000	40,000
4d 7P Tr Sed	1,500	4,550	7,600	15,200	26,600	38,000
4d Imp Tr Sed	1,550	4,700	7,800	15,600	27,300	39,000
4d 8P Tr Sed	1,550	4,700	7,800	15,600	27,300	39,000

	6	5	4	3	2	1
4d 8P Imp Tr Sed	1,600	4,800	8,000	16,000	28,000	40,000
4d Twn Car	2,250	6,700	11,200	22,400	39,200	56,000

1938 Series 90, V-16, 141" wb, Fleetwood bodies

	6	5	4	3	2	1
2d Conv	4,250	12,700	21,200	42,400	74,000	106,000
4d Conv Sed Trk	4,300	13,000	21,600	43,200	76,100	108,000
2d 2P Cpe	3,050	9,100	15,200	30,400	53,200	76,000
2d 5P Cpe	3,100	9,350	15,600	31,200	54,600	78,000
4d Tr Sed	2,800	8,400	14,000	28,000	49,000	70,000
4d Twn Sed	2,900	8,650	14,400	28,800	50,400	72,000
4d Div Tr Sed	3,050	9,100	15,200	30,400	53,200	76,000
4d 7P Tr Sed	2,950	8,900	14,800	29,600	51,800	74,000
4d Imp Tr Sed	3,100	9,350	15,600	31,200	54,600	78,000
4d Fml Sed	3,100	9,350	15,600	31,200	54,600	78,000
4d Fml Sed Trk	3,200	9,600	16,000	32,000	56,000	80,000
4d Twn Car	3,850	11,500	19,200	38,400	67,000	96,000

1939 Series 61, V-8, 126" wb

	6	5	4	3	2	1
2d Conv	2,650	7,900	13,200	26,400	46,200	66,000
4d Conv Sed	2,700	8,150	13,600	27,200	47,600	68,000
2d Cpe	1,200	3,600	6,000	12,000	21,000	30,000
4d Tr Sed	1,100	3,250	5,400	10,800	18,900	27,000

1939 Series 60 Special, V-8, 127" wb, Fleetwood

	6	5	4	3	2	1
4d Sed	1,600	4,800	8,000	16,000	28,000	40,000
4d S/R Sed	1,700	5,050	8,400	16,800	29,400	42,000
4d S/R Imp Sed	1,800	5,400	9,000	18,000	31,500	45,000

1939 Series 75, V-8, 141" wb, Fleetwood bodies

	6	5	4	3	2	1
2d Conv	3,100	9,350	15,600	31,200	54,600	78,000
4d Conv Sed Trk	3,200	9,600	16,000	32,000	56,000	80,000
2d 4P Cpe	1,400	4,200	7,000	14,000	24,500	35,000
2d 5P Cpe	1,450	4,300	7,200	14,400	25,200	36,000
4d Tr Sed	1,300	3,950	6,600	13,200	23,100	33,000
4d Div Tr Sed	1,350	4,100	6,800	13,600	23,800	34,000
4d Twn Sed Trk	1,400	4,200	7,000	14,000	24,500	35,000
4d Fml Sed Trk	1,450	4,300	7,200	14,400	25,200	36,000
4d 7P Fml Sed Trk	1,500	4,550	7,600	15,200	26,600	38,000
4d 7P Tr Sed	1,500	4,450	7,400	14,800	25,900	37,000
4d 7P Tr Imp Sed	1,500	4,550	7,600	15,200	26,600	38,000
4d Bus Tr Sed	1,400	4,200	7,000	14,000	24,500	35,000
4d 8P Tr Imp Sed	1,600	4,800	8,000	16,000	28,000	40,000
4d Twn Car Trk	1,650	4,900	8,200	16,400	28,700	41,000

1939 Series 90, V-16, 141" wb, Fleetwood bodies

	6	5	4	3	2	1
2d Conv	4,000	12,000	20,000	40,000	70,000	100,000
4d Conv Sed	4,400	13,200	22,000	44,000	77,000	110,000
2d 4P Cpe	3,450	10,300	17,200	34,400	60,000	86,000
2d 5P Cpe	3,350	10,100	16,800	33,600	58,800	84,000
4d 5P Tr Sed	2,800	8,400	14,000	28,000	49,000	70,000
4d Twn Sed Trk	2,900	8,650	14,400	28,800	50,400	72,000
4d Div Tr Sed	2,900	8,650	14,400	28,800	50,400	72,000
4d 7P Tr Sed	2,900	8,650	14,400	28,800	50,400	72,000
4d 7P Imp Tr Sed	2,950	8,900	14,800	29,600	51,800	74,000
4d Fml Sed Trk	2,950	8,900	14,800	29,600	51,800	74,000
4d 7P Fml Sed Trk	3,050	9,100	15,200	30,400	53,200	76,000
4d Twn Car Trk	3,600	10,800	18,000	36,000	63,000	90,000

1940 Series 62, V-8, 129" wb

	6	5	4	3	2	1
2d Conv	2,800	8,400	14,000	28,000	49,000	70,000
4d Conv Sed	2,900	8,650	14,400	28,800	50,400	72,000

2d Cpe1,2503,7006,20012,40021,70031,000

	6	5	4	3	2	1
4d Sed	900	2,750	4,600	9,200	16,100	23,000

1940 Series 60 Special, V-8, 127" wb, Fleetwood

	6	5	4	3	2	1
4d Sed	1,550	4,700	7,800	15,600	27,300	39,000
4d S/R Sed	1,650	4,900	8,200	16,400	28,700	41,000
4d Imp Sed	1,650	4,900	8,200	16,400	28,700	41,000
4d S/R Imp Sed	1,700	5,150	8,600	17,200	30,100	43,000
4d MB Twn Car	2,000	6,000	10,000	20,000	35,000	50,000
4d LB Twn Car	2,000	6,000	10,000	20,000	35,000	50,000

1940 Series 72, V-8, 138" wb, Fleetwood

	6	5	4	3	2	1
4d Sed	1,500	4,550	7,600	15,200	26,600	38,000
4d 4P Imp Sed	1,550	4,700	7,800	15,600	27,300	39,000
4d 7P Sed	1,600	4,800	8,000	16,000	28,000	40,000
4d 7P Bus Sed	1,500	4,550	7,600	15,200	26,600	38,000
4d 7P Imp Sed	1,600	4,800	8,000	16,000	28,000	40,000
4d 7P Fml Sed	1,650	4,900	8,200	16,400	28,700	41,000
4d 7P Bus Imp	1,550	4,700	7,800	15,600	27,300	39,000
4d 5P Fml Sed	1,700	5,050	8,400	16,800	29,400	42,000

1940 Series 75, V-8, 141" wb, Fleetwood

	6	5	4	3	2	1
2d Conv	3,200	9,600	16,000	32,000	56,000	80,000
4d Conv Sed	3,300	9,850	16,400	32,800	57,400	82,000
2d 2P Cpe	2,250	6,700	11,200	22,400	39,200	56,000
2d 5P Cpe	2,200	6,600	11,000	22,000	38,500	55,000
4d Sed	2,100	6,350	10,600	21,200	37,100	53,000
4d 5P Imp Sed	2,200	6,600	11,000	22,000	38,500	55,000
4d 7P Sed	2,150	6,500	10,800	21,600	37,800	54,000
4d 7P Imp Sed	2,250	6,700	11,200	22,400	39,200	56,000
4d 5P Fml Sed	2,200	6,600	11,000	22,000	38,500	55,000
4d 7P Fml Sed	2,300	6,850	11,400	22,800	39,900	57,000
4d Twn Sed	2,400	7,200	12,000	24,000	42,000	60,000
4d Twn Car	2,550	7,700	12,800	25,600	44,800	64,000

1940 Series 90, V-16, 141" wb, Fleetwood

	6	5	4	3	2	1
2d Conv	4,650	13,900	23,200	46,400	81,000	116,000
4d Conv Sed	4,700	14,200	23,600	47,200	83,100	118,000
2d 2P Cpe	3,450	10,300	17,200	34,400	60,000	86,000
2d 5P Cpe	3,350	10,100	16,800	33,600	58,800	84,000
4d Sed	3,300	9,850	16,400	32,800	57,400	82,000
4d 7P Sed	3,350	10,100	16,800	33,600	58,800	84,000
4d 7P Imp Sed	3,350	10,100	16,800	33,600	58,800	84,000
4d 5P Fml Sed	3,500	10,600	17,600	35,200	62,100	88,000
4d 7P Fml Sed	3,500	10,600	17,600	35,200	62,100	88,000
4d 5P Twn Sed	3,600	10,800	18,000	36,000	63,000	90,000
4d 7P Twn Car	3,600	10,800	18,000	36,000	63,000	90,000

1941 Series 61, V-8, 126" wb

	6	5	4	3	2	1
2d FBk	900	2,750	4,600	9,200	16,100	23,000
2d DeL FBk	950	2,900	4,800	9,600	16,800	24,000
4d Sed FBk	850	2,500	4,200	8,400	14,700	21,000
4d DeL Sed FBk	1,000	3,000	5,000	10,000	17,500	25,000

1941 Series 62, V-8, 126" wb

	6	5	4	3	2	1
2d Conv	2,400	7,200	12,000	24,000	42,000	60,000
4d Conv Sed	2,500	7,450	12,400	24,800	43,400	62,000
2d Cpe	1,150	3,500	5,800	11,600	20,300	29,000
2d DeL Cpe	1,200	3,600	6,000	12,000	21,000	30,000
4d Sed	750	2,300	3,800	7,600	13,300	19,000
4d DeL Sed	800	2,400	4,000	8,000	14,000	20,000

1941 Series 63, V-8, 126" wb

	6	5	4	3	2	1
4d Sed FBk	1,000	3,000	5,000	10,000	17,500	25,000

1941 Series 60 Special, V-8, 126" wb, Fleetwood

	6	5	4	3	2	1
4d Sed	1,550	4,700	7,800	15,600	27,300	39,000
4d S/R Sed	1,700	5,050	8,400	16,800	29,400	42,000

NOTE: Add $1,500 for division window.

1941 Series 67, V-8, 138" wb

	6	5	4	3	2	1
4d 5P Sed	900	2,750	4,600	9,200	16,100	23,000
4d Imp Sed	950	2,900	4,800	9,600	16,800	24,000
4d 7P Sed	900	2,750	4,600	9,200	16,100	23,000
4d 7P Imp Sed	1,000	3,000	5,000	10,000	17,500	25,000

1941 Series 75, V-8, 136- 1/2" wb

	6	5	4	3	2	1
4d 5P Sed	950	2,900	4,800	9,600	16,800	24,000
4d 5P Imp Sed	1,000	3,050	5,100	10,200	17,900	25,500
4d 7P Sed	1,000	3,050	5,100	10,200	17,900	25,500
4d 9P Bus Sed	1,000	3,000	5,000	10,000	17,500	25,000
4d 7P Imp Sed	1,050	3,100	5,200	10,400	18,200	26,000
4d Bus Imp Sed	950	2,900	4,800	9,600	16,800	24,000
4d 5P Fml Sed	1,050	3,100	5,200	10,400	18,200	26,000
4d 7P Fml Sed	1,050	3,100	5,200	10,400	18,200	26,000

1942 Series 61, V-8, 126" wb

	6	5	4	3	2	1
2d FBk	950	2,900	4,800	9,600	16,800	24,000
4d FBk	700	2,150	3,600	7,200	12,600	18,000

1942 Series 62, V-8, 129" wb

	6	5	4	3	2	1
2d DeL FBk	1,000	3,050	5,100	10,200	17,850	25,500
2d FBk	1,000	3,000	5,000	10,000	17,500	25,000
2d DeL Conv Cpe	1,700	5,050	8,400	16,800	29,400	42,000
4d Sed	750	2,300	3,800	7,600	13,300	19,000
4d DeL Sed	800	2,400	4,000	8,000	14,000	20,000

1942 Series 63, V-8, 126" wb

	6	5	4	3	2	1
4d FBk	750	2,300	3,800	7,600	13,300	19,000

1942 Series 60 Special, V-8, 133" wb, Fleetwood

	6	5	4	3	2	1
4d Sed	950	2,900	4,800	9,600	16,800	24,000
4d Imp Sed	1,000	3,000	5,000	10,000	17,500	25,000

1942 Series 67, V-8, 139" wb

	6	5	4	3	2	1
4d 5P Sed	750	2,300	3,800	7,600	13,300	19,000
4d 5P Sed Div	900	2,650	4,400	8,800	15,400	22,000
4d 7P Sed	800	2,400	4,000	8,000	14,000	20,000
4d 7P Sed Imp	900	2,650	4,400	8,800	15,400	22,000

1942 Series 75, V-8, 136" wb, Fleetwood

	6	5	4	3	2	1
4d 5P Imp	900	2,650	4,400	8,800	15,400	22,000
4d 5P Imp Sed	900	2,750	4,600	9,200	16,100	23,000
4d 7P Sed	900	2,650	4,400	8,800	15,400	22,000
4d 9P Bus Sed	900	2,650	4,400	8,800	15,400	22,000
4d 7P Imp Sed	950	2,900	4,800	9,600	16,800	24,000
4d 9P Bus Imp	900	2,750	4,600	9,200	16,100	23,000
4d 5P Fml Sed	1,000	3,000	5,000	10,000	17,500	25,000
4d 7P Fml Sed	1,050	3,100	5,200	10,400	18,200	26,000

1946-1947 Series 61, V-8, 126" wb

	6	5	4	3	2	1
2d FBk	1,000	3,000	5,000	10,000	17,500	25,000
4d FBk	800	2,400	4,000	8,000	14,000	20,000

1946-1947 Series 62, V-8, 129" wb

	6	5	4	3	2	1
2d Conv	1,900	5,750	9,600	19,200	33,600	48,000
2d FBk	1,050	3,100	5,200	10,400	18,200	26,000
4d 5P Sed	850	2,500	4,200	8,400	14,700	21,000

1946-1947 Series 60 Special, V-8, 133" wb, Fleetwood

	6	5	4	3	2	1
4d 6P Sed	900	2,750	4,600	9,200	16,100	23,000

1946-1947 Series 75, V-8, 136" wb, Fleetwood

	6	5	4	3	2	1
4d 5P Sed	1,000	3,000	5,000	10,000	17,500	25,000
4d 7P Sed	1,050	3,100	5,200	10,400	18,200	26,000
4d 7P Imp Sed	1,200	3,600	6,000	12,000	21,000	30,000
4d 9P Bus Sed	1,050	3,100	5,200	10,400	18,200	26,000
4d 9P Bus Imp	1,100	3,350	5,600	11,200	19,600	28,000

1948 Series 61, V-8, 126" wb

	6	5	4	3	2	1
2d FBk	950	2,900	4,800	9,600	16,800	24,000
4d 5P Sed	850	2,500	4,200	8,400	14,700	21,000

1948 Series 62, V-8, 126" wb

	6	5	4	3	2	1
2d Conv	1,700	5,050	8,400	16,800	29,400	42,000
2d Clb Cpe	1,000	3,000	5,000	10,000	17,500	25,000
4d 5P Sed	900	2,750	4,600	9,200	16,100	23,000

1948 Series 60 Special, V-8, 133" wb, Fleetwood

	6	5	4	3	2	1
4d Sed	1,000	3,000	5,000	10,000	17,500	25,000

1948 Series 75, V-8, 136" wb, Fleetwood

	6	5	4	3	2	1
4d 5P Sed	1,000	3,000	5,000	10,000	17,500	25,000
4d 7P Sed	1,050	3,100	5,200	10,400	18,200	26,000
4d 7P Imp Sed	1,200	3,600	6,000	12,000	21,000	30,000
4d 9P Bus Sed	1,050	3,100	5,200	10,400	18,200	26,000
4d 9P Bus Imp	1,100	3,350	5,600	11,200	19,600	28,000

1949 Series 61, V-8, 126" wb

	6	5	4	3	2	1
2d FBk	1,000	3,000	5,000	10,000	17,500	25,000
4d Sed	900	2,650	4,400	8,800	15,400	22,000

	6	5	4	3	2	1
1949 Series 62, V-8, 126" wb						
2d FBk	1,050	3,100	5,200	10,400	18,200	26,000
4d 5P Sed	950	2,900	4,800	9,600	16,800	24,000
2d HT Cpe DeV	1,200	3,600	6,000	12,000	21,000	30,000
2d Conv	1,750	5,300	8,800	17,600	30,800	44,000
1949 Series 60 Special, V-8, 133" wb, Fleetwood						
4d 5P Sed	1,050	3,100	5,200	10,400	18,200	26,000
1949 Series 75, V-8, 136" wb, Fleetwood						
4d 5P Sed	1,050	3,100	5,200	10,400	18,200	26,000
4d 7P Sed	1,100	3,250	5,400	10,800	18,900	27,000
4d 7P Imp Sed	1,250	3,700	6,200	12,400	21,700	31,000
4d 9P Bus Sed	1,100	3,250	5,400	10,800	18,900	27,000
4d 9P Bus Imp	1,150	3,500	5,800	11,600	20,300	29,000
1950-1951 Series 61, V-8						
4d 5P Sed	700	2,150	3,600	7,200	12,600	18,000
2d HT Cpe	900	2,650	4,400	8,800	15,400	22,000
1950-1951 Series 62, V-8						
4d 5P Sed	750	2,300	3,800	7,600	13,300	19,000
2d HT Cpe	950	2,900	4,800	9,600	16,800	24,000
2d HT Cpe DeV	1,050	3,100	5,200	10,400	18,200	26,000
2d Conv	1,400	4,200	7,000	14,000	24,500	35,000
1950-1951 Series 60S, V-8						
4d Sed	950	2,900	4,800	9,600	16,800	24,000
1950-1951 Series 75, Fleetwood						
4d 8P Sed	1,000	3,000	5,000	10,000	17,500	25,000
1950-1951 Series 75 Fleetwood						
4d 8P Imp	1,100	3,250	5,400	10,800	18,900	27,000
1952 Series 62, V-8						
4d Sed	750	2,300	3,800	7,600	13,300	19,000
2d HT	900	2,750	4,600	9,200	16,100	23,000
2d HT Cpe DeV	1,050	3,100	5,200	10,400	18,200	26,000
2d Conv	1,450	4,300	7,200	14,400	25,200	36,000
1952 Series 60S, V-8						
4d Sed	950	2,900	4,800	9,600	16,800	24,000
1952 Series 75, V-8, Fleetwood						
4d Sed	1,000	3,000	5,000	10,000	17,500	25,000
4d Imp Sed	1,100	3,250	5,400	10,800	18,900	27,000
1953 Series 62, V-8						
4d Sed	700	2,150	3,600	7,200	12,600	18,000
2d HT	1,150	3,500	5,800	11,600	20,300	29,000
2d HT Cpe DeV	1,300	3,850	6,400	12,800	22,400	32,000
2d Conv	1,700	5,050	8,400	16,800	29,400	42,000
2d Eldo Conv	3,300	9,850	16,400	32,800	57,400	82,000
1953 Series 60S, V-8						
4d Sed	1,200	3,600	6,000	12,000	21,000	30,000
1953 Series 75, V-8, Fleetwood						
4d 7P Sed	1,250	3,700	6,200	12,400	21,700	31,000
4d Imp Sed	1,300	3,950	6,600	13,200	23,100	33,000
1954 Series 62, V-8						
4d Sed	700	2,150	3,600	7,200	12,600	18,000
2d HT	1,100	3,250	5,400	10,800	18,900	27,000
2d HT Cpe DeV	1,200	3,600	6,000	12,000	21,000	30,000
2d Conv	1,700	5,050	8,400	16,800	29,400	42,000
2d Eldo Conv	2,300	6,950	11,600	23,200	40,600	58,000
1954 Series 60S, V-8						
4d Sed	1,050	3,100	5,200	10,400	18,200	26,000
1954 Series 75, V-8, Fleetwood						
4d 7P Sed	1,150	3,500	5,800	11,600	20,300	29,000
4d 7P Imp Sed	1,250	3,700	6,200	12,400	21,700	31,000
1955 Series 62, V-8						
4d Sed	700	2,150	3,600	7,200	12,600	18,000
2d HT	1,100	3,350	5,600	11,200	19,600	28,000
2d HT Cpe DeV	1,200	3,600	6,000	12,000	21,000	30,000
2d Conv	1,600	4,800	8,000	16,000	28,000	40,000
2d Eldo Conv	1,700	5,050	8,400	16,800	29,400	42,000
1955 Series 60S, V-8						
4d Sed	1,050	3,100	5,200	10,400	18,200	26,000
1955 Series 75, V-8, Fleetwood						
4d 7P Sed	1,150	3,500	5,800	11,600	20,300	29,000
4d 7P Imp Sed	1,250	3,700	6,200	12,400	21,700	31,000
1956 Series 62, V-8						
4d Sed	700	2,150	3,600	7,200	12,600	18,000
2d HT	1,050	3,100	5,200	10,400	18,200	26,000
4d HT Sed DeV	900	2,750	4,600	9,200	16,100	23,000
2d HT Cpe DeV	1,200	3,600	6,000	12,000	21,000	30,000
2d Conv	1,750	5,300	8,800	17,600	30,800	44,000
2d HT Eldo Sev	1,450	4,300	7,200	14,400	25,200	36,000
2d Brtz Conv	1,650	4,900	8,200	16,400	28,700	41,000
1956 Series 60S, V-8						
4d Sed	1,050	3,100	5,200	10,400	18,200	26,000
1956 Series 75, V-8, Fleetwood						
4d 7P Sed	1,150	3,500	5,800	11,600	20,300	29,000
4d 7P Imp Sed	1,250	3,700	6,200	12,400	21,700	31,000
1957 Series 62, V-8						
4d HT	550	1,700	2,800	5,600	9,800	14,000
2d HT	1,000	3,000	5,000	10,000	17,500	25,000
2d HT Cpe DeV	1,100	3,250	5,400	10,800	18,900	27,000
4d HT Sed DeV	750	2,300	3,800	7,600	13,300	19,000
2d Conv	1,500	4,550	7,600	15,200	26,600	38,000
1957 Eldorado, V-8						
2d HT Sev	1,100	3,250	5,400	10,800	18,900	27,000
2d Brtz Conv	1,450	4,300	7,200	14,400	25,200	36,000
1957 Fleetwood 60 Special, V-8						
4d HT	800	2,400	4,000	8,000	14,000	20,000

	6	5	4	3	2	1
1957 Eldorado Brougham, V-8						
4d HT	1,150	3,500	5,800	11,600	20,300	29,000
1957 Series 75						
4d 8P Sed	850	2,500	4,200	8,400	14,700	21,000
4d 8P Imp Sed	900	2,750	4,600	9,200	16,100	23,000
1958 Series 62, V-8						
4d HT Sh Dk	500	1,450	2,400	4,800	8,400	12,000
4d 6W Sed	500	1,550	2,600	5,200	9,100	13,000
4d Sed DeV	550	1,700	2,800	5,600	9,800	14,000
2d HT	900	2,650	4,400	8,800	15,400	22,000
2d HT Cpe DeV	950	2,900	4,800	9,600	16,800	24,000
2d Conv	1,300	3,850	6,400	12,800	22,400	32,000
1958 Eldorado, V-8						
2d HT Sev	950	2,900	4,800	9,600	16,800	24,000
2d Brtz Conv	1,500	4,450	7,400	14,800	25,900	37,000
1958 Fleetwood 60 Special, V-8						
4d HT	800	2,400	4,000	8,000	14,000	20,000
1958 Eldorado Brougham, V-8						
4d HT	1,100	3,350	5,600	11,200	19,600	28,000
1958 Series 75						
4d 8P Sed	750	2,300	3,800	7,600	13,300	19,000
4d 8P Imp Sed	850	2,500	4,200	8,400	14,700	21,000
1959 Series 62, V-8						
4d 4W HT	600	1,800	3,000	6,000	10,500	15,000
4d 6W HT	550	1,700	2,800	5,600	9,800	14,000
2d HT	800	2,400	4,000	8,000	14,000	20,000
2d Conv	1,900	5,650	9,400	18,800	32,900	47,000
1959 Series 62 DeVille, V-8						
2d HT Cpe DeV	1,050	3,100	5,200	10,400	18,200	26,000
4d 4W HT	650	1,900	3,200	6,400	11,200	16,000
4d 6W HT	600	1,800	3,000	6,000	10,500	15,000
1959 Series Eldorado, V-8						
4d HT Brgm	1,250	3,700	6,200	12,400	21,700	31,000
2d HT Sev	1,400	4,200	7,000	14,000	24,500	35,000
2d Brtz Conv	2,700	8,150	13,600	27,200	47,600	68,000
1959 Fleetwood 60 Special, V-8						
4d 6P Sed	1,000	3,000	5,000	10,000	17,500	25,000
1959 Fleetwood Series 75, V-8						
4d 9P Sed	1,100	3,250	5,400	10,800	18,900	27,000
4d Limo	1,150	3,500	5,800	11,600	20,300	29,000
1960 Series 62, V-8						
4d 4W HT	550	1,700	2,800	5,600	9,800	14,000
4d 6W HT	500	1,550	2,600	5,200	9,100	13,000
2d HT	850	2,500	4,200	8,400	14,700	21,000
2d Conv	1,550	4,700	7,800	15,600	27,300	39,000
1960 Series 62 DeVille, V-8						
4d 4W Sed	600	1,800	3,000	6,000	10,500	15,000
4d 6W Sed	550	1,700	2,800	5,600	9,800	14,000
2d HT Cpe DeV	900	2,750	4,600	9,200	16,100	23,000
1960 Eldorado Series, V-8						
4d HT Brgm	1,250	3,700	6,200	12,400	21,700	31,000
2d HT Sev	1,350	4,100	6,800	13,600	23,800	34,000
2d Brtz Conv	2,500	7,450	12,400	24,800	43,400	62,000
1960 Fleetwood 60 Special, V-8						
4d 6P HT	950	2,900	4,800	9,600	16,800	24,000
1960 Fleetwood Series 75, V-8						
4d 9P Sed	1,000	3,000	5,000	10,000	17,500	25,000
4d Limo	1,100	3,250	5,400	10,800	18,900	27,000
1961 Series 62, V-8						
4d 4W HT	400	1,250	2,100	4,200	7,350	10,500
4d 6W HT	400	1,250	2,100	4,150	7,300	10,400
2d HT	650	1,900	3,200	6,400	11,200	16,000
2d Conv	1,200	3,600	6,000	12,000	21,000	30,000
1961 Series 62 DeVille, V-8						
4d 4W HT	450	1,300	2,150	4,300	7,500	10,700
4d 6W HT	400	1,250	2,100	4,250	7,400	10,600
4d HT Sh Dk	400	1,250	2,100	4,200	7,350	10,500
2d HT Cpe DeV	700	2,150	3,600	7,200	12,600	18,000
1961 Eldorado Series, V-8						
2d Brtz Conv	1,400	4,200	7,000	14,000	24,500	35,000
1961 Fleetwood 60 Special, V-8						
4d 6P HT	600	1,800	3,000	6,000	10,500	15,000
1961 Fleetwood Series 75, V-8						
4d 9P Sed	700	2,050	3,400	6,800	11,900	17,000
4d 9P Limo	900	2,650	4,400	8,800	15,400	22,000
1962 Series 62, V-8						
4d 4W HT	450	1,300	2,150	4,300	7,500	10,700
4d 6W HT	400	1,250	2,100	4,200	7,350	10,500
4d HT Sh Dk	400	1,250	2,100	4,200	7,350	10,500
2d HT	650	1,900	3,200	6,400	11,200	16,000
2d Conv	1,200	3,600	6,000	12,000	21,000	30,000
1962 Series 62 DeVille, V-8						
4d 4W HT	450	1,350	2,250	4,500	7,850	11,200
4d 6W HT	500	1,450	2,400	4,800	8,400	12,000
4d HT Pk Ave	450	1,400	2,300	4,600	8,050	11,500
2d HT Cpe DeV	700	2,150	3,600	7,200	12,600	18,000
1962 Eldorado Series, V-8						
2d Brtz Conv	1,400	4,200	7,000	14,000	24,500	35,000
1962 Fleetwood 60 Special, V-8						
4d 6P HT	650	1,900	3,200	6,400	11,200	16,000
1962 Fleetwood 75 Series, V-8						
4d 9P Sed	700	2,050	3,400	6,800	11,900	17,000
4d 9P Limo	900	2,650	4,400	8,800	15,400	22,000

	6	5	4	3	2	1
1963 Series 62, V-8						
4d 4W HT	400	1,200	1,950	3,900	6,850	9,800
4d 6W HT	400	1,150	1,900	3,850	6,700	9,600
2d HT	500	1,450	2,400	4,800	8,400	12,000
2d Conv	950	2,900	4,800	9,600	16,800	24,000
1963 Series 62 DeVille, V-8						
4d 4W HT	400	1,200	2,000	4,050	7,050	10,100
4d 6W HT	400	1,200	2,000	4,000	7,000	10,000
4d HT Pk Ave	400	1,200	1,950	3,900	6,850	9,800
2d HT Cpe DeV	600	1,800	3,000	6,000	10,500	15,000
1963 Eldorado Series, V-8						
2d Brtz Conv	1,150	3,500	5,800	11,600	20,300	29,000
1963 Fleetwood 60 Special, V-8						
4d 6P HT	500	1,550	2,600	5,200	9,100	13,000
1963 Fleetwood 75 Series, V-8						
4d 9P Sed	600	1,800	3,000	6,000	10,500	15,000
4d 9P Limo	750	2,300	3,800	7,600	13,300	19,000
1964 Series 62, V-8						
4d 4W HT	400	1,200	2,000	4,000	7,000	10,000
4d 6W HT	400	1,200	1,950	3,900	6,850	9,800
2d HT	550	1,700	2,800	5,600	9,800	14,000
1964 Series 62 DeVille, V-8						
4d 4W HT	400	1,200	2,050	4,100	7,150	10,200
4d 6W HT	400	1,200	2,000	4,000	7,000	10,000
2d HT Cpe DeV	650	1,900	3,200	6,400	11,200	16,000
2d Conv	1,000	3,000	5,000	10,000	17,500	25,000
1964 Eldorado Series, V-8						
2d Conv	1,200	3,600	6,000	12,000	21,000	30,000
1964 Fleetwood 60 Special, V-8						
4d 6P HT	550	1,700	2,800	5,600	9,800	14,000
1964 Fleetwood 75 Series, V-8						
4d 9P Sed	650	1,900	3,200	6,400	11,200	16,000
4d 9P Limo	750	2,300	3,800	7,600	13,300	19,000
1965 Calais Series, V-8						
4d Sed	400	1,200	1,950	3,900	6,850	9,800
4d HT	400	1,200	2,000	4,000	7,000	10,000
2d HT	500	1,450	2,400	4,800	8,400	12,000
1965 DeVille Series, V-8						
6P Sed	400	1,200	2,000	4,000	7,000	10,000
4d HT	400	1,250	2,100	4,150	7,300	10,400
2d HT	550	1,700	2,800	5,600	9,800	14,000
2d Conv	750	2,300	3,800	7,600	13,300	19,000
1965 Fleetwood 60 Special, V-8						
4d 6P Sed	500	1,500	2,500	5,000	8,750	12,500
4d Brgm Sed	500	1,550	2,600	5,200	9,100	13,000
1965 Fleetwood Eldorado, V-8						
2d Conv	950	2,900	4,800	9,600	16,800	24,000
1965 Fleetwood 75 Series, V-8						
4d 9P Sed	650	1,900	3,200	6,400	11,200	16,000
4d 9P Limo	750	2,300	3,800	7,600	13,300	19,000
1966 Calais Series, V-8						
4d Sed	400	1,200	1,950	3,900	6,850	9,800
4d HT	400	1,200	2,000	4,000	7,000	10,000
2d HT	500	1,450	2,400	4,800	8,400	12,000
1966 DeVille Series, V-8						
4d Sed	400	1,200	2,000	4,000	7,000	10,000
4d HT	400	1,200	2,050	4,100	7,150	10,200
2d HT	550	1,700	2,800	5,600	9,800	14,000
2d Conv	750	2,300	3,800	7,600	13,300	19,000
1966 Eldorado, V-8						
2d Conv	950	2,900	4,800	9,600	16,800	24,000
1966 Fleetwood Brougham, V-8						
4d Sed	500	1,450	2,400	4,800	8,400	12,000
1966 Sixty Special, V-8						
4d Sed	500	1,450	2,400	4,800	8,400	12,000
1966 Seventy Five, V-8						
4d Sed	600	1,800	3,000	6,000	10,500	15,000
4d Limo	750	2,300	3,800	7,600	13,300	19,000
1967 Calais, V-8, 129.5" wb						
4d HT	400	1,200	2,000	4,000	7,000	10,000
2d HT	450	1,400	2,300	4,600	8,050	11,500
1967 DeVille, V-8, 129.5" wb						
4d HT	400	1,250	2,100	4,250	7,400	10,600
2d HT	500	1,550	2,600	5,200	9,100	13,000
2d Conv	750	2,300	3,800	7,600	13,300	19,000
1967 Fleetwood Eldorado, V-8, 120" wb						
2d HT	500	1,550	2,600	5,200	9,100	13,000
1967 Sixty-Special, V-8, 133" wb						
4d Sed	450	1,300	2,200	4,400	7,700	11,000
1967 Fleetwood Brougham, V-8, 133" wb						
4d Sed	450	1,300	2,200	4,400	7,700	11,000
1967 Seventy-Five Series, V-8, 149.8" wb						
4d Sed	500	1,450	2,400	4,800	8,400	12,000
4d Limo	500	1,550	2,600	5,200	9,100	13,000
1968 Calais, V-8, 129.5" wb						
2d HT	450	1,400	2,300	4,600	8,050	11,500
4d HT	400	1,200	2,000	4,050	7,050	10,100
1968 DeVille, V-8, 129.5" wb						
4d	400	1,200	2,050	4,100	7,150	10,200
4d HT	400	1,250	2,100	4,250	7,400	10,600
2d HT	500	1,550	2,600	5,200	9,100	13,000
2d Conv	750	2,300	3,800	7,600	13,300	19,000

	6	5	4	3	2	1
1968 Fleetwood Eldorado, V-8, 120" wb						
2d HT	500	1,550	2,600	5,200	9,100	13,000
1968 Sixty-Special, V-8, 133" wb						
4d Sed	450	1,300	2,200	4,400	7,700	11,000
1968 Fleetwood Brougham, V-8, 133" wb						
4d Sed	450	1,300	2,200	4,400	7,700	11,000
1968 Series 75, V-8, 149.8" wb						
4d Sed	500	1,450	2,400	4,800	8,400	12,000
4d Limo	500	1,550	2,600	5,200	9,100	13,000
1969-1970 Calais, V-8, 129.5" wb						
2d HT	400	1,150	1,900	3,800	6,650	9,500
4d HT	350	1,000	1,700	3,400	5,950	8,500
1969-1970 DeVille, V-8, 129.5" wb						
4d Sed	350	1,050	1,700	3,450	6,000	8,600
4d HT	350	1,050	1,800	3,550	6,250	8,900
2d HT	400	1,150	1,900	3,800	6,650	9,500
2d Conv	650	1,900	3,200	6,400	11,200	16,000
1969-1970 Fleetwood Eldorado, V-8, 120" wb						
2d HT	500	1,450	2,400	4,800	8,400	12,000
1969-1970 Sixty-Special, V-8, 133" wb						
4d Sed	400	1,200	2,000	4,000	7,000	10,000
4d Brgm	400	1,250	2,100	4,200	7,350	10,500
1969-1970 Series 75, V-8, 149.8" wb						
4d Sed	400	1,250	2,100	4,200	7,350	10,500
4d Limo	450	1,300	2,200	4,400	7,700	11,000
1971-1972 Calais						
2d HT	400	1,200	1,950	3,900	6,850	9,800
4d HT	350	1,050	1,750	3,500	6,100	8,700
1971-1972 DeVille						
2d HT	400	1,250	2,100	4,200	7,350	10,500
4d HT	350	1,100	1,850	3,700	6,450	9,200
1971-1972 Fleetwood 60 Special						
4d Brgm	400	1,200	1,950	3,900	6,850	9,800
1971-1972 Fleetwood 75						
4d 9P Sed	400	1,200	1,950	3,900	6,850	9,800
4d Limo	400	1,250	2,050	4,100	7,200	10,300
1971-1972 Fleetwood Eldorado						
2d HT	450	1,300	2,200	4,400	7,700	11,000
2d Conv	600	1,800	3,000	6,000	10,500	15,000
1973 Calais, V-8						
2d HT	350	1,000	1,700	3,400	5,950	8,500
4d HT	350	1,000	1,650	3,300	5,800	8,300
1973 DeVille, V-8						
2d HT	350	1,100	1,800	3,600	6,300	9,000
4d HT	350	1,050	1,750	3,500	6,150	8,800
1973 Fleetwood 60S, V-8						
4d Brgm Sed	350	1,050	1,800	3,550	6,250	8,900
1973 Fleetwood Eldorado, V-8						
2d HT	400	1,200	2,000	4,000	7,000	10,000
2d Conv	600	1,800	3,000	6,000	10,500	15,000
1973 Fleetwood 75, V-8						

NOTE: Add 20 percent for Pace Car Edition.

	6	5	4	3	2	1
4d Sed	400	1,150	1,900	3,800	6,650	9,500
4d Limo	400	1,200	2,000	4,000	7,000	10,000
1974 Calais, V-8						
2d HT	350	1,000	1,700	3,350	5,900	8,400
4d HT	350	1,000	1,650	3,300	5,750	8,200
1974 DeVille, V-8						
2d HT	350	1,050	1,800	3,550	6,250	8,900
4d HT	350	1,050	1,750	3,500	6,100	8,700
1974 Fleetwood Brougham, V-8						
4d Sed	350	1,050	1,750	3,500	6,150	8,800
1974 Fleetwood Eldorado, V-8						
2d HT	400	1,200	2,000	4,000	7,000	10,000
2d Conv	650	1,900	3,200	6,400	11,200	16,000
1974 Fleetwood 75, V-8						
4d Sed	400	1,150	1,900	3,800	6,650	9,500
4d Limo	400	1,200	2,000	4,000	7,000	10,000

NOTE: Add 20 percent for Talisman Brougham. Add 10 percent for padded top on Series 75. Add 10 percent for sunroof on DeVille/60/Eldorado.

	6	5	4	3	2	1
1975 Calais, V-8						
2d HT	350	1,050	1,750	3,500	6,100	8,700
4d HT	350	1,000	1,650	3,300	5,800	8,300
1975 DeVille, V-8						
2d HT	350	1,050	1,800	3,550	6,250	8,900
4d HT	350	1,000	1,700	3,400	5,950	8,500
1975 Fleetwood Brougham, V-8						
4d Sed	350	1,000	1,700	3,400	5,950	8,500
1975 Fleetwood Eldorado, V-8						
2d HT	400	1,200	2,000	4,000	7,000	10,000
2d Conv	650	1,900	3,200	6,400	11,200	16,000
1975 Fleetwood 75, V-8						
4d Sed	400	1,150	1,900	3,800	6,650	9,500
4d Limo	400	1,200	2,000	4,000	7,000	10,000
1976 Calais, V-8						
2d HT	300	950	1,600	3,200	5,600	8,000
4d HT	300	950	1,550	3,100	5,450	7,800
1976 DeVille, V-8						
2d HT	350	1,000	1,650	3,300	5,800	8,300
4d HT	300	950	1,600	3,200	5,600	8,000
1976 Seville, V-8						
4d Sed	400	1,250	2,050	4,100	7,200	10,300

	6	5	4	3	2	1
1976 Eldorado, V-8						
2d Cpe	450	1,300	2,200	4,400	7,700	11,000
2d Brtz Cpe	500	1,450	2,400	4,800	8,400	12,000
2d Conv	700	2,150	3,600	7,200	12,600	18,000

NOTE: Add 15 percent for Bicent. Edit.

	6	5	4	3	2	1
1976 Fleetwood Brougham, V-8						
4d Sed	300	900	1,450	2,900	5,100	7,300
1976 Fleetwood 75, V-8						
4d Sed	300	900	1,500	3,000	5,250	7,500
4d Limo	300	950	1,600	3,200	5,600	8,000

NOTE: Add 5 percent for Talisman on Fleetwood Brougham.

	6	5	4	3	2	1
1977 DeVille, V-8						
2d Cpe	300	850	1,400	2,800	4,900	7,000
4d Sed	300	850	1,400	2,800	4,900	7,000
1977 Seville, V-8						
4d Sed	300	950	1,600	3,200	5,600	8,000
1977 Eldorado, V-8						
2d Cpe	350	1,100	1,800	3,600	6,300	9,000
2d Brtz Cpe	500	1,450	2,400	4,800	8,400	12,000
1977 Fleetwood Brougham, V-8						
4d Sed	300	950	1,600	3,200	5,600	8,000
1977 Fleetwood 75, V-8						
4d Sed	350	1,000	1,650	3,300	5,750	8,200
4d Limo	350	1,000	1,700	3,400	5,950	8,500
1978 Seville						
4d Sed	300	900	1,500	3,050	5,300	7,600
1978 DeVille						
2d Cpe	250	800	1,350	2,700	4,700	6,700
4d Sed	250	750	1,200	2,450	4,250	6,100
1978 Eldorado						
2d Cpe	400	1,200	2,000	4,000	7,000	10,000
2d Brtz Cpe	500	1,550	2,600	5,200	9,100	13,000
1978 Fleetwood Brougham						
4d Sed	250	800	1,350	2,700	4,750	6,800
1978 Fleetwood Limo						
4d	300	900	1,550	3,100	5,400	7,700
4d Fml	300	950	1,600	3,150	5,550	7,900
1979 Seville, V-8						
4d Sed	300	950	1,600	3,200	5,600	8,000

NOTE: Add 10 percent for Elegant'e.

	6	5	4	3	2	1
1979 DeVille, V-8						
2d Cpe	300	850	1,400	2,800	4,900	7,000
4d Sed	250	750	1,250	2,500	4,350	6,200

NOTE: Add 5 percent for Phaeton Special Edition.

	6	5	4	3	2	1
1979 Eldorado, V-8						
2d Cpe	400	1,200	2,000	4,000	7,000	10,000

NOTE: Add 15 percent for Biarritz.

	6	5	4	3	2	1
1979 Fleetwood Brougham, V-8						
4d Sed	250	800	1,300	2,600	4,550	6,500
1979 Fleetwood Limo						
4d Sed	300	900	1,550	3,100	5,400	7,700
4d Fml Sed	300	950	1,600	3,150	5,550	7,900

NOTE: Deduct 12 percent for diesel.

	6	5	4	3	2	1
1980 Seville, V-8						
4d Sed	300	900	1,500	2,950	5,200	7,400
1980 DeVille, V-8						
2d Cpe	300	850	1,400	2,800	4,900	7,000
4d Sed	250	750	1,300	2,550	4,500	6,400
1980 Eldorado, V-8						
2d Cpe	400	1,200	2,000	4,000	7,000	10,000

NOTE: Add 15 percent for Biarritz.

	6	5	4	3	2	1
1980 Fleetwood Brougham, V-8						
2d Cpe	300	900	1,500	3,000	5,250	7,500
4d Sed	300	850	1,400	2,750	4,850	6,900
1980 Fleetwood, V-8						
4d Limo	300	950	1,600	3,150	5,550	7,900
4d Fml	300	850	1,400	2,850	4,950	7,100
1981 Seville, V-8						
4d Sed	250	800	1,300	2,600	4,550	6,500
1981 DeVille, V-8						
2d Cpe	250	750	1,200	2,450	4,250	6,100
4d Sed	200	650	1,100	2,200	3,850	5,500
1981 Eldorado, V-8						
2d Cpe	350	1,100	1,800	3,600	6,300	9,000

NOTE: Add 15 percent for Biarritz.

	6	5	4	3	2	1
1981 Fleetwood Brougham, V-8						
2d Cpe	250	800	1,300	2,650	4,600	6,600
4d Sed	250	700	1,200	2,400	4,200	6,000
1981 Fleetwood, V-8						
4d Limo	300	850	1,400	2,800	4,900	7,000
4d Fml	300	850	1,450	2,900	5,050	7,200
1982 Cimarron, 4-cyl.						
4d Sed	200	600	1,050	2,100	3,650	5,200
1982 Seville, V-8						
4d Sed	250	800	1,300	2,650	4,600	6,600
1982 DeVille, V-8						
2d Cpe	250	750	1,250	2,500	4,400	6,300
4d Sed	250	700	1,150	2,300	4,000	5,700
1982 Eldorado, V-8						
2d Cpe	350	1,100	1,800	3,600	6,300	9,000

NOTE: Add 15 percent for Biarritz.

	6	5	4	3	2	1
1982 Fleetwood Brougham, V-8						
2d Cpe	250	800	1,350	2,700	4,750	6,800
4d Sed	250	750	1,250	2,500	4,350	6,200
1982 Fleetwood, V-8						
4d Limo	300	850	1,450	2,900	5,050	7,200
4d Fml	300	900	1,500	2,950	5,200	7,400
1983 Cimarron, 4-cyl.						
4d Sed	200	650	1,100	2,200	3,850	5,500
1983 Seville, V-8						
4d Sed	250	800	1,350	2,700	4,700	6,700
1983 DeVille, V-8						
2d Cpe	250	800	1,300	2,600	4,550	6,500
4d Sed	250	700	1,200	2,350	4,150	5,900
1983 Eldorado, V-8						
2d Cpe	350	1,100	1,800	3,600	6,300	9,000

NOTE: Add 15 percent for Biarritz.

	6	5	4	3	2	1
1983 Fleetwood Brougham, V-8						
2d Cpe	300	850	1,400	2,800	4,900	7,000
4d Sed	250	750	1,300	2,550	4,500	6,400
1983 Fleetwood, V-8						
4d Limo	300	900	1,500	2,950	5,200	7,400
4d Fml	300	900	1,500	3,050	5,300	7,600
1984 Cimarron, 4-cyl.						
4d Sed	200	650	1,100	2,250	3,900	5,600
1984 Seville, V-8						
4d Sed	250	800	1,350	2,700	4,750	6,800
1984 DeVille, V-8						
2d Sed	250	800	1,300	2,650	4,600	6,600
4d Sed	250	700	1,200	2,400	4,200	6,000
1984 Eldorado, V-8						
2d Cpe	350	1,100	1,800	3,600	6,300	9,000
2d Conv	800	2,400	4,000	8,000	14,000	20,000

NOTE: Add 15 percent for Biarritz.

	6	5	4	3	2	1
1984 Fleetwood Brougham, V-8						
2d Sed	300	850	1,400	2,800	4,900	7,000
4d Sed	250	800	1,300	2,600	4,550	6,500
1984 Fleetwood, V-8						
4d Sed	300	900	1,500	3,000	5,250	7,500
4d Fml Limo	300	900	1,550	3,100	5,400	7,700
1985 Cimarron, V-6						
4d Sed	250	700	1,150	2,300	4,000	5,700

NOTE: Deduct 15 percent for 4-cyl.

	6	5	4	3	2	1
1985 Seville, V-8						
4d Sed	300	850	1,400	2,750	4,850	6,900
1985 DeVille, V-8						
2d Cpe	250	800	1,300	2,650	4,600	6,600
4d Sed	250	750	1,200	2,450	4,250	6,100
1985 Eldorado, V-8						
2d Cpe	350	1,100	1,800	3,600	6,300	9,000
Conv	800	2,400	4,000	8,000	14,000	20,000

NOTE: Add 15 percent for Biarritz.

	6	5	4	3	2	1
1985 Fleetwood, V-8						
2d Cpe	300	850	1,400	2,750	4,850	6,900
4d Sed	250	800	1,350	2,700	4,700	6,700
1985 Fleetwood Brougham, V-8						
2d Cpe	300	900	1,550	3,100	5,400	7,700
4d Sed	300	900	1,500	3,050	5,300	7,600
1985 Fleetwood 75, V-8						
4d Limo	350	1,000	1,700	3,400	5,950	8,500

NOTE: Deduct 30 percent for diesel where available.

	6	5	4	3	2	1
1986 Cimarron						
4d Sed	250	700	1,150	2,300	4,050	5,800
1986 Seville						
4d Sed	300	850	1,400	2,800	4,900	7,000
1986 DeVille						
2d Cpe	250	750	1,250	2,500	4,350	6,200
4d Sed	250	750	1,200	2,450	4,250	6,100
1986 Fleetwood						
2d Cpe	300	950	1,550	3,100	5,450	7,800
4d Sed	300	900	1,550	3,100	5,400	7,700
1986 Fleetwood 75						
4d Limo	350	1,000	1,700	3,400	5,950	8,500
4d Fml Limo	350	1,050	1,800	3,550	6,250	8,900
1986 Fleetwood Brougham						
4d Sed	300	950	1,550	3,100	5,450	7,800
1986 Eldorado						
2d Cpe	350	1,100	1,850	3,700	6,450	9,200
1987 Cimarron						
4d Sed, 4-cyl.	250	700	1,200	2,350	4,150	5,900
4d Sed, V-6	250	700	1,200	2,400	4,200	6,000
1987 Seville, V-8						
4d Sed	300	850	1,400	2,850	4,950	7,100
1987 DeVille, V-8						
4d Sed	250	750	1,250	2,500	4,400	6,300
2d Cpe	250	750	1,250	2,500	4,350	6,200
1987 Fleetwood, V-8						
4d Sed d'Elegance	300	950	1,600	3,150	5,550	7,900
4d Sed, 60 Spl	300	950	1,600	3,200	5,600	8,000
1987 Eldorado, V-8						
2d Cpe	350	1,100	1,800	3,650	6,350	9,100

	6	5	4	3	2	1
1987 Brougham, V-8						
4d Sed	350	1,000	1,700	3,350	5,900	8,400
1987 Fleetwood 75 Series, V-8						
4d Limo	400	1,250	2,100	4,200	7,350	10,500
4d Fml	400	1,200	2,000	4,000	7,000	10,000
1987 Allante, V-8						
2d Conv	750	2,300	3,800	7,600	13,300	19,000
1988 Cimarron, V-6						
4d Sed	200	650	1,100	2,200	3,850	5,500
1988 Seville, V-8						
4d Sed	400	1,150	1,900	3,800	6,650	9,500
1988 DeVille, V-8						
2d Cpe	350	1,050	1,700	3,450	6,000	8,600
4d Sed	350	1,050	1,700	3,450	6,000	8,600
1988 Fleetwood, V-8						
4d Sed d'Elegance	400	1,150	1,900	3,800	6,650	9,500
4d Sed 60 Spl	400	1,250	2,100	4,200	7,350	10,500
1988 Brougham, V-8						
4d Sed	450	1,300	2,200	4,400	7,700	11,000
1988 Eldorado, V-8						
2d Cpe	400	1,150	1,900	3,800	6,650	9,500
1988 Allante, V-8						
2d Conv	800	2,400	4,000	8,000	14,000	20,000
1989 Seville, V-8						
4d Sed	500	1,450	2,400	4,800	8,400	12,000
1989 DeVille, V-8						
2d Cpe	500	1,450	2,450	4,900	8,550	12,200
4d Sed	500	1,450	2,400	4,850	8,450	12,100
1989 Fleetwood, V-8						
2d Cpe	550	1,600	2,700	5,400	9,450	13,500
4d Sed	550	1,600	2,700	5,350	9,400	13,400
4d Sed 605	500	1,500	2,500	4,950	8,700	12,400
4d Sed Brgm	400	1,250	2,100	4,200	7,350	10,500
1989 Eldorado, V-8						
2d Cpe	500	1,550	2,550	5,100	8,950	12,800
1989 Alante, V-8						
2d Conv	800	2,400	4,000	8,000	14,000	20,000
1990 Seville, V-8						
4d Sed	400	1,200	2,000	4,000	7,000	10,000
4d Sed STS	500	1,450	2,400	4,800	8,400	12,000
1990 DeVille, V-8						
2d Cpe	400	1,250	2,100	4,200	7,350	10,500
4d Sed	400	1,200	2,050	4,100	7,150	10,200
1990 Fleetwood, V-8						
2d Cpe	450	1,400	2,300	4,600	8,050	11,500
4d Sed	450	1,400	2,350	4,700	8,200	11,700
4d Sed 605	500	1,550	2,600	5,200	9,100	13,000
1990 Eldorado, V-8						
2d Cpe	500	1,450	2,400	4,800	8,400	12,000
1990 Brougham, V-8						
4d Sed	500	1,450	2,400	4,800	8,400	12,000
1990 Allante						
2d Conv	800	2,400	4,000	8,000	14,000	20,000

NOTE: Add $3,000 for hardtop.

	6	5	4	3	2	1
1991 Seville, V-8						
4d Sed	400	1,200	2,000	4,000	7,000	10,000
4d Trg Sed	450	1,300	2,200	4,400	7,700	11,000
1991 DeVille, V-8						
4d Sed	400	1,150	1,900	3,800	6,650	9,500
4d Trg Sed	400	1,250	2,100	4,200	7,350	10,500
2d Cpe	400	1,150	1,900	3,750	6,600	9,400
1991 Fleetwood, V-8						
2d Cpe	400	1,200	2,000	4,000	7,000	10,000
4d Sed	400	1,200	2,000	4,000	7,000	10,000
4d Sed 605	400	1,250	2,100	4,200	7,350	10,500
1991 Eldorado, V-8						
2d Cpe	450	1,300	2,200	4,400	7,700	11,000
1991 Brougham, V-8						
4d Sed	450	1,300	2,200	4,400	7,700	11,000
1991 Allante, V-8						
2d Conv	800	2,400	4,000	8,000	14,000	20,000

NOTE: Add $3,000 for hardtop.

	6	5	4	3	2	1
1992 Seville, V-8						
4d Sed	500	1,550	2,600	5,200	9,100	13,000
4d STS Sed	550	1,700	2,800	5,600	9,800	14,000
1992 DeVille, V-8						
4d Sed	450	1,300	2,200	4,400	7,700	11,000
2d Cpe	450	1,300	2,200	4,400	7,700	11,000
4d Trg Sed	500	1,450	2,400	4,800	8,400	12,000
1992 Fleetwood, V-8						
4d Sed	500	1,450	2,400	4,800	8,400	12,000
2d Cpe	500	1,450	2,400	4,800	8,400	12,000
4d Sed 605	500	1,550	2,600	5,200	9,100	13,000
1992 Eldorado, V-8						
2d Cpe	550	1,700	2,800	5,600	9,800	14,000
1992 Brougham, V-8						
4d Sed	500	1,550	2,600	5,200	9,100	13,000
1992 Allante, V-8						
2d Conv	950	2,900	4,800	9,600	16,800	24,000

NOTE: Add $1,500 for hardtop.

	6	5	4	3	2	1
1993 Seville, V-8						
4d Sed	500	1,550	2,600	5,200	9,100	13,000
4d STS Sed	550	1,700	2,800	5,600	9,800	14,000
1993 DeVille, V-8						
2d Cpe	450	1,350	2,250	4,500	7,850	11,200
4d Sed	450	1,400	2,300	4,600	8,050	11,500
4d Trg Sed	500	1,450	2,400	4,800	8,400	12,000
1993 Fleetwood, V-8						
4d Sed	550	1,600	2,700	5,400	9,450	13,500
1993 Sixty Special, V-8						
4d Sed	500	1,550	2,600	5,200	9,100	13,000
1993 Eldorado, V-8						
2d Cpe	550	1,700	2,850	5,700	9,950	14,200
1993 Allante, V-8						
2d Conv	1,000	3,000	5,000	10,000	17,500	25,000

LASALLE PRICING

	6	5	4	3	2	1
1927 Series 303, V-8, 125" wb						
2d RS Rds	2,950	8,900	14,800	29,600	51,800	74,000
4d Phae	3,050	9,100	15,200	30,400	53,200	76,000
4d Spt Phae	3,100	9,350	15,600	31,200	54,600	78,000
2d 2P Conv Cpe	2,650	7,900	13,200	26,400	46,200	66,000
2d RS Cpe	1,600	4,800	8,000	16,000	28,000	40,000
2d 4P Vic	1,400	4,200	7,000	14,000	24,500	35,000
4d Sed	950	2,900	4,800	9,600	16,800	24,000
4d Twn Sed	1,050	3,100	5,200	10,400	18,200	26,000
1927 Series 303, V-8, 134" wb						
4d Imp Sed	1,150	3,500	5,800	11,600	20,300	29,000
4d 7P Sed	1,100	3,350	5,600	11,200	19,600	28,000
4d 7P Imp Sed	1,200	3,600	6,000	12,000	21,000	30,000
1928 Series 303, V-8, 125" wb						
2d Rds	2,950	8,900	14,800	29,600	51,800	74,000
4d Phae	3,050	9,100	15,200	30,400	53,200	76,000
4d Spt Phae	3,100	9,350	15,600	31,200	54,600	78,000
2d Conv	2,650	7,900	13,200	26,400	46,200	66,000
2d Bus Cpe	1,350	4,100	6,800	13,600	23,800	34,000
2d RS Cpe	1,600	4,800	8,000	16,000	28,000	40,000
2d Vic	1,300	3,950	6,600	13,200	23,100	33,000
4d 5P Sed	1,200	3,600	6,000	12,000	21,000	30,000
4d Fam Sed	1,100	3,350	5,600	11,200	19,600	28,000
4d Twn Sed	1,150	3,500	5,800	11,600	20,300	29,000
1928 Series 303, V-8, 134" wb						
2d 5P Cpe	1,500	4,550	7,600	15,200	26,600	38,000
4d Cabr Sed	2,900	8,650	14,400	28,800	50,400	72,000
4d Imp Sed	1,650	4,900	8,200	16,400	28,700	41,000
4d 7P Sed	1,600	4,800	8,000	16,000	28,000	40,000
4d Fam Sed	1,450	4,300	7,200	14,400	25,200	36,000
4d Imp Fam Sed	1,650	4,900	8,200	16,400	28,700	41,000
1928 Series 303, V-8, 125" wb Fleetwood Line						
2d Bus Cpe	1,550	4,700	7,800	15,600	27,300	39,000
4d Sed	1,450	4,300	7,200	14,400	25,200	36,000
4d Twn Cabr	2,900	8,650	14,400	28,800	50,400	72,000
4d Trans Twn Cabr	2,950	8,900	14,800	29,600	51,800	74,000
1929 Series 328, V-8, 125" wb						
2d Rds	2,950	8,900	14,800	29,600	51,800	74,000
4d Phae	3,050	9,100	15,200	30,400	53,200	76,000
4d Spt Phae	3,100	9,350	15,600	31,200	54,600	78,000
4d Trans FW Twn Cabr	2,650	7,900	13,200	26,400	46,200	66,000
1929 Series 328, V-8, 134" wb						
2d Conv	2,900	8,650	14,400	28,800	50,400	72,000
2d RS Cpe	1,750	5,300	8,800	17,600	30,800	44,000
2d 5P Cpe	1,650	4,900	8,200	16,400	28,700	41,000
4d Sed	1,500	4,550	7,600	15,200	26,600	38,000
4d Fam Sed	1,550	4,700	7,800	15,600	27,300	39,000
4d Twn Sed	1,600	4,800	8,000	16,000	28,000	40,000
4d 7P Sed	1,600	4,800	8,000	16,000	28,000	40,000
4d 7P Imp Sed	1,650	4,900	8,200	16,400	28,700	41,000
4d Conv Lan Cabr	3,350	10,100	16,800	33,600	58,800	84,000
4d FW Trans Twn Cabr 1	3,350	10,100	16,800	33,600	58,800	84,000
1930 Series 340, V-8, 134" wb Fisher Line						
2d Conv	2,950	8,900	14,800	29,600	51,800	74,000
2d RS Cpe	1,950	5,900	9,800	19,600	34,300	49,000
2d Cpe	1,750	5,300	8,800	17,600	30,800	44,000
4d Sed	1,550	4,700	7,800	15,600	27,300	39,000
4d Imp Sed	1,600	4,800	8,000	16,000	28,000	40,000
4d 7P Sed	1,650	4,900	8,200	16,400	28,700	41,000
4d 7P Imp Sed	1,750	5,300	8,800	17,600	30,800	44,000
1930 Series 340, V-8, 134" wb Fleetwood Line						
2d RS Rds	3,400	10,200	17,000	34,000	59,500	85,000
1930 Fleetcliffe						
4d Phae	3,300	9,950	16,600	33,200	58,100	83,000
4d 7P Tr	2,850	8,500	14,200	28,400	49,700	71,000
1930 Fleetlands						
4d A/W Phae	3,500	10,600	17,600	35,200	61,500	88,000
1930 Fleetway						
4d S'net Cabr 4081	2,800	8,400	14,000	28,000	49,000	70,000
1930 Fleetwind						
4d S'net Cabr 4082	2,800	8,400	14,000	28,000	49,000	70,000

1931 Series 345A, V-8, 134" wb Fisher Line

	6	5	4	3	2	1
2d RS Cpe	2,150	6,500	10,800	21,600	37,800	54,000
2d Cpe	2,050	6,100	10,200	20,400	35,700	51,000
4d Sed	1,600	4,800	8,000	16,000	28,000	40,000
4d Twn Sed	1,650	4,900	8,200	16,400	28,700	41,000
4d 7P Sed	1,700	5,050	8,400	16,800	29,400	42,000
4d 7P Imp Sed	1,700	5,150	8,600	17,200	30,100	43,000

1931 Series 345A, V-8, 134" wb Fleetwood Line

	6	5	4	3	2	1
2d RS Rds	3,400	10,200	17,000	34,000	59,500	85,000
2d Conv	3,100	9,350	15,600	31,200	54,600	78,000
4d Tr	3,100	9,350	15,600	31,200	54,600	78,000
4d A/W Phae	3,600	10,800	18,000	36,000	63,000	90,000
4d S'net Cabr 4081	2,800	8,400	14,000	28,000	49,000	70,000
4d S'net Cabr 4082	2,800	8,400	14,000	28,000	49,000	70,000

1932 Series 345B, V-8, 130" wb

	6	5	4	3	2	1
2d Conv	2,700	8,150	13,600	27,200	47,600	68,000
2d RS Cpe	1,950	5,900	9,800	19,600	34,300	49,000
2d Twn Cpe	1,750	5,300	8,800	17,600	30,800	44,000
4d Sed	1,350	4,100	6,800	13,600	23,800	34,000

1932 Series 345B, V-8, 136" wb

	6	5	4	3	2	1
4d 7P Sed	1,350	4,100	6,800	13,600	23,800	34,000
4d 7P Imp Sed	1,750	5,300	8,800	17,600	30,800	44,000
4d 7P Twn Sed	1,800	5,400	9,000	18,000	31,500	45,000

1933 Series 345C, V-8, 130" wb

	6	5	4	3	2	1
2d Conv	2,500	7,450	12,400	24,800	43,400	62,000
2d RS Cpe	1,600	4,800	8,000	16,000	28,000	40,000
2d Twn Cpe	1,500	4,450	7,400	14,800	25,900	37,000
4d Sed	1,300	3,950	6,600	13,200	23,100	33,000

1933 Series 345C, V-8, 136" wb

	6	5	4	3	2	1
4d Twn Sed	1,750	5,300	8,800	17,600	30,800	44,000
4d Sed	1,450	4,300	7,200	14,400	25,200	36,000
4d 7P Imp Sed	1,400	4,200	7,000	14,000	24,500	35,000

1934 Series 350, 8-cyl., 119" wb

	6	5	4	3	2	1
2d Conv	2,000	6,000	10,000	20,000	35,000	50,000
2d Cpe	1,300	3,950	6,600	13,200	23,100	33,000
4d Clb Sed	1,050	3,100	5,200	10,400	18,200	26,000
4d Sed	1,000	3,000	5,000	10,000	17,500	25,000

1935 Series 50, 8-cyl., 120" wb

	6	5	4	3	2	1
2d Conv	2,100	6,350	10,600	21,200	37,100	53,000
2d Cpe	1,200	3,600	6,000	12,000	21,000	30,000

	6	5	4	3	2	1
2d Sed	850	2,500	4,200	8,400	14,700	21,000
4d Sed	900	2,650	4,400	8,800	15,400	22,000

1936 Series 50, 8-cyl., 120" wb, LaSalle

	6	5	4	3	2	1
2d Conv	1,900	5,750	9,600	19,200	33,600	48,000
2d RS Cpe	1,100	3,350	5,600	11,200	19,600	28,000
2d Sed	750	2,300	3,800	7,600	13,300	19,000
4d Sed	800	2,400	4,000	8,000	14,000	20,000

1937 Series 50, V-8, 124" wb, LaSalle

	6	5	4	3	2	1
2d Conv	2,000	6,000	10,000	20,000	35,000	50,000
2d Conv Sed	2,100	6,250	10,400	20,800	36,400	52,000
4P Cpe	1,100	3,350	5,600	11,200	19,600	28,000
2d Sed	800	2,400	4,000	8,000	14,000	20,000
4d Sed	850	2,500	4,200	8,400	14,700	21,000

1938 Series 50, V-8, 124" wb, LaSalle

	6	5	4	3	2	1
2d Conv	2,000	6,000	10,000	20,000	35,000	50,000
4d Conv Sed	2,100	6,250	10,400	20,800	36,400	52,000
4P Cpe	1,150	3,500	5,800	11,600	20,300	29,000
2d Sed	850	2,500	4,200	8,400	14,700	21,000
4d Sed	900	2,650	4,400	8,800	15,400	22,000

1939 Series 50, V-8, 120" wb

	6	5	4	3	2	1
2d Conv	2,000	6,000	10,000	20,000	35,000	50,000
4d Conv Sed	2,100	6,250	10,400	20,800	36,400	52,000
2d Cpe	1,150	3,500	5,800	11,600	20,300	29,000
2d Sed	850	2,500	4,200	8,400	14,700	21,000
2d S/R Sed	850	2,600	4,300	8,600	15,050	21,500
4d Sed	900	2,650	4,400	8,800	15,400	22,000
4d S/R Sed	900	2,700	4,500	9,000	15,750	22,500

1940 Series 50, V-8, 123" wb

	6	5	4	3	2	1
2d Conv	2,000	6,000	10,000	20,000	35,000	50,000
4d Conv Sed	2,100	6,250	10,400	20,800	36,400	52,000
2d Cpe	1,200	3,600	6,000	12,000	21,000	30,000
2d Sed	850	2,500	4,200	8,400	14,700	21,000
2d S/R Sed	850	2,600	4,300	8,600	15,050	21,500
4d Sed	900	2,650	4,400	8,800	15,400	22,000
4d S/R Sed	900	2,700	4,500	9,000	15,750	22,500

1940 "Special" Series 52 LaSalle, V-8, 123" wb

	6	5	4	3	2	1
2d Conv	2,000	6,000	10,000	20,000	35,000	50,000
4d Conv Sed	2,100	6,250	10,400	20,800	36,400	52,000
2d Cpe	1,250	3,700	6,200	12,400	21,700	31,000
4d Sed	900	2,650	4,400	8,800	15,400	22,000

PRICE GUIDE ABBREVIATIONS

Alphabetical

A/C .... Air Conditioning
Aero .... Aerodynamic
Anniv .... Anniversary
Auto ..... Automatic Transmission
A/W or A-W .... All-Weather
Berl .... Berline
Brgm .... Brougham
Brn .... Brunn
BT .... Boattail
Bus. .... Business (as in Bus Cpe)
Cabr .... Cabriolet
cc .... Close-coupled
cid ..... Cubic Inch Displacement
Clb .. Club (as in Clb Cpe/Clb Cab)
Cpe. .... Coupe
Coll .. Collapsible (as in Semi-Coll)
Conv .... Convertible
Ctry .... Country
Cus .... Custom
DC .... Dual-Cowl
DeL .... Deluxe
Der .... Derham
DEx .... Dual Exhausts
Dly .. Delivery (as in Sed Dly)
Dtrch .... Dietrich
DuW .... Dual Windshield
DW .... Division Window
Edn .... Edition
EFI ...... Electronic Fuel Injection

Encl .... Enclosed
Eng .... Engine
FBk .... Fastback
Fcty .... Factory
FHC .... Fixed Head Coupe
FI .... Fuel Injection
Fml .... Formal
FWD .... Front-wheel Drive
GT . Gran Turismo (Grand Touring)
HBk .... Hatchback
H&E .... Hess & Eisenhart
Hemi .. Hemispherical-head engine
HD .... Heavy Duty
Hlbrk .... Holbrook
hp .... Horsepower
HT .... Hardtop
Imp .... Imperial
Int .... Interior
IPC .. Indy (Indianapolis) Pace Car
IROC .... International
                Race of Champions
Jud .... Judkins
KO .... Knock-off Wheels
Lan .... Landau
Lan'let .... Landaulet
LBx .. Long Box (pickup truck bed)
LeB or Leb .... LeBaron
LHD .... Left-Hand Drive
Limo .... Limousine
Lke .... Locke

LWB .... Long-Wheelbase
mph .... Miles Per Hour
M/R. .... Moonroof
nhp .... Net Horsepower
O/D .... Overdrive
opt .... Option(s)
orig .... Original
P ...... Passenger (as in 3P Cpe)
Phae .... Phaeton
PT ...... Power (Convertible) Top
Pwr .... Power
Rbt .... Runabout
Rds .... Roadster
Ret .... Retractable
RHD .... Right-Hand Drive
Rlstn or Roll .... Rollston
R/S .... Rumbleseat
R/T .... Dodge model
SCCA . Sports Car Club of America
S/C .... Supercharged
SE .... Special Edition
Sed .... Sedan
SMt or SMts .... Sidemount(s)
Spds .... Speedster
Spec or Spl .... Special
Spt .... Sport
S/R .... Sunroof
Sta Wag .... Station Wagon
Std .... Standard
SWB .... Short Wheelbase

T&C .... Town & Country
T-top .... T-top Roof
Trg ...... Touring Car (not Targa)
Turbo .... Equipped with
                turbocharger(s)
Twn ...... Town (as in Twn Sed)
V-4, -6, -8 .... V-block engine
Vic .... Victoria
W .... Window (as in 3W Cpe)
WW .... Wire Wheels
W'by .... Willoughby
Woodie .... partially
                wood-bodied vehicle
W.T .... Winter Top
Wtrhs .... Waterhouse

Numerical

2d .... Two-door (also 4d, 6d, etc)
2P .... Two-Passenger
                (also 3P, 4P, etc)
2S .... Two-Seat (also 3S, 4S, etc)
3W .... Three-Window
                (also 4W, 5W, etc)
4-cyl .... In-line Engine
                (also 5-cyl, 6-, 8-,)
4-Spd .. Four-speed Transmission
                (also 3-, 5-, etc)
4V .... Four-barrel Carburetor
4x4 .. Four-wheel drive (not FWD)
8/9P ... Eight- or Nine-Passenger

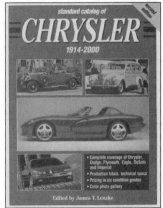
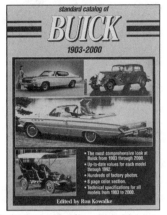

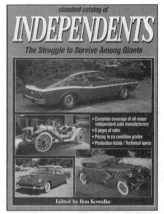
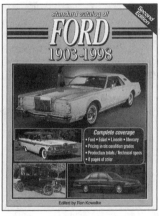
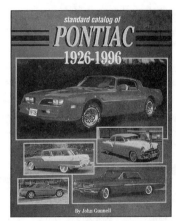

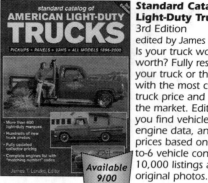
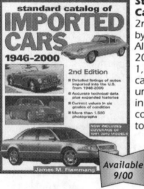

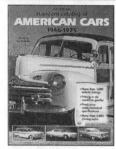